New Towns for the Twenty-First Century

THE CITY IN THE TWENTY-FIRST CENTURY

Eugenie L. Birch and Susan M. Wachter, Series Editors

A complete list of books in the series is available from the publisher.

New Towns for the Twenty-First Century

A Guide to Planned Communities Worldwide

Edited by Richard Peiser and Ann Forsyth

PENN

UNIVERSITY OF PENNSYLVANIA PRESS

Philadelphia

Publication of this volume was aided by a generous grant from China Vanke Company.

Published by
University of Pennsylvania Press
Philadelphia, Pennsylvania 19104–4112
www.upenn.edu/pennpress

Printed in the United States of America on acid-free paper
10 9 8 7 6 5 4 3 2 1

A Cataloging-in-Publication Data record for this book is available from the Library of Congress.
ISBN 978–0-8122–5191–3

publication supported by a grant from

The Community Foundation for Greater New Haven

as part of the Urban Haven Project

Contents

Part IV

New Town Futures

New Towns for the Twenty-First Century

Part I

Overview of New Towns in the Twentieth and Twenty-First Centuries

Introduction

Ann Forsyth and Richard Peiser

Exploring the New Town Idea in Practice

People have been building new settlements for thousands of years. The new town idea as presented in this book is more recent, a reaction to urbanization in the industrial and postindustrial eras. New towns are relatively large, comprehensively planned developments on newly urbanized land that boast a mix of spaces. In their ideal form they can provide opportunities for all the activities of daily life for a variety of people. From garden cities to science cities, new capitals to large military towns, hundreds were built in the twentieth century. Their planning and development approaches have also been influential far beyond the new towns themselves. While new towns are difficult to execute well, and their popularity has waxed and waned over the past century, their development is currently on an upswing, with major initiatives in the developing countries of East Asia, South Asia, and Africa. They continue to be built in developed countries as well, in part because they are seen as providing efficient and adaptable settings for a number of social goals, from technological innovation and environmental conservation to high quality of life.

In 1963, in the midst of the last golden age of new towns, Frederick Osborn and Arnold Whittick published *The New Towns: The Answer to Megalopolis*. This 376-page work has been the key reference for new towns scholars for over fifty years. Based on British experience but with a broader view, this book argued for new towns as a key solution to metropolitan growth. Covering history, policy, legislation, governance, finance, regional development, opposition, and international spread, cases from British new towns were supplemented by an international inventory. Balancing vision and practicalities, the book was both a visionary document and based in practicalities. In this period of a current upswing in interest in new towns, *New Towns for the Twenty-First Century* provides an updated view about the potential for new towns. It looks at the ideals behind new towns, the practice of building them, and their outcomes. It examines their design, planning, finances, management, governance, quality of life, and sustainability. It shows how they have taken form globally. It traces their past to understand their accomplishments and to frame challenges and

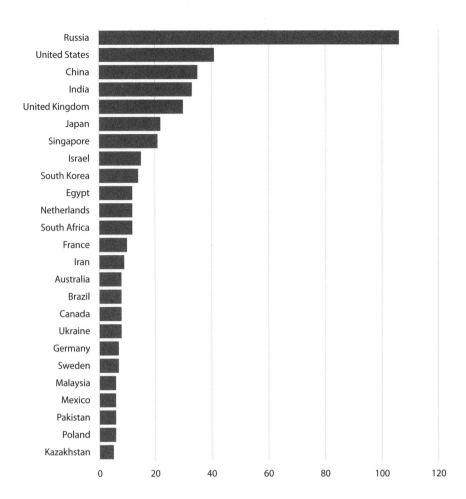

lessons for developing new towns. And it looks to the future—
how might they evolve in coming years?

While contemporary new town ideas emerged in the late
nineteenth and early twentieth centuries, the golden period internationally was from World War II through the 1970s. For
this book, we compiled an inventory of new towns in the twen-
tieth century, looking specifically at those that had reached a population of at least
thirty thousand by 2015—a cutoff used to make the inventory manageable in size.
More than 530 such developments have been located and appear in Appendix 1
(maps) and Appendix 2 (the inventory lists) (Figure 0.1). Many more have been
important in terms of making a design, planning, or real estate innovation but either have not reached thirty thousand in population or have fallen short in some
other dimension that would make them a full, multifunctional, planned new town.
Some of these are in the listing of classic new towns in Appendix 2. The inventory
has some limitations, as we describe there. New towns are by definition planned

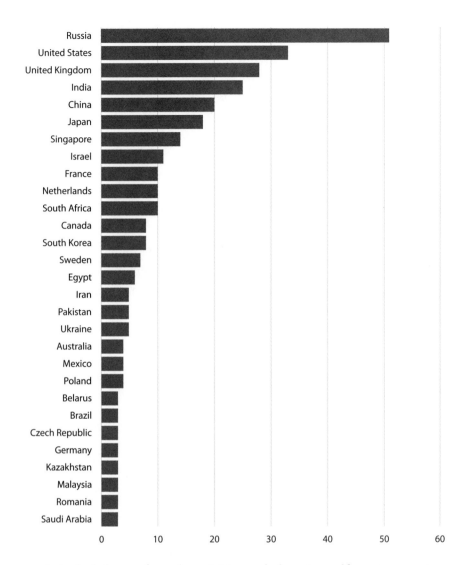

to mimic the balance of people, activities, and places in a self-contained town. However, it can be hard to tell whether a specific place had a high enough level of planning and infrastructure provision to be classified as a true new town. Where municipal boundaries do not exactly match the new town, estimating populations can be difficult. The inventory shows rough trends, however. It demonstrates that between 1945 and 1979, sixty-seven countries started at least one new town that succeeded enough to have a population of over thirty thousand people by 2015. Several countries built at least three such new settlements in this period of just a few decades. This group included countries from all inhabited continents (Figure 0.2). The new town movement in the twentieth century was a global phenomenon.

Figure 0.2. Countries with three or more inventory new towns in the first golden age (1945–79). *Source*: New towns database in Appendix 2.

After a lull in interest in the 1980s, new towns are again on the agenda. In the first fifteen years of the current century, over 140 new towns were started in countries such as Vietnam, India, Korea, Kenya, China, and Saudi Arabia. While it is unclear how many will be successful, it is apparent that this is a second golden age of new town development.

Why New Towns?

Why have these developments been proposed in so many different countries? This is a complex story, and new towns have fulfilled multiple purposes from housing workers to deconcentrating urban areas. Whatever their purpose, new towns were intended to create urban patterns that could better serve important social goals, lower long-term costs though efficiency, and demonstrate planning, design, and development innovations.

This book's Appendix 2 shows numerous socialist-inspired *industrial* new towns built in the twentieth century. It classifies over 240, or 45 percent, of the twentieth-century new towns as industrial—including ports and railways and in industries such as steel smelting and oil refining, manufacturing and mining, and agricultural and energy production. Of course, all new towns have employment, but this group puts resource extraction and manufacturing at the center. Another 5 percent were related to military and research purposes, including science cities and industrial cities producing nuclear weapons. We call these industrial-, military-, and research-based places as a whole *employment-based new towns*. Of these industrial, military, and research new towns, over one hundred were in Russia. Adding other countries in the Soviet Union and Eastern bloc, as well as China and India, that received Soviet help in industrial development, shifts the figure to 68 percent. That is more than 180 of the approximately 270 employment-based new towns started with a socialist impetus and aimed to house workers, develop regions, and build science capacity.

Of course, these broadly defined employment-based developments occurred throughout the world; the geography might also be different if the numbers also included smaller developments, which would likely include more resource extraction communities such as mining towns. In the twenty-first century, employment-led new towns remain important, with industrial new towns recently started in Algeria, China, Ghana, India, Kenya, Nigeria, Portugal, Saudi Arabia, and Vietnam. These are not the classic satellite new towns that have dominated professional debates; most are not likely to be well planned, with less comprehensive infrastructure.

In contrast, many other countries often developed new towns as a tool for *deconcentrating urban areas*. Of the twentieth-century new towns in the inventory, approximately 210 were developed for metropolitan deconcentration. For planned decentralization, new towns were seen as having advantages over incremental development in that they could provide infrastructure up front, balance jobs and housing, and coordinate growth regionally. They could accommodate the large number of housing units needed after World War II. Approximately 28 percent of these twentieth-century new towns were in western Europe (dominated by the U.K., but also in the Netherlands, France, and Sweden); another 24 percent in East and Southeast Asia (mainly Singapore, Japan, China, and South Korea); and 21 percent in the United States and Canada. Together these accounted for 153, or 73 percent, of new towns developed to deconcentrate urban areas. Removing China, the total would be 67 percent. In the current century, China dominates this category, with over half the recently started new towns built to deconcentrate urban areas. Fewer than 10 percent of new towns were developed for other reasons: as capital cities or to resettle people after political turmoil (e.g., the partition of India) or disasters such as earthquakes.

This book also looks to the future. The twentieth and early twenty-first centuries were dominated by two types of new town planning and production. The comprehensive phased new town, which is planned as a whole and developed over many decades, is perhaps the dominant type. In some areas of tremendous growth, or when needed for worker housing, the instant new town could be rapidly built in under a decade. In both cases, new towns were planned, infrastructure provided, and housing built, all in an integrated process.

In the coming century, two other forms may become important. On the one hand, many new towns are aging, increasing the need to redevelop, extend, or retrofit. What we call maturation planning can already be seen in many new towns from the golden period but will continue as the latest round of new towns, often in Asia, age. In addition, much urban growth is now happening in developing regions, particularly in Africa. It may be the time to revisit sites and services approaches that provide infrastructure but allow households to build their own dwellings. A new town approach to such development could provide infrastructure more comprehensively, and plan settlements with a mixture of activities including substantial employment, thus overcoming some problems with the type in earlier periods.

Because of climate change and demographic shifts to come, three other issues may become more important. First are developments that move whole populations away from a threat such as provided by coastal storms, floods, and rising sea levels from climate change. Many urban areas are vulnerable to flooding and storm surge. While some will be able to remain, using various technologies to protect them from and adapt to this new reality, in other circumstances planned retreat may be the best option, though not an easy one. Second, in the twentieth century, some new towns were built to resettle people after disasters, wars, or political upheavals; but the era of climate change, and climate-induced strife, is likely to make refugee resettlement a more compelling issue. This poses questions about how to achieve an appropriate mix of people and efficiently create higher-quality environments. In other cases, urban areas may need to adapt to new constraints—particularly land scarcity. In the twentieth century, land-scarce Singapore and Hong Kong built high-density new towns; in the coming centuries, other locations may use them to resettle refugees or intensify urbanization to protect nearby natural resources.

What Is a New Town?

This book focuses on comprehensively planned, mixed-use, freestanding, implemented new towns rather than new towns-in-town (large urban infill projects), planned extensions to existing developments, or largely residential developments. They may be satellites of an existing city, linked to it economically and via commuting patterns, or independent places, often sites close to natural resources and remote from existing urban areas. They may be developed by the public or private sector, or some combination of the two. Several parts of this definition deserve elaboration.

Comprehensive planning and mixed uses: New towns are typically large (in the tens of thousands or hundreds of thousands in population). They are also comprehensive in two senses. First, they are comprehensively planned, designed as a whole. Second, they have a comprehensive array of activities so that much of daily life can be conducted within them. This requires employment for those in the workforce, even when new towns' primary goal is metropolitan deconcentration. This distinguishes them from so-called packaged suburbs or large-scale residential projects. However, there is a continuum from residential developments through new towns to employment zones, and the boundaries can be murky. Some terms, such as the U.S. "new community," may mean a new town in one context but a master-planned, primarily residential community in another, making classification more difficult (Eichler and Kaplan 1967; Ewing 1991; Forsyth 2005; Griffin 1974).

Spatial location and independence: An important distinction between such places has been their spatial location in relation to the metropolitan area and their level of self-containment. All are freestanding, but only some are economically independent. Independent examples include towns developed for resource extraction and many capital cities. Others are freestanding satellites of metropolitan areas that, while of mixed use and with a jobs-housing balance, are economically linked. While large developments within the existing fabric of metropolitan areas have been called new-towns-in-town, these are different in many ways and are not the focus of the book (Griffin 1974).[1]

City extensions are a difficult category. For example, several of the areas in the inventory are planned extensions of Canberra, and many of the Chinese and Dutch new towns take this form (Nozeman 1990). We have included them when they were large and comprehensive, though it really is a matter of degree, and certainly there can be quibbles with what we have included and excluded. Even classic new towns on what is considered new land frequently include existing small villages within the fabric. In the twentieth-century new towns inventory, the vast majority of all new towns are satellites of existing cities—approximately 69 percent. Basically, all the new towns developed to deconcentrate metropolitan areas are satellites; industrial and military new towns are more mixed.

Size: While sometimes new towns are defined in terms of spatial size—in the United States it might be two thousand or more acres—the very high densities of many recent new towns make this problematic (Eichler and Kaplan 1967, 23; Ewing 1991, 2). Further, for the purposes of the inventory of twentieth-century new towns, we chose a threshold of thirty thousand population as of 2015—the size of the original garden city's town population (there were more people in the rural surrounds). This eliminates some recent new towns that will go on to become large and successful, as well as older new towns that do quite well with smaller numbers. Nonetheless, this cutoff is an attempt to filter out the struggling new towns, new neighborhoods, and the like. However, the threshold applies only to the inventory. New towns discussed in various chapters of this book may be smaller, though they need enough population to have viable mixed use.

Beyond a proposal: For this book, we are also interested in new towns that have been implemented and not just proposed. Many fail to get off the ground, and others abandon key parts of the plan such as comprehensiveness. The contemporary part of the inventory does contain some new towns that though started, have barely materialized.

It is possible to come up with more complex definitions. An Urban Land Institute (ULI) publication from the 1970s elaborated the definition of new towns, calling them new communities, as large developments that:

- were developed with a mix of land uses including housing; commercial areas; public and semipublic spaces (e.g., schools, places with municipal functions, and faith communities); recreation and open space; and employment,
- created opportunities for residents to be involved in neighborhood- and community-level governance,

- encouraged interaction between different "social, economic, age, and racial groups,"
- provided significant employment, with enough jobs for a "significant" proportion of residents to potentially work in the new town,
- supplied housing at various price levels for economic mix,
- planned the physical environment considering aesthetic values, open space preservation, human scale, and personal identity,
- encouraged, through physical planning, opportunities for both "social interaction at the neighborhood and community levels" and "privacy and individual flexibility." (Forsyth 2005; Griffin 1974, 3–4)

There are also related terms for communities that have some similarities with new towns but are not the same:

- The *planned community* or *master-planned community* includes new towns, but they are often primarily residential developments that lack employment. Some master-planned communities include retail, office, and industrial uses but lack the scale and full set of social and cultural institutions found in new towns. They may also be on redevelopment sites within the urban fabric.
- The *new-town-style neighborhood* or *planned neighborhood* is too small for comprehensiveness, though it may include some planning and design features, as well as community facilities and a mix of housing types and income levels, common in new towns.
- *Master-planned resorts, golf communities, and senior communities* may have many similarities to new towns but lack employment and the full set of uses that occur in a self-contained town.
- Some *employment-based developments* include a small amount of housing but for only a small part of their workforce.

Because largely residential and resort communities often share planning and development similarities with new towns, several authors in the book examine such places in their chapters. Some of these predominantly single-use communities were also included in the list of classic new towns and new-town-style developments that is a supplement to the twentieth-century and contemporary new towns inventories.

Questions about New Towns

Throughout their history new towns have raised questions for those proposing them (Cullingworth 1979, 367). These fall into several categories.

Scale: How big should new towns be to be appropriately multifunctional and efficient, viable as government or private investments, yet having a human scale? This is a complex question to resolve because people's views of a complete array of activities vary. Over time, however, the size has generally trended upward from Ebenezer Howard's ([1898] 2003) thirty-thousand-person towns. Land per person has varied greatly, with many contemporary high-density new towns having a comparatively small footprint.

Location: Particularly for satellite new towns, a question has been how far they should be from the parent city to balance self-containment, or its potential, and access to metropolitan opportunities. How should they relate to a wider regional vision?

Structure: Many new towns have been structured around neighborhoods or villages of a few thousand people to a few tens of thousands, with associated schools and shops. This is not the only way to create new towns—for example, Cumberland in Scotland deemphasized the neighborhood in favor of access to a town center (Forsyth and Crewe 2009a). The location and character of employment areas, green spaces, transportation networks, and civic facilities raise further questions. Is there an optimal structure?

Populations: A key idea behind of new towns has been population or social mix—for both residents and workers—to provide a town-like balance of ages, incomes, and other important social characteristics such as race and ethnicity. Reasons have included matching residents to jobs, promoting equity, and enhancing community stability. Indeed this book does not count as new towns developments aimed solely at one population group such as retirees. This balance has often been difficult to achieve in practice. Publicly developed new towns have often focused on lower-income populations; private sector new towns on the reverse. Newly built new towns may attract people at similar life-cycle stages; something similar may happen with maturing developments. Initiating and maintaining mix are thus key issues.

Design: From the layout of housing and employment areas to the detailed design of streets and housing units, new towns provide opportunities for innovation but also substantial challenges. Should design for private versus collective spaces have different treatment? How can design and planning evolve in later phases of the development? What about the redevelopment of aging new towns?

Governance: When should residents be involved in governing the development, and how? What should be the balance of standard local government activity and collective management of common spaces? Can involving residents undermine the plan that attracted them in the first place? What kind of social supports can and should new towns provide? Can new towns exist in very fragmented and decentralized governmental systems such as in many parts of the United States?

Financial viability: Are new towns profitable as investments? Even governments must have some kind of positive balance sheet to justify investing in a new town—though governments can factor in costs over a long time period or cover a range of topics.

Alternatives: Is a new town better than alternative new development options such as more incremental suburbanization? Do new towns draw attention away from existing urban areas that may need planning and redevelopment attention?

To address the array and complexity of these questions, the book combines insights from both academics and practitioners. It deals with these questions in four parts. Part I, including this introduction, provides a broad overview of how to define new towns, their history over the past century or so, and arguments for and against the type. As Robert Freestone remarks: "In the early twenty-first century, the new town is no longer the definitive touchstone for the planning project but retains relevance in settlement policies." Part II examines new towns in major parts of the world—in the United States, where the private sector new town has been a key type; in Asia, which has recently had a great deal of new town building activity; and in other parts of the world. Part III focuses on key practical issues in developing new towns, particularly looking at finance and organization. A key component of this part involves lessons from leading practitioners. Part IV looks to the future, focusing on challenges of environmental sustainability and resilience and how the new town movement will evolve in the twenty-first century. To traditional incrementally built new towns may be added residents building their own homes, via self-construction; more of the almost instant new towns typical of recent years in East Asia; and new towns for resettling populations away from hazards and threats. Not all towns are new, and an emerging issue is the need for aging new towns to be incrementally rehabilitated.

New Lessons from New Towns

The opportunity to make comprehensive master plans and to develop entire new cities from scratch remains a planning ideal. In theory, comprehensive planning allows one to anticipate all the future physical and social needs of the city and its inhabitants and to provide for them in the master plan. In reality, this dream has never been achieved because of the complexity of both predicting the future and coordinating multiple systems. However the new town movement has enabled some new towns to come close to achieving this ideal.

Each new town is different, depending on its context and the urban issues that were paramount when it was built. The various new towns across the world in the twentieth century exhibit a panoply of solutions for curing urban ills. They offer numerous insights for achieving the better urban forms and approaches to implementation based on their context.

Despite the ebb and flow of new town construction in many countries throughout the twentieth century, new towns are being built at a rapid rate in many developing countries where the pace of urbanization is straining the capacity of existing cities to accommodate the increasing populations. While the pace is slower in developed countries, new towns continue to be created both in satellite locations and in resort areas. The lessons of earlier new towns offer valuable guidance for new towns in the twenty-first century.

Note

1. New-towns-in-town, such as New York City's Hudson Yards, or Stapleton in Denver, are surrounded by long-standing urban neighborhoods and may not have the balance of different uses. While they certainly have many characteristics of new towns as described in this book, they represent a special case of large-scale urban redevelopment.

1

A Brief History of New Towns

Robert Freestone

Speaking for many of his generation, Lewis Mumford (1977, xv) held that new towns not only were a solution to urban problems but shone as "a victory for the rational, the human, the disciplined, and the purposeful." Advocacy for, achievements in, and analysis of planned new towns constitute a significant strand in the evolution of modern planning thought from the late nineteenth century. The enthusiasm has been cyclical, reflecting broader shifts in national and international economic conditions, narratives of national social progress, rates of population growth, cultural fashions, design innovation, urban policy, and community acceptance. Responses have been remarkably diverse, with different nations and cities claiming the limelight at various times from the 1900s. The overall trajectory has been from utopian salvation through major state enterprise and capitalist initiative to declining icon, albeit with enduring support in certain progressive circles and high-growth settings. In the early twenty-first century, the new town is no longer the definitive touchstone for the planning project but retains relevance in settlement policies.

This chapter attempts an abbreviated global overview of the new town phenomenon in planning history. It is constructed around a time line of the ebb and flow of initiatives from the early twentieth century, organized into seven main phases forming a layered and intersecting narrative. The chronology is preceded by a consideration of the concept of the ideal community and followed by an exploration of some key issues arising, notably cross-cultural manifestations and significance in the evolution of urban design. The treatment is high level and selective to convey an overall appreciation of the international scale of new towns from the early twentieth century.

The chapter draws from literature skewed toward major authored texts representing the tip of a vast and still growing body of work over more than a century. Descriptions, reviews, and case studies go back to the early 1900s. Much of it until the 1970s is partisan, quasi-official, and descriptive. Two indirect indicators of how new towns have captured the imagination of the planning and development communities across successive generations are bibliographic documentation (e.g., Clapp

1970; Golany 1973; McNamara 1948; Viet 1960) and specialist encyclopedic entries (e.g., Ashworth 1973; Forsyth 2011; Kafkoula 2009; Osborn 1974). Like other enduring planning concepts and processes, new towns have also remained as a staple of planning historiography (Sutcliffe 1981), recently attracting attention as experimental exemplars of future urbanisms (Meller and Porfyriou 2016; Wakeman 2016). A huge store of contemporary and historical documentation is testimony to their hold on the planning imagination though paradoxically disproportionate to their direct impact on urban life globally.

The Ideal Community

The new town has been long seen as an ultimate ideal in urban development and a laboratory for testing new planning concepts. A prevailing but not uncontestable view is that a more comprehensively engineered new environment ensures better outcomes compared to the ad hoc extension and renewal of the unplanned or pre-existing urban environment.

Stein (1951) assembled many of the recurring tropes and values involved in his American community-planning projects up to the 1940s into a general case for new towns. First and foremost was the need for a clean slate free from the archaic and obsolete constraints of the patchwork city. "Existing cities cannot fit the needs of this age without a complete rebuilding," he wrote (Stein 1951, 194). Reiner (1963, 34) later codified the spirit and purpose of the ideal community in modern urban planning, with a "prospect" of projects from seers such as Ebenezer Howard, Edgar Chambless, Frank Lloyd Wright, Le Corbusier, and Percival and Paul Goodman. These were intentional communities with roots in utopian thinking driven by social reform and conceiving a better urban society through manipulation of urban form, circulation, density, and growth. For both Stein and Reiner, the intent was primarily a beneficent democratic living environment, but new towns have also been the product of more utilitarian national and territorial development initiatives.

The "new town" label has been applied expansively. For example, Forsyth and Crewe (2009b) label a suite of comprehensively designed new districts: architectural villages, diverse communities, designed enclaves, neighborhoods, ecoburbs, ecocities and technovilles. Keeton's (2011) survey of new towns in Asia and the Middle East recognizes six types according to their major drivers: economic development, elite enclaves, hi-tech, housing/shelter, political capitals, and ecocities. In terms of urban form and location, two broad types can be identified, namely "metrotowns" and "regional cities" (Archer 1969).

The first relate primarily to metropolitan overspill. The new town as an idealistic expression for a new urban order has channeled a strong sense of anti-urbanism as an alternative to the big, bloated dinosaur city. The aim has been to decant a growing or in-migrating urban population away from established dysfunctional cities with all their shortcomings to peripheral new-start communities offering an enhanced quality of life. Suburbs also historically had this decentralist rationale but simply made the dormitory dimensions of the metropolis bigger. The new town ideal conceived as a stand-alone but connected satellite township with aspirations for self-containment is one dominant narrative. A more typical variant is the large-scale metropolitan extension driven by public and/or private investment. Many of the former have segued into the latter given the rate of metropolitan growth. A second variant is a cluster or corridor of new or expanded communities within the metropolitan field.

The second broad type of new town in regional settings addresses different spatial needs and opportunities. Crudely, there are also two main types. They are intended either to assist in the isolated exploitation of natural resources or to constitute a collective force to claim and valorize nonmetropolitan space in region- and nation-building programs. In the latter case, the new town has been a recurring settlement type in projects for industrial development, land reclamation, defense preparation, and advancement of scientific research, tourism, and rationalization of a fragmented settlement patterns.

In all contexts, shifting policy focuses reflect evolving political, demographic, economic, and spatial circumstances. This is exemplified in the British New Towns program from the late 1940s, which evolved through three clear stages: Mark 1 towns (1946–50), aimed at relieving overcrowding in cities, particularly London; Mark 2 towns in the early 1960s, when the focus shifted to relieving stresses faced by major regional centers; and larger scale Mark 3 towns from the late 1960s, to stimulate and rationalize regional growth (A. Alexander 2009; Prince 1995). The continued reinvention and promotion of the new town idea is evident in the pages of *Town and Country Planning*, the official organ of the British Town and Country Planning Association. Admittedly a partisan organization, the journal provides a remarkable record of ups, downs, tweaks, and byways spanning three centuries (Hardy 1991a, 1991b).

Timeline of New Towns

Temporal periodization of the new town idea is conventionally applied to the experience of individual countries. The global frame of reference adopted here is rarer because of cross-national and cross-cultural complexity (Gaborit 2010). The treatment below is thus simplified and compressed into a layered and unfinished story comprising seven major phases that are discussed in turn.

The Garden City and Other New Town Models

Several strands of advocacy and action converged at the turn of the last century to propel new towns into the vanguard of modern planning thought. One was the sheer awfulness of the new industrial city for millions of workers that underlined the need for decisive moves in public health, infrastructure, and the control of town growth. A second strand was the comparatively recent experience of colonization and the founding of hundreds of new towns in the process (Hamer 1990). A third was the actual building of planned communities showcasing ideas about housing, zoning, street systems, open space, and civic art. These were frontier towns such as Dalny (1903), regional capitals such as Belo Horizonte (1897), and industrial communities physicalizing progressive views on worker welfare such as Pullman (1880) and Port Sunlight (1888). There was also a significant prehistory through a long tradition of utopian schemes, though most remained unbuilt (Morrison 2015). From the mid-nineteenth century, these were stimulated by the unplanned and unforeseen urban malfunctions occasioned by the industrial revolution, for example, James Silk Buckingham's proposal for Victoria (1849).

Contemporary commentators were careful to distinguish between planning as amelioration of existing fabric versus incursions into completely new territory. The most decisive contribution in an era alive to the prospect of urban reform bridged these two arenas of reform. This was Ebenezer Howard's vision of a "better and brighter civilisation" (147) of new polycentric constellations of small, "slumless smokeless" (130) garden cities founded and reproducing themselves by populist insurgency as an alternative to the great "wen" (3) of London and other evil industrial centers (Howard [1898] 2003). Howard's "unique combination of proposals" (102) was the right package at the right time in the right company. Seeking to avoid the stigma of utopianism by elaborating in detail the practical bases for land acquisition, town finances, and governance, Howard was a determined pragmatist who did a remarkable job in founding the Garden City Association in 1899 to successfully advance his cause. While the appealing "garden city" label was applied liberally to suburban ventures that were its antithesis, Letchworth Garden City (1903) was almost the real deal. Howard's Victorian radicalism was inevitably diluted, but the successful design and construction of the first planned new town was a decisive historic moment.

There is nonetheless a profound ambiguity as to the legacy of Ebenezer Howard because no subsequent new towns, not even the two he founded (Welwyn came next in 1919), comprehensively transcribed his core social and economic vision of self-built and governed "co-operative commonwealths" (Hardy 1991a, 314). Other theoretical ideas for new settlements would follow, and Reiner's (1963) survey hints at how these intermingled and competed to develop more threads and starting points into the mid-twentieth century. Tony Garnier's *Cité Industrielle* (1915) became a reference model for the creation of new industrial cities. Antonio Sant'Elia's futuristic new city visions in the 1910s spoke of a brave new urban world. Le Corbusier's *Ville Radieuse* in the 1920s was similarly vertiginous. Soviet planners would develop their own distinctive ideas based around new linear city forms. Theoretical sources for new town thinking were thus quite diverse.

Campaigns for and Experiments with New Towns

The first four decades of the twentieth century were marked by rising engagement in the theory and practice of planning new towns to confront head-on the limitations of market-driven cities. Howard's Garden Cities Association led the charge in Britain, changing its name in 1909 to incorporate a new nexus with town planning and embrace a wider set of environmental and social issues. Arguments for a national program of new city building were articulated in sustained propaganda. Booklets by New Townsmen (1918, new edition in 1942) and Ex-Service Man J47485 (1934, republished 1944) encapsulated the case for accelerated housing production in livable and efficient new communities. Principal author of the former was F. J. Osborn, one of Howard's most influential disciples, and of the latter, the architect A. Trystan Edwards. They were remarkably similar manifestos for one hundred new state-constructed settlements but differed in Edwards's distancing from the garden city movement to advocate Continental-style medium-density apartment living.

The global mission and relevance of the garden city was signified in the formation of the International Garden Cities and Town Planning Association (forerunner of the present International Federation for Housing and Planning) in 1913, with Howard as president until his death in 1928. Its first conference outside of Europe in New York in 1925 was the prelude to a decade of experimentation in the United States. This commenced in 1929 with the influential design of Radburn as a "garden city for the motor age," with its strong connections to the Regional Planning Association of America advocating decentralized garden settlements, and culminated with the three small New Deal towns of Greenbelt, Maryland, Greenhills, Ohio, and Greendale, Wisconsin under the auspices of Rexford Tugwell's Resettlement Administration. American involvement continued with small but iconic communities servicing national development needs, such as Norris (1934) in the Tennessee Valley and Oak Ridge (1942) for the Manhattan Project.

Elsewhere, the new planned town took different forms reflecting varied political economies: two capital cities for the British Empire (New Delhi, 1911; Canberra, 1912); colonial settlements such as Bissau and Huambo in Lusophone Africa (Silva 2015b); many industrial centers conceived in the rollout of Five-Year Plans in the USSR (e.g., Magnitogorsk, 1929) with the idea diffusing to other Eastern European nations along with a less desirable legacy of major environmental pollution; and the five towns, including Sabaudia (1934), built in the Pontine Marshes outside Rome under Mussolini (Caprotti 2007). Through the interwar years there was growing awareness of the need for integrated metropolitan planning that helped advance the notion of satellite towns as vehicles for long-term urban growth (Purdom 1925). Foundations were being laid for decisive action.

Postwar New Towns and Public Enterprise as a Global Project

By the 1940s, conventional planning wisdom enshrined new towns front and center in battling the evils of unplanned metropolitan growth. This ushered in what Wakeman (2014b, 105) terms a "golden age," with sustained moves "to construct . . . a completely new world." This continued in fits and starts linked to cyclical political enthusiasm and population growth spurts until the 1970s. The signal moment was the U.K. New Towns Act of 1946, providing the legislative framework for twenty-eight new towns through Britain, the majority in England, commencing with Stevenage (1946) and ending with Central Lancashire (1970). This emanated from decades of campaigning by advocates such as Osborn, from influential government inquiries on population and employment distribution, from Abercrombie's iconic plans for London in 1943–44, from the bombing of English cities during World War II, and from a postwar socialist government committed to national enterprise. Decentralization and house-and-garden living became the lynchpins of planning policy. Howard was airbrushed from the reports of the New Towns Committee (Thomas 1969), and the top-down approach inverted his ideal of self-governing commonwealths (Hall 2014), but the genealogical momentum was undeniable.

The new town idea was a simple, attractive, and understandable formula which, wedded to welfare state ideals, was readily exported as almost a panacea for other nations striving for effective urban development strategies. Even when British interest seemed to flag through the 1950s, new towns were a beacon for big-thinking planning around the world. Iconic developments soaked up much of the publicity into the 1960s, including Tapiola (outside Helsinki), Vällingby (Stockholm), Petaling Jaya (Kuala Lumpur), Tama (Tokyo), and Elizabeth (Adelaide). More politically problematic but still capturing the garden city/new town as a technical ideal were the apartheid townships on the metropolitan fringe of South African cities (Lupton 1993). A major upscaling in density saw a distinctive city-state interpretation imposed on Singapore and then Hong Kong with extensive high-density public housing estates connected to impressive mass transit systems. The evolution in both centers was from housing satellites to mixed-use urban complexes increasingly attractive to private capital with hundreds of thousands of residents (Bristow 1989; Padawangi 2010). Other Asian cities followed suit. However, an overall assessment in the late 1980s of these new communities' degree of self-containment concluded that imperfect policy guidance was mostly producing dormitory suburbs dependent on established centers (D. R. Phillips and Yeh 1987). Shanghai's first ring of satellite towns proved an "unsatisfactory development experience," having a narrow industrial base poor design and amenity, and lacking good transport connections (Yeh and Yuan 1987).

Some nations embarked on or sustained new town construction as part of national urbanization and industrialization policies, including the USSR (Underhill 1990), Brazil (Trevisan 2014), and Malaysia (Omar 2008). In 1965, President Charles de Gaulle announced France's *villes nouvelles* as an ambitious, large-scale growth-center program. The most decisive imprint was reserved for Paris through the articulation of regional development corridors housing several major urban nodes such as Cergy-Pontoise that departed significantly from the garden city model and emerged through the 1970s as beacons of high-modernist urbanism (Cupers 2014).

New Towns and the Private Sector

Meanwhile, alternatives to the statist model were offering a different new town product, notably in the United States. Precedents there lay in some of the more substantial private developments of the interwar years such as John Nolen–designed Kingsport (1917) and Mariemont (1923). Bucking the overwhelming trend of "cookie cutter" suburban sprawl in the 1960s were several large-scale residential communities. These never challenged conventional patterns of urbanization nor amounted to a national urban policy, but progressive developers such as James Rouse and Robert Simon created distinctive places with high design values and environmental amenity that nurtured civic innovation. Rouse also had aspirations for racial and economic integration (Forsyth 2005). The peak business periodical *Fortune* depicted the private new towns as the "best of everything . . . transforming not just the physical landscape, inside and outside of cities, but the human affairs of millions of Americans as well" (quoted in Stowe and Rehfuss 1975, 223). The three showcases were Reston (1963) and Columbia (1964), deep in the East Coast "Bos–Wash" conurbation; and Irvine (1970) in Los Angeles (Bloom 2001).

In 1970, the U.S. Congress passed new legislation that provided federal support in the form of bond guarantees for new town developers through the Department of Housing and Urban Development. The small-scale program was a policy response to the urban riots of the 1960s, looking toward racial and income integration through new community development (Whelan 1984). Several private projects were funded, but the program was abandoned in 1978, with The Woodlands outside Houston one of the few substantial outcomes.

The scorecard for the U.S. experience in the 1960s and 1970s was uneven. A major study of the period drawing on extensive interviews concluded that new communities delivered major advantages in terms of housing choice, access to services, better recreational facilities, and overall livability (Burby and Weiss 1976). Forsyth's (2005) study of Columbia, Irvine, and The Woodlands acknowledges their innovative design and attention to the public realm in ways that anticipate later "smart growth" thinking but nevertheless point to shortcomings such as lack of affordable housing and car dependence. Continuities especially in design innovation can also be traced into the more substantial products of the new urbanism movement such as Seaside (1982) and Celebration (1994), both in Florida (Grant 2006).

Major private land developments on the suburban fringe billed as new town projects but almost invariably targeted at upper-middle-class consumption rather than broader reform objectives are found in many countries. This type of planned community often displays an uncomfortable liaison with the gated community concept. They have spread to developing regions including Southeast Asia, where they have tended to reinforce socio-spatial segregation (Firman 2004; Percival and Waley 2012).

Reassessment, Critique, and Redirection

The 1970s produced considerable global interest in the progress and fortunes of new towns, with a concomitant spike in research outputs as the postwar history could be more confidently assessed. Merlin (1971), in the first authoritative cross-national study, concluded that, regardless of chosen organizational style, new towns were the only viable solution to congestion, industrial expansion, and sprawl. Robinson (1975), in a three-nation study, was less ebullient but saw relevance when new towns were integrated into overall settlement policies. On the positive side, the achievements in Britain and France in quantitative terms were lauded by many commentators (Cullingworth 1979; Merlin 1971). Thomas (1969, 448) called the British new towns a "howling success." Alongside came more sober evaluations. Aldridge (1979, xii) identified weaknesses in the British new town program as the result of "lack of resources and resolve by central government." Robinson (1975) concluded that they had contributed little to solving urban problems. Drawing primarily from a critique of the privatized American experience, Clapp (1971, 287) concluded that new towns "may well be an idea whose time has passed." Corden (1977) similarly foresaw the demise of formal new town programs.

The watershed in the 1970s was the cessation of the British program. In the 1940s, Lewis Silkin, as minister for town and country planning, had presided over new towns legislation with its promise of a "fairer civilisation" (McCallister 1947, 20). Thirty years later, his son John, as minister of housing and local government, was instrumental in bringing the program to an end, with urban renewal the new priority (Prince 1995). Political support for new towns dried up, and the conservative Margaret Thatcher's prime ministership in the 1980s was the nail in the coffin. A perfect storm of circumstances contributed. The cost of such long-time projects and their call on the public purse seemed impossible to sustain (Peiser and Chang 1999). There was loss of faith in bureaucratic planning and a turnaround in favor of more contextualized interventions. Population growth slowed appreciably. Global financial restructuring changed the fundamental nature of urban economies. Neoliberal political ideology saw major threads of the postwar welfare state unraveled. What space existed for urban policy focused on the neglected inner cities (for which new towns partially copped the blame). It was the crest of a slump in Britain, but there were other narratives.

The mantle of leadership of the new town movement shifted to France with its *villes nouvelles*—the new world showpiece; and in 1976 the International New Towns Association was formed to help study and promote the cause. Best-practice principles globally were captured to provide guidance (Golany 1976). Galantay (1975) predicted a positive future based on colonization of marginal lands through technological innovation and continued development of industrial settlements; by 2000 he foresaw urban investment budgets monopolized by the founding of hundreds of new towns housing up to thirty million people. New town strategies remained in place as national policy to fortify this view in countries such as Egypt (Abou-Zeid 1979), Saudi Arabia (Anis-Ur-Rahmaan and Fadaak 1991), and Iran (Zamani and Arefi 2013). Australia explored a national program for urban-corridor-orientated "system cities" and ex-metropolitan "regional cities" but with extremely modest results (Freestone 2013). Other countries fostered individual new communities through bespoke intergovernmental mechanisms, for example Almere in the Netherlands (Van der Wahl 1997).

Megaprojects and the Asian Tiger Economies

In recent years, the new town frontier has migrated to the burgeoning postreform market economies of Asian powerhouses such as China, South Korea, and India.

Here, economic liberalization has been closely linked to intensified processes of urbanization. The "new town" label is loosely applied to a spectrum of projects, but definitively capturing this new trend are high-rise, high-density residential and corporate compounds of a scale fashioning multicentered metropolitan forms. The Asian new towns are different from those that preceded them (Joo 2013). Characteristically, they are property development vehicles reflecting the entrepreneurial city paradigm in which the national and/or local state play key facilitating and brokering roles. There is an explicit profit orientation with a powerful presence "of the corporate sector in their conceptualization, planning, development, and governance" (Shatkin 2011, 80). With some exceptions, noted in other chapters, they are gentrified urban environments striving for Western amenity standards. A global profile is paramount as they exemplify the "worlding" of urban space (Roy and Ong 2011). Their joint private-public delivery, large scale, extent of foreign investment, accent on marketing, comprehensiveness, and often spectacular urban design mark them as urban megaprojects. Notably missing are the aspirations for economic and social self-containment voiced by prominent independent advocates that led earlier urban reform initiatives globally (Provoost and Vanstiphout 2011).

Neatly encapsulating the directions these new cities signpost are banner slogans featured in "The Banality of Good" exhibition at the Venice Biennale in 2012: "from housing the poor to sheltering the rich"; "from public works to global finance"; and "from the common good to the postcard city" (Crimson Architectural Historians 2012). These hint at some frequently voiced concerns: the trending to social exclusivity, automobile dependency even where mass transit is provided, rampant speculative development and ownership, and loss of valuable agricultural land.

China exemplifies this new urban phenomenon. Here the state plays a vital role in leading and guiding new towns as "investment and financing" platforms in the interests of accelerated economic development (F. Wu 2015, 163). There are four main models: transmogrified satellite towns, regenerated industrial zones, complete greenfield centers, and expanded regional cities. Since the late 1990s, Shanghai has provided a definitive expression of new town ideology underpinning the cause of global competitiveness (Jie 2015). Here a ring of seven new suburban cities such as Songjiang has helped reduce the population density in the central city core, narrowed the urban-rural per capita income divide, and housed a rising middle class (Shi and Chen 2016). But attendant concerns have been identified: lack of integrated governance, little commitment to public participation, lack of affordable housing, limited job opportunities, "lagged regional rapid transit system construction" (Shi and Chen 2016, 65), and underoccupied speculative housing and commercial tenancies (Shepard 2015). Shi and Chen (2015, 54) conclude "the goal of new city construction is clear and the pace is fast, but the progress is uneven."

Green Towns and Sustainable Urban Forms

While new towns may have dimmed as cutting-edge development forms in the West, the ideal of the planned new community intermediate between suburban neighborhood and Asian-scaled megaproject has persisted. In this context, the new town has retained, or, more accurately, reinvented the human scale and green connotations associated with the garden city. There is convergence with new urbanism, but here advocacy is situated within a broader context of urban settlement and social reform built around sustainability. Hardy (2008) offers a normative spatial framework of "eco-places" comprising a hierarchy of eco-villages and eco-towns that parallels Howard's thinking and extends to the reengineering of existing settlements. While the foundation in eco-villages does not approach a genuine urban scale, the underlying principles of sustainability, self-sufficiency, low-rise housing, closeness to nature, community, cooperation, and democracy help articulate the requisite philosophical foundation in how best to start again (Freestone 2000). The nexus with the garden city might seem like a nostalgia-driven policy, but the remit is contemporary.

The dream is most obviously being kept alive in Britain. In theoretical terms, a compelling framework is the late Peter Hall's Sustainable Social City, first announced in 1996. This development envisaged compact, walkable, mixed-use communities comprising moderately high densities strung out in clusters along public transport spines offering good metropolitan access to be developed through partnerships between development corporations, local authorities, communities, and private developers. The vision is Abercrombie-like and converges ideas of thinkers such as Michael Breheny and Peter Calthorpe (Hall and Ward 2014). Broader interest was reaffirmed by the prestigious Wolfson Economics Prize in 2014, which sought answers to the question: "How would you deliver a new Garden City which is visionary, economically viable, and popular?" The winning entry used the fictional city of Uxcester to illustrate how garden city principles could still be constructively applied to the expansion of existing large towns (URBED 2014). Other campaigners have set down core principles revolving around economic productivity, community governance, and low-carbon design by which any community, not just new ones, could be considered a garden city (Cabannes and Ross 2014). Finally, on the back of a succession of thinkers and practitioners applying themselves to the task of recovering lessons from the new town movement relevant to latter-day urban policy came a major study in 2006 that identified over sixty transferable lessons across issues such as financing, community development, physical environment, and long-term sustainability (U.K. Department for Communities and Local Government 2006).

The Town and Country Planning Association (TCPA) has continued its campaign for new settlements for over a century through updating, adapting, and extending seemingly timeless goals to address modern planning challenges. Its working definition of a garden city liberalizes historic strictures: "a holistically planned new settlement which enhances the natural environment and offers high-quality affordable housing and locally accessible work in beautiful, healthy and sociable communities" (Town and Country Planning Association 2014b, 3). The TCPA continues to produce substantive advocacy documents (Town and Country Planning Association 2007, 2011, 2012a, 2014a, 2014b, 2017). The ruling idea that new towns still can contribute to advancing sustainable development is also promoted by international organizations (Gaborit 2014) and surfaced in discussions for a "new urban agenda" at the Habitat III conference in Quito in October 2016.

Actual outcomes of the green town movement point to continuing difficulties in challenging the path dependency of market-driven urban development. From the late 1970s, the TCPA propounded a scheme for a conservation-oriented and human-scaled "Third Garden City" of ten thousand residents within the grid of Milton Keynes. Hall (1980, 33) hailed it as "absolutely timely . . . at a period when both right-wing free enterprise and left-wing anarchistic philosophies are rejecting the notion of large-scale bureaucratic planning." It eventually transmuted into the Lightmoor "model urban village" project at Telford New Town with support from the Bournville Village Trust. The renaissance of garden city ideas led by TCPA campaigning was confirmed in 2007 when the British government committed to building a series of new, freestanding zero-carbon "eco-towns." Starts were made in places such as Whitehill and Bordern ("Hampshire's Green Town"), but flawed policy development hampered implementation (Warwick 2015). The concept of constructing new communities resurfaced at Ebbsfleet, east of London, in 2014. Regardless, there is a strong sense of Howard's legacy persisting as one guiding force in U.K. planning (S. V. Ward 2016).

The Global New Town

There are now hundreds of "new" planned settlements in countless countries with an aggregate population in the millions. This is still small fry compared to a total world urban population in the billions but nevertheless impressive. The pronouncement in the early 1950s that the British new towns had failed "socially, economically, and architecturally" (Richards 1953, 29) was rather premature given that they alone now house nearly three million people and over one million jobs. New towns are a genuine global phenomenon represented on every inhabited continent. The diffusion wave has spread from economically developed countries at the start of the twentieth century to newly industrialized and then developing countries at the beginning of the twenty-first (Tan 2010).

Like all planning systems and artifacts, their diverse forms essentially reflect the interaction of unique political economies with contrasting planning traditions (Sanyal 2005). Three junctures capture these contrasting cultural traditions. Before World War II, the major divide was between garden city and socialist new town modes. Garden city standards were based on Raymond Unwin's (1912) creed of "nothing gained by overcrowding" and embodied a strong ideology of home-and-garden within localized suburban neighborhoods. Soviet new town planners shared similar modernist ambitions but expressed them in different ways via a top-down ideological model favoring uniform multiunit housing in more compact communities and servicing industrial development (Underhill 1990; Wakeman 2014b). The pathway adopted by the USSR was taken up by Eastern European nations, as well as China (Bernhardt 2005). A second dimension of difference reached its zenith in the 1970s as comparative studies pinpointed governance, density, and tenure contrasts between the national British model and the decentralized American response, with the former deemed more successful (Corden 1977; Robinson 1975). A third divide evident today is the distinctive governance of most Chinese new cities, which reflect a higher degree of local state entrepreneurialism than countenanced in other jurisdictions (Jie 2015; F. Wu and Phelps 2011).

While frequently airbrushed from the historical record, the initiation, let alone subsequent evolution of new communities, has often been contested in both ideals and implementation. Turning first to ideals, much of the received wisdom through the literature celebrates new town advocates rather than their critics, but the latter have also shaped community and professional receptiveness. In 1939, when Clarence Stein lectured his peers with inspiring words on the need to start afresh rather than rebuild old cities, the reaction was decidedly mixed. Harland Bartholomew spoke for the majority in maintaining that Stein was ignoring "the great economic problems of the central city, and is concerned only with the ideal design of a certain small sector in the suburban territory" (Bartholomew in Stein 1939, 42). Of a later generation and from a different perspective that still resonates today, Jane Jacobs saw little value in the U.S. greenbelt town experience or Howard's "scheme for isolated towns" (Jacobs [1961] 1993, 568). And notwithstanding his involvement in Ciudad Guyana (1961), Lloyd Rodwin was a long-term academic critic of simplistic garden city ideals (Rodwin 1945), the limited achievements of the Mark 1 British new towns (Rodwin 1956), and the irrelevance of the U.S. new communities program given more pressing urban issues in the 1970s (Evans and Rodwin 1979). In terms of implementation, the new town in history seems often to be conveyed as peacefully colonizing terra nullius, but difficulties for original land owners and inhabitants have been endemic. Local opposition to the designation of Stevenage as the first British new town in 1946 was of such strength as to jeopardize the entire new town program (S. V. Ward 2015). Its renaming as "Silkingrad" by detractors recalled the negative branding of the U.S. greenbelt towns as "Tugwelltowns" as "the start of a socialist takeover" (Hall 2014, 142). Disgruntlement of displaced farmers is a story repeated widely even into the Chinese new city era and as dramatically captured by isolated "nail houses" stubbornly nailed down in holding out against the tide of modern progress (Keeton 2011). Here and in India, the dispossession process has occasionally turned violent (L. Wang, Kundu, and Chen 2010). The struggles of newcomers, pitted against longer-standing rural residents, authorities, architects, and developers, is undeniable (A. Alexander 2009; Llewellyn 2004). Yet the stories recovered by Clapson (1997) belie the stereotyped assessments of British new towns as bland, alienating subtopias. Evaluations by pioneering colonists of privatopias have tended to be more positive since the 1970s (Burby and Weiss 1976). The exclusivity of the newest new towns in Asia nevertheless remains problematic, with Jacquemin's (1999) analysis of the inexorable gentrification of Navi Mumbai anticipating an almost universal process. A counterprocess also heightening social division is the "inevitable encroachment of the excluded population on these new zones of exclusivity" (Bhattacharya and Sanyal 2011, 41).

New Town Design

A final attribute in this brief history is the significance of new towns in urban design terms. Forsyth (2011, 373) has already canvassed responses to design objectives and concludes that the "palette" has changed little in a century, with formulas revolving around neighborhoods, self-containment, balanced development, open space, and the automobile. Branch (1983, 147) codified a whole digest of design principles as testimony to a "consensus of city planning thought and learning from experience." The new town blueprint that crystallized in the 1940s proved particularly enduring with the neighborhood unit as the building block, with road hierarchies, land-use zoning, civic centers, employment zones, and greenbelts. This was a Western model that was vigorously exported and usually well received. While the British new town underwent a demonstrable metamorphosis from the 1940s to the 1970s—producing radical prototypes including Cumbernauld (1956), with its central civic megastructure and spread-city Milton Keynes (1970)—Osborn and Whittick (1977, 459) conclude that central ideas around housing, parks, town centers, and aesthetics nonetheless "stood the test of time." While there are remarkable similarities through particular phases globally, also evident is the variety of models sharing common goals. This is not surprising given that two wellsprings of modern thought, the garden city and the radiant city, shared fundamental aims of decongesting the city, increasing open space, and facilitating mobility.

One justification advanced for investing in new towns has been the opportunities presented for experimentation and education in demonstrating "alternate modes of urban living" (Galantay 1975, 80). There has been a succession of innovations and design refinements linked to new towns. The planned suburbanism of the two British garden cities was totemic. Later came application of Radburn principles, separating people from cars, and the further novelty of pedestrianized shopping centers. The French new towns were laboratories for bold design solutions brokered through architectural and planning competitions, and not always well received by the public, a situation emulated by the new vertical cities in Asia. Langford and Bell (1975) catalogue twenty-eight physical, twenty social, and two economic innovations associated with the fourteen funded Title VII new communities in the United States. Ecological planning breakthroughs were made in some developments such as The Woodlands through habitat conservation, natural drainage, and aquifer protection (Forsyth 2005). The city-state new towns pointed the way toward transit-oriented development. In these various ways, new towns thus "continue to capture the imagination of urban designers interested in building concepts from the ground up" (Forsyth 2011, 277).

Helping to frame understanding of how new towns became global and their variety in design is the emerging body of literature on the mechanisms and implications of urban policy transfer (Healey and Upton 2010), which welds onto a foundation of diffusion studies in planning history (S. V. Ward 2000). At the macro level, the new town movement can be caricatured as the product of geopolitics and market-driven globalization. This has been accelerated by the interconnectedness of the modern world but has been there from the earliest days of the planning movement.

World War II and its ending promoted diffusion of modernist ideas through the international dispersal of design and planning talent as well as receptivity among governing elites to technocratic problem solving. The new town as the "idyllic model of the urban future" was a centerpiece in the transnational circulation of knowledge through printed information, study tours, consultancies, conferences, and exhibitions (Wakeman 2014a, 157). Both the American and British governments actively promoted their nation's expertise through international activities in a planning version of postwar "soft power" (Amati and Freestone 2014). Thirty years later, both these nations demanded roles in the new International New Towns Association to ensure influence on the global stage. Britain even established a British Urban Development Services Unit in 1976, based in Milton Keynes, to export its expertise in new town planning and development (Baeten 2010).

Through the 1960s and 1970s many leading Western architects and planning consultants picked up new town design commissions. Prominent among them was Constantine Doxiadis, whose expertise in ekistics methodology was easily adapted to diverse contexts (Provoost and Vanstiphout 2011). By the 1990s a "global intelligence corps" of so called starchitects and international consultants was well placed to service design opportunities coming in Asia (Olds 2001). Chinese and Indonesian expertise was also exported through Asia and Africa. Indeed, a complete package was open to the most entrepreneurially minded development interests: the "city in a box" (Oosterman 2012).

Interspersed with the success stories and intriguing connections are the dysfunctional products of international knowledge transfer: the transplanted application of culturally incongruous British formulas in the 1950s (Y.-W. Wang and Heath 2010); the appeal of Singapore's high-density solution minus its social housing underpinnings paving the way for high-income enclaves (Huat 2011); the imposition of grandiose new city plans with little respect for local conditions (C. Q. L. Xue, Wang, and Tsai 2013); and ersatz reproductions of European quarters in Shanghai's new cities emulating the Dubai model (den Hartog 2010). Also evident is the sameness of many of the new city landscapes in Asia with "rigorous, rectilinear, and simplified urban design" in mass production (Keeton 2011, 37). The effect is to induce a certain placelessness in the outcomes even if residents themselves inevitably have coping mechanisms (Freestone and Liu 2016). So just as state-overseen postwar new towns were often critiqued as bland and desultory, so too can the free market create "remarkably similar places, wherever they might be" (Winton 2009, 185).

Conclusion

The high point of new towns with their roots in the social reform movement stretched from the 1940s into the 1970s. Through this period, they became established as components of national urban policies driven by the social reform of beneficent welfare states. Leading up to that were several decades of propaganda, advocacy, and experimentation holding that urban systems might be restructured in the public interest. Nevertheless, when these programs were implemented under state direction or at least financial involvement, it is surprising how little intensive study on the economic and social consequences was undertaken. These programs were thus ideological products driven more by rhetoric than undeniable evidence that they substantially improved social equity.

As the world fundamentally changed in the late twentieth century, so too did planning, although not always along optimal pathways (Castells 1992). The new town had to be rethought as part of this critical juncture. The idealistic strand has largely reworked the historic garden city model to apply to sustainable large-scale town extensions. In a postconsensus world, as social mission transformed into economic product, new towns were interpreted in different ways. Whereas the roots of the new town were a vehement condemnation if not "a deep hatred of the disorder and blight of big cities" (Wakeman 2014a, 159), the megaproject cities now testify to the "triumph of the city" (Glaeser 2011).

New towns today are not the pristine icons on a green baize backdrop suggested by the simplicities of traditional town and country planning. Urban territories today are a challenging mix of spaces, forms, and functionalities. Within that context they are but one constituent element. It is little wonder that even the main advocacy groups without exception have widened their ambit, for example the International New Towns Association, known as the International Urban Development Association since the early 1990s. Also, while new towns have not completely ceded claims to be innovative urban milieus, in that category they are joined and frankly overwhelmed by many different kinds of urban environments: witness the "grand tour" of European hot spots reported by Hall and Falk (2014, 4). New towns have been no match for old cities. In aggregate, the results are modest; they have not attained the numbers and significance envisioned by their proponents.

But three final observations about their continuing value in conceptual, developmental, and historical terms are proffered. First, and a step back from actual development, is a reaffirmation of the notion of tabula rasa towns and settlement systems as an invaluable heuristic device for conceptualizing, tracking, and evaluating urban futures (Reiner 1963; Wakeman 2016; Weller and Bolleter 2013). Visioning is a fundamental planning technique in establishing desired directions and scenarios (Freestone 2012; Hopkins and Zapata 2007). This value spills into planning advocacy, community deliberations, and planning education through design studios.

Developmentally, even with seemingly little prospect of a grand new town renaissance, new towns remain an urban artifact that cannot be ignored. They are not frozen in time and, throughout their lifetimes, have had to respond to new national priorities, technologies, consumer sentiments, design technologies, and financial mechanisms. They face urban renewal challenges comparable to conventional city and suburban zones (Gaborit 2010). They are major urban investments that must be maintained and enhanced (A. Alexander 2009). One important dimension is their heritage values, which need to be acknowledged and respected (Sies, Gournay, and Freestone 2019).

Historically, new towns provide a tremendous focus in urban studies for appreciating broader themes in urban development. They have metamorphosed from beacons of the welfare state—a veritable "essay in civilization" in the 1940s (McCallister 1946, 8)—to agents of "inter-city rivalry and globalized contingency" (Roy and Ong 2011, xv) in a neoliberal world. The time line at the core of this chapter tacitly captures the broader sweep of planning thought from experimentalism and innovation through the first half of the twentieth century, to the "golden years" driven by consensus as to rational-comprehensive planning, and to paradigm meltdown with planning pulled in different and often antithetical directions (Sanyal 2005). In these terms the new cities of China, for example, now illustrate the "new style" of postreform approaches "more than any other type of planning" (F. Wu 2015, 187). New towns are less and less places apart—their challenges, their lessons, their contribution to knowledge, and their rationale as places to study are now universal.

Acknowledgments

My thanks to Nicola Pullan for research assistance in the initial phase of this project; to Ann Forsyth for her critique of an earlier version of this chapter; and for the insights and feedback garnered at the New Towns Symposium at Harvard University in September 2016.

2

The Promises and Pitfalls of New Towns

Ann Forsyth

New Towns: Ideals and Experiences

Built from scratch, new towns can implement new concepts about efficient and affordable development, socially balanced communities, environmentally sensitive design, innovative industrial spaces, healthy place making, and supportive services. Even when new towns have been built much as planned, however, critics have often found them to fall short of their initial aims and general ideas about what makes a great place to live. It is easy enough to do an innovative subdivision or neighborhood, but a whole new town is far more complex. This chapter examines these two central issues: Given their potential, why have new towns not spread even further? Given their difficulty, why have they been attempted at all?

The contemporary era of new town development commenced in the late nineteenth century, but it was in the 1950s through the 1970s that new town starts reached their peak, as governments and developers around the world tried to realize the promise of the type. By the 1980s, however, they were in decline, attesting to both the difficulty of creating such developments and the uncertainty of their benefits. Indeed, for a decade or two it seemed that critics, who had also increased in numbers in the midcentury, were on the winning side. A recent resurgence in the type, particularly in East Asia, the Middle East, South Asia, and Africa, however, begs the question, is anything new? Are there new reasons why the benefits of such developments may be outweighing the costs?

The short story is that perhaps with so much urbanization happening, the balance has been tipped again toward planned developments. The most idealistic of the current wave of developments focus on topics of substantial current concern such as providing sustainability benefits and industrial innovation. Whether this contemporary upswing represents just slightly better-planned versions of contemporary suburbs remains an open question. Understanding the potential and pitfalls of new towns can help guide development in more positive directions.

Arguments about a topic require a subject. As noted in the introduction, there is no clear consensus on the definition of a new town, but this chapter focuses on satellite and freestanding or independent new towns rather than new-towns-in-town, planned extensions to existing developments, or largely residential developments (Alonso 1970; Forsyth 2003, 2005). New towns need to have substantial size so they can have mixed uses that could plausibly allow self-containment in jobs, residences, and other resources for daily living. For all but the most remote such towns, there is likely to be significant exchange with nearby areas, however. Because of their size and scope, new towns are relatively difficult to develop but also have potential to reap larger long-term benefits than smaller and more incrementally developed areas might. However, as the database of new towns in Appendix 2 demonstrates, between 1900 and the 1970s, many hundreds of such new towns were started and were successful enough that their populations today are now over thirty thousand. More have been developed since their resurgence in the 1990s. Of course, this list contains places of varied quality. Relatively few demonstrate the best features of the type, the result of aiming to be somewhat comprehensive in the listing.

The Rise and Fall of Twentieth-Century New Towns

The history of debates over new towns has some relation to the pattern of actual development. The inventory in Appendix 2 demonstrates that the early part of the twentieth century was dominated by new towns built in Russia, both before and after the Russian revolution. These were part of policies to limit city size, settle more remote areas, promote economic development, and create a Russian presence in other parts of the Soviet Union (Underhill 1990, 264). New towns really took off globally in the period starting at the end of the Second World War through the financial crises of the mid-1970s. Looking only at those developments that have reached thirty thousand in population by 2015, according to the inventory compiled for this book, approximately sixty were started in the 1940s, most in the latter part of the decade, over 110 in each of the 1950s and 1960s, and almost ninety in the 1970s. Of course, there is much debate about whether all these are good examples of new towns. Undeniably, however, this was the high point in activity about large-scale, comprehensive development (Figure 2.1).

In the peak period of the 1940s through the 1970s, new town starts not only increased in number, but they diversified geographically, reaching every inhabited continent. Table 2.1 shows that in the 1970s there were eight countries with five or more inventory new town starts. Given that many new towns failed early, developed slowly, or were never intended to reach populations as high as thirty thousand, the actual numbers of starts were likely significantly higher. New towns appeared

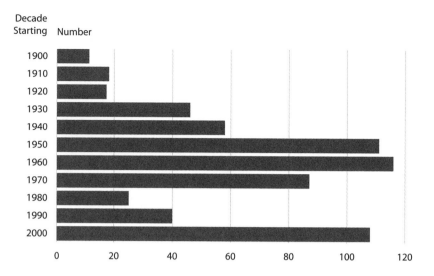

Decade Starting / Number

(chart showing bars for decades starting 1900 through 2000, with horizontal axis from 0 to 120)

throughout the world from Algeria, Argentina, Australia, and Azerbaijan, to the UAE, Uganda, Ukraine, Uzbekistan, Venezuela, Vietnam, Zambia, and Zimbabwe.[1] This is also a period that was a high point in debates about new towns.

By 1980, development had plummeted, however, with only twenty-six new towns started in the whole decade. Only one of these, Rancho Santa Margarita, was in the United States; the closest places to Western Europe were in Turkey and Russia; South Korea, China, and Egypt each started three new towns. Of course, some new towns that had been started earlier had gained enough momentum to keep going. The end, however, seemed to be near for large-scale new towns, replaced by smaller developments and less comprehensive planned communities in all but exceptional cases.

Table 2.1. Countries with Five or More New Towns by Decade

Decade	1940s	1950s	1960s	1970s	1980s	1990s	2000s
Total new towns	58	111	116	87	25	40	109
Countries with five or more new towns	Russia 14	Russia 26	U.S. 21	Singapore 10		China 11	China 50
	U.K. 10	India 11	U.K. 15	Russia 6		Singapore 5	India 11
	India 6	Israel 10	Russia 9	Japan 6			
		China 10	Japan 8	S. Africa 6			
		U.S. 7	Netherlands 5	U.S. 5			
			France 5	India 5			
				Egypt 5			
				China 5			

Source: New towns database in Appendix 2.
Notes: Prior to the 1940s there was only one country per decade with five or more new towns, Russia. China includes Hong Kong.

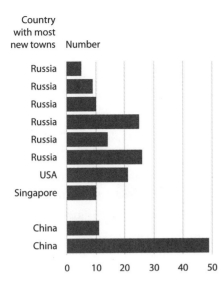

Country with most new towns	Number

Figure 2.1. Numbers of large-scale new towns by decade. *Source*: New towns database in Appendix 2. *Notes*: Includes only those that reached population of thirty thousand by 2015.

Starting in the late 1990s, the tide turned. Changing policy to encourage urbanization, China embarked on a large program. How large the Chinese program is depends on how one defines new towns. However, it includes at least dozens and perhaps hundreds of new towns, many of very substantial size. Elsewhere in Asia, the Middle East, and Africa still more new towns have been proposed. As indicated earlier, the golden period of new town development was littered with failed proposals, and it is likely the same will be the case in this period. It is notable, however, that the type has a major resurgence in some important and quickly growing countries. China has been dominant, but India, Saudi Arabia, Singapore, and Kenya are also representative of the kinds of places where new towns are being proposed and built. Even Russia has had new proposals. Why the resurgence? Which proposed benefits of new towns might be still relevant today, and which criticisms may have been overcome?

Why Attempt a New Town?

For innovations to spread widely, they either need to fulfill a very common human need or desire, or they must have multiple strengths so that different aspects appeal to different constituencies. To proponents, new towns have appeared to do both, providing basic living space and being a plausible way to achieve various goals from economic innovation to environmental balance. New towns could be more comprehensive, efficient, and potentially trouble-free than other types of development from suburban subdivisions to worker housing schemes. They have seemed to be a viable alternative to generic suburban development, or sprawl, criticized for a variety of reasons: social, aesthetic, environmental, economic, cultural, and infrastructural (see reviews in Eichler and Kaplan 1967, 4–10; Forsyth 2005, 2011; Gans 1963; Popenoe 1977, 2–8).

However, within the broad range of benefits or planned communities, different interests have emphasized a varied set of outputs. Table 2.2 presents a summary of the main benefits proposed over the last century or so in the English-language literature.

First, *demographic and economic* reasons include fostering and channeling growth. The central idea of many new towns has been to improve existing urban areas. New towns would provide attractive new alternatives where people and industries could find new space. Some have been in nearby satellite locations, but others have been developed more remotely for resource-dependent industries, or to foster innovation, such as the science city type. A contemporary alternative is to deal with populations displaced by climate change, providing new environments that maybe more attractive, resilient, and efficient than incremental development. This is one of the few really new purposes suggested in the twenty-first century (see Chapter 22). In the 1960s, James Rouse also suggested approaching the building of new towns as an industry in its own right, imagining a General Motors for city building (Rouse quoted in Breckenfeld 1971, 177–78).

Urban planners and designers have seen new towns as an alternative to urban sprawl, saving countryside, and creating better-quality urban environments, generally balancing the needs of people and nature, jobs and housing. Social and physical infrastructure could be provided in an efficient manner up front, with economies of scale, rather than retrofitted into incrementally developed areas at substantially more expense. Affordability could be enhanced by developing attractive whole communities on inexpensive land. Comprehensive planning could create opportunities for specific innovations from modernist megastructures and safety-supporting traffic separation to efficient green infrastructure and promising new housing types (Alonso 1970). Finally, planners and designers could achieve social goals. For example, parts of suburbia attract young families who first need schools, then colleges, wasting facilities. New towns could do better, improving function and also potentially fostering more interaction among groups. Alternatively, new towns might focus on supporting particular populations. In the U.K., many early new towns promised better housing for the working class. Less common among large-scale new towns, but of potential importance, are green developments for those inclined toward environmental conservation (Forsyth and Crewe 2011).

In *business* terms, new towns have the potential for inbuilt diversification. Real estate is very cyclical, but not every part of the industry is in decline at the same time—when for-sale residential demand is low, office and rental housing may be high. A new town can adjust its development phasing to take advantage of sectors that are in demand, though not all do it. Their comprehensive design is also thought

Table 2.2. Proposed Benefits of New Towns

Issue	Benefits
Demographic and economic	
Channel population increase	• Absorb general **population growth** in a planned way. • Redirect rural to urban or international **migrants** to new areas.
Shift population to better locations	• **Deconcentrate** existing very high density urban areas to compact new developments. • Foster climate change adaptation by providing attractive, efficient, and less vulnerable **alternative communities**.
Foster **economic growth** and innovation	• Provide housing for workers in industry in **remote** locations and/or decentralized out of core cities. • Create **new industrial space** for various industries with a balance of jobs and housing for different kinds of workers. • Create an **innovative milieu,** e.g., the science city. • Create a new kind of **city-development industry**.
Urban planning and design	
Solve problems with existing **urban patterns**	• Provide an **alternative** to incremental and uncoordinated suburban growth (sprawl)—phased and coordinated—preserving the countryside and structuring regions in a positive way. • **Relieve problems** with core city congestion and poor housing quality. • Provide better options for life in **remote** resource extraction areas.
Create **efficient** areas to save long-term costs	• Use nonurban (inexpensive) land to create an environment as attractive as urban areas, with some savings in the **cost of land**. • Provide **physical infrastructure** in a comprehensive/phased manner early in the development, making it less expensive to provide. • Provide infrastructure such as schools, shops, community centers, and employment, to **reduce social costs** of isolation etc.
Create more **balanced communities**	• Create balanced areas—with a mix of housing costs and types, social groups, jobs and housing, people and nature, industry and agriculture. This would create a place **supporting all aspects of daily life** and/or a microcosm of the region. • Balance and the relatively **smaller size** of new towns—compared with scattered generic development—would provide number of associated benefits from shorter trip lengths, to faster access to countryside, and a stronger sense of community.
Demonstrate/test **innovative** planning, design, and development	• Demonstrate innovative and **comprehensive** planning and design that would create better, more livable places and that could be implemented in developments beyond new towns. • Demonstrate **particular innovations** in areas such as aesthetics, social planning, economic development, transportation, open space planning, housing design, regulation, and real estate development processes. A recent iteration has been making sustainable or resilient communities through better planning, e.g., reducing energy use and greenhouse gas production.
Create environments that achieve **social goals**	• Develop in areas where land is inexpensive, **combining affordability with quality**. • Create **socially mixed** areas to provide beneficial interaction between key population groups (e.g., class, race, age) and help provide services in a phased manner. • Create enclaves for people with similar **needs or perspectives** to better tailor support (e.g., older people needing services, the working class needing low-cost housing, environmentalists wanting ecological performance). • Provide a **sense of community** due to small scale of residential neighborhoods and associated community facilities and resident groups.
Business	
Provide **market edge**	• The mixed use character of development creates inbuilt **diversification** to ride out real estate cycles in particular sectors. • Providing a range of housing options integrated with commercial and industrial space allows developers to **attract high-quality employers**.
Political	
Implement **political and colonial** policies	• Create viable and balanced towns in **colonial** settings. • Stake a **claim** to territory that is contested. • Develop **new capital** cities away from existing urban areas to unify a country or province. • Create a **visible product** of a regime typically with an outcome such as economic development.

Sources: Alonso (1970); Fava (1973); Finley (1969); Forsyth (2005, 2011); Osborn and Whittick (1977).
Note: Sources include proponents, critics, and analysts.

to attract employers interested in high-quality environments for a range of workers, and those across the workforce interested in short commutes.

Finally, some new towns have been built with *political* aims to claim and unify territories, from colonial settlements to new capital cities, and have less to do with the needs of urban areas or the aspirations of urban and regional planning. While physically similar to mainstream new town developments, these have caused some ambivalence among planners. Some have been controversial more generally—some Israeli settlements are large enough to be classified as new towns.

Why Have They Not Spread Further?

Efficient, balanced, innovative, and socially supportive, new towns have had great promise. Fairly early on it became clear, however, that new towns did not achieve all their aims. Even the most ardent proponents would admit that only a small proportion of the new towns in the inventory are really excellent examples of the type. In addition, their idealism and aims to create high-quality environments from the start brought on some additional problems (Table 2.3).

One of the most fundamental criticisms is that many of the benefits of new towns proclaimed by supporters have not been *proven*. Positive outcomes can be obtained, at least in part, by using other, less expensive and complex forms of development, including new neighborhoods or incremental redevelopment. Many new towns have failed to reach their target populations, indicating that potential residents are not sure the new towns can provide all the benefits proposed.

New towns are also notoriously *difficult to get off the ground*. It is a complex undertaking to find land to provide infrastructure early enough to make residents and business people confident in the new town's quality. Planning permissions can be incredibly tedious in all but the most authoritarian or laissez-faire situations; once overall permission is provided, typically numerous more specific approvals are needed. Because they are so complex, new towns also require coordination with many agencies and levels of government from transportation to education, and planning to health. This is difficult for both private developers and new town government development agencies. Except in the case of large centrally allocated public housing developments, which have their own problems, developments also need to be vigorously marketed to a relatively large proportion of a region's home buyers or renters. While the diversity of housing types in new towns can help this occur, it can only do so much. With these difficulties, it can be hard to obtain financing.

Like more generic suburbia, new towns in their first years are often physically distant from major population centers creating *social stresses*. Isolation is exacer-

Table 2.3. Proposed Problems with New Towns

Issue	Problem
Lack of overall success	
Benefits **not proven**	• While new towns may provide some of the proposed benefits, so do other forms of urban development, such as smaller planned neighborhoods that are typically **less expensive**.
Problems reaching target **populations**	• In many countries, new towns have **failed to attract the populations** they were planned for—owing to location, employment opportunities, high relative cost, etc. • New towns created using inexpensive government land distributed through nonmarket mechanisms can promote **speculation,** hurting the people they aim to help (Hegazy and Moustafa 2013).
Practical difficulties	
Difficulty **getting started**	• **Land assembly** is difficult and costly. • **High-quality up-front infrastructure** to attract population is expensive in the short term (even if efficient in the long term). • **Planning permissions** can take a great deal of time. • Financial entities are often **unwilling to lend** money.
Complex and expensive development	• It is expensive to buy and **hold land** for later development, even if what is held is an option to buy. • Once the new town has started, **additional land costs** rise. • Development involves **organizing multiple levels and divisions of government** over a long time.
Difficulty **Marketing**	• New towns need to capture a large percentage of **regional housing demand**. • New towns need to market **multiple products** and a complex overall package, much of which will be developed only fairly far in the future. They have to project an image of success (A. Alexander 2009).
Social concerns	
Social **isolation** and depression	• In their early years new towns are small and often **isolated** by distance and a lack of fully functioning transport systems—a problem for those stuck there such as children, teens, and stay-at-home parents. • Many people move to new towns seeking some life improvements; disappointment when this does not happen has been called **new town blues** (Forsyth 2005).
Social **communities** do not match expectations.	• Planners imagine that people will **interact** with those nearby, creating networks across social divides, but empirically they interact with those with common interests. • While people tend to shop for groceries nearby, as planned, many other activities happen **outside the neighborhood** (Biddulph 2000). • Designers and planners imagine some spaces will be **bustling** and vital, but physical design alone is often not enough for this to happen.
Lack of diversity	• It is hard to achieve real economic diversity as it can be difficult to provide new low-cost housing in private developments, compared with older and/or informal housing. • Conversely, public developments may aim to provide social housing, excluding some of those at the upper end. • New towns may become less diverse over time—if they are popular they may become more high-end, and if less successful they may tend to the reverse.
Problems with the new town idea	
Problematic **design approach**	• What for some may be an aesthetically orderly environment is for many **too homogenous, boring, or bland,** and indistinguishable from generic suburbia. • Greenfield development on new land has **inherent environmental problems**, even if the development uses "green" building and infrastructure approaches. • Those that are architecturally innovative—from prefabricated housing and underground tunnels to megastructures—often **failed** socially, structurally, or in marketing terms. • Design regulations needed to attract private owners, as well as overly complex attached designs, **constrain flexibility** over time.
Governance issues	• New towns are often run by independent development corporations—public or private—with separate local governments and different geographies making it difficult to have **coherent long-term governance** of the new town. • New towns are built in areas with little existing population and serve regional goals **undermining participatory planning**. • New towns need to have an overall vision somewhat locked in at the start—so developer and residents have some certainty—**limiting later public input**.

(continued)

Table 2.3. Proposed Problems with New Towns *(continued)*

Issue	Problem
Problems with the new town idea *(continued)*	
Spillover effects	• New towns can be expensive, pushing low-income workers or informal uses **into surrounding municipalities** with worse conditions. • New towns may **draw resources away** from other deserving places and populations.
Lack of quality	• Because of the development complexity, it is very **difficult to excel** in all dimensions. • New towns are frequently part of state or national **political agendas**, and their location and development processes may not necessarily reflect the best planning and design principles.

Sources: Aldridge (1979); A. Alexander (2009); Finley (1969); Forsyth (2005); Hegazy and Moustafa (2013); Oxford Brookes University (2006); Provoost (2010); Rumbach (2014).

bated by the expectations new residents have that the new town will improve their quality of life. Disappointment leads to disillusionment. While a clear aim of many planners is to improve social interaction within neighborhoods, assuming that people will make friends with those who are nearby, this outcome has not been convincingly demonstrated (C. Alexander 1965; Biddulph 2000). More practically, with a new development it can be hard to provide a full range of housing types, and thus to attract a very broad social spectrum. Even when this is managed, over time private properties in popular new towns will become more expensive, and the reverse will occur in those that are not as successful, making them less diverse.

Finally there are some fundamental *problems with the very idea* of creating a new town from scratch. Order can be unexciting and bland. Innovation may be unattractive to a wide population and may not age gracefully. While new towns can be built to conserve energy, land, water, and habitat, the core idea of developing on new land raises environmental concerns. In only a few places does the new town government cleanly match a local municipality, making long-term governance quite complex. New towns, being new and large, both impose an outside vision on existing residents and also need to maintain the vision newcomers have bought into. This can lead to inflexible design and planning regulation and a general lack of participation. Many are motivated by political agendas that may not coincide with optimal location and planning approaches, particularly the need to service and revitalize existing areas. Overall few achieve all their aims, undermining overall quality.

Why Has There Been a Resurgence?

By the 1980s it seemed the main question about building large-scale, comprehensively planned new towns had been settled—in general, they were too difficult to build. Many had been proposed but never quite got off the ground. Those that had been built were often slow to turn a profit or were not a big enough improvement on more incremental development to be worth the bother. Banks did not want to finance them, and governments had other priorities.

There were some exceptions. New towns might be needed in remote mining communities. They could be viable if a strong government wanted to use new towns as a growth strategy, perhaps as a science city or a planned satellite in land-constrained areas. But the trend was away from the type.

In the 1990s this started to change. The inventory in Appendix 2 lists over 140 new towns started since 2000 that are already, or potentially will be, over thirty thousand in population; perhaps fifty in China, twenty in India, seven in Kenya, and four each in Algeria, Vietnam, the United States, and Saudi Arabia. It could well be that many of these recent new towns proposed are not as comprehensive and visionary as the best of the midcentury models. Songjiang, a very large new town on the edge of Shanghai, is perhaps not as finely crafted as Vällingby in Sweden (Figure 2.2). But many are or will be much bigger, and some are very well made. In addition, not all proposed developments will be completed. Several large ecocities proposed seem to have ground to a halt or peeled back their more visionary components—from Masdar in the UAE to Dongtan outside Shanghai—but this is a broader problem (Appendix 2; Sze 2015).

In terms of debates, proponents may point to advantages for industrial development (e.g., in India, Kenya, Saudi Arabia, China, Algeria) and urban deconcentration (e.g., in China, Vietnam). Climate change adaptation, or generally green city building, might join the mix. Critics, including some of those in this book, focus on inequality (e.g., in India, Kenya), long commutes, and isolation (e.g., in China). One might also include a lack of overall quality and conflicts over governance and participation. This is perhaps a more realistic set of reasons for critiques of the concept.

Figure 2.2. Songjiang and Vällingby. Photos by Ann Forsyth.

What this means for the long-term future is hard to tell. Obviously, one should not overstate the benefits of new towns. In addition, population growth is slowing in many places, and where growth will continue, for example, in Africa, there may not be the regulatory and economic structure to support this kind of investment beyond a few key locations. That is, the current wave of construction may end.

However, there could also be potential for smaller developments in the twenty thousand to thirty thousand range—such as Hammarby Sjöstad or Izumi Park Town (Crewe and Forsyth 2011; Forsyth and Crewe 2010). This is not as risky as larger developments but still substantial enough. They can be part of a regional plan. Specialized new towns may find a niche as well, for example, as a way of maintaining communities if they need to be relocated from such places as low elevation zones or used to develop innovation economies. In sum, new towns continue to offer intriguing opportunities and challenging problems.

Note

1. Those countries in the database with at least five new towns started between 1945 and 1979 include Australia, Canada, China, Egypt, France, Germany, India, Iran, Israel, Japan, Mexico, the Netherlands, Pakistan, Poland, Russia, Singapore, South Africa, South Korea, Sweden, Ukraine, the United Kingdom, and the United States.

Quality of Life in New Towns

What Do We Know, and What Do We Need to Know?

Robert W. Marans and Ying Xu

Shortly after the modern new town movement began in the U.K. in the late nineteenth century with the establishment of garden cities (Howard [1898] 2003), the Garden Cities Association was created. It later evolved into the British Town and Country Planning Association (TCPA), an organization advocating sound planning for new and established towns and cities. On its ninetieth anniversary, the TCPA selected the theme "British Towns and Quality of Life" for its annual conference (Town and Country Planning 1989). Although many excellent papers were presented, few papers mentioned *quality of life*, and none attempted to define it or discuss its meaning to town residents. Yet the proceedings concluded that "the conference reinforced the argument that the quality of life in British towns can only be improved through effective planning, community participation, and sensitive development, which is what the TCPA exists to promote" (Hall 1989, 13.4).

This chapter discusses the meaning of *quality of life* in the context of cities and towns, or *quality of urban life*, and reviews literature on the quality of life in new towns.[1] It identifies factors or attributes associated with the quality of urban life and outlines key questions that still need to be answered for planners, developers, and government officials interested in creating new towns and other residential environments that enhance the residents' life experiences.

Quality of Life: What Is It?

Quality of life (QOL) generally refers to the well-being of societies and individuals and has been used with reference to international development, health care, employment, and places including countries, cities, and their neighborhoods. In the 1960s, scholars from various disciplines began to question its meaning and how it might be assessed and measured (Campbell and Converse 1972; Moore and Sheldon 1968). Over the years, there have been two approaches to assessing QOL: one using objective indicators and the other relying on more subjective measures (Andelman et al. 1998).[2]

The objective approach typically relies on secondary data aggregated by some geographic unit such as a country, city, or smaller grouping, including census tracts, police precincts, or school districts. These typically include records from governmental units or intergovernmental entities such as the United Nations, or the World Health Organization (e.g., U.N. Habitat 2013).

The subjective approach relies heavily on primary data collected at the disaggregated or individual level using social surveys that address people's behaviors, assessments, and evaluations of different aspects of their lives. Campbell, Converse, and Rodgers's (1976) seminal work best typifies this approach, arguing that quality is a subjective phenomenon and that quality of life assumes different meanings for different individuals. Their conceptual framework considered quality of life based on one's satisfaction with various domains of life: family, marriage, health, financial situation, spirituality, leisure, and place of residence including one's individual dwelling, neighborhood, and community. While community was not the most important predictor, the place where one lived was a factor in determining individual well-being (Campbell, Converse, and Rodgers 1976, 265). Recent research by Marans and Kweon (2011), though, demonstrated that satisfaction with community contributed to overall quality of life, but its impact differed depending on the type of community one lived in. For people living in cities, towns, villages, and rural townships outside metropolitan core areas, community satisfaction was a significant factor in determining their overall well-being.

Place-based conditions, whether human or physical, that are scale dependent (Mulligan, Carruthers, and Cahill 2004) more accurately reflect the quality of life in a *place*, or what has typically been referred to urban quality of life or quality of urban life (QOUL). Over the years, researchers from several disciplines including urban planning have examined QOUL and its associated factors (Marans and Stimson 2011). These factors include not only communities, neighborhoods, and dwellings, but also their social and environmental dimensions. Many are planning and design elements familiar to urban planners, urban designers, and architects, who shape places including new towns, contributing to the residents' well-being.

Quality of Life in New Towns

This section first examines the literature on efforts to measure the overall quality of life of new town residents and is followed by literature covering responses to new town living, including expressions of "community satisfaction" and its determinants. Notably, many of these studies erroneously equate positive sentiments about the community with the residents' overall quality of life.

Quality of Life—Life Satisfaction

The rhetoric among urban planners since the days of the garden city movement is that people living in new, highly planned communities will be happier and more satisfied with their lives than residents of less planned or conventional communities. Questions about the impact of living in new towns in terms of "life satisfaction," "overall well-being," and feelings about "life-as-a-whole" have appeared in surprisingly few surveys.[3]

An early attempt to test the hypothesis that new town living results in a higher quality of life was made in the late 1960s in the United States in a University of Michigan (U-M) study focused on travel patterns among new town residents and people living in paired, less planned communities (Lansing, Marans, and Zehner 1970). Findings showed little variation in levels of life satisfaction among residents in both the new towns and the conventional residential environments. The same conclusion was made in a 1970s University of North Carolina (UNC) study of residents in seventeen new communities including Reston, Virginia; Columbia, Maryland; and residents in a paired set of less planned conventional residential developments (Burby and Weiss 1976; Zehner 1977). It was found that there were no differences in overall life satisfaction between the residents in the new communities and those in the less planned communities. Nonetheless, respondents in the new communities expressed greater satisfaction than their counterparts in the traditional communities with *community livability* and with two important life domains—*use of leisure time* and *personal health*.[4] Moreover, the new community respondents expressed somewhat higher levels of satisfaction with their lives than the Campbell, Converse, and Rodgers (1976) U.S. national sample of participants with comparable household incomes.

Follow-up surveys required respondents in both the new communities and the traditional communities to express *in their own words* what was important to their lives. The results revealed that there were few differences in responses dealing with economic security, family life, and health. Key differences, however, were found with new community residents, who were more likely to mention their engagement in *leisure and recreational activities* and the *physical environment*—two attributes of new towns.[5]

Mixed uses and the provision of community services and facilities—two other features of new towns—were found to have had an impact on residents who moved to them. In the same study, new community residents were more likely to cite community features that improved their lives as a result of moving into the new towns. These include convenient access to schools, doctors, and other services; an improvement in health and medical facilities; more recreational opportunities with superior facilities; better shopping; and more attractive neighborhoods (Burby and Weiss 1976, 387). In particular, these new communities were in some ways able to address the racial and social disparities of the time. Low- and moderate-income families, blacks, and the elderly indicated in the survey that the new communities offered improvements to their living environment.

Quality of Urban Life

As discussed earlier, *quality of urban life* reflects one's feelings about his or her place of residence, including the domains of dwelling, neighborhood, and community. Those feelings are typically expressed in terms of satisfaction/dissatisfaction or likes/dislikes. More recently, the *quality of place* has been examined by looking at people's feelings of belonging, place identification, place attachment, and sense of community (Eng 1996; Jorgensen, Hitchmough, and Dunnett 2007; J. Kim 2001; Manzo and Devine-Wright 2013; Talen 1999).

Following conceptual models developed by Campbell, Converse, and Rodgers (1976) and Marans and Rodgers (1975), the degree of satisfaction with dwelling, neighborhood, or community is a function of one's perceptions and assessments of specific socio-physical attributes of each of the domains, which may be related to the objective measure of the attribute. For example, feelings of crowding in a neighborhood may be a function of the density of dwellings, the size of the buildings, the number of people on the street, and so forth. Community satisfaction reflects one's assessment of specific attributes of the socio-physical environment which may be associated with objective characteristics of those attributes. Those attributes could include the social mix of the community, crime rates, the number and quality of recreational facilities, and the availability of public transportation.[6]

Many of the early British new town studies did not explicitly ask about people's overall satisfaction with their lives. Rather, the studies focused on aspects of community satisfaction by examining residents' feelings about community life and identifying attributes that contribute to those feelings.

Community Life in British New Towns

During the 1960s, a series of empirical studies in postwar British new towns examined resident satisfaction and concluded that most participants were content with their lives. Positive comments gleaned from interviews related to pride in home ownership and improvements in housing quality (University of Strathclyde 1967;

Willmott 1962, 1967), a higher class of people and related higher levels of consumption (Willmott 1964), and clean and healthy surroundings (University of Strathclyde 1967, 1970). At the same time, residents complained about the lack of entertainment, public transportation, and other urban amenities (Willmott 1962, 1967; University of Strathclyde 1967). Community facilities, when they did exist, were unsuccessful in creating either social networks or a sense of place (Willmott 1967). It was suggested that the satisfaction expressed with the British new towns was more likely to reflect improvements to one's personal life rather than attributes of the new town (Hillman 1975). Another study conducted in Hemel Hempstead showed high levels of community satisfaction particularly among older residents and those representing a higher social class (Bardo 1977). However, a later survey in the same community found that levels of satisfaction had declined. The authors attribute this in part to regulations limiting the size of the community and restrictions on housing construction. Such restrictions did not accommodate changes in family composition, which prompted greater dissatisfaction and a desire to move (Bardo and Bardo 1983).

Community Life in U.S. New Towns

Community satisfaction was examined as part of the U-M and the UNC new community studies with comparable findings. Compared to residents in the less planned communities, new community residents, including those living in Columbia and Reston, were more likely to rate their communities as a good or excellent place to live and express high levels of satisfaction (Burby and Weiss 1976; Lansing, Marans, and Zehner 1970). In both studies, positive responses were associated with the concept of a planned community and the environmental and physical amenities imbedded in these communities—abundant open spaces and natural areas; availability of and accessibility to facilities for recreation, shopping, health care, and other community services; good schools; and attractive and quiet neighborhoods. In some instances, expressions of satisfaction with the community differed depending on the type of dwelling one lived in or housing tenure. For instance, health and medical facilities in the new communities were rated more positively by single-family home owners than by owners and renters living in townhouses and apartments. Expressions of dissatisfaction with the community often reflected residents' dissatisfaction with the dwelling and neighborhood (Lansing, Marans, and Zehner 1970).

Subsequent smaller surveys conducted two decades later in three of the new communities—Columbia, Irvine, and The Woodlands—showed levels of satisfaction comparable to those reported in the earlier North Carolina study (see Forsyth 2005, 259–60). In her comprehensive study of the three new towns, Forsyth (2005,

260) concludes that the urban design strategies in the three new towns seem to "have made the planned environments pleasant ones with high quality of life."

Community Life in European and Australian New Towns

New community and new town studies examining community satisfaction have been conducted in other countries with mixed results. While the availability of new housing and job opportunities were in many cases the primary attractions for residents, the planning concept and features of the new towns also contributed to feelings about the community as a place to live. For example, an examination of community satisfaction in two working-class new communities revealed conflicting findings. In the self-contained new town development of Kwinana in Australia, residents expressed a high level of satisfaction (Houghton 1976). On the other hand, Skarholmen, a planned Swedish satellite community consisting of high-rise, high-density dwellings and supporting shopping facilities, was disliked by some residents. Sources of dissatisfaction were the design, which was viewed as "anti-human"; its lack of housing-job links; the prevalence of vandalism in the shopping center; and the limited space and recreational opportunities for children (Gordon and Molin 1972). Hillman (1975) in his review of the new town literature indicates that, despite the criticism of Skarholmen by outsiders and some residents, others living there expressed satisfaction with the community.

More recent studies in the new towns of Almere in the Netherlands (J. Zhou 2012), Springfield Lakes in Australia (Rosenblatt, Cheshire, and Lawrence 2009), and Canberra, the planned capital of Australia (Nakanishi, Sinclair, and Lintern 2013), suggested high levels of community livability, satisfaction, and overall quality of life. The Canberra study examined quality of life in seven districts of the new city that were built at different stages of its evolution and according to different planning principles. Two districts consisting of older neighborhoods were built according to the early garden city principles. Another four districts consisted of neighborhoods built in the 1960s and 1970s following a more conventional new town model. Still another district was built in the 1990s and followed a new urbanism form of development. Using a quality-of-life index consisting of five satisfaction domains, the study showed that the early garden city districts had a relatively high quality of life as did the new urbanism neighborhood. Similar index scores were found in two districts representing the 1960s new town movement. However, two others built during this period had relatively low quality-of-life index scores. In one of the weak districts, access to health care and to social services and prevalence of drug use were rated poorly; while in the other having a low quality-of-life score, safety, housing affordability, and access to health care and social services were the most important factors contributing to the lower quality of life (Nakanishi, Sinclair, and Lintern 2013, 80).

Since the 1980s, several government-sponsored new communities have been built throughout Asia, which prompted researchers to examine living conditions and their impact on residents (Eng 1996; Foo 2000; J. Lee and Yip 2006; Omar 2009; Vasoo 1988; J. Zhou 2012). Although these communities have been referred to as new towns, some do not necessarily satisfy our definition. Rather, they were planned as satellite or residential environments adjacent to an older, established urban center (e.g., Singapore, Hong Kong). Accordingly, they have yet to accommodate the necessities of urban life such as entertainment and employment opportunities. Nonetheless, they offer insights into how new town residents representing different cultures respond to their new living situations.

In general, residential satisfaction is associated with the provision of high-quality community amenities. Most residents, especially those from low-income households, responded positively to their communities, citing improvements in services and facilities compared to where they previously lived. In cases where there were expressions of dissatisfaction (i.e., J. Zhou's (2012) study in Tongzhou, China), urban facilities were not available, and consequently, residents complained that the town lacked an urban vitality. J. Zhou (2012) concluded that urban amenities necessary to support housing should be in place in order to satisfy residents and improve their lives.

In another study assessing the quality of life in thirteen Malaysian state-sponsored new towns, Omar (2009) identifies attributes of each community that were rated on a satisfaction scale by residents. The twenty-two attributes are then ranked from those that are most satisfying (i.e., religious centers, electrical supply, telephone service, primary service, etc.) to attributes that are least satisfying (i.e., commercial services for higher-order goods, taxi services, entertainment centers, children's playgrounds, etc.). Finally, Omar assigned satisfaction scores to each new town and rank-ordered them from those having the highest quality of life to those having the poorest quality of life. Community satisfaction and those attributes contributing to it are equated with quality of life, a misnomer that is prevalent in many of the studies examined.

Sense of Community, Identity, and Attachment

As noted earlier, sense of community and related concepts of sense of place, place attachment, and place identification have been discussed in the new town literature. A comprehensive report on European new towns notes that "a lack of sense of community and shared identity are fundamental problems in new towns" (Gaborit 2010, 15). With respect to creating sense of community through physical design, a number of scholars have been critical of such efforts in British and European new towns (Brooks 1974; Burkhart 1981; J. T. Lang 1994; Talen 1999). Yet the empirical evidence to support these assertions is absent.

Several empirical studies suggest that sense of community does exist in new communities. In Australia's Springfield Lakes, a large master-planned community outside of Brisbane, researchers found that the developers' goal of creating a strong sense of community and building community identity had been realized (Rosenblatt, Cheshire, and Lawrence 2009). Residents responded positively to the development, and a significant number said they moved there because it offered a "sense of community." Similarly, Forsyth (2005, 77) noted an Irvine, California, survey that found a strong sense of community among the residents in each neighborhood.

Sense of community has also been examined in studies of new urbanism communities. J. Kim (2001) and Hashas (2004) used resident surveys and reported that compared to their suburban counterparts, those living in new urbanism communities reported stronger feelings of attachment. A survey in Seaside, Florida, reported similar findings. Most permanent residents and visitors recognized a strong sense of community as the most important attraction in their decision to move or visit (Plas and Lewis 1999).

There is empirical evidence suggesting that the pattern and design of physical features are associated with people's sense of identity and affiliation with a place. In his pilot study of Stevenage, Willmott (1962) reported that because of the low legibility of neighborhoods, residents were most likely to identify with the town and the smaller-scale housing clusters. Similarly, a study of Singapore new towns found that design features such as a pronounced skyline; housing block characteristics including building materials, colors, and artworks; and a distinctive town center and large park were central to place identity (Eng 1996). Finally, Ruggeri's (2009) survey in Irvine revealed that trees and an attractive landscape were major factors in residents' emotional attachment to the community. In sum, urban design strategies may help in creating a strong sense of community through greater legibility, aesthetic innovations, and the provision of public facilities that fosters community pride.

Although some new urbanism studies examined community satisfaction as well as sense of community and community identity, the linkage between these concepts was not made explicit. For example, both Hashas (2004) and Cropper and Brown (2001) found that in new urbanism communities, a strong sense of community among residents did not necessarily result in a higher level of satisfaction with the community. However, residents in the new urbanism communities were more satisfied with the overall design (i.e., inclusive development, mixed incomes, etc.) than their suburban counterparts (Cropper and Brown 2001; Hashas 2004; J. Kim 2001).

Some General Observations

Several observations about the quality of life in new towns can be drawn from the literature. First, compared to living in conventional communities, living in a new town does not have a major effect on the quality of life. It is unlikely that new town living directly contributes to the financial well-being, marriage and family life, living standards, social life, or health and physical well-being of the individuals and households that live there. However, given the location of new towns vis-à-vis employment centers, good transportation, and proximity to nature and facilities including medical and health care, recreation and leisure, and shopping, the quality of life of new town residents is likely to be enhanced. For instance, there may be major health benefits accruing to children and young and older adults who live in proximity to recreational and health-care facilities and programs. While such facilities are sometimes associated with conventional residential developments, they are more likely to be an integral part of new town planning and development, creating a self-sufficient living environment.

Second, people's feelings about living in new towns are attributed in part to their recognition that they live in a well-designed, planned community. Positive comments about living in a self-contained, mixed-use setting that is relatively new were prevalent, particularly in the U.S. new communities but also among residents in other countries.

Third, health and other individual benefits that contribute to quality of life may not be realized during the early stage of new town development when planned facilities and services are not yet available. Much of the research dealing with community satisfaction suggests that a lack of facilities, particularly during the early phases of growth, diminishes community livability. Fourth, opportunities for social engagement and community participation in new towns vary depending on the nature of the physical layout of the community, the auspices under which the community is built and governed, and the characteristics of the residents. Active social engagement is most likely to be found in places with homogenous populations or among people with a strong sense of community (i.e., community spirit). Community cohesion is established through common interests and shared values rather than physical proximity.

Finally, resident satisfaction with the housing unit and the neighborhood in U.S. new towns is comparable to housing and neighborhood satisfaction in conventional communities. Irrespective of country, the research on satisfaction with the residential environment indicates the primacy of dwelling over neighborhood and community. The saying that "a man's home is his castle" is applicable in all cultures.

Future Directions

New town studies focusing on the residents' lives were conducted during the early years of their evolution, whether in the U.K., in the United States, or elsewhere. Considering that new town and new urbanism developments have expanded during the past few decades, particularly outside of the United States, there are opportunities to learn more about the impacts of new community living on the residents' health and well-being. Several directions for future research can be considered.

Replication of New Communities U.S.A.

The seminal work of the North Carolina team in the mid-1970s was reported in *New Communities U.S.A.* (Burby and Weiss, 1976). The report was in part an evaluation of the federally sponsored Urban Growth and New Communities Act passed by the U.S. Congress in 1970. Some of the established new communities were reaching maturity while many were in their infancy and experiencing growing pains. Although there have been intermittent attempts to survey residents of some new towns since the North Carolina study was completed, such comprehensive studies of new towns residents have not been made in nearly a half century, either in the United States or elsewhere.

In addition to its scope, a strength of the North Carolina work was the research design and specifically the pairing of each planned new community including new towns with conventional residential developments of the same vintage. Indeed, the notion of comparative design and analysis from a research perspective gives greater validity and strength when interpreting findings, particularly with respect to people's assessments of their lives and the places they live.

Although a contemporary replication of New Communities U.S.A. would be useful to academics, its potential value is in understanding more about the quality of life of present residents and their responses to a more mature and aging physical and social environment. Such research could determine if the earlier conclusions still hold while informing contemporary policy makers operating in several realms (i.e., social welfare, public health, education, etc.), as well as planners and developers of new residential environments including new towns.

Following New Towns and New Town Residents over Time

Our review indicates that a longitudinal approach to research on quality of urban life and resident satisfaction in new towns has rarely been used (see Bardo and Bardo 1983). It would seem appropriate then to reexamine the earlier new towns to determine how life has changed for long-term residents and how responses to new town living for each demographic cohort differ from comparable cohorts covered in the earlier studies.

Similarly, longitudinal studies of residents living in new and emerging patterns of residential development (i.e., new urbanism communities) should be undertaken. Further efforts to test assumptions regarding built environment effects are needed.

Focusing on Targeted Populations

Consideration should also be given to examining the health and well-being of individuals living in new towns for an extended period. Attention should be given to people at both ends of the age spectrum. Residents could be asked to reflect retrospectively on how growing up in a new town influenced their childhood and teen years. Are they more appreciative of nature and living in a planned residential environment than people who grew up in more conventional communities? Do their early childhood experiences influence their quality of life in terms of long-term friendships and current social networks, career paths, and patterns of leisure? Has growing up in a relatively diverse socioeconomic and ethnic setting had a bearing on their political and social outlook including their views about different racial and ethnic groups? Longitudinal studies could also be conducted to track a sample of residents to assess life changes, housing histories, and their perceptions and evaluations of the socio-physical setting. Motivating factors for moving away from their original new towns would shed light on the inability of the new town to accommodate the changing needs of the individual or the family.

For older people living in new towns, how have their lives changed over time? To what extent has the socio-physical environment contributed to or hindered successful aging? Successful aging has been described as having three key components: a low risk of disease and disease-related disabilities, maintenance of high mental and physical functioning, and continued engagement with life including relations with others and productive activity—either paid or volunteered (J. Rowe and Kahn 1998, 2015). These components are related to overall well-being and quality of life, which can be influenced by the residential environment including its socioeconomic makeup and its man-made and natural features.

Exploring Physical Attributes Contributing to Community Satisfaction, Sense of Community, and Health

Campbell, Converse, and Rodgers's (1976) and Marans and Rodgers's (1975) conceptual models suggested how perceptions and evaluations of the socio-physical environmental attributes (i.e., recreational facilities, schools, shopping, landscaping, etc.) could collectively contribute to the understanding of quality of life and particularly the quality of urban life, including community satisfaction. The model also suggests that the perception and evaluation of each attribute vary depending on the characteristics of the attribute. Longitudinal studies focusing on the role of new towns in contributing to the quality of life of their residents would create opportunities to test and modify the model. Ideally, such studies would focus on residents prior to their moving into the new town and periodically after residency is established. At each period, measures would be made of their perceptions and assessments of various attributes in their surroundings, and the objective measures of the attributes themselves.

An early effort to measure both people's feelings and the objective reality in the context of new towns and paired conventional communities was reported as part of the North Carolina study (Burby and Weiss 1976; Zehner 1977). In addition to the comprehensive survey of residents, researchers inventoried commercial, recreational, health-care, and transportation facilities within each community. For the most part, new communities had many amenities, particularly recreational and leisure facilities. The objective measures provide one indicator of community livability; residents' perceptions matter as well (Zehner 1977, 54). Quantity, however, is an insufficient indicator of resident satisfaction. Other facility attributes would need to be taken into account as measures for resident assessments in subsequent new town studies. Further research will also be needed to determine aspects of the community and its neighborhoods that create a sense of community. Similarly, consideration should be given to examining associations between physical attributes of new towns and the physical health of its residents.

Summary

This chapter has examined what is known about the quality of life in new towns and suggested research that would expand the understanding of new towns and how they enhance their residents' quality of life. It has done so by first discussing the meaning of quality of life, an overused phrase that was explored by scholars in the latter part of the twentieth century. A conceptual framework was then presented showing how quality of life from an individual perspective is a function of assessments of different domains of life including the places where people live—their dwellings, neighborhoods, and communities. The challenge for planners, developers, and researchers interested in new towns and other residential settings is to determine the bundle of attributes that are most likely to contribute to the livability and ultimately the overall well-being of residents, irrespective of age, socioeconomic status, and ethnic background.

Notes

1. In the context of this book, new towns are meant to include comprehensively-planned developments on newly urbanized land that boast a mix of uses. They may be satellites of an existing city, linked to it economically and via commuting patterns, or independent places often sited close to natural resources and remote from existing urban areas. They may be developed by the public or private sector or some combination of the two (see Introduction).

2. More recently, approaches that integrate objective and subjective measures have been advocated and operationalized (see McCrea, Western, and Stimson 2011).

3. Several new town studies were conducted in Great Britain during the 1960s but did not explicitly ask about people's overall satisfaction with their lives. Rather, the studies focused on satisfaction with the community and factors liked and disliked about living in the new town. These are discussed in the next section.

4. Compared to those in conventional communities, new community residents also expressed greater satisfaction with recreation and health-care facilities.

5. While these differences were modest and not statistically significant, the new community residents were significantly more likely than those in the conventional communities to mention *social relations* as a factor contributing to their quality of lives.

6. For a more complete discussion of the models, see Marans (2003).

Part II
New Towns Around the World

4

New Towns in the United States

Alexander Garvin

In the United States, the development of planned new communities has been an ongoing activity since the sixteenth century. Assessing all of them is beyond the scope of a short essay. This chapter begins with a snapshot of nine iconic new towns and planned communities developed over the last 150 years: Riverside, Palos Verdes Estates, Country Club District, Levittown, Radburn, Columbia, Reston, The Sea Ranch, and New Albany (Figure 4.1). It then discusses the major issues that arose during their development.

These were private market ventures whose goal was making money, rather than encouraging regional development or some other public purpose, typical of new towns outside the United States. But whether a place is developed by a government agency, a nongovernmental organization (NGO), or a private business, that development entity must be able to finance and manage acquisition of a large enough site; make the necessary site improvements; install adequate infrastructure; create required community facilities and other amenities; and ensure

Figure 4.1. Town Center, Reston, Virginia (2010). Photo by Alexander Garvin.

production of housing that its future residents desire and can afford. Thus, examining the success and failures in the planning, design, financing, and management of these nine American new towns offers the opportunity to understand the problems of new town development anywhere in the world.

Nine Iconic New Towns and Planned Communities

Riverside, Illinois: Begun in 1869, this sixteen-hundred-acre planned community is located nine miles west of Chicago (Figure 4.2). It was designed for the Riverside Improvement Company by Olmsted, Vaux, and Company. The project went bankrupt in 1873. As of 2010, Riverside had just under nine thousand people living in approximately thirty-five hundred residences, mostly single-family houses, and retail businesses serving the community (Riverside Improvement Company 1871).

Palos Verdes Estates, California: This extraordinarily beautiful planned community was begun in 1913 as a $1.5 million land purchase of sixteen thousand acres, located twenty-three miles southwest of Los Angeles, by Frank Vanderlip, president of the National City Bank in New York (Figure 4.3). In 1923, the Palos Verdes Syndicate, which Vanderlip established to develop the property, commissioned Frederick Law Olmsted Jr. and Charles Cheney to create a master plan for a thirty-two-hundred-acre portion of the original land purchase (Beveridge and Hoffman 1987, 98). As of 2010, Palos Verdes Estates had more than 13,500 people living in just over four thousand residences, mostly single-family houses, and retail businesses serving the community (Fink 1966; Morgan 1982).

Figure 4.2. Scottswood Road, Riverside, Illinois (2013). Photo by Alexander Garvin.

Figure 4.3. Via Lazo, Palos Verdes Estates, California (2013). Photo by Alexander Garvin.

Figure 4.4. Crestwood residential neighborhood, Country Club District, Missouri (2010). Photo by Alexander Garvin.

Country Club District, Missouri and Kansas: In 1906, Jesse Clyde Nichols began assembling property four miles north of the Kansas City riverfront and eventually engaged the planning firm of Hare and Hare to prepare a master plan for what became a forty-eight-hundred-acre site (not including subdivisions in Kansas, developed after World War II) (Figure 4.4). As of 2010, Country Club District had just under sixteen thousand people. The southern end of the district includes the one-million-square-foot Country Club Plaza, America's first shopping center expressly designed for motor vehicles (Garvin 2002, 24–25).

Radburn, New Jersey: Arguably, America's most influential planned community was begun in 1928 by the City Housing Corporation to demonstrate of the effectiveness of combining city and country, using capital from investors who were

promised a "limited" return. Radburn was conceived by its architects, Clarence Stein and Henry Wright, as a genuine "garden city" for one square mile of rolling farmland in Fair Lawn, New Jersey, located ten miles west of the George Washington Bridge (Figure 4.5). The project succumbed to the Great Depression and went bankrupt in 1935. All that remains are 149 acres occupied by 430 single-family houses, forty-four two-family houses, ninety row houses, and a ninety-six-unit apartment house, along with a small cluster of convenience stores (Tennenbaum 1996).[1]

Levittown, Long Island, New York: Created between 1947 and 1951 by developer William Levitt and his brother, architect Alfred Levitt, on forty-seven hundred acres of potato fields located about thirty-five miles by parkway from Manhattan, Levittown supplied mass-produced housing at $7,990, a price that middle-class residents could easily afford (Figure 4.6). As of 2010, Levittown had a population of nearly fifty-two thousand people living in just under 17,500 residences, mostly single-family houses, and retail businesses serving the community (Gans 1967).

Columbia, Maryland: During 1962, the Rouse Company began assembling what was eventually eighteen thousand acres, thirty-two miles from Washington, D.C., and twenty-two miles from Baltimore, for a community designed by a group of planners including William Finley and Morton Hoppenfeld. It would eventually include nine villages with local retail facilities, an air-conditioned regional shopping mall with more than two hundred retailers, and a small lakeside town center (Figure 4.7). As of 2010, Columbia had nearly one hundred thousand people living in approximately forty thousand residences, mostly single-family houses. Its thirty-six-hundred-acre open space system includes three lakes, 114 miles of paths and trails, twenty-nine swimming pools, and a wide variety of recreational facilities. Nearly four thousand businesses employing seventy-eight thousand people are located in Columbia (Tennenbaum 1996).[2]

Reston, Virginia: First inhabited in 1964, this seventy-four-hundred-acre new town, located eighteen miles west of Washington, D.C., was designed initially for developer Robert E. Simon by Wittlesey, Conklin, and Rossant (Figure 4.8). As of 2010, Reston had more than fifty-eight thousand people living in some fifteen thousand residences, mostly single-family houses. In addition to a fifty-five-mile-long network of trails and a 476-acre lake park, Reston includes five village centers, a one-million-square-foot town center with shops, restaurants, offices, a cinema, and a hotel, and more than 750 businesses employing almost twenty-two thousand people (Grubisich and McCandless 2006).

Figure 4.5. Green spine, Radburn, New Jersey (2006). Photo by Alexander Garvin.

Figure 4.6. Levittown, Long Island, New York (2006). Photo by Alexander Garvin.

Figure 4.7. Town Center, Columbia, Maryland (2016). Photo by Alexander Garvin.

The Sea Ranch, California: Begun in 1964 as a fifty-two-hundred-acre second-home community located one hundred miles north of San Francisco, this site was developed by Oceanic Properties and designed by Lawrence Halprin and Associates (Figure 4.9). As of 2010, The Sea Ranch had a population of more than thirteen hundred people living in just over eighteen hundred residences; upon completion, there will be an additional six hundred homes. More than half the site consists of dedicated meadows and woodland, owned in common by the residents. The only nonresidential land use is the Sea Ranch Lodge (Lyndon and Alinder 2004).

New Albany, Ohio: Begun in 1985, this twelve-thousand-acre new town, located nineteen miles northwest of Columbus, was conceived by Les Wexner, president and CEO of The Limited, a conglomerate of retail stores. He established the New Albany Company to develop a diversified planned community (Figure 4.10). With the assistance of the Georgetown Company and designs by a combination of architects including Gerald McCue and Jaquelin Robertson and landscape architects Hanna/Olin Ltd., New Albany has evolved from a country club–based community established in the late 1980s to a diversified new town with a twelve-hundred-acre open space network including thirty miles of walking trails, creeks, wetlands, playing fields, a two-hundred-acre learning campus, Market Square (a regional retail hub), seven village retail centers, and a three-thousand-acre business park that, as of 2016, included more than fifty-eight businesses with fourteen thousand employees, occupying 9.8 million square feet. As of 2016 there were more than seventy-seven hundred people living in nearly twenty-seven hundred residences, mostly single-family houses in forty-six individual neighborhoods.[3]

Figure 4.8. Lake Anne Village, Reston, Virginia (2010). Photo by Alexander Garvin.

Figure 4.9. The Sea Ranch, California (2011). Photo by Alexander Garvin.

Figure 4.10. Keswick Drive, New Albany, Ohio (2016). Photo by Alexander Garvin.

Developing New Towns in America

In 1992, when the Urban Land Institute (ULI) prepared a survey of planned communities larger than three hundred acres then underway in the United States, it catalogued 522 projects (plus six in Canada), all of which were private real estate ventures (Urban Land Institute 1992). The same would have been true a century earlier because American planned new towns (with the exception of three very short-lived government experiments described later in this chapter) are the product of the attempt to earn a reasonable return on investments.

The developers' return on investment may come from purchasing inexpensive raw land and, once all necessary approvals for development have been obtained from local authorities or when the supporting infrastructure is essentially in place, selling individual parcels to future home owners for more than the cost of acquisition, site development, and the expenses of owning and managing the property up to its sale. A few new town developers also build houses for sale. Others sell large parcels of land in bulk to home builders, who, in turn, sell lots with newly built houses at retail prices or supplement their revenue with income from major retail facilities patronized by new town residents.

Despite a long history of private development of planned new towns, the U.S. government has occasionally entered the new town business because of either economic circumstances or pressure from crusading reformers advocating alternatives to suburban sprawl. The demand for worker housing was thought essential to boost production during World War I. Consequently, in 1917, Congress created two corporations that produced small planned communities. This program, which was terminated at the end of the war, produced residences for approximately fifteen thousand families and the same number of single workers (Urban Land Institute 1992, 467–68).

During the Great Depression, the Roosevelt administration embarked on a program of building one hundred planned new towns as a means of providing jobs, housing, and a suitable living environment for the unemployed. Only three new towns (Greenbelt, Maryland; Greenhills, Ohio; and Greendale, Wisconsin) were begun before the program was discontinued (Stein 1966, 119–87).

The third federal new town program was initiated by the Nixon administration in the late 1960s. It provided bond guarantees and interest-free loans to cover development costs prior to revenue flow from future town occupants. The program approved thirteen privately developed, greenfield projects plus two planned in-town districts. Only one of the new towns, the Woodlands in suburban Houston, Texas, was developed as initially conceived (Garvin 2013, 470–72).

New Town Design in America

New towns outside the United States tend to be built at a higher density and include high-rise buildings, often in mixed-use districts. While some American new towns include heavily used, concentrated business districts, retailing there is no different from auto-oriented shopping complexes throughout the country. Apartment towers, however, are rare.

Whether privately or publicly financed and developed, American new towns reflect the four basic residential layouts that are common throughout suburbia:

buildings fronting on either rectilinear or curvilinear streets, facing cul-de-sacs, or grouped around a shared open space framework. Rectilinear layouts are common because straight lines are easy to survey, lay out, and then combine into a grid of streets, blocks, and lots; easy to describe in property deeds; and easy to subdivide or recombine (Figure 4.11). Depending on the location and the development entity, however, these rectilinear plats differ in street width, block and lot size, and organization. Once Congress enacted the Northwest Ordinances of 1785 and 1787, most property outside the thirteen original colonies was developed on north-south, east-west grids, six miles square, irrespective of hills, mountains, cliffs, lakes, rivers, or other topographical features (Clawson 1968, 44–53). That is why so many new town plats are so similar.

Glendale, Ohio (1851), Llewellyn Park, New Jersey (1853), and Lake Forest, Illinois (1856) are early examples of American curvilinear planned communities. Nevertheless, it is the work

Figure 4.11. Queens, New York (2016). One of the most common street plats in American planned new communities is the rectilinear grid. Photo by Alexander Garvin.

of Frederick Law Olmsted that is primarily responsible for establishing the design principles for curvilinear new towns (Garvin 2013, 376–82). Starting with Riverside, Illinois, in 1869 and continuing to 1950, a total of 450 subdivisions and new communities were planned by Olmsted partnerships, forty-seven of which involved the senior Olmsted (Beveridge and Hoffman 1987) (Figure 4.12).

Roadways in Olmstedian communities follow the contours of the landscape or cross them at gently sloping inclines to provide vehicles with relatively flat rights-of-way and property owners relatively flat construction sites. The arteries usually are wide enough for at least two lanes of moving traffic with parked vehicles on either side. Streets dominate the appearance of Olmstedian communities because they are flanked with large shade trees that create an arch of foliage enclosing the right-of-way, making the houses, set back from the property line, less prominent.

Olmsted devised this site design because he believed that: "we cannot . . . control the form of the houses which men shall build, we can only, at most, take care that if they build very ugly

Figure 4.12. Plan of Riverside, Illinois (1869). One of the earliest curvilinear plans for a planned new community in America was designed by Frederick Law Olmsted and Calvert Vaux. Reprinted from Olmsted and Vaux (1869).

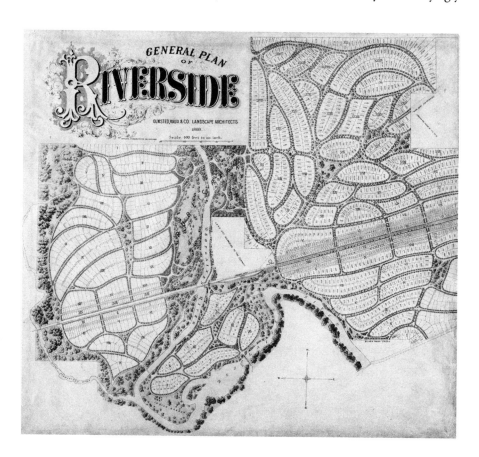

inappropriate houses, they shall not be allowed to force them disagreeably upon our attention when we pass along the road upon which they stand" (Olmsted, Vaux, and Co. 1992, 286). This dominant curvilinear, tree-lined public realm, often with smaller lots, has continued to be a model for suburban subdivisions and new towns to this day, although, only occasionally with the sensitivity or character of the communities designed by the Olmsted firm (Figure 4.13).

Figure 4.13. Tree-lined residential street, Columbia, Maryland (2016). As Frederick Law Olmsted predicted, a tree-lined curvilinear street from which houses are set back, lining green front lawns, keeps them from forcing themselves "upon our attention when we pass along the road." Photo by Alexander Garvin.

The third approach eliminates through traffic and increases privacy by extending straight or curving cul-de-sacs off other arteries (Figure 4.14). The resulting landscape of houses facing the cul-de-sac looks the same as the houses facing a rectilinear or curvilinear grid, except for the turnaround at its end. The absence of people or vehicles passing by the houses on their way somewhere else, however, reduces traffic, noise, and more important, potential social interaction.

The fourth design creates a dominant framework of open space (used in common, primarily by community occupants) (Figure 4.15). Often, the open space is not readily visible from public streets. During the second half of the twentieth century, developers of a growing number of these planned communities began to include swimming pools, tennis courts, and recreational and other community facilities. In some cases, they were gated, restricting use of the open space to residents. By the end of the century, it was estimated that there were twenty thousand such gated communities located in what Blakely and Snyder (1997) dubbed "fortress America."

Figure 4.14. *(Top)* Cul-de-sac, Lincoln, Nebraska (2006). The dead-end streets that are labeled cul-de-sacs increase the sense of privacy by preventing people and vehicles from passing by the houses on their way somewhere else. Photo by Alexander Garvin.

Figure 4.15. *(Bottom)* Cliff Trail, Sea Ranch, California (2011). Half of Sea Ranch is open space used primarily by community occupants. Visitors have nowhere to park, do not have lateral access to the Pacific coast (which is open to everybody), and drive by on their way somewhere else. Photo by Alexander Garvin.

In 1928, when Clarence Stein started designing the new town of Radburn, New Jersey, he had very different objectives in mind. The common open space at Radburn is not gated; it is open to anybody who is aware of its existence. It is set apart from vehicular roadways to provide protected recreational areas that are connected by underpasses, eliminating traffic accidents (Figure 4.16). As Stein explained: "The Radburn Idea" answered "the enigma 'How to live with the auto,' or if you will, 'How to live in spite of it,' . . . [by making] a radical revision of relation of houses, roads, paths, gardens, parks, blocks, and local neighborhoods" (Stein 1966, 41). Perhaps more important, it provided a place for people to do things together, nurturing civil society.

Figure 4.16. Cul-de-sac for motor vehicles and pedestrians and green spine for pedestrians only, Radburn, New Jersey (2006) *Top*: The cars coming to the houses in Radburn park at the back of the property. *Bottom*: Houses at Radburn are turned around so that they front onto a pedestrian spine leading to common open space. Photos by Alexander Garvin.

Figure 4.17. *(Top)* Residential neighborhood, Kentlands, Maryland (2012). Privacy at Kentlands is provided by locating houses close to picket fences that border the sidewalk, while community interaction is intended to be encouraged by the front porches that are a few feet from the sidewalk. Photo by Alexander Garvin.

Figure 4.18. *(Bottom)* Ashton Grove, New Albany, Ohio (2016). The red-brick houses whose appearance is inspired by Georgian-style Virginia provide a traditional trademark within middle America. Photo by Alexander Garvin.

Starting in 1979 with Seaside, Florida, and continuing in 1988 with Kentlands, Maryland, Andres Duany and Elizabeth Plater-Zyberk set out to promote an alternative to suburban sprawl. According to Leccese and McCormick (1999, vii–xi), they called for communities with identifiable centers and edges, yet "integrated with the existing urban pattern," including a "broad spectrum of public and private uses" and "housing types and price levels" occupied by "people of diverse ages, races, and incomes," all organized at a density that supports transit, pedestrian, bicycle, and other transportation alternatives to private automobiles (Figure 4.17). These admirable goals are shared by countless designers, social philosophers, and public officials. Despite the growing popularity of new urbanist desires, there are, with the exception of Celebration, Florida, few prominent new urbanist new towns (Garvin 2013, 479–81).

A desire for picturesque architecture is shared by new urbanist and other new town designers. New Albany, for example, requires houses to be Georgian in style and favors red brick as the predominant material (Figure 4.18). Palos Verdes Estates and other planned communities have design review panels to ensure that anything that is built will have an appearance that is consistent with the rest of the community—a brand that identifies all the buildings within that town.

The Business of New Town Development in America

While the goals and design of any new community can vary, its problems are always the same:

- Acquiring enough contiguous property
- Financing site and infrastructure development
- Providing community facilities and other amenities desired by new town residents
- Satisfying market demand for residential occupancy

Site Acquisition

Obtaining a site for a new town is easy if it requires the purchase of only one property, but very difficult if many transactions are required. Riverside, Illinois, involved the purchase of a sixteen-hundred-acre farm, surrounding a new train station on the Chicago, Burlington, and Quincy Railroad. The site of Palos Verdes Estates had been a vast sixteen-thousand-acre rancho, which included farms growing lima beans. Oceanic Properties acquired the five thousand acres that became The Sea Ranch in a single purchase in 1964.

Figure 4.19. Mission Hills section of Country Club District, Missouri (2016). It took the J. C. Nichols Company decades to assemble the thousands of acres that became this planned new town. Photo by Alexander Garvin.

Many planned new communities do not have the luxury of purchasing a site all at once. Assembling multiple properties at reasonable prices in a short period of time from a variety of owners usually requires secrecy, unidentifiable purchasers, and a purchasing strategy. The Rouse Company, for example, took nine months to make the 144 transactions needed to assemble the site for Columbia. Moreover, buying all the necessary land in a short period of time requires a great deal of money, in the form of either a huge equity investment or a large loan and somewhat less investment capital. For that reason, many new town developers purchase land in stages.

Country Club District, Levittown, and New Albany solved this problem by acquiring sites incrementally, while they were already generating revenue from land sales. In the case of Country Club District this was accidental. J. C. Nichols did not set out to create an entirely new town. He began as a residential developer and added retail centers as a way of competing for customers who were not eager to acquire homes that were far from the services they used daily (Worley 1990) (Figure 4.19). Levittown's incremental purchases were made in response to house sales.

As of 2016 the New Albany Company had purchased approximately 650 individual properties and was still adding land to its holdings (Ebbing 2016). Demand for residences and sites for businesses in New Albany and revenue from those sales is so steady that this new town outgrew its initial master plan years ago. The more that New Albany grows, the more diversified it becomes, illustrating both the importance of size to new town development and incremental acquisition of property to successfully finance its development.

Site Development and Infrastructure Installation

The costs of supplying residential sites for sale to home buyers in a new town include far more than just property acquisition and costs of carrying that investment to completion. The property occupied by a new town has to be graded; utility lines, traffic arteries, and street furniture installed; land for parks and playing areas landscaped; schools and community facilities created; and retail and business districts provided. These costs were not minimized for Reston or Columbia. Some other planned new towns have devised clever ways of reducing spending for site development or infrastructure.

Olmsted Sr. and Vaux transformed the banks of the Des Plaines River, which ran through Riverside, into public parkland, reducing site development costs (Figure 4.20). They excluded sloping river banks that would have been expensive to regrade, also eliminating the cost of restoring building that would be inundated during spring floods. Nevertheless, the plan required paying for the more than fifty thousand cubic yards of MacAdam stone, twenty thousand cubic yards of gravel, and twenty-five thousand cubic yards of excavated earth needed to open forty miles of carriage roads and eighty miles of walks, as well as planting forty-seven thousand shrubs, seven thousand evergreens, and thirty-two thousand deciduous trees (Riverside Improvement Company 1871, 17–18). These costs could not be recouped quickly enough from lot sales and, thus, contributed to Riverside's eventual bankruptcy.

Figure 4.20. Scottswood Road, Riverside, Illinois (2013). Photo by Alexander Garvin.

The plan that Olmsted Jr. and Cheney devised for Palos Verdes Estates reduced the cost of roadways and utility installa-

Figure 4.21. Sea Ranch, California (2013). Investment in infrastructure is minimized by placing clusters of houses on short cul-de-sacs, a short distance from the Pacific Coast Highway (Route 1), while leaving more than half the territory of this planned community undeveloped. Photo by Alexander Garvin.

tion by placing streets on thirteen flat terraces that had been created over millennia by the Pacific Ocean's tidal action. This simultaneously provided sites for two-story buildings on the uphill side of the street. Their second-story windows had views over the roofs of what appeared to be single-story houses on the downhill side of the street. In fact, those downhill houses had a second floor below the street level opening onto the slope below. The resulting waterfront views added to the sales value of sites on both sides of the street.

The cul-de-sac system that Clarence Stein and Henry Wright created for Radburn eliminated a portion of the paving, water mains, and sewers that would normally have been needed had the plan called for a complete grid of through streets. The Sea Ranch, like Radburn, capitalized on its system of cul-de-sacs to make far greater savings by leaving half the land undeveloped to be enjoyed in common by its residents (Figure 4.21). More important, no money needed to be spent paving and installing utility lines within the resulting natural grasslands.

By using natural drainage corridors (albeit in a different fashion from Riverside) and wetlands for runoff retention, New Albany has minimized operating costs. At New Albany, as in any new town, infrastructure and community facilities had to be installed and paid for before there were sufficient occupants to pay for their installation and operation. The company devised a clever way of reducing the initial cost of sidewalks. While streets are installed when a district is ready for development, sidewalks wait until the houses for the site are in construction.

The Ohio state government provides a mechanism for any incorporated city to finance required capital investments, by permitting the creation of a "community district" that can levy an annual fee paid by all occupants who move in after the district is established. The payments can be allocated to pay debt service on bonds issued to cover the cost of infrastructure and community facilities within the district. The New Albany Company initially guaranteed $16.7 million in infrastructure bonds that later would be repaid from proceeds of the city's income tax; further infrastructure and community facilities were financed with $53 million in community district bonds (Ebbing 2016). Thus, unlike any of the other developments discussed in this chapter, state legislation provided the mechanism to prevent capital investments from becoming a headache for New Albany.

Early investment in infrastructure, open space, and recreational facilities, however, also can be the source of problems, because they require major capital expenditures from the very beginning. The Palos Verdes Homes Association, for example, was responsible for maintaining the infrastructure and open space system, which included playgrounds, a country club with a golf course, and four and a half miles of beaches (Figure 4.22). Together they represented more than 25 percent of Palos Verdes Estates. The association had to collect fees to pay for these amenities as well as for the six miles of storm drains, fourteen miles of gas mains, two miles of underground conduits, and more one hundred thousand trees

Figure 4.22. Palos Verdes Estates, California (2013). Photo by Alexander Garvin.

and shrubs—upon their completion in 1924. During the Great Depression, many sites were unoccupied, and, where there were property owners, many were behind in their fees. Accordingly, the association had trouble covering all its expenses, and especially real estate taxes. Every property in this planned community was responsible for paying real estate taxes to Los Angeles County. That included properties occupied by private homes, vacant privately owned land, the country club, the beach, and other open spaces used by residents. By 1938, many privately owned parcels plus the open space that was owned in common by the association were in arrears on real estate tax payments. The solution the association devised included establishing a park and recreation district to which it could deed the parkland, incorporating as the city of Palos Verdes Estates, and deferring back taxes until there was enough revenue to pay them.

Amenities

During the nineteenth century, Minneapolis, Boston, New York, and other cities invested in acquisition and development of networks of open space and recreational facilities in advance of private property development. Cities such as Los Angeles and Atlanta, on the other hand, minimized investment in parkland. In suburban areas, however, where governmental jurisdiction is scattered, similar prior investment in parks and open space is most unusual. This is one of the areas in which planned new towns and planned communities excel. Major investment in public open space from the start provided the very essence of the conception of Palos Verdes Estates, Radburn, Columbia, The Sea Ranch, and New Albany. It provided them with a marketing edge over nearby subdivisions that were splattered across surrounding suburban counties lacking in public open space and recreational facilities.

The marketing edge for the Country Club District came from investment in country clubs and local retail centers, rather than parkland. Similar staged investment occurred at Reston

Figure 4.23. Education complex, New Albany, Ohio (2016). All the schools and their sports facilities are concentrated in a single two-hundred-acre complex patterned after Thomas Jefferson's design for the University of Virginia. Photo by Alexander Garvin.

and New Albany. In New Albany, for example, the two-hundred-acre education campus, inspired by the site plan of the University of Virginia, has developed in stages in tandem with population growth (Figure 4.23).

Time and Money

The business of planned new town development, like all businesses, is a matter of balancing expenses with revenue, with a view to maximizing ongoing net operating income. In the case of conventional real estate projects, revenue flow can begin as soon as a building is ready for occupancy. Generating net operating income from planned new towns, however, takes longer and involves much more than erecting a single building. New town developers must cover the costs of land acquisition, design, extensive site preparation, installation of infrastructure, creation of community facilities and other amenities, and marketing—prior to having sold all the sites to their users. Consequently, they usually seek equity investors and long-term lenders (banks or insurance companies) to provide them with the necessary capital.

This is not just a matter of obtaining adequate capital. Developers must cover the costs of carrying the entire site (debt service to lenders, taxes, operating costs, fees, insurance, etc.) for a long time before obtaining enough revenue from sales and then must keep covering those costs until the project is finished. If the developer does not have sufficient capital, the project will fail. This is one of the reasons that Riverside, Radburn, and Reston were financial failures. Even Columbia, which did not have to begin paying debt service to its financiers for ten years, could not come up with the needed revenue once the ten-year grace period was over. One reason The Sea Ranch did not have similar financial problems is that its scheme minimized carrying costs for site development and infrastructure installation.

Property at Riverside, Palos Verdes Estates, and the Country Club District was sold directly to future home owners. The Rouse Company primarily sold prepared sites to national and local home builders. The New Albany Company, on the other hand, sells primarily to Ohio home builders. But whether any new town developer sells sites to local or national home builders, by not developing any residential properties themselves, planned community developers avoid the problem of raising millions of dollars to finance the residential construction.

In some cases, as at Radburn and initially at Reston, the new town developer is also responsible for residential construction and sales. That had nothing to do with the ultimate failure of Radburn. In Reston's case, it was the reason the developer lost control of the project. Site acquisition at Reston took place all at once. Thus, its financing requirements kicked in immediately, as did the costs of taking care of the property, planning for the new town, preparing thousands of acres of land for development, and installing infrastructure and facilities. The added burden of also financing house construction was more than Simon could handle. Within three years Gulf Oil, one of his lender-investors, took over the project. In 1978 the Mobil Oil Company bought the remaining thirty-seven hundred undeveloped acres and became the master developer (Richardson 1996, 23).

The four-year development for Levittown was so rapid that revenue from sales began flowing within months. Site acquisition took place in stages. So, unlike Reston, Columbia, or The Sea Ranch, Levittown did not need to have all the money for the site at the beginning of the venture. More important, revenue from house sales was available to pay for land and site preparation as well as house construction. Even more important, houses were built and sold so quickly (eighty-four houses per week) that cash flow was not a problem.

New residential subdivisions are initiated every day. Planned new towns, on the other hand, are begun relatively infrequently because they also require a public realm of streets, squares, and parks; utility systems; supporting retail and community facilities; and places of employment, business centers, and (sometimes) entirely new downtowns. Not only do they require much territory, much money, and many more customers than live there; they will also experience many changes that were not considered in initial planning.

Satisfying Residential Demand

Because American new towns are not primarily established for ideological reasons, they are usually founded during periods in which market demand is high, cheap land has become accessible to that market, or easy money is available for financing both town expenses and individual home mortgages. But, whatever economic conditions may be, successful planned community development is dependent on steady demand for residences at an affordable market price.

Riverside, a largely residential planned community, was established during a period of suburbanization along railroad corridors. Within five years of opening of railroad service in 1863 to Chicago, Emery Childs understood the business potential of acquiring still inexpensive land and then selling sites at much higher prices on this newly accessible territory to a growing market of Chicago commuters (Figure 4.24).

Similar suburbanization along streetcar lines took place in Los Angeles over seven decades beginning in 1874, when the first streetcars were put into operation, until the network reached its peak of 1,164 miles in four counties (Bottles 1987, 28–32). The streetcars created a market for first- and second-home buyers. The cheap, mass-produced automobiles being purchased by millions of middle-class

Americans after World War I brought those customers to Palos Verdes. Thus, by 1924, when marketing of Palos Verdes got under way, there were tens of thousands of potential buyers who had settled in areas served by streetcars and could now use the newly developing road system to get to Palos Verdes in their own automobiles. At the same time, but on a smaller scale, streetcars and new roads had extended to the northern suburbs of Kansas City, where Nichols had begun transforming his subdivisions and retail center into a genuine new town.

Demand is not just a matter of accessibility. There are often downturns in the economy that, when they have not been prepared for as part of the planning for each new town, will result in financial difficulties. Problems for Riverside began with the Great Chicago Fire of 1871, four years after its purchase. The collapse of this planned community venture, however, came with the Panic of 1873, which lasted more than five years and resulted in a 33 percent decline in national business activity.

There were similar results when E. G. Lewis purchased the site of Palos Verdes Estates for $5 million from the Vanderlip Syndicate in 1922. Lewis expected the continuing expansion of the Los Angeles metropolitan area. Instead, the recession of 1923–24 led to a 25 percent decline in national business activity. Lewis was unable to finance his ambitious development schemes, forcing Vanderlip to repossess the property.

The City Housing Corporation had every reason to believe that Radburn would be a roaring success. Construction of the George Washington Bridge began in 1927, one year before the corporation purchased one square mile of property for development of a genuine garden city, ten miles west of the bridge. The bridge opened on schedule in 1931, but house sales at Radburn came to a halt in the aftermath of the stock market crash of 1929 and the Great Depression. The venture went bankrupt in 1935.

The New Deal took on the problem of balancing demand for housing with the supply of home mortgage money, the lack of which had contributed to the collapse of Radburn and other planned communities in the United States at the start of the Great Depression. The solution consisted of providing government insurance for standard, self-amortizing, long-term mortgages at predetermined moderate rates of interest for houses, which required down payments of as little as 10 percent, and sold at prices affordable to the middle class. The FHA (Federal Housing Administration) mortgage insurance removed most of the risk faced by banks and greatly lowered mortgage payments for home owners. Levittown was among the first American planned communities that made widespread use of FHA insurance.

Because of lending practice reforms that grew out of the Great Depression, the rate of home ownership in the United States went from 44 percent in 1940 to 62 percent in 1960 (U.S. Census Bureau 2011). Thus, obtaining a home mortgage was no longer an issue by the time that Columbia, Reston, and New Albany went into development. The only issue then facing developers of those and other planned communities was determining the adequacy of demand for their product.

Given the phenomenal growth of the federal government and of Washington, D.C., demand for residences in Columbia and Reston was certain. Continually rising incomes and available leisure time among residents of San Francisco Bay Area generated substantial demand for second homes in The Sea Ranch. The problem for the New Albany Company was not demand. Columbus, Ohio, already was one of the success stories of the midwestern Rust Belt when Les Wexner began thinking about creating this planned community.

Three New Town Fallacies

One of the great fallacies in planning is the belief that the objective of a master plan is to produce a superb, completed city, similar to a great work of painting or sculpture. Daniel Burnham understood that better than many other authors of so-called comprehensive plans. As he explained in the 1909 *Plan of Chicago*: "it is quite possible that when particular portions of the plan shall be taken up for execution, wider knowledge, longer experience, or a change in conditions may suggest a better solution" (Burnham and Bennett 1909, 2). This is particularly true of the process of acquiring the necessary properties to execute a plan. The plan for Reston, for example, called for the development company to build the town. When the primary investor, Gulf Oil, took over, construction was transferred to separate development companies. At The Sea Ranch, litigation forced a 50 percent reduction in the number of houses planned.

A second fallacy is that planned new communities can be self-sufficient. Reston, for example, suffered because it was planned to be independent of the surrounding metropolitan area. When it opened it had no direct connection to the highway that went from Dulles Airport through Reston to Washington, D.C. The federal government considered the highway to be *exclusively* an airport access road. The absence of highway on- and off-ramps at Reston greatly undermined marketing. Once direct access to Reston from the Dulles Toll Road opened in 1984, demand for residential and business sites accelerated, and the financial viability of this planned community as a real estate venture was assured. In addition, once residents of Fairfax County had convenient highway access to Reston, consumer spending in its mixed-use "downtown" greatly increased.

A third fallacy is thinking that planning should stop when all the components of a planned community are in place. Local retail centers so carefully conceived for the Country Club District, Palos Verdes Estates, Levittown, and other planned communities have changed numerous times since they opened and will continue to change as long as their customers change their buying habits (Figures 4.25 and 4.26).

Figure 4.25. Country Club Plaza (1981). Many of the stores that occupied sites in the mid-1940s had been replaced by national chains by 1981. Photo by Alexander Garvin.

Figure 4.26. Country Club Plaza (2011). Developers built new apartment buildings for customers who were attracted to ever more popular shopping opportunities. Photo by Alexander Garvin.

The Rhetoric and the Reality

What is the difference between the business of new town development and that of a conventional real estate venture? Are the results of new town and planned community development in America better than independent, incremental real estate ventures? They both require equity capital and long-term mortgages. New towns, however, require gigantic amounts of both. They both must cover carrying costs until occupants start generating enough revenue. New towns, however, with a few exceptions such as Levittown, require decades to reach full occupancy. During those decades, the country may experience several business cycles and consumer demand changes. No wonder five of the nine planned communities discussed in this chapter required financial restructuring. A sixth, The Sea Ranch, had to withstand political controversy and litigation before its target occupancy was forced to shrink by 44 percent.

The risk involved and the complexity of managing new towns' development process is similarly greater. Many developers tend to avoid making new investments when the market is oversaturated and begin exploring them only when they think the economy has reached a nadir.

Virtually all planned new communities, including the nine iconic new towns and planned communities in this chapter, provide impressive physical frameworks for low-density suburban housing that would otherwise disappear into sea of suburban subdivisions. The resulting networks of green recreational open space at Reston, Columbia, and New Albany greatly exceeds what are available in suburban areas where

the landscape is the product of a myriad of privately financed subdivisions (Figure 4.27). And at Palos Verdes Estates, the landscape is awesomely beautiful.

The reason that this is not true of most incremental real estate development is that suburban governments, even where they have jurisdiction, are loathe to use the power of eminent domain to acquire the what would be parkland or to raise the funds that its development would require. New town landscapes, however, are not necessarily superior to city park systems—as a visit to New York, Boston, or Boulder will demonstrate. In fact, the park system of Minneapolis is arguably the finest network of recreational green space anywhere in the world.

Figure 4.27. Columbia, Maryland (2016). Nearly 38 percent of this new town is devoted to open space and recreational facilities for residents. Photo by Alexander Garvin.

The commute to work can also be shortened when new town developers (as at Columbia, Reston, or New Albany) provide places of employment in proximity to residential districts (Figure 4.28). The result is less time spent traveling to work and back, less land devoted to the roads that provide access to regional employment centers, and lower automobile emissions. Not all planned communities include such business districts, and indeed this is a difference between a comprehensive new town and other forms of planned communities. Six of the nine examples in the chapter include only retail and service jobs.

Figure 4.28. Discover Card Headquarters, New Albany, Ohio (2016). Many new towns have difficulty attracting major national employers, whereas New Albany has succeeded. Photo by Alexander Garvin.

Figure 4.29. Via Arriba, Palos Verdes, Estates (2013). This planned community is more beautiful than most conventional real estate developments. Photo by Alexander Garvin.

The history of planned communities in America has included models of intelligent property development, efficient use of resources, healthy population diversity, civic engagement, and smart growth (Figure 4.29). New Albany, for example, is a case of intelligent property development; Riverside, Radburn, and Reston, however, had financial difficulties. Palos Verdes Estates is an example of efficient use of resources; at New Albany, however, outsiders are unable to enjoy access to the golf courses. The population of Columbia (50 percent white, 25 percent African American, 8 percent Hispanic, and 12 percent Asian and Pacific) is certainly far more diverse than

that of most suburban counties.[4] That diversity, however, does not apply to any of the other eight iconic planned communities discussed in this chapter. In fact, American planned communities can but do not necessarily produce places that are more beautiful, operate more efficiently, or supply residences at lower prices than conventional real estate development does.

But whether a planned community achieves one or more of these results, the advantages pale in comparison to the scale and complexity of managing a development process that includes acquisition of huge amounts of large property, installation of a vast complex of infrastructure and community facilities, and management of the complex operations needed to produce an entire new town. Thus, at least in the United States, planned new communities are not a practical alternative to incremental development by a myriad of independent real estate ventures.

Notes

1. Also Robert Tennenbaum, interview with author, August 15, 2016.
2. Also Robert Tennenbaum, interview with author, August 15, 2016.
3. William Ebbing, president of the New Albany Company, interview with author, April 25, 2016.
4. Robert Tennenbaum, interview with author, August 15, 2016.

5

Development Lessons from Today's Most Successful New Towns and Master-Planned Communities

Carl Duke and Reid Ewing

New towns are the largest and most complex real estate developments in the United States (Ewing 1991; Ewing et al. 1996). They dwarf residential subdivisions, apartment complexes, office parks, lifestyle centers, and regional malls, often containing multiples of these within their boundaries. New towns can be defined as developments of two thousand acres or more where people can live, work, and play without ever leaving the town (Ewing 1991, 2–3). Residents can shop and often go to school without ever leaving the community. They can also age in place, moving from one housing type to another within the same community as they grow old.

The very size and scale of new towns present unique opportunities and challenges. The opportunities arise from the fact that developers can achieve public purposes while they make a reasonable return on investment. The American Planning Association (APA) and Urban Land Institute (ULI) publication *Best Development Practices* has a subtitle, *Doing the Right Thing and Making Money at the Same Time*, that speaks to those public purposes (Ewing et al. 1996). Having hundreds or even thousands of acres to work with, new town developers can aspire to a jobs-housing balance within their boundaries. They can preserve wildlife corridors and natural drainage systems. They can (and often must) provide a complete mix of housing types from starter homes to retirement homes; the imperative to sell large amounts of land to diverse residential and nonresidential developers guarantees a mix of housing types and a mix of land uses. Developers can provide regionally significant roads, trails, storm water management facilities, shopping opportunities, and cultural facilities. They can donate land for schools and parks.

Many challenges also arise from the scale of new towns. Up-front expenditures for land, infrastructure, and amenities create huge debt burdens and require rapid land absorption to cover debt service. It becomes a "race between debt service and land appreciation . . . [in which] master developers are more likely to win if they can shift or defer costs through incremental development, special districts, and joint ventures—and if they can capture the residual value of the land" (Ewing 1991, 12).

The distinction between new towns and suburban sprawl can be thought of as revolving around the widely cited "D variables"—development density, land-use diversity, street design, destination accessibility, and distance to transit (Ewing and Cervero 2010). Even in the 1960s and 1970s, new towns such as Columbia, Reston, and the Woodlands had higher densities, more diverse land uses, more pedestrian-friendly designs, better accessibility to destinations, and more transit access than suburban bedroom communities (Ewing 1991). In the late 1980s and 1990s, under the influence of the new urbanism, designs evolved toward higher values of the Ds (except distance to transit, which moved in the opposite direction) in new towns and planned communities such as Rancho Santa Margarita, California; Southern Village, North Carolina; and Celebration, Florida. And in the twenty-first century, this trend, at least in the centers, has continued in new towns such as Baldwin Park, Florida; Stapleton, Colorado; and Daybreak, Utah. As the Ds have increased, the distinction between new towns and suburban sprawl has become increasingly pronounced.

Another observation by the ULI and APA is that the scale of new towns makes it possible to mix not only housing types and land uses, but conventional suburban elements and traditional urban elements, forming "hybrid" developments (Ewing 2000). Just as a housing and land-use mix appeals to different markets and accelerates land sales, a mix of conventional suburban neighborhoods and traditional urban centers appeals to different markets and accelerates land sales. All the new towns featured in this chapter are hybrids in this sense. Lake Nona in Florida, for example, started as a suburban golf course community but added traditional neighborhoods in a second phase. Daybreak has low-density suburban neighborhoods, albeit of traditional design, but will eventually have dense, mixed-use development around its rail stations.

Successful new towns can offer higher quality of life than conventional suburban subdivisions (Ewing 1991). This is the reason they often lead in home sales in their respective regions, as with every single community profiled below. The most successful new towns, by definition, are not examples of suburban sprawl (Ewing 1997; Ewing and Hamidi 2014; Ewing et al. 1996). Suburban sprawl is defined by low densities and intensities of development, single land uses segregated from other land uses, weak or nonexistent activity centers, and poorly interconnected streets that often end in cul-de-sacs. Instead, by virtue of a housing mix that includes townhomes and apartments, new towns have higher average densities than typical suburban subdivisions. They have a mix of residential and nonresidential uses, including retail and employment uses. They have centers of various types, often including town centers, village centers, and neighborhood centers. And in recent years, most have had more interconnected street networks than the typical suburb.

But, as already noted, new town developers also face challenges, and not all new towns live up to their social, environmental, and economic goals. Some challenges are pervasive and shared by all developers, while others are site specific. Nearly all developers face financial challenges: the rising costs of land, finding investors whose time horizons are as long as a new town takes to build out, and generating a sufficient return for the risk inherent in community development. Developers of new towns must address an increasingly difficult regulatory environment where they must preserve natural areas and open space all while seeking market-based entitlements to deliver housing that is affordable for various income classes. Many fall short, particularly in providing affordable housing. None of the challenges can even be addressed until the developer can find a parcel of land and a willing seller, and can emerge as the winning bidder in a competitive bidding environment. Clearly, community development is not for the fainthearted, and this is one of the many reasons why few new towns have started since the Great Recession.

This chapter cannot address all the challenges new town developers face. Instead, it focuses on three common problems and considers through case studies how these problems are being solved. Two relate to the D variables land-use diversity and distance to transit. First, new town developers are encouraged to deliver a sustainable balance between jobs and housing, when the traditionally community life cycle (starting with homes and adding jobs later) does not naturally facilitate this. Policy makers often want to regulate this balance, and yet developers are at the mercy of the market. Similarly, both new town developers and policy makers are engaged in expanding transit to new towns. While transit is a laudable goal, new town developers cannot bear the enormous cost of building fixed-rail transit to their communities. Finally, new town developers constantly struggle with finding the right mixture of amenities and deciding how to deliver them in a compelling yet affordable way.

This chapter explores these three themes in depth and provides examples of how new town developers have overcome these challenges. The examples draw from best-selling planned communities in the United States, meaning they sell well but are not necessarily comprehensive new towns. Best-selling planned communities, however, provide all new town developers with market-test guidance on these difficult challenges.

Economic Development and Jobs-to-Housing Ratios

In a perfect world, new towns would balance housing, services, and employment to reduce vehicle miles traveled (VMT) and promote alternative travel modes. An often-stated goal of new town development is to provide residents with a setting in which they can both live and work without leaving the community. Research has consistently shown that balancing jobs and housing, and locating services and shopping close to homes, both decrease VMT (Cervero 1989; Cervero and Duncan 2006; Ewing, DeAnna, et al. 1996; Ewing and Cervero 2010; O'Kelly and Lee 2004; Stoker and Ewing 2014). Cervero and Duncan (2006) found that jobs-housing balance reduces work-related VMT more than nearby retail and service employment reduce shopping-related VMT. However, what is more important is that both effects were significant. Attaining a jobs-housing balance has been recognized as a best practice, and this can reduce average travel time to work (Ewing, DeAnna, et al. 1996). Also, more people live and work in the same commute shed if there is job-worker balance and income matching, which is equally important (Stoker and Ewing 2014).

Community Life Cycle

Implementing a balanced community is extremely difficult in practice as uses are dependent on one another in a complex life cycle. Raw land becomes developed and either justifies redevelopment of underutilized areas or pushes out the suburban edge and spurs new residential construction. Consequently, commercial developers see an opportunity to provide services the new households demand (CCIM Institute 2012; DiPasquale and Wheaton 1996; Greer and Kolbe 2003, 312; Wheaton and Torto 1990).

The challenge for a new town developer is to create an economic engine early on where employment is created and the area can export goods and services and import dollars. However, until an area is proven to be a viable commercial or economic center, it can be hard to attract jobs of any kind. Two recent new towns—Lake Nona and Medical City in Orlando, Florida—have successfully attracted or capitalized on basic employment in large numbers far earlier than the household demand would justify.

The Lake Nona community was first envisioned in 1982 as a suburban golf community. The Estates at Lake Nona were made available in 1986, and the property struggled until it fell into distress. In 1994, Tavistock, a well-known developer with local ties, acquired the property and signed a development agreement with the city of Orlando where the bulk of the property was annexed (Levey 2007). Tavistock created separate new urbanist villages with unique identities and anchors such as the NorthLake Park Community School (Levey 2007). Since then, Lake Nona has been featured as the future of cities (Reingold 2014) and is still one of the best-selling new towns in America (Larue and Martin 2016).

Lake Nona benefits from close proximity to the Orlando airport but not much else. The property was bisected by the route 417 toll way, but the developer had to

Figure 5.1. Orlando Veterans
Affairs Medical Center.
Courtesy of Tavistock
Development Corporation.

fund millions of dollars for the primary interchange servicing the historic residential areas with the large medical jobs center called Medical City. It is against this relatively blank and nondescript backdrop that Tavistock created one of the largest economic development engines that survived the Great Recession, which still influences the remaining residential and retail lands (Caulfield 2016).

In 2002, Tavistock began working with Florida governor Jeb Bush on bringing life sciences to Lake Nona. After a focused three-year effort at local, state, and federal levels, Lake Nona saw a string of successes: the location of the University of Central Florida's fifty-acre health sciences campus and the creation of its medical school (2005); creation of the Stanford-Burnham Medical Research Institute East Coast facility (2006); announcement of a new Veterans Affairs Medical Center (2007) (Figure 5.1); and announcements of new Nemours children's hospital in Orlando (2008), the VA National Medical Simulation Center (2009), and an academic and research center for the University of Florida Research Institute (2009).

In seven years, Medical City absorbed 2.4 million square feet of just medical and research uses (Caulfield 2016). It has seen the construction of $3 billion in medical facilities and infrastructure that has brought five thousand permanent jobs to the region (Caulfield 2016; Burnett 2009). Medical City was able to create so much basic employment during a recession because Tavistock did not follow the traditional economic development model. First, they actively pursued a flexible entitlement that enabled them to respond to end users in a timely manner. The Lake Nona community was part of a Development of Regional Impact wherein the city of Orlando allowed for a flexible zoning category in certain commercial locations and only traffic impacts needed to be addressed (Levey 2007). Second, Medical City started with strong support at the state level and expanded upward to the federal level (Reingold 2014). Most developers focus on local economic development organizations with the goal of obtaining state support; Tavistock instead recognized the impact of federal support for uses such as the Veterans Affairs Medical Center and worked to gain support from federal entities. Finally, Medical City required a large amount of capital expenditures during the Great Recession to keep these deals alive. Tavistock took a long-term investment approach to this region and did not relent in their development efforts despite a broader economic slowdown.

Eastmark—Mesa, Arizona

While Lake Nona was successful in bringing a critical mass of jobs to a greenfield area, Eastmark offers an example of a community built around existing jobs. Both approaches bypass the traditional community life cycle of a new town to quickly arrive at a more sustainable balance of homes and employment.

From 1953 to 2009, the land was used as the General Motors Desert Proving Grounds, where the auto manufacturer tested its vehicles in extreme conditions (G. Nelson 2013). The property is thirty-two hundred acres, and while there are similarly sized land parcels in the Phoenix valley, few enjoy the proximity to existing infrastructure and a population base that Eastmark does (Leavitt 2015). In fact, suburban home buyers have leapfrogged this site in search of more affordable housing to the south of this site in Queen Creek.

Finally, what makes the Eastmark property most unique is the opportunity to defy the traditional community life cycle by balancing the existing employment base with residential housing and other services to quickly achieve a desirable jobs-housing balance. The Mesa Gateway Area Job Center as defined by the Maricopa Association of Governments had 4,727 jobs in 2014 (City of Mesa 2014). These are primarily basic jobs, meaning the goods and services provided in this job center are exported to other areas of the state and country as opposed to simply trading dollars between the homes and businesses of Mesa.

DMB Associates purchased the land in December 2006 and began working with community leaders and surrounding stakeholders to plan the site (Polletta 2015). The site was annexed into the city of Mesa in September 2008 with a flexible entitlement giving DMB an advantage as they sought additional commercial uses for the new town (DMB Associates 2014; Polletta 2015). General Motors abandoned the site in 2009, leaving the developer with an enormous task of removing the infrastructure from the prior use. Finally, homes began selling in 2013 through one local and six national home builders (Leavitt 2015; Reagor 2012).

All this occurred throughout the Great Recession in one of the hardest-hit housing areas in the county. To make matters worse, a few of the initial commitments fell through despite the passage of tax incentive packages. These included plans for a high-end resort by Gaylord Entertainment Company (Randazzo and Nelson 2013) and the development of a 1.3 million-square-foot manufacturing facility for Tempe-based First Solar. First Solar did not materialize, but in late 2013 Apple purchased the vacant facility for the manufacturing of sapphire glass for its products in an economic development deal that was awarded numerous national awards among site selector publications and associations (DMB Associates 2014). DMB, like Tavistock, was able to quickly arrive at a sustainable balance between jobs, housing, and services. While Tavistock had to convince medical users to locate in a greenfield location, DMB had to launch a new town in difficult economic circumstances on what was a stigmatized piece of land. The existing adjoining airport and surrounding industrial uses conjured up images of old testing fields. DMB reached out to the Sieb Organization to help them frame the story to consumers (Sieb Organization 2016) and then reinforced the message by bringing on board only high-quality builders. This strategy was highly successful. Eastmark was named the best-selling community in Arizona and the eleventh best-selling community in the United States in 2016 (Larue and Martin 2016).

Transit in New Towns

Consumers value transit, and home owners are willing to pay a premium to be close to transit stations (Debrezion, Pels, and Rietveld 2007; Hamidi, Kittrell, and Ewing 2015). Recent community preference studies continue to show that prospective home buyers and those evaluating their communities want transit. In a ULI study, 32 percent of respondents prioritize convenient public transit as a top or high priority (Urban Land Institute 2015). Similarly, a survey conducted by the National Association of Realtors and Portland State University revealed that 64 percent of participants believed it was important or very important to have public transit nearby when deciding where to live (National Association of Realtors 2015).

The mixture of land uses commonly found in new towns shortens internal trips within the community, facilitates walking and biking, and encourages the use of transit (Walters, Bochner, and Ewing 2013). And yet we see a paradox: people say they want to have access to and use transit, but in reality, a decrease in the transit mode share is occurring, and some are questioning the investment in transit (Freemark 2014).

Unfortunately, most new towns do not benefit from transit when they actually are the best candidates to capitalize on the benefits of transit. New towns in the United States commonly have pedestrian and bikeways for recreation, shopping, and school trips, but work trips are almost entirely by automobile. This section considers why transit is missing from new town communities and highlights two developments, Daybreak and Stapleton, that have been successful in attracting transit.

New Towns and Rail Transit

Of the fifty-eight new towns profiled in a 1991 ULI publication on successful new communities, almost all were auto oriented (Ewing 1991). Some of the better known, such as Reston, Columbia, the Woodlands, and Peachtree City, made an attempt at multimodalism by providing sidewalks or bike-pedestrian connections from neighborhoods to village centers, but none offered more than limited bus service.

Today, out of the top twenty best-selling U.S. new towns in 2015, only Daybreak and Stapleton benefit from any type of fixed-rail transit (Larue and Pawelek 2016). This is an illustration of how difficult it is for an area to justify bringing out rail improvements to the suburban fringe, where most new towns are developed. Rail transit to new towns is extremely expensive. The average, capital cost per mile for major light-rail transit initiatives was $79.9 million in 2012 dollars (Dobbs and Lyndon 2012). More recently, in a report released by Hillsborough County, Florida, the area immediately north of the successful new town of Lakewood Ranch, the average cost per mile for five light-rail projects in the United States was $87.8 million in 2014 dollars (AECOM 2014). Given their predominantly peripheral locations, this is one reason we do not see more new towns with light or commuter rail. Also, transit requires relatively high densities to achieve reasonable fare-box recovery ratios. Most new towns in the United States do not approach the fifteen to twenty or more dwelling units per acre required to support fixed guideway transit (Ewing and Bartholomew 2013; Ewing, Tian, Lyons et al., 2017).

The two successful new towns with transit, however, can be instructive for community developers trying to attract and incorporate transit into their plans. Interestingly, these communities offer similar lessons. First, timing needs to be right. Both communities show that without the confluence of several events, transit would not have come to fruition. Second, when timing is right, new town developers must work with numerous entities in a cooperative manner to make transit feasible. Finally, transit and planning is an iterative process, and the developer must remain flexible if the new town is to fully benefit from transit.

Daybreak—South Jordan, Utah

Daybreak is a 4,126-acre master-planned new town on the suburban edge of the Salt Lake valley in the city of South Jordan. The property owner, Kennecott Utah Copper, a subsidiary of the global mining giant Rio Tinto, began planning the site in the early 1990s (Rio Tinto 2009; Urban Land Institute 2007). This took place at the same time that the Utah Transit Authority was purchasing rights-of-way from Union Pacific for future transit lines (Associated Press 2002). It was fortunate for Kennecott that while they were considering the development of a large-scale new urbanist community, UTA was taking the first steps toward making transit a reality for this suburb.

Kennecott Land took advantage of this opportunity to work in conjunction with regional planners by spearheading an early feasibility study. In 2004, it was the first entity to make a large financial commitment to the initial feasibility study for the Mid-Jordan light-rail line. It was also the catalyst to bring together the other surrounding cities and encourage them and UTA to fund the remaining shortfall for the $3.2 million study (American Public Transportation Association 2004).[1]

Kennecott was also able to capitalize on this timing by having the results of the feasibility study fed back into their entitlement process with South Jordan. The study emboldened South Jordan to grant the controversial average density of five dwelling units per gross acre (with much higher densities near transit) and a greater amount of commercial zoning than would otherwise be realistic at this suburban location (Urban Land Institute 2007).[2] Kennecott would later go on to dedicate all the rights-of-way for light rail through the Daybreak community at no cost, and they upgraded the stations from a rural standard cross-section to elevated urban stations, at a cost to Kennecott of over $10 million.[3]

Finally, the Daybreak community is an example of how planning for transit in a new town is an iterative and constantly evolving process. In the initial planning stages, the market research indicated that the existing demographic valued education (Urban Land Institute 2007), so Kennecott actively worked to find a satellite higher education campus, eventually convincing the University of Utah to locate its 225,000-square-foot medical campus adjacent to one of two light-rail stops within Daybreak (Jackson 2010).[4] While this was not the original use Kennecott planned for the site, it fits well into the community and added momentum to the new town.

Stapleton—Denver, Colorado

Stapleton is another active new town that has attracted transit for its residents. The current Stapleton community was the home of the Stapleton International Airport and served Denver's commercial aviation needs for sixty-five years (Urban Land Institute 2004). In the early 1980s, it became clear that the airport could not be expanded to accommodate passenger growth, and in 1985, a multiparty agreement was announced to relocate it to the site of the current Denver International Airport (Stapleton Redevelopment Foundation 1995). This, along with the recent redevelopment of the eighteen-hundred-acre Lowry Air Training Center into a master-planned community, paved the way for the development of Stapleton (Urban Land Institute 2004).

Stapleton is a rare subset of new towns that are large-scale redevelopment or infill projects—new-towns-in-town. Others include Baldwin Park in Orlando and Atlantic Station in Atlanta. The forty-seven-hundred-acre Stapleton redevelopment is one of the largest in the United States (Godschalk 2004). As a redevelopment site, the land had over 170 structures that needed to be removed and $10 million in environmental remediation that needed to occur prior to any new town development (Schriener 1998). In addition, the area required $287 million worth of community-level infrastructure and improvements to support the proposed twenty-five thousand residents and thirty thousand employees (Stapleton Redevelopment Foundation 1995). Despite these costs, Stapleton has continually been a best-selling master-planned community because of the beneficial infill location and surrounding amenities (Forest City Stapleton 2016).

The property was transferred to the Stapleton Redevelopment Corporation, a private nonprofit, which oversaw the public-private partnership with Forest City, the developer (Urban Land Institute 2004). The redevelopment corporation is overseen by an eleven-person board with representatives from the public and private sectors (Urban Land Institute 2004). This structure allowed the developer to take advantage of tax increment financing for infrastructure, to purchase the large piece of land in phases, and to maintain close ties to the public sector, which proved valuable when transit discussions began.[5]

One of the lessons to be learned from Stapleton is the importance of timing. Stapleton was successful in attracting transit, in part, because planning efforts for the community took place at a time of transit excitement. The initial planning efforts for Stapleton began in 1989 and culminated in 1995. During this time, the Regional Transportation District (RTD) planned, constructed, and opened service on the Central Corridor light-rail line—the first modern light-rail service in the Denver area (Seattle Department of Transportation 1998). Because transit was prominent in policy discussions, it was easier to incorporate transit planning into the Stapleton master plan.[6] This is evident in the first planning document for Stapleton, in which an entire section of the property was characterized as an Intermodal Transit Center (Stapleton Redevelopment Foundation 1995). While the commuter rail station at Stapleton was not fully constructed and operational until 2016, planners and policy makers were clearly expecting transit from the early discussions.

Stapleton's success with attracting transit can also be attributed to the developer's ability to work with numerous interested parties. This was cultivated early on as the planning process involved so many stakeholders (Seattle Department of Transportation 1998). The success of Stapleton involved the Stapleton Redevelopment Foundation board and staff, Denver City and County elected officials and staff, a board of citizen advisers, a team of consultants, and numerous other public and private agencies that participated in the initial planning effort (Stapleton Redevelopment Foundation 1995). RTD had become so involved in the process, they along with Denver Regional Council of Governments and the Colorado Department of Transportation agreed to spend the eighteen months following the adoption of the initial Stapleton plan to study how to maximize future rail investment to reduce automobile reliance. The Stapleton planners also wisely recognized funding as a critical hurdle for transit and specifically addressed how the capital funding for the construction of transit could take place. This would have produced fixed guideway transit much earlier had the corridor not run into legal challenges, which changed the mode from light rail to commuter rail and delayed the entire process (Seattle Department of Transportation 1998).

Finally, the many people involved in the planning and development process for Stapleton understood the process was iterative and needed flexibility to respond to the market.[7] Transit was anticipated much earlier in the community life cycle, yet most of Stapleton was built out when fixed-rail transit opened in the community. Forest City was able to continue the new town development process while transit issues were resolved. The plan, and a patient developer, allowed an important thirty-five-acre piece of property to be held off the market in anticipation of transit. Prior to 2016, the site could have easily been developed for two-to-four-story mixed-use products. Now, with transit in place, Forest City believes this site will be able to support more density and a different mixture of uses. What would have likely been suburban office space will now possibly have a hospitality component along with some high-density residential space to take advantage of the transit amenity.[8]

New Town Amenities

Most American new towns we examined feature golf courses, tennis facilities, walking trails, and other amenities to attract higher-income residents, reflecting the private character of these developments. Developers seem to be engaged in an amenities arms race where each community must deliver every amenity the surrounding communities offer plus one new concept. These decisions have huge cost implications for new town developers, and if an amenity package is not well executed it could narrow the list of potential buyers.

Buyers complicate this problem by sending mixed signals to new town developers. There is no real consensus on what people want. A recent survey conducted by a large community development district in Florida shows how widely opinions range on seven proposed new amenities for the community (Berlin 2013) (Figure 5.2).

New town buyers have trouble agreeing on the ideal amenity package because the preferences of potential residents vary widely by demographics. A recent survey of twenty thousand new home shoppers revealed that Baby Boomers prefer walking trails while Generation Y shoppers would rather have a fitness center (Carmichael 2014). A National Association of Home Builders' survey of forty-three hundred prospective buyers across all housing types showed

Figure 5.2. Survey results from community survey on amenities. Adapted from Berlin (2013).

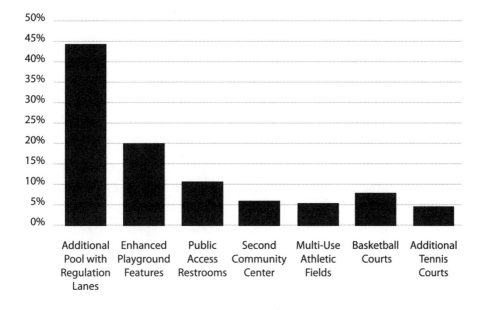

If additional community amenities were offered, what would be your top three choices?

that the top-three preferred amenities are a suburban feel, close proximity to parks, and access to trails (National Association of Home Builders 2016). Buyers, however, are consistent about one thing—they do not want to pay for many amenities and certainly do not want to incur the operational and maintenance costs for these facilities (Robles, Ross, and Sharpe 2012).

Amenities are a conundrum because they are extremely expensive and are needed at the worst time, early in the development process. A developer typically must construct a significant portion of the amenity package before a single home or lot is sold. These amenities must be constructed at the same time the developer is faced with large design and constructions costs for infrastructure. The standard model for paying for these amenities was a combination of charging higher prices for the lots and community associations. And yet amenities cannot be overlooked as they are one of the primary methods of conveying a lifestyle.

Rancho Sahuarita—Tucson, Arizona

Robert Sharpe began working on the idea of Rancho Sahuarita in the 1980s when he identified an area he felt would be suitable for developing a new town in Tucson, Arizona. He eventually came to control the property in the early 1990s and immediately began working to incorporate the town and obtain entitlements for the project (Leon 2016). This process took nearly four years, and the community of ten thousand planned residences and one million square feet of commercial space sold its first home in 2002 (Leon 2016).[9] By 2016, the community had sold fifty-four hundred homes, and it is recognized as one of the best-selling new towns in the United States.

The Rancho Sahuarita developer was required to install the initial amenity package but created a unique mechanism for funding future amenities. Any residential resale in the new town pays 1 percent of the sale price to a fund that pays for capital facilities related to amenities. At first this fund was quite small, but with fifty-four hundred homes it has grown to a significant sum of money. These funds are strictly used to construct new amenities or even repurpose existing amenities to better respond to the needs of the new town residents and employers. With the funds in place, these additions or alterations no longer fall on the developer.

The developers at Rancho Sahuarita also illustrate the importance of maintaining flexibility throughout the development process. It is important to keep in mind that the planning of amenities originally took place during the entitlement phase, over twenty years previously. Preferences have significantly changed over this period. With the emergence of more concern about health and wellness, for instance, a clubhouse originally constructed in 2008 was renovated to include a community

kitchen in 2015. This idea took off, and now the owners' association employs a full-time nutritionist on staff, with fifty health and wellness classes weekly.

Figure 5.3. Armed forces tribute at Entrada Del Rio, Rancho Sahuarita, Arizona. Courtesy of Rancho Sahuarita.

At Rancho Sahuarita, the developer noticed during the Great Recession that residents were facing financial stress and cutting back on vacations. Instead of cutting back on programming and social infrastructure, the developer increased offerings. Free camps were added throughout summer, free babysitting services were offered, and an active kids' club was created to relieve some of the stress on families.[10]

When evaluating amenities, it was noted that 40 percent of the community has direct ties to one or more branches of the armed forces. While most communities would not consider a tribute or monument to be an amenity, this community responded very favorably, with an armed forces tribute, possibly because there was already a substantial amount of public art in the community (Figure 5.3).

Victory/Verrado—Buckeye, Arizona

Victory is a good illustration of an experienced developer providing a compelling amenity package in today's economic environment. Victory is an age-restricted community within DMB Associates' larger Verrado new town. Verrado new town is an eighty-eight-hundred-acre development that opened in 2004, which could yield up to fourteen thousand homes and four million square feet of commercial space (DMB Associates 2016). After conducting market research, DMB identified the upcoming demand for an age-restricted community and began planning the Victory portion of Verrado (Gulick and Barefoot 2013). The community opened in February 2015 and continued to do well as the thirty-first best-selling community of 2015 (Kahn and Bachman 2016).

DMB's goal at Victory was to limit expenditures on amenities and infrastructure and try to time it such that they could take advantage of early home sales revenues.[11] Much of this desire came from the lessons learned from a grand opening of the broader Verrado project. The new town of Verrado is clearly on the exurban fringe of the Phoenix Metropolitan Statistical Area and had to convince people to accept the lengthy drive to Buckeye, Arizona. DMB delivered this with a fully constructed main street, town square, and grocery-anchored retail center. This strategy worked well from 2004 to 2006 but suffered in the downturn when the home buyer pool dried up. To avoid a similar scenario with Victory, DMB delivered the age-restricted new town amenities in a phased fashion.[12]

Victory used the climate and natural aesthetic of the land to create an open-air amenity that focuses on lifestyle. This overlooks a major fitness and recreation facility. At the location of the future amenity center was a large sign that read "Have Fun" to help show the type of lifestyle Victory was trying to offer and convince potential buyers that the planned amenity was coming.

DMB also intentionally delayed some of the key amenities for a year or more, including golf courses and an amenity center (DMB Associates 2015).[13] By delaying the completion of some amenities to coincide better with the first-year home sales revenues, DMB was able to defer some community development costs at the same time homes were being sold. The success of this approach has been recognized in the marketplace, and Verrado was named the number one place to retire in the United States in 2015 (Gulick and Barefoot 2015).

Conclusion

Clearly, developing a new town that sells well is a challenging endeavor. While the development community and policy makers can agree on an end goal, getting to that point can be complicated and difficult. Balancing jobs with housing can have a long-term positive impact on a community but is difficult to achieve as a new town is developing. Lake Nona provides valuable lessons on how developers can patiently work with various entities to create excitement and a critical mass of basic employment in an area. Eastmark teaches the importance of taking advantage of existing employment in adjoining areas to arrive at this worthy goal and the benefits for new town developers who are willing to take on the challenges of large-scale redevelopment opportunities.

Consumers, policy makers, and developers are in general agreement that transit benefits a new town, but the cost to developers for trying to influence the route of transit and attract it to their community is extremely high. Daybreak helps illustrate the idea that a new town developer can be the impetus for transit discussions in an area, and a new town can take steps after transit is in place to capitalize on the costly infrastructure. Stapleton provides a lesson on the importance of timing, flexibility, and the ability to work with the numerous agencies and entities involved in delivering a transit system.

Last, as prospective new town buyers become more segmented, developers face a challenge of delivering a comprehensive amenity package that has broad appeal, does not break the bank, and may even help achieve equity goals. Rancho Sahuarita provides some interesting lessons on how a developer can listen to residents in building and repurposing a community amenity package. Victory shows us how to phase amenities in a way that convinces people that they are buying into a highly amenitized new town but delays some of the costs to coincide better with home sales revenue.

Notes

1. Also Don Whyte, former president of Kennecott Land, telephone interview by author, March 24, 2016.
2. Also Don Whyte, telephone interview by author, March 24, 2016.
3. Don Whyte, telephone interview by author, March 24, 2016.
4. Also Don Whyte, telephone interview by author, March 24, 2016.
5. Jim Chrisman, senior vice president of Forest City Stapleton, telephone interview by author, March 24, 2016.
6. Jim Chrisman, telephone interview by author, March 24, 2016.
7. Jim Chrisman, telephone interview by author, March 24, 2016.
8. Jim Chrisman, telephone interview by author, March 24, 2016.
9. And Jeremy Sharpe, vice president of community development, Rancho Sahuarita, telephone interview by author, January 12, 2016.
10. Jeremy Sharpe, telephone interview by author, January 12, 2016.
11. Drew Brown, cofounder and board chairman, DMB, interview by author, October 7, 2015.
12. Daniel Kelly, DMB Associates senior vice president and general manager of Verrado, interview by author, January 27, 2015.
13. Also Daniel Kelly, interview by author, January 27, 2015.

New Towns as Laboratories
for Local Governance

Robert H. Nelson

In the United States, the new town movement historically has sought to surmount the limitations of traditional incremental development by pursuing the comprehensive design and coordinated development of whole towns. The leading emphasis has been on the physical design of the town, including the location and character of housing, transportation infrastructure, parks and other open spaces, and other design features of the physical environment. Less prominent but also important in many new towns has been an integrated social environment including adult education, community events, public performances, and other nonphysical features. There has been less attention, however, to questions of local governance. Innovations in American local governance have generally emerged elsewhere and then been extended to the process of creating a new town. New towns thus typically exhibit a complex mosaic of public and private governments, with varying implications for democratic engagement and service efficiency (see Chapter 18).

It might be possible, however, to consider new forms of local governance as part of the creation of a new town. Such innovations might be possible by taking advantage of flexibility found within the existing framework of state and local governance in the United States. Depending on the governance forms that might be under consideration for a new town, however, it might require specific action by state legislatures to authorize new forms of local governance that are not provided for in existing law. In the course of normal land development, a state legislature might be unreceptive to a request to make a significant—for one time in one place—change in local government law. A new town, however, might be able to marshal the resources and public visibility to engage the attention of a state legislature, thus potentially making greater local governing innovation possible. New towns might serve as laboratories for local governance experimentation, as well as innovating in other traditional areas of new town land-use concern.

At present, operating within existing state and local law, the default governance option for a new town would be a home owners' association—as it is often called, a "private government" (R. H. Nelson 2003, 2005a, 2005b, 2011). Indeed, one might characterize a large home owners' association as one form of new town, in that respect by far the most common form found today in the United States. Home owners' associations meet the criterion of integrating the physical arrangements, the social environment, and other details of communal living within a single planning and design process. In June 2016, the Community Associations Institute (CAI) released its first ever survey of what it called "large-scale associations." To be considered a large-scale association, the following criteria had to be met: the association had to have a minimum of one thousand housing or other units or a minimum of one thousand acres, and also have a minimum operating budget of $2 million. CAI chose four hundred such associations for its survey but estimated that there were six thousand to nine thousand large-scale associations in the United States. As the CAI report observed,

> These [large-scale] communities boast amenities such as golf, tennis, stables, ski runs, country clubs, leisure trails, fitness facilities, ball fields, playgrounds, parks, clubhouses, theaters, newsletters and other communications tools, garden plots, aquatic offerings and facilities to meet the needs of hobbyists for all manner of leisure pursuits.
>
> With all of these amenities and home offerings, many practical needs arose such as roadway maintenance, stormwater infrastructure, water and sewer plants, retention ponds, lakes, refuse pick up, security, shoreline management, along with numerous similar services. All of this infrastructure requires scheduled maintenance and the technical skills to keep these offerings operational. Thus, was born the large-scale community association, which in many ways operates as a mini-town. (Community Associations Institute 2016, 4)

The most relevant current body of law for the governance of a new town would thus be the existing state legal framework for the creation and operation of a home owners' association (also sometimes labeled a "planned community"). Each state has its own set of laws, often varying significantly from one state to another. Federal law, such as fair housing prohibitions on discriminatory practices against children and other groups, also can affect the governance of home owners' associations, but on the whole its role is much less than that of the individual state's laws. An important task for anybody seeking to establish a governance system for a new town would thus be to understand the specific laws relating to home owners' associations in the state in which the new town would be built.

Although it is a private form of government, a home owners' association would also be subject to public controls in many other matters such as zoning approval, taxation, water and sewer, basic public transportation infrastructure, public services, and so forth that remain the responsibility of state and local public governments. A new town would thus normally have a combination of private and public governance. This public-private relationship—such as the private common services the home owners' association provides and the public services provided by the local public governing jurisdiction within the boundaries of the association—can also vary significantly among individual home owners' associations and individual public jurisdictions. A home owners' association would be part of the development package that would have to receive initial public approval under the provisions of local land-use regulation. Indeed, local public jurisdictions have increasingly required the creation of a home owners' association as a condition of regulatory approval, a way of ensuring that key new public services will be privately provided, rather than a new financial burden on the local public treasury (Siegel 2006). Again, such public laws and rules may vary significantly from one state and locality to another.

In this chapter, I briefly survey the historical development of the existing legal framework for both public and private local governance in the United States. That is, the focus is on legal options rather than the functioning of such governments in terms of democratic participation and service outcomes. This is a large topic, so only a few highlights can be offered. I suggest some possibilities for new town innovations in governance that might be possible within the existing legal framework for home owners' associations and traditional local public governance. Whether determined publicly or privately, the key features in organizing a form of new town governance will be the following:

1. The long-term form of governance of the new town after it has been fully occupied by residents.
2. The manner of governance during a period of transition from an existing land use to a fully built and occupied new town community.
3. The collective arrangements for provision of common services in the new town.
4. The collective arrangements for determining and administering controls over the types of acceptable land uses, and changes in property exteriors. At present such controls are often very detailed and are the source of internal friction in many associations.[1]
5. The collective arrangements for regulation and maintenance of streets, including parking.
6. The possible inclusion of a federalism governance structure based on multiple units of collective subgovernance within the new town as a whole. Many existing larger home owners' associations have a master association for the entire

area and smaller neighborhood associations for appropriately sized clusters of homes—a form of "private federalism," as it might be called.

7. The provisions for making changes in the manner of governance of the new town—for amending or adopting "a constitution."

8. The provisions for terminating the new town if it ceases to be economically viable or no longer serves the best interests of its residents for other reasons.

The Corporate Legal Basis for Local Governance

Until the nineteenth century, "there was no legal distinction . . . between cities (municipal corporations) and business corporations" (Frug 1999, 32–33). Whether for city residents or businessmen, groups of property owners seeking to establish collective governance would seek corporate charters that were issued individually by a state (or colony) (Teaford 1975). As the requests to create business corporations increased in the nineteenth century, states moved to separate them from acts of municipal incorporation and to create formal procedures of business incorporation without requiring individual actions of the state legislature. In the residential sector, however, matters moved more slowly. It would not be until the 1960s that private nonprofit corporate governance—taking the form of a "community association" (a home owners' association, condominium, or cooperative)—began to spread widely to American housing. Starting from about 1 percent in 1970, more than 20 percent of Americans today live in residential community associations, around half of them home owners' associations (including most of the largest) (Community Associations Institute 2017). Private nonprofit residential corporations have thus been recently attaining to a comparable social and economic importance in American life as the private business corporation has long held (McKenzie 1994, 2011).

Reflecting in part their common corporate status, both business corporations and private residential corporations are at least nominally controlled by their "owners." The shareholders elect the board of directors of the business corporation by a direct vote; the unit owners elect the board of directors of a community association in a similar fashion. In both cases, the number of votes is directly proportional to the share of property ownership (like business shareholders, individuals in a residential corporation can own multiple units). If the owners of many business corporations and many community associations have a limited influence in practice in the actual governance and management of the common property, it is not for lack of a democratic framework of decision making. Rather, it reflects the large asymmetries of information between the legal owners and the actual managers as well as the problems of organizing large numbers of affected owners for collective action in the face of free-rider and other obstacles (Olson 1965).

In the public sector, a municipality is also organized as a corporation. Historically, many states continued to issue municipal charters of incorporation as individual state legislative acts well into the twentieth century. Some such as Georgia and Florida still do today (University of Georgia n.d.). But the majority of states now have procedures for municipal incorporation that do not require the direct involvement of the state legislature in each case. Such general municipal incorporation laws vary considerably from state to state. Typically, they establish a set of requirements that must be met before any act of incorporation can be officially considered. They often also include the approval of an incorporation vote by a county or other level of government. In most states, assuming those requirements are met, the residents of a proposed municipality then decide whether to approve the incorporation, normally requiring a simple majority affirmative vote.

In unincorporated areas of the United States, the instruments of local public governance are not incorporated municipalities but counties. While there are almost twenty thousand American municipalities, there are only 3,033 counties. If a new town were built in an unincorporated area, as perhaps the majority would be in the South and West, it would have to deal with a county as its immediate unit of local public government. Unlike corporate forms of governance, counties are direct creations of the states that are legally conceived as an administrative extension of state government. States established counties early in their history but later frequently created brand-new counties or otherwise changed county boundaries (*Counties USA: A Directory of United States Counties* 2006).

Because the public and the courts regard home owners' associations as legally "private" entities, these associations have wider legal flexibility to act collectively in some key respects, giving them governance options unavailable to counties or municipalities in the public sector. These potentially valuable legal powers of new towns governed as home owners' associations include:

1. Greater private flexibility in the assignment of voting rights, which do not have to follow the mandatory public sector rule of one person/one vote and do not have to give voting rights to renters (although a few, such as the new town of Columbia, Maryland, do).
2. Private flexibility to allow foreign nationals, people legally registered to vote in other political jurisdictions, nonresident property owners, and other types of unit owners the right to vote in the home owners' association, a right they are denied in a public setting, where voting *is* considered a right of public citizenship assigned to a person living there in an official place of residence.

3. Wider private flexibility to define a social environment by discriminating against and thus excluding others who do not meet the entry qualifications, as in a home owners' association of senior citizens that is legally entitled to exclude adults below the age of fifty-five or any residents with children.

4. Wider private flexibility to regulate even the fine details of neighborhood land use, such as house color, placement of shrubbery, parking of vehicles, building of fences, and other small alterations in property that public zoning has not traditionally controlled.

5. Greater private flexibility to regulate the entry of nonresidents into the neighborhood by the placement of gates and other barriers on streets and at other entrances to a home owners' association, creating, so to speak, a virtual private "visa" system.

6. Wider private flexibility to control the placement of political signs, regulate the holding of meetings, and limit other activities within the association boundaries that would be constitutionally protected in an officially public setting as rights of free speech and assembly.

7. Greater private flexibility to control the hiring and firing of home owners' association employees (and outside association management companies) than exists with respect to the hiring and firing of public sector employees, who typically have greater job security.

8. Greater flexibility in contracting out local government functions to private suppliers.

9. Greater flexibility to terminate the local government, as when the unit owners of a home owners' association might vote to sell all the units as a single package for comprehensive redevelopment of the neighborhood in an entirely new use (a potential step that home owners' associations have not often taken thus far, but one that might increasingly occur in the future as associations age and as the number of complete neighborhood land-use transitions rises in many rapidly changing urban areas).

10. In other matters as well, greater constitutional and other political latitude than public governance has traditionally had, often reflecting a past history of legislative and court decisions that have imposed tight constraints on local innovative capacity in the public sector. (Frug 1980)

The Rise of Private Collective Ownership of Residential Property

The legal form of the home owners' association dates at least as far back as the management arrangements for some private parks in London in the eighteenth century. By the late nineteenth century, some of the leading housing developers in America were creating large private communities. The developer would lay out the lots and bind the actions of future owners through a system of covenants in the deeds. However, it was difficult to write covenants that adequately specified future aesthetic concerns. Another problem was that the enforcement of covenants often proved burdensome; it might depend on some individual owner who was willing to shoulder the legal cost for the entire neighborhood. For these and other reasons, "covenants generally suffered from the lack of an effective enforcement mechanism" (Beito 1990, 283).

Another problem for private residential communities was the maintenance of recreational facilities, open spaces, and other common elements. It was much less expensive to build a common swimming pool to serve a community of two hundred residents than to build a separate swimming pool at each home. Some developers accepted the responsibility for assuring the upkeep of such common areas over the lifetime of the project. However, developers often found themselves subject to criticisms and complaints from the residents. Resolving such operating problems was a principal motive of J. C. Nichols—one of the leading builders of large private communities in the United States—in establishing the Country Club District Improvement Association in Kansas City in 1910 to assume the responsibility for maintenance and operation (Worley 1990). Membership in this association was voluntary, but Nichols in 1914 at the Mission Hills development pioneered the mandatory home owners' association. Each buyer of land was required as an initial condition of purchase to join the home owners' association, and to agree to comply with various requirements of collective ownership and management within the Mission Hills area.

Actively promoted by the federal government through tax advantages and other policies, individual ownership of homes soared in the United States after World War II. The Urban Land Institute (formed in 1936) and other builder organizations promoted the use of mandatory home owners' associations as a practical way of taking care of green spaces, playgrounds, swimming pools, tennis courts, and other common areas increasingly included in large private developments. The Federal Housing Administration (FHA) provided technical assistance to developers both in designing the physical layout of large projects and in establishing a suitable form of private collective governance to enforce use restrictions. Two FHA publications, *Planned-Unit Development with a Homes Association* in 1963, and *The Homes Association Handbook* in 1964 (produced in cooperation with the Urban Land Institute), were especially influential in setting future guidelines and standards (Federal Housing Administration and Urban Land Institute 1964).[2]

In the 1960s, most states passed laws authorizing for the first time in the United States the condominium form of collective ownership of housing. In the next few decades, most states also enacted legislation to clarify the legal status of home owners' associations (W. S. Hyatt and French 1998). By 1998, there were 10.6 million housing units in home owners' associations and 5.1 million housing units in condominium associations. In 2012, about half of residential private collective ownerships consisted of a home owners' association and more than 45 percent a condominium (Foundation for Community Association Research 2012).

Changing American Metropolitan Patterns of Local Governance

In the nineteenth century, good government at the local level in the United States was increasingly considered to mean consolidated government. In 1898, for example, the current city of New York was created by combining five separate boroughs into one much larger, centralized political unit. In the first half of the twentieth century, however, the tide began to turn. Small governments in the suburbs increasingly resisted being swallowed up by annexation by larger central cities. By the mid-twentieth century, the familiar northeastern and midwestern pattern of today was well established: a large central city surrounded by large numbers of small suburban municipalities, many with no more than a few thousand people.

Today, however, the manner of organizing local governance in the United States is once again changing. In California, Florida, Texas, Arizona, Nevada, and other rapidly growing areas, the rise of the private home owners' association is central to the newer urban models. In such places where private home owners' associations have proliferated, the small suburban municipality of the Northeast and Midwest is an uncommon occurrence. Instead the regulation of land use and the provision of neighborhood-level common services such as garbage collection, street cleaning, recreational facilities, and security patrols are being undertaken privately (McCabe 2011). This leaves local public governments at county and municipal levels to increasingly focus on wider responsibilities of a regional scope such as public education, water and sewer systems, arterial highways, rapid transit, courts of law, and other responsibilities that involve significant economies of scale beyond the neighborhood.

Because of the long lifetime of urban housing and infrastructure, the specific governance character of any metropolitan area is highly path dependent. As a result, the new governance trends are most visible in newly developing and rapidly growing metropolitan areas such as Las Vegas. In contrast to the hundreds of small public municipalities typically surrounding central cities in the Northeast and Midwest, there are only thirteen general-purpose local governments in the public sector in the Las Vegas metropolitan area. Almost all of metropolitan Las Vegas falls within one county, Clark County. The county includes large, unincorporated sections (including most of the "Vegas strip") where the county is the principal instrument of local governance in the public sector. In three large, incorporated municipalities—the city of Las Vegas (population of 575,000), Henderson (256,000), and North Las Vegas (202,000)—governing responsibilities are shared with Clark County.

At the same time, much of the traditional role of local government is now private. As Robert Lang and Jennifer LeFurgy note, "The bottom line . . . is that every new North Las Vegas development now has some form of common-interest development," and these home owners' associations have become "critical . . . to the basic functioning" of the system of local governance throughout the metropolitan area (Lang and LeFurgy 2007, 129–30).

New Towns: Municipal Incorporation Versus Home Owners' Association Nonprofit Incorporation

A new town could in concept be organized governmentally as a municipal corporation. This could happen in two ways. The creator of a new town might build it with the housing units individually sold to incoming residents and rental property owners. The instrument of public governance at that point initially would likely be a county, although it could also be a large existing municipality. At some later point, the residents of the new town would be expected to undertake the required process to newly incorporate the new town as a municipality itself (although this would not be possible in some states if the new town were already located within an existing municipality). Alternatively, the new town might be created initially as a home owners' association. Again, at some later point, the unit owners of the home owners' association might undertake the process to incorporate as a municipality as well. In the latter case, there would be two layers of collective corporate governance for the new town, one private and one public, as is the case for new towns such Irvine, California. Under either alternative leading to municipal incorporation, the designers of a new town should include a plan for the process by which the creation of a municipal government was expected to occur.

Transitional Issues

Each of these incorporation possibilities would pose its own transitional issues in moving from a large parcel of undeveloped land to a completed new town with an installed form of government. Consider, for example, a new town that seeks to become a new municipality without any prior home owners' association. Prior to some level of residency of the new town, it would not be possible to incorporate a new municipality because the normal state processes of municipal incorporation require an affirmative action by current residents, typically culminating in a vote of approval or rejection. Under current law a new town creator would have no legal ability to guarantee a later municipal incorporation (typically leaving a county government as the default public government). One possible legal innovation would be for a state to create new procedures allowing for this possibility at the initiative of a developer—putting a municipal government structure in place before there are any residents of a new town.

Whether the new town is located within an existing municipality, or within an existing unincorporated area of a county, could also make a big difference. If it is within an existing municipality, an act of municipal incorporation of a new town would be treated under state law as an act in effect of municipal secession. Some states would prohibit such an action altogether. If it were possible at all, one important consideration for an existing municipality would be the fiscal impacts—the tax revenues lost, versus the reductions in public service costs—of such an act of separation into two municipal jurisdictions. If the new town were in an existing unincorporated area, however, the relevant state law at present would deal with municipal incorporation within a county. In many states such as Maryland, a new municipal incorporation requires the consent of the county government and then a vote of the residents. Owing to such obstacles, municipal incorporation has been rare in Maryland in recent years. At present, there is no means by which the county approval could be guaranteed in advance—another area for possible legal innovation.

All this is in contrast to the state legal provisions for home owners' associations under which a developer can establish the association private governance system before construction has begun and before any homes have been purchased in a new town, for example. In the private model, there are also well-defined procedures for moving from initial developer control of the association to later control by the residents of a new town themselves (A. G. Hyatt 2004). Before development starts, all the members of the board of directors of a home owners' association are appointed by the developer. Then, as buyers make purchases and become unit owners in the association, they are gradually given an increasing number of seats on the board of directors. According to the standard association practice, full control of the association board shifts to the residents after 75 percent of the units have been sold and occupied. The developer is legally protected, however, in being able to complete the development plan.

Municipal and Home Owners' Association Taxation

Many home owners' associations deliver common services privately that elsewhere in the same local jurisdiction are provided publicly by local government. The association unit owners thus might be said to pay twice, first in the form of private assessments to cover the costs of their own privately provided association services, and second through property and other local government taxes to help to cover the costs of the same publicly provided services in other parts of the same local jurisdiction. Home owners' associations have often complained about this "double taxation," but New Jersey is alone among the states at present in legally limiting such taxing practices. One reason is that the fiscal benefits to local residents may be seen as a necessary "bribe" to win approval to develop the home owners' association in the first place—it is an informal but legal way for the local government to "sell" and the developer to "pay for" local zoning approval of new development such as a new town (R. H. Nelson 1977).

Moreover, the fiscal disadvantages of private association status extend to other matters. Local municipal governments, in part because they are regarded legally as appendages or extensions of state government, often receive large intergovernmental transfers of revenues. Overall, almost 40 percent of local government revenue in 2005 came from the states and the federal government. Although much of this local spending is for education and social services that home owners' associations typically do not provide, local public governments did spend $27 billion in 2005 for parks and recreation and $18 billion for garbage collection, areas of significant overlapping public and private responsibility. Federal and state funds generally are not available to home owners' associations, in part because they are regarded as a form of private sector activity not eligible for such public support. In one example, federal disaster assistance may be given to a municipal government in the aftermath of say a hurricane but largely denied to nearby private home owners' associations in similar circumstances. Adding to the incentives working against private sector provision, municipal property taxes are deductible for federal income tax purposes, whereas home owners' association assessments are not.

So it is reasonable to ask: Why do private home owners' associations exist at all when such significant financial advantages favor municipal public organization (R. H. Nelson 2009)? One answer is that, as discussed above, the private status of a home owners' association offers wider flexibility in the manner of neighborhood governance and other advantages that work to compensate for the additional financial burdens. There may also be no choice; absent a home owners' association, there may be no development permission forthcoming. There is admittedly one way to avoid double taxation. A home owners' association located in a county, municipality, or other public jurisdiction comprising only other home owners' associations will not be exposed to public taxation that mainly benefits local residents who live in the same jurisdiction but outside a home owners' association.

Terminating a New Town

A new town might be built today at a particular location and with a particular design to meet the economic and other needs of the present. Forty years later, however, it may be economically and otherwise outmoded for the location it occupies. The economically optimal solution might be to tear down the new town and build another form of development—possibly another new town—at the location. Few current home owners' associations have well-developed provisions in their founding documents for guiding such a process of land-use transition. But it would at least be possible to create such provisions in the future for a new town under the existing law of home owners' associations.

One might then imagine the following scenario. A developer might approach the board of directors of an aging new town with a generous financial offer to purchase the entire town to build something else at that site. There will normally be some home owners for whom almost any reasonable offer would not be enough. But what if a very high percentage of the owners in the new town would prefer to accept the offer—thus gaining a large financial windfall for themselves. The termination of a new town, for example, might be possible with an ownership vote in favor of say 80 percent. Some existing home owners' associations do have provisions for terminating their associations with less than unanimous consent. States might revisit this area of community association law, making the process of transition to a brand-new local land use less burdensome (if still requiring a substantial supermajority approval). By comparison, it would require a much greater legal departure to establish similar procedures in the public sector—to provide say for the "sale" of an entire municipality and all its property as a single development package transaction.

Differing Governmental Arrangements

In municipalities, there are two main governance models: the council/elected mayor and the council/hired city manager. Numerically, the latter type is most common. In a home owners' association, by comparison, legal authority lies with an association board of directors elected by the property owners (the "unit owners"), which may choose to delegate the operational responsibilities to an association management firm. With some differences, this arrangement resembles the council/town manager system of a municipality. One difference, for example, is that the dismissal of the private manager and administrative staff of the home owners' association—firing the association management firm—would likely involve considerably fewer transaction costs than the dismissal of a municipal city manager and all the civil service.

The level of "social capital" might be higher, and the transaction costs of governance therefore lower, in neighborhoods that are able to gather together a more homogeneous group of home owners (Fennell 2013). A strong new town culture, based on a powerful set of shared norms, is more likely in the private setting of a home owners' or residents' association. Although public municipalities can achieve substantial homogeneity of owner incomes through the exercise of their zoning powers, in other respects they have less authority than a private home owners' association to set individual entry requirements. For example, private home owners' associations of senior citizens (wherein at least one of the unit occupants usually must be at least fifty-five years old) have proliferated across the United States. It would be difficult—and perhaps legally impossible—for a public municipality to maintain a similar age restriction. There might be other forms of group association that could be served by a home owners' association. For example, although some people might reject a goal of residential religious homogeneity, others might see it as desirable to have possible private associations that serve as both a place of residence and a geographically based "church" in which unit owners must belong to the common neighborhood religion (R. H. Nelson 2005a). On a less exclusive side, new towns may attract people with similar aspirations—for everything from social equity to aesthetic quality.

Conclusion

Such differences in governing options between a small suburban municipality and a private home owners' association are not necessarily an intrinsic—and thus a permanently fixed—characteristic of the law. Indeed, to a large extent, they are the product of past state legislative decisions and federal and state court cases. In the future, courts could, in concept, modify the legal status of suburban municipalities to loosen current municipal restrictiveness and grant greater freedom of operation, thus coming to resemble the greater governance flexibility of today's private home owners' association. States could enact new laws with this purpose.

The developer of a new town may wish to go beyond existing law and practice to include creative governance solutions along with a creative physical design for the new town. In the case of a large new town, one might imagine, for example, the establishment of a new county in the state to encompass the full area of the new town, and then the public incorporation of each smaller individual neighborhood as a municipality or home owners' association within the county. If the new town is located in an existing large municipality, it might prefer to secede to form its own incorporated municipality with each neighborhood having its own home owners' association, as has happened in the Woodlands, Texas. Establishing a new county would require action by the state legislature, and a municipal secession might also require—or at least be more likely to succeed—with state legislative approval.

In establishing individual neighborhood governance within a new town, other innovative approaches might be contemplated. One possibility might be to establish the incorporated neighborhoods of a new town under the state laws of business incorporation, rather than the home owners' association legal regime. This would facilitate, for example, termination of the neighborhood home owners' association—more like selling a business corporation to a new owner. It might encourage the participation of outside directors receiving compensation on the board of directors of the private neighborhood association, just as business corporations have outside directors. Much like a cooperative, the individual unit owners would obtain the exclusive ownership rights to their units by legal agreement with the overarching "business/residential" corporation of the neighborhood.

An area where new towns might benefit from historic home owners' association experience is the perception of many current unit owners that existing association controls are unduly restrictive. Prohibitions or restrictions on the rental of units are maintained by some home owners' associations. They often have strict rules for the types of motor vehicles allowed—prohibiting house trailers, larger trucks, or even any kind of truck at all—and the manner of their parking on neighborhood streets and driveways. Many associations have restrictions on the ownership of pets, sometimes based on their size and weight. A common restriction in home owners' associations is a ban on any home-based businesses, in some cases prohibiting even personal businesses interior to a housing unit that generate little or no automobile traffic or other exterior impacts. The proper mix and manner of enforcement would be a key issue in establishing a new town governance regime. Perhaps there could be variations in restrictiveness among the individual neighborhoods in a new town. There could also be provision for newly flexible means by which a new town could revisit its initial development decisions and consider altering the types and degree of restrictions and other governance features, a problem area for many current home owners' associations. There could be provision for mandatory periodic new town "constitutional conventions."

One existing innovative governing arrangement is the Greensprings assisted-living community of several thousand people in northern Virginia, where the residents "purchase" their apartments but cannot sell them. If they leave, the original purchase price is returned to them by the private owner and manager of the whole Greensprings community. In this way, the residents provide the capital base for the community development but do not directly profit from increases in property values. The residents are also relieved of the responsibilities for collectively overseeing management and other details of facility operation—a particularly helpful feature in housing occupied by senior citizens, some of whom may be suffering from declining mental capacities. A new town might draw in part from this model in creating a governance regime.

Another possibility might be the establishment of a new town in which units are available only for rent—with the recent turn away from home ownership to rental tenures, there have been signs of growing developer interest in such "rental associations. These suggestions and examples are illustrative of a yet wider range of possibilities (Frey 2001; R. H. Nelson 2005b, parts 5–6; Oakerson 1999). If the creators of new towns are willing to seek state legislative approval, they might prove to be pioneers in the introduction of significantly innovative methods of local governance in the United States.

Notes

1. For example, in Colorado the South Creek Eight Homeowners Association demanded that a unit owner remove a hot tub. The Plantation Walk Homeowners Association in Tennessee regulates the height and edging style that must be followed by unit owners in mowing their lawns. Other associations regulate such details as the color of swing sets or even the size (to the sixteenth of an inch) of screws used to install balcony railings. See Franzese (2000, 674).

2. It might be noted that Byron Hanke, the head of land planning at FHA, was also the principal author of the ULI handbook.

7

New Towns in East and Southeast Asia

Peter G. Rowe

Setting aside precise notions about what constitutes a new town, post–World War II urban expansion in many parts of the world adopted the idea of creating new towns as the sites for the concentration of burgeoning metropolitan sprawl in a planned and integrated manner. East and Southeast Asia were no exceptions, even as these regions followed on from earlier Western programs, primarily and at different times in step with specific national developments. Apart from the city-state of Singapore, the Japanese were first in the 1960s, if not somewhat before, in planning new towns in the wake of almost total wartime devastation followed by massive resettlement and population boom. They were followed, in the early 1970s, by reformatory actions in Hong Kong in the aftermath of excessive laissez-faire and exploitative developments, along with slightly earlier national rebuilding in Singapore. Later, in the 1980s, more concerted efforts to reduce urban pressures on Seoul, South Korea, got underway at a sufficient distance from the urban area to be effective. Then, in the 1990s, new towns gained a new lease on life under legislative aegis as well as functional reshuffling in Beijing, China—a site of satellite developments from earlier times.

While similarities among these efforts certainly exist—almost all, for instance, were in public hands—each has its own character, peculiar to its time and place. Success has been mixed, as elsewhere, even among examples in a particular urban setting. New towns are still actively pursued in places such as China, Hong Kong, and Singapore, although discontinued and in need of substantial redevelopment in other places such as Japan. In what follows, background conditions, motivations, precedents, and outcomes in five national urban settings are discussed briefly, followed by outlines of specific examples at both the early outset and more recent occasions of new town building. These settings include Tokyo and other parts of Japan; South Korea with Seoul and Incheon; China, primarily with Beijing; and Hong Kong and Singapore. Other instances of large-scale planning and community development within the scope of broad metropolitan expansions are also briefly introduced in several other settings, the Philippines, and Malaysia, to round out discussion.

Two Turning Points in Tokyo and Other Parts of Japan

At the conclusion of World War II in 1945, Japan was physically shattered, not to mention demoralized and institutionally in tatters. Cities were on the brink of starvation, with around ten million people having lost their homes, primarily due to fire-bombing by the Allies that left many urban areas flattened and blackened wastelands (Sorensen 2002, 158–59). Recovery began quickly enough in 1945 with the "Tokyo Spring" and breaks with the past including land and local government reforms, among other measures, under American tutelage and insistence. The former led to the breakup of large land holdings to combat rural and tenant farmer disaffections, among other reasons, although the country still managed to maintain strong property rights and a weaker acceptance of public interest and good than occupying authorities might have liked. It also fragmented land ownership, paving the way, almost literally, for subsequent suburban sprawl (Sorensen 2002, 155–56). Then, in the 1950s the so-called reverse course set in, moving Japan away from earlier progressive agendas to forge strong economic and stable social developments as bulwarks against potential Communist aggression during the cold war (R. Sims 2001, 276–78). One consequence was the Income Doubling Plan of Prime Minister Ikeda in 1960, which promoted and eventually achieved a doubling of national economic production in a decade (Lu 1997, 527–29).

By 1960 or even earlier, a turning point had begun as a period of rapid growth and metropolitan concentration became established. The urban population rose from 38 percent of the national total in 1940 to 50 percent by 1960, on its way to 60 percent by 1970, and beyond that today. The Tokyo metropolitan region was accruing on the order of 285,000 persons of net in-migration per annum, roughly double that of Osaka, another sizable city to the south (Sorensen 2002, 171–73). Overall, about 36 percent or more of the Japanese population moved; this was in excess of similar booming periods of demographic movement and reconcentration in the United States and Italy after the war, and even in China today. Then, in 1963 the New Residential Town Development Act was passed, which, together with the earlier 1954 passage of the Land Adjustment Act—facilitating public takings of property—paved the way for new town development, beginning with Senri New Town outside Osaka in the early 1960s, Kozoji New Town in Nagoya, and Tama New Town on the western periphery of Tokyo around the same time (Hauk 2015). With a huge deficit in the number of suitable dwellings per household nationwide, the equalization of which was not reached until 1973, sheer housing production, including within affordable suburban locations, became an overwhelming goal. In fact, in this context the nascent new towns in Japan never managed to create a balance between local job opportunities and residences, becoming, instead, largely dormitory communities.

The second turning point, dating from the early 1980s, coincided with economic development away from older sectors of heavy industry and chemical manufacturing toward electronics, automobiles, and finance. Quickly this resulted in concentration of business activities in Tokyo. Globally, Japan had risen to become a leader in automobile manufacturing and in many aspects of the electronics industry. The rise of "Japan, Inc." during this time was chronicled widely as Japan took its place as the world's second-largest economy. Locally and with significant impacts in Tokyo, between 1980 and 1985 some 80 percent of all new jobs were in services of which fully 50 percent accrued to Tokyo (Sorensen 2002, 230). In short, the city and surrounding metropolitan area came to dominate Japan's educational, cultural, media, finance, and other business sectors. Further, increases in urban growth were accompanied again by governmental action to redress the distribution of employment opportunities. The Comprehensive National Development Plan of 1987, for instance, specifically focused on revitalizing peripheral urban areas. Its subsequent "technopole plans" led, among other measures, to the fuller establishment of Tsukuba City in the same year as a second generation of Japanese new towns.

Tama New Town

When Tama New Town was first planned around 1960–61, the expectation was that it would follow a British model, with relative independence from Tokyo in employment and other services (Tanabe 1978, 39; Figure 7.1). But when the project was finally adopted in 1964, the plan shifted to Tama being a dormitory town to meet urgent demand for housing in an affordable suburban location. Although the Japan Housing Authority moved into the area in 1958, some thirty-five kilometers

Figure 7.1. Tama New Town, Japan. Courtesy of Max Pixel (https://www.maxpixel.net/Tama-New-Town-Newtown-Countryside-Tama-Hachioji-2717379).

west of central Tokyo, fuller development began in 1961, with the Tokyo metropolitan government taking over in 1965. The total site development started in the east around Nagayama and Suma before moving westward during the 1980s. Before this development the site was very rural in the 1950s, even though it was considered to be in Tokyo. Two types of development occurred over time. One type, involving new largely single-family residences, was in the hills, and the other type, chiefly involving land readjustment—a process for public taking of property—and multifamily dwellings, was in the valleys. Of this development by far the majority took place on favorable hillside sites, housing 80 percent of the residents, with the remaining 20 percent living in the valley areas.

The expected population of Tama was 347,200 inhabitants on 28.92 square kilometers of often greenfield areas. Even with the demographic boom and outward suburban expansion of the 1960s and early 1970s, the population target was never reached, culminating in a population of 201,443 inhabitants in 2004 (Ducom 2008, 24). The overall density was 6,985 people per square kilometer, although spot densities varied among the various styles and types of development. These began with the basic *danchi* of 2DK and 3DK units (two to three rooms, a living room and a dining-kitchen area), primarily in the form of four-to-five-story walk-up slab buildings, followed, between 1975 and 1985, by multifamily dwellings, of *mansyons*, and then high-rise housing complexes further into the 1980s (Nakazawa 2011, 8; Tanabe 1978, 45–46).

The population per household in 1991 was 2.9 persons, declining to 2.3 by 2004. Tama's residents were mostly drawn from other parts of Tokyo and were largely in search of agreeable and inexpensive residential environments to raise families. However, commutes along the several rail lines that served the broader community or by vehicular transportation could take up to two hours. Indeed, over 25 percent of the working population traveled to the center of Tokyo, and fully 40 percent spent three hours or more per day commuting (Nakazawa 2011, 9). Development was undertaken almost entirely by the public sector, and the major developers were the Japan Housing Corporation, the Tokyo metropolitan government, and the Tokyo Housing Commission, with the remaining development undertaken by other operators (Tanabe 1978, 42). Without a doubt, as elsewhere in Japan at the time, this was a state-led undertaking.

As mentioned, the physical form of Tama took the shape of a chain of districts and neighborhoods, running from east to west, primarily centered on rail lines and ten station stops, with Inagi in the east and Tamasakai along with Hashimoto further to the west. Few jobs were offered on-site; those that were provided were usually associated with daily service activities. The broad land-use distribution was 47 percent residential, 17 percent parks and open space, 16 percent roads and streets, 12 percent public services, and 10 percent schools (Tanabe 1978, 42). There were some twenty-one neighborhoods of around one hundred hectares in area with about three thousand to five thousand dwelling units, seemingly respecting the thresholds of prevalent neighborhood unit concepts. These, in turn, were served by two elementary schools and one junior high school, and a neighborhood center of shops, a post office, a police station, and a clinic, all architecturally amalgamated with or near to the commuter rail station (Hauk 2015, 221). Beyond British new towns, those in Sweden, like Vallingby, and in Finland, like Tapiola, also appear to have served as models of appropriate low-scale modernity. Over time, one distinction emerged, and that was the location of sixteen university institutions, including a campus of Chuo University. Clearly in its heyday of the late 1960s and 1970s, Tama New Town proudly hosted the lives of the *sararimen* and their families as a symbol of a rising of Japan from its wartime ashes.

By contrast, today Tama is a conspicuous part of the graying outskirts of Tokyo and the site of noticeable population shrinkage together with economic crisis. With the bursting of the asset bubble in Japan, and especially Tokyo, in the early 1990s, property values in Tama, which had peaked in 1994, declined appreciably, in some cases below replacement costs. Population declinations occurred either through the natural process of aging and dying or by now more footloose residents of empty nesters leaving the community. Perhaps most dramatically, public school populations shrank from 16,779 students in 1988 to just 7,487 in 2002, with six of thirty-seven schools being closed completely (Ducom 2008, 9). Extrapolating in the same districts from present populations, fully 70 percent could be expected to be of age sixty-five years and older by 2050 (Ducom 2008, 8).

Physically, Tama now exhibits the ghost-town qualities of these declinations in abandoned schools and dilapidated and untended parks and open spaces. Tama Center—one of the oldest and once proudest—shows perhaps the strongest signs of reduced investment and decay. To be sure, there is something of note in the compressed cycle of growth and decline that took place in Tokyo, Tama, and other parts of Japan, between 1960 and, say, 2000. On the other side of the Koizumi government's urban regeneration reforms early in the new millennium, inner Tokyo became a more attractive location for both residents and businesses, probably reinforcing the plummeting of property values beyond a twenty-five- to thirty-kilometer radius of reasonable commuting and living. Indeed, at least two broad market failures have battered Tama. One was the early and long plunge into housing types that quickly became outmoded and underused, without successful replacement. The other was predicating the new town development almost entirely on an urban model of demographic increase and economic expansion, along with the programmatic requirements of earlier Baby Boomers.

Tsukuba City

Although often associated with Japan's program of technopoles, Tsukuba had earlier beginnings. In 1962, at much the same time that new towns were getting under way, the collective relocation of national research institutes in Japan was being proposed, and the Tsukuba Science Center, located in the Ibaraki prefecture about sixty kilometers northeast of Tokyo, came under consideration. Then in 1964 a blueprint for the Tsukuba Academic New Town Development was developed, and it was enacted into law in 1970. In 1973, the Japanese Diet initiated funding for the new town, and, by 1980, all forty-three designated national institutes were opened (Castells and Hall 1994, 65–67). In broad outline, Tsukuba bore some resemblance to Novosibirsk in the USSR at the time, with its concentration on academic and research facilities at the exclusion of industry and manufacturing (Birnbaum 1973, 25; Figure 7.2). Clearly, population decentralization was of only minor concern, as targets of one hundred thousand inhabitants or more were only drops in the proverbial bucket within the burgeoning Tokyo metropolitan area. The salient rationale for Tsukuba was redistribution of intellectual activities surrounding science in numerous fields of application. This was resisted by many in the research and development community out of a reluctance to leave behind circumstances of opportunity in Tokyo, along with a disbelief in ready cultural transfer to the satellite community and its potential for unbalanced

Figure 7.2. Aerial view of Tsukuba, Japan. Created by On-Chan. Courtesy of Wikimedia Commons (2012).

growth. For some families, the so-called Tsukuba syndrome of isolation even set in (Castells and Hall 1994, 72).

From 1987 onward, under the "technopolis plans" of the Ministry of International Trade and Industry, conditions began to change for the better. Tsukuba City's area of influence and diversity of normal activities expanded appreciably between 1988 and 2002 with the incorporation of several towns and villages into its jurisdiction. This was followed by the recognition of Tsukuba City as a "Special City" in 2009, with increased autonomy. Spread over 283.72 square kilometers, Tsukuba City had 223,151 inhabitants in 2014, an increase from eighty thousand people in 1973 (Takahashi 1981). Also, at the end of the 1980s, some 30 percent of all research agency employees, together with 40 percent of all researchers, were located in Tsukuba City. Several universities, including Tsukuba University—a national-level institution—located to the new town, with a large campus partially designed by Isozaki, a world-renowned architect. Over two decades, about 50 percent of Japan's public research and development budget was spent in Tsukuba. Although slow to materialize, the national institutes are now surrounded by several hundred private research facilities, producing finally the hoped-for government-led public-private collaboration (Castells and Hall 1994, 70).

Physically, planning of the Research and Development District in Tsukuba City was set out along a seventeen-kilometer-long diamond-shaped alignment in a plan of two north-south axes, about eight kilometers in distance at the widest point. Originally a one-hour train ride from Tokyo, with the advent of Joban Railroad and the Tsukuba Express in 2005, the commute has been lessened and, more important, become directly connected into the Tokyo metro system. This has also had something of a two-way effect, however, facilitating commutes by researchers to Tsukuba's laboratory facilities from outside the nearby community. The original plan had various national institutes and universities located adjacent to the two axes, as well as to southern portions where these axes flared out again in plan from a central midsection. Nearby neighborhoods of between thirty thousand and fifty thousand people were planned, to contain various dwelling types, including mid-rise and high-rise apartments and, later, single- and two-story units (Birnbaum 1973, 26). The complexes associated with the main infrastructure elements were themed along the lines of research and development activities such as university operations, agriculture and forestry science, and construction science. Well-equipped and large-scale laboratories and other research and testing facilities were constructed within each of the themed or purpose-built complexes. At the midsection of the plan, a town center was built, comprising shopping, service, and entertainment facilities; a city hall, a library, and a museum; and other supporting functions. Schools and playgrounds were then interspersed within the neighborhoods close to the research and development facilities. Overall, development was mixed in use and medium-to-low rise in scale, befitting the otherwise former rural area at the foot of Mount Tsukuba.

With the collapse of the asset bubble in the early 1990s and the subsequent economic downturn, further development and maintenance of Tsukuba's position in research and development has proven difficult to sustain (Castells and Hall 1994, 73). The extreme vertical integration of the various institutes also introduced unbeneficial rigidities among research programs. A sense of community lopsidedness has also persisted despite the broadening out of Tsukuba City after its municipal mergers. Universities have certainly begun to operate, although none has entered into the top ranks nationwide. More generally, the technopole idea seems to have been flawed. Tsukuba, because of its scale, is perhaps an exception in this regard, but its relatively narrow focuses represent only niches in a much broader entrepreneurial panorama, and it is less than a match, when it is all said and done, for nearby and dominant Tokyo.

Reform and Shifting Hong Kong's Center of Gravity

Established in 1973, the New Town Programme of Hong Kong was a response to population increases, severe overcrowding, and a need to relieve population and related pressures on well-established areas in the British Crown colony through decentralizing concentrated developments in the New Territories (Hayes 1993, 10–12; Figure 7.3). Originally intended to provide sites for public housing, following Governor MacLehose's sweeping reforms dating from 1971, the program also became bound up with an operating strategy of "collective consumption" that linked a stronger role by the state in housing and social services with economic production and capital accumulation (Castells, Goh, and Kwok 1990).

By 1971, Hong Kong's population had risen dramatically from 3.1 million inhabitants in 1961 to around 4.1 million (Welsh 1993, 470–73). One sign of the reformatory posture of the government was the 50 percent increase in government expenditure that took place between 1971 and 1972, along with a call for an additional 1.8 million housing units by the mid-1990s, all in an effort to come to grips with Hong Kong's squalid and increasingly dysfunctional condition. Another key ingredient of the program was a close connection to the MTR—the city's emerging mass rail transportation system—with new town developments through extensions beyond Hong Kong Island and Kowloon in the 1970s and 1980s (P. G. Rowe 2005a, 74–75, 81). Further administrative impetus was given by expanding the Housing Authority, originally founded in 1954, and by the creation of the New

Territories Development Department and provision of more authority to the Town Planning Division of Hong Kong's Land Department.

First mooted in 1949 by Sir Patrick Abercrombie of the London MARS Plan fame, expansion into the New Territories and the advent of new towns was slow to take place (Lai 1999). Some plans were prepared by the Town Planning Board in 1961 and by the Public Works Department in 1965. Tsuen Wan, Tuen Mun, and Sha Tin were the first generation of actual new towns to be undertaken as the Housing Authority began building dwelling units at a rapid rate (Hong Kong Lands Department 1984). With target populations in excess of five hundred thousand inhabitants, Tsuen Wan and Shatin, for instance, were studies in contrasts. Development in Tsuen Wan began earlier, and by 1975, it became the site of extensive public housing, high-rise factories, and other employment sites, while Sha Tin remained largely a bedroom community through the early years of its development.

The following generation of new towns, primarily from the 1980s, included Tai Po, Fanling, Yuan Long, and Tseung Kwan O. They all were slightly smaller in population size at around three hundred thousand to five hundred thousand inhabitants. The subsequent new town developments, including Tin Shui Wai and Tung Chung, were still smaller in population size, ranging up to three hundred thousand to three hundred and fifty thousand inhabitants, but no less dense in occupation (P. G. Rowe

2005b, 216–20). Overall, nine new towns account for around three million dwellers, closer to 50 percent of the new Special Region of China's population. One effect has been to shift the center of gravity of Hong Kong's population significantly, with 21 percent of it now living on Hong Kong Island, 41 percent in Kowloon, and 38 percent in the New Territories, where there were once only small market towns and a few villages (Hong Kong Information Services Department 2000, 216–20).

Sha Tin

The Sha Tin new town is in the Sha Tin district, one of Hong Kong's eighteen such administrative units. It is located north of Kowloon in an area around the mouth of the Shang Mun River and connected to the Tolo Harbor. Although people have lived and farmed in Sha Tin since the Ming dynasty, the district and new town site was largely rural and unoccupied until the 1970s. Tempered by rugged hilly topography, the river valley offered some purchase on flat land for development, enhanced by further channelization of the waterway itself (Figure 7.4). Developed significantly during the first half of the 1970s, Sha Tin new town was home to some 643,000 people as of 2013, with an average household size of 3.0 people. The site area of the new town was 35.87 square kilometers, with some twenty square kilometers of developable land (Hong Kong Census and Statistics Department 2015a). This yields an overall density of some 31,500 people per square kilometer, which is around the norm for most new towns in Hong Kong, which tend to range from twenty-five thousand to as high as sixty-seven thousand people per square kilometer.

While many of the population's daily needs could be served satisfactorily, balanced development with employment was slow in coming, largely owing to incremental rates of residential growth outstripping job opportunities available for residents. The continued development and expansion of the Chinese University of Hong Kong, originally established in 1963, located to the north of Sha Tin's Town Center has brought numerous jobs to the district and diversified employment, as has the racecourse, located between the university and the town center, although to a lesser extent. Today, it is probably hard to claim that Sha Tin has fully achieved the balanced development originally hoped for, but it has certainly made strides in that direction, including broadened expansion of its service sector.

Sha Tin's residential landscape is characterized today by high-density housing along the river channel, with lower-density housing and some village areas surrounded by or enclosed within an expansive greenbelt along the rising foothills on both sides of the river. Fully 58.3 percent of Sha Tin's housing is owner occupied, varying in distribution among the 212,800 households in 2013, with 33.4 percent in public rental units, 33.8 percent in subsidized flats for sale, and the remainder living

Figure 7.4. Aerial view of Sha Tin, Hong Kong (2005). Courtesy of Peter G. Rowe personal collection, Cambridge, Massachusetts.

in private residential areas (Hong Kong Census and Statistics Department 2015a). The general land-use plan resembles a linear development around a main railway and roadway spine, with pockets of high-rise development, almost exclusively with housing above and day-to-day commercial uses at the base, and often with above-grade links between buildings. In between are lower-density developments, recreational spaces, and community service functions, including primary and secondary schools, as well as about ten community halls. In 1982, the Prince of Wales Hospital was built, with a two-hundred-bed capacity along with four general clinics.

The Sha Tin Town Center, a fixture since the new town's founding, comprises a large and up-to-date mall connected to the railway station and intramodal transport hub; a town hall; law courts; a town library; a marriage registry; an outdoor performance space; and a museum.[1]

The Sha Tin Park runs beside the river in a double-decked configuration in places and along both sides of the waterway. It is crossed, in turn, by several pedestrian as well as vehicular bridges, knitting the town's communities together on both sides of the river. Access to the central and other districts in Hong Kong is offered by the MTR system, with station stops at Sha Tin, Racecourse, University, and Sha Tin Wai, with Che Kung Temple nearby. Service headways of less than five minutes during peak hours and only slightly more in more general operation provide uncommon levels of access and convenience. Multiple bus services also augment the MTR. At this juncture Sha Tin continues to expand, both within reasonably well-developed areas and by extension, such as in nearby Ma On Shan.

Tin Shui Wai

Located in the northwestern part of the New Territories, Tin Shui Wai was commenced in the late 1980s with plans dating from the early 1980s, as the second new town in the Yuen Long district (Figure 7.5). The overall area of the site was 4.3 square kilometers, with a population in 2014 of 292,000 inhabitants, on the way to scheduled build-out at 306,000 inhabitants (International New Town Institute 2010). This is the densest new town, at 67,906 people per square kilometer in 2006, and over twice the density of the next highest town. Built on reclaimed land, the town was developed next to the historic Ping Sha area of natural wetlands. The project was divided into two phases with two zones—the Development Zone and the Reserve Zone—with the latter of the phases starting in 1998. A constructed wetland was also completed between the Reserve Zone and the Mai Po Nature Reserve nearby. This then became the Hong Kong Wetland Park, which opened in 2006 (Tsang 2007, 301–20). The last public housing estate in the new town was completed in 2009, while the first was where the Housing Authority launched their Home Ownership Scheme of deeply subsidized flats in 1991. This was a program originally instituted in the late 1970s to provide an opportunity for home ownership for families unable to afford to buy in the private market and to encourage better-off tenants of rental flats to vacate in order to accommodate more needy families. This twinning of town development and housing provision has been and remains a consistent aspect of Hong Kong's New Town Programme.

The distribution of uses within Tin Shui Wai remained homogeneous despite efforts to achieve balanced development along with self-sufficiency. The early 1983 Master Development Plan for the new town, for instance, set aside 36.5 hectares for industrial development. However, nothing came of it. From its beginning in 1991, public housing production varied after a promising beginning with a new modular style of construction allowing for rapid building. By 2008, some seventy thousand publicly provided units were constructed in a series of housing estates, centered at and near ground level on community spaces comprising children's play areas, performance spaces, community halls, and recreational areas (Hong Kong Planning Department 2015).

The town center was constructed adjacent to the elevated MTR station, serviced by pedestrian links. Within this town center were various shopping opportunities, together with food and beverage establishments, and community services. Tin Shui Wai is also served by a light-rail system linking the town to outlying areas,

Yuen Long, and Sui Hong to the south. A station for the light rail was also located next to the at-grade bus station in the town center, in a manner similar to Japanese counterparts. Several malls and some other commercial buildings add to the urban architectural variety along the main axis of the town center. The

new town has seven secondary schools, nine primary schools, and a large hospital, now under construction. Although mostly a public sector affair, Tin Shui Wai also embraced some private sector residential development. Chief among this was the Kingwood Villas by Cheung Kong Holdings (later CK Hutchinson Holdings), providing fifty-eight high-rise blocks of housing, built in seven stages and comprising 15,808 dwelling units (Kingswood Villas 2018).[2]

Unfortunately, Tin Shui Wai was labeled the "City of Misery" in 2006 because of unusually high incidences of domestic violence, mental illness, and suicide.[3] This situation was attributed, by social workers, to the new town's remote location, the limited number of job opportunities available within the town, and the very high density of the public housing estates. Some also argued that the relatively large number of new mainland Chinese immigrants struggled to adjust to Hong Kong's culture and social dynamics, plunging them into social difficulties. Statistically, there is also evidence to the same or similar effect. As noted earlier, the residential density is actually very high and has risen over time. Average household income, at HK$13,750 per month in 2006, was demonstrably lower than the median or average in the New Territories of HK$17,250 per month. Further, in the recent decline of incomes, the drop in Tin Shui Wai was 20.5 percent compared to 7.8 percent elsewhere in Hong Kong (Hong Kong Department of Social Work and Social Administration 2008). Demographically, the population is young, with higher unemployment rates than many other places in Hong Kong, and is also accompanied by high crime rates. There also appears to be a disproportionate number of vulnerable groups in Tin Shui Wai, with associated issues of poverty, unemployment, and individual as well as family problems. Although none of this is necessarily directly attributable to poor physical planning, the specter of such a conclusion still rises along with less than effective social policies and poor economic conditions.

Past and Present Satellites in Beijing and China

During the mid-eighteenth century, if not before, the idea of satellite developments to the well-defined and walled precinct of Beijing in China began to emerge. This was a time when urbanization was burgeoning and overcrowding was overtaking the already cramped quarters of the Qing dynasty, necessitating the stationing of Bannermen of different colors and stripes outside the walls in the surrounding landscape. Much later, in 1957 and 1958, several satellite settlements were proposed for the capital, explicitly referring, according to some, to Saarinen's concept of organic decentralization and, at the time, to Abercrombie's Greater London Plan. For others, firmly under the tutelage of Soviet experts, satellite urban proposals were advanced in the manner of the 1935 plan of Moscow, with its road structure and greenbelts. In any event, the so-called Spider Plan for Beijing emerged, as a part of the overall master-planning activity, with satellites centered on industrial production ringing the city (P. G. Rowe 2005a, 144–48). This also coincided with an abrupt change in emphasis to the "production of the means of production" in official circles and rather wholesale conversion of cities, including Beijing, from sites of consumption to sites of industrial development.

In addition, the idea of building nearby or adjacent to well-established cities and urban areas in China had an even longer-standing record of occurrence. Certainly, in antiquity when settlement sites were abandoned for one reason or another, others often sprung up nearby. Again, the territory that became Greater Beijing comes to mind, with successive separate settlements by the Jin, Zhong, Yuan, and so on. Also, side-by-side development often ensued even in notable city-building situations such as in venerable Chang'an (Steinhardt 1999, 12–15). There the Daming Palace complex, for instance, was built by the ruling emperor for his father, adjoining the imperial compound, which, in turn, was subsequently expanded to the south into the now familiar 108-block gridiron of Chang'an and now Xi'an (P. Xue 2006). Both modern and contemporary examples have followed in Shanghai, for instance, during the 1950s with the building of Caoyang Xincun on the western outskirts, which eventually grew into a town within or beside a city in excess of one hundred thousand inhabitants. Certainly, expansion of Chongqing beyond its original walled redoubt in the Changjiang followed in a side-by-side manner, as did the east-to-west spread of communities making up Shenzhen today, like so many beads on a string. Throughout, in much of this successive side-by-side and satellite development, the need to respond to provision of newer and different functional urban requirements is evident, in addition to the need to release population and related pressures on cities and towns.

Tongzhou

Today, Tongzhou is the largest new town in the Greater Beijing region, well after emerging as a prosperous harbor town during the Ming and Qing dynasties. This was largely because of the Grand Canal making its way north up to the capital from Hangzhou far in the south and, much later on, as one of those towns designated an industrial satellite during the 1950s to 1970s (Shui 2008). Historically, Tongzhou was first authorized as a town in 1368, based on an existing settlement beside the Grand Canal. Expansion was then carried out in 1499 on the western bank of the canal (J. Zhou 2012, 244–49). Located between Beijing and Tianjin, the town had an advantageous trading position, which began to fade, however, by the mid-nineteenth century, with other improvements in modern transportation involving roads and, later, rail.

By the late 1950s, some forty state-owned and city-owned large-scale factories and enterprises were deployed to Tongzhou, primarily focusing on chemical, machine, printing, and textile industries. With little to no plan in place, these establishments were scattered into an ad hoc array, although never very far from the town center. Then, in 1978 the first multistory housing was built alongside the first department store. Further, in the 1982 Beijing Plan, the first edition after the historic opening up to the outside world, Tongzhou was designated as a growth pole. Adoption of a new industrial and land-use model followed in 1992, also with twenty-eight neighborhoods having been built by 1995 (Figure 7.6). In fact, a Special Economic and Industrial Zone was designated to further encourage entry by manufacturing industries. From 1978 and somewhat beyond 1995, Tongzhou was one of the most successful industrial towns in China. However, during this time

Figure 7.6. Aerial view of Tongzhou, China. Courtesy of Wikimedia Commons (2013).

the local government also began to lose control over development amid an array of multiple stakeholders and special interests. From then on, the town, by then a district of Beijing, became a market-driven, self-developing Chinese new town.

With the release of the Second Tongzhou Master Plan in 1996, emphasis shifted to technically intense but nonpolluting industry. Under the aegis of Beijing's polynuclei regional growth strategy, the number of new towns was also reduced from forty to fourteen but with Tongzhou still in an important position (J. Zhou 2012, 244–265). With top-down management still performing poorly, market-oriented real estate development boomed, with the most rapid acceleration taking place after 2001. This was attributable as much as anything to Tongzhou's proximity to Beijing's central business district in Chaoyang and to regional infrastructural provisions of expressways and light rail that opened in 2004. By 2003, the amount of housing for sale in Tongzhou approached almost half that for the Beijing metropolitan region, although after 2005 this share declined precipitously. Certainly, up until that time any goal of reaching a balanced satellite town was not achieved. Tongzhou became a dormitory town attached primarily to Beijing's central business district. Fully 93.6 percent of the constructed floor area built between 2001 and 2008 was for housing, with a further 5.5 percent in retail and only 0.4 percent in office commercial use (Tongzhou Municipal Local History Office 2003; J. Zhou 2012, 255). The most common form of housing at the time was mid-rise from six to nine stories in height built on former farm lands. Regeneration of the older historical town, an aim of the 1996 plan, was also sluggish.

Tongzhou's third incarnation occurred around the Beijing 2005–20 Master Plan, with which two urban axes and two urban corridors were proposed, alongside of a "central city–new town–new villages" arrangement for the broader regional network. Within this framework, Tongzhou was one of three major new towns sustained on the eastern development corridor of Beijing (J. Zhou 2012, 258–65). Here, it was to be developed as a multifaceted center with competitive finance and business sectors, as well as cultural activities. In the long run it was also designated to accommodate decentralization of municipal government bureaus from central Beijing. The plan, covering 135 square kilometers, proposed a population of one million permanent inhabitants by 2020. The plan's general spatial structure was to be defined by infrastructure mainly in the form of roads and light rail, public park spaces, and public facilities, as well as a network of "green-blue" corridors, greenbelts, and open spaces. Design at the largest scale, however, was still very weak. Demographically, the new town component of the broader Tongzhou district had 420,000 long-term residents and some 220,000 short-term inhabitants, without permanent resident status (*Beijing Tongzhou Government Statistical Yearbook* 2010). Most in-migrants came from central Beijing in an outward push, with the remainder from other provinces in China. Most were commuters, with fully 270,000 people living in Tongzhou and working in central Beijing, often causing serious congestion.

Within the cultural domain another conspicuous aspect of Tongzhou is the art community of Songzhuang and particularly Xiaopu Village. Located on the eastern side of the Grand Canal, northeast of the older central core of Tongzhou, Songzhuang and Xiaopu emerged in the early 2000s as artists moved out of the 798 art district further to the northwest because of high rents. In large part, they settled in nearby Songzhuang, renting from farmers among others. Then, as the larger town's economy rose, the farmers, the Songzhuang township leaders, and the artists came to an arrangement to combine development of art clusters with commercial real estate development. Under this arrangement Xiaopu Village, covering a relatively small area of 3.5 square kilometers, opened to some seventeen thousand artists, three thousand of whom were resident in the village at any one time, renting land for studios and residences, along with supporting some one hundred galleries and thirty museums or similar display spaces in the general area.[4]

Having gained the capacity to develop through a 1997 transfer of agricultural land into developable land, original plans for industry gave way to art production. Artists continue to find the location attractive because of affordable rents, good support services, proximity to the 798 art district for exhibiting, and access to township services and support for their families. In short, during the post-1990s, Tongzhou deindustrialized substantially, and real estate development became a dominant economic engine in the town. Productivity was not high, and employment opportunities—artists aside—were in lower-end services, compared to most of the reasonably well-educated population. Current plans, including construction of the vast municipal government facilities, appear to be focusing on attracting modern business, upgrading the spatial qualities of the town, and providing for missing public services.[5] Despite its dormitory quality, Tongzhou is one of the more urbane and lively towns within the broader Beijing region.

Yizhuang

Yizhuang began in the mid-1990s as an industrial park and industrially oriented district in the southeast of Beijing, south of the Fifth Ring Road. The development was backed by the Beijing municipal government in a manner similar to Zhongguancun near Tsinghua and Peking Universities, although with a different industrial orientation. Starting off as a low-density development, Yizhuang became more intensified, resulting in high-rise residential development, of more mixed use, and with higher occupancy of its spacious industrial sites (Figure 7.7). The population on the site thirty-eight or so square kilometers also expanded to around three hundred thousand in 2010 (China National Bureau of Statistics 2013). The degree of appreciation of property values has also been considerable, particularly among the relatively spacious and well-amenitized attached villa estates built to a height of two to three stories along curvilinear streets embedded within larger megaplots comprising the grid of roads and streets surrounding the project. Nowadays at costs of 36,000 CNY to 150,000 CNY for one hundred square meters, residential properties are expensive, particularly at this distance from the central city. In part this is also due to the proximity to non–service sector employment in Yizhuang itself.[6] This translates into about ten times an average salary, on a par with other major city prices. Generally, though, Yizhuang is regarded as being relatively successful if less and less affordable as a place to live. The industrial and related commercial development has become particularly well established, featuring light manufacturing, biotechnology, biomedical, and chemical production, although of a largely nonpolluting kind. Yizhuang also hosts numerous big-box showrooms, shopping centers, and malls.

Overall, physical development of Yizhuang is underlain by a gridiron pattern of roads and streets, with a relatively clear spatial hierarchy. This grid, in turn, parallels the G1 highway, which makes its way southeast toward Tianjin. The highway also serves as a central axis for the local road and street grid, with several under-highway crossings from west to east along its length. Residential development is largely confined to the western side of the G1, with industrial and related commercial development on the larger eastern side. Line 5 of the Beijing subway runs through and transects the town site, with nine stations stops, many of which are

Figure 7.7. View of Yizhuang, China. Courtesy of Huitu.

located above grade and serve as junctions below with commercial and day-to-day service uses. Most streets have ample sidewalks and are well vegetated. Park spaces, particularly along the western river front edge of the town, between various gated residential communities, and toward the north and the boundary with the Fifth Ring Road, are generally well manicured and abundant in recreational amenities. These areas, in turn, give off a feeling of a certain Western gentility, together with the pedestrian areas and plazas beside the subway stops.

The scale of the underlying grid of roads and streets is broad, yielding, as mentioned earlier, megaplots of on the order of five hundred meters on a side. This enables factory and office complexes to be combined in semi-campus-like formats, whereas in the residential areas, as noted earlier, the megaplots became frameworks for inserting more organically aligned gated communities. At the end of subway line 5, a station stop has been located adjacent to a high-speed train stop on the way to Tianjin. Once fully operational, this will add to Yizhuang's overall accessibility. The principal anomalies in the town development are the limited number of west-to-east crossings of the G1, causing a certain amount of traffic congestion; a solid waste site with methane extraction off to one side of the industrial development; and the uncertain impact of the high-speed train stop, if, and when, it finally opens.

Seeking Effective Deconcentration in Seoul and South Korea

From its earliest beginnings as Hanyang in 1396 under the Chosun dynasty, Seoul remained faithful to its original siting conditions almost up until the end of the Japanese colonization in 1945 and subsequent destruction during the civil war between 1950 and 1953. These conditions yielded an almost circular form of urbanization nestled into a basin surrounded by mountains and hills, with the Han River flowing to the south. It conformed to the Hyonsedo cartographic and geomantic tradition imported from China in the ninth century, which, among other attributes, reflected the flow of the earth's energies materialized by wind and water. In most respects, it was deemed an ideal site for human settlement (Jung 2013, 2–20; P. G. Rowe 2005a, 82–83).

Then, as South Korea made its remarkable recovery under military rule into the 1960s, Seoul's population expanded prodigiously, rising to around six million inhabitants from 1960 to 1980, at rates close to 6 or 7 percent per annum, year on year, among the fastest ever in a modernizing city of any scale (Kim and Choe 1997, 43–52). The city's attraction factors included production running at roughly twice the rate elsewhere in the nation, rapidly improving community services that exceeded in quality and opportunity anything on offer elsewhere, and a thriving informal economy, alongside of the booming official version. By 1966, the government passed its Comprehensive Development Plan for Seoul to decrease the overwhelming pressure on the central area, including plans to move southward across the Han River. By 1972 and 1973, multiple high-rise centers were developed in places such as Mokdong, Yongdongpo, Gangnam, and Jamsil (Kim and Choe 1997, 99–103; Kun-Hyuck and Ohn 1997, 89). Early satellite development had also been encouraged in the service of new industrial towns such as Ulsan as early as 1962, and Pohang later in 1968 (Jung 2013, 55–56; B. H. Lee 2012). Then, the aim was to lead needed economic growth, particularly in heavy manufacturing, somewhat after the fashion of China, although with very different ideological underpinnings.

Despite these efforts to deconcentrate development of the capital, Seoul continued to expand organically and often in place. On the eve of the rise of the democratic period, a decision was taken nationally to create five new towns beyond Seoul's active perimeter and with sufficient attractive opportunities and amenities to be effective in slowing the central city's growth (Jung 2013, 68–69; P. G. Rowe 2005a, 82–86). By then the continued growth pressure joined by rising housing prices made the city less and less affordable for many, compounded by a shortage of developable land, and management problems concerned with traffic congestion and environmental degradation. The five new towns were Pyeongchon, Bundang, Ilsan, Sanbon, and Jungdong, all some twenty-five kilometers from central Seoul but still inside the broader capital area. Unlike in the past, these new towns were relatively effective in circumscribing Seoul's urban growth and slowing the influx into the city compared to outward migration. Indeed, in recent times the city of Seoul's population has declined a little, whereas the number of inhabitants in the broader urban region has continued to increase, up to around twenty or more million people.

New town developments continued into the new millennium in a third phase, including new-towns-in-town. The aim of these efforts was to address multiple purposes for urbanization, to incorporate broader administrative and service functions, and to ride the trend toward so-called smart and innovative cities. To help improve the gateway to Seoul through Incheon on the western coast, the Korean government entered into an arrangement with private and government-linked developers to build the Songdo International Business District in 2001 (Henry 2012, 10–11). Later in 2009 and on the heels of the world economic crisis, low-carbon and sustainable urban development received stimulus, also affecting places such as Songdo that were then under construction. What the future holds for these more contemporary new town ventures remains to be seen, with some such as Pangyo appearing to fare quite well, but others, including Songdo, appearing to do less well.

Bundang

Located with good rail transit and automobile expressway access to Seoul and particularly to southern areas such as upscale Gangnam, Bundang's development spanned from 1989 to 1996. The new town covers an area of 19.6 square kilometers and has a population at present of about 390,000 and a density or around twenty thousand people per square kilometer, housing some 90,760 households (Jung 2013, 68; B. H. Lee 2012). It is and was the largest of the second round of satellite settlements and the first round of real new towns in a large-scale, planned, and aspirationally self-contained sense. The Korean Land Corporation acted as the primary developer and, until recently, was a strong government-run property developer working throughout the southern peninsula. Prior to the arrival of the new town construction, about twelve thousand people lived in the area, primarily involved in local business and a little agriculture. The natural setting for Bundang was a combination of a relatively flat valley around the Tancheon Stream, surrounded by well-vegetated and comparatively rugged hills typical of that part of South Korea. In short, with the Bundang rail line in place alongside other infrastructure, the quality of the natural and surrounding environment of the new town was and remains high. On a broader scale, the new town was also a part of Bundang-gu and Seongnam City, an administrative area of some 69.4 square kilometers and a

Figure 7.8. View of Bundang, South Korea. Courtesy of Wikimedia Commons (2006).

population of close to 450,000 people (Seoul Metropolitan Government 2017; Figure 7.8).

Bundang's overall configuration was a linear plan with offshoots and five dense urban cores, separated by green space in between. It incorporated various housing types from high-rise units to detached houses. In total, there were around ninety-four thousand apartments, principally in high-rise towers, and some 2,980 detached or semidetached units in the form of townhouses and single homes (Min Joo 2013). Generally, the denser urban cores were surrounded by and contained the high-rise apartments, with the townhomes and detached houses out on the periphery. Commercial uses were located in the distributed cores of activities and various community facilities, including schools. The central and largest commercial area had almost five hundred thousand square meters of facilities. The green axes running through the scheme also included a central park immediately adjacent to the central commercial core. Community streets, typical in some modern developments in South Korea, are of a pedestrian kind and provide convenient access to local amenities and community services. Overall, 32.4 percent of the land area is given over to residential development, 4.5 percent to commercial areas, 3.8 percent to schools, and 0.9 percent for public offices. In addition, fully 19.3 percent of the land is set aside for parks and recreation space, with a further 20.1 percent for roads and 19.0 percent for other functions (B. H. Lee 2012, 43–63). Commercial and nearby residential areas have a well-scaled urban feel to them, while the streamside environment is well landscaped, as is the central park, making both amenable venues for outdoor activities. The headquarters of several banks, together with the Korean Land Corporation and prominent IT firms, as well as notable shopping areas, also contribute to Bundang's relatively self-reliant character and success as a balanced community (Korea Land Corporation 1997).

Songdo

By contrast, the Songdo business district was contrived as the product of a public-private partnership between the city of Incheon and Gale International with Morgan Stanley and POSCO. Under this arrangement, some six hundred hectares of reclaimed land on Incheon's waterfront south of the city proper, along with infrastructure, is provided by the city, with the remaining development coming from the private sector. Within that sector, Gale International had the majority position at 61 percent, with POSCO at 30 percent and Morgan Stanley at 9 percent (McNeill 2009). An original master plan by OMA for a technology-manufacturing hub city floundered as a result of the financial crisis. Subsequently, the international consortium, headed by Gale International, was brought in, and Kohn Pedersen Fox developed the final version of the plan (Figure 7.9). More broadly, Songdo was a part of new development and public works used to reframe the gateway to Seoul and, by extension, to South Korea. This reframing also included the Incheon International Airport, the 12.3-kilometer-long sea link and bridge south to Songdo, and further developments, under the aegis of the Incheon Free Economic Zone in Yeongjong, adjacent to the airport, as well as in Cheongna on the eastern side, running into Seoul, sixty-five kilometers away. At the outset, considerable emphasis was placed on securing a foreign developer and

Figure 7.9. Street view of Songdo, South Korea (2012). Courtesy of Peter G. Rowe personal collection, Cambridge, Massachusetts.

master planner, ergo Gale International and Kohn Pedersen Fox, under the idea of enabling the attraction of foreign investment, particularly in the Songdo district (Gale International 2007). Songdo finally broke ground in 2005.

Overall, Songdo was envisioned to comprise eighty thousand apartments with a likely population of 180,000 or more inhabitants, five million square meters of office space, and nine hundred thousand square meters of commercial retail space. Fully 40 percent of the land area was to be set aside for green and park space, with an assortment of schools, hospitals, and cultural facilities. Incheon Line One, along with bus and roadway access, was to provide transport, although less directly back to Seoul. Several universities, including segments of the local university in Incheon, were to participate in the district, which was also billed early on as a "smart city" with substantial internet and data network linkages for various business and domestic functions (Chohan 2014). In addition, a vacuum trash collection and sorting system was to be installed, and LEED requirements were to be met by all buildings. The skyline of Songdo was to be dominated by the sixty-five-story Northeast Asia Trade Tower (NEATT), Korea's tallest (at the time of its construction) and a symbol of the general thrust of the overall development well beyond the peninsula toward the northeastern region of Asia (Kohn Pedersen Fox n.d.). The final master plan incorporated three reasonably distinct gridded urban areas alongside of three generously sized neighborhood parks, with a broad axis slicing diagonally through the site and terminating at the entrance to the highway to Incheon and to Seoul. To one side of this entry, government offices and institutions were to be concentrated. Part of the residential community was to feature canal and waterside development in a manner alluding to Venice, and the large central park within the scheme was intended to refer to its equivalent in New York City.

As of 2014, the population of Songdo was sixty-seven thousand inhabitants, well short of the final target to be attained that year. Overall, the project remained half complete. Although the private sector consortium got their equity back through fees, there was little profit available after twelve years of work. By and large, the condominiums sold well, but much of the planned commercial space remained either empty or unbuilt (Nam 2013). The 305-meter-tall Northeast Asia Trade Tower was completed, with its 423-room hotel, as well as offices, for a total of 139,000 square meters of built space. The striking convention center with its zigzag metal roof was also completed, although still reaching for business. Moreover, the attraction of commercial investment remained in short supply. Perhaps more telling from an urban design point of view, Songdo was roundly criticized as being mundane and generic in appearance (Chohan 2014, 20–25). While the initial developments—such as the NEATT Tower, the convention center, and the

First World Residential Towers—hewed closely to the master plan, subsequent developments completed by local developers, without the involvement of the international consortium or design team, reverted to the norm of Korean suburban residential architecture, with detrimental implications for the cityscape. The traffic regulations governing street design were also deemed to be relatively inflexible, resulting in unusually wide streets that also seemed to discourage pedestrian movement, with the exception perhaps of the canal-side paths. Gale International's idea of a "city in a box," as it was called, has proven to be overly controlling so far, even if the expansive deployment of digital technologies is enabling (Williamson 2013). Strategically planned, from the local perspective, to intervene into the world-city network, the new town has gained little traction. Indeed, Ahn Song-soo, the mayor of Incheon from 2002, lost his last election in 2010 reportedly because of entering the city into a range of expensive construction projects, including Songdo, which caused subsequent financial difficulties (Na 2012).

Building Singapore's Housing and Development Board Heartland

In 1959, Singapore, an island at the tip of what was Malaya, gained self-rule from Britain and became part of the Malay Federation, with the People's Action Party (PAP) in power and Lee Kwan Yew as prime minister. Having made strenuous efforts to remain in the federation on the grounds that Singapore was too small to make it on its own, it was summarily rejected from the federation, becoming a fledgling independent city-state in 1965. Faced with a nation-building process, Lee Kwan Yew and his colleagues confronted numerous stark and daunting realities (P. G. Rowe 2005a, 68–69). There was unemployment at levels of 17 to 20 percent, with a sharp decline in the entrepôt trade that Singapore had historically relied on. There was exploding population growth, with the population rising from around one million inhabitants in 1950 to two million by 1970. Living conditions were appalling, with some three hundred thousand people living in squatter settlements, and deteriorating infrastructure that had not been touched since the onset of World War II (Figure 7.10). Moreover, ethnic conflicts began to fester among the minority Malay and Indian populations against the majority Chinese, and during the political struggle in neighboring Indonesia, there was a mounting outside threat to Singapore's security and very existence.

Squarely facing these and other difficulties, the PAP elite set about to lay the foundation for a remarkable recovery of circumstances culminating in the modern state of Singapore today. Building on the statutory board legacy of the British, the young government capitalized on its assets of a low-wage, well-educated, hard-

China-town, Singapore.

Figure 7.10. Crowding in Singapore (1925). University of Washington Libraries, Special Collections, Postcard Collection. PH Coll 8.

working, and mostly English-speaking population, part of which also made up a squeaky-clean bureaucracy. Quickly the Housing and Development Board (HDB) emerged from the older Singapore Housing Trust and joined with other institutions, such as the Economic Development Board, to foster what was dubbed "collective consumption" (Castells, Goh, and Kwok 1990, 329–33). Under this developmental model, the state promoted and nurtured economic growth, capital accumulation, and direct foreign investment by underwriting labor costs and social stability through the provision of public housing and timely infrastructure improvements, especially for industry and transportation.

To spatially guide and help orchestrate the activities of the statutory boards and other developmental institutions, master-planning exercises were undertaken beginning in 1958 to 1962 with United Nations assistance and the work of E. E. Lorange—a Norwegian planner. This was followed in 1963 by another United Nations team of Koenigsberger, Abrams, and Kobe and the eventual contract to produce what became known as the Ring Concept Plan in 1965, with eventual promulgation by the state in 1971 (P. G. Rowe 2005a, 79–80). Under this plan a heavy belt of urban development was to be concentrated along the southern coast of the island, with Jurong in the west, the nominal downtown area at the center, and Changi to the east. Two corridors around a central catchment area moving up to the north provided spines for higher-density development of town centers and residential estates of public housing. These were also to be furnished with mass rail transit, as well as expressways, to ensure ready access to employment opportunities both within the towns and to the heavily developed southern belt. Different population targets were assumed, varying as high as four or more million inhabitants. Singapore's current population is about 5.4 million people. A massive state-supported housing program ensued. Today, some 85 percent of Singaporeans live in public housing, the highest in nominal terms in the developed world (Center for Livable Cities 2015, 10).

Toa Payoh

Toa Payoh was the first residential estate and town center built after Queenstown. Located on the north-south mass rail transit line (MRT), north of the older central and Orchard Road areas of Singapore, it was constructed from 1964 onward. Covering 8.17 square kilometers, it housed 125,000 inhabitants in 2015, with a residential area of 2.48 square kilometers and a density of around fifteen thousand people per square kilometer (Singapore Department of Statistics 2015b). Though it was planned to be developed as early as 1960, construction of Toa Payoh did not begin until later, owing to difficulties in relocating a *kampong* and squatter settlement on the site, both actively involved in agriculture. With an eventual target population of 250,000 people in thirty-five thousand dwelling units, along with numerous shops, schools, recreational amenities, and places of worship, Toa Payoh new town was envisaged to be self-sufficient at least with regard to daily goods and services (*Straits Times* 1966). With the HDB as developers, the first occupants began to move in by 1966. Subsequently, the new community was bordered by others, such as Bishan and Serangoon. Some measure of self-containment in the sense of on-site industrial and related commercial development did occur with the Royal Philips electronics establishment, including medical and electronic equipment manufacture. A HDB hub was also located within the town center and completed in 2002. In fact, the town center itself grew increasingly popular around an L-shaped open mall, with department stores at each end, along with two plazas with a branch library, a cinema, a post office, and some commercial offices (Figure 7.11).[7]

Modeled somewhat closely on British new town precedents, the layout of Toa Payoh consists primarily of the town center surrounded by separated, self-contained neighborhoods, each with its own shopping and commercial center. This spatial configuration is then contained in a more or less circular loop road called Lorong Toa Payoh, with direct access to the larger and busier Pan-Island and Central expressways. The MRT and bus stations are located adjacent to the town center and the mall, with the transit line extending to the north and the Braddell MRT stop

Figure 7.11. Street view of Toa Payoh, Singapore (2016). Courtesy of Peter G. Rowe personal collection, Cambridge, Massachusetts.

coterminous with Lorong Toa Payoh. This hierarchical and centered arrangement of both the components of community and infrastructure served, and still serves, as a basic spatial template for the construction of Singapore's new towns and estates. In Toa Payoh, it is further augmented by a substantial town park, replete with a pool, islands, and bridges, located to the south of the town center and hub. In addition, there is a sizable thirty-five-hundred-seat stadium and sports hall, drawing users also from elsewhere.[8]

Under an Estate Renewal Strategy run by the HDB, building replacements, redevelopment, and updating has taken place over the years, with the result that the estate appears to be in good physical condition (Han 2014). The once open ground-floor areas below the multistory housing slab blocks are now enclosed by local commercial retail and service activities, again enriching the lifestyles of inhabitants. In fact, many apparently prefer to shop closer to home in the neighborhood. Building stock is a mix of high-rise point towers, multistory shop houses, particularly near the mall, and mid-rise apartment slab blocks. Architecturally, many of the earlier developments in these regards were distinctly modernist in a subdued expressive form, clearly signaling when they were originally constructed. Over time, property values have appreciated substantially, with three-bedroom units selling for around 370,000 Singaporean dollars and with rental prices on the order of 2,000 Singaporean dollars per month all the way up to five-bedroom units selling for 750,000 Singaporean dollars and above (Housing and Development

Board 2013). This is quite expensive by local standards and attests in part to the success of the new town as well as to its central location. Until the 1980s, however, Toa Payoh, like Geylang, another early new town, was notorious for vice and the presence of gangs and criminal syndicates. Indeed, it was often referred to locally as "the Chicago of Singapore" in these regards (Han 2014, 1).

Punggol

With plans announced in 1996, the Punggol 21 Initiative started development in 1998, but with interruptions due to the aftermath of the 1997 Asian economic crisis, along with later local troubles in Singapore's construction industry. Finally, the project was initiated in earnest in 2007 by the HDB, becoming Singapore's latest round of housing estates and, effectively, new town construction. Located at the end of the northeast MRT line on the Tanjung Punggol peninsula on the northeastern edge of the island, Punggol has an area of 9.34 square kilometers and a population in 2015 of 107,750 inhabitants within a residential area of 3.74 square kilometers yielding a density of twelve thousand people per square kilometer, moderate for Singapore (Singapore Department of Statistics 2015a; Figure 7.12).

Figure 7.12. Bird's-eye view of Punggol, Singapore (2016). Courtesy of Peter G. Rowe personal collection, Cambridge, Massachusetts.

Originally the site was agricultural, and it was also the location of a notorious massacre during World War II. It was also occupied by several *kampongs*. In addition to the MRT line, Punggol is served by two light-rail transit loops, bringing more or less everyone in the estates to within three hundred meters of a station. These loops terminate in the MRT station. The new housing component of Punggol is a mix of private houses, extensive condominiums, and HDB flats grouped into distinctive estates of on the order of twelve hundred to twenty-eight hundred dwelling units and within an overall plan by the HDB. Crossing through the project is the 12.25-hectare linear Punggol Walkway Park, opened in 2011 (Singapore National Parks 2016). With a focus on a range of leisure-time activities, this park is operated and maintained by the National Park Board and includes splendid riverside walking areas, nature trails, cycling paths, and the distinctive Kelong Bridge spanning across the walkway.

Apart from its sporadic start, Punggol has also been relatively slow to get fully underway. Only sixteen thousand of the scheduled eighty thousand dwelling units, to house an eventual population of some 250,000 residents, were built by 2007, alongside only one of the three scheduled shopping malls and virtually no recreational facilities (Singapore Department of Statistics 2015a, 12–16). No doubt this uneven development with regard to self-sufficiency, let alone self-containment, has hampered the build-out and occupation of the new town (Meng 2016). Fortunately, as of 2016, Waterway Point and its MRT connection was launched, also providing a town square and gathering place for the community. The overall spatial layout of the plan for Punggol, in by now typical HDB fashion, comprises loose, grid-like layouts of megaplots, several hundred meters and more on a side. This certainly allows for the formation of distinctive communities within the plots, reinforced in many places by apartment buildings feeding off the central spines of community facilities and vegetated open space above the at-grade and below-grade parking areas. However, walkability beyond these verdant and well-manicured patches to MRT or light-rail stations is poorly defined and uninviting, at least at present. Also, there does not seem to be the interneighborhood convenience that is so evident in the earlier residential estates and town centers.

Furthermore, expressively the urban architecture, with significant amounts of multistory housing, especially adjacent to the larger walkway and park, has a distinctly commercial rather than residential feel and scale to it, further undermining the simpler clarity of the earlier schemes in Singapore.[9] With land available for further estate planning in short supply, the HDB is also shifting into more interesting architectural experiments and eventual fuller deployment of high-rise, high-density redevelopments of existing and other available sites. Except for some twinning with the Jurong Town Corporation industrial developments, or even because of this, the days of residential estate and town center developments seem to be over in Singapore.

Other Instances

Beyond this account of what might be considered mainstream modern new town developments in East and Southeast Asia, there have been others. This is certainly evident in broad municipal expansions within metropolitan areas in the form of side-by-side rather than satellite developments at a distance from central urban cores. Two instances in this regard that come to mind are the Bonafacio and Makati expansions of Manila in the Philippines during the 1990s and beyond (Zipporah 2014). Both areas are coterminous with older parts of Manila and also seem to be consistent with the institutional fragmentation within the broader metropolitan area, now comprising seventeen separate municipalities, particularly after the passage of the local government law of 1986.[10] On par, this event imbued the city with a populist but also "tribal" air of separate fiefdoms. With further development, or redevelopment, of sparsely settled military and other areas from the American colonial era still in the offing, this trend may well continue. At over twenty million inhabitants in Greater Manila, it is a primate city within its national setting, much like Seoul and Tokyo in theirs. Also as in earlier times in both those cities, the pull factors associated with Manila continue to be strong, pushing forward further adjacent development.

Finally, there have been some occasions of new town developments due to circumstances other than population pressures and servicing new employment opportunities. The construction of Putrajaya in Malaysia, which began in 1995, is a case in point. Conceived as the administrative center, although not capital, of the nation, it was located amid palm groves and water bodies, twenty-five kilometers south of Kuala Lumpur. The brainchild of Mohamad Mahathir, the prime minister, it was somewhat more than a vanity project, despite grandiose plazas, boulevards, and buildings, marshalling together efficiently a full range of government departments and bureaucracies (King 2008). Slowed by the Asian economic crisis in 1997, the population moved up from a few thousand to 88,300 by 2015. A low-density configuration by design, at eighteen hundred people per square kilometer, it had substantial areas devoted to open space and conservation reserves (Malaysia Department of Statistics, 2015). Planned, among other things, as a "garden-smart" city, Putrajaya is well served by sophisticated infrastructure, barely visible security precautions, and transit links. With the rail link to Kuala Lumpur in one direction and to the international airport in the other, the new town is also conveniently located regionally, particularly for its ostensible administrative and white-collar purposes (King 2008).

Summary Comments

Looking at these new towns, the particularities and even peculiarities of one place as distinct from another are often evident. Conceived in urban design terms largely in a modernist idiom, the results are rather more a collection of modernisms by way of local reflections and evolving circumstances. This divergence, however, has perhaps not gone far enough, as many of the towns still seem stranded somehow in the time and place of their early conception and where the "planned instantaneousness"—if it can be called that—has not yielded sufficiently to take on the seemingly inevitable, familiar, authentic, timeless, and even organic qualities of the cities with which they are associated. Most were bravely assembled in response to substantial and even massive migratory urban influxes. Many were expected to provide affordable accommodations at distances from well-established urban centers. Some were even intended to achieve functionally direct and novel mergers with transportation systems and assorted precisely programmed and explicitly specialized public services. All in some way hoped to be self-sufficient with regard to community if not lifestyle services, as well as balanced in development between resident populations and job opportunities on-site or nearby. Of the two aims, self-sufficiency was achieved at least at some basic level, although balanced growth was rarely if ever accomplished, resulting in long and crowded commutes, often with a feeling of dormitory conditions. Even in some Chinese examples where industrial development clearly led the way, it eventually if not rather quickly became moribund, stranding inhabitants far away from where they worked. In other places such as the technopoles of Japan, the difficulty in manufacturing sufficient attractiveness on-site stunted growth, especially for a clientele of well-educated, worldly wise, and technically accomplished citizenry.

For many inhabitants, though, all was not lost as they came to terms with their new town environments and began to find them satisfactory both as staging points in life before moving on and as permanent homes. Although high points of urban distinction were either absent or muted, neither did the town qualities slip into becoming slums or down-and-out places to reside. In most cases, a polite middle ground emerged, even if more on the side of a mundane ordinariness than a pointedly quotidian celebration of everyday life. Back then, there probably were no other alternatives, especially during an era strongly shaped by a technologically inclined temperament, pragmatic reckoning with need, and belief in the viability of big plans and their implementation. Today, by contrast, urban dynamics, development cycles, and aspirations in the region have changed or are changing, even in China. Rampant growth is giving way to spatial consolidation, diversification, and even withdrawal, as populations move into phases of aging and even declination. Like a proverbial tide that rolled in and began to recede, it has left some new towns stranded, probably most blatantly in Tokyo and other parts of Japan. In other circumstances such as those in Singapore, South Korea, and to some extent Hong Kong, redevelopment has begun to take over, preserving a status quo in some places, without promoting much in the way of expansion. In short, as much as anything, new towns in the East Asian region are becoming or have become largely vestiges of a hectic period in the near past, starting around the 1950s into the 1960s and extending to the later 1990s and into the new millennium.

Notes

1. Author's personal observation of the town center, June 2016.
2. Also author field visit, May 2015.
3. Labeled by the director of social welfare, July 2006.
4. Songzhuang town officials, interview and field trip with author, June 2016.
5. Songzhuang town officials, interview and field trip with author, June 2016.
6. Yizhuang town officials, interview with author, May 2015.
7. Author's site visit to Toa Payoh, June 2016.
8. Author's site visit to Toa Payoh, June 2016.
9. Author's field survey, June 2016.
10. Author's conversation with Senator Ed Angara, March 18, 2016.

8

A Governance Perspective
on New Towns in China

Fulong Wu

New towns are large-scale, mixed-use developments in suburban or peri-urban areas. Chinese new towns have a quite specific connotation as a government-led development with private-sector participation (see Chapters 6 and 7). In China, small "designated towns" are the lowest urban administrative unit below the county and above rural villages, but Chinese new towns may not have a single government that is responsible for their administration. New towns can take the form of development corporations or commissions, but a large estate alone without a government office is usually not referred to as a new town. This does not mean that Chinese new towns are ungoverned clusters of housing with a mode of private governance (Low 2003). Rather, their birth predominantly results from a formal planning process. In this regard, new towns are a planning phenomenon rather than a movement of "edge cities" (Garreau 1991) under the chamber of commerce, representing a neoliberal suburbanism (Peck 2011). In a way, they resemble more their socialist predecessor, the "industrial residential complex" or industrial satellite town (D. R. Phillips and Yeh 1987; Yeh and Yuan 1987), as a planned means to speed up state-led industrialization (Golubchikov and Phelps 2011) but combined with a more market-oriented approach to land development.

Although some gated communities are built into superlarge estates, literally as new towns, they are very different from formally designated new towns because the former are purely residential areas developed by property developers. Their governance is largely achieved through their property management functions. New towns, however, are mixed-use developments built through a financial model to achieve more orderly land acquisition. The primary developer is the government-backed development corporation. Thus, Chinese new towns represent a more organized approach to suburban development beyond urban sprawl.

In this chapter, I argue that Chinese new towns represent a particular mode of postreform urban governance that combines state capacity in planning and mega urban projects with the real estate market. The state promotes new town development as a new spatial growth-oriented strategy to inject city building and property development into industrial suburbs. Since 2000, new towns or literally "new cities" (*xincheng*) have become a strategy that "represents city governments' effort to consolidate the territorial authority over the rural hinterland in the 2000s" (Hsing 2010, 113). Hsing argues that "the city government's strategies for territorial expansion are intertwined with real-estate strategies of place production, consumption, and marketing" and that "this new urbanism is more than a real-estate marketing strategy. Compared with Maoist policy that associated urban agendas with industrial production, the new urbanism embraces a new regime of accumulation and legitimation founded on land rents" (Hsing 2010, 114).

Chinese new towns have a high population density and an atmosphere that resembles the urban rather than the industrial zone. This marks a departure from earlier urban sprawl through residential dispersal and scattered industrial projects (Deng and Huang 2004; T. Zhang 2000), in which the local government was willing to lease more to attract investors (T. Zhang 2000). New towns might epitomize a new phase of suburbanization that takes the form of polycentric metropolitan development with higher-density nodes surrounding mass transit (Feng, Zhou, and Wu 2008) or a Chinese version of postsuburbia (F. Wu and Phelps 2011). While Chinese suburbs show the wide spread of high-rise residential buildings, new towns are built into an even denser form than the sprawled suburb. New towns are themselves "mega" urban projects (Orueta and Fainstein 2008).

From Urban Sprawl to New Towns: The Context of Emerging New Towns

Because new towns are associated with suburban development, it is helpful to review the three general stages of suburban development in China (F. Wu and Shen 2015): first, the suburbs as state-invested industrial space, 1949–78; second, industrial decentralization and suburban resident development, 1979–2000; third, administrative annexation and the development of new towns, 2001 onward. This description distinguishes the earlier stage of industrial decentralization and the later stage of new town development.

After the establishment of a land market in China, the land rent gradient began to transform Chinese cities and relocate industrial land uses to the suburbs (F. Wu and Yeh 1999). In suburban areas, there were widespread illegal industrial and residential land conversions through scattered and sprawling development (Deng and Huang 2004; Y. Zhou and Ma 2000). Local governments in the suburban areas were often uncoordinated and competed with the central city to attract investment through the swift release of land. Intercity competition also occurred. For example, Shanghai competed with smaller cities such as Kunshan to industrialize its suburban districts of Jiading and Songjiang, in response to aggressive entrepreneurial development in Jiangsu province (Li and Wu 2012). Using land sales to subsidize road construction has been a common practice.

Population redistribution in the post-reform period has in practice been driven by excessively high population density in central areas that were simply too congested. The desire to improve living conditions with decent space together with urban renewal caused residents to begin to relocate to the suburbs. In addition, the desire for more privacy means that the gated community is now widely adopted (Pow 2009; F. Wu 2005; L. Zhang 2010). Suburbs have thus become places to pursue privacy, active citizenship, and community building, which is not too dissimilar from suburbanization in the West.

In terms of development finance, new towns are one of the most effective forms to operate the new financial model of infrastructure development. The model has been widely documented (Lin and Yi 2011; Tao et al. 2010; F. Wu 2016; F. Wu and Shen 2015; Shen and F. Wu 2019). The operation of a system of tax sharing between central and local governments means that the local government is highly dependent on land sales income, giving a strong incentive to the local government to secure rural land and resell it at a higher price. Collectively owned agricultural land represents a relatively weak form of governance for resisting state land acquisition. But more relevant is the innovation of infrastructure finance. As local governments are not allowed to issue bonds creating government debts, they created the so-called state-backed investment and capital mobilizing platform (*touzi rongzi pingtai*). These are essentially state-owned enterprises under names such as land banking center or new town development corporation. These investment platforms use their land as assets to borrow from banks, with implicit government credit guarantee. But recently because of the risk of local government debt, the government is no longer allowed to play such a role.

Individual residential projects, though large, could not afford to develop key infrastructure. Rather, the new town provides a platform for real estate development. The primary developer, usually a state-owned development corporation, organizes the development of infrastructure and sells the serviced land to property developers. The development of a new town thus becomes an operational model of land finance. Later, because of the increase in land value, this model operated even more efficiently because the development corporation needs to sell only a small quantity of land to finance transport infrastructure. This leads to a more compact form of development surrounding key transport nodes. This is known as transit-oriented development (TOD) (Shen and F. Wu 2019), recently encouraged in China.

In addition to the financial model, since the 2000s there have been rising concerns over environmental problems, including the loss of agricultural land. The discourse has effectively transformed the Chinese land management system. Management has once again been centralized in the central government, which allocates quotas for converting agricultural land into nonagricultural uses (Xu, Yeh, and Wu 2009). On the other hand, the land market is now required to be more transparent, obliging all commercial development to go through the formal primary land market (i.e., bidding and auction). This has strengthened land management and stopped underregulated land conversions and sporadic suburban developments. Development is thus more efficiently organized through mega urban projects. The introduction of TOD opens up new opportunities to integrate developments to achieve higher density in suburban development nodes. The new town as a TOD project matches well the environmental discourse of public transit–served so-called compact development, gradually replacing urban sprawl as a preferred metropolitan spatial strategy.

Chinese new towns represent a formal planning approach to suburban development. They are designed suburbs (F. Wu 2010). These new settlements are wholly planned through comprehensive strategies and branding tactics. For example, Songjiang, Jiading, and Lingang new towns in Shanghai are designated as major suburban growth centers. Songjiang new town was originally planned with an English townscape, but because of the cost of development only a very limited area was actually designed as an English market town, while Jiading new town is promoted as a German town with German-invested automobile projects. Lingang new town was inspired by the concept of a garden city with a distinctive artificial lake in the city center. Many of these new towns were associated with the development of packaged master-planned communities (Knox 2008; Shen and Wu 2012; F. Wu 2010) as a tactic to attract the upwardly mobile middle class (L. Zhang 2010). But the purpose of building new towns often goes beyond private sector developments. The Shanghai examples were designed by international architecture firms, which lent the credibility of their global vision. The development took a new-build approach, treating the original site as a blank slate. The former rural villages to a large extent have been removed, demolished, or secluded into their own communities. In the case of Lingang, the new town is largely built on land reclaimed from the sea. However, in the peri-urban region, the financial capacity of government is not sufficiently large. Some informal landscapes remain or are located outside the formally planned new town (Wu, Zhang, and Webster 2013). Although comprehensively planned, new towns as a place may see quite different formal and informal neighborhoods.

As mega urban projects, new towns show that the state and market are working together. They are not driven purely by "suburbia" as a way of life or by desires for gated neighborhoods, but rather by the strategic scale of the municipality and district government. Songjiang itself is a district government, but the new town project has been a joint venture between the state-owned enterprises belonging to the Shanghai municipal government and the district government. Lingang is driven by two major development corporations that belong to the municipal and district governments.

This mega urban project approach of new towns makes it easier to market and operate in both financial and land markets. In southern China, there was a tradition of superlarge estates that were developed by a single developer, such as property developer Biguiyuan (Country Garden). But these large estates are not new towns. New towns such as Lingang are able to use the government in the process of place making. The actual development might be orchestrated by state-owned enterprises (development corporations). The primary land market under the control of the local government is used for mobilizing development finance. For projects that have a strategy greater than housing, government support is particularly important. For example, the Sino-Singapore Tianjin Eco-City represents the Chinese national strategy of promoting ecologically friendly ways of development. The new town hence deploys tactics to promote eco-images (F. Wu 2015). The result of this eco-city project is a new town project rather than an industrial project like the earlier Sino-Singapore Suzhou Industrial Park.

Economic development is a key strategy for new towns. Chinese new towns are built for industrial development. For example, in Shanghai, Songjiang specializes in electronic manufacturing and creative industries, while Jiading focuses on automobile production. Lingang adopted a clear strategy of becoming an international shipping center, leveraging the international relocation of advanced manufacturing industries. Through an international design competition, the mega urban project attracted wide attention. Because of its strategic importance, it is now trying to associate with another state project—the China (Shanghai) Free-Trade Zone based in Waigaoqiao, Pudong area, a trade and logistics zone created in Lingang as part of the larger Shanghai Free-Trade Zone. Others such as Taihu New Town in Wuxi explore new opportunities in creative industries and has developed a film studio base (Wu 2015).

The mega project approach is reflected in the governance of new towns, which is through neither the business association (the chamber of commerce) nor the government. It is usually derived from existing administrative structures. Lingang, administratively located within the former Nanhui district and now under Pudong district government since Nanhui was annexed into Pudong, is not governed by a Lingang government. The new town is under the governance of a different development corporation that belongs to the Pudong district government, perhaps representing the interests of different government stakeholders. The new town serves the industrial zone to fulfill the spatial and economic strategies of the Shanghai municipality.

Dynamics of New Town Development

Chinese cities are economic powerhouses. A new wave of large-scale industrialization, started in the 1990s but accelerated since China joined the World Trade Organization (WTO) in 2001, has transformed Chinese cities. The emergence of Chinese new towns could be seen as an outcome of this economic restructuring. As mentioned earlier, this is different from the development of edge cities in North America, which has been interpreted as a flexible space of post-Fordism of production (Lehrer 1994), economic decentralization (Garreau 1991), and technological innovations that make suburbs into accessible locations (Fishman 1987). In China, new town development is associated with a new wave of industrialization of Chinese suburbs. Foreign investment has stimulated the establishment of development zones. However, there has been a significant pressure on local governments to build infrastructure to compete with others to attract investment. At the same time, demand for prime central city land pushed manufacturing industries and residents out to the suburbs. New towns became a key instrument to combine the processes of urbanization and industrialization to complete the circuit of investment. As a form of urban development, new towns aim to attract property investors to generate the demand for road infrastructure. This significantly increases the attractiveness of industrial zones adjacent to or within the new town. The relocation of universities, for example, provides a critical mass initially for underpopulated suburbs. The development of new towns therefore represents a more advanced phase of suburbanization. Different from its earlier stage of residential dispersal and industrial relocation from the central areas to the suburbs, new towns create a polycentric spatial structure of Chinese mega city-regions, as shown in the master plans of Beijing and Shanghai in the 2000s (see Figures 8.1 and 8.2).

First and foremost, suburbanization in the United States has been regarded as a lifestyle choice, although in Australia, Scandinavian countries, and to a lesser extent the U.K., the suburbs are also homes for the working class. But this vision of suburbia in China is seen only in some suburban developments, namely enclaves of upper-market residential areas or so-called villa compounds. Some new towns cater to these up-market villa compounds, as shown in Songjiang's Thames Town, but these residential areas are just a small part of the new town.

The Chinese suburb has a rather diverse population: local small-town residents, relocated population from the central areas, and rural-to-urban migrant workers

(Shen and Wu 2013). These groups come to the suburbs with different motivations and experience different processes of residential relocation. Some may be driven by cheaper housing prices, while others may be attracted to manufacturing jobs created in China's new wave of industrialization. Some residents in central locations may have invested in new town properties as second homes and come only on the weekends or for holidays. New towns provide a practical place to develop these gated communities because of the available infrastructure developed by the new towns. In addition, combined with new town development, these gated communities have adopted interesting planning and design methods to package and brand a low-density, private, and highly secured way of life (F. Wu 2010; L. Zhang 2010). However, a vast number of rural migrants came to the factories in the peri-urban areas, engaged in the process of production under global capitalism. These are the proletarian parts of Chinese suburbs. But within the strict boundary of the new town, some housing areas are specifically built for the middle class in the form of formally planned "commodity assets" (*new* housing for sale) in contrast to informal settlements of rural or urban villages. The suburb is therefore becoming a place of juxtaposed social classes, a place of significant spatial fragmentation but little social mix.

American suburbanization and new town development in particular have been seen as the urbanization of capital (Harvey 1978): through the secondary circuit, capital finds an outlet of investment in the built environment. This view of capital circuit is geographically defined within a particular nation or region. Perhaps seen more than a product of capital switch, Chinese new towns may represent the simultaneous opening up of spaces of accumulation in the primary circuit of global capitalism and the secondary circuit of infrastructure and the built environment that lays down the conditions for the former.

In short, Chinese new towns represent an urbanization strategy rather than a strategy of niche marketing of lifestyle choices. This shows the significant difference between new towns in China and those in Western advanced post-Fordist economies. If new towns in the West are seen as a "postsuburbia" phenomenon to resolve the deadlock of residential mass consumption (Phelps and Wu 2011), Chinese new towns are a more mainstream instrument to fix the conditions for global capitalism production in China.

Case Studies

The planning and development of new towns is a spatial strategy to transform the metropolitan region into a polycentric structure. In Shanghai's case, the master plan (1999–2020) proposed to consolidate satellite towns in the suburbs into larger new towns, to form a multi-axis, multilayer, and multinuclear structure (Figure 8.1). The purpose is to integrate industrial and residential development to increase the size of these settlements. In 2001, the Shanghai municipal government formalized the new town strategy into "one city and nine towns" (Shen and Wu (2012, 262), and each new town is designed into distinctively English, German, Scandinavian, Dutch, Italian, and North American townscapes. Connected with these spatial strategies are new urban policies to transform the suburban areas into more compact forms of development. Facing urban sprawl, the municipal government of Shanghai adopted a policy in 2004 to concentrate industries into planned industrial parks, suburban population into new towns, and land development into key development zones. The policy is known as "three concentrations," which laid down the basic principles of spatial development in Shanghai. In a way, the development of new towns can also be regarded as an effort to develop sustainable cities. In

Figure 8.1. The designation of "one city and nine towns" spatial strategy in Shanghai after its master plan (1999–2020). Adapted from Shen and Wu (2012, 262) by Antara Tandon.

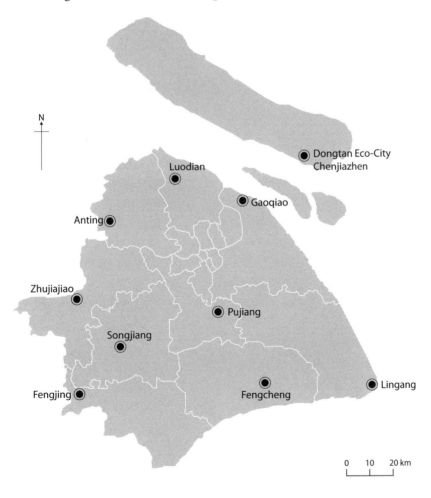

the remainder of this section, two new towns in Shanghai are examined as case studies.

Songjiang New Town

Songjiang is located forty kilometers west of central Shanghai (Figure 8.2). The new town is a composite city, made up of a university town, an industrial zone, an old town, a central business district, and a residential quarter. Within the residential quarter is a well-known one-square-kilometer master-planned community, Thames Town, following the English market town style. Songjiang new town was initially planned through an international design competition in 2001. A British-based architect and planning firm, Atkins, was the winner of the competition.

The development of Songjiang was organized by the Songjiang New Town Development Corporation, which is a joint venture of the district government and three large municipal development corporations. The municipal government of Shanghai provided a start-up fund of one hundred million Yuan, and the district government contributed the land. The new town development corporation is the master developer, which carried out the initial plan and development tasks. After the infrastructure was built, land was then released to the market for other development companies to carry out housing development. The town center of Songjiang was financed and managed by a domestic developer—Henghe

Figure 8.2. The layout of Songjiang new town. Adapted from Wu (2015, 151) by Antara Tandon.

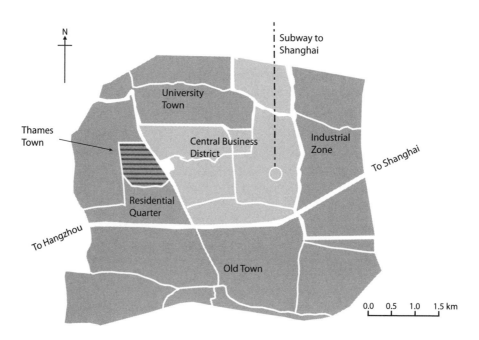

from Zhejiang province. Other developers paid a significant amount of capital to the new town development corporation for the land. The new town development corporation itself also developed a residential area and gained substantial profits.

By 2010, Songjiang had grown to a population of 684,000, from 271,000 in 2000. The annual growth rate reached 9.7 percent, among the fastest growth in metropolitan Shanghai. The new town has diverse residential forms, including villas and high-rise apartments. Many high-rise residential buildings are near the station of the number 9 metro line, which is relatively closer to Shanghai's city center, and the journey on the metro takes approximately an hour. Now, the high-speed intercity train also has a stop at Songjiang, which greatly enhances the accessibility of Songjiang new town.

The new town has seen a mismatch between property development for the middle class and that for the manufacturing industries that attract a blue-collar workforce. The lack of residential space for the latter has driven the relocation of manufacturing industries away from the new town. Residential development in Songjiang has been so successful that some industrial uses have begun to relocate to western China owing to rising land and labor costs, which have made it difficult to sustain the suburban economy. In the long run, the competitiveness of a suburban economy cannot rely on cheaper land costs but rather requires an accessible location within a global city such as Shanghai.

Lingang New Town

Lingang new town is located at the southeastern tip of Shanghai, about seventy-five kilometers from the city center. The area was initially developed into a heavy equipment manufacturing industrial zone. In the mid-1990s, to suit the needs of modern container ships, Shanghai decided to build develop the Yangshan deep-water port. This was seen as a new opportunity for industrial development. To support the port, the development zone strategy evolved into an urban strategy to combine industrial development and a new town. According to the population census, the population in Lingang increased from 156,000 in 2000 to 212,000 in 2010. This growth has been slower than expected, as in the Shanghai master plan Lingang was planned to accommodate some eight hundred thousand people by 2020.

A new governance structure was established in 2012. The two main governing bodies—Lingang Industrial Park Management Committee and Nanhui New Town Management Committee—were merged to form the Shanghai Lingang Region Development Management Committee. The new town is thus now under a unified governance framework. However, in practice, the new town areas are still managed by two respective development corporations: Lingang and Gangcheng (Harbor-

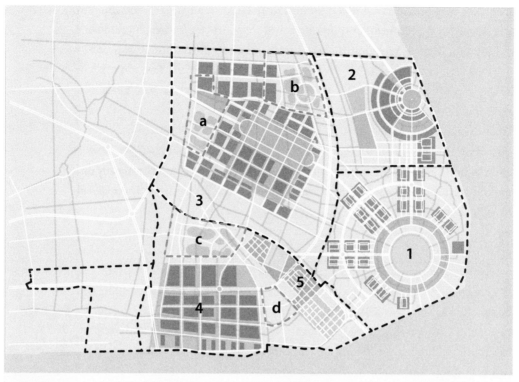

1. New Town Center 2. Comprehensive Area 3. Main Industrial Area 4. Heavy Equipment Manufacturing and Logistic Zone 5. Logistic Area
a. Wanxiang Community b. Academic Community c. Nicheng Community d. Luchaogang Community ▬ ▬ ·Zoning Limit ▬ ▬ ·Community Limit

Figure 8.3. The functional layout of Lingang new town. Adapted from Lingang master plan by Antara Tandon and Deni Lopez.

City) development corporations. Spatially, this division is reflected as the separation between the industrial zone and the new town proper, while the new town is functionally divided into three main areas (Figure 8.3).

The physical planning of Lingang was well organized, but the physical form of the new town is somewhat accidental because of its design vision. The conceptual plan was initiated through an international design contest organized by the municipality of Shanghai in 2002. The design of a German-based architectural firm, von Gerkan, Marg and Partners, was selected. The conceptual (master) plan was influenced by the idea of the English garden city. The circular zones surround a gigantic artificial lake, known as the "water drop lake" (*dishuihu*). The subsequent master plan made in 2003, together with the land use plan in 2008, tried to adapt the water ripple concept into more practical land uses. The huge lake at the center made transport connections very difficult. The main link between Lingang and Shanghai is in the northwest direction. The adapted plan allocates the main land uses to the northwest side of the lake, hence making the land use layout less symmetrical. The circular road system created difficulties for the preferred north-south orientation of residential buildings. Although influenced by the garden city idea, Lingang is car dependent, with superblock street layouts, segregated land uses, and wide roads.

Lingang new town's governance is also under transition from the streamlined structure of a management committee that supervises development corporations, typically seen in economic and technological development zones (enterprise zones), to a comprehensive form of urban governance that needs to manage social development and social affairs. Community development is a major responsibility of this new local governance structure. But the question is, who governs Lingang? It is not directly under the municipality of the Shanghai or Pudong district government. The regional management committee provides an overall governance framework, but development corporations are still the main stakeholders responsible for economic development.

Features of Chinese New Towns

Chinese new towns are planned and designed through master planning, but their development may not simply rely on state investment. From the perspective of governance, the government provides a framework to allow individual development projects to proceed. As a result, the new towns have two major features. First, Chinese new towns are often built as higher-density residential areas, with high-rise apartments. The landscape of high-rise and high-density development is mainly seen in central urban areas in the West. Although high-rise development can still be seen under TOD-style developments such as Sydney, or even edge-city style developments such as Tysons Corner in Virginia (Phelps and Wu 2011) or Canadian high-rise suburbs (Keil 2018), this kind of suburban landscape is regarded as an exception or known as postsuburbia. Historically, there have been state-organized high-rise housing development in suburbs such as the French *banlieues* or the former Soviet Union public housing estates (Golubchikov and Phelps 2011). The suburb in North America is ubiquitously characterized by single-family houses with gardens and garages. In retrofitted edge cities, a cluster of apartments may be developed near the mass transit station. This TOD is encouraged, but the overall density is still lower than in central urban areas. The landscape of new urbanism is also very much single-family oriented, with narrower streets and a small-town atmosphere. Chinese new towns, however, are planned mass housing developments. They bear some features of large-scale residential developments in the former Soviet period and resemble high-rise residential estates in Hong Kong. In fact, high-rise apartments are the norm, whereas single-family detached houses, or so-called villas, account for only a small fraction of the residential stock.

The attractiveness of Chinese new towns is that, compared with exclusively car-dependent suburbs, new towns are often supported by government-financed mass transit infrastructure and are usually developed as part of mega urban projects. For example, "university towns" are a common element for education-driven suburbanization. The relocation of a university campus into a suburban new town to build a single integrated residential and education entity replicates the earlier work units (*danwei*) landscape, characterized by multistory or high-rise apartment buildings. While there are some upper-income housing estates in new towns, the residential form of the new town is still a type of mass consumption. New towns are places from which residents can practically commute to the central area, rather than a destination of lifestyle choice. Low-density living space is often used for holiday homes or for an investment purpose rather than for everyday lives in the suburbs. For example, within the new town of Songjiang, Thames Town is a master-planned new residential area that accommodates several large gated communities. They have been built in the style of an English market town. But the actual occupancy is quite low, leading to empty streets, while high-rise apartments near the Songjiang and Jiuting metro stations are popular because of their practical locations for the middle class to commute to the city of Shanghai.

Second, the development of Chinese new towns is driven by the suburban economy. New towns are created to fulfill their economic functions, combined with industrial projects. They are rarely developed as purely residential areas as were the earlier generation of new towns in the U.K., where the development of public housing was a dominant element. Chinese new towns thus often combine industrial and residential development, particularly in manufacturing. The residential form of the new town is only an extension of existing industrial parks or development zones.

By contrast, the suburban economy in the United States, however, is largely associated with service sectors, and new towns are often linked with the development of edge cities (Garreau 1991) or the spread of back office functions into the metropolitan region (Knox 2008). As the so called workshop of the world, China is seeing its new towns develop as part of industrialization rather than postindustrialization. Hence, in Chinese new towns, there is still a significant proportion of industrial land uses. The concentration of manufacturing jobs in the new towns has led to a mismatch between jobs and affordable housing, and a lower level of services. Many management and professional workers have to commute from inner urban areas, while industrial workers are accommodated in dormitories near industrial areas. The latter, consisting of a large proportion of rural migrants, are not home owners. At the same time, property development in the new town targets the lower middle class, offering affordable housing within reasonable commuting times to the city center. Overall, the function of "town" is underdeveloped.

Conclusion

Chinese cities have initially experienced rapid urban expansion through the development of industrial areas and development zones in the suburbs. Driven by the land market, they began to release land in the suburbs to stimulate economic development, causing inefficient land uses and urban sprawl. To control the unregulated land development, a new land management system has been set up and consolidated since the mid-2000s. The central government issues quotas of development land to set a limit to the total amount of land that can be converted into built-up areas, which forces local governments to pursue a more compact and nodal form of suburban development.

Chinese new towns have been created in response to changing governance as a new metropolitan spatial strategy to bring together scattered industrial development zones in the suburbs. They also integrate industrial and residential developments and use the property market to generate capital for infrastructure investment. In this way, the new town can be seen as a type of property-led development along with industrialization. The new towns represent a more advanced stage of suburban development in China. They are mixed-use, large-scale developments. They have higher densities and more efficient land uses than uncoordinated urban sprawl. Operationally, new towns are governed through streamlined governance under development corporations or the commissions of new towns rather than the government, focusing on attracting inward investment and promoting property markets. From a governance perspective (Ekers, Hamel, and Keil 2012), Chinese new towns reveal the combination of state and market in suburban development. They symbolize the post-reform urban development that is deeply growth oriented but at the same time resort to a hybrid state and market approach to development organization (F. Wu 2018). In this sense, it is interesting to compare them to American suburbs, which symbolize a prosperous nation and distinctive suburban ideology that makes them an exception in the history of urban development (Beauregard 2006).

Chinese new towns are generally well planned with a higher quality of the built environment. For new towns entirely built under the real estate boom, it is a challenge for them to sustain their property markets. As for the new towns located in the periphery of large metropolitan regions, originating from industrial development, they are likely to be associated with economic development. The future of these new towns lies in whether they can continue to attract residents to make these places livable cities while maintaining their economic functions.

Acknowledgments

This research has been supported by U.K. ESRC research project "Governing the Future City: A Comparative Analysis of Governance Innovations in Large Scale Urban Developments in Shanghai, London, Johannesburg" (ES/N006070/1) and "The Financialisation of Urban Development and Associated Financial Risks in China" (ES/P003435/1). We would also like to acknowledge funding support from the Social Sciences and Humanities Research Council of Canada through funding from the Major Collaborative Research Initiative "Global Suburbanism: Governance, Land, and Infrastructure in the 21st Century (2010–2017)" and travel support provided by the New Towns Initiative at Harvard University. Particular thanks are given to Ann Forsyth and Richard Peiser for their constructive comments on an earlier version.

New Towns in China

The Liangzhu Story

ChengHe Guan, Richard Peiser, Shikyo Fu, and Chaobin Zhou

Why Is New Town Construction Relevant in Contemporary China?

The Liangzhu New Town has been a pioneer in Chinese new town construction since the 2000s. The experimental venture provides a well-balanced system of social, environmental, and lifestyle accommodations. In contrast to British new towns that were influenced by the garden city concept in the early twentieth century, and the American planned new communities of the late twentieth century, Liangzhu was built in an era of China's economic upturn and rapid urbanization. This case study describes the project's land acquisition, property buyout, public amenities, and infrastructure layout. It discusses Liangzhu's urban configuration in the context of international new town trends in the twenty-first century.

In China, contemporary new town construction emerged at the end of the twentieth century in response to rapid urban expansion. This gave rise to the term "new district" as an administrative status to areas adjacent to cities and towns to accommodate the growing population (C. Xue, Wang, and Tsai 2013). The administrative upgrading from suburban districts and counties to new districts helped to facilitate the rapid transition and land conversion from agricultural land to urban land. The scale and location of these new districts vary. They can be similar in scale to their Western counterparts or sometimes larger than the prototypical new towns. They can also be detached from the existing urban center as satellites or annexations of downtown areas. Sometimes, though, multiple new towns are included in a single new district boundary. For example, the Tianfu new district in Chengdu is composed of the high-technology new town, the Chengdu city Tianfu new town, and the Sichuan Province Tianfu new town. They are developed under a single master plan, but the actual operation is managed by different agencies.

China's new town phenomenon has given rise to a new type of urbanization. It is, in concept, related to the British and American new town developments that originated from the garden cities movement. At the same time, it also created a program that promoted the new regionalism concept. One advantage China has is the abundant precedents of new town developments around the world. The second similarity between Chinese and Anglo-American new towns is their shared aim to produce a better physical environment for the residents and the communities. A third similarity is the prolonged period of development that forces the new towns to survive through different economic cycles and jeopardizes their long-term economic sustainability.

Liangzhu New Town Concept

Liangzhu New Town is located twenty kilometers outside of downtown Hangzhou, the provincial capital of Zhejiang Province (Figure 9.1). It is part of the Yangtze River Delta region, one of the most urbanized areas in contemporary China. Since the 1990s, the region has developed its own typologies of urbanization. One of them is the core and periphery model (Guan and Rowe 2016). The Liangzhu New Town and Hangzhou resemble this model, Liangzhu being the new town and downtown Hangzhou being the core. The other quality is the urban continuum of densely packed towns and villages outside of the center city

Figure 9.1. The location of Liangzhu New Town in the Hangzhou metropolitan area. Map by Deni Lopez.

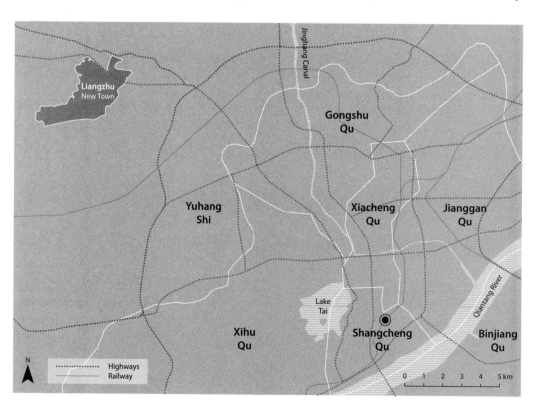

(Guan 2016). From the city center of Hangzhou to Liangzhu, the urban settlements are spread out continuously with no observable separation between urban and non-urban areas, like the suburbs of Los Angeles and other American cities.

The project covers an area of 832.3 hectares of existing agricultural and forest lands, among which 398 hectares was set aside for residential and tourism development (Ding, Fu, and Zhou 2013). At completion, Liangzhu will accommodate fifteen thousand households or thirty thousand to forty thousand residents (Ding, Fu, and Zhou 2013). The project is composed of five residential communities: the Bamboo Forest Valley, the Sunlight Vista, the Heronshire Residential District (HRD), the Chunmanli, and the Flower Rain Meadows (Table 9.1).

The Liangzhu Story

Narada, West Lake Exposition, and Land Acquisition

Liangzhu was developed by the Zhejiang Narada Real Estate Group (Narada), which was founded in 1993.[1] It is a local Hangzhou development company that had built over five hundred thousand square meters of real estate properties in the metropolitan Hangzhou area as well as some projects in Shanghai and Ningbo. The strong local presence helped the company to grow into one of the most successful real estate developers by the late 1990s. Preparing for the 2000 West Lake Exposition, Hangzhou's city and district governments proactively sought opportunities to collaborate with private developers to promote Hangzhou's urban expansion.[2] Narada took advantage of this opportunity and entered into a joint development agreement with the Yuhang Municipal People's Government in 2000 (Ding, Fu, and Zhou 2013). The land transfer for Liangzhu had a special "cultural promotion" designation, which reduced the purchase price dramatically to 95,800 RMB per acre on average, nearly half the market rate for other sites in the same district.[3] This low land purchasing price provided a favorable condition for Liangzhu's financial structure.

Integration of Narada Concept and Vanke Value

Compared with Narada, Vanke is a more sizable company. Founded by Wang Shi in 1984, Vanke has grown to be the largest residential developer in China in terms of revenue. In 2005, when the CEO of Narada expressed his plans to withdraw from the real estate market and go into the financial sector, Vanke moved quickly to put together a bidding package for the Liangzhu New Town project. The buyout and management transition went smoothly, and most of the original staff members stayed on.[4]

Table 9.1. Liangzhu New Town Land Use and Neighborhood Composition

Land Use	Neighborhood	Subneighborhood
Residential (market)	Festival Place	Residential
	Bamboo Forest Valley	(BFV)
	Sunlight Vista	(SLV)
	Heronshire Residential District (HRD)	North County
		East County
		South County
		West County (I)
	Chunmanli	Residential
Residential (relocation)	Flower Rain Meadows	
Residential (construction)	HRD	South County (II)
	Dignified Life	
Residential (proposed)	Golden Shores	
	Seven Sages	
	Chunmanli	
Total residential		
Commercial	Festival Place	Uniu market
Commercial (proposed)	Seven Sages	Commercial
Public	Liangzhu Museum	
	Narada Resort	
	Experimental school	
	Meilizhou church	
	Garbage center	
	Art center	
Public proposed	Youth hotel	
Total nonresidential		
Other construction	Landscape and public infrastructure	Quarry park
Total construction	Development zone	—
Forest land	No development zone	Including water
Total land	Purchased by Narada	—

Source: Vanke Hangzhou (2016).
Note: Numbers with underscores are estimated or based on construction phase data.

The original master plan borrows the concept of "jade," which is rooted in the local culture. Vanke retained the concept and the original master plan done by Civitas, a land development consultant hired by Narada. The plan envisioned eight villages connected by a major boulevard. In between the villages are green spaces connecting to the forests and the hills. Vanke typically undertakes rapid devel-

Completion	Land Area (m²)	Gross Floor Area (m²)	Floor Area Ratio (FAR)	Housing Units	Average Unit Area
2007	21,000	31,800	1.514	180	176.67
2007	247,000	89,000	0.360	369	241.19
2008	285,000	139,650	0.490	583	239.54
2006	159,000	131,000	0.824	858	152.68
2008	99,315	145,800	1.468	877	166.25
2009	134,000	145,376	1.085	1,514	96.02
2014	336,700	100,000	0.297	264	378.79
2010	5,544	6,820	1.230	50	136.40
2014	85,672	145,911	1.703	1,158	126.00
2018	303,030	95,000	0.314	250	380.00
2018	90,000	75,000	0.833	500	150.00
2020	480,000	400,000	0.833	3,200	125.00
2020	420,000	375,000	0.893	2,800	133.93
2020	145,000	150,000	1.034	1,500	100.00
—	2,811,261	2,030,357	0.722	14,103	—
2007	42,000	15,900	0.379	—	—
2020	100,000	30,000	0.300	—	—
2007	40,000	9,500	0.238	—	—
2007	183,000	73,000	0.399	—	—
2008	66,400	32,200	0.485	—	—
2010	10,000	958	0.096	—	—
2011	3,066	1,065	0.347	—	—
2016	14,000	7,000	0.500	—	—
2020	3,000	1,000	0.333	—	—
—	461,466	170,623	0.370	—	—
—	700,000	—	—	—	—
3,972,727	2,200,980	0.554	—	—	
—	4,350,000	—	—	—	—
8,322,727	—	—	—	—	

opment and sells the property in a speedy manner instead of holding onto it. For Liangzhu, the low purchase price allowed the project to be developed in phases over an extended period while still being profitable, enabling Vanke to realize many ideas that were not possible before (Guan 2016).[5]

Public Amenities and Community Building

Vanke's ideas include both tangible public amenities and intangible community building. Both are prerequisites for a successful new town construction. Liangzhu provides a variety of public amenities including the Meilizhou church, an art and cultural center, a senior housing complex, a hospital, a free market, the villager's cafeteria, and many other retail and commercial facilities. They all contribute to the sense of place for the residents.

The Meilizhou church was the result of extensive negotiations and craftsmanship. Under State Administration for Religious Affairs regulations, the permit for new construction requires a long and complicated application process. On the other hand, the two local Christian communities that were running independently were in great need of a new, larger facility for their members. At the same time, one of the donors expressed his willingness to pay for the construction cost if the project could be completed on schedule. To avoid the tedious permit application process, Vanke and the local communities creatively resolved this issue by consolidating the two existing religious groups into one entity. The new entity was able to build and expand its facility, that is, the Meilizhou church, under the license from the preexisting groups, greatly reduced the project completion time. The design director, Shikyo Fu, worked with Tsushima Design Studio to erect this 958-square-meter wood structure using glue-laminated cedar beams.

The Art and Cultural Center is a gift donated to the city in "good faith", according to the developer. The construction cost was estimated to be fifty million RMB. By the time of its completion in 2016, the total costs amounted to ninety-eight million RMB, all of which was covered by Vanke. Wang Shi, the chairman, who is a fan of the Pritzker Laureate Tadao Ando's architectural style, invited Ando to design the center. Ando approached the design with his signature cast-in-place concrete material, and he created a simple yet memorable space (Figure 9.2). The high-quality architecture not only provided an attractive space for Liangzhu, drawing locals and tourists alike, but also created a high-end image for the residents. There is a positive relationship between well-designed and well-maintained public facilities and the value of the real estate, as well as the well-being of residents (Voicu and Been 2008).

Senior housing is not a conventional component of new towns in China, and in the master plan Liangzhu provided no senior housing. With a rapidly aging society, however, accommodation for the elderly will become a trillion-dollar industry in China (A. Wu 2012). Again, with its forward-looking mentality and quick execution ability, the Vanke management committee decided to create a flagship senior housing project. The five-hundred-unit project took advantage of both the high-quality environment and convenient access to major cities of Hangzhou and Shanghai. The first one hundred units were released for purchase. Within a year, 80 percent of the units were sold, and the occupancy rate has reached 60 percent. The other four hundred units were for long-term rent. Of these, sixty units were designated for assisted-living or nursing-care service. The facility layout and management system were modeled after the Japanese Kaigo Hoken,[6] that is, the long-term-care insurance system. The senior housing project not only achieved the original goal of making Liangzhu a more comprehensively served community, but it also inspired others to incorporate senior housing as part of new town development in China.

Many new communities suffer from a lack of commercial services. On average, the commercial sector moves in three years or more after the residents. For Liangzhu, Vanke invited local farmers to sell their organic produce in a food market.[7] The Uniu food market began operating in October 2008 together with the rest of the Festival Place, which included retail and office space, food and beverage vendors, and a community cafeteria. Under Vanke Management Company's supervision, safety and health protocols were reinforced. However, the retail space has suffered from low sales and higher vacancies because of the low population in the immediate area.

Figure 9.2. Arts and Cultural Center by Tadao Ando (2016). Community building is enhanced by comprehensive public amenity facilities. Photos by ChengHe Guan.

Infrastructure and Property Management

A developer's own property management arm often provides better performance than a third-party agency. Developers assume more responsibility if they are responsible for their own properties. They also rely on customer satisfaction to establish their reputation, especially in a new market. In a society where *koubei* (word-of-mouth) is highly valued, and at a time when such word-of-mouth proliferates very quickly through social media, developers are investing more in property management to maintain their reputation. Hangzhou Vanke Property Management was established in 2008 and developed services unique to the needs and geographical characteristics of the area (Ding, Fu, and Zhou 2013). There are over four hundred employees servicing the four thousand property owners to realize Vanke's mission of providing "good housing, good services, and a good neighborhood."[8] Vanke's strategies have been well received by the residents, and the project includes a maintenance fund allocation plan, volunteer recruitment, and self-governance of the residents.

In China, real estate developers allocate a property maintenance fund to the local government department for land management. The government entity then creates a bank account for the pool of funds and supervises the distribution of it. For example, if a major facade maintenance project is necessary, the property management company will need to apply for the use of the fund, with the consent from the Residents' Committee. Then, the government representatives will perform an evaluation on the necessity and legitimacy of the request for funds. Only after such procedures are followed can the money be withdrawn and used for the project. The original fund is a one-time contribution, and its allocation throughout the lifespan of the project works more effectively if the management company has a long-term vision for the specific project. In the case of Liangzhu, the fund has been well used, and Vanke works closely with the Residents' Committee to make decisions.[9]

Volunteer participation is an effective way to involve the residents in property management, especially for recent retirees. A resident interviewed by the authors opined that the volunteer position provided an opportunity for him to apply his leadership skills as a former party secretary in a state-owned enterprise and facilitated his lifestyle transition from employed to unemployed.[10]

Liangzhu created a sense of self-governance by implementing the Villagers' Convention. The twenty-six provisions of the convention include regulations on citizen's behaviors that are often underaddressed in today's Chinese society. For example, provisions 12 and 16 call on residents to "queue up to board buses" and to "drive slowly and give way to pedestrians." Both provisions advocate for a more civil, pleasant interactions within the community. The goal is to create a harmonious village with communal order and respect. It is also part of an education system that includes the Waste Classification Promotion and Education Center, the Community Farm, and the Uniu market. The garbage center not only is equipped with a cutting-edge bio-waste treatment machine but also serves to raise awareness within the community. Since its opening in December 2011, the 1,065-square-meter facility hosts over one thousand visitors each month (Guan 2016). As explained by the design director, Shikyo Fu, the community farm provides opportunities for children to "gain food by labor" and "combine education with fun," by "getting back to and enjoying nature." Through education, the residents can gradually adopt, adapt, and improve considerate social behaviors that benefit the shared environment of the whole community.

Can Liangzhu New Town Sustain Itself?

Is Liangzhu a new invention of contemporary China, or a replica of its Western counterparts? It helps to answer the question by putting it in an international context of new town development. Milton Keynes and The Woodlands, two of the relatively successful new towns from the United Kingdom and the United States, respectively, are used as references for Liangzhu. The Woodlands is located 45 kilometers north of Houston along Interstate 45. It is a HUD-financed Title VII town influenced by the new community movement and Ian McHarg's *Design with Nature*, which promoted environmentally sensitive approaches for design. The Woodlands Corporation was sold in 1996 to Morgan Stanley and the Crescent Companies, and in 2011 the remaining undeveloped properties were sold to the Howard Hughes Development Corporation. Milton Keynes is located seventy-two kilometers northwest of London in the M1 growth corridor (Peiser and Chang 1999). The new town was developed to relieve housing congestion and was financially backed by the government. The management authority was originally delegated to the quasi-governmental organization Milton Keynes Development Corporation. In 1992, the government transferred control to the Commission for New Towns (CNT). In 2004, the Milton Keynes Partnership took over the management of Milton Keynes.

Milton Keynes, The Woodlands, and the Liangzhu New Town are all unique cases, but the comparison offers insights into new towns. Nevertheless, there are certain aspects shared by all three cases that can be distilled as useful lessons. Common to the three projects is the original low purchase price for land. This initial cost was low as Milton Keynes was largely a rural farmland (Peiser and Chang 1999) while The Woodlands was previously occupied by a lumber mill company (Cagle 2009).

Liangzhu also takes advantage of the low-price deal for the Hangzhou exposition. If the timing for land acquisition had been off by a year or even a few months, then Liangzhu's development would have been different entirely. Second is favorable regional growth. Phasing, especially, is related to the broader economic conditions and population growth of the region. Milton Keynes was developed for post–World War II growth. The Woodlands enjoyed 400 percent population growth from the 1980s to the 1990s. Liangzhu rode the wave of not only high economic and GDP growth for China, but also rapid urbanization in the Hangzhou region. The phasing of Liangzhu is basically in three parts: First, the early development by Narada from 2000 to 2006. This includes Heronshire North County and the basic infrastructure such as road construction, sewage system, and some commercial components. The second phase is the Vanke involvement, when most of the residential districts were completed from 2006 to 2016. Toward the end of this phase, the balance sheet for Vanke has already turned positive, and the cash flow from the development covered the operational costs. The last phase will be the following ten years, from 2016 to 2026. Most of the undevelopable land will be integrated into the ecological system for the Liangzhu New Town. Though some observers pointed out that Vanke could make more profit if the development period were shortened, the cost of holding vacant land did not offset the financial success of the project. Further, controlling the development is not all for profit but also for the well-being of the community.[11]

Future Growth of Liangzhu and New Towns Typology

Is the Liangzhu Model Repeatable?

Narada's local knowledge and well-established social network enabled the Liangzhu New Town to start with a very favorable land acquisition price. Vanke's long-term vision extended the original concept of community building and the celebration of cultural amenities. The combination of local knowledge and long-term vision resulted in Liangzhu becoming a self-sustained and financially successful new town development. In the coming decade, will Liangzhu stay attractive to the residents and maintain its high quality of living? In the areas around Liangzhu New Town, many land parcels have been auctioned and sold publicly to private developers. Most of the land is zoned for a higher density. Today the floor area ratio (FAR) for adjacent lands on the market can go as high as 3.0 for residential and commercial mixed-use parcels. This FAR translates into high-rise-dominated communities. Liangzhu, in comparison, has a much lower FAR of 0.67. It contributes to place making and community building. The picturesque and bucolic scenery undoubtedly differentiates Liangzhu from other more recent developments.

However, there are also concerns that Liangzhu may lose its competitiveness when its surroundings change from pastoral suburban to denser urban conditions. For example, a large shopping mall branded by a Japanese retail giant Japan United Stores Company (JUSCO) chose to locate a few kilometers east of the Liangzhu New Town. The new mall is located more centrally to serve a large population draw while Liangzhu is up in the foothills and retail tenants serve a much smaller drawing radius. Once the new shopping mall is completed, it will put pressure on the local retail shops, and some of them will inevitably go out of business. What will Liangzhu and Vanke do to keep a balanced development while holding on to the original concept of the new town? For Vanke, Liangzhu is its largest project in terms of number of residential units and land area. It has gone through three economic cycles as well as leadership changes. Even if Vanke cannot build another Liangzhu, the lessons learned from the past ten years will serve as valuable experience for the company's future development. As a private developer, Vanke will face more competition from new town developers backed by State-Owned Enterprise (SOE) and especially those that are owned directly by the central government.

A New Typology for China's New Town Construction

The Liangzhu story offers a sophisticated new town development framework and example of good decision making for others to learn from: what to do and what not to do. As China moves from a fast-paced urbanization stage to a slower and more sophisticated era, a new typology of new town construction has emerged and will reshape China's townization, urbanization, and regionalization. This new typology is not just an adaption of Western ideas of the *garden city movement* and *design with nature*, but also a blend of contemporary urban issues that are amplified by China's large population and rapid economic growth. The outcome of the new towns can create a type of spatial arrangements that satisfy economic, environmental, and social requirements. Further study of these spatial conditions will help us to better understand the integral structure of new town building in the modern age.

Lessons from Liangzhu

The Liangzhu story provides an opportunity to reflect on new town development in contemporary China. Liangzhu targets several different market segments and appeals to different age groups and demographics. The new town started with single-family homes and townhouses, which created a feeling of an upscale environment. It has managed to stay in the same market since then. Commercial areas, though managed by Vanke itself, are not so successfully operated. Retail activity is critical for creating a sense of community and place for people to interact. The conundrum is how to activate the community through retail in the early days of development when there are too few rooftops to support the retail profitably.

The Yuhang government and the developer provided new replacement housing for the villagers who farmed the land before the new town was begun. However, the new homes for the villagers are concentrated in areas that are not up to the standard of a new town. If attempts are made to provide more affordable housing and the village housing is raised to higher quality, the overall image of the new town can be enhanced. The solution raises the question of who should be financially responsible and accountable for what? Among involved parties, the initial

Figure 9.3. Liangzhu housing and neighborhoods (2016). *Top left*: Bamboo Forest Valley. *Top right*: Sunlight Vista (Yangguang Tianji), view from street (2016). *Bottom left*: Chunmanli residential community. *Bottom right*: Dignified Life senior housing (2016). Photos courtesy of Vanke Hangzhou and ChengHe Guan.

acquisition, total investment in infrastructure, and financial structure of equity and debt are all critical concerns for further investigation.

In the past thirty years, China has built many new towns, new districts, and large communities that exhibit uniform heights and similar functions. This process created a monotonous cityscape from town to town. Recently, planning policies have started to address this issue by promoting urban development with high diversity and mixed use. A guideline by the central government of China was published to encourage cities and towns to preserve and create their own identities. Liangzhu New Town, with its diversified building types and mix-use community, could also offer an alternative to monofunctional high-rise residences at risk of obsolescence. While Liangzhu's low density and bucolic setting help to make it very attractive visually, its pleasing mixture of housing typologies offers a useful precedent to all Chinese new towns.

Figure 9.4. Liangzhu community facilities (2016). *Top left*: Liangzhu Anjilu experimental school. *Top right*: Quarry park. *Bottom left*: Festival Place, Uniu market. *Bottom right*: Dignified Life senior housing common room (2016). Photos courtesy of Vanke Hangzhou and ChengHe Guan.

Notes

1. The data for the Liangzhu case study were collected from multiple sources including documents provided by the Vanke Hangzhou office and personal interviews conducted on site and online, as well as a special edition published by Shinkenchiku.

2. The first such exposition held in Hangzhou can be traced back to 1929. Although twenty years behind the exposition in Wuhan, it is still claimed to be the most innovative event at the time and has generated lasting impact on Zhejiang Province's economic development during the turmoil of this period of Chinese history.

3. S. Fu, Y. Shen, and H. Fang, interview by R. Peiser and C. Guan, Liangzhu New Town, March 9, 2016.

4. S. Fu, interview by P. Rowe and C. Guan, Shanghai, July 10, 2014; S. Fu, Y. Shen, and H. Fang, interview by R. Peiser and C. Guan, Liangzhu New Town, March 9, 2016.

5. And S. Fu, interview by C. Guan and Y. Lu, Liangzhu New Town, July 1, 2014.

6. Kaigo Hoken is a social insurance program in which society as a whole supports those who need long-term care, and everyone who is forty years of age or older must enroll in this mutual assistance program. Foreign residents are also eligible for this program.

7. S. Fu, Y. Shen, and H. Fang, interview by R. Peiser and C. Guan, Liangzhu New Town, March 9, 2016.

8. S. Fu, Y. Shen, and H. Fang, interview by R. Peiser and C. Guan, Liangzhu New Town, March 9, 2016.

9. S. Fu, Y. Shen, and H. Fang, interview by R. Peiser and C. Guan, Liangzhu New Town, March 9, 2016.

10. S. Fu, interview by C. Guan and Y. Lu, Liangzhu New Town, July 1, 2014.

11. S. Fu, Y. Shen, and H. Fang, interview by R. Peiser and C. Guan, Liangzhu New Town, March 9, 2016.

10

Successes and Failures
of New Towns in Hong Kong

Anthony Gar-On Yeh

New towns were actively developed in Asia after World War II, especially in the newly industrializing economies, such as Hong Kong, Singapore, and South Korea. They were a means to decentralize the urban population in their big cities, improve living quality, and provide land for industrial development (D. R. Phillips and Yeh 1987). The new town movement has slowed down a bit since the 1990s, but with a recent rapid increase in population in large Asian cities, especially those in China and India, new towns are reemerging again in the Asian urban planning arena. Among the Asian cities, Hong Kong has one of the oldest and largest new towns programs. The successes and failures of new towns in Hong Kong can help urban planners and policy makers in the planning and development of future new towns (Yeh 1987, 2003).

New Town Development in Hong Kong

New town development in Hong Kong can be dated back as early as 1953, when the first industrial satellite town was developed in Kwun Tong; the first new town was in Tsuen Wan in 1959. Kwun Tong and Tsuen Wan were meant to alleviate the congestion problem in the main urban areas due to a large influx of refugees from China after the revolution in 1949, and to provide land for industrial growth. Located at the urban fringe at that time, Kwun Tong was not planned to be self-contained but a satellite town. Tsuen Wan (including Kwai Chung) was planned to be the first self-contained new town in Hong Kong. However, as both new towns were developed in haste, their planning and development were ad hoc and chaotic.

In 1965, the government decided to proceed with the planning and development of two other new towns, at Castle Peak (renamed Tuen Mun in 1973) and Sha Tin. However, because of the slump in the property market after the bank crisis in 1965 and the riots in 1967, the new towns program lost its momentum (Leung 1980).

The major boost to the new towns program in Hong Kong came from the government's Ten-Year Housing Program introduced in 1972, which aimed to provide 1.8 million people with permanent, selfcontained accommodation in a decent environment (L. H. Wang and Yeh 1987). However, most of the developable land in the main urban areas had already been well utilized, and it was increasingly expensive and difficult to obtain additional land for public housing construction. Moreover, opportunities for comprehensive urban renewal were extremely limited because of the fragmented pattern of land holdings, the extremely high costs of land resumption, and the sporadic pattern of redevelopment that had already occurred (Pryor 1978). Although some sites had been made available in the urban areas by land resumption and reclamation, their values were so high that the government often sold them to generate revenue rather than use them for public housing development. Instead, new towns were actively developed in the New Territories, the once rural area of Hong Kong. It was estimated that 78 percent of the original target population of the Ten-Year Housing Program would be housed in the new towns there.

The development in the New Territories in the early 1970s could be identified on three distinct levels: (i) new towns of Tsuen Wan, Sha Tin, and Tuen Mun; (ii) market towns of Tai Po, Fanling/Sheung Shui, and Yuen Long and; (iii) smaller rural townships, such as Sham Tseng, Lau Fau Shan, Sai Kung, Tai O, Mui Wo, Cheung Chau, and Peng Chau in the outlying islands (Figure 10.1 and Table 10.1). Development plans and population targets for these new towns were constantly revised with a view to meet the requirement of the TenYear Housing Program. In 1979, the three market towns of Tai Po, Fanling/Sheung Shui, and Yuen Long were upgraded to new towns. Investigations of other possible sites for new towns development were also underway. In 1983, Ma On Shan was incorporated as an extension of Sha Tin New Town. The second-generation new towns developed in the 1980s are smaller in scale compared with the first-generation new towns developed in the 1970s.

After rapid development of new towns in the 1970s and 1980s, three other new towns were further developed. There are Tin Shui Wai, Tseung Kwan O, and Tung Chung (Figure 10.1 and Table 10.1). They are often referred as the third-generation new towns. Tin Shui Wai new town was built on reclaimed fish ponds and was a joint venture between the government and the private sector. Tung Chung is a new town to serve the new airport at Chek Lap Kok, and Tseung Kwan O is very close to the main urban areas. Although their target population is lower than that of earlier generations of new towns, they also have a high percentage of public housing.

In the late 1990s, the government stopped the old new town development model and instead developed well-planned new development areas (NDAs), adopting some successful planning concepts such as compact development and transit-oriented development (TOD) models with more sophisticated urban design. These NDAs are acted

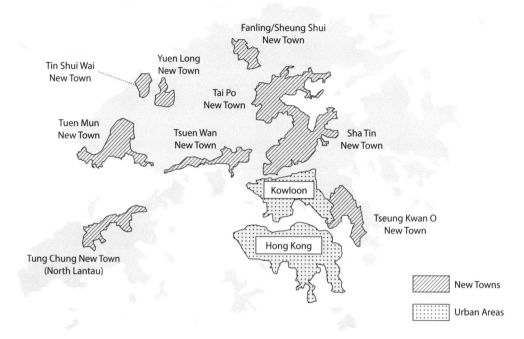

Mainland China

Fanling/Sheung Shui
New Town

Yuen Long
New Town

Tin Shui Wai
New Town

Tai Po
New Town

Tuen Mun
New Town

Tsuen Wan
New Town

Sha Tin
New Town

Kowloon

Tseung Kwan O
New Town

Hong Kong

Tung Chung New Town
(North Lantau)

New Towns

Urban Areas

Figure 10.1. New towns in Hong
Kong. Courtesy of Anthony Yeh.

Table 10.1. Characteristics of New Towns in Hong Kong

	First-Generation New Towns	Second-Generation New Towns
	Tsuen Wan[1]	Sha Tin[2]
Year of designation of new town status[4]	1961	1965
Distance from main urban area	5 km	5 km
Total development area[5]	3,286 ha	3,591 ha
Target population (approximate)	866,000	771,000
Target population in public housing (%)[6]	56%	67%
Original population (at the year of designation)[4]	80,000	24,000
2011 population	801,202	635,846

Sources: Bristow (1989); Hong Kong Planning Department (2002); Hong Kong Census and Statistics
Department (2012); Hong Kong Civil Engineering and Development Department (2016).
[1] Including Kwai Chung and Tsing Yi Island.
[2] Including Ma On Shan New Town.
[3] Combined figures of Yuen Long and Tin Shui Wai are from Hong Kong Planning Department (2002) while
the separate figures are from the Explanatory Notes of respective Outline Zoning Plans (OZPs); see Hong
Kong Civil Engineering and Development Department (2016).

as the extension of the existing new towns. In the medium to long term, there will be four NDAs development—Hung Shui Kui (HSK), Yuen Long South (YLS), North-East New Territories (NENT), and Tung Chung New Town Extension (TCNTE).

Planning and Development of New Towns in Hong Kong

In the new town development in the 1970s, a corporate planning approach was adopted with a New Town Development Office comprising a multidisciplinary team of engineers, town planners, and architects to carry out the planning, programming, and construction works of each new town under the New Territories Development Department that was set up in 1973 (Bristow 1989). Each New Town Development Office needed to liaise closely with the District Office of the New Territories Administration as the land authority in each new town and to obtain local feedback (Hayes 2012). Although most of the new towns were developed through land reclamation, which was much cheaper and eliminated the need to deal with land resumption and resettlement, some of the land was still owned by farmers and villagers. Existing villagers were either resettled or moved to public housing. Squatters that were cleared for new town development were resettled in public housing. These resettled public housing dwellers did not go through the normal income ceiling tests for public housing. They have created another class of public housing residents with income higher than those that were intended for the subsidized public housing (Keung 1985; Yeh 1990).

Third-Generation New Towns

Tuen Mun	Tai Po	Fanling/ Sheung Shui	Yuen Long[3]	Tin Shui Wai[3]	Tseung Kwan O	North Lantau New Town
1965	1979	1979	1978	1982	1982	1992
32 km	19 km	27 km	40 km[3]	5 km	n.a.	
3,266 ha	3,100 ha	667 ha	561 ha	430 ha	1,718 ha	780 ha
589,000	307,000	290,000	185,000	306,000	445,000	268,000
73%	53%	68%	53%[3]	44%	42%	
20,000	48,000	44,000	42,000	n.a.	7,000	n.a.
485,898	264,580	255,306	147,745	287,901	371,590	78,443

[4] Year of designation of new town status and original population are reference from Bristow (1989), except North Lantau New Town.

[5] The total development area (except North Lantau new town) are according to Hong Kong Civil Engineering and Development Department (2016); Figure for North Lantau new town is with reference to Hong Kong Planning Department (2002).

[6] Including government rental and subsidized sale flats, except Tsuen Wan (only includes public rental units).

To facilitate the resumption of land for developing the new towns, a transfer of development rights that was known as Letter A/B land exchange entitlements was used. Land owners were given a choice of either a cash payment at a stated rate or an entitlement to future grants of building land in any urban development area in the New Territories at some unspecified time in future (Nissim 2011). This arrangement was to avoid cash payment and prolonged debate about the compensation rate of land resumption. It was welcome by the villagers. The exchange was one square foot of building land for one square foot of building land and two square feet of building land for five square feet of agricultural land. The Letter A/B land exchange system was stopped in 1983 as it was found to be unsustainable. Since 1997, land exchange Letter A/B was totally replaced by monetized cash compensation. Although the Letter A/B land exchange system was unsustainable, it sped up land resumption for the development of new towns in the peak of land resumption in the 1970s.

The British new town planning concepts of "self-containment" and "balanced development" were adopted with an aim to reduce the need of commuting to main urban areas (Hong Kong Lands Department 1984). To achieve this, adequate provision of working opportunities, shopping, recreation, and community facilities was necessary (Hong Kong Lands and Works Branch 1984). New towns were also planned to provide an optimal split between public/private, ownership/rental, and high-/low-density developments. New towns developed after 1973 were more comprehensively planned than the early ones such as Tsuen Wan New Town. Segregation of land uses was advocated and made possible under comprehensive planning. As can be seen later in the chapter, the concept of "self-containment" was not attainable in the development of these new towns. There were many transport problems in their early days of development. Because of this, although "self-containment" is the hidden objective, it has never been mentioned again in the later development of new towns. Learning from these experiences, the Tseung Kwan O new town and Tung Chung new town are well connected by the Mass Transit Railway with transit-oriented development (TOD).

Successes of New Town Development

Meeting Population Needs

New towns in Hong Kong have decentralized the population from the traditional main urban areas of Hong Kong Island, Kowloon, and New Kowloon to the New Territories. In 1971, 81.1 percent of the total population of Hong Kong lived in the main urban areas. By 1981, after the active new town development of the 1970s, this figure had decreased to 73.0 percent and further decreased to 47.8 percent in 2011. Hong Kong's long-established single-nucleus urban form of the past has been replaced by several dispersed new towns.

New towns have witnessed the most rapid population growth of the major districts in Hong Kong. Between 1976 and 1986, almost 70 percent of the increase in population took place at the six earlier-established new towns (first- and second-generation new towns). The average population growth of these new towns was about 150 percent, of which 80 percent was from public housing developments (including public rental and government subsidized flats) (Table 10.2).

With the third-generation new towns of Tseung Kwan O and Tin Shui Wan in the 1980s, the total new town population increased by 70 percent while the population in the urban and other areas has slightly reduced. This illustrates the success of the New Town Program in decentralizing population from the main urban areas.

An early concern of new town development in Hong Kong was how to attract population to the new settlements. This has not in fact been a great problem, however, because 50 percent of the total population increase in Hong Kong during the period 1976–81 had moved to the new towns. The success in populating the new towns is mainly the result of the quasi-voluntary migration of the public housing program. Because there is a high demand for public housing (as reflected by the increasingly long waiting list) and a shortage of public housing in the main urban areas, it is easier to obtain a public housing unit in the new towns. In the 1980s, the average waiting time for public housing units in the main urban areas is eight to nine years, compared to only three to four years in the more remote new towns such as Tuen Mun. As of January 2003, the average waiting time in the main and extended urban areas[1] is about three to five years, while it is only about one year for allocation of a public rental unit in the new towns.[2]

In a study of the main reasons for living in Tuen Mun new town, 80 percent of the public housing residents indicated that easier access to public housing was an important factor (Leung 1980). Although there are few job opportunities in the new towns (with the exception of Tsuen Wan, which has a sound industrial base and is close to the main urban areas), the much cheaper rent and better living environment in public housing estates as compared with the congested private rental tenement housing in the urban areas make new towns quite attractive to people who have been on the public housing waiting list for a long time. The public housing residents have become pioneers of new town development quasi-voluntarily, with the hope that basic community facilities and job opportunities will be improved as the new towns gradually develop. New town development in Hong

Table 10.2. Public Housing Component of Population Growth in Hong Kong, 1976–2011

	Population				
	1976	1986	1996	2001	2011
First-Generation New Towns					
Tsuen Wan[2]	441,440	645,603	739,385	751,028	801,202
Sha Tin[3]	35,038	355,810	582,688	628,227	635,846
Tuen Mun	29,021	262,458	445,771	465,069	485,898
Subtotal	505,499	1,263,871	1,767,844	1,844,324	1,922,946
Second-Generation New Towns					
Tai Po	26,715	119,679	271,661	289,417	264,580
Yuen Long	39,226	75,740	130,992	140,359	147,745
Fanling / Sheung Shui	39,539	87,206	192,321	253,770	255,306
Subtotal	105,480	282,625	594,974	683,546	667,631
Third-Generation New Towns					
Tseung Kwan O (1982)	—	—	143,032	266,033	371,590
Tin Shui Wan	—	—	96,129	177,813	287,901
North Lantau	—	—	—	20,115	78,443
Subtotal	—	—	239,161	463,961	737,934
All new towns	610,979	1,546,496	2,601,979	2,991,831	3,328,511
Other Areas					
Main Urban Areas[5]	3,333,276	3,475,318	3,300,633	3,359,448	3,379,295
Other areas	399,535	336,903	304,754	351,215	362,582
Subtotal	3,732,811	3,812,221	3,605,387	3,710,663	3,741,877
Hong Kong total	4,343,790	5,358,717	6,207,366	6,702,494	7,070,388

Sources: Hong Kong Census and Statistics Department (1977, 1987, 1997, 2002, 2012).
Note: Total population of new towns includes only land population, including permanent housing and temporary housing.
[1] Public Housing includes Housing Authority (HA) public rental and aided housing, HA- and Housing Society (HS)-subsidized sale flats (home ownership).

Kong is public housing–led development (L. H. Wang and Yeh 1987), as can be seen from the high proportion of population growth from public housing in Hong Kong (Table 10.2).

Improvement of Living Environment

Compared with the living environment in the old urban areas, the new towns have a lower floor area ratio. They were well planned with a master layout plan before they were developed. The building density and open space are much better than that in the old urban areas. As a result, the new towns have provided a very good living environment for the residents of the new towns.

Balanced and Self-Contained Living Communities

Although there is a slightly higher proportion of public housing residents, because of the planned balanced development, there is also a good balance of private hous-

Public Housing Population (%)					Population Growth % from Public Housing Population			
1976	1986	1996	2001	2011	1976–86	1986–96	1996–2001	2001–11
71.2%	64.5%	58.8%	57.2%	55.5%	50.1%	19.9%	−47.0%	30.7%
23.0%	68.8%	68.1%	62.7%	56.6%	73.8%	66.9%	−6.6%	−439.3%
27.5%	82.7%	71.8%	65.7%	55.7%	89.6%	56.1%	−74.1%	−167.6%
65.3%	69.5%	65.1%	61.2%	56.0%	72.3%	54.2%	−29.8%	−67.4%
—	57.1%	68.9%	59.8%	52.0%	—	78.3%	−79.9%	143.5%
28.7%	23.6%	36.2%	28.9%	22.0%	18.2%	53.4%	−72.4%	−109.2%
—	55.0%	72.5%	65.5%	61.0%	—	87.0%	43.3%	−674.9%
10.7%	47.5%	62.9%	55.6%	48.79%	69.4%	76.8%	6.4%	−339.7%[4]
—	—	90.1%	82.0%	62.0%	—	—	72.6%	11.5%
—	—	74.7%	77.4%	81.9%	—	—	80.5%	89.3%
—	—	—	74.5%	65.4%	—	—	—	62.2%
—	—	83.9%	79.9%	70.1%	—	—	75.6%	53.6%
55.9%	65.5%	66.4%	62.8%	57.7%	71.7%	67.6%	39.2%	11.8%
41.4%	39.9%	41.4%	40.9%	40.4%	3.6%	10.8%	11.4%	−36.6%
—	2.1%	2.6%	4.3%	3.7%	—	-2.9%	14.8%	−14.9%
37.0%	36.5%	38.1%	37.4%	36.9%	15.4%	8.7%	12.9%	−28.7%
39.6%	44.9%	50.0%	48.7%	46.7%	67.3%	82.0%	33.6%	8.4%

[2] Includes Kwai Chung and Tsing Yi since 1986.
[3] Includes Ma On Shan since 1996.
[4] Both total population and the population living in the public housing decreased, the minus sign (−) indicates the decrease.
[5] Includes Hong Kong Island, Kowloon, and New Kowloon.

ing residents. The residents in the new towns are not stigmatized as lower-income residents.

Failures of New Town Development

Self-Contained Work Communities and Jobs-Housing Balance

Employment is one of the crucial elements in new town development. Inadequate employment in new towns will force people to commute daily to work. This will increase the traffic load on the transportation network and create additional burden on new town residents in terms of the time and cost involved in commuting. More important, employment opportunities will affect the ability of new towns to attract residents, especially private housing residents, which in turn will affect the social mix of the new towns.

The ability of employment to decentralize to the new towns will have a significant impact on new town development and the welfare of the rapidly growing new town populations. It affects job availability in the new towns, the attractiveness of the new towns as a place to live, and the volume of traffic between the new towns and the main urban areas.

Despite the effective population decentralization in Hong Kong's new towns, there was no concomitant policy to actively decentralize employment. In Britain, new town development corporations often play an active role in attracting industries by offering incentives such as building grants, low-interest loans, low tax rates, investment grants for plants and equipment, and housing provision for workers. In contrast, it was left to the free market to determine the location of businesses and the associated employment opportunities in Hong Kong. If there was any policy, it was mainly through the supply of land, which is a scarce resource there, and infrastructure to facilitate development.

In the planning of new towns in the 1970s and 1980s, the emphasis was on self-containment. Hong Kong was then at its peak in manufacturing industries (Table 10.3). The general principle was that industrial land in the new towns should match the industrial labor force, with some flexibility in taking workers' mobility into consideration. It was hoped that the provision of industrial land would attract industries to the new towns and create employment opportunities for new towns' residents. As the calculation is based on the needs of the population, it does not reflect the actual demand for industrial land in the new towns.

The general practice of incorporating shopping centers and related facilities into the development of major residential and town center projects in the new towns

Table 10.3. Economic Restructuring of Hong Kong, 1961–2011

	Employment (%)					
	1961	1971	1981	1991	2001	2011
Agriculture and fishing	7.3	3.9	2.0	0.0	0.0	0.0
Manufacturing	43.0	47.0	41.2	28.2	12.3	4.0
Construction	4.9	5.4	7.7	6.9	7.6	7.8
Wholesale, retail and import/export trades, and restaurants and hotels	14.4	16.2	19.2	22.5	26.2	30.6
Transport, storage, and communications	7.3	7.4	7.5	9.8	11.3	12.2
Financing, insurance, real estate, and business services	1.6	2.7	4.8	10.6	16.1	19.2
Community, social, and personal services	18.3	15.0	15.6	19.9	25.5	25.4

Source: Hong Kong Census and Statistics Department (1982, 1993, 2002, 2012).
Note: 2011 Population census data, Hong Kong Standard Industrial Classification version 2.0; the above table converted the data in the 2011 population census to Hong Kong Standard Industrial Classification (HSIC) version 1.1 based on the information in the HSIC version 2.0, published by the Census and Statistics Department, p. 4.

also provides some job opportunities. However, the main purpose of such provision is to serve the needs of the local population and to decentralize employment.

The industrial estates in Tai Po and Yuen Long, developed and managed by the Hong Kong Industrial Estates Corporation starting in 1977,[3] have had little impact on local employment. Owing to the shortage of suitable sites in the main urban areas, these industrial estates were forced to be located in the New Territories (Hong Kong Industrial Estates Corporation 1982). Because they catered to selected industries specializing in new products or involve a higher level of technology that cannot operate in ordinary multistory industrial buildings, industries located there were generally land and capital intensive and had little demand for local labor from the new towns.

In general, the government policy toward employment provision in the new towns has been passive. It is hoped that employment in new towns can be generated by the private sector through the provision of cheaper industrial land, abundant labor supply, and good infrastructure. However, these conditions alone are not sufficient for the location of industries and firms. Some other factors such as industrial linkages, accessibility to markets, and agglomeration economies may have a stronger influence in determining the location of a firm.

The employment structure changes with the development of any economy, and such changes will affect the relative importance of the locations of employment in different economic sectors. Since 1971, Hong Kong's economy has gradually changed from the postwar dominance of manufacturing industries to an Asian financial center with the establishment of internationally oriented financial firms and foreign banks focusing on the Asian Pacific region. An increasing proportion of workers are now engaged in wholesale, retail, and office employment, constituting 49.8 percent of the workforce in 2011 compared to 16 percent in 1961. As a result, the relative importance of manufacturing has declined dramatically since the 1990s, employing only 4.0 percent of the workforce in 2011 (see Table 10.3). Hong Kong has changed into a service-oriented economy because factories have relocated into the Pearl River delta for cheaper land and labor supply (Yeh 1997). The locations of the wholesaling/retail/ restaurant and hotel sector and of the financing/insurance/ real estate/other business services sector are more important than the manufacturing sector, which was important in new town development in the 1970s and 1980s, determining the place of work and the level of self-containment.

Despite the intention of self-containment, there is a great mismatch between the population's residence and place of employment. There are not enough jobs for the three major economic sectors in the new towns because employment did not decentralize with the population, which was mainly led by public housing develop-

Table 10.4. Distribution of Labor Force and Employment (2011)

District	Manufacturing		
	Employment (%)	Labor Force (%)	% Employment Less % Labor Force
First-Generation New Towns			
Tsuen Wan[1]	21.7%	13.6%	8.1%
Sha Tin[2]	5.5%	9.9%	−4.4%
Tuen Mun	6.4%	8.2%	−1.9%
Second-Generation New Towns			
Tai Po	7.0%	4.9%	2.1%
Yuen Long	3.4%	2.4%	1.0%
Fanling / Sheung Shui	1.3%	3.9%	−2.6%
Third-Generation New Towns			
Tseung Kwan O	2.6%	5.4%	−2.9%
Tin Shui Wai	0.1%	4.3%	−4.3%
North Lantau	0.1%	0.9%	−0.8%
All new towns	48.0%	53.6%	−5.6%
Other Areas			
Main Urban Areas[3]	42.2%	41.6%	0.6%
Other areas	9.8%	4.8%	5.0%
Hong Kong total	100%	100%	

Sources: Hong Kong Census and Statistics Department (2015b, 2015c).
Note: 2011 Population census and the table E009 used Industrial Classification version 2; the above table combined based on the information in the Hong Kong Standard Industrial Classification (HSIC) version 2.0 published by the Census and Statistics Department, p. 4. Public administrative sector is not included in the calculation of the total working population to match the number of persons engaged, which is without the civil services.

ment of the new towns. As can be seen in Table 10.4, there is an overall deficit of manufacturing, wholesale and retail trade, restaurants and hotels, as well as finance, insurance, real estate, and business services jobs in the new towns, except Yuen Long, which has a slight surplus in manufacturing, and Tsuen Wan, which has a surplus in manufacturing employment with its strong industrial base. The most severe mismatch is in wholesale and retail trade, restaurants and hotels, and financing, insurance, real estate, and business services. There is a surplus in the three employment sectors in the main urban areas, ranging from 18 percent to 32 percent. Among the three employment sectors, financing, insurance, real estate, and business employment has the greatest surplus, 32 percent, which illustrates the high concentration of office activities within the main urban areas.

Because of this jobs-housing mismatch, intra-district work trips in most new towns have decreased from 1981 to 2011 (Table 10.5). Interdistrict work trips from

Wholesale, Retail, and Import/Export Trades, Restaurants and Hotels			Transport, Storage, and Communications			Financing, Insurance, Real Estate, and Business Services		
Employment (%)	Labor Force (%)	% Employment Less % Labor Force	Employment (%)	Labor Force (%)	% Employment Less % Labor Force	Employment (%)	Labor Force (%)	% Employment Less % Labor Force
12.6%	11.7%	0.9%	16.6%	12.9%	3.7%	5.4%	10.4%	−5.0%
5.5%	9.1%	−3.6%	2.7%	9.2%	−6.5%	2.6%	8.5%	−5.9%
2.9%	7.2%	−4.3%	1.6%	8.8%	−7.2%	1.1%	5.5%	−4.4%
1.9%	3.9%	−2.0%	2.0%	3.9%	−2.0%	1.2%	3.2%	−2.0%
2.0%	2.2%	−0.1%	0.6%	2.2%	−1.6%	0.6%	1.8%	−1.1%
1.6%	3.8%	−2.1%	0.7%	3.8%	−3.1%	0.5%	2.9%	−2.4%
1.4%	5.5%	−4.1%	1.9%	5.8%	−3.9%	0.6%	6.0%	−5.4%
0.7%	4.0%	−3.2%	0.3%	4.7%	−4.3%	0.2%	2.9%	−2.8%
0.3%	1.1%	−0.9%	0.8%	1.9%	−1.1%	0.1%	1.0%	−0.9%
28.9%	48.4%	−19.5%	27.2%	53.3%	−26.1%	12.2%	42.2%	−30.0%
68.9%	46.8%	22.0%	59.7%	41.5%	18.2%	86.4%	53.5%	32.9%
2.2%	4.8%	−2.6%	13.1%	5.3%	7.9%	1.4%	4.3%	−2.9%
100%	100%		100%	100%		100%	100%	

¹ Includes Kwai Chung and Tsing Yi since 1986.
² Includes Ma On Shan since 1996.
³ Includes Hong Kong Island, Kowloon, and New Kowloon.

the new towns to the main urban areas should have decreased rather than increased if the new towns were "self-contained." Instead, many workers now commute between the new towns and the main urban areas. This phenomenon is more noticeable in Tsuen Wan/Kwan Tsing, Tseung Kwan O, and Sha Tin/Ma On Shan because these towns are located closer to the urban area, enjoying good accessibility. Tseung Kwan O, for instance, was under rapid development at the time, and there were no industries to provide manufacturing jobs, but only limited office and retailing employment opportunities with few commercial/retailing facilities. The percentage of total work trips from the new towns and other areas to the main urban areas has increased from 9.6 percent in 1981 to 22.3 percent in 1997. The total in-commuting work trips to the main urban areas has increased from 302,174 in 1981 to 1,034,082 in 1997, an increase of 242 percent, although the total work trips in Hong Kong has only increased by 48 percent. This has greatly increased the

Table 10.5. Comparison of Intradistrict and Commuting to Main Urban Area Work Trips, 1981, 1997, and 2011

	1981			1997		
	% Intradistrict Work Trips[1]	% Interdistrict Trips (MUA)	Work Trips (MUA)	% Intradistrict Work Trips	% Interdistrict Trips (MUA)	Work Trips (MUA)
Main urban areas (MUA)	87.4	—	—	93.8	—	—
Tsuen Wan /Kwai Tsing	45.1	84.3	159,240	41.1	86.1	272,838
Tuen Mun	20.8	46.7	21,125	22.1	54.5	131,089
Yuen Long/Tin Shui Wai	6.7	20.2	6,962	14.0	37.8	49,337
Fanling/ Sheung Shui	22.1	44.2	10,123	9.7	53.8	33,149
Tai Po	19.3	48.3	11,993	17.0	58.9	91,631
Sha Tin/Ma On Shan	14.2	81.8	64,292	20.7	67.7	237,003
Tseung Kwan O	n.a.	n.a.	—	7.1	78.9	79,694
North Lantau	n.a.	n.a.	—	n.a.	n.a.	—
Other areas in the New Territories	20.5	26.9	28,439	14.9	52.3	139,341
Total of work trips to main urban area	—	—	302,174	—	—	1,034,082
% Total of work trips to main urban area/total work trips	—	—	9.6	—	—	22.3

Sources: Hong Kong Census and Statistics Department (1984); Hong Kong Transport Department (1997, 2014).
[1] Work trips mean home-based work trips.

traffic pressure in the main urban area. It was fortunate that Hong Kong has a well-managed and efficient modern transport system (L. H. Wang and Yeh 1993; Yeh, Hills, and Ng 2001). However, there is still congestion during peak hours in the main urban areas because of the increased volume of commuting between the new towns and the main urban areas.

The trends in employment location from 1976 to 2011 suggest that the location of manufacturing employment poses less of a problem in new town development in Hong Kong than wholesale, retail, and office employment, which are of increasing importance because of the changing employment structure in Hong Kong (see Table 10.3). Most of the wholesale and retail establishments and office firms are still concentrated in the Tsim Sha Tsui and Central districts. Unlike manufacturing, which has a long history of decentralization to the New Territories, their locations are independent of population location. They are also less inclined to disperse to the new towns. However, with an increasing proportion of the labor force employed in these sectors and the decentralization of population into the new towns in the future, the jobs-housing mismatch will be exacerbated. This will increase the

Difference Between 1981 and 1997		2011			Difference Between 1997 and 2011	
% Intradistrict Work Trips	% Work Trips (MUA)	% Intradistrict Work Trips	% Interdistrict Trips (MUA)	Work Trips (MUA)	% Intradistrict Work Trips	% Work Trips (MUA)
6.4		69.7	—	—	−24.1	
−4.0	1.8	30.3	61.0	225,373	−10.7	−25.1
1.3	7.8	32.0	46.8	84,951	9.9	−7.7
7.3	17.6	21.2	37.9	61,896	7.1	0.1
−12.4	9.6	12.7	41.5	44,425	2.9	−12.4
−2.3	10.6	16.1	48.5	60,224	−0.9	−10.4
6.5	−14.1	24.4	63.8	177,518	3.7	−3.9
n.a.	n.a.	10.4	79.4	134,796	3.2	0.5
n.a.	n.a.	17.6	46.8	39,197	n.a.	n.a.
−5.6	25.4	17.7	42.8	85,544	2.8	−9.5
—	—			913,924	—	—
—	—			18.2	—	—

pressure on transport and will affect the attractiveness of new towns for private housing development.

With regard to the future employment situation in the new towns, the outlook for retail employment is probably less gloomy than for office employment. Retail activities, in part, are influenced by consumer demand (Shepherd and Thomas 1980), so some retail employment may decentralize to new towns when they grow to be sufficiently large and reach a threshold that can support more retail activities and result in the gradual opening of more shopping centers in the planned new town centers. At present, new town residents still maintain strong social and economic ties with the main urban areas, and they often find it easier to shop there than in the new towns. Nevertheless, because of the good accessibility in Mong Kok, Yau Ma Tei, Tsim Sha Tsui, Central, and Causeway Bay, these districts will remain strong magnets for retail activities, particularly for specialist and non–convenience goods.

Office employment locations are not expected to change much because the key locational factor is the need for a central location and ease in accessibility to clients and business associates (I. Alexander 1979; Daniels 1975). It is thus less likely than other economic activities to decentralize, even if the increasing use of information technology renders it relatively more footloose. The demand for home-to-office work trips will therefore increase with further decentralization of the population to the new towns.

Social Issues

Despite the new town planning principles of self-containment and balanced development, the former is difficult to achieve. This is a great problem for third-generation new towns that are more remote from the main urban areas. The lack of job opportunities in these new towns and the time that it takes to travel to main urban areas for work has created many social problems for them. The most notorious is Tin Shui Wai, which was widely called the "city of sadness" in the late 2000s (also see Chapter 7). The Planning Department commissioned the Department of Social Work and Social Administration at the University of Hong Kong to conduct a study on Tin Shui Wai to identify the issues and the implications for future planning of new development areas (NDAs).

The study identified the lack of local economy, distance from the urban center, inorganic management of commercial and retail outlets, high living cost as caused by the lack of competition in the retail outlet, and high traveling costs to the main urban areas for jobs as factors making life difficult for the residents in Tin Shui Wai, who are mainly composed of low-income immigrants as compared with other new towns (Law et al. 2009). Lau (2010) found that owing to the high commuting cost (more than 10 percent of their income if the job is in main urban area), low-income workers tend not to choose the jobs in the main urban area. The low-income workers also lack social networks to seek job opportunities, and their limited choice of transport mode also hindered their employment. The jobs-housing imbalance was severe in Tin Shui Wai as only 11,220 out of the 102,000 working population living there found a job locally (Lau 2010).

To encourage the unemployed and low-income residents to seek employment across districts and to reduce their travel costs, the Hong Kong government launched the Pilot Transport Support Scheme in mid-July 2007 (Hong Kong Legislative Council 2007). The scheme comprised the Job Search allowance and Cross-District Transport Allowance and received application from four districts (Yuen Long, Tuen Mun, North District, and Island District) to reduce their heavy travel costs. This was replaced by the Work Incentive Transport Subsidy Scheme (WITSS) in 2010, in which the program was no longer limited to the four districts but available to other districts in Hong Kong (Hong Kong Legislative Council 2015). The travel subsidies may help to increase the incomes of the low-income families in the remote new towns. However, their long commutes to work reduce their time with their children and families as compared with residents in new towns that are closer to the main urban areas. With less attention to their children and families, some of the social issues related to juvenile delinquency and family problems cannot be solved by the travel subsidy schemes. Better jobs-housing balance, which may be difficult to achieve, may still be needed.

Conclusion

Hong Kong's new town development has basically been intended to supply land for public housing, which is otherwise expensive and difficult to obtain in the main urban areas. Since 1973, this has been spectacular in terms of pace and scale. It is unquestionably a major planning achievement for Hong Kong. By the early 1980s, about one million people (almost 20 percent of the population) had been housed in the new towns; by 2011, the figure grew to over three million people, representing about 47.1 percent of the total population. The population has successfully decentralized to the new towns because of the high demand for public housing. However, there has been only limited success in private housing development. With the predominance of public housing, new towns have often become working-class communities with a high percentage of their working population engaged in production work and a low percentage in professional and managerial work. Their unattractiveness stems from the difficulty in attracting white-collar jobs. Although there is a tendency for manufacturing industries to decentralize to the new towns, employment in wholesale, retail, and office activities remains centralized in the main urban areas. This has deterred white-collar workers from moving to the new towns and has therefore affected the development of private housing.

In the development of new towns, too much emphasis has been given to public housing construction, but the provision of social facilities and transport has been overlooked (D. R. Phillips 1987). The emphasis on public housing is understandable in Hong Kong, where it has long been a major social problem. More important, the government has an overt public housing program to improve the living conditions of its people. Public housing development in new towns is rapid and always on schedule because the Housing Department has an annual production target to fulfill. Other departments, however, are not subject to this pressure. Although there have been improvements since the early new town development program, the provision of public facilities and internal/external transport in new towns often lags behind the population growth. Tuen Mun, for instance, saw a persistent shortage of primary schools in the 1980s and 1990s, and the Tuen Mun

Highway, linking the new town with urban areas, was only partially completed despite substantial occupancy in the new town. In Sha Tin, internal and external transportation facilities were also poorly developed in its early stage of development. Drawing on these experiences, a transport-led approach has since been taken in the development of newer new towns. The recently developed Tseung Kwan O and Tung Chung new towns are well connected with mass transit railway in their early stage of development using transit-oriented development (TOD).

Because of a lack of employment decentralization policy, new town development has caused an increasing jobs-housing discrepancy. A high percentage of people in the new towns have to commute to the main urban areas for work, overloading the transport network linking the new towns with the main urban areas. There is greater demand for door-to-door direct bus links, which has contributed to traffic congestion in the Central Business District (CBD) and the main urban area.

Much as new towns provide low-income families with low-rent public housing in a good living environment, they also increase the commuting time and costs for these families. Although the concept of "self-containment" is good in theory, it is difficult to accomplish in practice (Ogilvy 1968; Thomas and Cresswell 1973). Neither the "stick" of restricting new industrial and office development in the main urban areas nor the "carrot" of inducing firms through subsidies to move into the new towns has been used by the government. A clear and consistent policy toward new town development that integrates public housing and employment decentralization may be needed. There are arguments that the government should not interfere with the market because of its laissez-faire policy. However, there is evidence that nonmarket forces play an important role in its economic growth. With the government's involvement in the prices of rice, public utilities, transport, medical and health, education, and housing provision, Hong Kong is able to provide cheap labor for its economic development (Schiffer 1991). Without a proactive employment decentralization policy, the traffic problem in the main urban areas will increase, and the public housing residents in the new towns will have to bear the cost of time and money in commuting to the main urban areas for work.

Hong Kong is reviewing its Territorial Development Strategy in the Hong Kong 2030—Planning Vision and Strategy. It is about time to consider formulating an employment decentralization policy in relationship to employment and commuting problems of the new towns. With further integration with the Pearl River Delta (Yeh 2002), it may be possible to decentralize some of the office activities to the new towns in the New Territories such as Tuen Mun and Yuen Long in the northwest and Sha Tin and Tai Po in the northeast. They are located closer to the border between Hong Kong and the Pearl River Delta than the existing CBD in the main urban areas. Such decentralization may help to facilitate and promote the development of producer services between Hong Kong and the Pearl River Delta in addition to providing the much-needed white-collar employment in the new towns in northwest and northeast New Territories. The provision of land and infrastructure alone as with past new town development may be inadequate and take too long in promoting office development in these areas. A more proactive approach with fiscal incentives may be needed to speed up such needed development.

In order to improve the quality of life of new town residents, especially the low-income families living in public housing, who pay a large proportion of their income for transport costs, and to increase the attractiveness of new towns, the government may have to play a more active role in decentralizing employment to bring it closer to them. Moreover, as total "self-containment" in employment is difficult to achieve, the transport network between the new towns and the main urban areas will have to be improved to facilitate the daily work trips generated by the rapidly growing population in the new towns. The progress and success of new town development in Hong Kong will very much depend on the transportation network service with the main urban areas and the provision of jobs in the new towns.

Acknowledgments

I would like to thank Timothy Lam for his kind assistance in the collection and analysis of the data. I would also like to thank the Chan To Haan Endowed Professorship and the Distinguished Research Achievement Award of the University of Hong Kong for partial funding of this study.

Notes

1. Includes the main urban areas (main Kowloon and Hong Kong island) and the extended urban areas (Sha Tin, Ma On Shan, Tseung Kwan O, Tsuen Wan, Kwai Tung, Tsing Yi, and Tung Chung).
2. Includes Tai Po, Fanling/Sheung Shui, Tuen Mun, Yuen Long, and Tin Shui Wan.
3. The Hong Kong Industrial Estates Corporation merged with the Hong Kong Industrial Technology Centre Corporation and the Provisional Hong Kong Science Park Company Limited to form the Hong Kong Science and Technology Parks Corporation (HKSTP) in May 2001.

11

Right Place, Right Time

The Rise of Bundang

Kyung Min Kim and Jongpil Ryu

New town development in South Korea started in the 1970s, when rapid industrialization spurred a mass influx of people into the capital city of Seoul. This led to several developments being built at or near the edge of what was a far smaller city than it is today; one of the most notable was new-town-in-town Gangnam. Planned as a high-density urban center south of the Han River, it quickly became the region of choice for middle- and high-income earners and was an integral part of the city by the end of the decade.

During the 1980s, Korea's economic success intensified with annual GDP growth rates of over 10 percent. This prosperity had a huge impact on land price, which experienced a year-over-year increase of 28 percent in 1987, 32 percent in 1988, and 27 percent in 1989. Combined with the population growth in Seoul, which grew from 8.3 million to 10.6 million over the decade, a housing shortage was quickly becoming a critical issue. Not only did a newly emerging middle class have difficulty finding housing in the city; the cost of that housing was quickly climbing above what they could afford. In the first quarter of 1989, the rise of housing prices in Gangnam stunned the nation; within only two months, the price of a medium-sized condo increased more than the annual salary of ordinary office workers (G. Lee 1999, 430).

Concerned that the housing price increases in Gangnam could set off a trend in other regions, the Korean government made it a priority to stabilize housing prices in Gangnam. They believed it would be possible if they provided home buyers (especially the middle class) with new opportunities for housing in the form of not just one, but several new towns (Korea Land Corporation 1997, 54). The centerpiece of this massive new town project was Bundang. The rise of Bundang from scattered settlements and farmland to a bustling job center was meteoric. It could be thought that much of the success of Bundang is based on its fortuitous location, its ample size, and the economic and demographic conditions during the time of its development. It is important, however, not to discount the major impact of the then-powerful centralized government and its focused planning and construction initiatives. All told, it was really the exploitation of good circumstances through proper centralized planning that led Bundang to become the most successful new town project in Korean history.

Locating the Centerpiece

Believing that it was imperative to begin providing alternative housing options for the growing urban middle class, the Korean government decided to get involved in the housing market directly. The original plan was to build around three hundred thousand new homes for one million people, which represented 10 percent of the population of Seoul. To choose the optimal locations across the Seoul metropolitan area, the Korean government decided on four mandatory criteria (Korea Land Corporation 1997, 56):

1. The area was to be located within ten kilometers of Seoul for commuting purposes.
2. The area needed an adequate transportation system or good accessibility to Gangnam.
3. The area had to be larger than 990,000 square meters for the construction of at least one hundred thousand houses.
4. The area had to have a comparatively low land price.

Based on these criteria, the central government selected five locations, and in April 1989, they announced their Five New Towns Development Plan, which would involve new town construction in Ilsan and Joongdong to the west of the city, and Bundang, Pyeongchon, and Sanbon to the south.

A cursory glance at the location of the five towns in Figure 11.1 may be enough to see why Bundang was considered the centerpiece of the project. At 19.6 million square meters, it had the largest development area of the five and would be able to accommodate the greatest number of housing units and thus the highest number of people (Table 11.1). Accessibility to Gangnam was clearly its best feature, however; to reach Gangnam, it only took an hour by car during peak hours, and 30 minutes during off-peak hours. Also, because it was located near the Gyeongboo highway (the central transportation axis of Korea connecting Seoul, the largest city, and Busan, the second largest), it was convenient for getting to the other major cities. While all five towns had similar development durations, much of the attention of the planning and development agencies was fixed squarely on Bundang, as it provided the best opportunity to resolve the housing crisis.

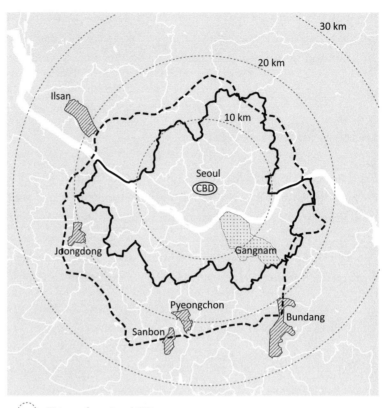

Figure 11.1. Location of five new towns. Map by SukJoon Lee.

○ Distance from Seoul CBD

Gyeongboo Expressway

Seoul Outer Circular Expressway, completed in 2007

Top-Down Development

Because reining in housing prices was a priority, the full capacity of the government was brought to bear on accomplishing the plan. Powerful support from the president, the prime minister, and administrative offices was provided, and several practical organizations were newly established. The government felt that rapid construction was the key to alleviating this national problem, and the presence of a powerful institution was needed to control conflicting interests among related governmental organizations (Korea Land Corporation 1997, 65).

The Korean political system of the time was centralized, hence the authority of the Blue House (the president's office) was very strong. To accelerate the development process, President Roh Tae-Woo presided over all housing-related ministerial meetings and controlled diverse tasks of many of the organizations involved. He

Table 11.1. The Five Korean New Towns

Category	All	Bundang	Ilsan	Pyeongchon	Sanbon	Joongdong
Location		Sungnam	Goyang	Anyang	Goonpo	Boocheon
Area (1,000m²)	50,140	19,639	15,736	5,106	4,203	5,456
Population (10,000 people)	116.8	39.0	27.6	16.8	16.8	16.6
Population density (people/area, population/ha)	1,406	199	175	329	399	304
Development density (people/development area, population/ha)	3,231	489	425	795	844	678
Housing (1,000 units) (Number of apartment units)	292 (281)	97.6 (94.6)	69 (63.1)	42 (41.4)	42 (41.4)	41.4 (40.5)
Average ratio of floor area (%)		184	169	204	205	226
Length of road (km)	232.2	82.8	51.4	69.6	0	28.4
Subway (km)	62	25.1	21.1	15.7		
First resident move-in month		Sept. 1991	Aug. 1992	Mar. 1992	Apr. 1992	Feb. 1993
Development duration		Aug. 1989~ Dec 1996	Mar. 1990~ Dec.1995	Aug. 1989~ Dec. 1995	Aug. 1989~ Jan. 1995	Feb. 1990~ Jan/ 1996
Development cost (100 billion KRW)	104.7	41.6	26.6	11.8	6.3	18.4
Main developer		KLC	KLC	KLC	KHC	Boocheon, KHC, KLC

Source: Korea Ministry of Land, Infrastructure and Transport (2016).

established the Affordable Housing Plan Task Force, which became responsible for the overall development plan as it controlled the interests of related players while asking for support from many public organizations. A separate task force, called the New Town Development Task Force Team, was formed within the Ministry of Construction. This team was to manage the specific plans for new town development (Korea Land Corporation 1997, 67). Although this team was deactivated after the five new towns were completed, it exercised the greatest authority during the development period.

While the central government provided blueprints and guidelines for the new town development, the Korea Land Corporation (KLC) executed the plans. This public enterprise held exclusive rights over land acquisition and supply in all public developments. As Bundang's main developer, it was responsible for land acquisition, allocation, and construction of the infrastructure and the arterial transportation system.

Besides the central government and the KLC, several major organizations participated in the planning and development of Bundang. The Korea Research Institute for Human Settlements conducted the land-use planning and the impact evaluation. Other public corporations, including the Korea Railroad Corporation, the

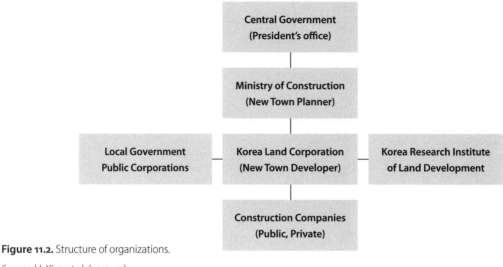

Figure 11.2. Structure of organizations.

Source: H. Kim et al. (1993, 93).

Seoul metropolitan government, the Korea Electric Power Corporation, the Korea Telecommunication Corporation, the Korea District Heating Corporation, and the Korea Housing Corporation, participated in the construction of the houses, infrastructure, and the arterial transportation system (H. Kim et al. 1993, 51). In short, new town development in Korea hinged on the collaborative effort of many public institutions and organizations (Figure 11.2).

Land Acquisition and Compensation

The plan was for Bundang to house three hundred thousand people within just seven years. To do it, the planning body could spend little time developing a consensus among affected parties. The process of land acquisition and compensation for Bundang was thus done stealthily. Only seven days after the government announced in April 1989 that they would build five new towns somewhere in the Seoul metropolitan area, they declared that Bundang and the other four areas had already been chosen. There had not been any prior public discussion or consultation, and very little information about compensation had been decided on. The local residents of Bundang (mostly farmers) were afraid they would be forced to leave their hometown with little compensation, which led to serious public outcry almost immediately. Several protests erupted, and in May 1989 about two thousand people occupied city hall to request for fair compensation and to prevent Bundang from becoming solely a town for the middle class (Bae 2008, 106).

The fact that their methods caused such a backlash may have been an oversight on the part of the central government, or perhaps they had expected it and were willing to deal with problems as they evolved. Certainly, nobody would confuse the planning agency for a democratic body. While the government tried to compensate land owners and tenants fairly afterward, there was no doubt that the government planning strategy was negligent in respecting the rights of local citizens, and at least some of these problems could have been avoided with better foresight.

Within two months of the initial project launch, the KLC announced their plan to provide market-rate compensation for land owners. The government did not attempt to deny that Bundang was being created as a middle- and upper-class town, but they calculated that if land owners and tenants were satisfied with the compensation they received, they would relocate without too much resistance.

Because Bundang was mostly farm land, it had been restricted from development by law, leading to static land prices and low property turnover for several decades. As a result, it was hard to make proper appraisal estimates. To persuade land owners, KLC applied land prices from neighboring areas, which land owners considered to be reflective of the market-rate price of their land (Korea Land Corporation 1997, 362). The government finished land price appraisal in August 1989 and completed most of its compensation in December 1989. Although most of the compensation was completed within eight months, revisions were made about ten times up until 1995 (Korea Land Corporation 1997, 373). Eventually, 4,045 households were compensated (1,665 landlords and 2,380 tenants) a total of 1,256 billion won (equivalent to 1,878 million USD as of 1989) (Korea Land Corporation 1997, 171).

Land Distribution

After KLC acquired the land, they divided it into several blocks. To minimize public investment, the government sought the participation of several big private companies using the "Early Parceling-Out Method."[1] Accordingly, unit blocks averaged about 110,000 square meters, varying from about 18,000 square meters to 353,000 square meters (1.8 to 35.3 hectares), big enough to allow private developers to build large condo complexes, which would ensure huge profits. Seventy-three blocks assigned for residential use were purchased by private developers and three blocks by public organizations (Oh and Yim 2014, 143).

Companies purchasing land from the KLC could pay for it in four installments. However, the payment schedule was tight; the land buyer had to pay 10–40 percent of the sale price when the contract was signed, 15–20 percent within six months, another 15–20 percent within twelve months, and the remainder when

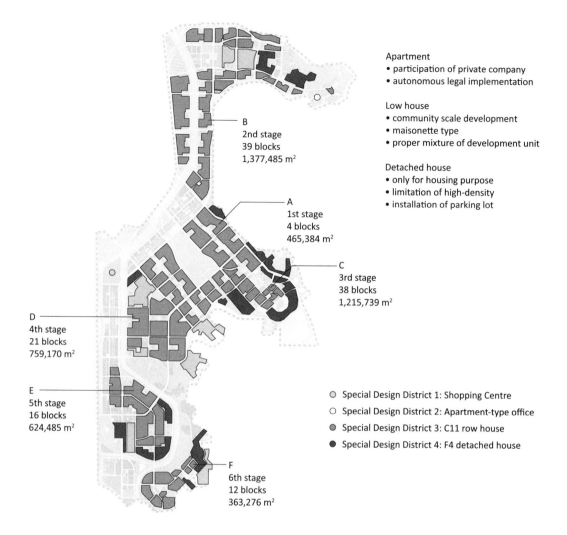

Apartment
- participation of private company
- autonomous legal implementation

Low house
- community scale development
- maisonette type
- proper mixture of development unit

Detached house
- only for housing purpose
- limitation of high-density
- installation of parking lot

B
2nd stage
39 blocks
1,377,485 m²

A
1st stage
4 blocks
465,384 m²

C
3rd stage
38 blocks
1,215,739 m²

D
4th stage
21 blocks
759,170 m²

E
5th stage
16 blocks
624,485 m²

F
6th stage
12 blocks
363,276 m²

○ Special Design District 1: Shopping Centre
○ Special Design District 2: Apartment-type office
◉ Special Design District 3: C11 row house
● Special Design District 4: F4 detached house

Figure 11.3. Bundang housing complex plan. Reprinted from Oh and Yim (2014, 143) with permission.

land clearing was finished. For land designated to affordable housing, a portion of the initial payment was reduced. Private companies developing affordable housing only had to pay 10 percent of land price when the contract was signed (Korea Land Corporation 1997, 247).

Land sales started in November 1989 in the center of the town (District A in Figure 11.3), followed by land in the north of the city (B), and then later in the south (C, D, E, and F). The size of the whole development area was 18.3 million square meters. The total land area for residential use was 6.5 million square meters (35.9 percent), 80 percent of which was assigned to large-scale condo construction. Retail and office use was allotted 1.7 million square meters (9.5 percent), and 10.0 million square meters was used for public areas (Oh and Yim 2014, 134).

Successful land sales within a very short time provided the KLC with substantial profits. Land sales income (5,998 billion KRW, equivalent to 4.95 billion USD as of 1998) far eclipsed land compensation costs (1,256 billion KRW, equivalent to 1.03 billion USD as of 1998). Even when considering other development costs (i.e., transportation and infrastructure costs), the KLC achieved quite a windfall.

Development Finances

The financial success of Bundang's development is noteworthy not only in Korea, but also globally. In comparison, many American new towns developed by private developers failed because of poor site selection, inadequate sponsorship (lack of experience in large-scale community development), and funding issues (Chapter 17). Unlike American new towns, British new towns were driven by public corporations that had much more support from the government. Consequently, broader site selection could be facilitated, land could be acquired with eminent domain, and there was sufficient funding. Still, when analyzing the economic returns of British new towns, many were failures. For instance, Milton Keynes, touted as one of the most successful British new towns, suffered a loss of more than five hundred thousand pounds. This kind of financial deficiency is typical of American and British new town projects (Peiser and Chang 1999, 1693).

The main problem in Britain may be that the new town development corporations (NTDCs) tried to develop both land and buildings, meaning that they competed with the private sector in the real estate market. If they were not as competitive as private real estate developers/operators, vacancies of publicly owned property would ensue, leading to financial destabilization. The KLC was an actual developer like the NTDCs, and as a "master developer," the KLC oversaw planning, land acquisition, land sales, and infrastructure construction. However, the KLC did not construct and manage buildings (Table 11.2). For example, both KLC and Milton

Table 11.2. Financial Breakdown of Milton Keynes and Bundang

	Milton Keynes (in USD, Undiscounted, Through 1992)	Bundang (in USD, Undiscounted, Through 1998)
Land development operations	$5,500,000	$3,110,000,000
Community services	−$436,500,000	−$1,430,000,000
Property operations	−$784,500,000	n.a.
Miscellaneous income and expenses	$113,000,000	n.a.
Net profit	−$1,102,500,000	$1,680,000,000

Sources: Korea Land Corporation (1999, 135); Peiser and Chang (1999, 1686).

Keynes generated a profit in land sales and a loss in community services as expected. However, KLC did not gain any operating income nor suffer any operating losses from property operations during the development period. This partly explains why Milton Keynes suffered a net loss of over $1.1 billion USD, while Bundang garnered an impressive $1.68 billion USD profit.

Peiser and Chang (1999) concluded that the key factors to successful new town development are quick land disposal, segregation of the land development and building development operations, and some government-backed financing. They argued that developments may become vulnerable if the development period is too long; for instance, if the period is several decades, the development is prone to pass through economic cycles that can include severe economic downturns. These changes in economic conditions have proven to bring financial ruin to many a new town developer.

Bundang experienced favorable circumstances: in the early and mid-1990s, Korea's economic growth was very high, and there was plenty of demand for housing, especially in the Seoul metropolitan area. Consequently, private construction companies were eager to participate in the land-bidding process operated by the KLC. These companies knew that the housing demand was so high that sales could be completed even before the real construction started. The construction companies were thus able to pay the land purchase cost to the KLC expediently.

By acquiring a vast amount of land in Bundang at a fairly low price within a short time, KLC earned substantial profits from the land sales very quickly. Because Bundang became a middle-class town, land price increases could have burdened KLC if they had taken more time or done their land acquisition in several phases. KLC acquired most of the land within the initial three years of development. As a result, even in 1989, the first year, KLC earned a net profit.

Figure 11.4. Surplus of fixed assets disposal. Reprinted from Korea Land Corporation (1999, 135) with permission.

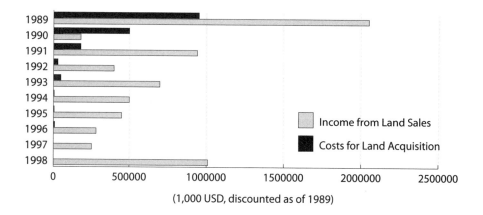

(1,000 USD, discounted as of 1989)

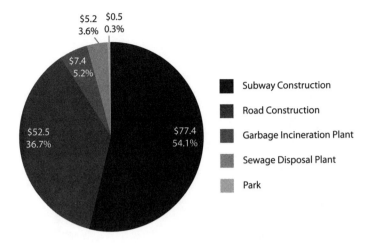

$5.2 $0.5
3.6%   0.3%

$7.4
5.2%

$52.5
36.7%

$77.4
54.1%

■ Subway Construction

■ Road Construction

■ Garbage Incineration Plant

■ Sewage Disposal Plant

■ Park

Figure 11.5. Expenditure on infrastructure provision. Reprinted from Korea Land Corporation (1997, 447, 448, 453) with permission.

Except for a net loss in 1990, every other year saw a net surplus, which gave great stability and momentum to the development process (Figure 11.4).

Based on its huge surplus, KLC could splurge on community services. Among their major infrastructure projects was a subway linking to Seoul's main system, major roads, a sewage disposal plant, and a garbage incineration plant (Figure 11.5). And while KLC invested lots of money into these community services, the operating incomes belonged to other organizations managing those services. KLC spent about 93.9 billion won (equivalent to 77.4 million USD as of 1998) on the subway system and 63.7 billion won (equivalent to 52.5 million USD as of 1998) on road construction. This only enhanced the town's allure and ensured that the demand for housing in Bundang would always be there.

Design Principles

The long-term vision for Bundang was for it to become a self-sufficient city, with a balance between employment and housing. However, the most pressing need was simply for Bundang to supply housing for middle- and upper-class households. A newly developed city could not be expected to provide enough jobs for the people moving in, which meant that most jobs would still be in Seoul.

On a regional scale, the development plan needed to provide several transportation modes to job centers (Gangnam and the central business district of Seoul): an inner-city highway, a subway, and several high-speed bus routes were provided to connect the new town with its central city. Within Bundang, five commercial areas were planned along the major road, which would contain entertainment,

shopping functions, and transportation nodes for inter-city travel. The elementary schools were located away from the commercial areas so that commercial activity did not affect the school environment.

At that time, the average household size was four, mostly composed of two parents and two children. Planning and design principles in Bundang thus focused on accommodating two-parent households with kids. Each superblock of five hundred by five hundred meters was considered a neighborhood unit for family living and was surrounded by secondary roads that bypass the town, generating a car-free safe walking environment. Within neighborhood units contained shopping and educational facilities, including schools that were located at the center of a block, generating a safe walking environment for the children. Planners arranged twenty-seven elementary schools within the city, and each school covered about thirty-six hundred households. Parks and neighborhood living facilities were located adjacent to each school to stimulate community activities, while parkways connect community centers with residential complexes.

Clarence Perry's ([1929] 1998) classic "neighborhood unit" theory formed the basis of Bundang's design, and the project satisfies most of the principles Perry suggested:

- Center the school within the neighborhood.
- Place arterial streets along the perimeter.
- Design internal streets using a hierarchy that easily distinguishes local streets from arterial streets.

- Restrict local shopping areas to the perimeter.
- Dedicate at least 20 percent of the neighborhood land area to parks and open space.

With a desire to provide enough green space and other neighborhood facilities for a growing population, the primary housing type was the high-rise condo complex. By the mid-1980s in Korea, high-rise condos had become the favored housing type and a symbol for middle-class living (Gelézeau 2007, 155) (Figure 11.6). There was strong demand, and by building more units within a given land plot, high-rise condos promised more profit for housing suppliers than low-rise or single detached homes. Essentially all the stakeholders in the housing market—planners, home buyers, and construction companies—welcomed the development of high-rise condos. Condos represented more than 90 percent of housing units built by the Five New Towns Development Plan, and naturally, they were the dominant housing type in Bundang. As Bundang was designed to give middle-class families exactly the kind of elegant, modern family lifestyle they were looking for, it is no surprise that they flocked to the new city in droves (Kang 2000).[2]

Conclusion

The prerequisite for successful new town development is favorable economic and demographic conditions within the main city. In addition, geographic conditions are essential—there must be an appropriate area close to the main city on which to build the new town. In the case of Korea's new town development in 1989, the capital city of Seoul provided robust economic growth and a high demand for middle-class housing, while the town of Bundang supplied the favorable location. But this was really only a starting point. For Bundang's development to be successful, these favorable conditions had to be capitalized on by proper decisions every step of the way:

Authority. The full support of the powerful central government was important. The authority they bestowed on KLC through targeted legislation allowed the development agency to literally steamroll through the land acquisition and land clearing phases, creating the conditions for the construction of a new town in record time.

Planning. The plan to divide the land into large parcels to be sold to private construction companies led to the rapid construction of high-density housing, much of it in the form of high-rise condominium complexes. Given that this form of housing was popular with the middle class and demand was high, the construction companies were able to go full steam ahead. In 1992, only two years after the official announcement of the Bundang project, the first settlement was established. Three years later, the population of the town reached 296,000, over 75 percent of the planned target.

Profitability. The plan executed by KLC was the right one under the circumstances. Rapid land acquisition at a fairly low price, coupled with the decision not to compete with private construction companies in the construction and management of buildings, led to rapid profits. An ample portion of these profits were reinvested in the town, improving its already compelling features and infrastructure.

Design. When the government built Gangnam in the 1970s and 1980s, several top high schools relocated to Gangnam to attract the middle class (Ogino 2004). Following this model, there was a focused intent on designing Bundang to accommodate the typical middle-class family of four in Korea. A focus on education, which is of primary concern to Koreans families, led to Bundang's designation as a special independent education district. The design of blocks and plots followed highly respected neighborhood planning schemes that promoted safety, education, and family life.

Branding. Although it is hard to say that the planning authority was really "branding" Bundang rather than just following market demand, it nonetheless became clear to a growing middle- and upper-class citizenry that Bundang would be a great place to live for lower-cost housing, with reasonable proximity to Seoul's established business hubs, and with beautiful new infrastructure and amenities.

By all accounts, the strategies implemented brought about the desired results. Based on a 1993 survey on the educational background, origin, and average income of new Bundang residents, they were characterized as a mostly well-educated middle class, where 33 percent had migrated from Gangnam and the average income was 40 percent higher than the national average (Koh and Park 1993). The Population and Housing Census of Korea in 2000 showed that 47 percent of Bundang residents were either college students or college graduates, twenty-one percentage points higher than the national average at that time.

Of course, the town went through some growing pains. Infrastructure provisions, especially public transportation, had not been completed in time for the first settlement, which occurred in 1992. Before the subway line connecting Bundang to Seoul was built in September 1994, Bundang residents who commuted to Seoul encountered severe traffic congestion. A survey by Korea Research Institute for Human Settlements in 1993 showed that residents were satisfied with housing and living conditions, but unsatisfied with commuting (Koh and Park 1993).

Soon enough, public transportation improved, and two subway lines and several bus routes gave commuters to the city a host of good options. But this was not the most important development brewing through the second half of the 1990s. This "dormitory town" serving the megacity of Seoul was already preparing for the next stage of its evolution: to become self-sufficient.

Bundang in the Twenty-First Century

Before the late 1990s, there were few large department stores in Bundang, as residents shopped in Gangnam (C. Lee and Ahn 2005). However, in the 1990s the growing number of middle-class residents made many retailers start to see Bundang as a profitable market. By the turn of the century, several luxurious department stores and regional-scale malls had begun to locate in Bundang to help them dominate the southeastern part of the Seoul metropolitan area. As of 2016, the largest department store in the Seoul metropolitan area was in Bundang.

At the same time, industry began to see Bundang as an attractive option. Because of lower rents and a well-educated population there, several of Korea's big IT companies such as Naver started to relocate their headquarters in Bundang. As Figure 11.7 shows, firms and employment in finance, insurance, and IT sectors grew very fast. The number of workers in these three industries grew from 21,040 in 1994 to 164,412 in 2012 (a 743 percent increase) (Korea Statistical Information Service 2016).

Correspondingly, the Bundang office market has grown rapidly. In 1996, the total floor area of office buildings was only seventy-six thousand square meters, but it grew to 1.4 million square meters in 2012 (Savills Research 2010, 4). This indicates a nineteen-fold increase in office space from 1996 to 2012. Today, Bundang is the fourth-largest office district in the Seoul metropolitan area in addition to the traditional CBD, the financial district in

Figure 11.7. Growth of finance, insurance, and IT sectors in Bundang. *Source*: Korea Statistical Information Service (2016).

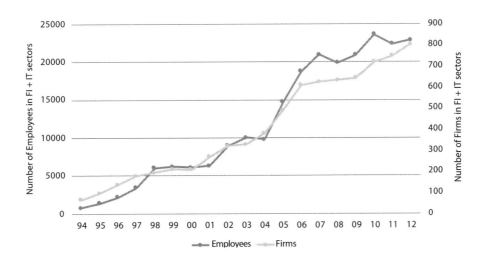

Table 11.3. Summary of Bundang's Finances by Activity Through 1998 (100 Million KRW)

	Undiscounted	Present Value as of 1989
Property operations	n.a.[1]	
Net operating income before adjustment		
Less: loan charges		
Less: loan write-offs		
Subtotal		
Land development operations		
Land sales income	59,984	46,353
Land compensation costs	12,555	11,817
Surplus from disposal of fixed assets	47,429	34,536
Less: general administration	9,700	7,493
Less: loan charges for land development, etc.	n.a.[2]	
Subtotal	37,729	27,043
Community services		
Income from road grant	n.a.[3]	
Less: contribution to local and public authorities	−17,350	−13,057
Less: other accounts	n.a.[4]	
Subtotal	−17,350	−13,057
Miscellaneous income and expenses		
Income from nonproperty	n.a.[5]	
Debt redeemed adjustment	n.a.	
Depreciation provided	n.a.	
Sums receivable from secretary of state	n.a.	
Subtotal		
Total Net Present Value (adjusted by CPI)	20,379	13,986

Sources: Korea Land Corporation (1997, 447, 448, 453); Korea Land Corporation (1999, 135).
[1] Korea Land Corporation sold all the acquired lands to private developers and did not involve itself in property operations.
[2] Korea Land Corporation did not issue any bond for Bundang development, although it was allowed to do so.
[3] Income from road grant and subway operation belonged to either the city government or the Korean National Railroad Administration.
[4] Miscellaneous development costs for community services are included under the land development operations expense.
[5] Korea Land Corporation was established to provide lands for the development and did not generate any income from nonproperty.

Yoido, and Gangnam, which was known as a Korea's Silicon Valley in the 1990s and the early 2000s. Bundang's proximity to Gangnam was what made it such an attractive new town for the middle class, and it is becoming more of a hub that serves as a focal point for new development.

When Korea experienced another housing price increase in the early 2000s, the government used the same policy to stabilize it. It planned to develop several new towns in the Seoul metropolitan area. The centerpiece of this new development was a town called Pangyo, which was located in a limited development district within the borders of Bundang.

Because Bundang had become a thriving middle-class town with a strong infrastructure, it was not a difficult decision for the government to build a new town within a new town. Pangyo new town development started in 2003, and large-scale condo development was completed in 2010. One important aspect of Pangyo is that the Korean government designated the central area of the Pangyo office district an IT-oriented cluster called Pangyo IT Techno Valley, contributing to its becoming a strong national IT hub.

A new town can be considered financially successful if its development was profitable, its construction was sound, it attracted enough people to live in it, and it had reasonable transportation access to the big city. Bundang is one of the few new towns in the world that not only can boast all these elements, but has also rapidly become a self-sufficient urban center that is attracting its own new town development around its periphery (Table 11.3). To have seen Bundang reach maturity so quickly is perhaps what the planners of Bundang can be most proud of.

Notes

1. Private companies were to pay 40 percent of the land price when signing a contract with the Korea Land Corporation and the rest within four months.

2. Initially, Bundang was planned to be a middle-class town. However, the Korean government constructed 11,479 units of social housing, representing 13 percent of the total apartment supply. In addition, the private developers constructed 17,695 units of small apartments (gross floor area smaller than sixty-two square meters) (Korea Land Corporation 1997), resulting in almost 40 percent of the apartments in Bundang being suitable for the lower middle class.

12

New Towns in India

Sai Balakrishnan

New towns are not a new idea in India. Starting in the 1950s, the newly independent Indian state had the daunting task of building the nation. One of the ways of realizing this vision was to build a nation of new towns (Kundu, Misra, and Meher 1986; Sivaramakrishnan 1976–77; Wakeman 2016). The country had recently been torn apart both by colonialism and by a debilitating partition from Pakistan, and the new towns were part of a national plan to remake a modern India. To jump-start industrialization, the central government financed the building of 120 new industrial townships, and one of the most familiar and well-known types of these is the steel townships. To integrate the flood of refugees pouring into existing cities from the newly formed Pakistan, the central government also financed and built some thirty-five satellite towns, many of them in or near the border regions between the newly divided countries.

These towns were built with the modernist ideal of national integration in mind, where religious and ethnic groups could start rebuilding their lives in modern built environments that turned their backs to the past. India at the time, under the leadership of Nehru, was one of the core countries in the nonaligned movement, but this did not stop the Nehruvian state from relying on both the United States' and the Soviet Union's technical expertise and financial assistance. The steel towns were largely built with Soviet aid, while the satellite towns relied on U.S. aid. The Ford Foundation played a key role in the latter, and the main urban planning consultant for the foundation was Albert Mayer, who had built a reputation for himself as a leading protagonist in the American garden city movement and by having worked with Clarence Stein.

Contemporary India is also on a massive new town building mission, but these new "new towns" are responding to a different set of planning challenges. India officially liberalized its economy in 1991, and the new "new towns" are part of a new paradigm of urbanization. Policy makers argue that the new towns—mainly in the form of Special Economic Zones (SEZs) and smart cities—are a pragmatic solution for India (Joshi 2009; Menon and Mitra 2009; Mukhopadhyay and Pradhan 2009). They point out that India is not just a liberalizing economy, but the country is unique in that, unlike countries in the West, it is attempting to liberalize its economy within

Table 12.1. Comparing Jamshedpur and Lavasa New Towns

	Location	Size	Governing Structure
Old "new town": Jamshedpur Steel Town	In the economically poor state of Jamshedpur	15,320 acres (6,200 hectares)	Jamshedpur Notified Area governed by an unelected committee headed by the chairman of the Tata Iron and Steel Company
New "new town": Lavasa	In the economically prosperous state of Maharashtra; located around 90 kilometers from the financial capital, Mumbai.	25,000 acres (10,117 hectares)	Governed by Lavasa Corporation Limited, a Special Purpose Vehicle floated by the construction firm Hindustan Construction Company (HCC).

the context of an electoral democracy. Existing land, labor, tax, and other laws that were put in place during an earlier agrarian-dominated, state-led era, they argue, had to be rapidly rehauled to regulate an urban and globally oriented economy. And instead of an economy-wide liberalization policy, policy experts see these new towns as pilot projects and enclaves of liberalization that can then be scaled up.

In contradistinction to existing cities with their creaking infrastructure and bloated public sectors, the new towns are expected to deploy information technology to solve urban problems and to rely on various mixes of public-private partnership financing. The prime minister, Narendar Modi, promised to build one hundred smart cities as part of his 2014 election campaign: "Cities in the past were built on riverbanks. They are now built along highways. But in future, they will be built based on availability of optical fiber networks and next-generation infrastructure" (Tolan 2014). His newly formed government has set aside Rs. 70,600 million in the 2014 budget and is in conversation with the Singapore foreign minister and other private sector players to form "vibrant" partnerships that can help realize the dream of one hundred smart cities.

This chapter compares India's old and new iteration of "new towns." It starts by outlining two cases of old and new "new towns": the steel town of Jamshedpur and the private city of Lavasa (Table 12.1). It then analyzes some key differences between the old and new iterations of India's new towns, organized into the themes of land assembly, service provision, and governance. It concludes by drawing some comparisons with the new town experiments in the United States and articulates some of the key and unresolved planning questions, specifically revolving around democratic governance, posed by India's new towns.

India's Old and New "New Towns": Jamshedpur and Lavasa

Old "New Town": Jamshedpur Steel Town

The old "new town" of Jamshedpur was first set up in 1907 by Jamshedji Tata (from whom the town takes its name), the founder of the Tata company. Tata was inspired by the new town movement that was then sweeping across the U.K., and he aspired to set up a steel company town that not only represented an urban utopia, but also exemplified the Tata company as model employers. Tata's vision for the town is evident in these words: "Be sure to lay wide streets planted with shady trees [and] space for lawns. Reserve large areas for football, hockey and parks. Earmark areas for Hindu temples, Mohammedan mosques and Christian churches" (Crabtree 2015; Sivaramakrishnan 1976–77, 45). Tata took his social vision seriously and, over the course of half a century, invited leading socialists, architects, and urban planners to help plan the township. The British socialists Sidney and Beatrice Webb visited the township in 1916. Inspired by the new town movement in the U.K., Tata wanted the Jamshedpur new town to be "self-contained," "self-containment" having a dual meaning. The first refers simply to the facilities that exists in a town. A self-contained area can be defined as one that has a complete range of urban facilities, that is, sufficient employment, shopping, health-care, educational, and other facilities adequate for the number of residents; but in general usage this definition has been overlaid by the second meaning, that is, a social purpose. A self-contained town is seen as one in which the residents can live while satisfying all their daily needs within the boundaries. "The town provides the environment for the life of a complete community: it is an experiment in social living" (Sivaramakrishnan 1976–77, 54). Following these ideals of social living, the steel firm in Jamshedpur was the first to introduce an eight-hour work day in 1912, marking it as a pioneer company town that was way ahead of its time. In 1944, Tata commissioned the architect Otto Koenigsberger to prepare the first master plan for the township.

For its governance, in 1924, the provincial government under the British raj carved out the Jamshedpur company town as a "Notified Area" or industrial township that would be governed by a Notified Area Committee. The present-day Notified Area Committee is made up of twenty-two nonelected representatives, with the chairman of the TISCO (Tata Iron and Steel Company) serving as the director of the company town. The other members include seven TISCO employees, four employees of other companies, and ten people from the public. Jamshedpur Notified Area Company is now part of the Jamshedpur Urban Agglomeration, which is made up of other Notified Areas, municipal corporations, and rural local governments (or gram panchayats, as they are called in India).

New "New Town": Lavasa

Around ninety kilometers from Mumbai, along the Pune-Mumbai Expressway, and on the backwaters of the Warasgaon Dam in the Sahyadri mountain range is India's largest privately financed new town, Lavasa. Lavasa is of an ambitious scale: spanning twenty-five thousand acres, it is approximately one-fifth the land area of the Municipal Corporation of Greater Mumbai. Lavasa represents a new breed of new towns, built entirely from scratch, with private financing. The private sector promoter of Lavasa—Ajit Gulabchand, the CEO of the prominent Mumbai-based firm Hindustan Construction Company (HCC)—sees Lavasa as the model for the new public-private cities that India needs as it transitions from a predominantly agrarian to a more urban economy: "[Lavasa] is a grand project in response to the Maharashtra government wanting to build a hill station city near Pune. It actually looks at the needs of India's urbanization—an estimated 400 million people will move to urban centers in the next 30–40 years. So, we really need to consider our urbanization needs and this project couldn't have come at a better time to create a kind of replicable model of a new city. The speed with which we will have to build these urban centers or enhance existing ones would need some kind of public-private partnership. And Lavasa is a model, an experiment in making that happen" (Iyer 2011). Ajit Gulabchand's bold new experiment took the organizational form of Lavasa Corporation Limited (LCL), a Special Purpose Vehicle (SPV) floated by the parent company, Gulabchand's HCC.

Lavasa is an experiment in both urban finance and urban governance. It is the first urban development that will be financed by tapping into India's newly liberalized equity markets. Private sector developers have, to date, financed their large-scale urban developments either through land disposition (lease/sale of land) or, more recently, through private equity. Real estate developers such as Lavasa's are setting a new precedent of forming new companies that finance and operate the new cities, and in offering the shares of the new companies to the public (Fontanella-Khan and Lamont 2010; Chadha 2014). LCL has regulatory approval to raise capital for the Rs. 33 billion ($492 million) project from public equity, including foreign institutional investors (FIIs). The new "new town" is also unique in having a private sector firm as the Special Planning Authority (SPA). In a controversial move, the state government delegated its land-use planning powers to LCL, in effect granting regulatory control over Lavasa to a private firm. Gulabchand recognizes that these governance changes are necessary to package the city as an initial public offering (IPO), as a brand that is seductive and sellable to investors.

What Is Different About India's New "New Towns"?

Land Assembly

Jamshedpur company town was formed when India was still under colonial rule. India's eminent domain law, the Land Acquisition Act, promulgated by the colonial state in 1894, enabled the colonial state to acquire private land for public purposes. One may argue that it was easier for the state to coercively acquire land from one private landowner to transfer to another private (industrial) landowner during colonial times, but the land acquisition for later postcolonial steel towns also relied extensively on the coercive powers of the state.

The steel towns of the Nehruvian era were part of a spatial strategy of balanced economic growth. The largest public sector townships set up in the 1950s and 1960s were concentrated in the most economically backward states of Madhya Pradesh, Bihar, and Uttar Pradesh (Kundu, Misra, and Meher 1986). Nationalist planners expected "the steel plants and other industrial projects [to] provide the basis for the development of small and medium industries and programs of education and training and other activities" (Planning Commission 2012). These steel towns then were to become the "nuclei of regional growth."

This was an important nationalist goal for a country that had just emerged from colonialism and that had deep spatial disparities where there were economically developed cities (such as the port cities) that had been beneficial to the imperial economy but also vast regions that had been left behind. Jamshedpur is in the economically backward state of Jharkhand.[1] Many of the steel towns were organized around recently completed multipurpose dams that were modeled on the United States' Tennessee Valley Authority. The big dams, which Nehru famously memorialized as the "temples of modern India," were the infrastructural scaffolding around which the edifice of steel towns were expected to rise. It is now extensively documented that the big dams took their heaviest toll on the lives and livelihoods of some of India's most marginalized and disfranchised Adivasi groups (Fernandes and Paranjpye 1997). Because the developmental projects of the big dams and steel towns were concentrated in economically backward regions, it was easier for the state to coercively acquire land from some of the most politically disorganized constituencies, the Adivasis.[2]

In contrast, in the new era, new towns are concentrated in some of the country's most prosperous regions. The one hundred smart cities proposed by the newly elected prime minister are expected to emerge along the Delhi-Mumbai industrial corridor, which connects the political capital of Delhi to the financial capital of Mumbai, and which passes through some of the most agriculturally productive regions of the country. In a study conducted by the Center of Policy Research in New Delhi, the author found that as of 2009, 154 SEZs had been approved by the central government (Mukhopadhyay and Pradhan 2009). Not only were all these SEZs concentrated in a few states; even within these states, they were concentrated in and around the largest city-regions of Delhi, Hyderabad, Bangalore, and Chennai. The concentration of SEZs around some of the country's leading economic nodes adheres to the market principles of agglomeration, but unlike the earlier steel towns that had a planning goal of balanced regional development, the new towns are exacerbating regional disparities by clustering around already developed cities. Lavasa is located in what the state government has designated as the Golden Triangle region, a premier regional destination for investment that is hemmed in by the industrially thriving cities of Mumbai-Pune-Nashik.

Land acquisition for the new "new towns" is a more volatile affair. As the new "new towns" are concentrated in economically prosperous regions, these lands are owned by organized agrarian constituencies that have reacted to the coercive acquisition of their land with a vociferous public backlash. The protests against land acquisition have escalated to such a degree of frequency and violence that the central government decided to finally amend the antiquated Land Acquisition Act of the colonial era and replace it with the Right to Fair Compensation and Transparency in Land Acquisition, Rehabilitation, and Resettlement Act (LARRA). As it becomes more and more politically untenable for the state to use conventional and coercive instruments such as eminent domain to assemble the vast swathes of land needed for new towns, public agencies are experimenting with new land-assembly tools—such as land pooling—for preparing agricultural land for the contemporary new towns.

Lavasa is a rare case where more than ten thousand acres of land were assembled by the promoter through voluntary market transactions. Lavasa, however, has been mired in legal disputes and protests. One of India's most successful social movements, the National Alliance of People's Movements, has taken up the claims of Adivasi landowners who charge the Lavasa company with purchasing their land through legal artifice and even fraud. Lavasa's promoters, on the other hand, stress that no coercion or manipulation went into these land transactions. Lavasa's land disputes continue to be fought in the courts and on the streets, but they point to the wider challenge of land assembly for new towns in a context where coercive land-use instruments, such as eminent domain, which could be justified as being used in the public interest during the earlier era of old new towns, are now becoming more and more politically fraught and untenable.

Service Provision

With its high quality of basic infrastructure, Jamshedpur company town stands in sharp contrast to its surrounding region. Its roads are pothole-free. In a country known for its power cuts and water shortages, the company town has 24/7 power and water supply. Residents can drink water directly from their taps, a feat unheard of in any other Indian city. Residents can avail of good-quality schools and world-class sporting facilities. The high-quality infrastructural services for the company town are provided by Jamshedpur Utilities and Services Company (JUSCO), a subsidiary company set up by Tata Steel in 2004. Tata Steel now has a contract with JUSCO for service provision. Before the setting up of JUSCO, these services were provided directly by Tata Steel, and the capital and maintenance costs for infrastructural services came from the steel plants' budget. Before the 1980s, the financial viability of the township was not a concern: the "womb-to-tomb" corporate ethos assumed that services like water, sewerage, electricity, and housing were not commodities to be sold to consumers but were amenities to be provided to labor for increasing their productivity. The company town had billboards that proudly proclaimed: "We also make steel."

Now, after the 1991 economic liberalization reforms, conditions are different, with heavy-manufacturing firms no longer protected from outside competition by import substitution policies. A recent article by the *Economist* questioned the Tata Company's role as a developer and asked, "Does Tata Steel know when to say no? Or will it be constantly pulled into new CSR activities that will divert too many resources from its core mission?" (Economist 2011). The setting up of JUSCO reflects these changed conditions. Earlier, employees were promised housing, schools, and utilities as free benefits in their employment contracts. But the setting up of a separate subsidiary company allows JUSCO to have its own policies that can limit these free services. JUSCO's website confirms this shift by stating its mandate as "convert[ing] an obligatory service into a customer focused sustainable corporate entity (Jamshedpur Utilities and Services Company n.d.). The timing of JUSCO's establishment also coincided with Tata Steel's foray into foreign capital markets. In order for a company to list abroad on stock exchanges such as NASDAQ, it has to comply with international accounting standards that require is to estimate future liability of all utilities, which in India is called contingent liability and need not be separately spelled out. JUSCO has an annual budget of $30 million per annum, and it is headed by a vice president of corporate services, who is akin to a mayor in any other municipal corporation. Even though Tata Steel may have scaled back its subsidies and the utility company is now more "customer focused," Tata Steel continues to pay a key role in financially supporting its subsidiary company, retaining the company town's reputation as one of the highest-quality and lowest-cost (to citizen/consumer) service providers in the country.

Lavasa is also a stark contrast to its surrounding region. LCL promises its residents world-class urban amenities: "abundant access to nature, a cosmopolitan lifestyle, good schools, a functional and clean city, an uninterrupted power supply, high-speed internet, e-governance, drinkable tap water, and a walkable city in which the need for cars is minimal" (Collings n.d.). In contrast, until recently, the surrounding villages around the new "new town" lacked even the most basic services of electricity and health-care centers. Children had to trek almost an hour each way to reach the nearest primary school. Like Jamshedpur, Lavasa relies on private service providers. LCL has formed forty subsidiary companies (Figure 12.1)

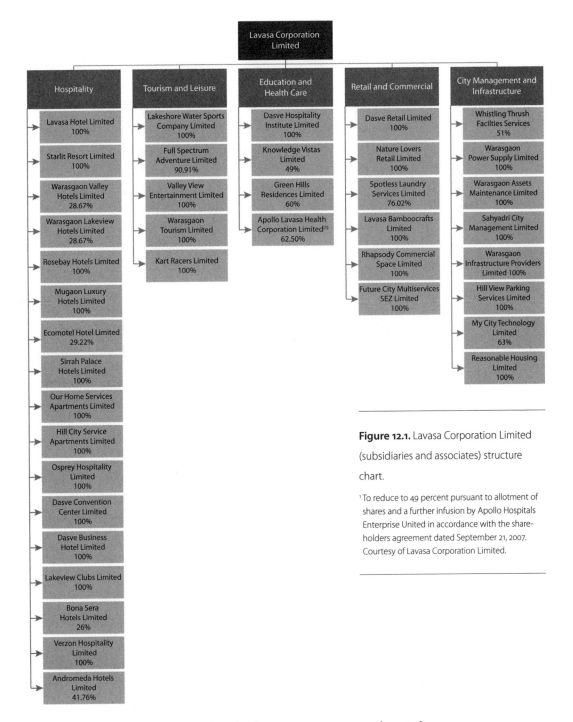

Figure 12.1. Lavasa Corporation Limited (subsidiaries and associates) structure chart.

[1] To reduce to 49 percent pursuant to allotment of shares and a further infusion by Apollo Hospitals Enterprise United in accordance with the shareholders agreement dated September 21, 2007. Courtesy of Lavasa Corporation Limited.

that are the main service providers for the new city: seventeen hospitality companies, five tourist and leisure companies, four education and health-care companies, six retail and commercial companies, and eight city management and infrastructure companies (Lavasa Corporation 2014). The eight "city management and infrastructure companies" provide services ranging from water supply, sanitation, electric power, and natural gas. The city is managed by a professional team of salaried employees, with the city manager, Scott Wright, having vast experience in city management through his previous work as a municipal official in different U.S. states such as Illinois, Kansas, and Missouri.

Though both Jameshedpur and Lavasa rely on private service providers, there is a crucial difference between them. Though Tata Steel formed JUSCO as a way of moving away from "obligatory services," it is clear that the core business for Tata Steel is steel manufacturing, and the parent company continues to heavily subsidize JUSCO. LCL and its forty subsidiary companies, on the other hand, represent a model of real estate development where the promoter sets up separate utility companies that can become the source of a continuous revenue stream after the development is completed. JUSCO's main "customers" are its city residents. For LCL, the main customers are distant shareholders whom LCL hopes to attract through the IPO. When the city is geared toward distant investors, the land uses that increase shareholder value may often be at odds with those that enhance residents' quality of life. Lavasa, for instance, does not have any schools, markets, or other basic amenities for daily living, but LCL had succeeded in attracting Oxford University to set up its first satellite campus in India within Lavasa. The presence of a world-class university, but the absence of basic schools, speaks to a branding strategy where these globally recognized brands can enhance Lavasa's brand image (Oxford University has since backed out of the deal pursuant to the controversies dogging Lavasa). The forty subsidiary companies provide high-quality services, but these come with an expensive price tag. Residents who bought flats, as opposed to the investors who are buying shares in the city, have expressed their ire through blog sites. One such site—"Lavasa Is the Highway to Hell" (Lavasa Investor 2015)—has flat buyers who feel misled and cheated by Lavasa's advertisements and hoardings. In short, though both Jamshedpur and Lavasa are private cities, the former is oriented toward its residents and the latter toward distant investors, which then affects the type, price, and quality of infrastructural services within these cities.

Governance

Private cities pose key planning questions of governance. Jamshedpur company town is designated as a Notified Area Committee, a constitutional provision—article 243Q—that allows "industrial townships" to be governed by manufacturing firms that take over the functions of local governments and become the sole public authority for that carved out area (Sivaramakrishnan 2009). Though Jamshedpur and the other steel towns were tightly bounded within the Notified Area boundary, these boundaries set up stark inequalities between the company town and its surrounding areas. The Jamshedpur Urban Agglomeration, for instance, consists of the following jurisdictions: Jamshedpur Notified Area Committee, Adityapur Notified Area Committee, Mango Notified Area Committee, Jugsalai Municipality, and the surrounding village panchayats of Bagbera, Gadhra, Ghorabandha, Parsudih, Kitadih, Sarjamdah, Haldubani, and Chotagovindpur. Jamshedpur Notified Area occupies an area of fifty-six square kilometers, while the urban agglomeration stretches beyond into an area of nearly 150 square kilometers.

A common criticism against the Notified Area Committee is that it leads to the model of industrial township–slum (Sivaramakrishnan 1976–77; Wakeman 2016), where the company towns are islands of prosperity with high-quality services amid an impoverished and underserviced region. Even within the well-serviced company towns, many argue employee-residents do not pay property taxes and are not bound to their governing authorities in the same way that other urban residents are, which undermines, or even negates, the rights of representation and accountability that other urban citizens enjoy.

Article 243Q is a provision introduced in the early decades of following independence when India was struggling to establish itself as a self-sufficient industrial economy in the wake of colonialism. In 1991, almost half a century after India gained independence from colonial rule, the central government introduced decentralization reforms to devolve decision-making power to the already present urban and rural local governments and further empower local governments as the primary sites of democratic decision making. The decentralization reforms were operationalized through the seventy-third and seventy-four constitutional amendments, which required the setting up of municipalities and panchayats for the governance of urban and rural jurisdictions respectively. Article 243Q was not mentioned in the report of the parliament committee, but it was belatedly added to the new decentralization laws. Senior policy makers involved in the making of the decentralization laws argue that the Tata company, "anticipating problems in the future, might have suggested to the Government of India that a special dispensation should be made in regard to Jamshedpur" (Sivaramakrishnan 2009, 98). The notified area clause has been one of the points of contention in ongoing jurisdictional turf wars in Jamshedpur since the 1980s (Bisoee 2014; Seetha 2006; *Telegraph India* 2016).

In 2005, under pressure from elected representatives of the Jamshedpur region and the state government of Jharkhand (in which Jamshedpur is located), the Jharkhand government issued a notification for the dissolution of the Jamshedpur Notified Area Committee and for the formation of an elected municipal corporation for Jamshedpur. The Tata company retaliated by filing a petition before the

Supreme Court of India, challenging the Jharkhand government notification. During this time, residents and organizations within Jamshedpur organized themselves into the Jamshedpur Citizens' Forum, and fifty thousand people submitted a petition to the district-level government against the proposed formation of a Jamshedpur municipal corporation. These petitioners cited the fear of a decline in the quality of public services if Jamshedpur were to become a municipal corporation. In September 2014, the state government's urban development bureaucrat convened a meeting of representatives from Jamshedpur, including elected representatives of the region, Tata Steel, NGOs, and trade organizations. NGOs pointed to the stark disparities between the formal and informal areas within Jamshedpur, and Tata Steel agreed to provide infrastructural services to the eighty-six slums within its jurisdiction. In December 2016, the supreme court disposed of the case as the Jharkhand state government and Tata Steel had arrived at a consensus on retaining the industrial township status for Jamshedpur.

The political consensus on Jamshedpur does not resolve key governance questions that underlie these jurisdictional turf wars. When the Jamshedpur Citizens' Forum assumes that the incorporation into the municipal corporation will mean a decline in public services, does that not imply a distrust of one of the most fundamental institutions of representative democracy, the elected local government? The jurisdictional turf wars that Jamshedpur is embroiled in have reached a head in Lavasa. Lavasa is located within the jurisdictional boundaries of eighteen gram panchayats. In 2008, the state government granted LCL the status of Special Planning Authority (SPA). As a SPA, LCL has the legal authority to prepare proposals for land-use development for the new town zone. The SPA is mandated to invite and consider the suggestions and objections from the public, and then submit its plans to the state government for approval. As LCL is a private company, it is questionable how genuine the public consultations are. LCL's SPA status has been challenged in a public interest litigation on the charges of the improper delegation of planning powers to a private company. Unlike Jamshedpur Notified Area Committee, Lavasa is not an "industrial township," and its promoter is not a manufacturing firm. The LCL promoters, however, argue that the new town is not a real estate project, but an employment-generating enterprise that is not too different from industrial townships: "Lavasa is not a township or a huge real-estate project such as the Sahara group's Amby Valley. It is a complete town that is self-sufficient and meets residential and living needs of poor, middle-class, and elite people. The hill station itself will create more than 50,000 jobs over the next 10 years. Hence, citizens residing here can enjoy the walk to work lifestyle" (*Business Standard* 2008). Lavasa, however, is mired in litigation and protests because the SPA rules contravene the environmental and land-use regulations that otherwise apply to other cities and urban regions. These jurisdictional turf wars raise questions of conflict of laws: when the same jurisdiction is overlain by rules made by different public authorities, which set of rules should prevail?

Conclusion

India's old and new "new towns" are responses to the specific political, economic, and social challenges of their times. In newly independent India, the steel towns were expected to be the paradigm of model industrial townships that could spur the national economy from a dependent colonial past into an economically self-sufficient industrial future. In the newly liberalized India, the smart cities are expected to become globally competitive hubs that can successfully attract private capital and position urban India as a top destination for investment. After more than a century of new town planning, what lessons and insights do these two eras of new town experiments hold for contemporary urban planners? Should planning continue with these utopian ideals of creating model towns, or should it focus on how existing cities, with all their seemingly intractable problems, can be incrementally improved? If the former, what are the institutional arrangements for scaling up these model towns into some replicable idioms of urbanization? When new towns are set up as gleaming islands of high standards within an otherwise poor and poorly serviced region, the spatial disparities can provoke social unrest. For instance, even within the steel towns, the level of services is starkly disparate between the formal and informal areas. The famed British sociologist Ruth Glass visited the Durgapur company town in the 1960s, and she applied her trenchant critiques on what would later become popularly known as gentrification to the workings of India's steel towns (Sivaramakrishnan 1976–77, 154–55):

> In the steel colony, there is no chance for anyone ever to forget his station. Differences in space standards alone range from 3/4000 sq. ft. for the top level managerial houses to 300 sq. ft for the lowest grade of laborers houses. . . . Each rank in this hierarchy of the steel works has better housing standards and more space than the next level just below. As the Township has expanded, its hierarchical pattern—accentuated by the fragmented, low density layout—has been most effective in keeping people apart. At work, at home, even in their recreation people are kept in their place. . . . Walking around in the enclaves of the steel townships, one gets claustrophobic that there are few signs of the buoyancy which is characteristic of much poorer urban areas in India.

One can argue about Glass's uncritical optimism about India's "poorer urban areas," but the socio-spatial hierarchy between the "top level managerial houses" and "the lowest grade of laborers houses" can incite retaliation. When a major labor dispute broke out in Durgapur steel town in the 1960s, the streetlights and gabions of the meticulously maintained management's areas became the target of the protestors' ire. Spatial inequality is more visible than other forms of inequality (such as income inequality), and the new towns create visible walls between themselves and their surrounding region, which could have politically volatile consequences (Ravindran 2015).

If the new towns have political costs of inciting resentment and social unrest, they are also underpinned by a more normative question of democratic governance and what it means to be a citizen in these new towns. If, for their effective governance, new towns have to rely on unelected organizational forms such as Jamshedpur Notified Area Committee or the Special Planning Authority, what is the relationship between these unelected organizations and elected municipal corporations? JUSCO has now started levying user charges; LCL's subsidiary companies work on a consumer model where access to services is denied to all those who cannot afford them.

This mode of governance, where zones are carved out from within local government jurisdictions and the functions of local governments within these zones are handed over to private organizations, bear similarity to the home owners' associations in the United States. The explosive growth of home owners' associations[3] in the United States led scholars to characterize this trend in sweeping terms as the "transformation of local government" (R. Nelson 2005b) and the "dominant aspect of the late twentieth century contribution to American residential group life" (Alexander 1989, 5). Home owners' associations have staunch and sharply divided advocates and critics. Robert Nelson, for instance, argues that home owners' associations take us back to a form of private local governments that were popular in the United States until the nineteenth century, when the municipal corporation functioned exactly like a business corporation (R. Nelson 2005b). Nelson argues that these home owners' associations solve many collective-action problems by shifting the unit of sovereignty from the local government to these neighborhood associations. Just as shareholders in a business corporation have voting and decision-making control, those who opt to move into an area regulated by a home owners' association have similar voting rights. The only difference between the business corporation and the home owners' association is that the latter is allowed to tax their members. Depending on the covenants, conditions, and restrictions (CC&Rs), the home owners' associations can privately tax residents for the private provision of services; many times, they also have regulatory authority and can make rules on building, land-use, and zoning regulations. Home owner associations also have their fair share of critics.

Robert Reich (1991) calls this trend the "secession of the successful" and argues that the wealthy are seceding from public services and public life into their own privatized enclaves. Blakely and Snyder (1997) argue that home owners' associations exclude renters, and they also legitimize home owners' parochial interests of enhancing their property values. They also undermine the social contract of citizenship by allowing home owners to keep out groups that they fear will lower property values: "gated areas . . . [represent] a concrete metaphor for the closing of the gates against immigrants and minorities and the poverty, crime and social instabilities in society at large" (Blakely and Snyder 1997, 152).

These debates about home owners' associations have relevance to India's old and new "new towns." There is, however, a crucial difference between the U.S. home owners' associations and the private corporations governing India's new towns. The U.S. home owners' associations are still vested within local and state government laws. For instance, the city of Boston has inclusionary zoning to ensure that the housing market in the city remains affordable and accessible. The home owners' associations are not exempt from these laws and have to conform to them. Article 243Q in India's constitution allows the new "industrial townships" to be exempt from laws that would otherwise govern cities. It is this legally enabled disjuncture between the company forms that govern the new towns and the municipal corporations that govern cities that poses crucial challenges to democratic governance. A pressing issue for planners and policy makers in India is to address the relationship between the companies and cities and, in keeping with the normative spirit of democratic decision making, to ensure that urban laws made by elected institutions prevail whenever there is a tussle between company and city.

Notes

1. Jharkhand was a part of the state of Uttar Pradesh until 2000.
2. The term *Adivasi* is a self-appellation that translates into "first inhabitants"; India's Adivasis are recognized by the United Nations as indigenous people, but the Indian government continues to count them in the census under the colonial category of "schedule tribe."
3. Also commonly referred to as common interest communities (CIDs), proprietary communities, and property owners' associations.

13

European New Towns

The End of a Model? From Pilot to Sustainable Territories

Pascaline Gaborit

Were European new towns foremost "utopias" and transformation projects for the suburbs? Can they be a replicable model for other parts of the world, where urbanization and demography are booming, or are they obsolete as a concept? Will they disappear and be merged into the current metropolis and agglomeration reforms in Europe? Created mainly after World War II, though earlier in Britain, European new towns have faced multifarious challenges in terms of urban planning, sustainable development, social inclusion, and image. This chapter identifies different paths for their adaptation to current challenges and examines the capacity of European new towns to manage their transition toward sustainability and livability at a time of dwindling local budgets, economic crisis, and territorial reforms. The chapter develops a comparative analysis of new towns development in Europe, based on several years of work and engagements with new towns stakeholders. These include the New Towns as Sustainable Communities (NEWTASC) project, the *New Towns' Study* report, the *New Medina Project*, and the *European and Asian Sustainable Towns: Satellite Towns in their Metropolises* (EAST) project (European New Towns Platform. 2006; Gaborit 2010, 2012, 2014). The case studies are drawn from the European New Towns and Pilot Cities Platform (ENTP)—a knowledge hub on new towns. The chapter outlines the key lessons and recommendations that could be integrated in future theories of urban sustainable development.

New towns were created in Europe to prevent anarchic urban development and as a way to cope with the demographic growth experienced after the Second World War and until the mid-1970s. They were initially conceived as a planning option to alleviate the congestion of metropolitan areas and to achieve balanced territorial development. However, they were often (wrongly) labeled as unwelcoming suburban areas, if not dormitory towns. It turned out that physical planning did not necessarily create ideal environments and communities, as has been foreseen by the initial urban planners and decision makers. But the fact that they were not "models" does not mean that they were failures. They reflected a specific context in the period of European urban planning influenced by the legacy of the Athens charter and the garden cities movement. As a result, they embedded low densities, a high percentage of green areas, and a relative monofunctionality of spaces. European new towns are the results of now several decades of political and economic choices directly linked to the economic and demographic contexts. For residents, they also epitomize the choice to live in peri-urban areas, between dense agglomerations and rural hinterlands with perceived better quality of life, far from the "compact cities."[1]

Currently, European new towns in general face similar challenges in the transition to sustainable and energy-efficient towns, and in social cohesion or social inclusion, as well as in the regeneration of some areas, including the redesign or renewal of their town centers. Not only have physical planning and social patterns transformed and shaped cities, but the local economies have been directly confronted by a more global and competitive environment. The role of these territories in the regions has slowly evolved from housing and business locations to innovative and sustainable peri-urban areas. The territorial reforms occurring in most European countries have also been important. Previously autonomous new towns have merged into larger entities (merger of local authorities), meaning they are parts of more multifunctional local government areas.[2] Although this is not the case of U.K. new towns that are self-contained communities, do we see the end of the new towns model in France, the Netherlands, and even eastern Europe? What will come next? How can new towns "reinvent themselves"? Will the new trends of sustainable and regenerative cities give them opportunities of reconversion?

New Towns

The European New Towns and Pilot Cities Platform (ENTP) defined new towns as "towns created in the periphery of large agglomerations, following a master planned approach" (European New Towns Platform 2015) (Table 13.1).

In western Europe, after World War II, new towns were created around major capitals such as London, Paris, or Amsterdam but also around Helsinki (Vantaa, Tapiola), and in the outskirts of Stockholm (Hässelby-Vällingby). These new towns aimed to provide housing to the larger cities, some of them destroyed during the war, and to other towns expanding from industrial sites. At that time, these new towns were mainly dependent on the larger cities for service provision, leisure, cultural events, and retail. Not all countries, however, invested in new town programs. New towns were mainly designed in the countries that had a centralized system and an interventionist approach toward territorial development. Germany

Table 13.1. Selected New Towns in European Countries: Designation and Current Population

New Town	Date of Designation	No. of Inhabitants, 2011–14	Country
Stevenage	1946	85,997	United Kingdom
Cwmbran/Torfaen	1949	48,535	United Kingdom
Basildon	1948	107,123	United Kingdom
Marne-la-Vallée–Val-Maubuée	1972	86,422	France
Sénart	1973	123,704	France
Zoetermeer	1960	121,521	Netherlands
Harlow	1947	84,564	United Kingdom
Spijkenisse/Nissewaard	1977	72,545	Netherlands
Cergy-Pontoise	1969	199,143	France
Evry	1965	52,349	France
Hässelby-Vällingby	1954	71,042	Sweden
Vantaa	1974	204,545	Finland
Tatabanya	1947	67,753	Hungary
Stalowa Wola	1937	64,189	Poland
Nieuwegein	1971	61,486	Netherlands
Almere	1976	198,315	Netherlands
Lelystad	1967	75,745	Netherlands

Source: European New Towns Platform (2006, 2015).
Note: The table provides an overview of a sample of new towns.

and Italy had programs of reconstruction without new towns. In Belgium, the creation of Louvain-la-Neuve new town was directly the result of the linguistic division of the country and remained an exception.

This chapter examines the new town programs in the U.K., France, the Netherlands, and eastern Europe as they were the most important in Europe (Table 13.2).

In the U.K., the Department of Environment put in motion a new towns program whereby twenty-one new towns were established after 1946, following a top-down interventionist approach. Rehousing on this scale meant that alternative settlements had to be designed in addition to existing settlements. The main influence was the garden city movement,[3] which aimed to tackle the problems of the unhealthy settlements in Victorian industrial cities (Watson 1991, 17) (Figure 13.1).

In France, the new towns program (French *villes nouvelles*) was set up in 1965. Nine *villes nouvelles* were designed, including five new towns around Paris. Other new towns were developed: L'île d'Abeau (around Lyon), Villeneuve d'Ascq in the surrounding area of Lille, and L'Etang de Berre in the region of Provence. The town of le Vaudreuil was planned in the western part of France but never took off because of its remote location and dependence on industry, and it epitomizes how new towns projects can fail.

In the Netherlands, the Groeikern growing centers plan established the program for new towns' development in the 1970s. Growth centers were towns designated by the central government to undergo considerable growth in the 1970s to 1980s. Additional financial resources for housing and amenities were allocated to these towns to compensate for the costs of growth during the years 1975–85. That plan was followed by the Vinex plan in 1988, meant to stretch the growth center policies to the period 1995–2005. As the name "growth center" underscores, most of these towns were created around existing villages, and not all are new towns as defined in this book. A counterexample, however, are the towns of Almere and Lelystad in the Flevoland region, which have been designed on reclaimed land.[4] In the Netherlands, the idea that new towns are "growing towns" did not grant them a specific fixed statute, as happened in such town in France and the United Kingdom. On the contrary, later programs such as the Ortega plan in 2008 still designated future growth centers with housing provision targets (Public Result 2012).

Western European new towns resulted from national governments' funded, interventionist projects. However, budget cuts occurring in the 1980s, especially in the

Table 13.2. British, French, and Dutch New Towns

United Kingdom	First Generation: 1946 Designed New Towns	Second Generation: End of the 1950s to Beginning of the 1960s	Third Generation: End of the 1960s to Beginning of the 1970s
	Basildon	Redditch	Milton Keynes
	Bracknell	Runcorn	Northampton
	Crawley	Skelmersdale	Peterborough
	Harlow	Washington	Telford
	Hatfield		Warrington
	Hemel Hempstead		
	Stevenage		
	Welwyn Garden City		
	Corby		
	Cwnbran		
	Newton Aycliffe		
	Peterlee		
France	**New Towns Around Paris**	**Other New Towns**	
	Cergy-Pontoise	Villeneuve d'Ascq (Lille Agglomeration)	
	Marne-la-Vallée	L'Ile D'Abeau (Lyon Agglomeration)	
	Sénart	Le Vaudreuil	
	Evry	l'Etang de Berre	
	Saint-Quentin-en-Yvelines		
Netherlands[1]	**First Generation: 1950s**	**Second Generation: 1960s and 1970s**	
	Hoogvliet	Alkmaar	Helmond
	Lelystad	Almere	Hoorn
		Capelle aan de IJssel	Houten
		Duiven-Westervoort	Huizen
		Emmen	Nieuwegein
		Etten-Leur	Purmerend
		Haarlemmermeer	Spijkenisse
		Hellevoetsluis	Zoetermeer

Source: Adapted from Gaborit and Nguyen (2009).
[1] Compiled with assistance from Michelle Provoost.

U.K., reduced the ambitions of new towns. They had to forego their initial plans, targets, and sometimes ideas to become full-fledged cities. Table 13.3 offers a summary comparison of European new towns.

New towns in central and eastern Europe followed a different path, although some of them have been more "iconic" garden cities models. During the communist period, new towns were built in Hungary (e.g., Tatabanya), the Czech Republic (e.g., Havirov), Slovenia (Velenje), and Poland (Nowa Huta, Nowe Tychy, Stalowa Wola), around large heavy industrial and mining areas to alleviate pressures on the capital regions.[5] Other new towns were glorifying the former regimes: in Bulgaria, the town of Dimitrovgrad was designed around the slogan "we build the town and the town builds us," whereas in eastern Germany the town of Eisenhüttestadt, later called Stalin Stadt, embodied the principles of garden cities. These towns, built as icons for the regimes, were meant to be modern, to be well equipped, and to facilitate the emergence of a new "workers" equal society (Kladnik 2005).

Also, in many central and eastern European countries, the main capital and regional cities expanded with the construction of large high-rise housing estates. This was done more vigorously than in western Europe during the 1970s because high-rise apartments were considered to be the ideal for a communist worker. With the collapse of communism, mining and heavy industry experienced a major downturn. Eastern European new towns were faced with serious problems related to obsolescence, maintenance, governance, and even retention of their populations. Increased

Table 13.3. The Planning of New Towns in the U.K., France, and the Netherlands: Similarities

Country	
All	**Method**: Centralized management of the state, public central financing and planning strategy. Provision of affordable housing to respond to growth, control of urban development, importance of quality of life and green spaces. National programs: Balance between jobs and housing. Shift away from "dormitory cities." Forecast of demographic and economic growing trends.
U.K.	**Location**: British new towns were conceived as "self-contained communities" and therefore independent from large cities. **Management**: British new towns were managed by new towns development corporations with simple mechanisms. These organizations were wound up at the end of the 1970s.
France	**Location**: French new towns were located at the periphery of larger cities in order to attract more residents, retail, and businesses. They merged existing villages in an intermunicipal organization/body. **Management**: The national committee of French new towns set up a complex system of EPA (Etablissement Public d'Aménagement du Territoire)/Public organization in charge of the new towns' design, development, and master plan. Later on, city councils were represented in an intermunicipal body "syndicat d'agglomération nouvelle" (SAN). The division of competences and financing between the EPAs and SANs created conflicts. Master plans integrated the relocation of universities on new towns' territories.
Netherlands	**Location**: Growing centers were created around existing villages. The new town of Almere was created on a polder (land reclaimed from the sea). Some of the new towns such as Capelle aan den Ijssel were built partly below sea level. **Management**: New towns were managed by city councils. Financing was decided by the national government with contractual agreements between the state and the local authority.

Sources: Gaborit (2010); Merlin (2005, 141).

unemployment in the new towns prompted an out-migration to capital cities, such that some eastern European new towns quickly became "shrinking cities."[6]

Throughout Europe, new towns gradually saw their role as a housing supplier diminish. They had to find ways of regenerating their housing stock,[7] creating or renewing their town centers, attracting and retaining retail, consolidating and re-aligning the urban spatial structure,[8] and accommodating changes in population, expectations, and lifestyles. How were they to create useful and efficient amenities, services, and infrastructure when densities were capped low?

Mobility, Transportation, and Accessibility

Mobility is the possibility to access one point or the other while located *within* the town. Accessibility is the capacity to reach a town *from the outside*. Accessibility is key to a new town's location and development. Almere and Lelystad in the Netherlands, for instance, are new towns located in the same region, but they had different development outcomes. Almere attracted many newcomers and has become the fifth-most-populated city in the Netherlands (the road and rail connections to Amsterdam were one of its success factors), while Lelystad, overshadowed by the success of Almere, remained a second-tier town (Fouchier 2010a).

Mobility is still a challenge in European new towns. Several decades after some towns' creation, investments were still not sufficient to develop an entire integrated public transportation system connecting all parts of the territory of many of them. Marne-la-Vallée–Val-Maubuée[9] in France, for instance, is well connected to Paris by the regional express network (RER), which has saturated in ridership and is perceived as unsafe. Its only other transit option is a low-frequency local bus service.

The "Grand Paris" initiative, launched in 2008, was the first attempt to improve the connection of the capital's surrounding areas, including new towns. Within this framework, each of the five Parisian new towns will get a new metro, regional, or national (TGV)[10] train station, except Sénart, which benefitted nonetheless from a new bus rapid transit system.

Dutch new towns are also investing in better transportation infrastructure; Zoetermeer, for instance, set up a smart light-rail system with its surrounding cities. Other Dutch new towns are well served by a metro/subway system such as those in Nissewaard (formerly Spijkenisse) and Capelle aan den Ijssel near Rotterdam.

However, most new towns are dominated by automobiles because of long distances and nonoptimal public transportation (Fouchier 2010b). This is exemplified in the prevalence of conspicuous car parks near city centers, particularly in British and French new towns, whereas Dutch towns have opted for underground parking spaces (Almere), or light-rail system accessibility (Zoetermeer). In new towns, more than anywhere else, urban experts have recommended that cars be "tamed" to facilitate a smoother urban development (Harlow Renaissance Ltd. 2007).

In Milton Keynes, the prevalence of private cars has unfortunately further shaped the already car-dependent urban structure. Milton Keynes, like Cergy-Pontoise or Sénart, has separate residential and industrial grid squares. Employment was dispersed across the town in different locations, and population density was lower than in the surrounding areas, requiring people to travel long distances between activities. To benefit from living in this new town, as in most new towns, a car was essential. Over the decades, the creation of a bus system has necessitated the entire redevelopment of some streets in the center to avoid compromising the cultural heritage of the new town that is being enhanced.[11] Moreover, the town of Milton Keynes has developed activities to promote a greener image with environmental activities such as the setup of a carbon offset fund to decrease the greenhouse gas emissions, and by "taxing" the creation of new buildings. Because of these visionary policies, the town has now a better air quality than other towns of the region (Milton Keynes Council 2016).

Of course, considering their rapid construction, new towns sought to provide limited-cost infrastructure and transportation systems. Early on, sidewalks were not considered necessary in the "new towns" model, but this has changed over time, especially in town centers. Bicycle lanes are currently emerging in Scandinavian and even French new towns. In Dutch new towns, they have been part of the initial master plans but still have had to be regularly adjusted to new urban plans. Regional governance problems have often hindered the improvement of transportation infrastructure and internal connections within new towns (e.g., in the Paris region).

Population Patterns: A Town for Whom?

The original aim of new towns national programs was to respond to intense population growth in a short time (Gaborit 2010; Merlin 2005). Consequently, providing homes at affordable/moderate prices was a priority for national governments to accommodate growing housing needs. The decision makers were also aware at that time that they needed to provide a good jobs-population ratio, to minimize commuting. In France, the Netherlands, and the United Kingdom, new towns development stemmed from an interventionist state approach that distinctly defined growth targets beforehand.

This original aim has led to a predominance of sometimes monotonous or even too-experimental housing that largely accounts for new towns' disparaged image as "dormitory towns." Most of the time, new towns have managed to accommodate increasing needs. The demographic trends that were anticipated when those towns were created proved, however, to be exaggeratedly high, which required several adjustments over the years (Gaborit and Nguyen 2009). This was particularly the case in France, but also in the Netherlands, where the target figure of 20 percent of new building in growth centers was never achieved; the highest was 15 percent in the early 1980s (Netherlands Social and Cultural Planning Office 2001).

The dwelling units built in the first decades of the new towns were designed to answer to the demographic patterns of that period: separated large housing estates (that recently have become mainly social housing), attached houses, and scattered villas. Most of the dwellings were designed to host nuclear families (two parents and two children), mainly from middle-class populations.

Over time, however, housing patterns have needed to accommodate new realities:

- The arrival among the residents of poorer populations, including from migrant and vulnerable groups with larger families.[12]
- Aging populations, and the necessity to adjust infrastructure and facilities (lifts and elevators, for instance, in the housing estates, such as in Hässelby-Vällingby, Sweden). In some new towns, such as in Harlow, U.K., public authorities have invested in equipment and facilities for senior citizens.
- Diversifying housing needs, given that more people live alone or without children).
- Regenerating infrastructure. As new towns were created in a short amount of time, the housing stock and facilities need to be refurbished or replaced in the same time range.

These problems are particularly acute for eastern and central European countries, where most of the housing stock is composed of condominiums. In this situation, how can one foster public awareness and action, especially when urban regeneration is so badly needed? Another crucial issue introduced by regeneration is the quality of the improvement, that is, the operational sustainability and its benefits derived.

Population patterns were, in part, affected by transportation availability. Residents became car dependent because of the distance between housing and other facilities and services. This was especially so for families with children, as access to schools and child care was not facilitated for the first residents.

Housing prices have also increasingly affected already vulnerable households in many new towns. Although prices remain relatively low compared to those in large cities' centers, there has been a steady increase due to the new towns' proximity to the centers. This is particularly true for the British, French, and Dutch new towns (Gaborit and Nguyen 2009). Harlow (United Kingdom) has experienced massive house price increases out of proportion to people's incomes (European New Towns Platform 2006). This is also why some new towns such as Almere invested in social and affordable housing programs to make home ownership available to lower-income families and individuals.

New Towns and Social Cohesion

In new towns, social cohesion is a process rather than an end state. According to the Council of Europe in 2001, "a strategy of social cohesion refers to any kind of action which ensures that every citizen, every individual, can have within their community the opportunity of access to meeting their basic needs, to progress, to rights and protection, and to dignity and self-confidence" (Jenson 2002). At the local level, we would need to add the right to have access to facilities, clean water, electricity, sewerage, schools, child care, and public services. Indeed, the residents' quality of life and their perceptions are at the core of new towns developments and future (see Chapter 3). But the perceptions and exceptions of what was expected of new town environments, and what the towns should provide, vary over time.

The ambitions of the first-generation new towns were to create good housing conditions for the working class (as for Stevenage or Harlow in the U.K.), and for the higher middle class (as for the French or Dutch new towns). However, during the recession starting at in the 1970s, poorer residents, including migrant communities, have moved into new towns and suburban areas in Europe such as the French "banlieues." Locating new towns in suburban areas (as they are in Europe) has led to (among other outcomes) the relegation of less well-off residents, and of the ethnic minorities (Donzelot 2004; European New Towns Platform 2006). Poverty indicators suggest that some of the European new towns face numerous and increasing challenges (Harlow, Basildon, Stevenage, Marne-la-Vallée, Evry). Other new towns have remained outside this "impoverishment" trend (Cergy-Pontoise, Almere, Zoetermer, Milton Keynes, Appeldoorn). Disparities are also present within new towns. Cergy-Pontoise illustrates this contradiction, as it hosts a well-off Parisian population, students, and vulnerable poorer groups. It also happens to be the town where over-sensationalized urban riots occurred in 2005.

Other new towns report high unemployment levels, social deprivation, or even teenage pregnancies. In the British new town of Harlow was the "the third most deprived district in the region."[13] A recent report of Milton Keynes also reports that "many residents still face multiple deprived areas, and life expectancy of those living in deprived areas is shorter than in most communities'" (Milton Keynes Council 2016, 23).

Social housing represents an important percentage of new towns' housing stock. In the Netherlands, it can be up to 30 percent, as a part of contractual obligations between central and local governments (Harlow Renaissance Ltd. 2007). In addition, new towns that are politically left leaning have developed services, such as social centers, to welcome youngsters with difficulties. "The foyer" located in the town center of Harlow is proposing accommodation and support for teenagers and youngsters at risk. Indeed, European new towns have tended to be left-leaning. This also explains why social cohesion and inclusion are important to European new towns' stakeholders.

Table 13.4 shows that unemployment may be slightly higher than average in new towns, but not to the extent that these areas are "deprived" by official measures. According to urban planners, the challenge may be in the coexistence of different economic and social groups, and the opportunity to create mixed and so-

Table 13.4. Unemployment Rate in Some of the European New Towns Compared to Country Average

New Town	Unemployment Rate (%)	Country Average (%)	Country
Cergy-Pontoise (2019)	7.6 (12.5 in 2014)	9.6 (2012), 10.3 (2015), 8.5 (2019)	France
Evry (2019)	7.3 (128 in 2012)	9.6 (2012), 10.3 (2015), 8.5 (2019)	France
Harlow (2019)	4.7 (9.9 in 2013)	7.1 (2013), 5.1 (2015), 4.1 (2019)	United Kingdom
Lelystad (2017)	6.5	4.5 (2009), 9.5 (2014), 3.9 (2018)	Netherlands
Marne-la-Vallée–Val Maubuée (2012)	13.6	10.3 (2015)	France
Sénart/Lieusaint (2015)	9.0	10.3 (2015)	France
Stevenage (2019)	3.9 (7.9 in 2013)	7.1 (2013), 0.1 (2015), 4.1 (2019)	United Kingdom
Vantaa (2018)	9.0 (12.6 in 2015)	9.4 (2015), 8.2 (2018)	Finland
Almere (2017)	6.1	4.5 (2009), 9.5 (2014), 3.9 (2018)	
Zoetermeer (2017)	9.7	4.5 (2009), 9.5 (2014), 3.9 (2018)	Netherlands

Source: European New Towns and Pilot Cities Platform and Eurostat.

cially diverse areas: "Social diversity is not easy to achieve. A significant number of inhabitants want to live where this social diversity does not exist. They want to have their own house in an area of houses only."[14] The case of Almere is also insightful: the creation of different themed neighborhoods such as the Muziekwijk, Almere, Buiten, Rainsbow neighborhood, and Homerus wijk proved to be a bit experimental.

Can social policies counterbalance this disharmony on the long run? This question is debated. "It is not established that social exclusion in the new towns is more or less extensive than in ordinary places. The association's observation is that the new towns generally achieved their objective of accommodating all varieties of households and those most in need of a home and a job" (Town and Country Planning Association 2012b). This perspective is shared by civil servants working both for urban planning and for social welfare in French new towns such as Cergy-Pontoise and Marne-la-Vallée–Val-Maubuée.

For some new towns such as Milton Keynes, the economic growth has created employment, and the town has even achieved a "faster economy than any other place in the UK" (Milton Keynes Council 2016, 23). In addition, if we look at the jobs/active population ratio in French new towns, they mainly have achieved their ambition with ratios of 1 or close: Cergy-Pontoise and Saint-Quentin-en-Yvelines (each 1.0); Marne-la-Vallée (0.85); Marne-la-Vallée–sector 4 (4.0); and Sénart (0.6).[15]

The percentage of the population living and working in the new town is around 60 percent for Cergy-Pontoise,[16] suggesting considerable levels of commuting, with the need of a better match between the skills of the local workforce and job opportunities.[17]

Urban Space, Ecology, and the Environment

Although sustainability was not at the core of new towns' creation, the idea of "green cities," closer to nature, has been prevalent since new towns' emergence in Europe. It is interesting to recall this in the current context of green cities or nature-based solutions in cities.[18]

New towns in general have a higher percentage of green spaces and lower densities than other medium-sized cities (Gaborit 2010). For instance, 70 percent of Basildon (U.K.) is rural, while 40 percent of Marne-la-Vallée–Val Maubuée is composed of green spaces, and the percentage is higher in Sénart (these proportions are to be considered cautiously, as each new town has its own system to map green spaces).

New towns are characterized by a mix of centrality and polycentricism. New towns have often merged, within a same local entity, different centers from the periphery originally constituted by burgs and villages. Moreover, within new towns such as Sénart in France different new centers have been created related to consumption (shopping malls), work (technopoles), and entertainment (cinemas, green parks, leisure centers, and sport stadiums). These patterns have become more pronounced recently with the integration of the European new towns within larger agglomerations, as is the case in France and in the Netherlands where new towns have become one district of a larger metropolis (Paris, Rotterdam, etc.).

The Environment: From Pilot to Sustainable Towns?

Most European towns nowadays wish to be labeled as sustainable and green (Figure 13.2). Dutch new towns have especially been aware of global warming challenges, and the rise of sea levels, as there are number of settlements that are below sea level (Capelle aan den Ijssel, Almere, Lelystad, Zoetermeer).

Although new towns were inspired from the garden cities movement, some new towns were planned with low densities, green areas, and a scattered urban pattern that would be categorized today as urban sprawl. Similar projects, if they were designed today, would be declared unfit or would be eliminated because of their economic cost and environmental footprint. This trend was less sharp in towns located nearby larger metropolises, such as Spijkenisse, and Capelle aan den Ijssel (near Rotterdam) or Zoetermeer (near The Hague), which have always had higher densities.

Despite the low densities, public transportation was planned and developed in many new towns, especially the latest ones such as Almere, but was never seen as a real alternative to private automobiles.

Environmental and energy challenges provide good opportunities for European new towns to recover their function as urban laboratories or "crucible of ur-

Figure 13.2. Pedestrians in Cergy-Pontoise. Photo by Ann Forsyth.

ban innovation" (see Chapter 18). It gives them opportunities to invest in environmentally innovative, smart, and pilot projects as a leverage for employment and branding. Indeed, the questions of climate change, environment (including biodiversity), transportation, and reduction of GHG emissions or other pollutants (e.g., those responsible for air pollution) have become central in the aftermath of the 2015 Paris Climate agreement. Each new town has a dedicated department for the environment, although identified investments vary from one new town to another (Table 13.5). In Marne-la-Vallée–Val Maubuée, investments have been developed for geothermal energy, and a cluster for sustainable construction is hosted by the Descartes University (the Advancity cluster). Zoetermeer has chosen to pilot eco-construction (Oosterhem eco-district), whereas Milton Keynes has set up a carbon offset fund. Some new towns try to reconvert the energy produced by public transport or highways, while others, such as Peterborough project, invest in waste management and "circular economies."[19]

New Towns' Image of "to Be Built": Urban Plans and Residents' Feelings

When new towns were created, newcomers were typically attracted by their greener environments and lower costs. New towns also aimed to develop better housing and

Table 13.5. Examples of Current Environmental/Ecological Projects in New Towns

New Town	Example of Environmental Project(s)	Country
Basildon	Transformation of an industrial park into an ecological park; work with small and medium-sized enterprises (SMEs) to reduce use of chemical products; waste management and recycling.	United Kingdom
Cergy-Pontoise	Transformation of waste incineration into thermal district heating; biomass heating system; Local 21 agenda; sustainable management for ecosystems.	France
Evry	Ecosystems protection program.	France
Harlow	Green waste service.	United Kingdom
Marne-la-Vallée--Val-Maubuée and Spijkenisse/Nissewaard	Geothermal district energy provision; integrated management of landscapes and green areas.	France and Netherlands
Milton Keynes	Carbon offset fund; air pollution lower than in country's average.	United Kingdom
Nieuwegein	Air-quality agenda and climate agenda, Natuurkwartier Nieuwegein.	Netherlands
Peterborough	Ambition to become the first city for circular economy.	United Kingdom
Zoetermeer	Reconversion of oversized roads and railways into green areas; energy retrofitting programs; wind energy programs.	Netherlands

Sources: European New Towns Platform (2006, 2015); Milton Keynes Council (2016).

educational services. It is generally acknowledged, however, that new towns suffer from a problem of image and identity (Gaborit 2010). There was the real image of the town in construction and the fictional image of the town to be built (or as it would be after the master plan was completed). This fictional city presented to the promoters, future residents, and regional population was instrumental, if not necessary, to sell the town and attract newcomers by emphasizing the role as pioneers of the first inhabitants.

Problems with place identity meant that new towns are often disparaged as a concept in Europe, not among urban planners, but among decision makers and stakeholders. Place identity is here understood as "a multifaceted gradient," which "encompasses the emotional attachment that emerges from individuals' bonds with place, the satisfaction experienced as their needs are fulfilled, the legibility and image ability of their environment, and the social imageability and values that they share with other residents" (Ruggeri 2009, 1). It is a concept that affects the arrival of newcomers and the sense of belonging among the inhabitants, as well as the economy and external perceptions of the town.

Business in New Towns

Whether some of the population moved to new towns for employment and in what proportion is still uncertain. Some of the new towns, such as Vantaa in Finland, or Haarlemmermeer, accommodated many job opportunities because they are airport cities. Similar examples include Espoo (the town where Nokia is headquartered and Tapiola located), or Marne-la-Vallée (because of Disneyland Paris). The existence of strong employment poles, however, led to a subsequent "commuters" trend (European New Towns Platform 2006), as the jobs created did not necessarily match the residents' main skills and education profiles.

Since 2010, new towns have invested in their local economies as they have enjoyed greater autonomy from the central state. Besides increased tax revenues to most local authorities (depending on the national tax system), a dynamic local economy was also necessary to foster the links between the local decision makers and residents. Innovative clusters, industries, and locally based universities are assets for many new towns. Paradoxically, the image of dormitory towns remained, while various government incentives supported the creation of thriving business centers and employment areas (Figure 13.3).

Figure 13.3. Harlow renovated shopping street—town center. Photo by Pascaline Gaborit.

New towns attracted businesses by offering good infrastructure, tax incentives, and facilities. Most new towns opened, for instance, a business one-stop shop, as in Basildon, or Val Maubuée. Clusters such as Advancity in Val Maubuée also proved to be interesting pilots for local economic development. Business parks facilitated the diversification of activities. There were also disparities among new towns, which made it difficult to compare their local economies. Some towns hosted service-oriented economies such as new technology companies (e.g., Nokia, Espoo Finland), while others such as Sénart clustered logistic and transport companies because of the availability of land.

Culture and Image

European new towns developed an assortment of culture and leisure activities to address their relatively negative image. This boom in cultural activities, widespread in the French and Dutch new towns, is in sharp contrast with their external perceptions as residential areas (European New Towns Platform 2006; Gaborit 2010, 2012). As underscored by one of the decision makers in Cergy-Pontoise: "Integrating cultural dimension is necessary to any project of development."[20] It is acknowledged that culture generates employment, contributes to social cohesion and the image of territories, and promotes a new form of economy.[21] In 2010, the culture sector in the European Union employed 6.7 million people and contributed to 3.3 percent of the GDP (European Commission, Directorate General for Regional Policy 2011).

The variety of cultural activities includes innovative architecture in Almere's Homeruskwartier neighborhood, where residents or architects can self-build (custom build) houses in one of the larger self-build areas in Europe.[22] Since 2010, Sénart and Nissewaard/Spijkenisse have opened new theaters and libraries; Almere opened an urban planning museum, and the city is investing in the Floriade 2022 (flowers exhibition) world event.[23] Other towns such as Milton Keynes and Hässelby-Vällingby have developed programs to enhance their cultural heritage. Compared with those of other medium-sized cities, new towns' stakeholders are highly aware that they need to brand their cities, and to propose activities, entertainment, and services, in order for their local population to retain young people (Table 13.6).

Cultural investments, however, have become more difficult since the 2008 economic crisis. Local authorities saw dwindling budgets, a decline that has sharpened after 2012. They had to balance the needs of reflecting the "future city," without

Table 13.6. Examples of Investments for Culture and Leisure

New Town	Main Investment for Culture and Leisure	Country
Almere	Floriade 2022; theaters.	Netherlands
Basildon-Harlow	Olympics and Paralympics Games infrastructure, 2012.	United Kingdom
Cergy-Pontoise	Bid to welcome one of the annexes from "Le Louvre" that has not succeeded (annex has been open in Lens); Museum Pissaro; cinemas; living and street arts yearly festival; involvement of the students' community; touristic itinerary with a dedicated tourist book.	France
Cwmbran	Library; 2 museums; jazz festival; international book festival.	United Kingdom
Evry	Concerts; carnivals; living arts; involvement of the students' community.	France
Harlow	Festival "Sparks will Fly" in 2012; playhouse theater; Victoria Hall theater; performing arts; Gibberd garden and gallery; youth festival; Museum of Harlow.	United Kingdom
Marne-la-Vallée– Val-Maubuée	La ferme du buisson (cultural center); chocolaterie meunier (museum/heritage); local castles (heritage); national school of music and performing arts; library bus (concerts, exhibitions, conferences, tells, music workshops).	France
Milton Keynes	Milton Keynes heritage project; bid for the prize of European cultural capital; international festival of creative urban living; designing a grid square of sport, arts, music, and dance.	United Kingdom
Nieuwegein	Education to culture; library; Geinbeat Festival (spring); blues festival (fall); platform for pop music, cinema, and theater.	Netherlands
Sénart	Opening of a new national theater (scène nationale), 2001, Festival "fête du carré" open to all residents.	France
Spijkenisse/ Nissewaard	Opening of a new theater and library.	Netherlands
Vantaa	Vantaa/Helsinki world design capital events, 2012.	Finland
Zoetermeer	Museum; sport and leisure as cultural investments (Snow World, Water Dreams); stadstheater; de Boerderij (performing arts); art school; music café; Baztille visual arts gallery; cinema; food festival (Zoetermeer culinair); Culture on Sunday initiatives; Sweet Vibes dance; blues festival; dragon boat festival.	Netherlands

Source: European New Towns Platform (2006, 2015).

losing scope of the "present city." This why some new towns developed promotion campaigns, "soon-to-be developed," such as Apeldoorn in the Netherlands.

Finally, Almere's slogan, "Everything is possible in Almere," exemplifies the ambitions of the first city planners. In a city developed on reclaimed land, everything was indeed possible, be it positive or negative. New towns had to cope with rapidly changing contexts due to economic crises, demographic shifts, dwindling budgets, and lifestyle changes. But this slogan truly shows the innovation potential of some of the new towns (Figure 13.4).

Figure 13.4. Residential area in Almere, Netherlands. Photo by Ann Forsyth.

In addition, current urban reforms in France and in the Netherlands have led to a major restructuring of metropolises, including the end of many European new towns as separate entities. This trend may positively affect their image as icons of past urban planning within the larger agglomerations. The town of Hässelby-Vällingby could be a good model. It became a part of Stockholm's agglomeration in the 1990s and has preserved its initial architecture and design as a protected urban neighborhood (buildings, front houses, but also apartment interior design) from the 1950s and 1960s. The current program of cultural heritage in Milton Keynes is also a promising initiative for other new towns and is part of the new city's vision (Milton Keynes Council 2016).

Conclusion

Before the economic crisis, national governments in Europe such as those of France (Attali 2008) and the U.K. proposed to build new "eco-towns"[24] despite new towns' current disparaged image. These never materialized as other priorities emerged. There are currently no real national projects of building new towns in

Europe anymore, not even in the form of "smart cities," as is the case in India (see Chapter 12)[25] and in other parts of the world. In this sense, this is the end of a model in Europe. With respect to "maturing" new towns, most observers would agree that they have been ambitious and innovative urban laboratories that accommodated unforeseen constraints, emphasized resilience, and were maybe not completely prepared to face so many pitfalls (see Chapter 2).

The main challenge over the decades has been what has been called the *reinvention of the new town mindset* (Gaborit 2010). This reinvention should focus on the development of a collective, long-term, sustainable, intragenerational vision stressing new towns' role in the wider region, addressing the question of whether a new town should be an entity in itself, a self-contained district, or a part of a larger agglomeration. In this regard, the current territorial reforms occurring in Europe have faced the necessity of new towns to cope again with new frameworks and realities. The environmental and energy transitions in a context of climate change offer opportunities for innovative projects, if they are not hindered by economic crisis and governance challenges. The disappearance of new towns as models in Europe does not mean that they were failures, nor that they cannot be sustainable, but that they were recaptured by realities, that the initial plans shifted, and that they generated headaches for their planners and developers. Their merging into larger entities, for the future, may also give them a new chance to emerge as continuous territories with their own specificities.

Notes

1. Peri-urbanization is defined as the process by which cities grow by increasing their suburbs.

2. This is the case in particular for the French new towns such as Val-Maubuée, but also for new towns such as Spijkenisse, which was merged with another local authority to become the municipality of Nissewaard.

3. Ebenezer Howard (1850–1928) is the author of the book *Tomorrow: A Peaceful Path to Real Reform* (1898), reprinted as *Garden Cities of To-Morrow* (1902). In his book he called for the creation of new suburban towns of restricted size, planned in advance and surrounded by an agricultural green belt. These garden cities were used as a model for new towns. In Howard's vision, garden cities were the perfect blend of city and nature. His ideas have had a direct impact on the creation of European new towns.

4. These polders are currently facing new challenges of flooding linked to climate change and the rise of sea levels.

5. Similarly, new towns were created in Russia, but these will not be part of this study.

6. This is, for instance, the case of Hoyerswerda in eastern Germany.

7. The housing stock was built at the same period of time and started ageing simultaneously.

8. New towns started with very low densities and had to make their territory more dense and compact in a later phase.

9. Marne-la-Vallée, was one of the French new towns initially designed in 1965. Four sectors have been planned for its implementation, each one with its own local authority, planning department (Etablissement Public d'Aménagement) and master plan. Val-Maubuée is the sector II, designed as a New Town in 1972. It was merged in 2014 into the new metropolis (local authority) communauté d'agglomération Paris Vallée de la Marne.

10. Train à Grande Vitesse (high-velocity national train).

11. Milton Keynes has a program of valorization of cultural heritage.

12. This has been the case in the U.K., but also in France, the Netherlands, and Scandinavia. This reflects the history of migration and city planning in western Europe especially in the 1960s and 1970s.

13. British local government improvement program, author's visit to Harlow District Council, March 19–23, 2001.

14. Jukka Kullberg, director of planning, Vantaa, Finland, at ENTP Workshop discussing the "Top 8 Specific Challenges for Urban Regeneration," Brussels, May 2005.

15. Hervé Dupont, former secretary general of the Secretariat of Urban Regeneration Major Operations, interview with author, Paris, France, May 2016.

16. Ibid.

17. See also Milton Keynes Council (2016, 8) report that mentions as a challenge: "the resident workforce is less qualified than in many other cities, and the educational attainments below average."

18. Green walls, green roofs, etc.

19. According to the European Commission, Directorate General for Regional Policy (2011), "the circular economy is an economy where nothing is wasted and where natural resources are managed sustainably, and biodiversity is protected, valued and restored in ways that enhance our society's resilience."

20. Luc Raimbault interview with Lauriane Lahery, April 2013, DGA Cergy-Pontoise.

21. AWARD project 2011–14, http://www.awardproject.eu.

22. Self-build or custom-built area. See also Collinson (2011).

23. See Almere's Floriade 2022 website, http://floriade.almere.nl/en/.

24. There was in France a proposal from the government of Sarkozy in this direction in May 2008. In 2007 in the U.K., the Department for Communities and Local Governments (CLG) announced a competition to build ten eco-towns, but by 2012 only four sites had been approved, and none of them completed.

25. Narendra Modi has a vision of building one hundred smart cities in India.

14

Governing an Adolescent Society

The Case of Almere

JaapJan Berg and Michelle Provoost

The many new towns built in western Europe after World War II were public projects initiated by national governments as part of their spatial policies. Institutions were organized in a top-down manner, and built with the help of subsidized housing corporations. Almere, the largest new town in the Netherlands, is no exception. Though Almere's governance structure was initially influenced by the new town's unique origin (built in a new polder), its development over the past four decades is typical of many other European new towns.

In Almere's governance history, three phases can be identified in the relationship between local government and residents. During the first phase, beginning in 1976 with Almere's inception by the central government in The Hague, a powerful top-down organization ruled the small city. Attempts at resident participation had little success, but the pioneering spirit of the first inhabitants compensated for this shortfall. The National Office for the IJsselmeerpolders (RIJP) and a *landdrost* largely called the shots during this first period, which included the development of a spatial plan for the city and the construction of the first three urban cores.[1] The city was based on a target population of 125,000 to 250,000 inhabitants (Salomons 1975, 12).

A second phase began in 1984 with the establishment of the municipality of Almere, ending the city's "special status." Three urban cores were constructed during this phase, and the city was home to almost thirty-four thousand residents and about seventy-five hundred dwellings. The municipal organization took over Almere's development, and the previously initiated policy aimed at expansion. In this period of pressure cooker democracy, unexpected events, such as the rise of an extreme right-wing party, were signs of an adolescent and unstable society (van Duijn and Huis 2004). The question remains whether the somewhat clumsy political maneuvers that occurred during this phase were coincidental or the result of a combination of a young city experiencing growing pains and the inexperience of its leaders. A schism between municipality and residents, partly based on different expectations and ambitions, was unavoidable. The political ambition was to expand the city, while residents felt that this compromised their neighborhood's livability, leading to a major crisis in the 1990s. Nonetheless, Almere's ambitions and growing self-awareness culminated with the decision to have OMA, the office of Rem Koolhaas, develop the new city center, thus taking a great leap forward to become an independent and "complete" city.

The most recent phase, since 2006, is characterized by increasing confidence and persuasiveness, mixed with bravado and recklessness. It all matches the image of an adolescent city. Almere's clearer profile is no longer based solely on growth but puts the emphasis on involving residents in shaping it and the city's long-term sustainability. Almere's increasingly professionalized political apparatus has drawn a conclusion from the ceaseless dissatisfaction and growing NIMBY-ism of its residents. The year 2006 saw the start of a large self-built (i.e., custom-built) housing project, efforts to minimize regulations, and, in general, a more positive attitude toward residents' initiatives. In 2008, a list of ambitions, *Almere Principles*, aimed to create an ecologically, socially, and economically sustainable future for the new town (Municipality of Almere 2008). This participatory approach is a sign of the times in Europe since the demise of the welfare state and is especially valuable for new towns, which often excel in control and regulations but have difficulty tapping into their residents' dynamism and entrepreneurialism. When Almere's municipality and residents succeed in adapting to their new roles and can come to a balance that is both sustainable and inspiring, it will be a valuable example for other new towns (Table 14.1).

Table 14.1. Key Dates in Almere's Development

Year	Event
1973	Working group focused on "Social Aspects management" set up by the National Office for the IJsselmeerpolders (RIJP)
1975	Foundation for Housing Almere initiated by the RIJP, which became responsible for housing in the Almere Haven, the first urban core
1976	Beginning of first phrase Keys delivered to Almere's first residents
1977	First Advisory Committee Almere (ACA) elections
1984	Beginning of second phase Establishment of the municipality of Almere, ending the city's "special status"
1989	Deadlock in city's development due to urban densification and parliamentary inquiry into abuses with construction grants
1995	Board of mayor and alderman decided to realize new city center designed by OMA, the office of Rem Koolhaas
2002	Newly founded political party Leefbaar Almere won the municipal elections
2006	Beginning of third phase Arrival of Adri Duivesteijn, social-democratic alderman for planning Start of self-building housing project in the Homeruskwartier district
2008	*Almere Principles* published, aiming to create an ecologically, socially, and economically sustainable future for the new town

Phase 1: The Birth of a National Project

Planning for Almere took place in the early 1970s, just as the large-scale urban expansion and monotonous high-rise architecture of the 1960s came increasingly under fire. In response, Almere sought to create small-scale, low-rise, recognizable urban patterns and an architecture that was rooted in the historic towns of the western Netherlands with canals and detached buildings. It was also shaped by ideas from the garden city movement. Almere is arguably one of the first postmodern projects in the Netherlands where architecture and urban design throughout the twentieth century was marked by functionalism and modernism.

The spirit of the 1970s was characterized by an emphasis on participation, democratization, individualization, and openness. The National Office for the IJsselmeerpolders (RIJP) set up a working group focused on "Social Aspects management" (1973), to advise on how the city could responsibly grow toward a target of 250,000 inhabitants (Pasveer et al. 1973). The working group noted that the call for participation and openness was related to the "stressful transition" to a hybrid welfare state. The Dutch social-democratic welfare state, strongly linked to the country's reconstruction after World War II, took the state's guarantee of a "civilized life" as its starting point. In the 1960s, reduced emphasis on the collective and growing prosperity resulted in a social transformation (evident throughout western Europe) where the primary aim was to provide every individual with optimal opportunities to develop his or her talents and personality.

This transformation could easily have led to a crisis of authority, and to avoid this, politicians wanted to encourage the building of a democratic society in which everyone had the right "to help determine and influence the communal policy in freedom and equality," and where the political leadership had a duty "to justify policy to the members of the community" (Salomons 1975, 12).

A new town such as Almere faced a relatively greater danger of alienation between government and citizens than a historic city because of the authoritarian tendencies of powerful government departments and the unpredictability of young communities. In this light, a three-step participatory decision-making model was proposed corresponding with the three scales of the urban structure: (1) for the whole of Almere, (2) per urban core,[2] and (3) per micro living environment.

When the keys were delivered to Almere's first residents in 1976, Minister Tjerk Westerterp (Transport, Public Works, and Water Management) indirectly referenced public participation: "Some will say that everything in this new city has already been imagined for you, that you as new residents of this land, end up in a kind of super welfare state where no more space exists for any private enterprise."[3] That space was indeed available in principle, although the first inhabitants had to fight hard for it. The

designers and RIJP often claimed the last word, alleging that they were busy building a city, rather than a democratic system.

Figure 14.1. Skating on the Kerkgracht in Almere Haven, the first built part of Almere. Courtesy of Stadsarchief.

The RIJP constructed the polder and owned the land; it also developed the land and infrastructure. In 1975, it was again the RIJP that initiated and controlled the Foundation for Housing Almere, which became responsible for housing in the first urban core, Almere Haven (Figure 14.1). Seventy percent of this housing consisted of affordable rental housing. No residents or private parties were involved, nor was there a special development corporation such as is the case in the United Kingdom. In the concept of the welfare state, it was the government that provided not only housing but also all other public services. Shops, offices, bars, and restaurants were supposed to be built by private parties, but when they hesitated, the RIJP built these. Furthermore, the most important decisions were made by civil servants who were not accountable to residents; administrators were appointed, not elected. This lack of democratic standards changed only in 1984, when Almere became a full-fledged municipality.

The Right Man in the Right Place

Thoughts about the relationship between government and residents were idealistic in those early years, but how did this play out? Besides RIJP, an Openbaar Lichaam (Public Entity) was established. The Public Entity was charged with overseeing management, public order, security, and education. At the head was the landdrost, a role that was filled by former Amsterdam alderman Han Lammers, a born-and-bred bureaucrat. The landdrost's power was substantial and corresponded to that of mayor, aldermen, and city council at the same time. In the 1960s, Lammers had previously criticized the "imperial" politicians of his time and advocated for far-reaching democratization. But in his role as "super regent," he could not always resist the temptation of power. Later, he was described as "the most outspoken imperial anti-regent in public administration in recent decades" (Pruntel 2013).

But in general, the Public Entity and Lammers were fully aware of the added value that a direct relationship with residents could have in creating a new urban identity and culture. That is why an Advisory Board and Executive Advisory Committee (DAC) were established from the outset. The Advisory Board and DAC advised Lammers and together formed a quasi–city council.[4] The Advisory Committee Almere (ACA) also existed, albeit only for a short while, as an additional advisory body that represented the residents of the first core, Almere Haven, and advised the DAC.[5] It was unusual, but understandable, given the small population of a few hundred people, that some members of the board were also employed by RIJP and so exerted their influence as both professionals and residents. Eleven candidates signed up for the first ACA elections in March 1977. In their presentations, the candidates highlighted personal motives that simultaneously reflected the situation in the fledgling Almere Haven: "This is not a matter for the government alone."

Despite attempts to establish a dialogue with the population, the task to build a city and to find ample means to realize it remained a government project. Administrative ambitions and temptations created—even in later years—certain authoritarian symptoms that could not be suppressed. Lammers kept strict control: residents were allowed to engage during Advisory Council meetings, but he determined the discussion duration and whether or not to answer questions.[6] This approach maintained the friction between the needs of a high-speed, energetic expansion of the city, on the one hand, and community building and democratization on the other. The head of the design team, Dirk Frieling, realized this as the first homes were constructed in Almere Haven: "For me, a . . . thorny problem is the way decisions are made in a society—and soon also in Almere. In one way or another, the occupants must act as producers of the town and not just as consumers. It may even be necessary to compel them to do so, for example, by not making simple things that should come anyway" (National Office for the IJsselmeerpolders 1975). The idea was that when residents became sufficiently annoyed by missing public facilities, they would take control and begin to play an active role.

Phase 2: Democracy in the Pressure Cooker

In those first years, local politics in Almere were "intense and sincere, democracy in a pressure cooker," according to those directly involved (van Duijn and Huis 2004). As of January 1, 1984, the city was entitled to call itself a municipality, but at the first city council meeting, Almere was startled by unexpected election results. The extreme-right and xenophobic political party Centrum Partij (viewed with suspicion throughout the Netherlands) claimed 10 percent of the votes and thus won two seats on the council.[7] According to a study conducted at the time, the reason for this political reckoning was not Almere's barely present ethnic minority, but rather a fear of loss of employment, housing, or benefits (Te Raa 1989).

In the years leading up to the election, Mayor Lammers fought hard for a quick municipal status instead of the *status aparte* (special status) desired by RIJP and the Public Entity. With that aim, Lammers revealed himself to be a democratic politician who recognized the shelf life of Almere's unusual governance structure. After the election outcome was announced, Lammers saw with dismay how national attention focused on the rise of the extreme right and how this led to negative perceptions of Almere. Consequently, his expectations about the added value of a municipal structure for realizing a "normal society" suffered considerable damage.

The directors, however, picked up the thread again and continued with their main goal: to expand the city, which already had more than forty thousand residents. At Almere municipality's inception, the city received 142 million guilders from the national government as start-up capital. The next two decades proved that it was the growth-oriented focus of Almere politics and the relationship with residents that would eventually lead to significant moments of crisis. Around 1989, two factors created a deadlock in the city's development. First, the central government decided to stop construction of new cities, shifting emphasis to better utilization of space within existing cities.

This urban densification continues today and has been exacerbated by the ever-growing popularity and appeal of cities in general over the last few years. Almere, therefore, seemed to be a less important factor in national policy. But the fear that the city would lose a substantial part of its revenue for new construction because of the collapse in housing production was short-lived. The pressure on the Dutch housing market, and the insufficiency of housing supply in the northern part of the Randstad to meet the demand naturally, returned the focus to Almere. That city had (and has) an unprecedented surplus of available space.

The second factor played out simultaneously at the national level: owing to a parliamentary inquiry into abuses with construction grants (1986–88), a new subsidy scheme for rental housing construction was introduced. In 1989, the document called *Volkshuisvesting in de jaren negentig* (Public Housing in the 1990s) proposed far-reaching changes to housing policy (Netherlands Ministry of Housing, Spatial Planning and the Environment 1989). It decided to strengthen the housing market, decentralize decision making, and privatize housing corporations. This brought an end to the typical organization of housing under the welfare state in which the national government was central (Klijn 1995). Almere was also affected.[8]

The housing dip of 1989 proved very temporary, as the economic upturn beginning in the early 1990s created a boom in Almere's housing production. From that moment, an average of three thousand homes were built annually. Most politicians considered the city's growth and the stability of building production levels to be beyond doubt. And yet, critical voices also began to grow during this period. As early as 1985, the journalist (and later politician) Frits Huis commented: "Build, build, and build again. The odd thing is that our city council still drinks that kool-aid, while a child can now see that urgent attention is needed for other social problems" (Huis 1985). These statements were a prelude to the subsequent creation of the local political party Leefbaar Almere (Livable Almere).

The unilateral managerial preoccupation with growth and construction led to a major political crisis in the early 1990s. A political argument over unjustified claims made by the mayor led not only to his departure, but also to that of three aldermen, the town clerk, and a handful of councilors. One of the aldermen, André Tierie, left because he initially lied about taking unethical, "gifted" tips from project developers: a sign that the relationship between politicians and commercial developers had become cozy during the construction of Almere. To the outside world, an unedifying picture of a diseased political climate, where favoritism, backroom discussions, political amateurism, and opportunism set the tone, swiftly began to emerge. The conclusion was soon drawn that Almere's politics had not managed to keep pace with the city's stormy growth. Planning and urban experimentation in Almere had produced politicians who managed the business themselves or acted incredibly headstrong. Skeptics saw plenty of evidence that the politicians had completely forgotten their role as the people's representatives (van Wijnen 1993).

Almere in the Region

As an overflow city, Almere was closely linked to Amsterdam from inception; there was talk of a "double city" in administrative, spatial, and planning rhetoric, but the relationship was marked from the outset by competition. Alderman P. M. M. de

Jonge said in 1988: "For Almere, it's important that things go well with Amsterdam. And if we can build enough, that's also good for Amsterdam; that promotes the flow in the housing market" (Lindelauf 1988, 6). The administrative struggles that came with the establishment of the Regional Organ Amsterdam (ROA) showed, however, that these relationships were not always so simple and positive. The extreme (financial) demands put on the table by Amsterdam were, in hindsight, perhaps a lifeline for Almere's political-administrative self-esteem. Through a strong power play in the direction of the national government, the Almere city council was able to successfully undermine the requirements. The government's threat to force Almere to join the ROA and make the corresponding payments was withdrawn. Almere received approval for a target of thirty thousand homes; maintained, and even strengthened, its relatively independent aura because of the resistance it had shown; and also landed a state guarantee for additional housing and financial coverage. The euphoria over the victory pushed the administrative crisis into the background. Almere suddenly felt strong and confident, and that it could continue its success story thanks to low land prices.

The first new council after the government crisis wanted to capitalize on the regained self-esteem with a project that would decisively position Almere as an autonomous city: a new city center designed by OMA, the office of Rem Koolhaas. In October 1995, the board of mayor and aldermen decided to carry out the costly and far-reaching plans. With the scale leap into a full-fledged urban center, the city wanted to offer serious alternatives to the facilities in nearby Amsterdam. Moreover, the implementation of OMA's controversial plan served as therapy to wash away the hangover of the administrative crisis and avoid a repeat of paternalistic behavior from Amsterdam in the future. The plan gave politicians another purpose: just as before, they would satisfy the population with promises of construction, square footage of new facilities, and growth plans.[9]

The Bill Is Presented

In the municipal elections of 2002, the victory of the newly founded Leefbaar Almere did not as much follow national trends as it did represent a bill presented to the politicians for overaccentuating the components of growth, construction, and development. Of course, much was also invested in the city's social and cultural structure, but in the residents' eyes, this was insufficient. The prestigious sports complex Omniworld, the high cost of the new city center, and the introduction of paid parking (partly intended to cover those costs) were all seen as points of con-

Figure 14.2. Train station and square in Almere center (2010). Courtesy of Wikimedia Commons.

tention. Aside from that, there were more general doubts about the sustainability of the implemented growth policies. The visible decline of some older districts also played an important emotional role (Figure 14.2).

The successful attack on the sports complex hit home especially hard. The city council had wanted to put Almere on the map with a prestigious sports complex that would also be the hub of the new expansion core, Almere Poort. Leefbaar Almere ensured that the project was put on hold, and the effects were far reaching. The signal from the residents was clear: politicians had concerned themselves too little with the opinions and the needs of the growing population. For a long time, the inhabitants had shown little interest in political decision making and were somewhat indifferent—an attitude that is sometimes seen as symptomatic of the bourgeois suburban environment. Each citizen was mainly concerned with his or her own interests and comfort. Through Leefbaar Almere, however, the residents managed to organize themselves and express their dissatisfaction in a powerful way. Citizens had recovered contact with politics, but not in the constructive way that had been hoped for in the 1970s: the sentiment inside Leefbaar Almere and the other major populist party, PVV, is mainly aimed at stopping major projects and growth. In that sense, these parties are an institutionalization of the powerful NIMBY-ism that exists in the city.

Phase 3: Participation and Private Commissions

Since the emergence of Leefbaar Almere in local politics, Almere must increasingly consider its residents' opinions. This is a common trend in the Netherlands and even in Europe overall, where local and/or populist parties are growing in popularity. In addition, the search for a new interpretation of the relationship between government and residents is underway as part of a wider development that began as early as the 1970s, where the government as the guardian of collective interests gradually makes way for a society of active, articulate individuals. This can partly be seen as a process of emancipation, but it is also, above all, an effect of neoliberalization since the 1980s, the retreat of the state, and the promotion of what is called "Big Society" in the United Kingdom and *de participatiemaatschappij* (participation society) in the Netherlands—a convenient convergence of economic and social objectives. In Almere, the consequences of these developments are seen not only in the composition of the council, but also in the way the city continues to be developed.

Almere's vanguard role is remarkable, because the governance structure in new towns is always based on a strong national and local government. The shift to a model in which power is shared with the residents is therefore a particular challenge in new towns. By contrast, the spirit of pioneering and inventing things often develops strongly, especially because of the lack of tradition and ingrained habits among both the residents and institutions. That was previously apparent in the structures Almere founded to provide health care and education in the 1970s, in the experimental Building Expos in the 1990s, and most recently in the embrace of private commissioning in housing: the first manifestation of greater freedom and empowerment for residents. Houses in Almere are now self-built. This requires the direct involvement of residents in the conception and realization of their homes, and for the Netherlands, this is a groundbreaking development.

The decisive factor in the shift to another form of urban development was the arrival of the social-democratic alderman for planning, Adri Duivesteijn, in 2006. His arrival made clear that the inexperienced politics that had characterized the adolescent phase of the city were now gone. Drawing on his experience with self-organized settlements in the global south as director of the Dutch Architecture Institute (NAI), Duivesteijn started his career in Almere by enabling self-built (custom) housing in the new Homeruskwartier district. Based on a master plan, lots in this district were made available to prospective residents, who could build to their own taste and desires (though typically using professional builders). Duivesteijn pursued a deliberate break with previous planning and building practice by distancing himself from the semiprivate housing corporations and private developers that had, until then, controlled the housing market. He advocated for a reconsideration of what he called the essential values of urbanism, with the citizen as the beginning and end of the process, and the idea that all enterprising men and women are driven by "their own power, their own needs, their own dreams, their own initiative" (Berg 2007, 40). This reorientation was particularly damaging for the institutions and large-scale private real estate companies. Duivesteijn opined: "The city facilitates construction and citizens build and no one needs to sit between them. People make their own city" (Berg 2007, 40).

Given the projected scope of private commissions, this could be a guarantee for very active participation from a large group of Almeer residents in the near future. The nature of that participation seems to be focused on the individual, and less on collective interests. By treating private commissioning as a guiding principle, the municipality hopes to meet the needs of current and future residents, as well as build a distinct profile for the city. Almere will thus cater to a desire for highly individualized forms of housing that are determined by social factors such as "lifestyle" and "independent and conscious" life. From this perspective, housing is no longer a necessity, but an image (Berg et al. 2007, 136).

Development of the Homeruskwartier was not an isolated project: in 2008, at Duivesteijn's instigation, an ambitious policy manifesto, *Almere Principles*, was published. This groundbreaking document was compiled with the input of the American sustainability expert William McDonough. This set the tone for an ecologically, socially, and economically sustainable future for Almere. The most important principle is undoubtedly that "people make the city," a claim that citizens should be the driving force in creating, maintaining, and preserving the city. City councilors and urban administrators exist mainly to support the efforts of the citizens where possible.

The Oosterwold project, a large expansion area of approximately forty-five hundred hectares, which will be developed "organically," is another step in distancing the government's controlling and regulatory role. Under the plan, based on a set of rules rather than a true master plan (MVRDV 2011), not only are people allowed to buy a piece of land and build their dream home; they are also responsible for collective facilities and infrastructures: roads, water, energy, schools, and shops. The city government now leaves these classic domains of public duty to the citizen. This step can be understood only as belonging to the ideology of empowering citizens and the government's relinquishment of traditional powers. It might also seem a pragmatic choice to reduce government costs, but the absence of a descriptive blueprint master plan means that civil servants must facilitate any planning application and each participant individually. The handing over of power by the municipality does not mean less labor; nor is it easy for civil servants to adapt to the new mentality in which they facilitate rather than dictate.

Why, then, did Almere bring all this trouble on itself? Projects such as the Homeruskwartier and Oosterwold carry a promise that is of great importance for the young city. With the focus on private commissions, residents' involvement in the city is increased, because their relationship with place and house is much stronger than that of a tenant or traditional buyer. This not only creates a new impetus for a sustainable building practice in Almere; it is also a clever tactic to strengthen the relationship between city and citizen. It also attracts a new category of residents that normally would not choose Almere, but change their minds because of the unprecedented freedom in building, realizing a far better price-quality ratio than any market development could deliver.

Will Duivesteijn's orchestrated enthusiasm resonate and draw responses from society? His unshakable faith in the power of individual citizens to participate and his confidence in the "make-ability" of Dutch society is indeed something of a flashback to the 1970s. For the time being, however, both Homeruskwartier and Oosterwold enjoy great popularity. A new group of residents is attracted by the opportunity to act as producers of the city and not just as consumers.[10] While residents play an active and creative role, it is questionable whether the local municipal apparatus can manage the turnaround. In a young city with no tradition other than top-down-driven growth, the principle of "people make the city" requires adaptation on all fronts: for designers and planners, financial services, licensing authorities, and other bureaucrats. If the city succeeds in that difficult step, it will become an example to all the other new towns that must necessarily develop from adolescent to adult city.

Figure 14.3. The new self-built area Oosterwold (2017). Courtesy of Municipality of Almere.

Notes

1. A *landdrost* is a Dutch public official who governs a particular area. The function goes back to the Middle Ages. In Flevoland, the new polder was not immediately classified as a municipality but instead had the status of public body with a landdrost as the head for quite some time.

2. The first three cores (or boroughs) were Almere Haven, Almere Stad, and Almere Buiten, with numbers of residents varying between twenty-two thousand and one hundred thousand.

3. (Former) Minister Westerterp on November 30, 1976, on the occasion of awarding the first keys in the Almere City Archive and the archive of Dirk Frieling.

4. The first Advisory Board had twenty-one members and was comparable to a city council. The Executive Advisory Board (DAC) had four members of the Advisory Board, in addition to the landdrost, who were regarded as full-time directors. The Advisory Board was comparable to a board composed of a mayor and aldermen. Elections for the Advisory Board took place in 1978, 1980, and 1982.

5. An Advisory Board for the "area of Almere" was chosen in 1978. It subsequently took over the role of the advisory council and residents.

6. André Tierie, interview by JaapJan Berg, January 10, 2007.

7. The first Almere city council had twenty-three members. The distribution of seats was as follows: PvdA 10, VVD 5, CDA 2, Centrum Partij 2, D'66 1, CPN 1, PPR/PSP 1, and Stap '84 1.

8. As of 2014, most of the houses in Almere are on their own land (76 percent), have a floor area of between 75 square meters and 125 square meters (69 percent), and are row houses (60 percent). In 2014, Almere had more than seventy-eight thousand homes, of which 76 percent were ground-floor family homes. Two-thirds of the properties were privately owned, but the remaining quarter of the stock were subsidized rental housing units with rents below €700. See Municipality of Almere (2014, 56).

9. See also Gemeente Almere, Teun Koolhaas Associates (TKA), and Goudappel & Coffeng, *Concept Ruimtestudie Westflank van Almere* (Almere-Pampus); and the study *ROSA 2015* (1996) under the leadership of Riek Bakker (BVR). The documents referred to are all in the collection of the Almere City Archive (Stadsarchief Almere). https://www.almere.nl/over -almere/historie/stadsarchief/.

10. Group development has become increasingly popular in the Netherlands as part of the bottom-up urban movement Het Nieuwe Stadmaken (the New City Making).

15

Ex Novo Towns in South America

A Genealogy

Felipe Correa

South America's history of urbanization is inextricably linked to the concept of ex novo cities and towns. From the foundational cities of the Spanish crown (Quito, Lima, Cartagena) to the conception and quick implementation of new republican city plans (Belo Horizonte, La Plata) to the physical inscription of a new federal capital in the heart of the continent's interior (Brasilia), the idea of a city planned anew has been an integral part of South America's cultural and urban imaginary. In fact, most of the major and capital cities that make up the more-consolidated South American urban landscape were founded as a physical manifestation of a new social order. While an expansive and continuously growing bibliography exists on the origins and evolution of the South American metropolis, a much newer and less-known parallel history exists on the evolution of the ex novo town as an urban model that emerged out of nineteenth-century urban planning theories as a counterpoint to large-scale metropolitan expansion. In the South American context, this model was the basis for agricultural and resource extraction settlement towns, facilitating the gradual exploitation of natural resources throughout the continent's hinterland.[1]

This essay examines—through a series of late nineteenth- and twentieth-century case studies—the genealogy of the ex novo town in South America and its relationship to larger geographies of resource extraction. The text charts the evolutionary arc of the resource extraction town in South America through three case studies, each sited in one of the three periods of greatest economic growth in the region. The town of Santa Ana and the sugar mills of Tucuman (Argentina) manifest the role of the new resource extraction town during the consolidation of South American nations in the late nineteenth century. The case of Maria Elena and the nitrate towns in northern Chile exemplify new towns in the context of an early twentieth-century export-led economy. Finally, the case of CESP and Vila Piloto (Brazil) places the resource extraction town in the context of a developmental state during the 1960s. These three case studies serve as a backdrop to argue for the need to reinvent the concept of the ex novo town, and for how this can help in the development of a new urban planning agenda in the context of the current urbanization pressures that are shaping the South American hinterland.

The Town of Santa Ana and the Sugar Mills of Tucuman (Argentina)

The Consolidation of South American Nations, 1880–1910

Nestled in the core of the Andes Mountains, the Ingenio de Santa Ana (Santa Ana Sugar Mill) exemplifies one of the first and most ambitious resource extraction towns of South America's early industrial era. Pioneered by French industrialist Clodomiro Hilebert in 1889 (Mercado 2003, 212), the sugar mill and its accompanying town were inscribed in the Argentine northwest as a new economic engine and a symbol of national progress, at the time when Argentina was one of the top ten wealthiest countries in the world (Horowitz 2008, 12). The figure of its plan, a square within a square, represented a new settlement model that through the virtues and efficiencies of industry and technology could put the economically forgotten hinterland of Tucuman to work (Figure 15.1). The plan successfully brings together two different scales, the agricultural and the urban, through the superimposition of two squares. The outer square, two kilometers by two kilometers, set the rhythm for the organization of the agricultural plots while also accommodating a *colonia*—a housing enclave given to field workers in exchange for working the land—in each corner. The secondary square inside it, approximately six hundred meters by six hundred meters, contained the factory, basic services, and housing for factory workers. All this was at the center of a twenty-seven-thousand-hectare sugar plantation. Erected in a neo-Renaissance style and with all the technological upgrades available at the time, Santa Ana had all the parts and pieces required for urbanity amid a sea of sugar fields.

The inner square, carefully defined by a wall of worker housing along the edges, contained the primary functions of the new town. Within this square, the factory and its adjacent programs—primarily "el canchon" or the main working plaza—represented the heart of the new town. The chimney stacks, standing as the tallest elements in the landscape, marked the new epicenter of industrial sugar production. The "canchon" adjacent to the factory served as the main drop-off point for freshly cut sugarcane branches. Chimney and plaza branded the physical, programmatic, and symbolic center of the town, and all other spatial elements where organized in relation to these two pieces. The inner square also contained the main

VISTA AEREA "PUEBLO DE SANTA ANA"

Ex Ingenio Santa Ana

residence for Hilebert—an impressive chalet with an accompanying garden and private chapel. The industrial village too was sited within the square, occupying its southwestern corner. While rudimentary, the village provided basic services including an infirmary, a dining hall, workshops, and a library. A massive row of housing for factory workers defined the square's

Figure 15.1. Aerial view of the Ingenio de Santa Ana (circa 1940). Courtesy of collection of Felipe Correa.

edges, establishing a clear distinction between city and field and making of the *ingenio* a highly distinguishable object in the landscape. The spatial continuity between the inner and outer square was maintained through a grid of roads and irrigation canals that set the framework for the sugarcane planting lots. The outer square was demarcated by a wider road and a *colonia* in each of the four corners acting as citadels outside of the walled city. This relationship between town and citadel established by Santa Ana's original plan exemplified the new relationship between industrial frontier and agrarian landscape, where the former was put in place to reinvent the latter.

Despite the peculiar organization of Santa Ana's plan, the spatial model of the plantation/company town pioneered by Hilebert and other industrialists of the late nineteenth century became the prototypical unit of development for the province of Tucuman and the Argentine Northwest. While sugarcane had been a staple crop of this region since the Jesuit missions of the sixteenth century, it was only with the arrival of rail in 1876—connecting the province of Tucuman with the port of Buenos Aires—that the large-scale industrial sugar mill town proliferated. The effectiveness of rail for transporting French and British manufacturing equipment uphill eased the upgrading of presses into industrial facilities, expanding the scale of the plantation (Juarez-Dappe 2010, 25–32). Rail also allowed for larger quantities of processed sugar to be carried out to Buenos Aires and exported to global markets.

More important, the implementation of rail, the new model of industrial sugar mill/company town, and the systematic reorganization of irrigation canals became the three crucial elements that reorganized and rebranded the province of Tucuman. The new town became the epicenter of a larger territorial and economic model that modernized a province that had been deemed economically defunct compared to the littoral provinces and their burgeoning economies. The sugar mill's modernization and its transition from an artisanal to an industrial production model involved a complete territorial reformatting, involving processes of consolidation and decentralization at different scales.

The new town was the element that brought these two processes together. The cost of new manufacturing technologies spearheaded a consolidation of presses into a smaller number of larger industrialized facilities (Sanchez Roman 2005, 157). In turn, this forced a scaling up of the company towns, allowing for these to operate as more autonomous urban enclaves in the landscape. The newly implemented rail network drastically improved the movement of goods and people, making it no longer essential for mills to be close to San Miguel de Tucuman—the provincial capital and main urban center in the region. New towns could be easily distributed throughout the province and far away from the city center, as long as they were connected to the main rail line or one of its multiple branches. The Santa Ana model of factory, town, *colonia*, and agricultural plot became the dominant model through which the Argentine state along with landowners set the framework for agro-industrial development in the region. By the turn of the century, a province of approximately twenty thousand square kilometers had been transformed into a sugarcane garden with approximately sixty thousand hectares planted and thirty-two new sugar mill towns implemented (Juarez-Dappe 2010, 42–43).

While the Argentine sugar boom was short-lived, the resilient urban framework put in place by the sugar mill town has adapted and evolved and continues to be an important element in this mostly agricultural landscape. The arrival of the sugar mosaic virus in 1916 (Juarez-Dappe 2010, 5) put an end to Tucuman's sugar rush. The destructive plague set the stage for a major agrarian reform in the region—one that focused on moving away from the sugar monocrop and finding other products that could appeal to a national and international market. Throughout this process, many of the original sugar mill towns had already established their own local economies and by now had incorporated into actual towns by buying out the original landowners. Such is the case of Santa Ana, where today a vibrant urban community exists over the ruins of the original canchon and chimney stacks.

The Town of Maria Elena and Nitrate Extraction
in the Atacama Desert (Chile)

Export-Led Economies, 1910–30

In the desert of present-day northern Chile, the combination of extreme aridity with mild topography yielded a massive concentration of sodium nitrate, which in raw form is better known as *caliche*. Nitrate, an essential product used in fertilizers, in gunpowder, and in entertainment through its use in magic tricks, was one of Chile's staple exports at the turn of the twentieth century until it was replaced by a synthetic version in the 1940s. While short-lived, Chile's nitrate boom and the implementation of hundreds of *oficinas salitreras*—also known as nitrate extraction towns—set off an extraction and urbanization process of an unprecedented scope and scale throughout the Chilean desert, reshuffling economic, migratory, and urban patterns nationwide.

The quaint town of Maria Elena, the grand dame of oficinas salitreras, exemplifies the role of the new town in the context of a much larger and ambitious territorial project spearheaded by nitrate extraction (Figure 15.2). Planned for seventy-five hundred workers, the town was founded in 1926 by the Guggenheim brothers (the company later became the Anglo-Chilean Nitrate Company), implementing a design by New York City–based architect Harry Beardslee Brainerd (1887–1977) working in collaboration with engineer Hjalmar Ejnar Skougor (1884–1932) (Morisset 2011, 15). Brainerd and Skougor brought to the Atacama Desert the ideals of the "city beautiful" movement, paired with a desire to improve the quality of life in the remote mining town. While by no means the first oficina salitrera, Maria Elena was by far the largest and most ambitious of all the oficinas built in Chile. It was conceived as a hexagonal superblock with two diagonal streets that intersected at the center, defining its main square. The plaza, diagonals, and orthogonal streets served as the main armature of the town, subdividing it into smaller districts. The central square contained most common collective services including a school, a supermarket, the worker's union, a theater, a museum, and a library. These facilities went well beyond basic subsistence, offering goods and services that would not be available in other nearby cities and making Maria Elena a desirable destination in terms of both labor and urban life. Offering a comfortable lifestyle was a crucial objective of the town, because the Guggenheims believed this was the only way to attract skilled laborers and their families to such a remote location.

Maria Elena stands as a synecdoche of a much more expansive resource extraction network that through the first half of the twentieth century facilitated the implementation of an experimental urban model in the barren grounds of the Ata-

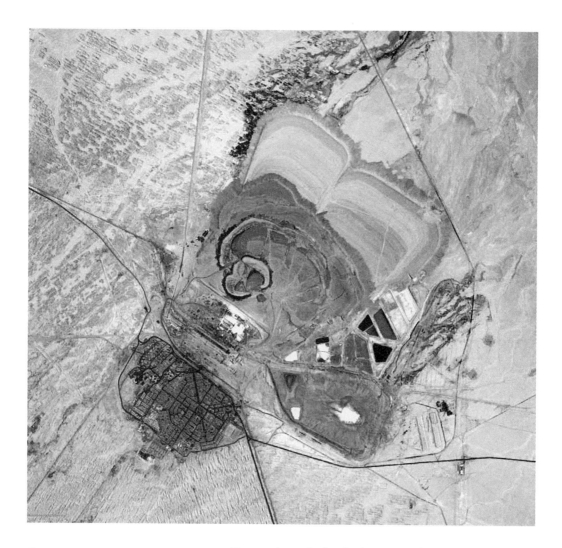

Figure 15.2. Aerial photograph of the nitrate extraction town of Maria Elena. Courtesy of Google Earth.

cama Desert through the deployment of hundreds of oficinas salitreras across the cantons of northern Chile. A constellation of new towns focused on bringing urban life to a geography that for centuries had been deemed uninhabitable.

Previous literature about these nitrate walled cities—all sharing an organizational and programmatic framework similar to Maria Elena—has highlighted the resemblance of the salitreras to the Renaissance military cities of the sixteenth and seventeenth centuries such as Scamozzi's Palmanova and Vauban's Neuf Brisach. Other references are the social utopias of the nineteenth century, such as Robert Owen's New Harmony (Garcés Feliu 1989, 3). The systematic repetition of a seemingly self-sufficient urban unit easily lends itself to this analogy. Yet the gradual translation of these ideas across the Atlantic Ocean and their implementation within a capitalist economic model resulted in a much less autonomous and less insular urban system than the one proposed by the references. While both the referenced cities and the nitrate towns relied heavily on single, large-scale pieces of real estate and were implemented in one piece, the oficinas were primarily organized and financed as private entities with a single purpose, establishing no distinction between public and private realms. The architecture of the salitreras was not about defense or about providing a new spatial model for a more just society but rather served as a device to improve productivity and profit in relation to a single resource.

While innovative, the spatial organization of the oficinas salitreras primarily followed the most prominent company town models at the time. It is in their aggregation and their larger territorial organization that their greatest urban contribution lies. Specifically, they were instrumental as midpoints between port cities along the coast and agricultural villages along the Andes mountain range, setting up a regional framework for the urbanization of the Atacama Desert. The Atacama is an arid band of desert that had traditionally divided this scarcely populated region of northern Chile. This rift was quickly erased through the systematic deployment of more than seventy oficinas salitreras in the years between 1890 and 1920. Despite the fact that the oficinas were conceived as autonomous ready-made cities complete with mining facilities, office space, and full-service residential quarters, the distribution of these towns created a middle landscape throughout the desert pampas that allowed for a new east-west regional network to unfold. Relying on rail infrastructure, this network connected four key urban elements—the oficina salitrera, the coastal city, the railroad hub town, and the Andean oasis town. The salitreras were the basic unit for nitrate extraction. Yet both the port city and the oasis town were also essential to the process of extraction and distribution. The port city guaranteed access to global markets while the oasis provided food and water to the railroad line and mining towns. This resulted in a constellation of desert communities, with varied purposes and ambitions, that relied on each other to survive in such an extreme environment.

With the proliferation of German synthetic nitrate shortly after the end of World War II, the demand for natural nitrate rapidly declined. Today all nitrate mining towns, except Maria Elena, have closed and become desert ghost towns. Maria Elena continues to produce natural nitrate at very low levels, and its dwellers are in conversation with the current owners to incorporate Maria Elena as an actual municipality. Only a few such towns have become world heritage sites and have been preserved as Chilean national treasures. Yet the coast-to-mountain regional framework set forth through the implementation of rail has survived. This infrastructure has been adopted by other industries, primarily copper extraction, which also relies on ports along the Pacific Ocean for global distribution.

The Town of Vila Piloto and Hydroelectric Energy (Brazil)

The Developmental State, 1950–70

Brazil throughout the first half of the twentieth century undertook intrepid efforts to claim, domesticate, and "make productive" its expansive interior territory. Crucial to this agenda was an expansive energy policy that could put in place the necessary infrastructure to provide a large amount of steady electricity to a nation that was rapidly industrializing. While the intent to transform Brazil's rivers into a productive machine can be traced back to the late nineteenth century, it was only during the presidency of Juscelino Kubitschek (1956–61) that government-sponsored, large-scale hydroelectric projects gained momentum. Kubitschek ran on a platform that targeted four strategic areas: energy, transportation, agriculture, and industry in relation to national integration (Steinberg 1985, 31). Given his campaign's promise, hydroelectric projects became an ideal vehicle to integrate the interior of the country with the coast. Despite the expense of the initial investment required for hydroelectric energy, the turn to large-scale dams as a source of electricity made sense in a nation that at the time believed itself to have limited resources in terms of oil. Furthermore, the larger organizational requirements of a hydroelectric network—dams, roads, towns, reservoirs, and so on—served as an underlay for a much larger and ambitious territorial restructuring that could link the resources of the interior with the urban economies along the coast.

While the national electrification plan sponsored by Kubitschek implemented large-scale dams throughout most of Brazil's interior, the Paraná-Uruguay basin on the western edge of the state of Sao Paulo became the site of one of the most expansive midcentury regional planning experiments in the Americas. The Comissão Interestadual da Bacia Paraná-Uruguay (CIBPU)—in collaboration with a group of experimental architects and engineers and sponsored by the Companhia Energética de São Paulo (CESP)—produced a collection of studies, plans, and projects that took advantage of the investment in hydroelectric infrastructure in order to set the stage for a comprehensive regional vision. These projects relied extensively on the concept of the new town as the basic element that could transform the Brazilian interior from passive hinterland into a productive backyard. The quaint temporary town of Vila Piloto became the first urban experiment in the region.

Described by the *Hartford Courant* in 1966 as "sitting like a giant's play thing in the middle of prairie lands covered with shoulder-high grass," Vila Piloto was the first and most ambitious new town built by CESP in the lower Paraná River basin (Erbsen 1966). A perfect circle inscribed in the landscape, the "Pilot City" consolidated many of the urban ideas that transformed this remote hinterland into a hy-

CELUSA

Figure 15.3. Aerial view of Vila Piloto (1962). Courtesy of the Acervo Fundaçao Energia e Saneamento.

droelectric playground. A temporary encampment designed to house approximately fourteen thousand construction workers and their families, Vila Piloto was the showcase piece of the Usina Hidroelétrica Jupia, one of the first and most ambitious hydroelectric complexes in the region. Constructed in 1961 with the objective of being disassembled in five to seven years, Vila Piloto became the first experimental project to provide housing for the massive migration of workers needed to build the dam. While the supply of housing for temporary workers in remote locations had traditionally been resolved through the systematic deployment of prefabricated barracks, at Vila Piloto, its authors, Ernest Mange and Araki Kato, saw an opportunity for a new urban model. It was a project that could strive to more than just "technical favelas," or shantytowns, built next to the construction site of the dam. Heavily influenced by the "neighborhood unit," Mange and Kato opted to construct a self-sufficient town organized around a gradient of residential typologies. The two authors argued in favor of a perfect circle on both technical and qualitative grounds. For one, they saw the concentric ring strategy as the most effective way to lay out infrastructure (electricity, potable water, sewerage). Also, this configuration allowed for a more calibrated overlap between vehicular and pedestrian traffic. Radial streets would accommodate vehicles while the concentric rings would be mostly for pedestrians. Mange and Kato also argued that the circle provided a clear town center where activities such as administration, commerce, and recreation could be placed, giving the town a true "sense of belonging." The circle was organized in seven sectors that contained all the basic infrastructure for an instant city. Sector 1 predominantly contained housing for bachelors, sectors 2 and 7 were left open for sports and recreational activities, and sectors 3 to 6 aggregated most of the housing. Each sector also included a neighborhood center that contained an elementary school. Following the construction methods of typical Brazilian *casinhas*, or cottages, the buildings were built with standardized timber framing and had high-pitched roofs with long overhangs to mitigate the heat. Despite its temporary nature, Vila Piloto became an example of how urbanity and quality of life could be constructed in Brazil's new hydroelectric frontier.

Disassembly was a critical component of Vila Piloto. From the start, the residential units were conceived with the objective of being dismantled and reassembled in future CESP projects. Once the Jupia Dam opened in 1968, Vila Piloto was gradually disassembled, slowly eroding the strong circular figure. Yet the town of Vila Piloto could never be shut down. By the time the dam opened, Vila Piloto had a life of its own, and the basic infrastructure defined by the plan, primarily roads and parcels, guided a gradual infilling process, first informally, and then as an annex to the neighboring city of Três Lagoas. Throughout the 1970s and 1980s, local dwellers built their homes within the circle guided by the traces of the Vila Piloto plan. Today, the circle is once again fully built, and the town has taken full advantage of the infrastructure Vila Piloto left behind.

Architects and planners involved in Vila Piloto's design and implementation used this experience to advance their ideas regarding the role of the new town in the context of an ever-expanding hydroelectric network, and their ideas evolved as they planned additional cities for CESP. An important lesson was the idea that once a town was implemented, it developed its own life, making it very difficult, if not impossible, to shut it down completely. For Ilha Solteira, a second town built by CESP in 1973, the model shifted from a provisional town into a permanent-growth pole city model (Perroux 1970, 94). Ihla Solteira was meant to house construction workers for the hydroelectric plant of the same name. From the start, the city was planned with the idea that over time it would become its own administrative unit. Through the introduction of industry, commercial services, and agricultural support programs the city was to be the epicenter and engine of a new and diversified regional economy. Today, it is an autonomous municipality and has further expanded its economic base into education and service economies. Porto Primavera, the third city built by CESP, in the early 1980s, followed a similar model. Yet in the case of Primavera, private citizens not affiliated with the construction of the dam could purchase property from the start. The ability of independent entities to purchase land within the state-sponsored town was a critical component of its success.

From the implementation of Vila Piloto until today, CESP has been responsible for introducing a constellation of more than thirty dams, along with reservoirs and towns that have set the stage for urban development in the region. While the new town was only one of the many different scales that CESP's planning strategies engaged, it was planners' unassailable belief in the importance of a foundational structure for urban life—a new town—that guaranteed their continued regional planning success from the early 1960s until today. While many of these towns are no longer associated with CESP, their foundational principles continue to organize the urban life they facilitate.

From Resource Extraction Town to Extraction Hotel

Throughout the late twentieth century, the idea of a new town as an integral part of extractive industries gradually eroded. Large corporations—generally foreign companies that had bought from national governments the rights to extract resources—were no longer interested in constructing worker towns or pairing a larger social project to their extractive activities. A case in point was Standard Oil in Venezuela. Owned by the Rockefellers, the company had built multiple worker camps and oil towns throughout the 1940s and 1950s around Lake Maracaibo, South America's oil Eden. Towns such as La Salina and Judibana were pioneers in bringing American lifestyle and culture to remote yet oil-filled regions of Venezuela.[2] By the 1970s, Standard Oil had no interest in investing in towns to house their workers. For one, corporate management argued that company-owned towns created an unhealthy relationship between employer and employee, where professional disputes affected all aspects of the worker's life, and, vice versa, domestic quarrels would also have a direct effect on an employee's performance. Furthermore, the Rockefellers also contested that given the price they were paying for extraction rights, it should be the government's responsibility to provide housing and basic services to employees. Standard Oil's sentiments in Venezuela became mainstream throughout South America. The general attitude of corporations was to involve themselves in housing families of high-ranking executives in capital cities such as Caracas or Quito, relying on government-sponsored programs to house workers and their families on-site. As these international extraction corporations changed their mindsets, the notion of a full-service city that would bring urban models to remote destinations in South America came to an end.

Perhaps the only exception to the resource extraction town's decline is the copper industry in Chile, which until today continues to reinvent the worker town typology to continue providing workers with good-quality facilities in extremely barren geographies of the Atacama Desert. Copper, another mineral found in abundance throughout northern Chile, has also left a significant imprint of resource extraction towns along the northern portion of this slim but long South American nation. Capitalizing first on the port cities and rail infrastructure set up by the nitrate industry, and later linked by newly implemented highways, new towns deployed by the copper industry have a legacy that traces an important evolutionary arc of the resource extraction town from the early 1900s until today. Many of the copper extraction towns up until the 1960s responded to the need of creating full-fledged desert cities, similar to Maria Elena.

Throughout the last forty years the industry has completely reinvented its settlement model by shifting to a mining hotel model with full-service dormitories that accommodate workers only on a temporary basis, while their families reside in more established cities along the Pacific coast. Projects such as San Lorenzo, Pabellón del Inca, and Los Pelambres all reformulated the notion of the mining city into high-quality temporary encampments, creating temporary utopias in the middle of the desert, each accommodating approximately two thousand dwellers (Garcés Feliu 2010). While the copper industry has dismissed the idea of a new full-fledged town, the mining hotel model does present a compelling alternative to housing employees. Of high design and construction quality, these hotels offer extremely comfortable accommodations with full amenities to its residents—swimming pool, restaurant, cinema—showing a strong commitment to staff that many other extraction industries have abandoned.

New Towns in the Context of IIRSA

As represented by Santa Ana, Maria Elena, and Vila Piloto, the concept of the new town in the South American hinterland throughout the late nineteenth and twentieth centuries has an expansive history. The motivation for the implementation of new towns varies drastically—they vary from agricultural settlements to mining camps, and from private enclaves to government-sponsored cities. Yet what remains constant in each of these new town stories is their instrumentality in organizing space at multiple scales, from plaza to region. As political agendas wane and natural resources expire, the spatial organization and formal structure of these towns remain operative, evolving and adapting to new uses and programs, and helping format in space new economies and social mores. The careful design and implementation of the new town model has become one of the longest-lasting capital investments in the South American hinterland.

Today, as South America embarks on its most aggressive regional integration plan ever proposed for the continent, an updated conceptualization of the new town is more relevant than ever. Through the vehicle of IIRSA (the Initiative for the Integration of Regional Infrastructure in South America)—a comprehensive energy, transportation, and communication network, the most aggressive transcontinental project ever planned for South America[3]—a revised version of the resource extraction town could once again have agency in regional integration. The IIRSA plan, set forth by Brazil and endorsed by the eleven other South American nations, proposes the gradual deployment of ten east-west corridors that would link the burgeoning economy of Brazil with multiple points across the Pacific to shorten trading times with Asia. IIRSA has been cast predominantly under the positive light of economic development, yet its many side effects provoke powerful caveats to the project, specifically the effects that such an expansive collection of highways, ports, and airports will have on the urbanization of the South American interior. This is particularly problematic in the heart of the Amazon, where IIRSA is providing access to remote areas that until now were environmentally protected simply because they were disconnected from the national highway grid.

The emergence of new regional nodes is drastically changing the physical and economic character of once small and mostly forgotten regional cities and towns. Iquitos, deep in the Peruvian Amazon, is a case in point, where upgrades on the Amazon's navigability are bringing significant investment to the city since it was designated an important regional hub of the Manta–Manaus corridor. It is in contexts such as Iquitos that a revised new town model could be instrumental to the IIRSA agenda. Evolving beyond the paternalistic model of the agricultural and resource extraction towns of Argentina and Chile, and the developmental approach of Brazil's Vila Piloto, the new town model for twenty-first-century South America can be one that strengthens municipalities in response to major national and transnational investment in mobility corridors. In this context, the new town model is about reinventing existing cities rather than creating cities from scratch. The key question regarding IIRSA is how governments at municipal and local levels can capitalize on investment that as of now only serves global trade. In doing so, cities that directly or tangentially touch the IIRSA plan can take advantage of an investment source that otherwise will only serve myopic resource extraction objectives and leave no cultural, environmental, or social investment for the region.

Notes

1. For a more expansive overview of resource extraction and urbanism in South America, see Correa (2016).

2. For additional information on Standard Oil and its company towns in Venezuela, see Correa (2016, 65–88).

3. For additional information, see the IIRSA website, www.iirsa.org.

16

New Towns in Africa

Rachel Keeton and Michelle Provoost

Many people who have never set foot in Africa think of it as a verdant land, dotted with roaming herds of wildlife and villages where children run barefoot. This romantic but misleading image of a rural arcadia persists despite the continent's incredible diversity of people and landscapes, and its growing urban centers (Pieterse 2015, 10). Africa is currently urbanizing faster than anywhere else on the planet, and city-scale changes are happening in concert with that growth. Although precise data is notoriously hard to come by, the United Nations estimates that the number of Africans living in cities will grow from 471 million in 2015 to 1.33 *billion* by 2050 (United Nations 2014). The speed at which these changes are now occurring exacerbates existing challenges: uncontrolled growth leads to land mismanagement, a depletion of natural resources, and the spread of informal settlements and related social issues such as crime, poor sanitation, and lack of access to services.

The same diversity that characterizes the inhabitants of this giant land mass can be seen in varying approaches to city building (Heine 2000). Among the different regions in Africa, geographically divided as northern, eastern, western, central, and southern Africa, urbanization is taking place at different rates and in different ways. Except for central Africa, all the other regions have seen extensive urbanization over the last two decades, particularly in coastal areas.[1]

While this urban growth takes various forms (mostly uncontrolled), in countries with higher GDP rates it often includes the construction of new towns. This correlation is significant because it suggests that contemporary African new towns, unlike postwar European new towns, are not built to accommodate the ever-increasing population overflow, but rather for rising middle-class markets and economic incentives.

Africa will be the main stage for urbanization in the twenty-first century, but the nature of that urban growth has yet to be determined. If things go on as they have been going, informal settlements will continue to proliferate as most people continue to build in the only way available to them. There is therefore a clear and urgent need for innovative urban, design, financial, and governance models tailored to the needs of African countries as they enter this phase of rapid urbanization. This is formulated in a call to order by Edgar Pieterse, director of the African Center for Cities, who states: "As a continent that will be disproportionately shaped by the way in which society thinks about cities, Africa must assume an increasingly central position in the urban imaginary of theorists and practitioners" (Parnell and Pieterse 2014, 15). This chapter attempts to answer the question: Do the new towns currently under construction across the continent offer these inventive solutions? If not, what is needed?

History and Present

African new towns are not a new concept. They are heirs to master-planning legacies that were widely imposed across Africa under colonial administrations, as well as spatial-planning techniques that informed settlements prior to European involvement. Planning, in fact, was part of African urban development long before colonial powers began importing European models.

Ideas differed inherently from one colonizing power to the next and were reconciled with the reactions of native people—with major differences between them. Planning approaches and implementation changed considerably over time in individual places, but segregation between European, African, and Asian residents was a constant factor in urban planning. As the garden city model gained popularity in Europe during the early twentieth century, it became the preferred model for African colonies. As preferences changed in Europe, that shift was also reflected in African colonies: following the Second World War, it was the modern movement and Congrès Internationaux d'Architecture Moderne (CIAM) discourses that became most influential on urban planning practice (Silva 2015a).

In the early years of independence, new towns were seen by national governments as a way of affirming national identities. Political ideology drove the construction of new capitals such as Dodoma, Tanzania; and Abuja, Nigeria. Ideas about equal representation and national unity were especially important in young countries where political allegiances roughly correlated to tribal identity. New economic policies led to the creation of new towns such as Tema, Ghana, an industrial port city, and Julius Nyerere's African Socialist Ujamaa villages, Tanzania. New socio-spatial policies in the postcolonial period contributed to the construction of both South African townships and the Egyptian new towns that followed the unpopularity of Anwar Sadat's *infitah* ("Open Door") economic policies.[2]

Despite this legacy of groundbreaking ideas about urbanism and its power to bring together or keep apart, contemporary African new towns are shockingly mundane. Privately developed new towns, tech cities, economic cities, and gated communities accommodate the wealthy, and little, if any, public expenditure is made to relieve the housing burden on the urban poor. Some countries, including Kenya, Rwanda, and Nigeria, have shown interest in building new towns to encourage international investment and to support IT development. Examples of these, such as Konza Techno City and Eco-Atlantic, propose high-tech new cities as a means of leapfrogging toward the digital infrastructures now supported in many Asian cities.[3] Another type of development is large-scale government-driven social housing development, such as Morocco's state-led project to resettle *bidonville* (slum) residents in fourteen new satellite cities, and Ethiopia's ambitious Integrated Housing Development Program (IHDP), which has completed more than two hundred thousand new condominium units in large-scale communities around Addis Ababa. These projects are publicly funded interventions in places that sorely need low-income housing options, but including them in a compilation of "new towns'" stretches the definition a bit too far. In practice, this development type is also notorious for missing its target. Low-income residents who are unable to pay their mortgages are forced to rent out the apartments to higher earners and return to informal settlements. This type of housing is also often far from jobs and existing social networks, forcing residents to pay more for transportation and extended child care because of long commutes. There may also be stricter regulations on informal entrepreneurial work, including outlawing kiosks, street hawking, or unregulated work.

In Africa, there is a real and rising middle class, although the substance of this group varies from country to country and includes a much smaller percentage of the population than many news outlets would have us believe. As Melber points out, the optimism of the African "middle class" rhetoric sometimes gets in the way of a real discussion of development challenges and increasing inequality (Melber 2016). It also perpetuates a false image of western middle-class lifestyles (broadly characterized by car and home ownership, and health and retirement security) in an African context.

The myth of the African middle class does, however, have its roots in reality. While most Africans are either very rich or very poor, a small group of Africans have enough spending power to support the new wave of air-conditioned shopping malls and supermarkets. However, the African middle class is something very different from its European or North American counterpart and should not lead to the same imagery (Figure 16.1). Economists at the World Bank, OECD Development Centre, African Development Bank, and Center for Global Development define the African middle class as earning or spending between $2 and $10 per day. That definition includes a huge number of Africans and thus supports the narrative

Figure 16.1. Kilamba café culture. Courtesy of Rachel Keeton.

of a continent with growing economic prowess. However, the group that can actually afford to buy real estate in the new developments is generally estimated to be only 6 percent of the continent's population. These are the clients snapping up homes in new towns such as Appolonia City (Ghana), Kilamba (Angola), and Sheikh Zayed City (Egypt) (*Economist* 2016).

New towns such as these are good examples of the mismatch between the reality of the housing market and developers' projects. Developed by Rendeavour, Appolonia is a planned new town that offers "a serene and well-planned space dedicated to your lifestyle" (Appolonia City 2016). Prices start at US$75,000, and mortgage rates in Ghana run around 24 percent. In 2014, the average gross annual salary in Ghana was US$10,500. This means that Rendeavour will have a hard time reaching its self-imposed ambitious goal of making Appolonia "meet the pockets of a larger number of Ghanaians" (Gadugah 2015).

Sheikh Zayed was originally conceived as a full-scale, mixed-income city for five hundred thousand residents, but because of increased sales by the state-run New Urban Communities Authority (NUCA) to private developers, this area has evolved to become little more than a collection of "compounds" (gated communities with varied housing stock) serviced by a few shopping plazas. Because of the disconnect with the actual housing demand, the new town had a vacancy rate of 69 percent in 2006 (D. Sims 2014, 150).

When national governments are involved in new town construction, those projects are often conceived as economic kick-starts to provide a framework for further development and attract foreign direct investment. This is the case with Kenya's Konza Techno City development (2016), "a sustainable, world-class technology hub and a major economic driver for the nation," as well as Nigeria's Eko-Atlantic development (2016)—"the new economic capital of Africa"—as these cities are characterized by their respective developers.[4]

New town development on greenfield sites is attractive because it avoids the messy business of urban regeneration and piecemeal planning. With heavily congested roads and a widespread lack of basic planning tools such as land ownership information or utility infrastructure maps, upgrading or densifying existing urban fabric can be difficult. Many older African cities simply do not have detailed records of how those cities function. What lies below the ground is often an even greater mystery. As both spending power and urban populations increase, however, the market for upscale housing, more comfort, and better safety grows accordingly. As elsewhere in the world, anyone able to afford it wants a safe place to raise children, surrounded by their peers. In such situations, politicians and planners find fertile ground for new town development. Starting fresh has obvious appeal: the satisfaction of good organization, reliable services, quality housing, safety, and the possibility of foregoing the chaotic existing city for a clean, controlled urban environment.

One of the dangers in this approach is that enclave developments such as these new towns exacerbate spatial segregation. New towns are seen as islands with high-quality services (their strongest selling points), while many existing African cities continue to suffer from unreliable electricity provision, limited access to clean water, and other ineffectual municipal services (trash collection, security, etc.). The *real* African middle class cannot afford to live in these new towns. Because of limited access to mortgages and other home-financing models, only a very small percentage can actually access real estate in these new towns.

There are other reasons why this form of development is problematic in the African context. New town development redirects resources that could be used instead to upgrade or densify existing urban areas. When enough resources are routed out of the existing cities, these places will become even more congested and stagnate. Next to that, many new towns currently do nothing to acknowledge specific ecological realities. While many African countries have a wealth of natural beauty and resources, most new town designs simply ignore this bounty and tend to avoid dealing with questions related to climate change issues (flooding, desertification), water insecurity, or environmental degradation. The following two case studies—Kilamba, Angola; and Sheikh Zayed, Egypt—further illustrate these challenges. Both new towns were conceived in the neoliberal era as state-initiated projects built by private developers.

Kilamba, Angola

Just a few years ago, Kilamba was reported to be a failed city, a ghost town, a trick played by the Chinese on poor Angola.[5] But now, if people on the street in Luanda are approached and asked about their impressions of Kilamba, eyes begin to gleam, and voices turn wistful. In four short years, Kilamba has become the national symbol of an aspirational lifestyle (Figures 16.2, 16.3, and 16.4). How did this happen? How did a "ghost town" become what most Angolans refer to as "the most popular place in an entire country"?[6] The answer begins with the peace treaty in 2002, ending a period of twenty-seven years during which a tripartite civil war ravaged the country. The war created a staggering housing deficit of two million units,[7] caused by a complete lack of real estate construction and a huge rural-to-urban migration, the result of people fleeing the rural areas that were vulnerable to ranging militias. During the war (1975–2002), the population of Luanda grew tenfold from four hundred thousand to more than four million (Luanda Urban Poverty Programme 2010). An estimated 70 percent of them now live in *musseques*—informal settlements (Luanda Urban Poverty Programme 2010).

In the early days of peace, the Chinese government offered help in reconstructing the war-torn country, and Angola welcomed new credit lines backed by oil sales to China. After close consultation with the Angolan president José Eduardo Dos Santos, the Chinese government sent CITIC (a state-owned developer) to Angola to begin feasibility plans for a new city: Cidade do Kilamba, a flagship project presented to the public in 2008 as a key part of President Dos

Figure 16.2. Street view of Kilamba high-rise, Angola. Courtesy of Rachel Keeton.

Figure 16.3. Informal settlement, Kilamba, Angola. Courtesy of Rachel Keeton.

Santos's electoral promise to combat the housing crisis with one million new homes over the next four years (Almeida 2009).

CITIC completed the construction of Phase 1 (710 towers with twenty thousand apartments) three years later. It was designed by a team of Chinese architects employed by CITIC, and its Chinese origins are immediately recognizable. Located thirty kilometers from the center of Luanda, Kilamba occupies a rectangular footprint, orthogonally divided by roads in building sites, which showcase a repetition of similar apartment blocks of four to ten stories, each with characteristically Chinese saddle roofs and different colors to identify different neighborhoods.

Midway through construction, Chinese president Xi Jinping made an official trip to Angola in 2010 to visit Kilamba and publicly reinforce Angola's value to China. Despite talk of a replicable urban model in its early days, Kilamba is now considered a one-off: a presidential prestige project. To counter this, President Dos Santos ordered in 2013 that the Kilamba apartments be made more affordable and state-backed mortgages to be made available to all qualifying Angolans. The price of the smallest apartment immediately dropped by almost half: from US$125,000 to US$70,000. Still, Kilamba is far out of reach for the vast majority of Angolans. Residents in Kilamba have clean water, reliable electricity, new infrastructure, and a responsive—if underfunded—urban management team. Wherever else one might

Figure 16.4. A villa in Sheikh Zayed New City, Egypt. Courtesy of Rachel Keeton.

choose to live in the entire country, power outages, traffic jams, and poorly treated water are the norm. Kilamba is unique. When asked about the negative early international press the new town received, Mayor Israel Marques shrugs: "BBC, CNN, they all came during the time after the opening when we were trying to figure out how to sell the apartments to Angolans without access to bank mortgages. They never came back."[8]

That was four years ago. By 2016, the city had one hundred thousand residents and was 97 percent occupied. There is a waiting list for apartments that runs into the thousands, according to Mayor Marques.[9] With its large, attractively designed apartments, it appeals to a group of Angolans that is upwardly mobile but without many housing options. Like the postwar new towns in Europe that were popular because they offered an attractive housing alternative, Kilamba is popular in a country where the majority of citizens live in corrugated sheds. One questions, however, whether Kilamba will face the same reversal of fortune that has seen postwar housing become Europe's most maligned housing solution after other more desirable housing options became available.

A top-down, centralized governance model still characterizes most African nations. This often means that any tax revenue collected at the city level is routed to the national coffers before a significantly lower operating budget is approved and made available to city authorities. This financing model applies to many new towns, including Kilamba. As Mayor Marques explains: "For two years, no one collected the rent from the shops or from the residents. We were here the whole time. We could have collected that and used a percentage to reinvest in the management of the city. But each party wants the best piece of the cake. In fact, the municipality is the one who sees the problems and should be able to deal with those problems with our own resources. People don't understand that."[10]

Because its identity is based on a "middle-class lifestyle," the informal economy is closely regulated within Kilamba. Activities that are the norm outside of this development are not allowed. Mayor Marques recalled the story of one family reported by their neighbors for using their apartment as a place of business: "At the beginning, we found one family selling homemade ice creams from their apartment. And we said, come on, you cannot do that. We are going to close this. But then we saw the [economic] reality of the family, and we thought, it's not possible, so we let them continue doing that, but we helped them to make a deal with the canteens in the schools, to sell the ice creams there instead."[11]

In an effort to create a mixed-income development, approximately 25 percent of all apartments (five thousand) were given to civil servants, many of whom could not otherwise afford to call Kilamba home. For those with lower incomes, a district at the southeast corner of the new town was developed with the name KK5000. This so-called social housing district was designed with lower-quality materials and no services, amenities, or public space, and again no facilities for informal economic activities. In fact, this area offers just housing. Residents are required to travel farther to access schools, shops, or employment. "You go there, you will be shocked," says Mayor Marques. "The quality of design is so bad. . . . KK5000 looks like a military camp."[12]

While KK5000 is the lowest-income area officially part of Kilamba, just across the road defining the periphery of the rectangular new town, a sprawling *musseque* has formed. The symbiosis between the two interdependent opposites—one characterized by a hyperfunctional grid, the other by the intuitive spatial planning of the urban poor—should come as no surprise. Residents of Kilamba depend on the informal settlement for service providers such as mechanics, cleaning personnel, and handymen, as well as foodstuffs and products cheaper than those sold in the nearby supermarket. The informal settlement's residents likewise depend on Kilamba for employment, schools, and certain services, such as health clinics. The relationship is like the one that exists between the two income groups in other Angolan cities but is made strikingly visible by the sharp spatial divide between the two areas.

The main problem with social housing in Angola is that access to it has yet to be regulated and defined by national legislation. In 2010, President Dos Santos raised the maximum price for social housing from US$50,000 to US$60,000 at the national housing commission meeting (Croese 2012, 138–40). The lack of an accessible mortgage system, another critical shortcoming, has had widespread ramifications on the housing market. A mortgage loan from a private bank currently comes with an interest rate of 27 percent, and at the personal discretion of a loan officer.[13]

Since its completion, African heads of state from Liberia, Mozambique, East Timor, and Namibia have all visited the project, giving their collective stamp of approval to a development model that is entirely new on this continent. While the oil-for-a-new-town exchange that brought Kilamba into being may not be replicable, the idea of outsourcing the entire process of city making has gained popularity in recent years. One size fits all: is that the urban imaginary that will guarantee vibrant African cities in the coming years?

Sheikh Zayed City, Egypt

Sheikh Zayed is one of two Egyptian new towns situated in the desert west of Cairo. Thirty kilometers west of downtown, it was established by presidential decree in 1995 and completed around 2002 (although new compounds continue to be added). It was initiated by the governmental New Urban Communities Authority (NUCA) and named after its main investor, Sheikh Zayed bin Sultan al Nahyan of Abu Dhabi. While the official population target for the new town is now 675,000, there are currently only 233,000 residents living in close to sixty compounds (Egypt New Urban Communities Authority n.d.). The curvilinear form of the urban plan, based on the prototypical American suburb with individual plots for villas, is peppered with private, gated compounds where vigilant guards check identity cards before allowing access. Curving streets calm traffic, and private gardens peek invitingly over concrete walls. The public realm in Sheikh Zayed is limited to the main roads; at the entrances to plazas, guards turn away groups of street children, allowing access only to those who look like they "belong" and thus creating semiprivate spaces for commerce, restaurants, and international chain stores.

Sheikh Zayed came into being at a time when neoliberal ideology was just beginning to permeate Egyptian politics. In the older Egyptian new towns, the state provided subsidized housing to the working and lower-middle classes. In the early 1990s, as David Sims writes, "a much more 'state capitalist' mode of development was applied. Large private real estate developers became the main agents of progress, enhanced by an extremely friendly relationship with NUCA" (D. Sims 2014, 288). Although it was originally planned to be a mixed-income city, Sheikh Zayed City quickly transformed as NUCA discovered the profit-making potential of land sales to private developers. As a result, what was intended to be a real reflection of Egyptian society has instead become synonymous with an aspirational life-style of brand consciousness.

NUCA originally built 9,938 public housing units in Sheikh Zayed, of which about half were intended for high-, medium- and low-income groups and half classified as "youth" or starter housing.[14] Many of those apartments have since been privately upgraded and now attract mostly upper-middle-class residents. The private sector has built another fifty-eight thousand units (nearly all within the confines of gated communities) and continues to build more (Egypt New Urban Communities Authority n.d.).

In public discourse, the Egyptian new towns, and Sheikh Zayed in particular, are continuously presented as diametrically opposed to Cairo. Cairo is dirty, overcrowded, unsafe, polluted; Sheikh Zayed is clean, quiet, well organized, and safe. The comparison is repeated to the point that it has become gospel for most Sheikh Zayed's residents. They appreciate their separation from low-income groups; an inclusive society is not part of the cultural consensus. It is no coincidence, then, that NUCA has managed its new towns with much stricter enforcement of regulations than Cairo or other Egyptian cities.[15] Informal economic activities are outlawed in Sheikh Zayed; the ubiquitous *tuktuks* (three-wheeled mini-taxis), street vendors, and kiosks are nowhere to be seen. In contrast to the utter whirlwind of downtown Cairo, the lack of these urban actors gives the new town a somewhat sterile aspect that its inhabitants seemingly love. As in a U.S. suburb, no one walks in Sheikh Zayed as distances are far and walking would imply that one cannot afford a car.

Nazih Hallouda, a resident of the "Zayed 2000" compound, recalls his parents' reasons for moving there: "They liked that it was a quiet place, outside of the city. We could have a bigger house there, so that was better for us. We already knew that our lives would still be in Cairo; all our activities would be in Cairo. Even after twelve years, there is no interaction with our neighbors; there's no social activity inside the gated community."[16]

The compounds vary in terms of their relative luxuriousness, but all of them are beyond the reach of the average Egyptian earning US$92 per week (*Daily News Egypt* 2015). The older compound of Al Rabwa offers the most complete amenities, including a school, shopping mall, mosque, golf course and club, medical services, and twenty-four-hour security. There is a choice from 970 villas, designed according to twelve different plans, ranging in size from 220 to 637 square meters. The entire compound is encircled by a ten-meter-wide horse track (Al-Rabwa 2006). All this goes to show that new towns such as Sheikh Zayed are actually exacerbating segregation by creating exclusive, high-security communities that turn their backs on the reality of Egyptian demographics. Even "youth housing" or other forms of social housing are unavailable to the very poor. Because of Sheikh Zayed's strictly enforced building regulations, the very poor, in turn, are forced to remain in rural communities or in Cairo's labyrinthine *ashwa'yat*, where the basic amenities of water, electricity, safety, and public services are scarce. Working as maintenance workers, cleaners, or taxi drivers, they commute to their service jobs in Sheikh Zayed.

As in Angola, the Egyptian real estate market is largely a cash market. Although mortgages have been available since 2001, the mortgage system is inefficient, and there is cultural resistance to long-term loans. Interest rates (currently around 14.5 percent) are seen as doubling the total cost of the investment over time. As a result, only 37 percent of the Egyptian population is able to buy a house (Housing Finance Information Network 2016).

Conclusion

History has taught us that new towns attract not only those who can afford their relative luxuries, but also those who cannot: the poor who follow new developments looking for opportunities to improve their quality of life. This is the case with Tema, Ghana, and its neighboring shantytown Ashaiman; Konza Tech City, Kenya, and the adjacent villages that mushroomed with informal housing after the project was announced; Kilamba and its bordering *musseque*; and nearly every other new town around the continent. The reality of this twin phenomena of informal settlements and planned new towns gives us an opportunity to reflect on the current approach to city making in Africa. As African countries become increasingly unequal, and increasingly urbanized, informal settlements will continue to grow if governments fail to meet the demand for affordable housing. Self-construction will continue to be the only available housing option for families and communities without recourse to capital or loans. If urban development continues as it has, we might imagine an endless sea of informal settlements, dotted with islands of planned urbanization—accessible only to the privileged few.

How can we anticipate this development instead of being forced to repair the damage later? Especially in developing countries, the right to the planned city should be central to guarantee a basic quality of life: *planning is essential in creating livable cities*. Every new town should expect an influx of low-income residents, and respond to this certainty in ways that accommodate, incorporate, and respect the needs of the urban poor. This assertion puts forward questions for the design, finance, and governance of future African new towns. It also requires strong political statements as there is currently no consensus on the necessity of building inclusive cities and no financial system to support it. With continued focus on neoliberal policies, it is hard to imagine that developers will be asked to provide for groups when they cannot make a profit.

Given the scale of African urbanization, the question of what the next African city will be needs to be paramount in the imaginations of urban planners and designers. Presently, many new towns are copied from European, Chinese, Singaporean, or Korean models. This is not a valid approach for Africa. Models need to be customized to the reality of people's lives. Conscious inclusion and mixing income groups can be part of a recipe for sustainable growth, but cultural acceptance will inform the appropriate scale of that mixing. Flexible planning, combining commercial and informal housing development by leaving areas open to self-building, but providing basic services such as water, roads, sewage, and energy, may be one solution. By approaching planning as a tool to build social sustainability, one imagines different degrees of completion for different income groups within a single development. Combining cost-effective self-building with well-designed infrastructures can decrease spatial segregation and give the urban poor access to the same urban amenities available to the wealthy.

Home-financing models that work with people's cultural expectations and financial limitations are tools that are desperately needed in the movement to increase access to tenure security and improve land management. New financial constructions are also needed to support the construction of services and facilities for low-income groups that are not traditionally profitable.

Governance in these new towns must be undertaken at different levels (national, regional, municipal, and local), but not in ways that foster competition or create overlaps among governing bodies. National Urbanization Policies (NUPs) are needed to steer regional growth, but also to ensure that the urban poor are not abandoned. The European experience with requiring percentages of private development to be social housing may be a useful reference. Regulations for developers to include low-income housing options need to be written into law and enforced. Furthermore, decentralization is needed to empower local municipalities and new towns and overcome national-level complexities, corruption, and weak governing structures.

Chronic poverty must for now be accepted as a reality in many African cities. Until new towns are planned with consideration for the majority, they will be seen and experienced as enclaves that perpetuate feelings of otherness, apartness—*apartheid*. A mentality change is needed. The top-down, hierarchical approach that is typical in African urban planning must be adapted to include the vitality and dynamics of the informal sector. In Africa, it is difficult to imagine an inclusive and fair urban model without including the informal economy and self-built tradition. Governments—and the private sector—must begin accepting the existence of the informal sector before real change can be made. By combining master-planned new towns with semiplanned areas for the urban poor, African new towns can become more inclusive, resilient, and vibrant places to live.

Notes

1. Central Africa has largely missed the recent wave of new town construction that has spread along the continent's coastline. This may be attributed to continued ethnic violence and political unrest in Chad, Sudan, South Sudan, Democratic Republic of the Congo, and the Central African Republic.

2. Sadat's *infitah* policies opened socialist Egypt up to foreign investment and liberalized the economy. The resulting destabilizing effects on Egypt's poor majority were highly criticized. After the so-called bread riots of 1977, Sadat announced the first new town, Tenth of Ramadan, would be a planned city for working-class Egyptians offering industrial jobs and a better quality of life than that of crowded Cairo.

3. The first example of an African smart city is Ebène Cybercity, Mauritius. It has had numerous problems, mostly related to poor urban planning, but houses twenty-five thousand residents as well as the internet registry platform for the entire continent of Africa. High-speed internet and back-up generators ensure uninterrupted connectivity.

4. These quotes are from corporate websites https://www.konza.go.ke/vision-mission/ and https://www.ekoatlantic.com/.

5. In 2012, the BBC reported on "Angola's Chinese-built ghost town"; see Redvers (2012).

6. This impression is based on street interviews in Luanda, Angola, January 12–18, 2016.

7. Antonio Gameiro, national adviser on urbanism and housing policy for Angola, interview by R. Keeton, January 14, 2016.

8. Israel Marques, Mayor of Kilamba Ciudade, interview by R. Keeton, January 18, 2016.

9. Israel Marques, interview by R. Keeton, January 18, 2016.

10. Israel Marques, interview by R. Keeton January 18, 2016.

11. Israel Marques, interview by R. Keeton, January 18, 2016.

12. Israel Marques, interview by R. Keeton, January 18, 2016.

13. The state does offer a mortgage program for public servants at 3 percent interest. Antonio Gameiro, national adviser on urbanism and housing policy for Angola, interview by R. Keeton, January 14, 2016.

14. Youth housing refers to a specific form of social housing designated for Egyptians between twenty-one and fifty, and meeting certain income requirements (i.e., a family's income must be less than EGP 3,000 per month [US$337]). See Fahmi (2008, 281).

15. In Egypt, the quality of life in different *ashwa'yat* (informal settlements) ranges across a broad spectrum from the vulnerable position of families without access to services, schools, or a social safety net to stable, working-class families and professionals living in apartments that simply happen to have been built without permission. Both are considered *ashwa'yat*, or slums, and both are considered by the government to be undesirable.

16. Nazih Hallouda, resident of Sheikh Zayed, interview by R. Keeton, December 14, 2015.

Part III

Lessons on How to Build New Towns

17

Why Is It So Difficult to Develop Financially Successful New Towns?

New Town Finance: Problems and Solutions

Richard Peiser and Andrew Stokols

New towns represent the grandest visions of city planning, and many have been developed throughout the world. Many countries have had national policies to develop new towns led by the government. Other countries such as the United States have instead left new town development up to the private sector. Both approaches have largely been successful in providing housing for millions of families. However, they have been less successful as financially profitable enterprises. Indeed, the history of new towns is littered with bankruptcies.[1]

And while government-sponsored new towns do not go bankrupt, as investments in social enterprise, they have often failed to meet economic return objectives, even using lower social rates of return appropriate for government investment.

This chapter examines the economic and financial outcomes of eleven new towns in the United States, Great Britain, Netherlands, China, and South Korea. Because financial data is very limited, case studies combine financial information with interviews and published information. The experience of each country differs depending on the extent of government or private sponsorship, urban growth rates, and institutional factors including governance, public-private sophistication, property rights, social policy, and other factors.

The economics of new towns are important because new towns consume vast amounts of capital, and this can lead to a misallocation of resources when new towns are poorly planned and implemented. Significant infrastructure investment is underutilized if demand and construction lag behind expectations. Poor planning for parks and open space, boring and homogeneous buildings, too much or too little density, lack of diversity in age groups, absence of commercial centers for place making, and poor recreational opportunities may cause the new town either to grow slowly for lack of demand or to age quickly. At worst, new towns can become blighted neighborhoods with many social problems, deflecting investment from existing urban areas.

Short-term profitability for the developer does not necessarily ensure long-term success for the community as overly homogeneous communities have aged poorly and new towns with too much social housing have failed to attract a sustainable economic base. Furthermore, poor financial performance hurts government commitment to new towns, as occurred in the United States when the Nixon administration withdrew support for the Title VII new towns program, only three years after it was started (Peiser and Chang 1999, 1680).

We proceed with a literature review of scholarly articles on new town economics and finance, followed by case studies of several new towns in the United States and abroad where financial information was available (most dealt with elsewhere in the book as well). The article concludes with lessons from the experience of these new towns and recommendations concerning how future new towns can achieve financial success, or at least avoid the financial pitfalls that have plagued many new town programs. Comprehensive planning that accurately forecasts market demand, low land cost, generous open space, phased infrastructure investment, good governance, and marketing to a broad spectrum of residential and commercial buyers and firms is the key to success. However, the long development time horizons (often thirty years or more) and multiple economic cycles that most new towns outside of Asia must survive make financial success all the more difficult.

Literature Review

The literature on new town economics has been relatively limited. A primary reason for this is that detailed accounting of new town finances is generally not publicly available, especially in the United States, where most of the new town projects were undertaken as privately owned ventures. The best-documented evidence of the finances of new towns exists in the United Kingdom where the long-standing government-run new towns program accumulated a wealth of reports and findings about the success and failure of the program. Some early literature on new town financing emerged in the 1960s and 1970s, as postwar governments in Europe and America began looking toward the concept of new towns as a viable strategy for suburban development as well as affordable housing and job creation. However, early scholarly literature consisted mostly of descriptions of "best practices" or general recommendations for developing new towns, often written as perspectives from developers or planners involved in the projects themselves (Bailey 1973), or was on financial strategy in large real estate projects generally (Borut 1976; Wilburn and Gladstone 1972).

British New Towns

As the British New Town Program drew to a close, several reports and articles eval-uated the success along a series of different metrics. A 2006 report commissioned by the Department for Communities and Local Government (Oxford Brookes University 2006), came up with a series of lessons learned from the program. The report stated that while many of the early new towns closer to London, including Harlow and Bracknell, were profitable, "many later new towns suffered from high interest rates, inflexibility over borrowing rules, and changes in housing subsidy regimes. . . . Many later new towns also had to spend much more on infrastructure and at an earlier stage in their development, with less spending on rental housing which brought in valuable early direct returns in rents and subsidies" (Oxford Brookes University 2006, 29). The financial success of Bracknell was attributed pri-marily to its location in the vibrant western region of London.

The British new towns did not have an explicit hurdle rate of return, but they were expected to achieve a *social rate of return* appropriate for government investment. The social rate of return is below the market rate of return. Nevertheless, it should be greater than the government borrowing rate because the new town investments take the form of equity when the government buys the land and develops the new town. The original developers of Letchworth and Welwyn Garden City were private devel-opers who accepted a below-market rate of return called "5% philanthropy" (Town and Country Planning Association 2014b, 10). Government social rates of return have typically been in the 10 percent range, but many British new towns actually lost money. Only by including nonquantified estimates of social benefits such as better quality of life did the new towns overall achieve positive rates of return (Social Value UK 2016).

Milton Keynes has been the object of investigations that used standard real es-tate accounting procedures to get a more accurate picture of the true financial suc-cess of the project. These studies showed that the project was not a financial success owing to several factors: the high cost of land acquisition, limitation of the type of financing available, dominance of social housing for lower-moderate-income resi-dents that made it harder to attract higher-income buyers, and political pressures that forced a sell-off of assets when the market was at a low point (Peiser and Chang 1999). This investigation also showed that the costs of providing social services and infrastructure as well as the costs of holding land without developing it may have added to the financial burdens. One of the lessons from Milton Keynes is that new town developers should try to sell off land as quickly as possible to provide cash to cover the enormous up-front infrastructure requirements and to achieve a positive cumulative cash flow, preferably within seven years.[2]

Because the British New Town Program was long running, political changes in the U.K. had a definite impact on the new towns' financial accounting. The increasing pressure for new towns to be financially self-sustaining meant that the time frame in which the overall accounts of the new town corporations were expected to move into surplus was shortened (Turok 1990). The new conservative administration in 1979 hastened this pressure and also deprived the government of future income from this long-standing investment. Turok notes that the forced sell-off of new town assets was not necessarily at an optimal time, and may have resulted in lower-than-expected profit margins than if the sales had been phased gradually.

U.S. Experience

While the British new towns were the result of a large public commitment, the majority of U.S. new towns were financed through the private market. A chief problem for U.S. town developers has been raising sufficient capital to manage the complexity and take on the risks of a large-scale new town project, and achieving positive cash flows early enough to offset the huge up-front investment in infrastructure. Few private developers have been willing to do that on their own. The Title VII program, which began with the passage of the Urban Growth and New Community Act in 1970, sought to provide government loan guarantees for up to $50 million. However, these loan guarantees were not sufficient to guarantee financial success. An early work on this topic explored how risk analysis could better

Table 17.1. Summary Data of New Town Case Studies

New Town	Opening Date	Population	Main Developer	Country
Almere	1970	198,315 (2016)	Netherlands government	Netherlands
Celebration	1994	7,427 (2010)	Disney	United States
Cergy-Pontoise	1966	205,742 (2014)	French New Towns Program	France
Columbia	1967	103,467 (2015)	Rouse Corporation	United States
Irvine	1960	256,927 (2015)	Irvine Company	United States
Las Colinas	1973	28,294	Ben Carpenter Southland Financial	United States
Milton Keynes	1967	178,809 (2014)	U.K. New Towns Program	United Kingdom
Mission Viejo	1966	97,156 (2015)	Phillip Morris	United States
Reston	1963	60,070 (2016)	Robert Simon/Gulf Reston	United States
Songdo	2009	96,290 (2015)	Gale International	South Korea
The Woodlands	1974	114,625 (2016)	George Mitchell/Mitchell Energy	United States

Sources: Data were compiled from national census web sites and other similar sources used to compile the new town inventory (Appendix 2). As census data do not always overlap new town boundaries they should be treated as approximations only.

account for uncertainty in financial models for new town developments, as such large-scale developments are more impacted by exogenous factors outside the control of the developer—such as metropolitan economic trends (Peiser 1984). This study showed how sales volume, initial sales prices, and inflation rates dominate cost estimates in financial modeling of new towns. Furthermore, the demand side of the equation carries greater uncertainty than the cost side.

Several subsequent studies have explored just how developers of large-scale projects such as new towns can be financially successful (Mouchly and Peiser 1993; Peiser and Yu 1998). These articles explored the case of Green Valley as an example of minimal debt and appropriate phasing, and the case of Reston as an example of many of the problems that plagued U.S. new towns: their large size, both in acreage and projected development, infrastructure obligations, initial cash flow difficulties, inadequate long-term financing, and lack of a market segmentation program.

Case Studies

With the rapid urbanization of developing countries such as China and India, the new town model has proven globally adaptable and relevant again. Nonetheless, it is important to take stock of the financial success of new towns worldwide. There has been no comprehensive, comparative analysis of the financial success of new towns around the world. But, by examining the financial situation of new towns in the United States and Europe alongside those in the United Kingdom and elsewhere, we can get a more accurate picture of the specific factors that influenced why certain new towns were profitable and others were not. Summary data for the case studies is in Table 17.1.

Reston

The first major new town project in the United States, Reston, commenced in 1961 when Robert E. Simon Jr. purchased 6,750 acres in northern Virginia, later expanded to 7,400 acres, for $13.15 million, or $2,000 an acre (Gulf Reston 1970; Reston Museum 2018). Dissatisfied with suburban development trends, Simon envisioned a "unique private real estate venture which would integrate residences, industry, commerce, schools, churches, cultural institutions . . . in an independent community structure which would be economically viable and socially desirable" (Gulf Reston 1970, 9). To accomplish this, Simon had to adopt a new zoning code, permitting areas of higher density (sixty people per acre) and residences above stores. The master plan of Reston called for seven villages, organized around elementary schools, with village centers serving commercial needs of each village of ten to twelve thousand. The plan envisioned a population of seventy-five thousand, and one thousand acres in the heart of the property were set aside for industry. A loan from the Gulf Oil Corporation in 1963 allowed Simon to begin construction on his dream city, with the first resident arriving in 1964 (Reston Museum 2018).

Reston was officially dedicated on May 21, 1966. Although sales were brisk, development costs were outstripping revenues. By early 1967, only 370 townhouses, 400 apartments, and 325 homes had been sold or rented, far short of projections—the population was only twenty-five hundred. Convinced that the project was nearing bankruptcy, Gulf Oil assumed management of the town in 1967 (Bloom 2001, 26).

In an editorial in the *Washington Post*, the president of the American Institute of Architects reflected:

> It would be a mistake to believe that Reston's current problems raise questions about the viability of the New Town movement or about Reston's design.... Rather, they reflect the fact that in the U.S. we have not yet faced up to the special kind of financing needed by New Towns.... Contrary to other construction projects, a New Town by its nature must provide for a long lead time between investment and returns—a time when costly community facilities and amenities, plus payments, taxes and land carrying cost in general will deplete early capital and there will be insufficient income to replace it. (Durham 1967)

The high cost of infrastructure development and the failure to generate adequate cash flows early on seem to be the main reasons why Reston was nearly bankrupt just three years after breaking ground. In addition, a federal law prohibiting access to the Dulles Airport freeway limited access to the new town at a critical time.

Gulf Oil created a subsidiary, Gulf Reston, to manage the project. Gulf Reston "filled the high and medium density corridors with more typical suburban garden apartment complexes and town-house clusters, and increased the rate of construction and sales" (Bloom 2001, 26). This approach helped the company achieve financial stability after only a few years. But a county moratorium against new sewer development in the 1970s as well as the national recession of 1974 slowed sales. In 1978, Gulf sold the project to Reston Land Corporation, a subsidiary of Mobil Oil. By the 1980s, Reston was profitable again, and many large-scale projects were completed, including Reston Hospital Center, a county branch library, and high-tech office parks. The town center, which originally was located inside the new town, was moved to a location next to the airport freeway to which access finally became available in 1984.

Columbia

Columbia, Maryland, is one of the most well known of the American new towns because of its broad and idealistic vision for a mixed-income, mixed-race community, and because of its founder's wide-ranging promotion of his ideas in academic and public circles. Developer James Rouse began the process of accumulating land for a new town in 1962. He envisioned a project of approximately twelve thousand acres, developed over ten years with a price tag of $42 million and a pretax profit of $67 million. By the end of the early land-accumulation process, Rouse's newly created Howard Research and Development Corporation (HRD) had accumulated 15,500 acres for around $23 million (Forsyth 2005, 114). From an early phase, Rouse invited well-known scholars from public policy, public health, and even psychology to advise on the project as part of a "social planning work group" (Tennenbaum 1996).

Financing the project became a challenge, and initial profit projections were gradually revised. Some advisers estimated a profit as low as $4 million because of initial infrastructure costs—this led to an increased amount of commercial and industrial land, a reduction of open space, and an increase in overall residential density from 2.1 to 2.3 units per acre (Forsyth 2005, 136). In 1965, Rouse refinanced the project, which included a new projection of a before-tax profit over a fifteen-year period of over $100 million. Rouse received $50 million in loans from Connecticut General ($25 million), Chase Manhattan Bank ($10 million), and the Teachers Insurance Annuity Association ($15 million). Construction finally broke ground in 1967. As part of the complex financing arrangement, the Rouse organization would run HRD while Connecticut General put in most of the financing and controlled three-fifths of the seats on the board (Forsyth 2005, 113).

The Columbia project used innovative new financing models, such as PERT (program evaluation and review technique), but even so, early development was not a smooth process. In a bid to attract employment, Rouse acquired an additional 2,139 acres of land for $19 million for a new General Electric office site. Connecticut General provided the loan for this purchase, which brought debt to above $100 million in 1970 (Forsyth 2005, 139). The recession of 1974 also reduced sales in Columbia from $22.6 million in 1973 to $6.3 million in 1974. Columbia went through a technical foreclosure with Connecticut General in which most of the interest in the new town of the holding company, HRD, was transferred to the life insurance company. In 1985, the Rouse Company bought back Connecticut General's interest in HRD, making it a wholly owned subsidiary of the Rouse Company (Forsyth 2005, 108). In November 2005, Chicago-based General Growth Properties acquired the Rouse Company, continuing development activities in Columbia.

Irvine

The largest of the American new towns in terms of current population, Irvine, California, now has over 250,000 residents. An important difference between Irvine and Columbia or Reston is that the land for this new city was already in the possession of one owner: the Irvine family, who acquired it in the 1860s. The plan for creating a new community began in the 1950s, when the University of California called for a new campus south of Los Angeles in Orange County, a rapidly growing suburban region. The Irvine Company donated one thousand acres to the university in the hopes of building a vibrant community around the campus. While the city is considered a success, and is often ranked as one of the safest and most prosperous midsize cities in the country, the early development history was not without troubles. A much-publicized fight between the Irvine family and eventual president of the Irvine Company Donald Bren underscored the difficulty of attaining profitability while balancing the revenue need for commercial and industrial development alongside the desires of new and prospective residents.

A tentative agreement between the University of California and the Irvine Company was reached in 1959, when a plan by architect William Pereira and Associates (who would also design much of the early university campus) called for a college town of around one hundred thousand residents on ten thousand acres. A final plan in 1970 envisaged 430,000 people on fifty-three thousand acres, although this would include land outside of what became the city of Irvine when it incorporated in 1971. Raymond Watson, a planner, was hired by the Irvine Company and became responsible for shaping much of the new town's design over the next few decades. The core design principles of the plan included architecturally distinct residential villages with accompanying shopping centers, a road hierarchy system, a town center around the university, and large office and light industrial complexes around the north and south ends of the city, the Irvine Business Center and the Irvine Spectrum.

Despite Irvine's early success, a change of ownership in 1977 revealed the difficulties of appraising the value of a huge new town and the difference in development strategy between the Irvine family and new investors. Then the Irvine family sold the company to a consortium of developers. Joan Irvine Smith, the head of the family's foundation that had a controlling stake in the company, was forced to partner with auto heir Henry Ford II, shopping center magnate A. Alfred Taubman, and a Southern California developer Donald Bren, to outbid a takeover proposal by Mobil Oil. The group bought the company for $377 million. When Bren subsequently bought out the shareholders, a rift ensued with Smith, who refused Bren's offer. He had valued the company at $1 billion compared to her valuation at $3.3 billion.

According to historian Spencer Olin, "Bren's takeover led to the drafting of a new comprehensive plan designed to dramatically increase the pace of development on the ranch" (Kling, Olin, and Poster 1995, 80). This included 740,000 square feet of new office space in the John Wayne Airport area, a two-hundred-acre medical complex on the western edge of Irvine Center, and three new shopping malls. In 1987, Bren claimed he had increased cash flow 327 percent from $246 million in 1983 to $1.2 billion (Flynn 1987). But Bren was still worried about climbing vacancy rates in office buildings and opposition from antigrowth activists. The Irvine Company has continued its success at developing what is arguably America's largest new town. But the problems plaguing other new towns were also present in Irvine's development process. The tensions between commercial and residential development and between private profit and community will, and the differing strategies of maximizing cash flow versus developing infrastructure were all present.

Interestingly, Bren's critique of the consortium's management of Irvine's development (Berkman 1987) discusses problems opposite those seen at Reston and Columbia. Bren had criticized the company's management from 1977 to 1983, claiming that by maximizing cash flow with land sales too quickly and not investing in long-term infrastructure, the company would soon exhaust its vast land resources, although with around one hundred thousand acres, they had a long way to go.

This is different from Reston, where investing in infrastructure and initial public amenities threatened to outstrip revenue from early residential sales. However, the Irvine Company's initial successes and scale were probably a result of the contiguity of the land holdings, and the fact the entirety of the original ranch was already in the company's possession at a very low basis with no debt. Among contemporary U.S. new towns, only The Woodlands had a similarly low cost. Both new towns demonstrate that successful new town development requires that land be owned with little or no debt.

The Woodlands

Like Columbia, The Woodlands, Texas, was the product of an idealistic visionary developer, George Mitchell. And, like James Rouse, Mitchell brought in planning and landscape design experts, namely Ian McHarg, who advocated harmonizing urban development with natural systems. The Woodlands received $50 million in loan guarantees from the Department of Housing and Urban Development in 1972 and remains the only Title VII new town[3] that avoided bankruptcy. However, The Woodlands' finances were not without problems (Galatas and Barlow 2004).

Even with the loan guarantees, money was going quickly. About $23 million was spent to pay off mortgages and owners of the land, $3.6 million went to pay predevelopment costs incurred by The Woodlands Corporation, and $27 million would be left to pay for infrastructure. When the project finally opened in 1974, the country was already in a recession. The oil embargo further decreased demand for suburban homes far away from Houston's city center. The Woodlands, like the other Title VII new towns, found it very difficult to raise additional financing under the stringent terms of their loans. If not for George Mitchell's commitment to the new town and his agreement to inject $15 million in additional equity from his oil company, Mitchell Energy, The Woodlands would likely have declared bankruptcy. However, by the end of the 1970s, The Woodlands was on a more profitable track. Houston subsequently led the nation into the savings and loan crisis in the early 1980s. Despite the slowdown in the economy, Houston's master-planned communities, including The Woodlands, were able to achieve almost half of the entire market share for new home sales during the 1980s.

In 1997 Mitchell decided to sell The Woodlands because of pressure from the market to divide his oil and gas business from his real estate business. The Woodlands was sold for $545 million to a partnership of Crescent and Morgan Stanley. While the sales price was within the higher range predicted by Goldman Sachs, the sale amounted to a before-tax loss of approximately $75 million. According to Galatas, "the sale occurred before The Woodlands assets had reached financial maturity . . . and because of George Mitchell's charitable nature and his belief that the community required contributions of assets and funds to make it a better place like the funds and grants to Houston Area Research Center, John Cooper School, and other institutions" (Galatas and Barlow 2004, 160). While these donations could be seen as investments in creating long-term value for The Woodlands, they did not generate any current income for the company. However, the increase in profitability of Mitchell Energy more than compensated for the loss of sales revenue. However, the loss generated by the sale points to the fact that the enormous investments required for new towns development make it very difficult to realize adequate returns if the owner is forced to sell the new town before time has progressed to realize them.

Songdo, South Korea

The city of Songdo was conceived by the South Korean government as both an "eco-city" and an "aerotropolis." After the new Seoul Incheon airport opened in 2001, the national and Incheon city government unveiled plans to create a new business hub that would allow residents and travelers "access to 700 million people or 50 cities with a population over 1 million within a 3.5-hour flight from Incheon" (Segel et al. 2012, 3). The Korean government granted the domestic firm POSCO development rights to the fifteen-hundred-acre site reclaimed land, with instructions to partner with an international developer. In 2001, Gale International was invited and eventually agreed to a 70 percent controlling interest with POSCO taking 30 percent for the project (Segel et al. 2012). Overall, Songdo was envisaged to comprise eighty thousand apartments with a likely population of 180,000 or more inhabitants, five million square meters of office space, and nine hundred thousand square meters of commercial retail space (see Chapter 7).[4] But a host of financial problems has led to Gale International's stake being significantly reduced, and as of 2014, there were only about one-sixth of the planned employees and half of the planned residents there.

The project's completion date was pushed back from 2014 to 2018, largely because of the 2008 global financial crisis. The project had not earned a profit in twelve years for the developer, except for initial equity recouped, less than $100 million (Nam 2013). In 2010, Gale and POSCO had to restructure their debt, giving up 50 percent of future profits to the city of Incheon. Gale Company's deal with POSCO was also restructured because of slow sales and leasing to foreign corporations. The government's objective in inviting Gale Corporation into the deal in the first place was predicated on their leasing or selling an equal amount of floor space for commercial development as for residential development. Not surprisingly, demand for residential was far greater than commercial space, so they were unable to sell and lease commercial space fast enough to service their debt, and the government was inflexible about changing the requirement.

The profits have fallen far short of initial expectations of the developer, which had anticipated making $400 to $500 million profit in five years. While that has not happened, they believed that they will do very well in the long run (Stokols 2014). Residential sales at Songdo have begun to accelerate, but commercial tenants have been much slower to move into a new city that is still over an hour by train from Seoul's city center. The government has given incentives to foreign firms but not to domestic ones, meaning that the necessary business ecosystem of service industries such as tax and accounting firms has not materialized to support the firms the government would like to attract.

Cergy-Pontoise, Paris, France

Cergy-Pontoise is one of five new towns that were built outside Paris beginning in the late 1960s. Original plans called for towns of five hundred thousand to one million, while today the town has 185,000 inhabitants and is a thriving regional center in the Ile de France region, which surrounds Paris. However, in 1979, several years into the construction of the city, scholars were already writing about the heavy costs of constructing new towns and the associated debt the government was undertaking to do so. The loans and grants from the national government were expected to total 2.454 billion francs from 1976 to 1980 for the entire New Town VII Plan, most of which was devoted to infrastructure projects. Developers were acquiring land and premises more slowly than anticipated, making the repayment of loans to finance land purchase hard to repay (Tuppen 1979).

The French new towns differed from those in the British program in the stronger central control from the beginning. New Town Public Development Bodies took over the functions of land purchasing, plan preparation, selling land to private sector developers, and coordinating infrastructure development. According to Hervé Dupont, former general secretary of the Secretariat of Urban Regeneration Major Operations, all French new towns achieved a financial balance except for Le Vaudreuil, which reached only thirty thousand inhabitants versus the one hundred thousand initially planned.[5] National taxes and business taxes were used to pay for public facilities and construction of national roads, highways, public schools, public services, regional transit, and local buses. The local authority (SAN)[6] paid for municipal roads, sewage, waste/refuse collection, and maintenance.

Land for Cergy-Pontoise was purchased from agricultural owners between 1968 and 1970 by the Land and Technical Management Agency of the Parisian Region. Land for the future new towns had originally been classified as ZAD[7] (postponed planning zones), which froze land prices and helped the new towns buy land at a lower basis. The site was then sold to the New Towns Corporation (EPA),[8] the new town development corporation. Loans for land development were private but were backed by state guarantees, which justified lower interest rates.

Unlike many new towns, Cergy-Pontoise achieved the targeted population/jobs ratio equal to 1. Sixty percent of the population lived and worked on-site within the new town. When the EPA was rolled up in 2002, the balance before liquidation was 7.4 million euros—a profitable outcome. The remaining land plots were transferred to the SAN that comprised the eleven original municipalities originally combined to create the new town of Cergy Pontoise. In addition to the six case studies described above, we studied five additional new towns. The results are described in the next section.

Financial Outcomes

Table 17.2 summarizes the financial outcomes for eleven new towns that are part of the present study. All the U.S. new towns are privately sponsored and financed—with substantial support from patient capital industries such as insurance, oil, and

Table 17.2. Financial Outcomes

New Town	Sponsorship	Financial Outcome	Country
Almere	Government	Government paid back	Netherlands
Celebration	Private	Loss	United States
Cergy-Pontoise	Government	Government paid back	France
Columbia	Private	Loan default	United States
Irvine	Private	Profitable—sold far below market value	United States
Las Colinas	Private	Loan default	United States
Milton Keynes	Government	Debt write-off	United Kingdom
Mission Viejo	Private	Profitable	United States
Songdo City	Private	Profitable—American partner forced out	South Korea
Reston	Private	Loan default	United States
The Woodlands	Private	Profitable—book loss[a]	United States

[a] The Woodlands was sold for a $75 million write-off, but Mitchell Energy common stock went up $300 million, and the subsequent purchasers have realized profits in excess of $350 million (Roger Galatas, author phone interview, 2018).

farming—although The Woodlands received a government-guaranteed loan. Songdo City in South Korea is also privately sponsored. All three of the European new towns are government sponsored. The advantage of government financing, of course, is that the government does not run out of money. However, as happened in Milton Keynes, the new town can be so much in debt that it is unsustainable, forcing a write-off of some or all of the government investment. Of the eleven new towns studied, eight either went bankrupt or incurred a loss on their investment. Of the three that were profitable, only one—Mission Viejo—was an unqualified success in terms of meeting the developer's profit objectives.

Financial success depends on sufficient cash flow to cover all debt obligations and ultimately to return a competitive profit on the developer's/government's investment. The enemy of success is the real estate cycle. Recessions have occurred in the United States every five to seven years. When they do occur, housing sales drop precipitously. Construction loans for home building become very difficult to get as banks raise credit standards and reduce lending, often caused by bad loans from overbuilding prior to the recession. Consequently, sales of homes to home buyers, and the upstream sales of land to home builders are greatly reduced, and with them, revenues.

The key to financial success is rapid sales. New town developers can increase sales by offering a broader range of housing types and price ranges, as they did in Mission Viejo. Developers also can raise cash quickly or reduce land debt by selling off undeveloped land, although this may cause competition down the road (see

Mouchly and Peiser 1993). A common problem is filling up the pipeline of lots to homebuilders who are not able to sell finished homes to buyers. Ultimately the home builders either return the lots to the new town developer or default on the construction loans, in which case banks take over the vacant lots or unfinished homes. In either case, excess inventory of developed lots reduces future land sales and revenues.

Certain Asian new towns such as Bundang in South Korea have avoided the cash-flow difficulties of most American new towns by speeding up development and by higher volume of sales. Whereas the typical American new town takes thirty years or more to be fully developed, some Asian new towns have been fully developed in ten years. The faster economic growth rates in Asia have also reduced the frequency and depth of recessions. Understanding the lessons from those new towns that experienced poor financial outcomes is critical for avoiding similar problems in the future. The reasons for financial failure of the new towns in this study are summarized in Table 17.3 and financial results and population in Table 17.4.

Table 17.3. Reasons for Financial Failure

Early land and development cash flow
Acquisition costs too high
Acquisition financed by debt
Failure to sell off land quickly to generate cash and reduce carry
Government financing with inflexible terms, subject to politics
Selling or dumping of property at low prices during recession
Excessive hiring and management

Poorly phased construction
Excessive construction of up-front infrastructure—poor phasing of infrastructure
Housing and building construction (vertical development) not separated from land development, making it difficult or impossible for developer to know where the company is making and losing money
Overbuilding and excessive inventory
Inflexible planning unable to meet market demand

Public image
Excessive concentration of social housing
Image as place for low-income housing
Failure to attract middle- and upper-income residents
Excessive residential development leading to employment imbalance
Failure to achieve diverse demography—overconcentration of young families; absence of mixed age groups
Lack of amenities, recreation opportunities, and open space
Absence of sense of place and community due to poor urban design and lack of social organizations

Table 17.4. New Town Statistics and Financial Information

	Opening Date	Master Plan Acreage	Bankruptcy/ Sale Event	Sale Price	Current Acres	Population
Columbia[1]	1967	14,000	1965		20,608	103,467 (2015)
Reston[2]	1966	6,500	1967		11,136	60,070 (2016)
The Woodlands[3]	1974	17,455	1997	$543 million	27,000	114,625 (2016)
Irvine[4]	1971	53,000	1977	$337.4 million	42,528	256,927
Las Colinas[5]	1973	12,000	1986		9,333	28,294
Cergy-Pontoise[6]	1972				20,800	205,742 (2014)
Songdo[7]	2009	1,500	2010		1,500	96,290 (2015)
Mission Viejo	1966	10,000	n.a.	n.a.	11,596.80	97, 156 (2015)
Milton Keynes[8]	1967	21,900				171,750

Sources: Data were compiled from national census web sites and other similar sources used to also compile the new town inventory (Appendix 2). As census data do not always overlap new town boundaries they should be treated as approximations only.

Notes on fate of original developers

[1] Rouse was forced to refinance the project, with Connecticut General and Teachers Life Insurance taking large stakes in the project.

[2] After initial sales fell short of expectations, Gulf Oil assumed management from Robert Simon, the initial developer, in 1967.

[3] George Mitchell sold The Woodlands in 1997 because of problems with a lawsuit against his oil business. The sale amounted to an after-tax loss of $67 million.

[4] Joan Irvine Smith, the heiress to the Irvine Company, sold to a consortium of outside investors for $377 million.

[5] The 1986 Dallas economic slowdown slowed sales and forced Ben Carpenter to step down and let his son take over. Debt was restructured by Teachers and JMB Realty.

[6] Publicly owned Établissement public d'aménagement (EPA) remained the developer from inception in 1969 to completion in 2002.

[7] In 2010, Gale and Posco had to restructure their debt, giving up 50 percent of future profits to the city of Incheon.

[8] The quasi-autonomous nongovernmental organization Milton Keynes Development Co. remained the developer until all the undeveloped lands of the British new towns were transferred to the Commission for New Towns in 1992.

Conclusions

New towns hold the promise of achieving the highest quality of life among urban settlements. They represent the largest scale of development and the highest level of urban planning. Financial success in new town development is critical if new towns are going to survive and thrive.

This chapter has examined the financial performance of eleven new towns throughout the developed world. Taken together, the new towns present a sobering picture of financial performance. The vast majority either went bankrupt or failed to deliver competitive financial returns. While cheap land is a requirement for success, need for appropriate timing with respect to the economic cycle, phasing, early disposition of land to generate cash, strong market demand, and residential and commercial product offerings serving a broad and diverse spectrum of the market are among the lessons learned from the new towns investigated here.

Globally, many countries have had new town development initiatives. Numerous developing countries in Asia, the Middle East, and Africa currently have extensive new town programs. Because of their rapidly growing economies and high levels of rural-to-urban migration, they may avoid the most common problems of new towns in American and Europe—slow sales and long development periods that extend over several real estate cycles. While financial success is not impossible, it requires superior development management and very deep pockets. Oversupply, too much infrastructure investment, too little demand, poor planning, poor market analysis, inadequate equity, financing land with debt, government inflexibility, poor governance, poor quality of life, inadequate amenities, poor transportation, and boring, homogenous design all contribute to the failures. New towns are among the most complex urban development projects to be found. While there is no magic bullet for all new towns, financial success requires careful balancing of investment in infrastructure and amenities with accurate demand forecasts and sales to generate sufficient cash flow to withstand economic downturns and ultimately generate a profit.

Notes

1. While the incidence of financial failure among new towns is extremely high—in the 80–90 percent range in the United States—a number of new towns have succeeded such as Green Valley, Nevada; Kingwood and Clear Lake City outside of Houston; and the London ring new town of Bracknell. See Turok (1990).

2. The longer it takes for a project to reach positive cumulative cash flow, the lower the rate of return. To the extent that infrastructure investment (negative up-front cash flow) is financed by long-term debt or by special districts, cumulative positive cash flows on equity investment will be easier to achieve. The longer the payback period is, the higher will be the rate of return required by equity investors because of risk.

3. Title VII of the Housing and Urban Development Act of 1970 provided government loan guarantees for up to $50 million to fifteen new towns, fourteen of which went bankrupt.

4. Earlier build-out projections called for $20 to $26 billion for the planned city of 65,000 residents and 250,000 workers and 50 million square feet of office space (Segel et al. 2012).

5. Hervé Dupont, interview by Pascaline Gaborit.

6. The local authority was called SAN, Syndicat d'Agglomération nouvelle.

7. Zone d'Aménagement Différée.

8. Etablissement Public d'Aménagement, the French equivalent to the British New Town Corporations.

18

Organizing and Managing New Towns

Sandy Apgar

New towns are crucibles of urban innovation. Their structures foster systemic improvements in organization, financing, and operations. Their management processes incubate changes in physical form (land uses, building designs, and construction) and in institutional relationships among staff, consultants, employers, affinity groups, local officials, and the myriad other constituents who make up the community.

In current parlance, "management matters." Nowhere is this truer than in organizing and managing new towns. From origination through land assembly, planning and design, entitlements, financing, construction, and operations, new towns take fifteen to fifty years to complete and engage thousands of professionals and workers to create thriving places for living, working, and playing.

New town management requires a fundamental evolution from the original developer's vision, through planning and construction, to community operations, resident services, and continuing attention on the economics of capturing value from the developer's assets and activities. In the American context, new towns must synthesize profit-oriented business concepts and techniques with the delivery and administration of public services.

This chapter is based on my research into the British New Towns and experience in supporting the developer of Columbia, Maryland, in the 1960s; leadership of the U.S. Army's Residential Communities Initiative (RCI) in the 1990s; and advisory services to more than one hundred other new community organizations and projects during the past fifty years. From this research, experience, analysis, and casework, I have distilled three principles for organizing and managing new towns:

1. New towns require a unique management philosophy that embraces the development "process" and the property "portfolio," as well as the physical "products" of the built environment.
2. The new town must be managed as a holistic enterprise, deriving its goals and structure from the developer's vision and its economics from the land uses and the occupants' activities.

3. New town operations initially entail a developer-led and developer-staffed enterprise management function that transitions to an independent, autonomous, community facilities- and service-provider organization.

The "Enterprise" View

New town management differs from traditional real estate development because the new town developer's aim is to create an entire human community that is more than a collection of individual buildings. Business and government executives are realizing the importance of viewing their real estate holdings as a portfolio, more valuable than the sum of its building parts. They employ corporate strategy to go beyond the static snapshots of sites, structures, and land uses, framing a dynamic "enterprise" view of the organization's real estate requirements over time. To create a large-scale real estate development that not only accommodates tens of thousands of people but also accounts for their activities in the local environment and economy, the enterprise view is essential.

The new town enterprise is designed to guide long-range planning, arrange sizable financial and staffing commitments, oversee and control multiple projects, and organize and lead a wide range of specialties. Its basic objectives and policies determine the character of both the community and the organization, setting the stage for myriad decisions. The roles it assumes must reconcile the eventual community's need for a full range of activities and services with the developer's capability to provide them directly, or arrange for others to provide them, effectively and efficiently. The systems for planning, executing, and controlling the development and operating process must weave routine, predictable, day-to-day activities into the longer-term, more organic, and dynamic tapestry of urban life.

Therefore, the organization design begins with, and must be built on, the developer's vision for the enterprise, at least until people come to live and work in the new town. This new town vision must be exceptionally creative, robust, and broadly based. The Rouse Company, developer of Columbia, Maryland, articulated its corporate and community mission this way: "To conceive, design, and bring into being better places for people to live, to work, to shop, . . . a better environment for the growth of man and his family, . . . a product for which the world hungers and for which it will richly reward the successful producer. We seek to build a corporate institution which is capable of undertaking and successfully completing real estate development built and managed to high standards of taste, beauty, human fulfillment, and profitability" (McFadden 2015).

As corporate objectives, these are at once broad and vague, but they infused the organization with a sense of ideals and purpose that founder James Rouse hoped would transcend the crises of day-to-day decision making and ongoing pressures for profit. In his own prophetic words, "We can choose new communities that provide for people and the services they need, for the conservation of energy, and for the economical use of scarce capital resources. . . . The gathering together of community services and facilities creates a sense of place; provides a feeling of scale in human dimension; enlarges relationships among people; encourages a community of mind, expectation, action" (Rouse 1976, xvii).

Similarly, in Reston, Virginia, founding developer Robert Simon "envisioned a Northern Virginia community that blended the serenity of an Italian hill town, the urban attractions of San Francisco and the social equality of Finland," further articulated as "a racially integrated, economically diverse mix of urban and suburban lifestyles, with high-rise apartment buildings, town houses and single-family homes; youth and senior centers; swimming pools; tennis courts; woodland paths; lakeside shops; industries and businesses" (Rouse 1968, 3).

The Woodlands, Texas, largest and arguably most successful of the U.S. federal government's Title VII New Communities[2], thrived in large part because of the vision of its founder, George Mitchell. Roger Galatas, The Woodlands' longtime CEO, sums up Mitchell's vision: "Our early mission statement was informal, but it was an important factor in our success. George [Mitchell]'s vision was 'to create a real home town for people and companies, with a better quality of life than they were finding in the cities amid the turmoil of the 1960s'. . . . He didn't just want to create a residential or commercial development, he wanted to create economic value, and he wanted people who lived in The Woodlands to be participants in the program, to buy into its goals, and to feel a part of it."[1] By focusing primarily on people's needs and aspirations—rather than on building form and use—new towns can succeed where conventional approaches have failed in humanizing the faceless bureaucracies of many government-provided services and refining the sometimes rough-and-tumble results of market-driven, large-scale construction.

New towns' organizations exhibit five key management factors for success:

1. *Clear roles* to delineate all property assets that are owned or controlled by the developer, articulate the developer's analysis and assumptions of human needs and its vision to meet them, define the desired outcomes of the development process, and establish metrics to assess the organization's performance in meeting them.

2. *Mutually beneficial relationships* with all major stakeholders, including customers, regulators, constituents, and suppliers, as well as investors and

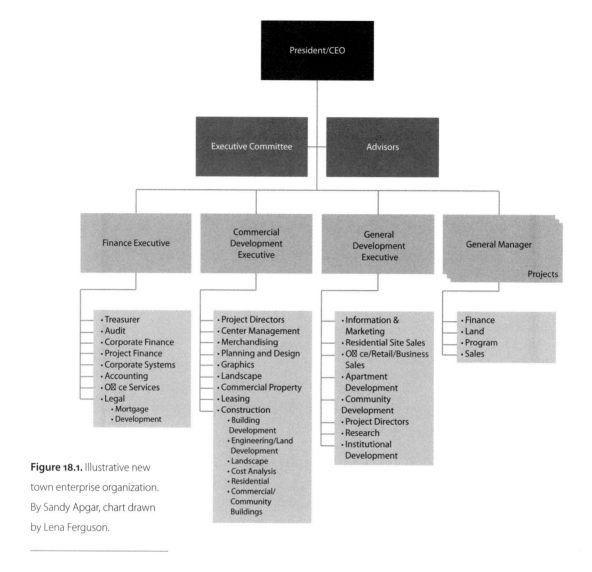

Figure 18.1. Illustrative new town enterprise organization. By Sandy Apgar, chart drawn by Lena Ferguson.

employees, who, together, assure the management and financial strength to deliver a complex, long-term megaproject, while ensuring that rewards to the private partners are commensurate with their financial contributions and their organizational and reputational risks.

3. *Lifecycle "end-to-end" planning and management*, with continuous engagement of major stakeholders in the decision-making process, from the project's visioning through its final disposition, hallmarked by long-term capital budgeting and resource allocation systems that elude most governmental and many business organizations.

4. *Comprehensive communications*, incorporating community outreach, frequent conversations among stakeholders throughout each stage, progress reports at

key milestones, and outcome-based reports on the long-term value for money to be realized.

5. *Entrepreneurial stewardship* to encourage proactive, but disciplined, leadership and direction over the project's life, provide effective fiscal and public oversight, yet avoid adversarial, contract-driven, procedural governance.

The art of new town management lies in tailoring these factors to the vision for each project. The proponent's primary responsibility is to ensure that each new town incorporates the full range of factors but weights them to reflect the specific needs that drive its strategy and structure. Wise judgment, infused with common sense, ultimately should prevail (Figure 18.1).

Managing the Enterprise to Capture Value

While new towns are built according to the developer's vision, they also are businesses that must create economic value. This section describes the "value economics" in new towns produced through the development and use of land and buildings, which provide the financial base for realizing overall project objectives. Mastering this concept and associated techniques is one of the most important management skills required of the community development enterprise.

Figure 18.2 illustrates a prototypical economic model to support new town management decision making. Both strategic and operational executives address tradeoffs between short- and long-term financing commitments; test alternative scenarios for single, multiple, and mixed land uses; design adaptations and conversions of capital and operating leases; negotiate structures for fee ownership and ground leases; and assess other issues as the development team moves the new town from the developer's original vision through detailed planning, construction, sales and leasing, operations, and, ultimately, restructuring. While the illustrative model's basic architecture was framed in the pioneering Columbia Economic Model, this design has since been adapted to various greenfield and urban renaissance new towns (Apgar 2015).

The relationships among real estate uses may change radically during the project's life to accommodate new needs, shifts in taste, and location preferences. The key to unlocking a project's economic potential is therefore to manage the timing, phasing, and mix of uses that will best realize the development concept while responding to unforeseen opportunities, risks, and constraints. The development cycle is simply too long, the multiplicity of objectives too complex, and the operating environment too uncertain to permit a single, static financial plan. The private

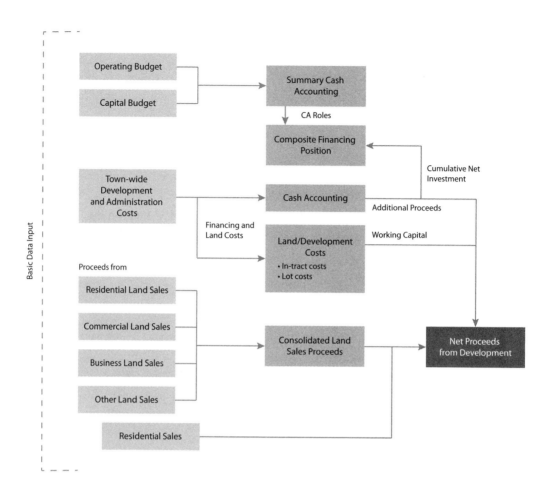

Basic Data Input

Operating Budget

Capital Budget

Summary Cash Accounting

CA Roles

Composite Financing Position

Town-wide Development and Administration Costs

Cash Accounting

Cumulative Net Investment

Financing and Land Costs

Land/Development Costs
• In-tract costs
• Lot costs

Additional Proceeds

Working Capital

Proceeds from

Residential Land Sales

Commercial Land Sales

Business Land Sales

Other Land Sales

Consolidated Land Sales Proceeds

Net Proceeds from Development

Residential Sales

Figure 18.2. Illustrative new town economic model. By Sandy Apgar, chart drawn by Lena Ferguson.

developer, for instance, may choose a product mix that initially will maximize cash flow and shift to an asset-appreciation goal once cash flow has stabilized. The public developer, on the other hand, may pursue short-term asset growth at the start to increase the taxable revenue base while allocating a high proportion of space to nonearning public uses.

Thus, land uses that are prescribed in the project plan should be seen only as an initial definition to be modified as new patterns of demand and the cost or availability of capital emerge. Regrettably, too many financial staff pay scant regard to the importance of this dynamic, continuing process, when they focus solely on the initial financing structure, the subsequent implementation, and the budgets, status reports, and cash management tools of prudent financial control.

In short, creativity in structuring project economics is required not only in planning the new town, but also whenever significant changes in direction or additional investments are decided. Imaginative ideas, however, must be grounded on a solid understanding of both the possibilities and the pitfalls in using leverage. The project that achieves planned revenue and cost targets, and is seen as a secure investment opportunity, will have excellent prospects of sustaining the investors' interest and attracting fresh, affordable funds as unforeseen needs arise.

Figure 18.3 illustrates the design of a land development model. The clarity of assumptions and data for this model supports new town management decision making by identifying *structural* relationships between land, financing, and development; and the *sequencing* of cash sources, availability, and requirements. Whereas the economic model informs management about the new town's overall performance, this model highlights the efficiency and utilization of the "fuel" that managers use to drive it.

Figure 18.3. Illustrative new town land development model. By Sandy Apgar, chart drawn by Lena Ferguson.

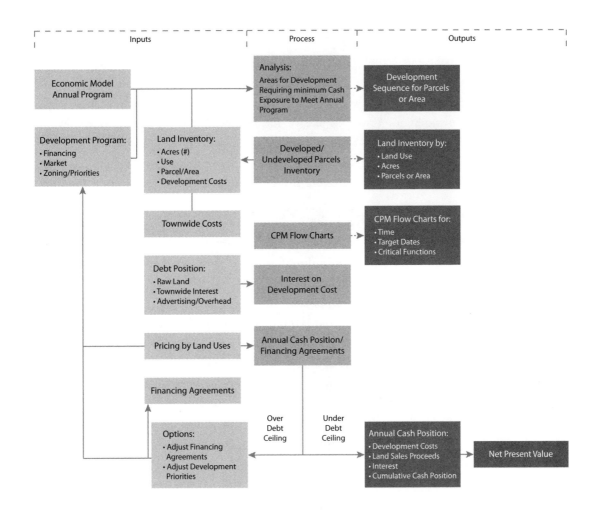

Sources and Measures of Investment Return

The types of return on investment must be carefully classified and thoroughly evaluated based on the project's financing requirements. The attractiveness of large-scale development depends not only on the proper use of land and buildings to generate market volume, and on effective leverage, but also on an acute understanding of the sources of profitability and risk.

Investment returns are derived from two interlocking sources: capital appreciation on land and buildings attributable to the value created by development; and cash flows generated by land sales, building development, refinancing, and the operation of income-producing properties. Full capital appreciation on land is not normally realized until the entire project is completed, some fifteen to twenty years after the land is acquired, but cash flows on individually marketed subprojects can and should be structured almost from the start.

Capital Appreciation

The primary financial objective in most projects is to increase property values as rapidly as possible through the development process, and to derive the cash flows resulting from sales of developed land parcels, plus the investors' proceeds from partial, typically minority and passive, interests in selected operating businesses which occupy them. This distinguishes the community developer from the property speculator. While this distinction is oversimplified, it highlights the criticality of fully and completely managing the capital appreciation cycle in new town development.

Both the scale and the type of value created in any project depend on its financial structure (the mix of debt and equity and the terms and interest rates of mortgages) and on the timing of cash flows resulting from financial decisions (especially, phasing of the initial equity investment, refinancing, and the sale of subprojects), as well as on its marketability.

Because they offer a concentrated mix of uses, new towns may enjoy higher land values after development than traditional single-use ventures. Residential viability is generally the key to a new town's success because most other community and public service demands spring from housing; easy access to available jobs, though, is essential to sustain housing demand. According to Roger Galatas, "One advantage The Woodlands [had] over most other master-planned communities in the Houston area [was] its commitment to creating jobs as well as homes. The Woodlands Corporation has nurtured that advantage not only by luring companies—and their current decision makers—but also by identifying and courting future corporate leaders, especially people working at lower levels in energy companies who already lived in The Woodlands and could advance as corporate decision-makers." Similarly, the U.S. Army's Residential Communities Initiative (RCI), while rooted in housing, has created thousands of jobs in both military bases and surrounding civilian communities.

Cash Flow Measures

The evaluation of cash flow is simple in principle, but complicated in new towns by the need to compute all cash flows over the duration of the entire project rather than year by year. In the planning and land development phases, annual cash flow will understate the project's profit potential because actual land sales will be far below their anticipated future pace, and revenues from building development and operations will be limited.

Whichever measures are used, a new town's financial performance depends largely on the accuracy of assumptions in the economic model. Negative deviations, even if small in absolute terms, can seriously affect the arithmetic because interest and other holding costs will be compounded over the prolonged development cycle. A constant watch over the break-even indicator is essential to effective project management and to avoid overoptimistic assumptions about demand.

Capturing the Economic Values of Social Investment

Social investment—that is, in infrastructure, schools, health clinics, fitness facilities, community centers, and the like—benefits the new town in tangible, though nonfinancial, ways and can result in real, albeit unrealized, savings for the local government and/or community association in the long term. Indeed, community impact studies show conclusively the net positive impact from planned development. In total, cash expenditures are substantially lower. Funds for parks and open space may be higher, but expenditures on roads, water, and sewers are generally lower, because more rational land-use relationships and higher planning densities permit more compact infrastructure and the provision of basic services at lower per capita investment. Moreover, sound, community-scale planning can generate substantial savings in public programs—savings that should be possible in existing communities but that often go unrecognized.

In Columbia, Maryland, for example, the simple fact that most children can walk to school was expected to save the state $1 million annually in transportation and operating costs that would have been mandatory within most traditional patterns of development. In The Woodlands, the U.S. Title VII new communities program[2] provided for grants to support basic utilities (e.g., sewer, water), without which development could not proceed, and other services (e.g., public transportation, child care) which are important to fulfilling a new town's objectives but are not essential to its physical structure.

Existing institutions and foundations may be eager to participate in a new town, particularly if they might derive some competitive advantage from it. In Columbia, for example, the local bank president chose to live in the community. The developer recognized this fortuitous circumstance and requested that, in view of its identification with the community and assured market growth, the bank allocate 10 percent of its earnings to the Columbia Foundation. This contribution provided seed money to local institutions, supporting a wide variety of community services. The initial contribution was expected to increase tenfold within fifteen years of the community's launch, and so it did.

The special economics of large-scale development, and the difficulties of accurately calculating and communicating them through conventional accounting and management information, underscore the need to thoroughly evaluate each project on its own merits. It is essential that the financing concept for a project clearly distinguishes development uses that have commercial real estate market potential from those that are designed to meet community objectives. In contrast to European new towns, a critical shortcoming of much U.S. community development financing to date has been confusion between their commercial and social objectives. This has placed a burden on the underlying financing structures of the programs, on the institutions that have supported them, and, ultimately, on the new towns' residents.

As capital markets increasingly recognize the value of long-term investments in this low-interest, low-inflation era, the relative attractiveness of real estate generally, and new towns specifically, is likely to grow. Japan's current consideration of fifty-year bonds, to be issued through its central bank, indicates the perpetual horizon that European new towns have long enjoyed but has eluded American new town developers. When long-term, "patient" capital is fused with the public-private partnership model summarized below, the potential for value capture in new town management is exponential.

Managing the Community

Developing a community includes providing community facilities and services, embracing diverse activities that supplement the community's main function as a place for living and working. These include primary social services, such as education and health care; infrastructure, such as roads and sanitation; leisure programs for sports and entertainment; and services for groups with special needs, such as youth and the elderly. Because their home is most people's largest single investment, and its location is a decision of paramount importance, it is essential that the community reflect where and how its residents choose to live. Whether it will do so depends significantly on the scope and quality of these community programs.

As the main force behind the project, particularly in its early years, the new town enterprise must keep a firm grasp on community activities that influence the concept definition. Typically, the larger and more diverse the new town, the less homogeneous the social values and lifestyles of residents are likely to be—and, therefore, the requirements for community service support will be more wide ranging. Moreover, service needs and demands vary substantially with community demographics and socioeconomic factors. A community designed mainly for young professionals, for example, will obviously make greater use of fitness, entertainment and recreation facilities, and may enjoy lower operating costs; a predominantly older community will face higher health-related capital and operating costs.

The cost implications for infrastructure, land and facilities, and operations, and the availability of the requisite program specialists, can be substantial. In project plans I have reviewed, the range of error has been as high as $16 million (20 percent) in excessive costs and one hundred unproductive acres (15 percent) because the demand estimates were inflated. The political repercussions from such improvident planning also are likely to be significant.

Strategies for efficient service provision will benefit from close analysis of linkages across geographies, programs, budgets, and organizations. When a new development is grafted onto an existing town or city—as in new-towns-in-town, suburban satellites, "cluster cities," and even "edge cities"—numerous opportunities emerge for linking services and programs between the two. For example, in one project to expand a small town of ten thousand existing residents by adding twenty thousand new residents, analysis revealed that in addition to the local government's services, there were already some one hundred twenty local organizations providing more than fifty different services to the community.

For most community services, the developer will be well advised to reinforce existing links rather than forge new ones. Close integration between newcomers and existing residents is likelier to emerge from informal interplay among local organizations than from structured competition and formal negotiation of terms. This also can help to reduce tensions between old and new residents, encouraging a more constructive approach to community needs.

The forms these linkages could take may be suggested by surveying the local organization structure, program by program; identifying their coverage, strengths, and limitations from informal local discussions; and then evaluating the cost-benefit results of a partnership between the existing and new communities. Incentives (usually geared to their limitations) may be needed to encourage their participation.

The French *villes nouvelles* program has refined and broadened this concept through a focused policy for new town innovation to embrace a range of community activities, from standard civic forums and cultural services to voluntary groups for welcoming newcomers and comforting seniors. The principal aim has been to relieve the isolation and anonymity of urban life and to "animate" the new community with programs and institutions that will help generate and develop social relationships (Roullier and Apgar 1976).

In addition to organizational links between the new and existing communities, possible links between users and facilities are worth close evaluation. Attention should be given at the earliest stages of program planning to leverage resources through shared use of buildings and services, such as schools, health clinics, clubs, churches, and community centers. To aid in the arduous process of negotiation and persuasion, the analysis should show not only the possibilities for multiple uses, but also the marginal costs of providing them and the potential means of financing and managing these extra requirements. For example, it is often possible to integrate commercial, profit-making activities with public nonprofit ones serving the same general needs. A public library in one project was combined with a bookstore, clothing store, discotheque, and coffee shop around a central service core. Not only was the library considerably enlivened and its usage quadrupled, but the total complex was financed at a greatly reduced net cost to the local government. In both the United States and the United Kingdom, local churches and even local school boards generally are willing to make their facilities available for community use outside congregational and school hours, as long as the overhead and operating expenses are allocated proportionally, or at least partially subsidized.

Setting Up the Community Management Structure

Because the community management structure must provide a variety of avenues for action to match the residents' diverse needs and interests, community organizations will do well to emulate the fine mesh of social institutions in mature, well-established communities, rather than replicate the monolithic structures found in some traditional, deterministic new town planning.

The optimal management structure will need to be flexible to allow organic growth and response to new conditions. Because the ultimate range of needed services and facilities cannot be anticipated with certainty at the outset, the developer should allow for the possibility of adding or removing programs, adjusting financial arrangements, and changing organizations over the life of the project.

Other things being equal, services should be managed to offer the greatest value for money in delivery—for example, through efficient use of scarce staff and facilities. However, the enterprise should impose the least control compatible with its own interests, and surrender complete control to the community as early as possible. As residents' interests in creating and maintaining value in the community normally will be compatible with its own, the enterprise will thus escape the charge of paternalism, without risking political exposure or overcommitting its financial and managerial resources.

Although each community's structure should be uniquely matched to its needs, four components are likely to be required in some form, in addition to the *development organization* itself: (1) *a community association*, to provide and operate services for community-wide benefit; (2) *neighborhood (or home owners') associations*, to perform more restricted services (primarily maintenance and service delivery within groups of residential units) at a level closer to their users; (3) *residents' councils and advisory groups*, to represent residents' views on community issues of immediate concern to them; and (4) *a builders' guild* to hear and consolidate residents' complaints, ensuring that they are properly directed and monitored for responsive service during the massive construction process. (Table 18.1).

The community association (CA). The community association is the centerpiece of new town community management (see also Chapter 6). As the principal organization for supplementing conventional services provided by the local government, it should manage and maintain common properties and services for the community, and sponsor and encourage various community activities. Being close to the community and endowed with wide powers, the CA is better placed than any other entity to identify community needs and ensure that they are met. It should have the scope to provide, either directly or indirectly, any services that the community may require in addition to those already provided by local agencies, commercial operators (including the developer), and non-profit voluntary organizations.

The CA's second purpose is to safeguard and enhance property values in the community by maintaining a high-quality environment. To this end, it should maintain common properties deeded by the enterprise, and any other properties it acquires. Maintenance standards and guidelines for each property will be specified by the enterprise before the property is conveyed.

It is important for the CA to embrace the entire new town area and reflect its internal structure. For instance, the Columbia Association adopted a two-tier representational and administrative structure, consistent with the town-wide and vil-

Table 18.1 Illustrative New Town Community Management Structure

	Community Association	Neighborhood Associations	Residents' Advisory Groups	Builders' Guild	Development Organization
Scope	Community-wide	Neighborhood/subdivision	Housing cluster	Community-wide	Community-wide
Role	Provide community service programs, facilities: stimulate provision by outside organizations Provide central maintenance to NAs Form interest groups Carry out architectural review Stimulate resident involvement in program planning/operation	Supplement CA services Decide maintenance policy Monitor CA maintenance contract Organize selected local activities, e.g., welcome teas	Advise CA on program priorities Consult NA on specific issues Channel complains to Builders' Guild Represent residents to developer Identify opportunities for resident participation	Coordinate builder activities to minimize disruption Manage cooperative action where feasible—e.g. bulk purchase, storage Respond to resident complaints Review design/construction standards Coordinate/police sales programs to avoid complaints	Plan/organize start-up programs—e.g. child care Organize community management structure Provide initial staff support to CA Operate selected services Plan/build start-up community facilities for CA Stimulate community "identity" actions through marketing program
Membership	Residential and commercial property owners/tenants Developer	Residential owners/tenants	Residential owners/tenants	Developer Builders Resident representative	
Financing	Annual property assessments Special assessments User charges Developer/external loans Foundation grants	Proportional block grant from CA User changes in selected activities	Grants Subscriptions	Developer assessment	
Staffing	Community manager Professional program staff as required Developer staff support	CA staff support Paid resident volunteers	Volunteers CA staff support on ad hoc basis	Developer staff support	Project team

Source: Apgar (1971).

lage structure in the new town's master plan. In The Woodlands, three associations provide all the services normally expected of city government in the absence of a municipal or county authority. In Reston, the original CA structure was based on neighborhood units, on the assumption that the only significant concern would be property maintenance; but emerging community-wide demands made the original structure obsolete, entailing a painful process of amalgamation in 1970.

A unified approach will be needed for managing services that will be used on a community-wide basis—for example, walking trails, bike paths, and fitness facilities. Besides ensuring economies of scale, such an approach will also reduce the risk of conflict between different parts of the community. At the same time, the enterprise will be better able to avoid the invidious role of arbitrator in intracommunity disputes.

The CA's membership should reflect the new town's main interest groups: residential tenants and owners, owners of developed or undeveloped commercial sites, and, of course, the enterprise itself. The CA should be governed by a board of directors, small initially but expanding as development proceeds and as control passes from the enterprise to the association. The association's staff should be lean at first, to preserve flexibility and contain costs. As the community matures, however, it could become a substantial organization resembling a small municipality.

Neighborhood associations (NAs). Besides community-wide programs and services, further common services will be required for the use of residents living in their respective development subdivisions or tracts—particularly for external and internal maintenance.

Because these services are most valued and best controlled at the point where they are used, that is, the neighborhood, they should be managed by an independent association for each neighborhood, not by the CA. NAs probably would find it economical to contract for the CA's maintenance facilities and to share administrative overhead and costs. However, it would be fully within their rights to change contractors in the case of inadequate performance. This should provide both owners and renters with far more control over important basic services than most other community governance structures.

In addition to maintenance, the NAs should manage any local programs utilizing common properties (such as swimming pools) and provide any local facilities or services for the use of their members that supplement facilities already being provided by the CA—for example, children's play areas.

They will also provide a valuable channel of communication between residents and the CA on issues of local concern—for example, the use of community recreation facilities adjacent to the subdivision and the quality of CA maintenance.

Thus, two types of NAs are most likely needed: (1) to administer common properties (a legal requirement in the United States wherever a condominium is established); and (2) to provide local services and represent the residents' mutual interests in any street or cluster of dwellings. It is neither necessary nor desirable for the developer or the CA to prescribe covenants and operating mechanisms for NAs. Particularly in large suburban subdivisions, experienced residential developers may have their own formulas based on their previous experience. The developer should, however, provide guidelines to individual builders and to residents, particularly where neighborhood associations impinge on the CA.

Both the CA and the NAs should be established as management entities, but there is a distinct and equally important need for the community organization—to provide opportunities for grass roots representation of residents' interests. Without an adequate "safety valve" to direct pressures that are inevitable in a new town, opposition is likely to be focused directly on the advocates, and potentially constructive community contributions thereby dissipated. Experience suggests that bodies conceived as service providers are unlikely to be effective vehicles for this additional representational safety valve function, particularly during the critical early years of development.

The developer should therefore anticipate the emergence of unofficial residents' groups to supplement the official service-providing entities. These groups are likely to take two forms: (1) a community-wide residents' council, and (2) ad hoc advisory groups on specific community issues.

Residents' council. A residents' council, on behalf of those in the new town, engages with the developer on town-wide development issues, with the local government on identifying and meeting needs, and with the CA on services for which the CA is responsible. It also provides a vehicle for enabling community participation in the planning process and for citizen advice and participation in local government.

The demand for a residents' council is not likely to be apparent for the first two or three years of the new town's lifecycle, until a sense of community has developed among the residents themselves. When the demand does build up, the developer should leave the definition of roles and the precise form of the council to the residents themselves. It would be desirable for the electoral basis of the council to be aligned with that of the local government, if close working relationships are to be established.

The council also could well have a fixed life. Once the community has assumed control of the CA, they may find that it can serve as an adequate representative vehicle, in addition to its management functions.

Residents' advisory groups. The formation of ad hoc residents' advisory groups has often proved valuable for enlisting community help on specific issues and for resolving points of conflict with residents. Many opportunities will arise for the formation of such groups—for example, to decide the most appropriate uses for a neighborhood center, to plan additional tennis facilities, or to expand the pre-school child-care program. Without attempting to impose a formal structure, the CA should encourage the formation of advisory groups to study issues of acknowledged community concern and to make recommendations to the Community Association Board. The CA should support their activities on a low-key basis with staff and material resources.

The creation of ad hoc advisory groups need not await the formation of the residents' council. On the contrary, they should be established as soon as residents express an interest and believe they have a contribution to make.

The builders' guild. One of the most trying aspects of living through a community development process is the intensive building activity it entails. It is therefore not surprising that resident complaints are so prevalent, not only about the noise, dirt, and confusion caused by large-scale construction, but also about the performance of the building contractors. Indeed, in a survey of community leaders in the Irvine, California, new town, 60 percent complained of poor quality, shoddy materials, insufficient landscaping, and inadequate follow-through by the developer.

Normally, complaints are directed either to the community development organization, which does not have direct responsibility for construction, or to the CA, which is unable to take remedial action. The purpose of the builders' guild is to provide an effective channel for organizing and responding to complaints, and to promote coordination among the builders' on-site programs, economies of scale in bulk purchasing, control of materials, and overall resource management. Cooperatives, of course, already exist in many areas. But the key feature here is the organization of multiple builders' activities within a single, multidimensional project. Moreover, the concept can be adapted to specific needs: at Flower Mound New Town in Texas, the builders' guild has the special purpose of coordinating the supply of prefabricated housing units.

To realize such benefits, the guild should undertake several tasks. To manage residents' suggestions and complaints about housing deficiencies, resident and community opinion should be monitored and problems promptly tackled. Architectural standards should be reviewed, with particular consideration to escalating housing costs, and recommendations should be made to the developer for possible incorporation as guidelines for subsequent development on-site. The potential benefits and scope of a builders' warranty program should be evaluated, and a program set up if the developer and builders agree on its merits. On-site activities should be integrated where economies of scale can be achieved—for example, materials purchasing and storage, and site surveillance (individual builders would be charged by the guild for these services on a proportional basis). Marketing and sales programs should be coordinated—for example, avoiding inconsistencies in sales approaches and preventing duplication of tasks between the developer and the builders. And on-site operational problems should be resolved through the guild—for example, access obstructions, labor difficulties, and coordination of delivery schedules.

The builders' guild should be a distinct entity with its own budget, but under the new town developer's leadership and control and possibly with developer staff support. It should also include a residents' representative.

The community developer. The intention of the new town's community management structure is to spread the basis of power and responsibility through the community. Nevertheless, the developer—as initiator of the project—will remain a decisive influencer in community management. The primary tasks for the developer in the initial stages are therefore to control the form of development through architectural review, to exercise specific guidance over the CA, and possibly to direct the initial operations of community facilities and support services to ensure effective performance. Over time, the developer gradually will cede development and operational control to various entities, as above. However, the wise, effective developer will not use its majority board and designated executive positions to veto any decision that is backed by community opinion.

The Woodlands' developer envisioned that Houston eventually would annex the property to protect its tax base from natural outward migration and thus provide its infrastructure and basic municipal services. Short of that future, the developer advanced funding for water and sewage services, to be reimbursed when growth was sufficient to support conventional infrastructure bond financing. As other needs for facilities and services emerged, individual financial and management structures were installed. On paper, the result is a complex web of interrelated, though not interconnected, organizations which might be foreseen as a bureaucratic nightmare. But in Galatas's words, "The Woodlands might well remain far into the future with a government that is not a government at all, but a collection of nonprofit corporations and special purpose districts. It does seem to work. In recent years, The Woodlands entered into a 50-year lease agreement with the City of Houston which would allow incorporation of the development as a city, subject to the vote of its residents."

Public-Private Partnerships: A New Way Forward?

An important lesson from the new towns experience is that weaving together social, economic, and environmental goals, diverse constituencies, and numerous programs to achieve the community development concept is a task too mammoth and intricate to be entrusted to either the public or the private sector alone. Moreover, the plural interests to be accommodated demand the widest possible combination of perspectives and capabilities if both the individuals and the community are to benefit.

In the United States, basic services such as health care and recreation are provided only sporadically by established public authorities. Thus, several developers have negotiated arrangements with nearby hospitals to provide on-site ambulatory and clinical care at no added cost. Columbia's famed community-wide health-care program, partnered with the Johns Hopkins University Medical Institutions, has been widely copied. In The Woodlands, George Mitchell committed more than $12 million of his personal fortune as a guarantee against operating losses to ensure that a hospital would be built there.

In short, new town development warrants a combined public and private response, based on an objective assessment of the capabilities and potential contributions of each. Indeed, public-private partnerships (P3s, for short) have become a central component of urban policy in the United States, the United Kingdom, Australia, Canada, and other countries as government leaders face limits on resources while business leaders recognize the strategic potential of new town markets.

New towns exemplify the ideal of achieving public purposes through private enterprise by defining their objectives, missions, structures, and financing to serve both public and private interests. In 1970, the U.S. National Urban Policy and New Community Development Act[2] (known as "Title VII") specified that the U.S. private sector would lead a national program to create new towns—in contrast with Britain's government-led strategy. The Woodlands remains one of the most (perhaps the only) successful Title VII new towns in that it is being built much as it was planned. This was due to the private developer's persistence in adhering to the government's stringent requirements, resisting the pressure to recoup investments too quickly, and committing private funds to enhance residents' quality of life where public funds fell short.

In a current example that was launched over twenty years ago, the U.S. Army engaged the home-building industry as "partners" to meet an acute need for adequate on-base family housing, and to stretch the military budget. Using long-term ground leases, the Army's Residential Communities Initiative (RCI) has attracted $12 billion of private capital from ten developer groups, alongside $1.9 billion of public investment—a seven-to-one multiplier of private to public dollars. This program package produces $1.5 billion in annual portfolio revenue to fund short- and long-term housing reinvestments. The planned end-state of this public-private investment is eighty-six thousand new and renovated family housing units on forty-four Army installations, or 98 percent of the Army's military family housing stock in the U.S., to a higher quality standard than government-built housing had achieved for comparable public expenditures. RCI, by my estimate, also has created some two hundred thirty-five thousand construction and permanent jobs. In the U.S. Department of Defense as a whole, including the Navy, Marine Corps, and Air Force, as well as the Army, the military privatization and partnerships program, formally known as the Military Housing Privatization Initiative (MHPI)[3], is producing similar, proportionally larger-scale, outcomes: over two hundred thousand family housing units are being built, renovated, and maintained to achieve nearly $32 billion in development value with less than $4 billion in federal funding, for a total defense-wide "budget multiplier" of eight-to-one private to public dollars. In addition to this significant fiscal outcome, the privatized military homes incorporate energy-saving features, community and recreational enhancements, and faster, better maintenance. Despite operational challenges in the program's second decade that are now being resolved, these results mark RCI and its sister military P3 programs as an unusually successful public policy and private business design for neighborhood-scale new towns, and a stage-setter for P3s in other government functions.

Conclusion

Given wide predictions of substantial urbanization, the global imperative for new towns is clear. There is, however, no playbook to guide new town leaders on what to do or how to do it. As one of the most complex management challenges in business or government, the new town defies easy or formulaic solutions. When an enterprise must scale up rapidly after its first successful project(s), the old rules may obstruct the developer's and community's essential progress or simply may not apply. However, that possibility offers enterprise executives and major project managers the freedom to innovate and, where necessary, to reinvent the rules.

Notes

1. All quotes attributed to, and verified by, Roger Galatas come from author's interviews by telephone, by email, and in person, between August 2015 and July 2016.

2. National Urban Policy and New Community Development Act of 1970, Public Law 91–609, Title VII, 1970–12–31, 84 Stat. . . . § 4501 et seq.

3. The Military Housing Privatization Initiative (MHPI) was incorporated into, and authorized by, the National Defense Authorization Act, Fiscal Year 1996, Public Law 104–106 (110, Statute 186, Section 2801).

19

Reflections from International Practice

Paul Buckhurst, Tony Green, Todd Mansfield, Pike Oliver,

Jamie von Klemperer, Gene Kohn, and Elie Gamburg

Paul Buckhurst (Perkins Eastman Architects, New York)

Demographic, public policy, planning, and economic trends are fueling a new generation of new towns and even cities. There is also growing evidence that recent new town developments, because of their size and density, are better suited for the environment while creating a better quality of life for urban living. Many of the most interesting and informative new community projects are located outside the United States.

The recent resurgence of interest in new towns, chronicled elsewhere in this book, offers significant opportunities to explore new directions in the design of new town developments. It is likely that a large percentage will be initiated by governments and public authorities anxious to cater to growing urban populations and rapid urbanization. In China, for example, plans call for almost three hundred million people to be moved from rural regions into the country's urban areas over the next twenty to thirty years. Future designs will take advantage of the experience gained from the past few decades of new town development, in addition to responding to the challenges presented by new technologies, climate change, and the decreasing availability of readily developable land. Some of these influences are summarized below: higher density and mixed uses, smaller and capital cities, and new towns as testing grounds for innovation.

Higher Density and Mixed-Use Development

New towns in much of Asia have been built at significantly higher densities than those developed in Europe or the United States. Satellite towns developed around Seoul, Beijing, or Shanghai, for example, involve population densities in excess of ten thousand residents per square kilometer (one hundred per hectare), compared to Milton Keynes in the U.K. (about three thousand per square kilometer) or The

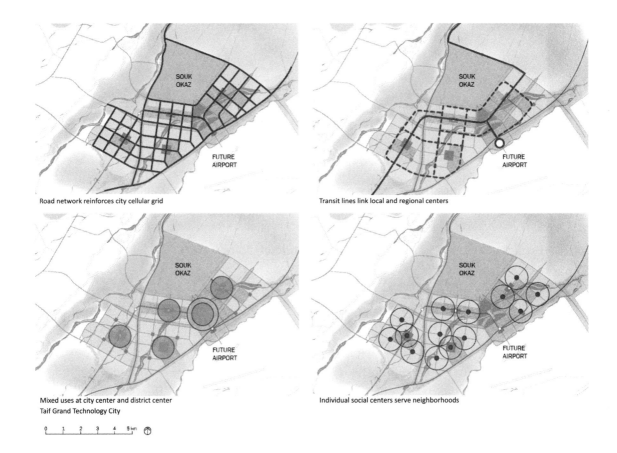

Road network reinforces city cellular grid

Transit lines link local and regional centers

Mixed uses at city center and district center
Taif Grand Technology City

Individual social centers serve neighborhoods

0 1 2 3 4 5 km

Figure 19.1. Taif Grand Technology City. Proposed public transit will link mixed-used neighborhood centers. Courtesy of Perkins Eastman Architects.

Woodlands in the United States (eleven hundred per square kilometer). Higher-density development reduces land acquisition costs, is more energy efficient, and can better respond to future housing needs with the demographic shift toward smaller families and single-person households. In this regard, a focus on low- and mid-rise high-density development rather than a focus on high-rise buildings can result in a more active street frontage and opportunities for shaping public open space. In addition, compact new town development is more likely to encourage transit service given the goal of reducing dependency on private automobiles.

Higher-density development can also be seen in future expansion of existing new towns. For example, recent proposals to expand Milton Keynes include plans for an additional twenty-eight thousand homes at densities of around ten thousand residents per square kilometer, a figure far above current levels in the town's neighborhoods.

The blending of residential, commercial, cultural, institutional, or light industrial uses provides an effective way to create compact urban environments that are pedestrian friendly. It can provide a greater variety of housing types and programs; reduce traffic congestion; and produce a stronger neighborhood character. However, successful examples of mixed-use centers have generally been restricted to in-town development sites or to modest-scaled core areas serving residential neighborhoods. Expanding the concept of mixed uses to a town-wide scale would reinforce the advantages inherent in this form of development and establish a network of mixed commercial, social, and employment cores that would be distributed throughout the new town development. Aligning the cores of these neighborhoods in a linear arrangement would also allow for more efficient transit linkages.

This concept can be seen for Taif Grand Technology City, one of several high-tech urban centers under study in Saudi Arabia (Figure 19.1). The multicenter plan is based on a grid of mixed-use modules, each roughly 750 meters in length. These modules are grouped to create a series of defined neighborhoods with centers containing a concentration of technology uses. These specialized centers will in turn be linked by transit to provide convenient access to the existing university and to a future airport.

New Political Centers and Smaller New Towns

As in the past with Canberra, Brasilia, Abadan, and Chandigarh, the creation of new provinces or states as well as national capitals continues to be a factor. India is currently planning a new capital for the state of Amaravati, and preliminary plans have been prepared for New Cairo, a new city to be developed on the east side of Egypt's capital. In Vietnam, the Hanoi master plan calls for five new communities, of which one will be the relocation site for the national university and several government ministries.

Smaller new towns with population in the range of twenty thousand to thirty thousand are also likely. Smaller-sized towns may be less comprehensive in scope, resulting in residents having to rely on transportation links to larger urban centers offering specialized attractions and services. However, smaller-scaled towns offer several advantages. Land needs (and acquisition costs) are reduced, especially if plans incorporate higher-density development with a focus on mixed land uses. More important, smaller new towns can be built out more quickly, reducing the development risks given the unpredictability of long-range economic, social, and political futures.

An example where a smaller-scale new community has been successfully developed can be seen in Jinan, China. South Jinan Luneng City is a satellite town encompassing an area of approximately 3.5 square kilometers (Figure 19.2). Developed to the south of the main city, the town was envisaged to accommodate approximately eighty thousand to one hundred thousand inhabitants, equivalent to an average density of

Figure 19.2. South Jinan Luneng City, China. Housing includes a mix of mid-rise and high-rise buildings. Courtesy of Perkins Eastman Architects.

around twenty thousand people per square kilometer. South Jinan Luneng City was completed in 2014 within an eleven-year build-out period.

New Towns as Testing Grounds for Innovations

Since World War II, new towns have spearheaded new ideas and innovations in planning and urban design practice, in part to help differentiate themselves from urban sprawl development. In practice, many of these efforts have had mixed results, with proposed programs often being overly ambitious in scope or being curtailed by financial restrictions. Despite the setbacks, new towns will continue to explore innovative planning and design concepts. In many cases the thrust of future demonstration programs will continue to concentrate on sustainability and resilience goals, including topics such as transit operations, responses to climate change, and issues related to reducing future energy needs. A small sample of the growing number of recent plans aimed at demonstrating future ideas in the planning of new towns is noted below.

Masdar City, Abu Dhabi

Masdar's initial concept plan was prepared in 2006 with the aim of developing a specialized research- and technology-intensive new community. Although the project is unlikely to meet its earlier ambitious goals of establishing an urban zero-carbon, car-free city, current innovative programs include operation of electric cars for transit use within the community and extensive use of solar panels for all buildings

Tianjin Eco-City, China

The city is a collaborative effort between the Chinese and Singaporean governments and is envisaged as a model for sustainable development for other Chinese new towns. The plan emphasizes light-rail transport and pedestrian and bicycle accessibility to limit the use of motorized transportation.

Lavasa New Town, Pune India

Lavasa is one of several new planned townships currently under development in India (see Chapter 12; Figure 19.3). The one-hundred-square-kilometer site in western Ghata

Figure 19.3. Lavasa New Town, India. First phase development is focused around existing lakes. Courtesy of Hindustan Construction Company.

preserves existing hills and lakes, and this has largely dictated the new town's layout and character. The master plan proposes five urban villages, each containing between thirty thousand and fifty thousand inhabitants. The design responds to many of the "new urbanism" principles, with a focus on walkability and a human-scaled urban environment, and development limited to low- and mid-rise buildings.

Milton Keynes, U.K.

Although planned over forty years ago, Milton Keynes continues to be developed, with recent proposals to expand the site area by almost twenty square kilometers. It is one of four urban centers that are experimenting with driverless car technologies in the U.K. This pilot project will in turn be developed into a larger-scale program designed to provide a fleet of self-driving cars connecting downtown to the main rail station.

Summary

Historically, new towns have played a prominent role in the development of new and expanding urban environments. Unlike typical suburban developments, new towns are aimed at establishing comprehensive, self-sufficient communities that are socially balanced and are sensitive to their local environments. Twenty-first-century new towns will continue to pursue similar goals, with the likelihood that their role and design will consider additional factors such as (1) higher-density and more intensive mixed-use development; (2) new provincial or state capitals along with smaller-scale sites and population targets; and (3) opportunities to explore innovative design and planning concepts.

Tony Green (The Pinehills)

The Pinehills, Plymouth, Massachusetts

In 1997, nearly 380 years after the pilgrims landed in Plymouth, over 5.5 square miles or three thousand acres of pine forest remained untouched, covering ancient glacial moraines. Part of Plymouth's original Ten Great Lots, it was never settled because of the depth (fifty to three hundred feet) to groundwater in soils too sandy to support a well. Two families held this land as a private estate for recreation from the 1880s to the sale in 1981 to Digital Equipment Corporation (DEC). Old Sandwich Road, the oldest unpaved road in continual use in the United States, was the only access until Route 3 was built along the westerly border in 1963. Despite rezoning for twenty-four million square feet of office space for DEC, by 1996, no building had started, and the land adjacent to the underutilized highway interchange, just forty-five miles from Boston was for sale, with no water, no sewer, no gas, and only enough power to run a 1792 tavern and 1929 farm estate home—the only buildings on the three thousand acres.

New Town

In this place, we saw the opportunity to create a new town and to build a community. We started entitlements in 1997 and purchased the land in 1998, and the first home owners closed in June 2001.

In 2020, The Pinehills is a new village center of Plymouth and home to five hundred thousand square feet of mixed use, some twenty-eight hundred households, miles of trails, and acres of trees. Total zoning build-out is 3,065 homes and 1.3 million square feet of mixed use. The premise of the community is to build on only 30 percent of the land, preserving two acres of open space for every built acre. Residential density ranges past fifty per acre and averages ten times the underlying zoning of one home per three acres.

Town Center

The cultural heart of this new town is the Village Green, The Pinehills' 175-acre, mixed-use commercial town center, organized around a two-acre park. The Village Green feels like it has always been here with its natural rolling topography and large (preserved) pine and oak trees. This image of the Green (Figures 19.4 and 19.5) with its trees and buildings beyond is what resi-

Figure 19.4. Village Green at The Pinehills, a community home to some twenty-five hundred families. Photo by Dan Cutrona Photography, courtesy of The Pinehills.

Figure 19.5. The Village Green (*top*), a mixed-use commercial town center. Biking Pinehills on Old Sandwich Road (*bottom*), the oldest unpaved road in continuous use in the United States. Courtesy of The Pinehills (*top*); image by Jeff Vallee, courtesy of The Pinehills (*bottom*).

dents think of as home. By Massachusetts standards Plymouth is a rural place. Even rural people like to walk and the density in the mixed-use Village Green makes walking easy.

Today, The Village Green has 150,000 square feet of commercial space and 762 residences, from apartments and assisted living to townhomes, condominiums, and single-family cottages. A new mixed-use building with 178 apartments, underground parking and 17,000 square feet of ground floor amenity and retail begins construction in 2020. Fourteen of The Pinehills' forty-two neighborhoods are a short walk to the Village Green. The Village Green's twenty-five shops and services are open to the public, including a post office, two banks, a gas station, a grocery store, a wine and spirits store, a dry cleaner, a hairdresser, a furniture store, doctors' and dentists' offices, a fifty-room inn and spa, a coffee shop, and five restaurants. The intentional location of the Village Green near the highway interchange encourages two-thirds of the business to come in from outside The Pinehills.

Market Research

The first question we asked when we began planning: "What do customers want that we can uniquely provide given the character of this hilly, wooded land? Or, why would people prefer this new town to the one in which they already live?" The high-profile permitting process instigated many inquiries, and we invited them to workshops over breakfast. We asked them to describe their ideal home and neighborhood by making collages with glue sticks and scissors. Each participant individually presents their collage, showing their heart's desire with the mutual reinforcement possible only in an unplanned group setting. We did not present what The Pinehills would offer, except in response to questions at the end, resulting from the desire nurtured by the workshop.

From these workshops, we knew that demand, in terms of both price and housing type, was much broader than the existing home inventory in Plymouth. And that customers across price ranges valued views of open space. Most collage photos were of the outside, especially from the inside looking outside. Finally, we learned that they desired the feeling of small-town America—alongside modern amenities and conveniences. During permitting, these workshops expanded our marketing premise to include a wider range of people who would want to live (and work) here. Now we use workshops as a research and selling tool: to find amenities and activities people really want the old-fashioned way, by asking them through workshops similar to those with home buyers, all deepening the relationship by our listening to the customer.

Permitting

The permitting process incorporates flexibility to accommodate inevitable changes in housing demand over time. Reflecting today's demand, The Pinehills has eleven independent builders offering different types of homes (apartments, condominiums, living for those fifty-five and older, assisted living, townhomes, cottages, single-family and custom) ranging in price from the high $300,000 range to over $2 million. The Great Recession proved the importance of this flexibility. In late 2006, we platted three large custom lots near the Summerhouse, the sales center in the Village Green district. Postrecession, a ten-minute planning board meeting changed the three lots into sixteen Nantucket-style cottages on homesites as small as twenty-five hundred square feet. The neighborhood's visible construction on the way to the sales center showed activity in spite of the market.

Regulatory flexibility from Plymouth also alters the relationship between the auto and the home: narrow, twenty-foot roads with existing mature trees right at the edge (compared to the standard forty feet of pavement in a sixty-foot layout cleared of trees) follow existing topography with a twenty-mile-per-hour speed limit, and homes are oriented to views on lots with as little as nineteen feet of frontage. These differences ensure that almost every home has a view of open space, whether it is a small condominium or a large, custom, single-family home. Often walking trails are a faster route than driving.

Planning

Planning the Village Green required understanding how to grow in a way that made good economic sense, and how to appeal both to residents and to the larger Plymouth community. Plymouth is a rural place, yet the town has well over twenty thousand rooftops. Almost half of those rooftops are close enough to The Pinehills that the commercial center is a choice for them. The key decision in the planning process was locating the Village Green at the edge of the community, adjacent to an existing highway interchange, rather than at the geographic center of the community, where planning officials in Plymouth originally thought it should be. This proximity to the highway made the Village Green a very convenient option for neighboring areas around The Pinehills.

Marketing

Early on, two signature golf courses at The Pinehills reinforced a brand and a reputation for quality. Today, marketing through unique programming attracts local and regional visitors. Artisan markets, food truck festivals (the first in New England), concerts, and holiday events (one hundred dogs and owners entered 2019's "Holiday Reindog" Parade) all build demand for commercial businesses by drawing people to the Village Green. These events are open to the public.

This widespread sense of ownership is key. The Pinehills is large, but three thousand homes and families do not show up all at once. Their numbers are not sufficient to support a real village center. So the stores and restaurants in the Village Green see most of their business coming from outside The Pinehills. That has been critical to growth, ensuring that the businesses remain economically viable. We operate the branch of U.S. Post Office (on a contract), the Market, and the Summerhouse sales center. All other commercial spaces are leased and earn competitive rents.

The Summerhouse, the first building constructed, continues as the welcome center. Creating a place with a positive reputation requires a consistent message, so all builder advertising drives traffic to the Summerhouse first. Potential residents' first impression happens here (our mothers were right: we have only one chance to make

Figure 19.6. Activities in Pinehills Village Green (*top*) appeal to both residents and the Plymouth community. The Stonebridge Club (*bottom*) resident amenity center includes two pools, tennis courts, a fitness room, and an adjacent cabana building with meeting space and lockers. It is the hub for more than sixty clubs and hosts daily activities. Courtesy of The Pinehills (*top*); photo by Eric Roth, courtesy of The Pinehills (*bottom*).

a first impression), and these potential residents often return multiple times for guidance as they explore and compare Pinehills home choices (Figure 19.6).

Recession and Recovery

While not immune to the Great Recession of 2008, we had some foresight and the financial strength to keep our ownership and bank relationship intact. We track home sales and match our projections with each builder annually. The New England volume peak was 2005, and in 2006 while prices continued to rise, the number of sales decreased enough to cause us to open our January 2007 meetings with two messages: (1) no more unsold starts, and (2) time to think about changes in product line. In recession, it is better to be selling a new home different than those homes up for resale. Every builder stopped speculative starts, and by 2010, all but one builder had entirely new product offerings. To stay current with the bank loan, we put millions back into The Pinehills. We paid off that $60 million loan in 2018.

Additionally, our antirecession program included a 2008 investment in a fourteen-thousand-square foot grocery store, which "proved" to buyers that we were here to stay, buoying sales. The Market has a focus on fresh, local produce, meats, and other products, and it averages over one thousand customers per day.

While the Market was under construction, we continued to prelease the commercial building meant to link the businesses near the post office on the Village Green to the Market. The recession overpowered that preleasing strategy, leading to one of the biggest mistakes. The result was a gap of empty land from the Market to the post office retail, which we then filled with a terraced grass venue for music and events.

Today, continued success with rental housing in the Village Green (including a national record-breaking apartment lease-up and sale to John Hancock) has encouraged building the next mixed-use residential building ourselves. Those 178 apartments and retail on three acres is 178 times underlying zoning density. The job of the rural new town builder is to disguise that density by the way topography and existing trees to literally root the place.

Utilities and Association Management

All utilities in The Pinehills are private. Eight miles of new gas line and a new "take" station at the Cape Cod Canal provide natural gas. The Pinehills built new private water and sewer facilities, regulated by the state, with resident user fees paying for water, operating, and capital costs. Private associations manage roads and common areas. The master association deals with connector roads, trails, and common amenities that link neighborhoods to each other and the Village Green.

Any neighborhood with its own amenity must form its own district association. Most decisions that affect residents' day-to-day lives are made by local (district) neighborhood associations. Local association guidelines are set by the master association covenants, conditions, and restrictions (CC&Rs), but each neighborhood district independently manages road and landscape maintenance; snow removal from streets, driveways, and front walks; and trash pickup, as well as design review for building and landscape approvals, subject to the master rules.

During the first year, The Pinehills established resident advisory committees that continue today. Resident representatives are chosen so various members get the experience and opportunity to serve. The association's accounts are open for any resident to review. The resident advisory committees of the master association and the neighborhood associations meet quarterly to review budgets and policy. These advisory committees act as market research: they provide feedback and help ensure that we are building what residents value, and that people are happy. Satisfied residents are the essence of reputation, and especially important as many who move to The Pinehills know someone who already lives here. Massachusetts law permits developer control of each association until 95 percent sellout. At 95 percent, a board of directors is elected to govern the association, from revising guidelines and setting budgets to choosing management companies. To date, five district associations have transitioned to owner boards.

Reputation, Recognition, and Community

The Pinehills has received over one hundred awards, including "Community of the Year" for the entire nation in the 2015–16 Best in American Living Awards by *Professional Builder* and the National Association of Home Builders. Collectively, having already added new assessed value of $1.35 billion to the town's tax base. Collectively, The Pinehills is also the largest taxpayer in Plymouth. The town of Plymouth's consultant, John Connery, reported The Pinehills as the most productive economic development return that he has seen in his career, with ninety cents of every revenue dollar to bottom line. In fiscal year 2019, Pinehills owners paid $24 million in annual property taxes and, after expenses, nearly $22 million to Plymouth's bottom line.

Community is difficult to describe and even harder to measure. The desire for connection and social interaction is palpable in the market. In The Pinehills some of this feeling of community results from interactions built into the design of the place: there is no mail delivery to the home, so getting the mail is a social activity. Ten miles of paved walking trails run through the woods along main roads and are lit at night (roads are not; cars have headlights) and, along with another ten miles of dirt trails, prompt a lot of walking.

Residents also participate in eighty clubs and activities at the community clubhouse, where every resident from custom owners to renters is a member. The clubhouse was one of the first places we built at The Pinehills to provide meeting space for these groups. As the clubs grew, now four different spaces host groups of different sizes. These clubs have built connections and each club or group is led by a resident. Community can also be seen in the number of residents who volunteer outside Pinehills, at such places as Pilgrim Hall Museum and Plymouth Plantation, and the food pantry and schools, as well as in The Pinehills having the highest voter turnout of any precinct in Plymouth.

Having a choice of places to eat or meet without driving makes the Village Green a unique place to work. The Pinehills' focus on both community image and design engages prospective residents to pursue dream fulfillment. Developers and new town builders provide people a place and choices that heretofore did not exist. If successful, that new place will meet the hopes and dreams of diverse people who come together to form a community.

Todd Mansfield (Crescent Communities)

Commercial Development and New Towns Centers

Commercial development is vitally important to the gestation of new communities. In addition to the obvious lifestyle benefits, our practitioner-style research supports the critical social and economic importance of a commercial center in new communities; the ability to create a social and commercial center in a master plan is fundamental to creating true "community" among residents.

Pursuit of a "commercial" center presents an economic conundrum for developers. Premium residential valuations of about 25 percent (plus or minus) occur in communities that have a successful mix of uses and a town center. However, occupied residences are required for a full range of food, retail, recreational, and institutional uses to be supportable. Consequently, the residential sector must lead, and the economic benefits that the retail development provides accrue heavily to the original home buyers. This is not necessarily a bad thing, but it leads some developers to conclude that it is not worthwhile to pursue retail because they will not be the primary economic beneficiary and because such pursuit requires capital and entails economic risk.

At Crescent Communities, we are the midst of planning a fourteen-hundred-acre new community adjacent to the Charlotte Douglas airport in Charlotte, North Carolina. Currently, the community site, while well located and accessible, has limited surrounding population and is perceived to be somewhat isolated. For these reasons, it cannot initially support significant town center commercial uses. This has led us to think about alternative paths to seed and create a commercial center from the beginning of the planning process before traffic will support conventional uses. Our planning includes the following steps:

1. Assume no land cost basis on the initial town center phase.
2. View the initial components of a center to be amenities and treat them as another form of marketing and not directly economically supportable.

3. Use the land plan to create a place, and use the site's natural features and landscape to bring people to that place. The center will become the hub for mail, some residential and community pool and club amenities, and planned institutional uses. In our case, this may include a farm and, in time, religious and other institutions as well. Investment in place making is essential.
4. As a first step, create an attractive public space at the center as a hub for extensive walking and biking trails to maximize the benefit of a beautiful site, and use programming, such as events, art, food trucks, and concerts, to bring visitors from the region.
5. Identify an operator for a simple food and beverage facility to offer items such as beverages, ice cream, prepacked food, and sundries. This is an aspiration for us at the moment.

We have not found a formula but are using an entrepreneurial effort to bring traffic and energy to the site. We believe that social media will be an important tool to drive visitation. As the four-thousand-home community builds out, we will have space for and be able to support conventional town center uses on an economic basis.

Mixed-income affordable housing is in the first phase of the town center in Charlotte. We have a shortage of affordable housing in the Charlotte region, and the government is making housing affordability a criterion for approval of new large-scale development. We are very excited about the initial mixed-income housing initiative because in supplying multistory, multifamily housing, it presents the opportunity to build density at the town center early on, making it easier to attract other retail and facilitate the town center's growth and development, and because it signifies an inclusive community.

The Celebration Story

There is a push-pull as to the location of town centers. Planners and the potential for long-term benefits often suggest a central location that can be surrounded by other uses, notably residential, but commercial factors would drive the location to one offering the most exposure and traffic. At Celebration, Florida, where I was president of the development company, the town center was essentially sited in response to the land plan and less so by commercial considerations. The ability to do this was perhaps a luxury afforded by Disney's financial capacity to take the long view.

The planning objective for Celebration was to make the town center the heart of the community. It covered approximately twenty-five acres and was set on a small lake. It included traditional food and retail uses, the post office, town hall office space, a movie theater, apartments, the school, recreational uses, a small hotel, and a church.

The mix and abundance of early uses, surrounded by residential development, was highly successful from a community-building and place-making perspective.

While it is physically successful, it was not as successful from an economic standpoint as it could have been because of the lack of exposure associated with the internal siting. Had the town center been located at the outer edge, it would have been more dynamic and would have included other uses that were ultimately developed on the commercial thoroughfare.

In addition to the location siting, being a part of The Walt Disney Company also allowed us to make an investment early on of around $15 million for the town center. The early investment was made because we had the luxury to be able to look at the long-term returns and justify making the investment, not because we were devoid of the responsibility to be profitable. Ultimately, Disney sold the town center for a financial gain.

While Celebration's town center architecture was very supportive, in my opinion, it was the land plan that made the difference. It moved the needle, brought people together, and created visibility, walkability, and all the other things that allow neighbor to connect with neighbor. In turn, I do not believe a town center necessarily has to be elaborate.

From the beginning, we had philosophically and idealistically believed that community institutions and groups would be the community's glue, and we did a few things to help foster them. We created and funded the Celebration Foundation to facilitate the organic creation of community institutions. We also created a community-wide internet, which was unusual at the time. Today, community connectivity has morphed into apps such as Nextdoor, and it allows neighborhoods to have an online network where they can post items to sell, offer services, or create forums to talk about whatever they like.

The capital structure required for successful community development also is quite critical. Large master-planned communities have a long tenure likely to include one or more economic cycles. Many of the great historical master-planned communities were economically unsuccessful for their first owners because of capital structures that did not accommodate the long-term nature of these investments.

We believe large-scale new communities require public-private partnerships to have economic success including municipal financing districts, road or utility funding, and recreation investments. Celebration, for example, benefited from two community development districts, as well as significant public investment in roadways and utilities. These public partnerships have proven to be wise given the very substantial tax base that has resulted that otherwise would not have occurred.

That said, establishing private-public partnerships can be challenging because the scale of master-planned communities can be a double-edged sword. While scale affords many opportunities to create amenities, quality, and comprehensive planning that in the end are proven to be beneficial to all stakeholders, the scale of large-scale communities can also be frightening to surrounding landowners and home owners. It can be challenging for elected and other officials to feel comfortable approving and supporting large-scale communities simply because they are so large. For example, the development in Charlotte, which was unanimously approved, was the largest single land-use approval in the history of the community.

Significant early investment also is required to plan and prepare the land prior to revenue production. Ideally, the landowner will be a partner in the development because carrying significant investment in land makes it very difficult to produce competitive returns on capital. At Celebration, the land itself was purchased by Walt Disney in the 1960s at low cost but required significant fill and had limited infrastructure nearby, so there were high development costs. The ending real estate values and the sales price of homes fortunately were quite high, so we could afford to invest in the land. Otherwise, it would have been difficult to justify.

Absent of a landowner partnership and public-private partnerships, the upfront costs and relative dearth of capital for land development drive most developers to create small-scale subdivisions as the only means of balancing capital and risk parameters. Such outcomes are not necessarily beneficial from an overall community policy perspective. In our situation in Charlotte, we are fortunate to have a sophisticated municipal government and elected officials who understand the public benefits of such economic collaboration.

I believe most successful large-scale community developments require a combination of an experienced developer with a compelling vision, expert and creative master planners and engineers, a well-located property, and a supportive regulatory environment. Creating a real place with adept place making that is attractive to residents and commercial uses is likely to ultimately drive higher sales velocity and price premiums, unlike more traditional developments, and ultimately a successful "community."

Pike Oliver

Lessons Learned from Irvine Ranch:
Early Retail Development and Governance

Irvine Ranch, located about forty-one miles southeast of downtown Los Angeles, is a large landholding that comprised about ninety-three thousand acres before urban development began. The city of Irvine's boundaries encompass 47,360 acres of the ranch property, which consists of master-planned neighborhoods and commercial areas along with substantial permanent open space and habitat preserves with a 2015 population of about 250,000. Two of the major lessons learned from nearly a decade of working for the Irvine Company have concerned developing retail early on in development and issues of governance.

Early Retail Development

A key issue that I have observed in master-planned communities is how to bring retail into the community when starting out. This is a challenge because retail is driven by rooftops—dwellings that house the critical mass of people needed to support retail development. For example, even though the average grocery store size has fluctuated from the 1970s to the early 2000s, to an even wider range now of forty thousand to more than sixty thousand square feet, what has been consistent is that it takes a minimum of five thousand households (about 12,500 people with current household sizes) to support a grocery store. So, when master-planned communities get started, it is a challenge to bring a grocery store to the community.

A question that I often receive is at what point in development can master-planned communities attract major retailers? Some of these have substantial requirements, such as Starbucks, which has a target of five thousand residents in a three-mile trade area, or TJ Maxx, which has a target of seventy-five thousand residents in a five-mile trade area. Trader Joe's, for instance, looks for about eighty thousand to ninety thousand higher-income people in a five-to-ten-mile radius to support one store.

When significant development began on the Irvine Ranch in the early to mid-1960s, the large landholding had a varied topography. It had only about ten thousand people by 1970, half located south of the 405 freeway, which bisects the property. Therefore, the issue was that Irvine's earliest retail development only had that small population to support it.

University Park was Irvine's first residential village. It is located near the University of California, Irvine, which was founded in 1965. University Park began its first phase of development in 1966 with 250 homes. Development also began on the University Town Center, which was always envisioned as the community's town center. The area essentially had nothing on it when we at the Irvine Company started and it developed slowly. The challenge was that there was a lot of pressure from the university, its students, and the emerging community to bring in retail to University Town Center to serve the population while the village was still very much in its earliest stages of growth.

We decided to build the initial retail hub, called Campus Plaza, away from the core of University Town Center so we did not disturb it or limit its development and vision. Campus Plaza thus got the grocery and drugstore. Today, it comprises 8.5 acres and supports 77,500 square feet of retail space. Because we developed Campus Plaza first, when the development of the core of University Town Center got underway in the early 1980s, there was not enough demand to develop another grocery or drugstore that would attract daily shoppers. Therefore, University Town Center was left to focus on specialty retail along with some food and beverage uses. Specialty retail, however, is quite volatile and not well capitalized, and restaurants tend to experience high turnover and failure rates, even in markets that have a lot of disposable income. These uses also tend not to be well supported by student populations. Retail in the core of University Town Center struggled for a long time because it was unable to attract local community-serving retail to begin with. Developing Campus Plaza first turned out to undermine the retail component of the core of University Town Center.

The core of University Town Center also struggled because of its environment, location, and design. First, the specialty retail environment is quite competitive. University Town Center had to compete with coastal locations such as Laguna Beach. Regional retail destinations such as South Coast Plaza in Costa Mesa and Fashion Island in Newport Beach also emerged at the same time as University Town Center, and these much larger developments could offer more amenities to attract more people.

Given that University Town Center is somewhat distant from the freeway, it could draw only from the relatively small nearby population. Its design was largely inwardly oriented, with no main street cutting through it, meaning the auto-oriented public had no way of seeing what was there to encourage them to stop. With these challenges and without the draw of community-serving uses such as a grocery and drugstore, along with related daily attractions, University Town Center just did not attract enough traffic to make it a viable town center.

So how can master-planned communities do a better job attracting retail in the early stages? Verrado, located twenty-five miles west of downtown Phoenix, is a successful example. Verrado is a large eight-thousand-acre community with a fifty-two-hundred-acre development area for ten thousand to fourteen thousand planned dwellings and four million square feet of commercial space. The developers prioritized a phase 1 district commercial core in their master plan and designed and built a one-block main street district and retail area along a major street. They put the grocery store and other important retailers there rather than dispersing the retail and trying to fill it in later as the community developed. Main Street Verrado was built early in the community's development around 2005.

The key lesson here is that Verrado's developers viewed this center as an early amenity investment and as part of the place making for phase 1 of the community. They provided the services the community needed, and they had to subsidize them.

The rationale was that they would see an increased land value for the adjacent parcels and get higher-intensity development. This strategy works because it is now something that the market supports even though it was not the case back in the 1970s.

Verrado is now developing another commercial core called South Town Center. It will be located near the freeway and will be programmed as an integrated regional center rather than a compilation of commercial uses. The developers avoided developing this center too early to ensure that it did not undermine Main Street Verrado. This new development will be able to draw regional retails because of its location and Verrado's increased population.

Issues of Governance

I see two primary issues regarding the governance in master-planned communities from my experience at the Irvine Company. First, municipal jurisdictions can present development challenges, meaning that developers do not always get to do what they want to do when they want to do it. Second, there are several political issues that arise when home owners' associations get too large and begin to compete with municipalities.

Irvine's geographic position on the edges of the greater Los Angeles metropolitan region and adjacency to the existing jurisdictions of Costa Mesa, Santa Ana, and Tustin to the northwest has meant development has not always gone according to plan. While incorporating Irvine as a municipality was always part of the Irvine Company's vision, we did not wish to do it too early in the new town's development because the company was allowed far more land-use flexibility under the county's jurisdiction than it would under a city's. In the late 1960s, however, just when Irvine's development was beginning, the city of Santa Ana tried to do a finger annexation, which was legal at the time, across the Irvine Ranch property to annex a retirement community called Leisure World. The proposed narrow strip would have run through the middle of what became the city of Irvine and would have foreclosed having a unified municipal government for the central area of the Irvine Ranch. The finger annexation failed, but essentially the Irvine Company capitulated and in 1971 the city of Irvine incorporated—probably about fifteen years earlier than what the company viewed as the ideal time for that to occur. It was a defensive move that preserved comprehensive municipal governance, but strains between the company and the Irvine city council did interfere with the developer's original plans.

Pursuant to state law, the new city of Irvine was required to have a general plan. The Irvine Company's development plan envisioned an ultimate population of more than four hundred thousand. When a slow-growth city council finalized its first general plan in 1977, they selected a medium-intensity plan that reduced the ultimate population by about 20 percent minus build-out in favor of designating land for open space and habitat preserves. A 1989 amendment incorporated a program to restrict approximately one-third of the ultimate city area from development. This affected projects such as the Quail Hill development, which got derailed and scaled back by the city council as a result of a citizen-led "Save Quail Hill" initiative. These types of negotiations, however, can make a better community in the long term with more focus on preserving open space.

Today, the relationship between the company and the city is far less fraught than it was in the 1980s. As the Irvine Company's ownership evolved, it became more supportive of efforts to preserve open space and entered an agreement with the Nature Conservancy for preservation management. Nevertheless, the nature of the relationship between the two parties is that the company "proposes" and the city "disposes," which is in stark contrast with the company's complete development control in Irvine's pre-incorporation days.

The size and political power of home owners' associations also posed a significant challenge in Irvine, namely in the Woodbridge village in the 1980s. Woodbridge comprised seventeen hundred acres and had a population of between twenty seven thousand and twenty-eight thousand—a minicity within the city, so to speak. In the 1980s, when the population was about half of the current total, the village's home owners' association, the Woodbridge Village Association, was primarily in charge of maintaining the village's parks and other recreation facilities. The association represented such a large portion of the population within the city that it became a competing entity with Irvine's city council. This caused a lot of political problems especially for the developer because the city was working against implementing aspects of the general plan.

Essentially, what happened was that instead of people first serving on the municipal planning commission or a similar citywide entity and then moving on to city council, they instead served on the Woodbridge Village Association board and then moved on to the council. This meant that the council eventually represented a minority of the community both spatially and population-wise and became a force that dominated the politics of the community and diminished a broader perspective on the future of the city.

Learning from the lesson of Woodbridge, the Irvine Company limited the geographic size and scope of responsibility of master associations in developments initiated from the mid-1980s going forward. We switched from overall associations to maintenance associations with limited scopes clearly outlined in their bylaws and divided the associations up into smaller geographic areas to limit their ability to become a problematic dominant representative force. It is important to establish a clear hierarchy of governance that goes from the city council to the master-planning association to the maintenance associations.

Concluding Thoughts

I believe that there is much to be learned from Irvine's successes and mistakes made, especially when it comes to developing retail in the early years and governance and strategic jurisdiction. Overall, I would say that Irvine got retail development wrong but jurisdictional issues right.

When it comes to retail, first, the reality is that to create a strong retail core, new towns need to subsidize retail at the outset because it is not initially going to have the users to support it. Second, if a new town wants to create a retail-oriented main street, it is important not to locate key uses in another nearby retail center as Irvine did, but instead phase in those uses directly on the main street. It also is important for the design to lay the foundation for an active main street. Early retail developments should be oriented so that they create a main street block with surface parking behind that could later be converted into a parking structure. New towns such as Verrado, as I mentioned earlier, and Stapleton in Denver have been able to do this successfully. They incorporate a mix of specialty and everyday uses.

Governance issues involve endless negotiation and renegotiation. As in Irvine's case, when challenges arise and long-term opportunities are foreclosed, new town developers might need to take actions to preserve the long-term vision for the new town. I believe Irvine did the right thing when the issue with the finger annexation arose. The developers had to support early incorporation, as the finger annexation and expanded city of Santa Ana would have been a greater loss of opportunity in the identity and branding of Irvine as a new town. It was a strategic decision that had to be made, and, all in all, it was the right call.

Jamie von Klemperer, Gene Kohn, and Elie Gamburg (Kohn Pedersen Fox)

Songdo—Vision to Realization

The idea of the new city is in part an outgrowth of the concept of the ideal city, that which can be conceived as a complete geometry, a well-considered distribution of functions, or even an image of heaven and can be realized according to a complete plan, and implemented without hesitation. Such examples include Chang'an, Kyoto, and Nicosia. Often such efforts have effectively provided a central nucleus around which a larger more diverse city has grown.

The impetus for new cities can also be traced to societal needs. A government or a corporation might seek to achieve protection from attack (Vauban fortified

Figure 19.7. Bird's-eye view of Songdo City. Courtesy of KPF.

towns), military mobilization (Miletus, Priene), industrial advancement (Port Sunlight, Pullman), central governmental administration (Brazilia, Chandigarh), or environmental progress (Masdar). Though these cities may have morphed into urban areas with a broader purpose, they started with more singular aims.

It is the sheer rapidity and scale of development that sets apart new towns in the contemporary context, particularly in Asia, from historical new towns. Their rapid development makes it difficult to ensure that the elements of successful urbanism, which normally evolve over time, are present—but it is precisely in those cities that having these elements "out of the box" is most important.

The new city we examine here is neither an ideal town nor a place answering to a specific collective goal. Songdo City (Figures 19.7–19.9) arises from a perceived need to create a generally high quality of life. This example fits into a category of planned cities whose goal is to find a balance of characteristics that together create a vibrant place including urban density; connections to international networks; a varied mix of programs; a diversity of scales; walkability; and an engaging design both urbanistically and architecturally. Part of this experiment's objective was to apply a set of engineered systems, including systems that facilitate efficient traffic, waste removal, and energy use, that will optimize the operations of the community.

Nearly 40 percent complete, Songdo is arguably, the world's most complete large-scale new town initiated in the twenty-first century, and, at an estimated $40 billion, also one the single largest private developments in history. The result of a close collaboration between KPF architects, ARUP engineers, and the client (a consortium of Gale International, Posco, and Morgan Stanley), Songdo offers a valuable opportunity to assess the elements of urban design necessary to create vi-

10	OFFICE MIXED-USED
27	RETAIL MIXED-USED
23 35 82 125	RESIDENTIAL MIXED-USE
54 56	RESIDENTIAL BLOCKS
38	PRIVATE SCHOOL
	PUBLIC SCHOOL
21	CULTURAL CENTER
36	CONVENTION CENTER
37	HOTEL
22	GOVERNMENT CENTER
112	HOSPITAL
33	PARK + LANDSCAPE
106	GOLF COURSE

Figure 19.8. Land-use map of Songdo City. Courtesy of KPF.

tal, energetic urban environments intrinsic to economically, socially, and environmentally sustainable new towns. The various challenges and successes in Songdo's execution also allow an assessment of the results of policy actions or inaction by developers, governmental entities, and designers.

Several principles guided KPF's design, based on the belief that these are intrinsic to all successful cities—past and present. These principles resulted in a number of planning and policy decisions including the city's urban form/organization, phasing, program distribution, and special elements/programs.

Connectivity

1. *Leveraging adjacent urban density*—Successful new towns are parts of larger urban agglomerations, integrated into cultural and economic networks already present as nodes of activity. Songdo is part of a program of new towns encircling Seoul and is an extension of Incheon, an industrial city that is a "sister town" to Seoul. Once conceived of as a "city of technology," Songdo was reimagined after the 1998 financial crisis as a "city of trade" intended to leverage Korea's proximity

to China. Well-connected to both Seoul and Incheon by sub-way and road, Songdo included housing and office space along with support programs such as schools, hospitals, and retail and cultural centers.

 2. *Connecting to international networks*—Towns connected to airports, high-speed rail corridors, important ports, or free trade zones are easily able to leverage connectivity to interna-

Figure 19.9. Bird's-eye view of Songdo City. Courtesy of KPF.

Figure 19.10. Songdo's international networks. Courtesy of KPF.

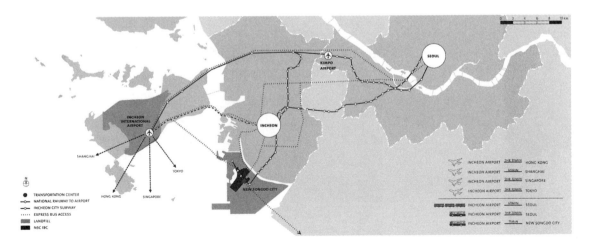

tional flows of people, goods, ideas, and services, benefitting from a "commerce" that is both economic and cultural.

Songdo is directly connected to the Incheon International Airport by a new bridge 12.3 kilometers long and is near the port of Incheon, Korea's main port. The first major completed building in the city was Songdo Convensia, a major convention and exhibition center. The Korean government's commitment to building this connective infrastructure was a key component of the city's early success.

Lifestyle

3. *Culture and entertainment*—Those elements that attract people need to be present in new towns, from day one. Verdant parks, stimulating cultural venues, and exciting places for entertainment and social gathering are the catalysts encouraging people to live and spend significant amounts of time in new towns. A rich mix of

Figure 19.11. One-hundred-acre park that features a navigable canal, a museum, a performing arts center, and other cultural amenities. Courtesy of KPF.

Figure 19.12. Songdo's first phase was formed by a rich mix of lifestyle elements. Courtesy of KPF.

lifestyle elements formed part Songdo's first phase. These include a one-hundred-acre park built at the city's center, featuring a navigable canal, museum, performing arts center, and other cultural amenities. A major objective of the park design was to make a central place where people would participate in a multitude of informal activities relatively rare in Asian cities (Figure 19.11). The park follows an urban tradition of large, central parks in many successful cities (e.g., Central Park in New York; Hyde Park/Kensington Gardens in London; Boston Common).

Placing a park at the center of the city was initially counterintuitive from a real estate point of view, but it increased the value of sites abutting the park and enhanced the value of the entire development. Another first-phase element was the Canal Walk, a series of mixed-use blocks featuring retail, entertainment, and live-work spaces flanking a one-kilometer-long canal and series of networked gardens (Figure 19.12). This open promenade and permeable public space allowed for social activity to occur within an activated environment from the earliest moments of the city's development, even as many of the remaining sites were under construction.

4. *Schools and education*—Schools, universities, and research/educational venues generate economic activity, encourage residents to come (and stay), and attract business. Songdo was organized around two residential neighborhoods bisected by the central park, each of which was centered on a large block containing a school and assorted cultural amenities and open spaces. In the context of Seoul, good schools are especially important in attracting residents. The school campuses also

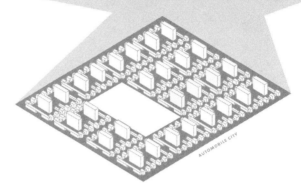

Figure 19.13. Variety of
building typologies and
densities in Songdo. Courtesy
of KPF.

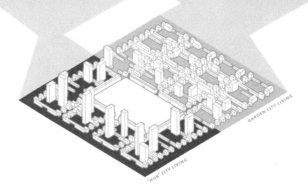

provide a mix of sports fields, performance venues, community facilities, and cultural programs open to neighborhood residents.

Variety

5. *Mixed scales/densities*—Density is a prerequisite for activity and energy within the urban realm, but successful contemporary cities are not all one scale. Typically, they feature low-rise, low- and high-density neighborhoods, mid-rise block-type neighborhoods, and places with high-density and high-rise buildings. Densities can be mixed within one neighborhood.

A tent-shaped density gradient inherent in the Songdo plan places the highest-density zones in Songdo toward the center of the city, around the central park. This puts the greatest mass of people, retail, and employment there and creates a legible skyline The gradient is not uniform: each block contains residential buildings at various scales: mixed low-rise "perimeter block" and mid-rise "slab block" buildings define courtyards and residential precincts while high-rise towers achieve high density with more open space (Figure 19.14). This approach contrasts with most Korean exurban residential developments comprising repetitive residential slabs, all the same scale, featuring the identical facades, and all south facing rather than considering street wall and neighborhood definition. Throughout Songdo, a

Figure 19.14. Section building gradient of Songdo. Courtesy of KPF.

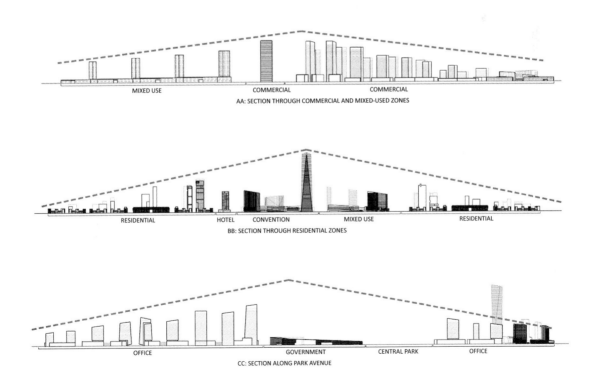

MIXED USE   COMMERCIAL   COMMERCIAL
AA: SECTION THROUGH COMMERCIAL AND MIXED-USED ZONES

RESIDENTIAL   HOTEL   CONVENTION   MIXED USE   RESIDENTIAL
BB: SECTION THROUGH RESIDENTIAL ZONES

OFFICE   GOVERNMENT   CENTRAL PARK   OFFICE
CC: SECTION ALONG PARK AVENUE

similar mix of heights is also proscribed for commercial buildings. Early stages of the city successfully mixed scales; later developments have sometimes reverted to standard Korean development models, with negative impacts to the feel of the city in these areas.

6. *Mixed programs*—Programmatic heterogeneity fosters activity throughout the day and attracts people. While residential neighborhoods can form genteel precincts within a new town, they benefit from local activation. In Songdo, this is achieved by mixing retail and social/educational programs, such as schools, into each neighborhood. Songdo's Park Avenue CBD serves as the connective tissue between the residential neighborhoods and is itself activated by the close proximity of cultural and retail programs. Similarly, the Canal Walk runs the length of Songdo and stitches together the more residential and commercial portions of the city with its lively program mix.

Sustainability

7. *Scaling cities for walkability and transit*—Cities with the appropriate mix of density and programs located in proximity become more economical to supply with mass transit and become more walkable. The scale of Songdo is designed around a multimodal transit strategy focused on walkability at multiple scales: the individual courtyards within the individual blocks, residential neighborhoods, spacing of office boulevards, position of the central park, and location of the schools, subways stations, and shopping. Various scenarios were mapped, capturing permutations of how residents would experience the city in their daily lives— whether staying local or commuting out of town to neighboring districts or into Seoul itself. The city's walkability has led to lower automobile use and a more active streetscape than is typical in the Korean context. While secondary streets have a pleasant neighborhood scale, Korean regulations concerning roadway width often proved intractable so that many of the major streets in Songdo feel less pedestrian friendly.

8. *Density and efficiency leading to sustainability*—While much is made of new sustainable design technologies in areas such as energy production and efficiency or water collection and efficiency, building cities to a high density with efficient, long-lasting buildings remains one of the most sustainable urban design strategies available. Dense cities use less energy for transportation and building heating and power, while high-quality buildings last longer, are reusable, and use less energy. Songdo's design employed a number "smart" sustainable technologies and systems: mass transit is plentiful; trash is removed by a pneumatic system; building gray water is harvested, centrally treated, and reused for irrigation and toilet water; the central park is entirely irrigated with harvested rainwater; the canal uses saltwater

that is passively channeled; and extensive systems for energy monitoring and control are integrated into the buildings. However, basic decisions regarding the right density, location of buildings for proper solar orientation (and using passive solar shading on many of them), and proximity to transit or degree of encouraging walkability all have provided the largest downstream savings in terms of energy use and resource consumption. The city contains one of the highest concentrations of LEED-rated buildings in the world and 40 percent of Korea's certified office space.

Policy

9. *Design matters*—Strong architectural, urban, and landscape design creates a sense of place and gives new towns an identity, making for more memorable, attractive places to live. Buildings such as the strikingly curvaceous Convensia and NEATT provided new Songdo City with a set of iconic landmarks from the start, and these were also complemented by an equally strong set of early projects that created a high-quality and architecturally meaningful fabric, rich both spatially and texturally. Residential precincts such as First World Towers and Canal Walk were designed to provide visual interest while also creating a sense of context that defined them as a neighborhood. However, subsequent projects in the city diluted this commitment to design quality. Repetitive designs, lacking scalar elements and featuring homogeneous flat facades, were consolidated on singular blocks—giving many of the later phases an ersatz quality.

10. *Government and private sector working together*—New towns succeed only with a strong and clear vision articulated and held jointly by all involved (both private and public partners). Songdo was initially conceived in response to the 1998 Asian financial crisis, as a way of diversifying Korea away from a purely manufacturing base (especially considering strong Chinese industrial growth) and to serve as a portal for foreign direct investment. In place of a failed development as a technology city, Songdo emerged as the joint vision of an enlightened client team, investors with a long-term time horizon, and a strong group of designer and engineers, all with a strong commitment to sound urban design principles and a desire to build quality architecture. This vision was developed in tandem with both the local government and several key national Korean ministries. The successes of land reclamation, rapid development of critical infrastructure, and the quality of the initial building phases of the city (Convensia, Central Park, Canal Walk, First World Towers, Chadwick School, and NEATT) speak to the ability of coordinated efforts between government and private sector to engage in urban development at a truly city scale.

Subsequent changes both at the national level and at local levels of government resulted in the delayed opening of several important project elements despite their completion (including NEATT and Chadwick School). Over time, there seemed to be a reluctance to encourage foreign direct investment, and a preference for local developers.

The dual nature of Songdo as speculative commercial development and national economic project explains its rapid construction, early success, and current challenges. The ability to execute the project profitably was predicated on the support and investment of government entities in reclaiming the land, being flexible with regulatory control, and building the airport and road and mass transit connections. The innovations in the city that make it unique within the context of typical East Asian and Korean exurban development could not have been done without the participation of globally innovative design, finance, and development firms seeking to attract a global clientele of companies, people, and institutions through sound urban design. Where the intentions and aspirations of the private and public sector aligned, the results, in terms of speed, quality, and profit, are noteworthy. Where these interests diverged, development floundered. As economies and national aspirations evolve across the Pacific Rim, Songdo will continue developing toward its ultimate completion. Currently, the success of the city is as much in the hands of the players continuing to develop it as it is in the invisible hand of economic cycles and transnational flows of people, capital, and culture.

New towns have always been projects with long time horizons, whose successes, failures, and ultimate character are hard to assess while in progress. Similarly, Songdo as a semicomplete new town development presents an open question: does the commitment remain to pursue a truly well-planned, and economically, socially, and environmentally sustainable, mixed-use, mixed-density city that is more than a bedroom community to Seoul? The critical early ingredients of sound urban design—featuring defined streets, neighborhoods of various scales, educational and cultural amenities, open space, variable densities, walkability, environmental sensitivity, and good architectural design—are there. Now, only time will tell.

Part IV

New Town Futures

20

The Twenty-First-Century New Town

Site Planning and Design

Steven Kellenberg

L ooking at the trajectory of new town development, there appear to be several essential components to a new town's basic function and its residents' optimal well-being. These timeless framework elements are: (1) cores and centers, (2) connectivity, (3) green infrastructure, and (4) civic/public realm. Although there is much more to designing a new town than these, they provide a structure for discussing how key design paradigms of the past might be reassessed when applied to the twenty-first-century new town. This chapter draws on U.S. and international case studies, framed largely against the backdrop of climate change and its implications for new town design.

Cores and Centers—New Tools for Optimizing Reduced Carbon Footprint

New towns typically provide (1) employment, (2) a variety of housing types for various income levels, and (3) support services to meet residents' everyday needs. Jobs and services are typically concentrated in a higher-density, multiuse core that allows more convenient access to components of daily living. Such cores have been developed at various scales and levels of complexity. Historically, most new towns included either a central activity core (downtown) or a combination of both primary and secondary cores in a multinodal pattern (Figure 20.1).

If twenty-first-century new towns aim to emit lower levels of greenhouse gases (GHG), then having a higher-density, multiuse core is fundamental because proximity and interaction between jobs, housing, and support services will not only reduce vehicle miles traveled (VMT), but also allow daily needs to be accessible with less energy and time investment. Of course, what would qualify as high density should be appropriate to the new town's context, and this will vary from center city to suburban settings.

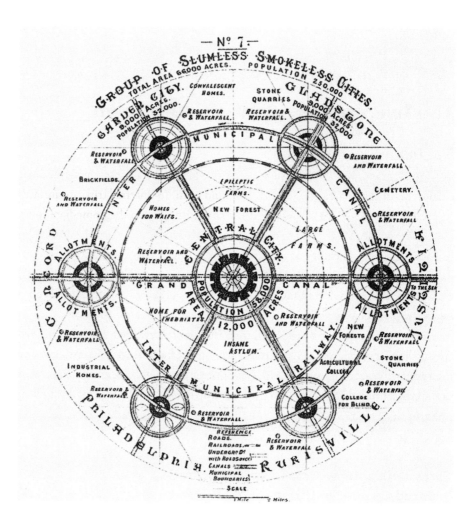

Figure 20.1. The garden city movement led by Ebenezer Howard acknowledged the importance of a town design organized around a series of service cores of relatively higher density (1902). Reprinted from Howard (1902).

The "Golden Mean" Methodology

Determining the appropriate land-use mix and density in the core is thus key. One of the tools used for calculating this land-use mix and density is the "golden mean" methodology developed by Fehr and Peers of Roseville, California. This approach first identifies a control area within the subject region large enough to have achieved full self-sufficiency and calculates the mix for a "perfect economy," that is, a balance in terms of jobs, housing, and retail. This land-use mix is then used as a guideline for individual cores; the area within a half-mile radius from the district's boundary is considered because it is close enough to interact directly on the core.

For example, in a predominantly residential area, the strategy would be to add just enough employment and retail uses so that there are sufficient jobs to serve the persons who already live in the area. If too many jobs are added, then workers have to be imported, and the project is out of balance. Theoretically the resulting core should have the highest potential internal trip capture with proportional reductions in off-site VMT, GHG, and congestion impacts.

The tool has been used in numerous large-scale projects, including the plan for the Jurong Lake District in Singapore. Here the Golden Mean was used as guide in refining the land-use program of a major transit-oriented development multiuse district. Although it is assumed such a district will not literally mirror the land-use balance in the larger area of reference, it should optimize internal trip capture after adjustments are made for specific land-use concentrations in the immediate (one-kilometer-radius) area. Through adjustments to land-use balance and other measures total vehicle kilometers/miles traveled (VKT/VMT) was reduced by over 9 percent (AECOM 2010b).

Optimal Multinodal Framework—Using Spatial Analytics

Another approach to lowering GHG is to have a multinodal development in the new towns. Work on new towns at AECOM's studio for SSIM (sustainable systems integration model) showed a clear pattern of GHG reduction by optimizing multinodal development patterns in both suburban and core city projects. In suburban locations where from 60 percent to 80 percent of GHG emissions were from vehicles, reductions of up to 35 percent VMT could be gained leading to reductions of up to 25 percent of total new town emissions (AECOM 2002).

The same AECOM studio developed a Geographic Information System (GIS) based spatial analytics tool to test various new town urban patterns for best resident and worker access to services. They found that the most effective pattern was a larger central core, where services supportable only by the full project size were provided, along with a system of subcores allowing access to distributed services at a district/neighborhood level (AECOM 2010a). When the subcores in this multinodal network were arranged in a manner supportive of light-rail, trolley, or shuttle service, the project-wide GHG was further decreased.

When used at the conceptual master-planning stage, these GIS analytic models can evaluate accessibility from:

a) home to job
b) home/job to local retail services
c) home/job to medical
d) home/job to child care and schools
e) home/job to primary and secondary transit

By combining services proximity with land-use density on a block-by-block basis, the degree to which density variations further reduce total average trip lengths can be shown (AECOM 2010a, 2011a). By linking some rudimentary traffic modeling and building energy data by product type, a preliminary carbon footprint can be calculated. This allows multiple design alternatives to be tested for the highest accessibility and GHG footprint at a very early stage of planning. If meaningful carbon reductions are going to be achieved, this type of evaluation must be part of the conceptual planning and design process.

VMT reductions also reduce more localized traffic impacts, and the master developer cost associated with off-site mitigation and on-site road sizing. These reductions can save tens of millions of dollars that can go to other more meaningful community components or simply to the bottom line. It goes without saying that any land-use balance programming must also be consistent with market forces and standard economic feasibility analysis.

Figure 20.2. GIS spatial analysis study leading to increases in pedestrian access to retail services and park land in a proposed expansion area of Marina Bay, Singapore (2012). Courtesy of AECOM.

This GIS spatial analytics model was applied in the master plan for Canon Station—a twelve-hundred-hectare (three thousand acres) TOD in the "capital corridor" of towns connecting Sacramento and San Francisco. Refinements from

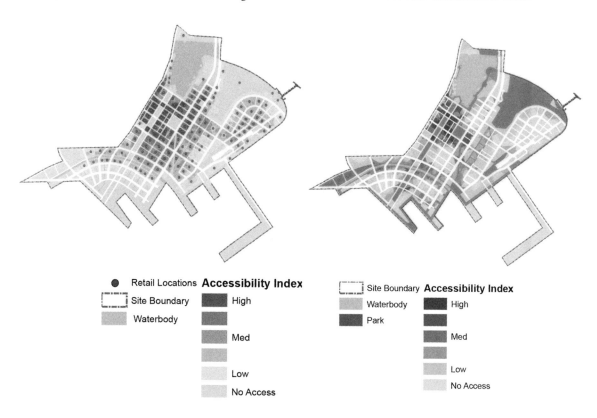

the model helped to enhance access to the train station. A linear, multinodal land-use pattern was identified that helped support a possible shuttle program in what is an automobile-oriented context. Also, product densities were gamed to provide the highest level of access to key services.

The GIS spatial analytics was also used in AECOM's master plan for Marina Bay, possibly the most aggressive new-own-in-town project in Southeast Asia covering over 480 hectares of land adjacent to the Central Business District in Singapore. The modeling helped to boost access between jobs and housing, access to transit, bicycle and pedestrian connectivity, and access to parks and open space (Figure 20.2). This allowed Singapore's Urban Redevelopment Authority (URA) to make master-planning decisions based not just on aesthetic, economic, or social justification, but also on quantified metrics related to quality of life and GHG reductions.

Connectivity—Transport Networks Driving Urban Form

Historically, most new town master plans are based on a well-organized, hierarchical network of streets based on either radial or grid patterns. One can argue the merits of each, but both have what count: (a) predictability, (b) alternative routing capability, (c) an efficient system of land division, and (d) modular growth ability. More quasi-romantic street networks have dominated several postwar new towns, seeking the garden cities vision, but often resulting in compromised orientation, less efficient travel, and greater difficulty in dealing with eventual redevelopment pressures. Public transit was added to the mix in the early twentieth century when regional planning in many countries began using public transit as a form giver to land-use patterns.

Sustainable Mobility as Master Plan Framework

The master plan of the twenty-first-century new town will be formed by low-energy, low-emission, time-efficient connectivity. Two primary strategies for achieving this are (1) increasing the percentage of local trip capture, and (2) reducing the percentage of trips utilizing single-occupancy vehicles. Local trip capture is best achieved when land-use/density patterns provide as many jobs and services as possible within the bounds of scalable, walkable cores as discussed in the previous section.

Achieving the second metric of less single-occupancy car use occurs more easily when urban form supports transit from the outset: by creating nodes of higher

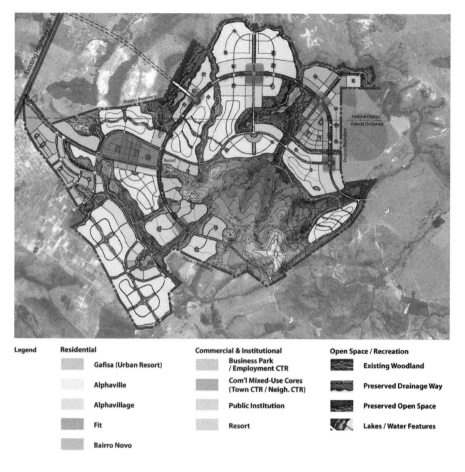

Legend

Residential	Commercial & Institutional	Open Space / Recreation
Gafisa (Urban Resort)	Business Park / Employment CTR	Existing Woodland
Alphaville	Com'l Mixed-Use Cores (Town CTR / Neigh. CTR)	Preserved Drainage Way
Alphavillage	Public Institution	Preserved Open Space
Fit	Resort	Lakes / Water Features
Bairro Novo		

Figure 20.3. The Brasilia 2 new town consists of a series of district cores organized on a transit loop connecting to a town and jobs center (2009). Courtesy of AECOM.

density, typically in a liner arrangement, along which transit networks can (ultimately) be economically developed. Such multinodal and/or linear city models should be included in any set of initial master plan alternatives.

Transit-ready planning ensures the reservation of non-auto rights-of-way linking key destinations, even in early development phases, allowing multimodal connectivity to evolve over time at lower costs. Initial modality could be limited to bicycle, walking, and/or shuttle programs. As the town develops and higher densities are achieved, streetcars, Bus Rapid Transit (BRT), and light rail may or may not become feasible, but the basic form is in place for more robust implementation at a lower cost. Brasilia 2 (Brazil), for instance, has transit corridor–based plans where transit spines connect a series of district cores and centers. Located thirty kilometers from Brazil's capital, this 995-hectare new town housing over two hundred thousand will have at least 75 percent of its population within walking distance of a transit station and/or hub of services and activities (Figure 20.3).

New Frontiers in Connectivity

New towns also present an opportunity to rethink connectivity. There are three basic tiers of vehicular connectivity (Sturgis 2016):

Tier 1 = Local (30 mph)
Tier 2 = Metro/regional (70 mph)
Tier 3 = National/global (600 mph)

According to Sturgis, new towns are an opportunity to rethink the transport grid, especially at the tier 1 (local) level. The current tier 1 network is based on oversized, inefficient cars on 15 percent to 30 percent of land area (for streets and parking). Instead, new town designers could consider *capillary* movement networks at the local level with much smaller (probably electric) vehicles. Rancho Mission Viejo in Orange County, California, is exploring aggressive local networks based on neighborhood electric vehicles (NEVs). They have already developed a *reduced auto impact* village, Terramor, a more contemporary, land-efficient version of the Radburn model, where most homes are pedestrian accessible to village cores without encountering a car or crossing a street (Figure 20.4).

Figure 20.4. Images of the Terramor internal, auto-free pedestrian system (2004). Courtesy of EDAW (2004) and AECOM (2004).

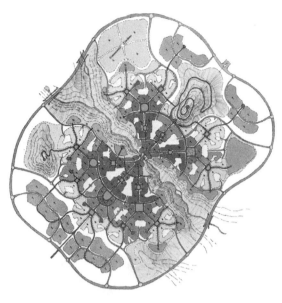

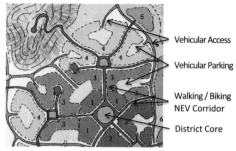

Vehicular Access

Vehicular Parking

Walking / Biking
NEV Corridor

District Core

Figure 20.5. The *Town* concept removed the impacts of the auto from everyday village activity. Vehicle corridors accessed building clusters from the rear with all development oriented to auto-free *capillary* movement corridors (1994). Courtesy of Chris Lawrence /Steven Kellenberg.

The Terramor concept was inspired by Christopher Laurence's work on Town, a hypothetical community of fifty thousand residents where all homes had garages, but the car was completely removed from its visual, social, and pedestrian fabric (Figure 20.5). Such models need to achieve financial parameters, but the reduction in local street costs and the recapture and conversion of 10 percent to 15 percent of a project's land area for additional revenue-generating uses could provide an initial basis for consideration.

Autonomous Vehicles

Road network traffic capacity is often the largest limit to scale and density in new town development. Increases in traffic capacity due to autonomous car *platooning* will allow land-use densification as the benefits become evident and acknowledged by local governments. Unfortunately, this will take decades to manifest, but opportunities for future densification should be built into entitlement strategies allowing long-term intensification if the opportunity eventually presents itself.

Green Infrastructure—Reviving Open Space as a Framework Element

Early new town planners recognized the need to have easy access to farmland and open space. The family plot was either adjacent to the house or around the town periphery. As farming faded, the importance of accessible open space remained a primary element with the garden city movement seeking a balance between the fresh air and clean water of the countryside and cultural benefits of the city (Figure 20.6). A maximum town size was even established to guarantee a balance between built and open lands.

For American new towns of the federal and entrepreneurial eras (1930s to 1960s) constructed and natural open space were key framework elements. At Greenbelt, Reston, Columbia, and the Woodlands, planners ensured that proximity and access to open and natural lands was a key feature.

The preservation of peripheral open space had the secondary benefit of defining a new town's *edge*. This allowed a sense of place and geography, unlike many contemporary suburban landscapes that do not have clear edges.

Two current movements have prompted a reevaluation of the role of open space in the twenty-first-century new town. First, the increased understanding and value placed on healthy ecological systems and their role *within* the urban realm; and second, the *healthy city* movement with its increasing documentation on the link between mental and physical health and access to usable urban open space (Maller et al. 2005).

Figure 20.6. Raymond Unwin's plan for Hampstead was an early interpretation of the role green infrastructure played in the garden city vision for the ideal, healthful city (1906). Reprinted from Parker and Unwin (1906).

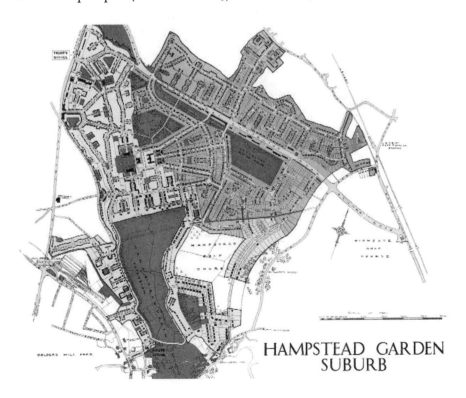

HAMPSTEAD GARDEN
SUBURB

Rather than a hodgepodge of internal parks with natural lands occurring in the distant hinterlands, the emerging concept of green infrastructure creates a network of multifunctional green space, both new and existing, both rural and urban, which supports the natural and ecological processes and is integral to the health and quality of life of sustainable communities (Town and Country Planning Association 2008). This represents the broad, European definition of green infrastructure, which goes beyond the U.S. definition focused on storm water management.

The green infrastructure concept differs from a traditional city park and recreation system in three ways: (1) it emphasizes ecological values and systems, not just recreation; (2) it becomes part of a larger citywide and regional system, ideally connecting to external natural lands; and (3) it provides an internal framework to help guide growth and urban form at the community and neighborhood levels.

Why Do It?

Using a green infrastructure network as a key component of the master plan has several benefits:

Open space access and trail connectivity. The link between open space access and mental and physical health is complex, but multiple studies have found correlations between natural and constructed open space exposure and (1) general physical health, (2) cognitive functioning, (3) physiological or mental health, (4) social interaction, and (5) physical activity and obesity (Wells and Rollings 2012).

The greater a green infrastructure network's surface area, the greater the access afforded to a district. For every additional .8 kilometers (half mile) of network, at an average density of thirty dwellings per hectare (twelve dwellings per acre), more than six thousand residents would be within a .5-kilometer (one-third of a mile) walking distance. This is increasingly relevant given current social equity issues and the growing separations in economic class structure.

Biodiversity and wildlife movement. The connectivity found in a green infrastructure network allows free movement of wildlife, even of an urban or quasi-urban species, allowing a robust gene pool maximum interface between people and nature to be maintained (Tzoulas et al. 2007). In turn, a high level of biodiversity guarantees longevity, genetic health, important interactions between species, and resilience in the face of climate and artificial influences (Tzoulas et al. 2007). The Stapleton North Trunk Park in Denver, Colorado, for instance, incorporates a high level of connectivity and biodiversity (Figure 20.7).

Carbon sequestration and urban heat island effect. Having a green infrastructure network in place to the extent that plant surface is increased will help to absorb more GHG. Most large development projects have not sought credit for increased carbon

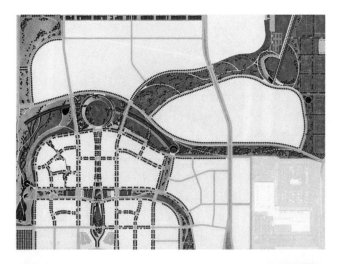

Figure 20.7. Stapleton North Trunk Park designed by Civitas for the Denver Park Creek Metropolitan District (2016). This incorporates a high level of connectivity and biodiversity, both traits of a strong green infrastructure network. Courtesy of Civitas.

sequestration through landscape and open space development. This is changing as calculation methodologies have been developed, and total project carbon footprint reductions of between .5 percent and 1.5 percent are projected (AECOM 2007). This does not sound like much, but when the equivalent GHG reduction could cost millions of dollars in solar arrays it becomes worth consideration.

In addition, the urban heat island effect has been identified as a key contributor to increased energy consumption, let alone human discomfort, in larger dense cities. Again, having a green infrastructure network can make a notable difference to the urban heat island effect. For instance, dynamic modeling by AECOM for the Marina Bay project indicated that increasing street trees, vertical vegetation on buildings, and carefully located open spaces to increase natural ventilation can lower urban heat island effect by up to one degree centigrade (AECOM 2012). Again, a small increment, but the reduced energy cost and emissions associated with such reductions are material in a total sustainability and strategies for emissions reduction.

How to Do It

A healthy green infrastructure utilizes both natural and constructed open space consisting of "hubs" and "links." Hubs are sizable areas of natural lands and/or community and regional parks that anchor the green infrastructure network. These provide origins and destinations for wildlife and ecological processes as well as trail and bikeway termini. Links are the connections tying the system together, consisting of drainage ways, greenbelts, parkways, and other linear elements (Figures 20.8, 20.9).

According to the U.K. Town and Country Planning Association (Town and Country Planning Association 2008), green infrastructure should:

1. Be designed as a varied, widely distributed, strategically planned and interconnected network.
2. Preserve the highest-value existing ecological resources with sufficient buffer for their continued health and protection.
3. Be factored into land values and decisions on housing densities and urban structure prior to and during the master-planning process.
4. Be accessible to local population and provide alternative means of transport (riding, hiking, etc.).
5. Be designed to reflect and enhance the town's locally distinctive character utilizing local habitats, eco-tones, wildlife, and recreation priorities.
6. Achieve physical and functional connectivity between sites at all levels and across the entire new town and ultimately the subregion.

One of the most comprehensive programs for green infrastructure can be found in the U.K. Eco-Town Program, where 40 percent of the total land in a new town, including private open space, is recommended to be earmarked for green infrastructure, with the additional following criteria (Town and Country Planning Association 2008):

Figure 20.8. Basic construct of green infrastructure network is a series of natural or man-made open space hubs linked together by corridors allowing movement in various forms and systems. Reprinted from McMahon and Benedict (2012) with permission.

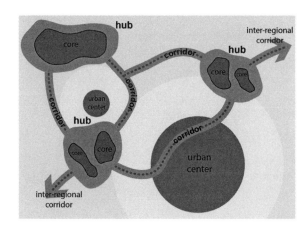

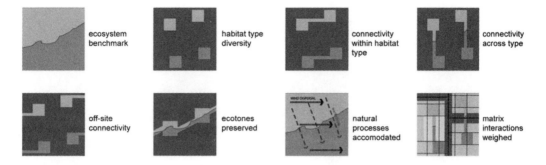

Figure 20.9. Robust green infrastructure networks result from the interplay of habitat diversity, connectivity, and natural processes. Courtesy of Isaac Brown (2011).

- No resident should be farther than three hundred meters (one thousand feet) distant from a natural open space.
- At least one hectare (2.5 acres) of nature reserve should be provided per one thousand residents
- At least twenty hectares (fifty acres) of natural open space should exist within two kilometers (1.5 miles) distance of residents
- At least one hundred hectares (250 acres) of natural open space should exist within five kilometers (three miles) distance of residents
- At least five hundred hectares (twelve hundred acres) of natural open space should exist within ten kilometers (six miles) distance of residents

International new town examples where these criteria have been approached include Amersfoort, Netherlands; Drieburg, Germany; and Zaragoza, Spain. In the United States, the new communities developed on the Rancho Mission Viejo and Irvine Ranch in southern California routinely achieve at least a 50 percent natural and man-made open space ratio.

Multifunctionality in Green Infrastructure

Green infrastructure can be a key implement in the tool kit for climate change mitigation because of its multifunctional nature and ability to act as a buffer to extreme events. The reductions it brings about of urban heat islands, storm water accumulation, and flooding, and its improvement of the ability of species to move and to adapt to changing climate forces all increase a new town's resiliency.

To reduce the amount of land required to achieve these values, the concept of *multifunctionality* is used to provide for the integration and interaction of various

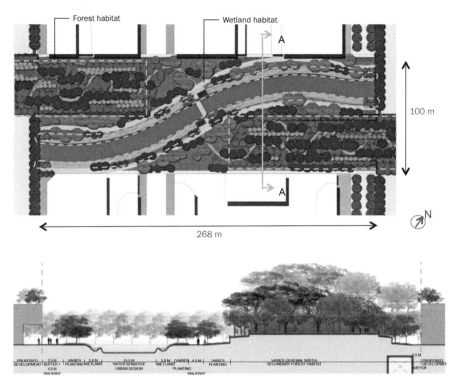

Figure 20.10. Conceptual study for an eco-corridor in Singapore demonstrating multifunctionality providing trails, biofiltration, biodiversity, flood control, and carbon sequestration (2012). Courtesy of AECOM.

Figure 20.11. Conceptual study for an eco-corridor illustrating extension of eco-zone into private development blocks. Integrating vegetation into building form is becoming more common in Southeast Asia (2012). Courtesy of AECOM.

values in the same open space component (Grant 2010). Designing a segment to provide flood control, hiking and biking, wildlife movement, and native species regeneration in the same area is an example. The eco-corridor proposed in a concept study to link the Gardens by the Bay urban park to the core of the new Marina Bay district in Singapore, for instance, was designed to be highly multifunctional by providing usable park space, bike and pedestrian trails, storm water biofiltration, and biodiverse eco-tones to achieve ambitious ecology enhancement targets (Figures 20.10, 20.11). The corridor as studied would help increase biodiversity within the overall district by over 400 percent from baseline conditions (AECOM 2012).

The Jeffery Open Space Trail (JOST) corridor that links the Irvine Ranch, California, to outlying major open space preserves is another good example of multifunctionality. It overlays uses of recreation, native habitat, bike and trail connectivity, and historical and natural systems education (Figure 20.12). This extensive green infrastructure system is the result of conservation and open space networking efforts over the last fifty years.

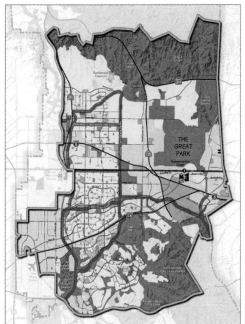 

Figure 20.12. The green infrastructure of Irvine, California (2016). The design reflects an early bias in the master planning of the original 110,000-acre Irvine Ranch. Spines are more recent trails and corridors linking open space hubs. The Jeffery Open Space Trail corridor on the right is an example. Courtesy of Irvine Company.

Civic/Public Realm—the Value of Intentional Urban Space

Besides creating healthy, efficient, and sustainable town form, it is just as important that the new town of the future be designed as an engaging, fruitful, and pleasant place.

Central public places have been the essential heart and soul of new towns. Garden city planners Raymond Unwin and John Nolen, for instance, used classical Beaux-Arts design structure in suburban settings to create strongly connected public spaces, boulevards, and parks around which neighborhoods could be perceptibly organized. Their use of axial organizing principles and formal spaces resurrected the power and integrity of ancient classical public space as shown in Nolen's plans for Mariemont, Ohio, and Venice, Florida (Figure 20.13).

However, in postwar Europe and the United States, the art of great place making took a hiatus with extensive suburban development occurring without strong urban design elements. The advent of new urbanism was a call to arms on the issue, and several new towns in the recent decades have sought to create attractive, interactive, and livable town. The iconic towns of Seaside, Celebration, and Kentlands are examples. Their use of form-based zoning has shifted two-dimensional Euclidean zoning into three dimensions with hopes of forming a higher-quality street space and comfortable sense of human scale.

Figure 20.13. Raymond Unwin's plan for a hypothetical suburban new town (1912). The plan exemplifies his focus on interconnected public space, a principle that more recently became a core construct for the new urbanism. Reprinted from Unwin (1912).

As laudable as the new urbanism doctrine is for creating attractive public spaces and charming streets, a debate continues, in the United States at least, regarding its higher cost and market feasibility, in part owing to the required diver-

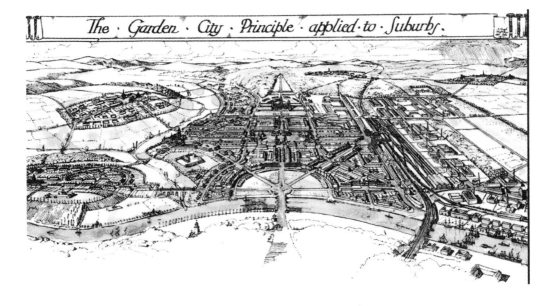

The · Garden · City · Principle · applied · to · Suburbs.

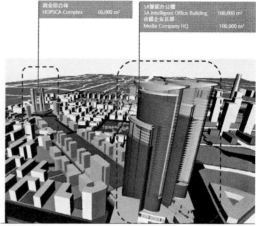

sity of product and complexity of building design. Progress has been made in new communities such as Stapleton, Colorado, in applying the concepts to larger-scale, noncustom projects that achieve many of the public realm and place-making benefits at an attainable price.

Historic precedents suggest that the twenty-first-century new town will be best when built around a strong *urban design framework* that transforms otherwise mundane land uses into balanced networks of boulevards, avenues, urban parks, iconic buildings, and striking public space. In addition to creating a highly engaging and memorable town form, such a framework helps to mitigate the impacts of volatile economic cycles and the damage they can do to well-laid-out plans.

Figure 20.14. At an urban density a study for a district in Tongzhou New City on the edge of Beijing shows strong urban design intention with a linear central park terminated by iconic high rise buildings (2011). Courtesy of AECOM.

As market shifts occur, the planned land uses may need to adapt, but the core character of the master plan is maintained because of its strong public realm "bones." As in any living organism, these bones are manifest as a connected series of elements: some linear (civic boulevards, natural drainage corridors, enhanced parkways, linear parks) and some nodal special destinations (civic plazas and buildings, community and neighborhood parks, and iconic architecture).

In a higher-density, context, the Tongzhou New City in southeast Beijing has also developed a strong-boned urban design framework with links between well-defined public space and various urban parks and plazas. The overall framework is perceived as *intentional* and transmits a concern for the quality and sequence of public space around which standard, built product is placed (Figure 20.14). This public realm framework is of sufficient definition that specific adjacent uses can shift with economic cycles and the new town still maintain identity and place-making integrity.

Figure 20.15. The first phase of Verrado outside of Phoenix (2005). The phase broke housing types into smaller groupings than typical of the market (left plan) with the master plan achieving the "every street tells a story" goal as shown in the various street typologies (right plan). Courtesy of AECOM.

A strong urban design framework is the basis of the Verrado master plan, a new town forty-eight kilometers (thirty miles) west of downtown Phoenix, Arizona. Its strong bones were created with a series of civic boulevards, natural drainage ways, and neighborhood and pocket parks (Figure 20.15). Open spaces were sized to be both intimate and flexible and located to be *formative*, that is, perceived as the origin or seed core of the surrounding neighborhood.

The Neighborhood Crafting Toolbox

Within the urban design framework discussed above, the smaller scales of district and neighborhood deliver the day to day tactile surroundings that most directly affect residents' quality of life. Guiding developers on the scale and proportion of human space, view alignment, natural light, and focal architecture helps users make sense out of the world while exciting their senses and creating memorable experience. Design guidelines often focus on the building, but district and neighborhood need also be addressed in order to create effective and enticing surroundings. The following are examples of district and neighborhood scale design principles:

- *Streets designed to tell a story*—Ideally, no two streets in a neighborhood are the same. Views, alignment, architecture, and landscape interventions provide each street with a slightly individual personality. Ideally, each street has a special element along its course or at its terminus, for example, a park, special view, landscape element, or community service.
- *Diversity of building type*—Although developers require economies-of-scale in large projects, they are best broken into smaller increments. Using multiple architects and builders creates a more natural, organic texture. These strategies shift character from production building to a more authentic, fine-grained character.
- *Reduced presence of the car*—Recessed, rear-loaded garages have a material impact on street character and the overall personality of a neighborhood. Avoiding exposed garages and using ground floor "liners" along primary streets result in more walkable and intimate street scenes leading to higher real estate values.
- *Focal vs. background architecture* – Some buildings should be more visually important than others, allowing opportunities for special buildings to accent a district while others fade into a tasteful but more neutral background.
- *Special places deserve special treatment*—Whether core city or suburb, each district has locations that are more strategic and should be treated accordingly. Focal architecture, special treatments on street corners, and enhanced architecture along important edges increase visual interest and sense of authenticity. Including gathering and social spaces in central locations are critical to a districts social and cultural health.

For the Town Center District in Diyar Al Muharraq, Kingdom of Bahrain district guidelines were developed by AECOM to ensure walkable streets, people gathering places in key locations, focal architecture, terminating view corridors and a variety in neighborhood character.

The Third Place

What is the role of public space for a digitally and Wi-Fi connected population? How does the shift away from bricks-and-mortar retail affect activity in urban cores? Although technology has created the highest level of social connectivity in the history of our species, the new connections and people groupings that result

Figure 20.16. Effects of demographic, technological, and sociocultural change.

		Less	→	More
Demographic	Growth of millennial cohort	Predictability/formality		Uncertainty/flexible
		Manicured/finished		Natural/organic
		Monumental space		Varied-scale social spaces
	Aging populations	Separated/district land uses		Local/accessible services
		Age segregated		All-age community
		Simple security systems		Layered levels of openness
	Increasingly mixed ethnicity	Single-themed space		Multithemed spaces
		Corporate retail/food tenants		Regional/local tenanting
		Conventional size shops		Diverse shop size
Technology	Advent of internet shopping	Larger retail centers		Mod/smaller retail centers
		Larger anchors		Smaller anchors (less stocking)
		Long tenant duration		Higher tenant turnover
	Experiential vs. comparison retail	15–25% food and beverage		35–50% food and beverage
		Mundane place making		Intentional place making
		Auto/parking oriented		Pedestrian scale
	Visual technology	Static signing		Digital sports/music
	Growth in social media	Commercial function		Social function/gathering
		Simplistic spatial design		Nuanced/multiscaled
Social/Cultural	Intensified socialization	No/little public seating		Varied types seating pockets
		Fixed seating		Movable seating
	Increased community engagement	No/little event space		Flexible event space
		No/little event infrastructure		Flexible/moveable infrastructure
		No/little event programming		Ongoing/multicultural programming
	Focus on visual arts	No/little public art		Robust arts programming
		Fixed/static displays		Changing/interactive events

ultimately seek and need real-world interaction. It follows that new town design has a role in providing a network of places that are accessible, comfortable, engaging, and varied, designed in a manner that encourages gathering of various sizes of social groups.

Ray Oldenburg, in his book on the importance of creating places for social engagement, differentiates the *third place* from the two dominant environments of home ("first place") and the workplace ("second place") (Oldenburg 1989). Cafés, active streets, plazas, clubs, and parks are examples of the third place, where a certain level of energy and sensory and social engagement naturally occur. Oldenburg suggests that for a community to maintain mental and physical health, such social places are essential and often overlooked in the more function-driven processes of town design. The *third place* ideally has at least these characteristics (Oldenburg 1989):

- Perception of neutral ground
- A leveling place between class and ethnicity
- A place for conversation
- Accessibility
- Opportunity to become a "regular" place
- Low profile and wholesomeness
- Playful mood
- Homelike feel

Shifts in demographics, retailing, technology, and social engagement require urban space to be more flexible to morph into expressions of the constituent cultures, ethnicities, and stages of life. The notion of (un)intentional space as defined by Gavin Shaefer acknowledges that most urban spaces are used, in fact, differently than originally planned, which results in a freshness, authenticity, and spontaneity not found in overly programmed and structured spaces. Designing (un)intentional space is an emerging art form, but the first step is recognizing its value and providing third places within the urban design framework that exhibit sound spatial form but allow a multiplicity of uses, activities, and community expression (Figure 20.16).

Summary

Based on a review of new towns through the ages, several key consistent elements can be identified providing cues for foundation, and innovation, for the future:

1. As people push back on climate change, the organization of towns around well-composed *cores and centers* is an effective, low-cost tool for reducing

emissions as well as freeing time and energy for higher levels of individual and societal development.

2. Multimodal *connectivity* is not a new idea but will become increasingly fundamental to town form using transit-ready planning techniques and seeking new forms of local movement to gain greater land and energy efficiencies.

3. It is time to rethink the role of *green infrastructure* in the organization of the town to break sprawl, to provide greater equity in open space access, to increase choices for active, healthy living, and to increase ecological diversity *within* the fabric of the town.

4. Building "good bones" with a strong *urban design framework* will result in the city plan having staying power over time. However, greater thought needs to go into the design of places for gathering, as this will be increasingly critical in the quickly emerging uberconnected society.

These are exciting times in new town design, and hopefully the above discussion has tickled the thought process as people engage in designing and building new towns deserving of the moniker "twenty-first-century town."

21

Environmental Concerns and New Towns

Four Paths

Ann Forsyth

Since early experiments to create cleaner company towns and harmonious garden cities, the natural environment has been an important theme in new town development. In the past decades, new towns have taken three main approaches to designing with nature, and a fourth may be emerging in the current period. Some new towns continue to create a traditional *garden* setting, typically for pleasant aesthetics and to balance the social, economic, and health benefits of town and country. The *compact city* approach is efficient in terms of energy and land use, placing people in relatively high-density communities; this is also an approach valued for mitigating climate change. *Eco-villages* or eco-burbs create a closer connection between people, natural systems, and agricultural practices in a low-impact format at typically lower densities. Finally, an emerging type, *resilient new towns*, potentially meld components of other versions, integrating natural systems with the compact city, while adding useful redundant infrastructure, robust safety systems, and mechanisms for change over time. Some of these resilient places may be part of a strategy of planned retreat from hazardous areas, as described in Chapter 22, leaving less adaptable locations behind. While some such places have been proposed, few truly resilient new towns have been built. They, however, are obviously an important future direction for new town development.

This chapter outlines these four approaches that have emerged over the past century and a half, responding to an evolving set of environmental problems and changing understandings of how to combat them (Beatley 2009; Carson 1962; Crewe and Forsyth 2011; Healey and Shaw 1994; Leopold 1949; Meadows, Randers, and Behrens 1972). Early examples were part of a nostalgia for the preindustrial past and horror at the environmental degradation of the industrial city. By midcentury this evolved to a somewhat more sophisticated but still human-centered approach to growth management (Healey and Shaw 1994). From the 1970s, a more firmly ecological approach saw nature as a source for resources, a sink for pollutants, and a functioning structure of support systems such as flood control, all helping urban areas contribute to human well-being (Alberti 1999; Healey and Shaw 1994). Both the compact city and eco-village approaches are part of this latter tradition but differ in emphasis—on the one hand promoting efficiency and minimizing disturbance outside the urban area, and on the other hand connecting people and natural systems. Resilience is a relatively new approach that started off as a concept related to the ability of systems to persist after disturbance and now also emphasizes a capacity to adapt to changes (Meerow, Newell, and Stults 2016).

Table 21.1 The Four Approaches to Incorporating Environmental Issues into New Town Development

	Garden Tradition	Compact Ecocities	Eco Villages or Ecoburbs	Resilient New Towns
Emblematic Case	Letchworth, UK (1900s)	Punggol Eco-town, Singapore (1990s)	The Woodlands, TX (1970s)	
Human Well Being				
Access to green spaces	Balance town and country in a green environment	Compact but well-designed green spaces within developments	Integrate extensive green spaces near residences bringing people close to nature	Green spaces perform multiple functions including managing disturbances
Connection to Nature	Compact new towns surrounded by rural areas; substantial greening within the town	Natural systems tend to be more dominant on edges of development; they often look less "green"	Natural systems are interwoven into the fabric of development; often have substantial environmental education	Manage a dynamic natural system undergoing long-term change; may have significant greening for well-being
Sources				
Resource use— energy, water, agricultural land	Balance town and country	Higher densities conserve land, water, and energy	Water infiltration often a priority; may have on-site local food production	Redundant efficient systems minimize environmental footprint and maximize adaptation
Habitat and ecosystem protection	Rural context for new towns	Compact design uses less land preserving habitat outside development area	Try to preserve onsite habitat; often use land in similar amounts to typical suburbs	Deals with changing habitat context
Sinks				
Pollution—air, water, soils	Separates people from sources of pollution	Many use brownfield sites; may increase urban heat island and impervious surfaces	Attention to green infrastructure for treating water, air pollution, soil remediation	Developed in a context of significant damage to natural systems— designed to manage this
Environmental Support Systems				
Climate change	Devised before climate change awareness	Transit-oriented to save energy; higher density Housing is efficient in terms of heating and cooling	On site energy production e.g. solar panels; may support some alternative transportation (bicycles, buses)	Direct response to climate change using multiple systems to reduce environmental footprint, mitigate, and adapt to change

Adapted from Crewe and Forsyth (2011).

Table 21.1 outlines these four approaches showing their key features. Of course, some new towns do none of these, but, because of the dominance of the garden city approach in the history of new town development, the cases are rare where these are totally absent. This is also the case in terms of the three other environmental traditions—there is typically something of the garden tradition in most of them, and there are many hybrid traditions. Of the four traditions, resilient new towns are the least well developed; indeed, within the new town tradition, social resilience, or the ability to deal with changes in demographics and the economy, is better represented than its environmental counterpart.

Garden Tradition

As many others have explained, Ebenezer Howard's ([1898] 2003) *Tomorrow: A Peaceful Path to Real Reform* is a central work in the history of new town development. While often treated as a starting point for the new towns movement, the central proposal of the book drew on earlier, nineteenth-century planned suburbs, colonial cities, and company towns, along with wider debates about social reform including improved housing, social welfare provision, and better employment opportunities. The idea also evolved over time as the new town idea was taken up by a movement involved in garden city and town and country planning associations and general debates about how to improve urban areas (Forsyth 2011; Hall and Ward 1998; S. V. Ward 2002).

As is well known, Howard's core idea was a network of self-contained towns of one thousand acres and about thirty thousand in population set in a wider context of five thousand more acres with another two thousand rural residents. These towns were linked to others by railways and canals; along with the core city this network would create what Howard termed the social city, combining the best of town and country (Forsyth 2003, 2011; Howard 1902). The idea of cities limited in size and density along with comprehensive planning that balanced urban and rural life allowed closer contact with nature. It created a compelling image of a melding of town and country in a garden-like environment that underscored new town development subsequently. As Howard outlines:

> The town is the symbol of society—of mutual help and friendly cooperation, of fatherhood, motherhood, brotherhood, sisterhood, of wide relations between man and man—of broad, expanding sympathies—of science, art, culture, religion. And the country! The country is the symbol of God's love and care for man. All that we are and all that we have comes from

it. Our bodies are formed of it; to it they return. We are fed by it, clothed by it, and by it are we warmed and sheltered. On its bosom we rest. Its beauty is the inspiration of art, of music, of poetry. Its forces propel all the wheels of industry. It is the source of all health, all wealth, all knowledge. But its fulness of joy and wisdom has not revealed itself to man. Nor can it ever, so long as this unholy, unnatural separation of society and nature endures. Town and country must be married, and out of this joyous union will spring a new hope, a new life, a new civilisation. (Howard 1902, 17–18)

Howard's was obviously a multifaceted vision, looking broadly at nature as a resource for urban life but also grappling with the substantial movement of people from rural to urban areas seeking their many opportunities. By building smaller cities in the countryside Howard was trying to bring together these two dimensions—resources and opportunities.

Of course, the success of the garden city movement was not in its vision but rather in that developments were built inspired by the ideas. These varied from fully fledged garden cities such as Letchworth and Welwyn near London to a variety of smaller, less comprehensive neighborhoods of garden suburbs that popped up around the world featuring leafy environments and robust services, to larger ideas of satellite cities (Chapter 22). As I have outlined elsewhere, even in its first decades, the movement was international in scope: "They ranged from the philanthropically sponsored garden suburb of Forest Hills Gardens in suburban New York (1910–), the early public housing neighborhood of Daceyville Garden Suburb in suburban Sydney, Australia (1912–), the privately developed middle-class enclave of Den-en Toshi in suburban Tokyo (1918–), to cooperative and worker initiated developments of Floréal and Logis in Brussels, Belgium (1921–)" (Forsyth 2011, 372 :2003; Hall and Ward 1988; Ward 1992). Garden city ideas were spread further through the work of the Regional Planning Association of America (RPAA), including such participants as Lewis Mumford, Clarence Stein, and Henry Wright. Key was their neighborhood prototype, Radburn, New Jersey, which used a super-block to more extensively intertwine green space into the heart of each neighborhood, using the open space system as the primary pedestrian network (Stein 1957). This was further promoted after the Second World War and was much used in new town and planned community designs around the world to embed development in green areas.

The garden tradition creates pleasant, leafy environments with clear open space networks (Figure 21.1). Many examples do quite a lot more, incorporating larger ideas about the place of urban areas. Thus, over time the garden tradition became a source for the other approaches in this chapter—with the difference mainly in emphasis.

Figure 21.1. Examples of the garden city tradition. Letchworth Garden City, U.K. (*top*); Caoyang Xincun garden suburb, Shanghai (*bottom*), has high densities (over six hundred persons per hectare) (Rowe et al. 2016, 26). Photos by Ann Forsyth.

Compact City

The compact city idea takes a different tack, inspired by the need to make urban areas more efficient in terms of land, energy, and water and thus allow rural and wilderness areas to remain intact. Crystallizing in the 1970s at a period of substantial environmental concern and reform, this has been a wider movement beyond new towns. Compact city approaches include programs of metropolitan densification and urban containment along with transit-oriented neighborhoods and mixed-use districts. The compact city idea has been criticized as not accounting for individual, social, and economic behaviors, but it has remained attractive in urban planning and design (Neuman 2005).

Figure 21.2. Examples of compact new towns. Toa Payoh, Singapore (*top*); Almere, Netherlands (*bottom*), has lower densities than its Asian counterparts but is designed explicitly to favor nonmotorized transport. Photos by Ann Forsyth.

Of course, many new towns and neighborhoods in the garden tradition were relatively efficient and oriented around transit, and they aspired to self-containment, where the activities of daily life can be carried out locally (Forsyth 2003). The compact city idea, however, makes this central and is less nostalgic about the benefits of rural life. While the highest-density versions, for example in Singapore or Hong Kong, look superficially like classic Corbusian modernist developments, compact new towns tend to mix activities closely together so that they are more walkable than the classic modernist examples that rigidly separate uses.

High population densities provide a critical mass of people to support local services accessible by foot, bicycle, and transit. It should be noted that they are not all high-rise; low-rise, higher-density forms are common particularly where the alternative would be detached homes on larger lots. Because new towns are planned from scratch, automobiles can be channeled away from residential areas and nonmotorized modes favored. Higher-density housing is often more energy efficient than lower-density approaches; compact development can allow innovative garbage collection and recycling. Open spaces within the urban fabric are necessarily smaller, but good design can make them perform well, and the pattern of development protects land outside the new town and many have substantial greenbelts and interwoven open spaces (Crewe and Forsyth 2011).

Compact new towns are typically developed in places where governments have a substantial role in actual new town development or a strong land-use and infrastructure planning system, from the Netherlands and Singapore to China and Korea.

Eco-burbs

While the garden and compact city traditions are the most common approaches to incorporating environmental considerations and natural systems into new town planning, the eco-burb has been important in key developments such as The Woodlands (Crewe and Forsyth 2011). This approach typically combines larger-scale landscape analyses in the tradition of McHarg and others, with more detailed ecologically sensitive design at the new town, neighborhood, and site scale (McHarg 1969; Spirn 1984). These aim to identify areas of most ecological value and protect them from urban development while also using natural systems as a green infrastructure for on-site water treatment, food growing, and energy production and low-impact development principles that mimic and use natural processes in site design.

In doing this, the approach also taps into deep-seated attachments of people to nature, dubbed by Schroeder (1996, 13) "the ecology of the heart." Environmental psychologists have pointed to the positive emotional responses of people to savannah-like natural settings. While there is some cultural variation in terms of specific preferences (e.g., for tree shape or levels of maintenance) numerous studies show reduced stress, improved sense of well-being, and better cognitive functioning resulting from exposure to nature (Crewe and Forsyth 2011; Maller et al. 2005). Of course, the garden tradition also provides some of this effect, but the eco-burb idea combines it with more a contemporary environmental awareness.

Eco-burbs are typically lower density and can be automobile based—like the Woodlands—though in an ideal world they could take advantage of modes such as the bicycle. While some lower-density new towns in the compact city tradition can have eco-burb components, as densities get higher it is more difficult to incorpo-

Figure 21.3. Eco-burb examples. Civano planned suburb, Arizona (*top*), and the Woodlands, Texas (*bottom*). Photos by Ann Forsyth.

rate features such as substantial on-site food production, natural storm water treatment, or solar energy production. As such eco-burbs allow a more back-to-nature approach that may be more household based and less collective than the compact city; they are also more interested in ecology than the garden tradition.

Resilient New Towns

Less an identifiable style than an overall approach that looks to a complex and changing future, resilience is an emerging approach in new town development. It has several dimensions. On the one hand is the issue of social and economic resilience. The maturation planning challenges faced by older new towns are related to this issue; are these mature new towns resilient enough to be viable as economies and social arrangements have changed?

Environmental changes are a further challenge, highlighted by the issue of climate change. Resilient new towns might minimize contributions to climate change, as described in Chapter 20. However, such new towns need to respond to changes that are already in process. Resilience in one place will emphasize resistance to storm surges, and in another place resistance to drought, integrated into the overall design. New towns may be used as parts of major programs to relocate populations away from hazards, as Godschalk suggests in Chapter 22. However, in many parts of the world new towns are being built in areas vulnerable to climate change effects; many coastal new towns in China come to mind. That is, like other development, new towns can contribute to vulnerability if not well planned and located.

All told, this is an area where new towns can play an important role, most notably in planned resettlement.

22

Regional New Town Development

Strategic Adaptation to Climate Change

David Godschalk

Intersecting global forces of climate change and massive population growth are creating unprecedented twenty-first-century problems for contemporary urban areas, especially those situated on ocean shorelines. Revisiting Ebenezer Howard's nineteenth-century proposal for developing new towns as components of regional urban systems may suggest one potential solution to the looming problems.

In response to obsolete and overcrowded central cities, Howard proposed building regional new town networks (Howard [1898] 2003). His idea was first taken seriously at a large scale in the mid-twentieth century following World War II in Britain, Scandinavia, France, and the Netherlands (Merlin 1971; Strong 1971). The idea resurfaced in the twenty-first century, in the form of eco-towns or cities that responded to concerns about global sustainability (Ecocity Builders 2016; Sze 2015).

This chapter reviews the history of regional new towns and argues that their time has come again in situations where existing settlements are no longer viable because of climate change hazards, particularly sea-level rise. While the chapter's premise could be applied globally, it looks solely at the U.S. case, exploring possibilities for proactive government policies to encourage regional new town development.

The idea is simple, although both ambitious and radical. Rather than wasting resources on piecemeal mitigation efforts in threatened coastal communities, the United States and governments more generally should initiate a program of *strategic adaptation to sea-level rise* based on a planned network of regional new towns in safe locations. Over time, vulnerable coastal populations and economic activities would be relocated to these regional new towns, which are not only less hazardous but also built to be sustainable and resilient from the start.

The new regional new town networks could both *mitigate* climate change pollution through green construction and design, and *adapt* to climate change impacts through relocation and reorganization of basic functions in safer locations. Evidence-based advance planning and implementation could ensure sustainable and resilient outcomes (Godschalk 2003). If Ebenezer Howard were alive today, he might well have applauded this bold adaptation of his idea.

Regional New Towns: Impact of an Idea

Howard's original new town concept pictured a regional set of publicly planned small but complete communities within greenbelts, linked by transit to each other and a larger central city (see Chapters 1, 2, 20, 21, and 23). These communities' purpose was to ease the pressure on overcrowded central cities while offering an improved quality of life (Howard [1898] 2003). Since then, many variants of the concept have appeared, including both complete "garden cities" with their own employment bases, and residential "garden suburbs" housing workers in nearby central cities (Hall 2002, chaps. 4 and 5). Clearly, that early idea has had a powerful and lasting impact over more than a century (Hall and Ward 1998).

Adaptations of Howard's Model

Howard's design concept has diverged into two main streams: one focusing on the form of individual new towns (Godschalk 2009) and one focusing on new towns within a comprehensive regional plan (Merlin 1971). The regional stream is where new towns contribute to important regional growth and economic goals. These regional new towns are explicit *instruments of regional development strategy*, as well as being relatively complete garden cities with significant on-site employment as well as housing. Important examples of such regional new towns range from Abercrombie's 1944 Greater London Plan (Merlin 1971, 5) and Delouvrier's 1965 master plan for the Paris region (Merlin 1971, 146) to Shanghai's 1990s "One City, Nine Towns" plan for a ring of new towns to ease overcrowding in the central city (Sze 2015).

The original regional design has been adapted from the concentric circle form into linear sustainable development corridors in Britain (Hall and Ward 1998, 162–70) and the United States (Calthorpe and Fulton 2001, 151–58). Original purposes have moved from alleviating central city congestion to increasing sustainability with eco-towns in China, India, South Korea, and the United Arab Emirates (Sze 2015). The scale and shape have grown to accommodate contemporary economic demands. British "super towns" such as Milton Keynes were planned for a population of 250,000 with high-density, mixed-use centers within a grid plan and located sixty miles (96 kilometers) from London, outside of commuting distance (Hall and Ward 1998, 57). Regional new town concentrations in China and Korea are considerably larger, up to a million in population (see Chapters 7, 8, 10, and 11).

Despite the adaptations, the underlying concept of developing new towns as planned interventions in the urban growth process has persisted (Calthorpe and Fulton 2001; Freestone 2016; Hall and Ward 1998). Regional new towns might become the centerpiece of a strategy to respond to the challenge of climate change.

The Climate Change Crisis: Sea-Level Rise

Global climate change is expected to set off a series of negative impacts, including more severe storms, droughts, hurricanes, and tsunamis (U.S. Global Change Research Program 2009). Climate change–induced sea-level rise has already begun to create problems for coastal cities and is projected to become increasingly severe (Beatley 2009; Blakely and Carbonell 2012; Kolbert 2015; Pilkey and Pilkey 2011).

Sea-Level Rise Projections

Coastal settlements have enjoyed some two thousand years of relatively stable sea levels, but in the twentieth century the sea level rose by about eight inches. In the twenty-first century, that rate has doubled (U.S. Global Change Research Program 2009, 18). Projected future changes are being revised upward as more evidence accumulates. Recent estimates suggest a sea-level rise of between three and four feet during the twenty-first century (U.S. Global Change Research Program 2009, 150). Some scientists go even further, suggesting five to seven feet in the next one hundred years (cited in Pilkey and Pilkey 2011, 73).

Global warming causes the sea level to rise in two ways. First, ocean water expands as it warms and takes up more space. Second, warming melts glaciers and ice sheets, which adds water to the oceans. Although these ice sheets are not expected to completely melt during this century, they pose enormous potential problems. If the entire Greenland ice sheet melted, it would raise the sea level by about twenty feet; melting of the West Antarctica ice sheet would raise the sea level by sixteen to twenty feet; and complete melting of the East Antarctica ice sheet would raise the sea level by about two hundred feet (U.S. Global Change Research Program 2009, 18).

A map of potential impacts from complete melting of the world's ice sheets (an extreme and unlikely case, but one that illustrates the very long-term vulnerability of the U.S. coast) illustrates the catastrophic submergence of existing U.S. coastal cities. Florida's major cities would be completely underwater, as would Norfolk, Charleston, New Orleans, and Houston. Boston, New York, Philadelphia, and Washington, D.C., also would face significant flooding (National Geographic 2013).

Vulnerable Coastal Areas

Sea-level rise will affect millions of people; about one-half of all Americans live in counties immediately bordering ocean coasts. Twenty-three of the nation's twenty-five most densely populated counties and ten of the most populous cities are found in U.S. coastal areas (Beatley 2009, xiv, 14–15). Meanwhile, the vulnerability of coastal settlements continues to grow as more development and population increases take place in the coastal zone. This problem extends around the Atlantic, Pacific, and gulf coasts in varying degrees of risk.

The mid-Atlantic and gulf coasts are especially vulnerable, owing to geology and hydrography, facing substantial increases in the extent and frequency of storm surges, coastal flooding, erosion, property damage, and loss of wetlands. In the South, sea-level rise coupled with increased hurricane intensity and storm surge can have catastrophic consequences. Some communities will be inundated permanently by the advancing sea (U.S. Global Change Research Program 2009, 114). Globally, Miami, the lowest U.S. city at an average elevation of six feet, is the most threatened city in terms of the property that will be flooded by a three-foot sea-level rise (Pilkey and Pilkey 2011, 85–86).

Other U.S. coastal areas are also vulnerable. New York state has more than $2.3 trillion in insured coastal property, and some major insurers have withdrawn home owner coverage in coastal areas, including New York City (U.S. Global Change Research Program 2009, 109). The entire Sacramento–San Joaquin River delta system from San Francisco nearly to Sacramento is now below sea level, protected by a thousand miles of levees and dams, a problematic situation (U.S. Global Change Research Program 2009, 133). Within Puget Sound, beach erosion and bluff landslides will be exacerbated by sea-level rise (U.S. Global Change Research Program 2009, 137).

Strategic Adaptation to Sea-Level Rise: Relocating Threatened Coastal Cities

Coping with sea-level rise is taking place in three ways: (1) protecting the shoreline by building hard structures, such as levees and seawalls, which can increase risks and worsen beach erosion and wetland retreat in some cases; (2) accommodating rising water by elevating or redesigning structures, enhancing wetlands, or renourishing beaches, which can wash away during the next storm; and (3) planned retreat from the shore as sea level rises (U.S. Global Change Research Program 2009, 152).

Of the three approaches, only planned retreat represents a long-term, permanent solution. Seawalls and other hard structures are brittle and subject to failure, while increasing collateral damage to beaches and wetlands. Elevated buildings can raise habitations above rising sea levels but will not be habitable if the sand beneath them is eroded away leaving them standing in the surf. Sand pumped up in beach renourishment projects may not outlast the next coastal storm. Relocating settlements to higher land, while expensive and challenging, is the safest solution in the long run.

Planned retreat is recommended by the National Research Council (2014) report to the U.S. Army Corps of Engineers on reducing coastal risk. The report calls for a national vision for managing risks from coastal storms that includes a long-term view, regional solutions, and recognition of the full array of economic, social, environmental, and life and safety benefits from risk reduction efforts (National Research Council 2014). They recommend benefit-cost analysis as a framework for evaluating investments in coastal risk reduction. They caution that extensive collaboration and policy changes will be necessary to move from reacting to coastal disasters to investing in risk reduction and resilience.

Planned Retreat

My proposal adopts the Corps of Engineers' safest vision—planned retreat: to gradually relocate threatened coastal city populations and physical components to new towns in safer locations through a program of *strategic adaptation to sea-level rise*. Under this approach each region would prepare a new towns plan attuned to the evidence of forthcoming sea-level rise. Vulnerable populations would be eligible for federal buyouts of their at-risk property. Government grants would be provided for construction of new town infrastructure. Resilience agencies would prepare neighborhoods and businesses for the necessary social and economic adaptations (Godschalk 2003). Clearly this would be a unique and costly program. An outline strategy to pay for planned retreat is discussed below.

While the fundamental idea is simple, implementation will be complex and demanding. Only two small U.S. communities have been substantially relocated in recent times—Soldiers Grove, Wisconsin, in 1979, and Valmeyer, Illinois, in 1993 (Schwab 2014, 166; Freudenberg et al. 2016, 26–27). Both incorporated green building techniques in their redevelopment following floods, as did Greensburg, Kansas, which had to be completely rebuilt in 2007 following an EF5 tornado (Schwab 2014, 162). Some coastal areas have moved threatened houses back from eroding beaches (Pilkey and Pilkey 2011), but there is not a major body of experience to guide the planned relocation of major cities as a public safety initiative.

Planned retreat calculus. To weigh the costs and benefits of planned retreat, the expected losses from remaining in place could be compared with the expected gains from strategic relocation. The exercise would be similar to assembling a large pro forma for a development project, with the loss avoidance outcome in place of anticipated profit. An analysis performed for Congress to compare the costs of avoided losses from natural hazards with those of Federal Emergency Management Agency (FEMA) hazard mitigation costs found that every dollar invested in grants to mitigate natural hazards resulted in reducing expected losses by four dollars (Godschalk, Rose, et al. 2009; Rose et al. 2007). The same four-to-one ratio would not necessarily be expected in the case of relocated coastal communities with their new land and infrastructure investments and other costs. However, a foresighted new town investment strategy should result in long-term payoffs due to reductions in costs of insurance,[1] emergency response, evacuation, debris removal, displacement, infrastructure repair, and environmental damage.

While a specific benefit-cost analysis is beyond the scope of this chapter, it is possible to identify some of the major components:

Benefits	*Costs*
Losses avoided (death, damage)	Site acquisition and preparation
Continuity of operations	New town planning
Green development opportunities	Infrastructure and services
Reduced flood insurance premiums	Residential and business moving expense
Lower flood insurance program liability	Buyout and relocation expenses
	Abandoned assets
	Loss of historical/cultural value of places

Two major types of funding would be needed to pay for strategic adaptation to sea-level rise. The first is funding for buying out and relocating home owners and businesses in the high-risk "sending" areas. The second is funding for developing the "receiving" regional new towns and their infrastructure.

Buyouts in sending areas. The United States has substantial experience in removing vulnerable individual properties from hazard areas. Under FEMA's buyout program, qualifying home owners in threatened areas can voluntarily sell their property to the government, which then demolishes the structures, reducing future risk (Federal Emergency Management Agency 2014; Godschalk, Beatley, et al. 1999; Polefka 2013). The home owners can then use these payments to relocate. For eligible communities, FEMA typically funds 75 percent of the cost of property acquisition, with the municipality and state contributing the remaining 25 percent. Buyout projects are initiated and administered by local and state governments with grant funding support from FEMA. Additional federal funding may also be provided by the Community Development Block Grant program administered by the Department of Housing and Urban Development (HUD).

States participated in federal buyouts in the New York metropolitan area in the aftermath of Hurricanes Irene and Sandy (Freudenberg et al. 2016, 28–29). New York state established the New York Rising Buyout and Acquisition Program in 2013, which designated enhanced buyout zones giving home owners additional incentives to participate. New Jersey made use of state bonds to finance the Green Acres/Blue Acres program established earlier to acquire open space to widen the application of buyouts. Morris County, New Jersey, set up a buyout program using funds from a county open space tax. Overall, some $750 million was spent on buyouts, which alleviated the flood risk for more than fifteen hundred homes (Freudenberg et al. 2016, 4).

Expanding buyouts to cover major relocations of urban areas threatened by sea-level rise would require changing buyout programs from short-term recovery tools to long-term adaptations to flood risk. A small buyout program of this type is underway in southern Louisiana to move the people of Isle de Jean Charles away from a disappearing coast (Barth 2016). According to a study of the recent New York area buyouts, "the pervasive threats of flooding brought on by climate change necessitate a restructuring of buyout programs, including redefining long-term goals and strategies, and implementing viable time frames" (Freudenberg et al. 2016, 57). Alternative models will need to spread the funding over many years and scale up state and federal funding sources. Managing the growing flood risk will be very costly—but not as costly as the price of inaction.

The buyout program makes fiscal sense for both the property owner and the government. A recent report for FEMA found that sea-level rise is projected to increase the flood hazard area in our nation's coastal floodplain by 55 percent by 2100 (cited in Polefka 2013). If the United States fails to adapt to rising seas, the study projects that the number of coastal flood insurance policies will increase by 130 percent over the same period, owing largely to growth in the coastal flood hazard area. Such an increase would devastate the underfunded National Flood Insurance Program in which U.S. taxpayers currently underwrite flood insurance for $527 billion on properties in the coastal floodplain.

Developing receiving areas. Building the regional new towns would require funding for major land acquisition and infrastructure construction. Here the United States lacks experience in such public sector programs. In Europe and Asia, the national governments provided both the wherewithal and the necessary land for large-scale regional new town development. Applying that same approach in the United States on grounds of protecting the public safety would reduce the challenge considerably. It is possible to envision state and federal new town development corporations with the power to issue bonds undertaking this task, if the threat of inaction was sufficient to overcome the opposition to such a government initiative.

Without a federal government mandate, the other approach would be to devolve the initiative to combinations of individual state organizations and private sector developers. For example, states with both the public powers and the billion-dollar stake in vulnerable property might well be motivated to take the lead in such a program. They could partner with deep-pocket private development firms to plan and build safe new towns. Basic transportation, communication, and sanitation facilities frameworks in the new towns would be publicly funded. Firms providing employment would be recruited with economic incentives, such as low-interest loans and tax increment financing. Developers would receive assistance for green building and sustainable development.

New town site acquisition would have to be carefully managed. In many cases, new towns could be colocated with existing small settlements, as was done with many of the British new towns. In other cases, new town development corporations could be formed to assemble property, as was done with some U.S. new town developments. The challenge would be to avoid raising the specter of government running over the property rights of citizens; the use of eminent domain would be extremely unpopular.

Building consensus. To succeed, strategic relocation also would need to build solid social support. The increasing difficulty of maintaining normal living and working arrangements in the face of damaging flooding and breakdowns in public facilities would motivate residents and enterprises to move. Agreement on new town plans would be built by extensive participation of residents, businesses, and social and cultural organizations in strategy development. Conflicts and tensions over social and environmental changes would be resolved through extensive facilitation and consensus building.[2]

The most effective approach for gaining public support for relocation might be through use of participatory scenarios. Scenario planning is a process of integrating technical hazard analysis and public workshops, leading to a resilience strategy (for a scenario model approach, see American Planning Association et al. 2016). Scenarios compare the pros and cons of planned action versus denial and business as usual. The U.S. Climate Resilience Toolkit recommends a five-step process to resilience, shown in Table 22.1.

Pros and cons. The advantages of this strategic adaptation approach include:

1. Flexibility to respond to the unique sea-level challenges of each city and region, in recognition of the fact that a one-size-fits-all approach could not possibly deal with the myriad circumstances of each threatened area.

Table 22.1. Five-Step Process Toward Resilience

Step 1: Explore climate threats	Build a team, explore your regional climate trends and projections, and consider if things you value are threatened by climate.
Step 2: Assess vulnerability and risks	Determine which of your assets are most likely to be damaged or lost to climate impacts. Decide if you can tolerate the risk.
Step 3: Investigate options	Brainstorm possible solutions and explore what other groups have done. Narrow your options to a list of actions stakeholders are willing to support.
Step 4: Prioritize actions	Consolidate actions and determine the best sequence to protect your full range of assets. Align your resources to focus on your largest risks.
Step 5: Take action	Implement your plan and monitor your results. Modify your approach as needed.

Source: Adapted from U.S. Government (2016).

2. Comprehensive planning and development of new towns to gain the advantages of compact form, best urban design practices, efficient land use, green construction, sustainable development, provision for business growth, and conscious maintenance of community social and cultural bonds.

3. Scheduling to allow the staging of relocation in sync with the progressive stages of sea-level rise over time, rather than requiring a draconian full-scale movement of the entire city at one swoop.

4. Prioritization to make possible the planning and budgeting for relocation of critical infrastructure on a pragmatic, multiyear schedule with opportunities for issuing bonds, obtaining grants, and so on.

5. Regionalization to provide for coordinating area-wide adaptation by multiple municipalities, firms, organizations, economic clusters, and social systems.

6. Involvement of publics and stakeholders to ensure that the goals, objectives, and procedure of relocation and new town development are widely understood and that the wisdom and insights of the citizens and leaders are incorporated into adaptation plans.

7. Resilience in the face of a known but slowly arriving threat with time to plan and carry out a coordinated package of social, economic, and environmental responses to develop a new community fabric while adapting to the conditions of retreat.

By contrast, an approach based on ad hoc rebuilding of damaged existing threatened cities would face several drawbacks:

1. Reshaping the existing urban form to accommodate submerging civic and economic functions would be a never-ending process—a long-term challenge without a clear end.

2. Reengineering and refinancing fixed investments in urban systems would be an expensive drain on the public treasury simply to continue the status quo without improvement.

3. Progressive relocation of threatened residential neighborhoods would be a painful and expensive process, putting community social bonds under continuing stress.

4. Businesses would face uncertain economic futures with shrinking client bases and difficulties in finding adequate new space at safe distances from projected rising water levels.

5. Municipal fiscal and economic prospects could be dimmed if continuing natural hazard threats discouraged banks and investors.

6. Community morale would suffer as continuing disasters took their toll.

Assuming that necessity to respond to the flooding threat might be the deciding factor, it makes sense to explore a more strategic adaptation approach in the form of a comprehensive coastal region new town system.

Developing a Coastal Region New Town System

To implement a safe regional new town system, public and private roles and responsibilities must be allocated, and a sequence of planning stages must be carried out. Justification for the program would be protection of the public health, safety, and welfare. While it is not possible to describe fully such a program, some salient aspects can be identified.

Roles and responsibilities. At the federal level, FEMA would coordinate and fund planning, buyouts, and relocation. HUD would coordinate regional planning, housing, public facilities, and green development. The National Oceanic and Atmospheric Administration (NOAA) would analyze risks and publish maps of threatened areas and safe locations for new communities.

State governments would adopt legislation and financial assistance programs. They would empower new town development authorities to assemble and develop land and collaborate with government agencies to provide infrastructure. They would approve regional relocation plans and coordinate them with state programs of economic development, environmental protection, hazard mitigation, and social services.

Regional planning and transportation agencies would be forums for new town planning and relocation. As the platform for voluntary cooperation of municipal governments, these regional agencies or some metropolitan or multistate consortium of them, such as the New York Regional Planning Association, could ensure that regional new town development serves overall economic development and environmental protection goals.

Local governments, in collaboration with new community authorities, would work with stakeholders to develop and implement plans and schedules for relocation; manage transitions in land use and transportation; issue design guidelines; and operate public information services. They would be the forums for resolving community fears and concerns about strategic adaptation.

Private firms would develop the new town commercial and residential areas, working with governments in public/private partnerships, constructing projects under contract, and operating as standard real estate development companies. They could be encouraged by favorable land leases and financial terms and by streamlined development regulations to reduce red tape for new construction that followed the new town plan.

Some large development firms with new community experience might undertake both planning and development of regional new towns. Others might work directly with relocating commercial firms to develop their new facilities, including offices, retail areas, or neighborhoods as joint or individual ventures.

Nongovernmental, charitable, and religious organizations would play a major role in assisting groups and individuals to cope with the social and behavioral changes involved in community relocation. Existing organizations and institutions would be forums for involving stakeholders in transition planning and implementation, serving as communication channels, and providing social services as needed.

New organizations based in the relocated communities would be developed to help integrate relocated firms and residents into the new community fabric. They might take familiar forms, such as home owners' associations and chambers of commerce, or their functions might be pulled together in new types of organizations designed around specific adaptation needs.

Planning stages. The first stage would be to identify the expected threat (timing and extent of projected sea-level rise) and to locate safe and feasible areas for relocation. Safety will be a matter of analyzing land elevation and proximity to rising waters for various future new town sites. Feasibility will be a matter of finding and acquiring land parcels with favorable conditions for town development, including adequate size, reasonable topography and soils, access to water supply, and transportation connections. Sites must be chosen that do not infringe on wetlands and other critical natural areas that can help to mitigate natural hazard damage. Land assembly will be a critical and challenging early task, as exemplified in the experience of new communities in the United States and Britain (Forsyth 2002; Hall 2002).

The second stage would be to conduct a comprehensive new town planning process. An important consideration will be the feasibility of providing basic infrastructure and social services at the available sites, including water and sewer systems, roads, railways, transit lines, and schools, parks, and health services. Alternative land-use plans will need to ensure that receiving commercial and residential neighborhoods can accommodate relocated populations and enterprises. New infrastructure and community facilities should incorporate contemporary green building and sustainable design practices, following the precepts of eco-towns.

The third stage would be to analyze prospects for economic development, including both relocated and new enterprises, employment opportunities, and business organization. Much of the necessary economic base would come from relocated businesses and facilities, with the benefit that already employed workers could obtain housing near their workplace locations. Newly arriving enterprises would be encouraged to choose locations in the new towns, as in the British new towns.

Example Application: Southeast Region

An example can illustrate the application of planned regional new towns as a form of strategic adaptation to sea-level rise. To take the case of the Southeast region of the United States, where many coastal settlements are vulnerable: very high-risk areas focus on the coasts around Virginia Beach, Charleston, Miami, and New Orleans, but the entire coastline has some degree of vulnerability. A regional strategic adaptation plan could look to relocating the highest-risk settlements.

Guiding future growth and relocation of existing threatened areas into safe planned new community locations not only will permit ongoing adaptation to future hazards, but also will reduce sprawl and protect shrinking biodiversity. As Figure 22.1 shows, the North American coastal plain, including the floristic province with its

Figure 22.1. Coastal plain as a designated world biodiversity hotspot (2016). *Source*: Adapted from Noss (2016).

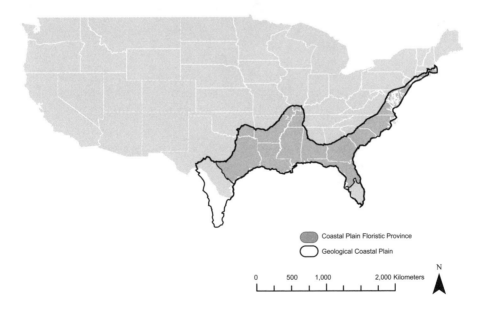

Coastal Plain Floristic Province
Geological Coastal Plain

0   500   1,000   2,000 Kilometers

N

unique array of plants and animals and the larger geologic coastal plain, has been designated as a world biodiversity hotspot (Noss 2016). Protecting natural areas such as forests and wetlands will allow them to function in their natural roles as sponges to absorb flooding.

Safe inland sites. One way to visualize safe locations for relocating threatened cities would be to select inland sites along existing interstate highway corridors that parallel the coast. Typically, these routes were placed along ridgelines, which would put them well above low-lying coastal cities; they also are connected with other major roads leading to the coast. The regional adaptation pattern resulting from taking advantage of such locations would be a network of gradually developing new communities parallel to the coast but located a safe distance from rising sea levels and connected by existing expressways to each other and to their base cities on the coastline.

For example, the southeast Atlantic coast is paralleled by I-95, which could become the axis for a cluster of linear regional new towns (Figure 22.2). Connected by new transit lines, these new settlements could become safe havens for relocating threatened populations from Norfolk to Jacksonville.

Figure 22.2. Interstate 95 axis for southeastern Atlantic new towns. Map by Kevin Chong.

Relocating Charleston

To step down from the regional to the state level, we can look at South Carolina's vulnerable coastal cities. Charleston faces serious flooding from sea-level rise. It is already subject to monthly "sunny day" tidal flooding (Gillis 2016). According to researchers from Climate Central, a nonprofit group focusing on climate change and sea-level rise, more than eight hundred square miles of land lie less than four feet above the high tide line in South Carolina, including $24 billion in property value and fifty-four thousand homes—mostly in Charleston and Beaufort Counties—that would be threatened by a four-foot rise in sea level (Bowers 2014). If a parallel new community to gradually replace the vulnerable Charleston areas were started in a safe inland location, a possible site might be near the intersection of Interstate 95 and Interstate 26, where the Norfolk Southern Rail line running northwest crosses I-95 (Wilbur Smith Associates 2009).[3] This might be one of three new town sites at interstate intersections, as shown in Figure 22.3.

Charleston is surrounded by water. As depicted by NOAA's (2016) Climate Explorer tool,[4] the threat from sea-level rise is

Figure 22.3. Potential network of South Carolina and Georgia regional new towns. Map by Kevin Chong.

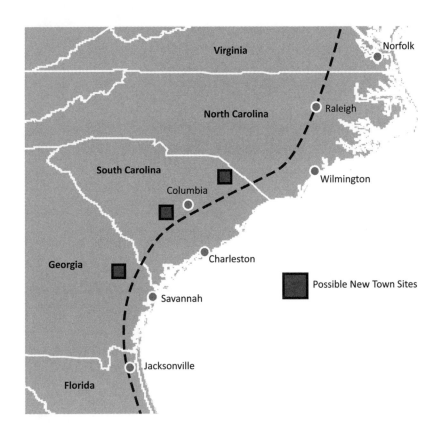

evident. Four rivers envelop the city, along with Charleston Harbor, resulting in a very vulnerable, low-lying, watery landscape. The historic city center is located on a peninsula with water on three sides. Flood insurance risks and commensurate costs obviously will be high.

When the Climate Explorer is set to illustrate the inundation from the projected turn-of-the-century three-foot sea-level rise,[5] parts of the barrier islands disappear under water. The riversides and wetlands are flooded. The land-use and transportation systems are disrupted. Not only will day-to-day functions be affected, but vulnerability to severe coastal storms and hurricanes will be greatly increased. Insurers will be aware of the high risks and will require extreme premium payments, if they are even willing to provide coverage.

Still, even with the threat of massive destruction from sea-level rise and future hurricanes, gaining agreement to relocate a historically and culturally significant city such as Charleston is almost an unimaginable challenge. However, some tactics could be used to build acceptance. Charleston began life as a new settlement some three hundred years ago, and that history could become part of the new town narrative. The new town design could incorporate familiar elements of the existing city to make relocation more comfortable. Layout of the new town center might reflect the square grid layout of historic Charleston. New neighborhoods could include architectural references to both historic and contemporary structures. The pioneer spirit of the early settlers could be revived in the new town planning process, as those bought out in flooding areas participated in creating their new sustainable environments.

This would not be a quick fix. Exploring the feasibility of relocation will take years. Detailed studies, analyses, and public consultation processes will be needed. Benefit-cost analyses to compare the savings from avoided damages will be necessary but not sufficient. The public debates and politics will be turbulent. Champions for strategic adaptation will need to step forward. However, numbers from existing studies indicate that relocation could have major benefits if the projected damage from sea-level rise proves accurate.

Regional New Towns: An Idea Whose Time Has Come Again

New towns have always attempted to serve a societal purpose. The twenty-first-century rationale for regional new town development is protection of the public health and safety from climate change calamity. While the specifics of the threat are still being determined, it seems very clear that climate-induced sea-level rise will bring staggering human risk and property damage to coastal regions. Short-term mitigation measures, such as seawalls and elevated structures, may delay the impacts, but they will not prevent them.

Strategic relocation is a bold but reasonable response to the threat of catastrophic sea-level rise, both in the United States and globally. Resilient regional new towns, built with green technology to carry on in safe locations, can both adapt to coming hazards and help to mitigate them. The scale is great, but Ebenezer Howard's compelling concept, in the realization of which 2.7 million British residents now live in thirty-two planned new towns (Town and Country Planning Association 2014b), can once again inspire a program of socially important new town development.

Notes

1. An important benefit of the strategy would be substantial reductions in hazard insurance premiums for the property owner and in costs of insuring coastal property against sea-level rise for the federal flood insurance program. Coastal flood insurance is increasingly expensive, and property risks due to climate change are significantly underinsured (Holzheu, Lechner, and Turner 2015). Early reductions in insurance premiums would immediately benefit home owners and businesses, contributing to the strategy's short-term effectiveness. Longer-term reductions in disaster preparation, response, and recovery costs would benefit governments and first responders.

2. For an example of successful implementation of an even more challenging planned retreat, see Waterman (2016) on the Dutch Room for the River program. Expenditure on this long-term green infrastructure project, nearing completion, is approaching 2.3 billion euros ($2.6 billion) to adapt to projected sea-level rise impacts on the Rhine, Meuse, Waal, and Ijssel Rivers, which make up the estuary of the southern half of the country. The project involves creating new river channels, adjusting dikes, and "depoldering" previously protected agricultural lands to allow them to absorb floodwaters.

3. The Norfolk Southern Rail line carries containers from the port of Charleston to the town of Greer in the state's "inland port," a warehouse, industrial park, distribution, and manufacturing hub called the "Upstate," two hundred miles inland in the Greenville-Spartanburg area. The port of Charleston is dredging its harbor to be the deepest on the East Coast in order to capture shipping traffic from the newly expanded Panama Canal (E. E. Phillips 2016).

4. NOAA's Climate Explorer is a research application built to support the U.S. Climate Resilience Toolkit; see http://toolkit.climate.gov/tools/climate-explorer. The tool offers interactive visualizations for exploring maps and data related to the tool kit's Taking Action case studies. Base maps (imagery, street maps) come from ESRI Web Services. Map layers in the tool kit represent geographic information available through climate.data.gov. Each layer's source and metadata can be accessed through its information icon. The user can explore the effects of climate change, such as inundation from one-, two-, and three-foot sea-level rises, on specific cities.

5. A three-foot rise may prove to be conservative. Current evidence suggests that the actual rise by the year 2100 could be somewhere between three and four feet, and if a more rapid ice melt occurs, sea-level rise could begin to approach the worst-case scenario, which puts the entire Charleston area under water.

23

New Towns in a New Era

Richard Peiser and Ann Forsyth

What is the future of new towns in the coming decades and even the coming century? This is a complex issue with overlapping questions. What problems will new towns need to solve in coming decades? What types of new towns will have the best fit in terms of solving those problems? What entities can provide the strong coordinating role, with a substantial coordinating vision, and the long-term financial horizon needed for new towns to succeed? Given the demand and potential methods for delivering new towns, will they come to be at any sort of large scale?

Answering these questions requires relying on assessments about plausible futures in different parts of the world. Assuming that new towns continue to go ahead, there will not be a one-size-fits-all solution. In some cases, new towns will be incremental. New developments may involve residents in building their own homes, via self-construction, at a level greater than has been in the past. Aging new towns will need to be incrementally rehabilitated. However, in other places those creating new towns may use the full force of government coordination to deal with a growing need for resettling populations away from hazards and threats. While new towns will likely remain a modest part of overall development in most areas, they will provide important test cases for planning innovations that can be more broadly influential.

The Twenty-First Century

Twentieth-century new towns largely responded to the need to industrialize and innovate in new locations, extract resources in remote areas, deconcentrate or expand large metropolises, and reconstruct after wars and disasters. A few were for other purposes—largely, political and military. Many of these circumstances continue in some form, but the twenty-first century brings several new concerns affecting urban areas where new towns have some potential for helping with the solution (Forsyth 2014a, 2014b).

Table 23.1 provides an overview of likely challenges in the twenty-first century along with the implications for new towns, using a language of new town purposes

Table 23.1. Twenty-First-Century Trends and New Town Implications

Issue	Trend	New Town Implications	Purposes	Styles
Urban growth	Continuing in Africa and parts of Asia	Lower-income countries: less expensive models that coordinate infrastructure Higher-income countries: deal with local land shortages; respond to demands for increased quality of life.	To channel growth/for deconcentration To solve land shortages	Comprehensive, phased Instant Sites and services
Urban shrinkage	Already evident in places where population has peaked or economies are slowing, e.g., East Asia, former Soviet Union, rustbelt U.S.	New towns provide a model for good planning.	To deal with demographic shifts/aging	Maturation planning
Population aging	Evident in most of the world except Africa; East Asia and parts of Europe are the leading edge. From 2000 to 2100 the population over 60 will increase from 10% to 30% globally.	New forms: hybrid intergenerational retirement communities taking advantage of new research on aging and environments, and new assistive technologies, could create a second generation of age-friendly new towns as a living/employment center.	To deal with demographic shifts/aging. To provide employment	Maturation planning Comprehensive, phased
Climate change and environmental damage	Increased floods and droughts, heat waves, and continued problems from polluted air, water, building materials, and soil will continue. Stresses from climate change are at the base of many armed conflicts.	Planned retreat from the most problematic areas could be efficiently conducted via new towns. Eco new towns: To date tend to be small or to focus on a narrow range of environmental goals. More comprehensive versions could pilot major innovations.	For planned retreat For resettlement	Comprehensive, phased Instant
Poverty and inequality	While absolute poverty has been decreasing, providing housing affordable to those with very low incomes will remain an issue.	Lower income countries: Less expensive new town models Higher income countries: large scale new towns allow cross-subsidy between lower income housing with employment development.	To channel growth/for deconcentration	Sites and services Comprehensive, phased
Technological change	Changes in communications technologies reshape personal transportation and assumptions about location. Assistive technologies can help older people. Science city–type new towns can create innovative milieu (Forsyth 2014a).	New town locations may be more flexible, with more distant links to major centers, though this is complex (people may travel less but goods more). A new generation of science cities would be more successful with more humanistic design. Both could be the silver lining in dealing with a need for planned retreat.	To provide employment To deal with demographic shifts/aging	Comprehensive, phased Planned retreat
Governance	The roles of different levels of government and of the public and private sectors are likely to be rethought.	This may affect new town financing and ongoing management.		Comprehensive vs. phased

and styles elaborated later in this chapter. Issues include urban growth but also shrinking urban areas; aging populations as well as continued inequality; environmental changes; technological opportunities; and shifts in governance and, in particular, the balance between the public, private, and civic sectors.

Purposes of New Towns

Larger trends shape the purposes of new towns. As noted in the introduction, in the twentieth century and up to the current period, most new towns were built for *economic and research* reasons (for resource extraction, as science cities, even for tourism); as what we call *employment* new towns; or to help *channel growth* away from cities that are already built up (that is, for metropolitan deconcentration). They were comprehensive in terms of having a mix of activities, a diverse population, and being comprehensively planned from the start.

These purposes will remain. In the coming century, however, some other reasons for new towns may take on a larger role. New towns have been used in the past to *resettle refugees* after political upheavals or after substantial disasters such as earthquakes or repeated floods. A number of Delhi's satellite cities, for example, were founded to resettle refugees from Pakistan. However, such new towns have been relatively unusual, as the inventory demonstrates. With increasing potential for disasters—given increasing populations in vulnerable areas, climate instability, and geopolitical strife—resettlement new towns could potentially become much more important. This is already being seen in refugee streams from Africa, the Middle East, and South Asia and may well continue and in various locations globally.

Because some of the forces that lead people to become refugees can be predicted or may build up somewhat slowly over time (e.g., from chronic droughts) there is time to have a more considered approach to resettlement. As Godschalk proposes in Chapter 22, in the context of climate change, *planned retreat* to new towns could be important. This would involve a considered program by governments assessing where it is worth defending existing settlements and where moving populations may be the most efficient and acceptable approach.

As we note below this may need new forms of new towns that can be built more incrementally using resident labor; or the instant new town could be refined for these new circumstances. Of course, finding large areas of land for a new town is much more difficult than piecemeal development, as is the coordination needed to pull off a new town. However, the comprehensive physical, economic, and social infrastructure of new towns could do much to help those being relocated more quickly become contributors in their new environment.

A related topic is the problem of lack of developable land as expanding urban areas bump up against natural barriers. Alternatively, in some locations such factors as food security, energy efficiency, or infrastructure cost savings may prompt governments to implement urban growth boundaries and green belts. While it may seem contradictory to promote large-scale new towns as a solution to *land shortages*, they have several benefits in these situations. Such developments can use available land more efficiently. This is something of the case of Singapore and Hong Kong in the twentieth century. In addition, because of their comprehensive nature they can be placed further from existing urban areas while still attached via transportation. New towns can also be built on "new" land such as is the case in the Netherlands, where new towns have been built on filled polders (e.g., Almere). The scale of the new town makes such land reclamation feasible.

Finally, some new towns will create models for dealing with demographic shifts, particularly *population aging*. The retirement community to date has not provided a truly comprehensive model for new towns, even when very large, as age restrictions require many workers to live outside. Smaller models—the serviced apartment building, for example, or service cooperatives at the neighborhood scale—provide models for integrating support for older people into a comprehensive new town. Such hybrid models—with smaller concentrations of older people in new towns open to a complete age range—hold great promise.

While new towns will be found in greater numbers in developing countries in Africa and Asia, primarily to accommodate urbanizing populations, they are likely to continue to be developed in the United States, Europe, and Australia to meet demand for exurban growth. Resort towns and other more specialized new towns will likely emerge in rural locations with good access to nearby metropolitan areas as well as more remote locations. These new towns will need to address problems of employment and homogeneity if they are to become balanced communities over the long run.

In emerging markets, new towns will confront problems of incorporating unplanned informal development on their borders. In addition to providing badly needed infrastructure for informal settlements, Michelle Provoost predicts that new towns in the twenty-first century will celebrate less planning. "The purely formal planning we are familiar with from the twentieth century has resulted in cities that many critics now consider over-determined. They are planners' constructs which, in all their model-like perfection and correctness, have proved to be quite vulnerable. They are too much the embodiment of one idea, too much the product of one system, too much a reflection of one moment in time, and too inflexible" (Provoost 2010, 8). Providing urban infrastructure to informal development and regularizing land ownership is an imperative in many developing countries. New towns are uniquely equipped to facilitate this process because of their framework and super-structure for providing infrastructure to new development. However, Provoost also takes aim at what she calls "over-determined" planning. The need for greater flexibility in land use and density is one of the lessons learned from twentieth-century new towns. Real estate markets and preferences for housing and commercial space change over time. Master plans that accommodate future changes and build in flexibility will help to reduce the overdetermined planning that Provoost criticizes.

While new towns in the twenty-first century will serve different needs, they will also likely have different styles from the dominant paradigm in the twentieth century. These are addressed in the next section of this chapter.

Styles of New Towns

The classic new town was what we have called the *comprehensive, phased new town*, developed over a long period so that a large part of what was challenging about the new town was how governments and private sector players could keep delivering the initial vision over time, often several decades. After all, this comprehensive vision of a mixed-use, human-scaled, socially cohesive, and efficient place was a large reason many had moved to the new town. Departures from the initial plan needed to be well-thought-out responses to changing circumstances. Many of the new towns in this book are of this type—with the best of them being triumphs of urban planning and real estate development (Figure 23.1). Not all were successful, however. Indeed, one of the failures of the United States new towns program of the

Figure 23.1. Vällingby in the Stockholm suburbs is a comprehensively planned new town from the 1950s that remains a classic. Photo by Ann Forsyth.

Figure 23.2. Songjiang on the outskirts of Shanghai is the site of much instant new-town-type construction. Photo by Ann Forsyth.

early 1970s was that developers picked locations where they controlled land—often in locations that were too far removed from metropolitan growth corridors to have sufficient market demand to cover the up-front cost of infrastructure investment. Consequently, the developer-driven government loan program was cancelled after three short years.

A second type, which had always been around but became perhaps more visible with the recent wave of new towns in China, is what we might call the *instant new town*. While still comprehensive, it could be built much faster because it was smaller, or because the pace of urban growth was fast, or because a strong government could channel a large amount of urban growth into a limited number of areas (Figure 23.2). These new towns might be built in under a decade, or even just a few years. At a time of need—quickly taking advantage of a natural resource, or managing massive population growth—they could potentially provide higher-quality housing with better access to jobs and other resources than more incremental or fragmented alternatives could.

Looking toward the future, these types may endure, but two other issues may reshape what are seen as new towns. On the simplest level, many new towns of the last century have reached a stage where redevelopment is needed and, indeed, already under way. Of those that were successful in attracting population, some have been successful enough to have additions planned and even built. Milton Keynes outside

Figure 23.3. Higher-density town center commercial space has been developed in Milton Keynes forty years after the new town was started. Photo by Richard Peiser.

London, for example, benefitted from a wave of Japanese companies moving there (Figure 23.3). The town center was redeveloped, and many higher-priced homes were added in recent years, along with more upscale office and retail centers. Similarly, The Woodlands outside Houston has recently added a San Antonio–like river walk with mid-rise commercial, residential, and retail buildings bringing much more vitality to its town center (Figure 23.4). With major investment in the town center and close-in locations, The Woodlands is becoming one of the most sought-after subcenters in Houston, attracting a cosmopolitan crowd such as late-night Salsa dancers.

Those that were not successful may need work to make a smaller development fully functional. This work of redeveloping, extending, and retrofitting is called *maturation planning*. There has really been very little thought put into maturation planning in the context of new towns, though Chapter 13 covers some important initiatives. Part of the reason for developing a new town is to more quickly and efficiently create something mimicking the best vernacular places that have evolved over time. However, new towns raise particular issues for redevelopment and revitalization. Those that have used very robust architectural controls to provide certainty and control to residents may find that these controls constrain needed upgrades. Maturation planning would involve modifying regulations and processes for the new context. Alternatively, many new towns aim for a social and economic

mix that may be undermined over time by new town success (attracting those with the most resources) or new town
problems (doing the opposite). Either case—success or failure—can lead to more homogeneity over time without a
concerted effort to maintain diversity. A demographic and
income mix helps urban areas function better and also helps
promote equity, so maturation planning would need to deal

Figure 23.4. New river walk taking shape in The Woodlands, Texas, as the town center attracts more mid-rise and high-rise office buildings, hotels, and condominiums. Photo by Richard Peiser.

with these challenges. Instant new towns are developed quickly and could well suffer from failures of various infrastructure systems at about the same time—redevelopment needs to be carefully planned.

There may well be a need to push quite a bit further beyond these existing new
town types where new towns are wholly produced by governments, developers,
and builders. While new towns have been constructed largely by governments in
lower-income countries, the cost of creating a new town from whole cloth limits
their application. Often, they have reached only those with middle incomes, with
the poor either excluded or inhabiting nearby shanty towns (e.g., Brasilia, or the
new towns around Cairo). In other cases, they have been too expensive to replicate
widely. Perhaps this means that new towns should be rejected and that different
models of development are better. However, in cases of rapid urbanization, refugee
resettlement, and retreat from increasingly disaster-prone areas, the new town
model promises benefits in terms of efficiency and quality.

Thinking of major areas of potential urbanization, such as Africa and South Asia, what can be done? This may be the moment to revisit the approach called *sites and services*—where governments provide infrastructure, and often the wet core of a home, and users construct the buildings over time. Such programs, popular in the 1970s, were criticized for several deficits. They were too expensive for the very poor and often poorly located. These are all valid criticisms, but such developments were often at the scale of a residential neighborhood or subdivision, and the infrastructure provision focused on basic physical components such as water, streets, and electricity. A new-town-style scheme for sites and services would be more comprehensive, involving physical infrastructure, social services, and economic activities. This would cost more up front than a squatter settlement but would avoid later costs to the residents and society as a whole, as such areas need to be upgraded. Compared with a classic, fully built new town, it could provide a more affordable version while maintaining the benefits of self-containment or a balance of uses. While self-built housing is not always the most efficient use of land, densities could certainly be high enough to support public and collective transportation systems, and other infrastructure benefitting from a critical mass of people.

Innovations are occurring. Similar programs are being used to create mass economy housing in China on the outskirts of major cities such as Beijing and Shanghai. Building on government-owned land, developers are limited to a 3 percent profit margin (She, Chen, and Wang 2016, 226). The apartments are delivered in shell condition, to be finished out later by the home buyers. Other innovations of this type could be tried.

Both maturation planning and sites-and-services new towns represent substantial recasting of the new town idea for the twenty-first century.

New Town Coordinators

No matter what the purpose, new towns had to provide an initial vision; a plan for practically achieving that in physical, social, and financial terms; and a long-term organization to execute that planned vision. Few new towns manage to be an overall success. By this we mean combining all three—a substantial vision that mixes public planning goals such as sustainability, equity, jobs and design quality; a realistic implementation strategy where benefits exceed costs in a reasonable time; and a town-scale development and governance structure that balances positive initial aims with new circumstances including the desires of new residents, and does this while being financially stable.

The classic problem for private developers of new towns has been insufficient capital to weather the economic downturns. Government-sponsored and government-financed new towns have not faced similar cash constraints but still have had to survive the political ups and downs of different administrations. Public-private partnerships on government-owned or government-financed land will help bridge the financing problems of privately sponsored new towns. The challenge, as in twentieth-century new towns, will be one of providing enough flexibility for development to change as market demands change.

Also, social services require special attention and focus. Left to themselves, the social fabric of new towns lags behind the physical fabric, making them cold and unfriendly places to live. Indeed, one of the problems in China's new towns is that even though all the units are sold, they remain uninhabited. The early involvement of nonprofit organizations and strong focus on social organization development, as happened in The Woodlands and Almere, help to provide the boost that new towns need in their early days to be more welcoming to new residents and to help them achieve a better quality of life.

New Towns Versus New-Town-Style Planning Innovations

A large question remains whether new towns as such will be built in large numbers or if their planning innovations will be mainly dispersed to other kinds of planning projects and areas. The answer to this depends in part on the purpose. For example, resettlement, planned retreat, and land shortages could be more compelling reasons for new town development while other purposes such as fostering employment, channeling growth, and dealing with aging may be well done more incrementally.

Overall, it is likely that, as in the twentieth century, new towns will be part of the solution but in many ways will be most important as urban laboratories. They will show what is possible when urban areas are designed from the ground up with good planning and public and private financial viability as the main criteria. Some of these ideas can be transferred into locations where the inertia of existing patterns of ownership, development, and governance make innovation more difficult.

In the United States and the United Kingdom, and even much of the rest of Europe, the twentieth-century new towns have been car dependent with relatively low densities dominated by single-family homes, townhouses, and low-rise apartments. In developed countries, new towns in the twenty-first century will be more varied. Their design will start with an emphasis on lifestyle. They will have more vibrant town centers, designed around transit-oriented developments. Driverless cars and car sharing will reduce parking requirements and may support more urban lifestyles, even in new towns located on the urban fringe.

New towns in the United States such as Columbia, Reston, Irvine, and The Woodlands have maximized recreation and open space. Twenty-first-century new towns will have even better public realms with more walkable neighborhoods and greater ranges of housing types for different demographic groups, serving older residents who want to age in place, more single parents, people who are less car dependent, and people with a greater range of incomes. New towns that have focused on providing economy (social) housing need to have greater economic diversity. Financial success requires attracting a better cross section of residents with more higher-income home owners and workers. New towns will also see more public-private finance including tax increment financing arrangement (TIFs), business improvement districts (BIDs), and nonprofit ownership of affordable housing.

By contrast, in developing countries, where most new towns will be developed, there will be more government involvement and sponsorship. African new towns, which today are enclaves for the wealthy, will need to provide social housing. But they cannot be exclusively towns for workers (even foreign workers) as is being proposed in places such as the United Arab Emirates. From twentieth-century experience, it is clear that successful new towns must be diverse, heterogeneous communities in terms of both age and incomes. Indeed, one of the most important lessons of new town development is that market absorption is maximized by providing the full range of housing opportunities, from small apartments to estates, catering to all age groups, household structures, and incomes. While achieving a proper balance between residents and workers has been a perennial problem everywhere, it remains a critical component of success and that necessitates a range of both housing and employment. Indeed, commuting times and carbon footprints are minimized when people can live and work in the same small town, and commute by bicycle. In summary, while new towns will continue to provide efficient infrastructure for servicing homes and workplaces, they will need to do a better job of providing social services and promoting the evolution of local clubs, activities, and organizations that are essential for better quality of life.

Toward Twenty-First-Century New Towns

It is very difficult to predict the future, and indeed new towns may fade away. But if they continue, in coming years there may well be an expansion of new town purposes beyond economic development, worker housing, and urban deconcentration toward increasing amounts of refugee resettlement, planned retreat from potential disasters, and efficient responses to localized land shortages. This will involve traditional comprehensive, phased new towns, developed over decades, as well as their close relatives, instant new towns, developed in a few years. However, in the coming century, existing new towns will increasingly face the need for maturation planning, including redevelopment and extension. Finally, to match resources to needs, new models that provide comprehensive infrastructure while allowing incremental building by users show some promise, as the sites-and-services new town.

New towns in the twentieth century have housed millions of people worldwide under different circumstances. At their best, new towns provide a superior physical environment that allows their residents and workers to achieve a better quality of life than they can find in most traditionally planned and incrementally developed towns and cities. The many new town programs that have evolved in different countries described in this book offer important lessons for twenty-first-century new towns. There are limits to government-led new towns with their top-down approach to planning and development. As Chapter 14 on Almere in the Netherlands discussed, local residents and other stakeholders want to have a greater role in what gets developed, for whom, and at what price. Governance will become more participatory, sometimes making it harder for the developer to achieve the original vision. While many of the original company and resource extraction new towns were developed entirely by a single company, experience has shown that having multiple designers and builders is healthy for providing a diverse urban cityscape that resembles traditional towns. To succeed, twenty-first-century new towns must serve the full range of purposes that modern cities provide. If the lessons of the twentieth century are fully absorbed, one can look forward to better and more varied, interesting, and successful new towns in the new century.

Appendix 1

Location Maps

New Towns and Planned Communities

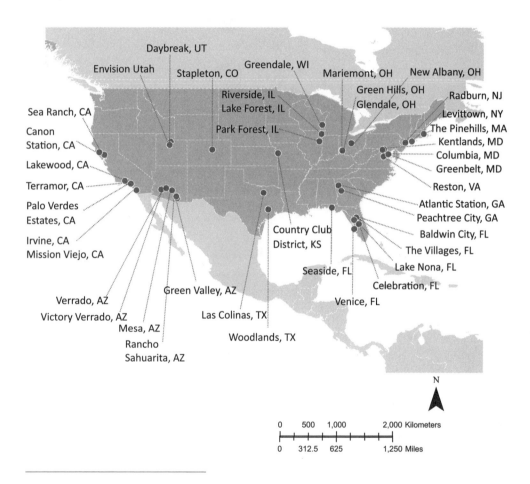

Map A.1. United States.

Map by Antara Tandon and Kevin Chong.

Map A.2. South America.

Map by Antara Tandon and Kevin Chong.

Map A.3. Western Europe.

Map by Antara Tandon and Kevin Chong.

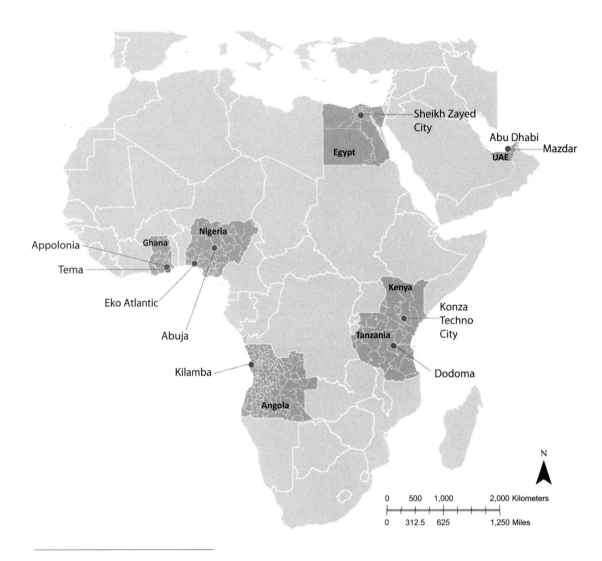

Map A.4. Africa and the Middle East.

Map by Antara Tandon and Kevin Chong.

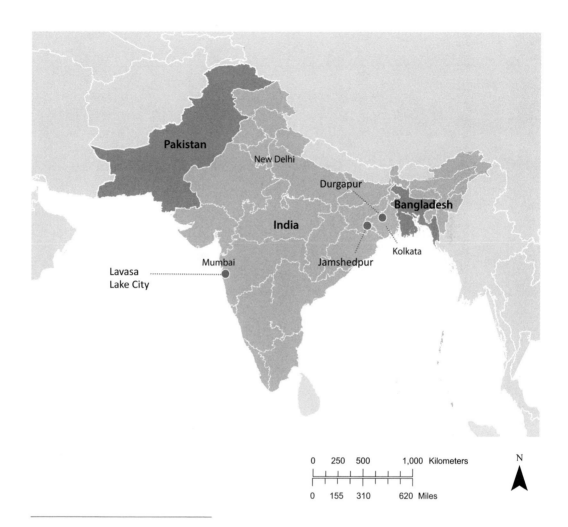

Map A.5. India.

Map by Antara Tandon and Kevin Chong.

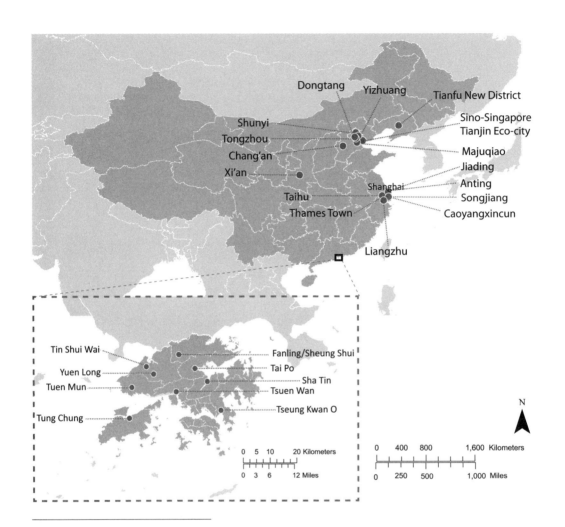

Map A.6. China and Hong Kong.

Map by Antara Tandon and Kevin Chong.

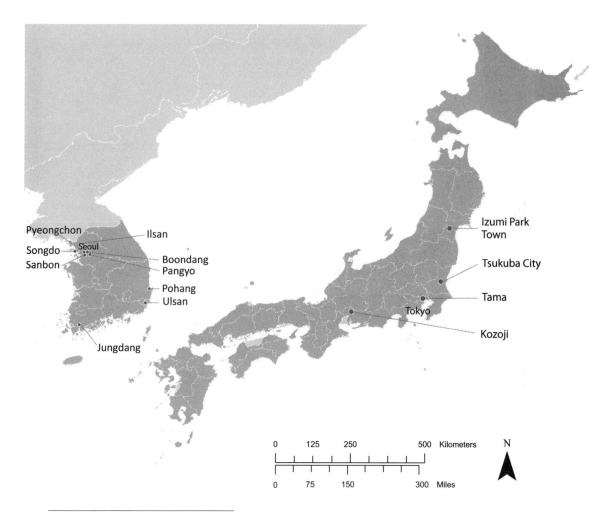

Map A.7. Korea and Japan.

Map by Antara Tandon and Kevin Chong.

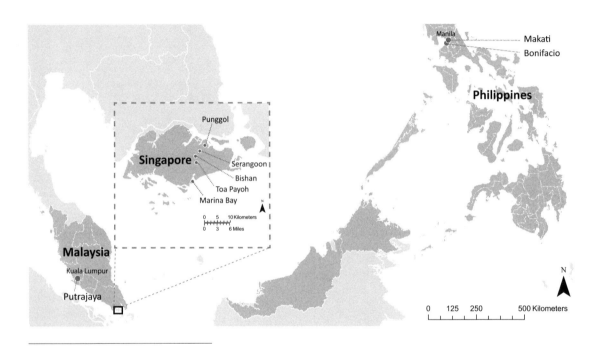

Map A.8. Southeast Asia.

Map by Antara Tandon and Kevin Chong.

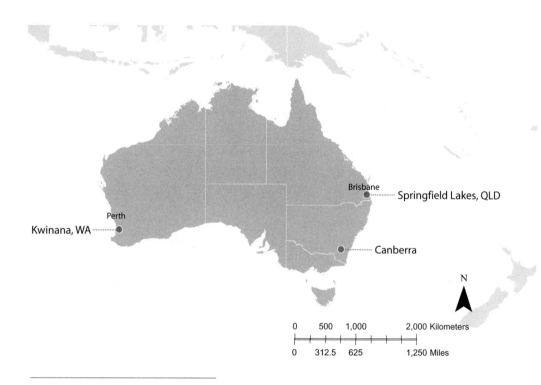

Map A.9. Australia.

Map by Antara Tandon and Kevin Chong.

Appendix 2

New Towns Inventory

Adam Tanaka and Ann Forsyth

with Richard Peiser, Silvia Danielak, Har Ye Kan, Jihoon Song, Peter G. Rowe,

Rachel Keeton, Felipe Correa, Reid Ewing, Carl Duke, Kyung Min Kim,

Alexander Garvin, Robert Freestone, Pike Oliver, and Sandy Apgar

Overview

The full inventory of new towns with sources and further details is accessible from the website: https://research.gsd.harvard.edu/new-towns/. Attempting to create a global inventory of new towns is an exceedingly complex task, and such lists will always be partial. For the purposes of the book we thought it was worth trying. There were lists to build on. Osborn and Whittick (1963; 1977) had included a listing in their compendiums, but it was obviously out of date. The International New Towns Institute (2010) had an online database, but they included new towns through history and many entries had just a name.

We wanted to update the list with a more specific definition. In the introduction we defined new towns as relatively large, comprehensively planned developments on newly urbanized land that boast a mix of spaces that, in their ideal form, can provide opportunities for all the activities of daily life. For the purposes of the main inventory we added two additional criteria, that they were started in the twentieth century and have populations as of 2015 over thirty thousand.

This *population cutoff* reflects the population of Ebenezer Howard's garden city; the date reflects developments initiated after the first edition (1898) of his classic work. Many excellent smaller cities and towns exist, but this cutoff made the inventory manageable. It also meant that the new towns in the inventory have been successful enough to have reached this population threshold. By limiting to the *twentieth century* we focused on the period when the contemporary new town was developed and brought to scale. In addition, it is difficult, though not impossible, for a new town to reach thirty thousand people in under a decade, so limiting the main listing to the twentieth century gave time for us to know if the new cities were in some sense successful (Table A.1).

The inventory may well have missed some new towns—though many that might be seen to be missing are not on the list because of population levels. However, there are many difficulties.

- At times it can be difficult to judge *what is a new town and what is just an urban expansion or a large-scale housing development, perhaps part of some of the same government programs as new towns.* This is the case with Ede in the Netherlands,

432

which makes some lists but is often not included as it was a quickly growing town rather than a comprehensively planned new town. It is included in Chapter 13 as the author of that chapter, Pascaline Gaborit, has a capacious view of new towns; those with stricter definitions would not.

■ It can also be difficult to determine what is merely an *industrial growth center with basic housing and very broad planning of land uses, and what would be seen as a comprehensively planned new town* that involves more detailed design and implementation of social and physical infrastructure. This is the situation with a number of proposed new smart city and industrial development areas in India as well as many early twentieth-century industrial settlements in Russia.

■ A related issue was new developments that were *deliberately exclusionary* such as labor camps or gulags and deliberately segregated areas such as apartheid townships. We hope we have excluded all these, but we may have included a few by accident.

■ A more positive example are *large-scale retirement communities*. While they have many features of comprehensiveness, they need to import substantial amounts of workers each day who do not have any option to live there, so we did not include them.

■ Sometimes *new towns are phased, and some accounts treat sections separately*, as each section can take decades to complete. But in other cases the new towns are treated as a whole. We tried to clear up these inconsistencies but some will remain. An example is Canberra, where the initial 1911 new city was completed and then new satellites are treated as separate new towns.

■ Sometimes a *small new town was later expanded in a less planned way*, and we may not have been able to tell this, so we have included the less planned areas in current population numbers.

■ We may also have *estimated the populations incorrectly* in other ways. In some cases municipalities with the same name as the new town may not actually share the same boundary. This is the case for Irvine in California, where the city is just a small part of the whole Irvine Ranch new town (Forsyth 2005). In other cases we had to estimate from zip codes and census tracts and may have introduced errors.

■ We had a team who could read Chinese, Japanese, Korean, German, French, Spanish, and English but may have missed sources in some *other languages*.

The *twentieth-century* list of *larger* new towns creates an incomplete picture in other ways as well. Many important new towns and new-town-style developments are smaller than thirty thousand—including many that are household names among new town experts. Others are infill development, or the new-town-in-town, which we also excluded from the main list. The list of *classic new towns and neighborhoods* includes those famous developments, as well as some *other developments mentioned in the book* that are at the neighborhood scale or that include planning later in their developments (Table A.3).

A second omission from the main list is recent or *twenty-first-century new towns*. A number of developments have been started in the current century, some even making it over the thirty-thousand-person threshold. Others may become important in the future. The twenty-first-century new towns list is an attempt to list this current wave though we tried to include only those where substantial construction had commenced, not those that were at present only proposals (Table A.2). This is, of course, a moving target. We will have missed some substantial developments that had little coverage in the press. We were conscious of the work of Osborn and Whittick (1967). There were scores of new towns in the inventory to their book that we could not find—presumably many did not go ahead, at best having parts swallowed up in nearby urbanization. There were many others that had not reached the population threshold of thirty thousand people.

The inventory has several components.

First is the original name. Where this was in a different language we used the current version in English. The country is the country in the current period, so Hong Kong has been included in China, for example. The date started is complex as in some cases it was the date of first planning or designation, and in others the date of opening. This is quite rough. Current populations are our best guess and included in the online listing. Purposes are best guesses.

Methods

Adam Tanaka completed the first draft of the inventory starting from listings compiled by Ann Forsyth based initially on the Osborn and Whittick inventory. The listing was then checked by authors of the chapters and Peter Rowe (Asia), Rachel Keeton (Africa), Felipe Correa (Latin America), Reid Ewing and Carl Duke (United States), and Kyung Min Kim (Korea). Alexander Garvin, Robert Freestone, Pike Oliver, and Sandy Apgar provided helpful updates. In addition, Har Ye Kan then checked the Chinese cases; Jihoon Song, the Korean and Japanese ones; and Silvia Danielak, those in Africa and elsewhere.

Checking involved trying to complete the list, find current populations from reliable sources (beyond Wikipedia), and ascertain other information such as new town type. We also tried to assess how mixed-use the developments were.

Table A.1. Main Inventory of Twentieth-Century New Towns with Populations over 30,000

Original Name	Country	Date Started	Purpose
Abu Nuseir New Town	Jordan	1977	Resettlement
Abuja	Nigeria	1976	Capital
Agadir	Morocco	1960	Reconstruction
Ahwatukee	United States	1971	Metropolitan deconcentration
Ajax	Canada	1948	Industrial
Akademgorodok	Russia	1960	Military/research
Akhtubinsk	Russia	1959	Industrial
Al Shorouk	Egypt	1995	Metropolitan deconcentration
Alamar	Cuba	1970	Metropolitan deconcentration
Al-Badr	Egypt	1982	Metropolitan deconcentration
Albury-Wodonga	Australia	1973	Industrial
Ali Mendjeli	Algeria	1988	Metropolitan deconcentration
Almere	Netherlands	1970	Metropolitan deconcentration
Almetyevsk	Russia	1953	Industrial

Original Name	Country	Date Started	Purpose
Amursk	Russia	1958	Industrial
Andisheh	Iran	1990	Metropolitan deconcentration
Ang Mo kio	Singapore	1972	Industrial
Angarsk	Russia	1949	Industrial
Angered	Sweden	1968	Metropolitan deconcentration
Anyang	South Korea	1949	Industrial
Anzhero-Sudzhensk	Russia	1928	Industrial
Apatity	Russia	1935	Industrial
Aprilia	Italy	1936	Metropolitan deconcentration
Aranya Community Housing	India	1989	Satellite
Arsenyev	Russia	1902	Industrial
Artyom	Russia	1924	Industrial
Ashdod	Israel	1956	Resettlement
Ashkelon	Israel	1951	Industrial
Ashok Nagar	India	1964	Metropolitan deconcentration
Asmara	Eritrea	1930	Capital
Astana	Kazakhstan	1994	Capital
Atlantis	South Africa	1972	Industrial
Baharestan	Iran	1990	Metropolitan deconcentration
Ballymena	United Kingdom	1967	Metropolitan deconcentration
Bandar Baru Bangi	Malaysia	1974	Industrial
Bandar Mahkota Cheras (BMC)	Malaysia	1999	Metropolitan deconcentration
Banja Luka	Bosnia and Herzegovina	1969	Reconstruction
Baoshan District	China	1959	Industrial
Basildon	United Kingdom	1949	Metropolitan deconcentration
Batikent	Turkey	1983	Metropolitan deconcentration
Bedok	Singapore	1971	Industrial
Beer Sheva	Israel	1951	Resettlement
Beilun District	China	1970s	Industrial
Beit Shemesh	Israel	1950	Resettlement
Beitar Illit	Israel	1984	Metropolitan deconcentration
Belconnen	Australia	1966	Metropolitan deconcentration
Belogorsk	Russia	1926	Industrial
Belovo	Russia	1938	Industrial
Berezniki	Russia	1932	Industrial
Berlin-Hellersdorf	Germany	1950s	Metropolitan deconcentration
Beryozovsky	Russia	1965	Industrial
Beslan	Russia	1950	Industrial
Bhadrāvati	India	1941	Industrial
Bhilai	India	1956	Industrial
Bhubaneshwar	India	1948	Capital
Bidhannagar (Salt Lake City)	India	1958	Industrial
Bijlmermeer-Gaasperdam	Netherlands	1960	Metropolitan deconcentration

Original Name	Country	Date Started	Purpose
Binhai New Area	China	1995	Industrial
Birobidzan	Russia	1931	Industrial
Bishan New Town	Singapore	1995	Metropolitan deconcentration
Blanchardstown	Ireland	1972	Metropolitan deconcentration
Bobigny	France	1969	Metropolitan deconcentration
Bokaro Steel City	India	1965	Industrial
Bolshoy Kamen	Russia	1947	Industrial
Bor	Serbia	1903	Industrial
Bracknell	United Kingdom	1949	Metropolitan deconcentration
Bramalea	Canada	1957	Metropolitan deconcentration
Brasilia	Brazil	1957	Capital
Bratsk	Russia	1952	Industrial
Bukit Batok New Town	Singapore	1998	Metropolitan deconcentration
Bukit Panjang New Town	Singapore	1981	Metropolitan deconcentration
Bumi Serpong Damai (BSD)	Indonesia	1994	Metropolitan deconcentration
Bundang	South Korea	1989	Metropolitan deconcentration
Canberra	Australia	1913	Capital
Cancun	Mexico	1973	Resort
Caoyang Xincun	China	1951	Metropolitan deconcentration
Capelle aan den IJssel	Netherlands	1960s	Metropolitan deconcentration
Castle Peak	China	1967	Metropolitan deconcentration
Castries	Saint Lucia	1949	Capital
Central Lancashire New Town	United Kingdom	1970	Metropolitan deconcentration
Cergy-Pontoise	France	1966	Metropolitan deconcentration
Chandigarh	India	1950	Capital
Changchun	China	1906	Industrial
Changwon	South Korea	1977	Industrial
Chapayevsk	Russia	1911	Industrial
Chaykovsky	Russia	1955	Industrial
Chayuan New Town	China	1998	Industrial
Chelyabinsk-70	Russia	1955	Military/research
Chernogorsk	Russia	1936	Industrial
Chervonohrad	Ukraine	1951	Industrial
Chiba	Japan	1957	Metropolitan deconcentration
Chimbote	Peru	1948	Industrial
China-Singapore Suzhou Industrial Park	China	1994	Industrial
Chisinau	Moldova	1947	Reconstruction
Chittaranjan	India	1950	Industrial
Ciudad del Carmen	Mexico	1970s	Industrial
Ciudad Guayana	Venezuela	1961	Industrial
Ciudad Ojeda	Venezuela	1937	Industrial
Clear Lake City	United States	1963	Metropolitan deconcentration
Clementi New Town	Singapore	1973	Industrial

Original Name	Country	Date Started	Purpose
Columbia	United States	1963	Metropolitan deconcentration
Comodoro Rivadavia	Argentina	1901	Industrial
Coral Springs	United States	1963	Metropolitan deconcentration
Corby	United Kingdom	1950	Industrial
Craigavon	United Kingdom	1965	Metropolitan deconcentration
Crawley	United Kingdom	1947	Metropolitan deconcentration
Cuautitlán Izcalli	Mexico	1971	Metropolitan deconcentration
Cumbernauld	United Kingdom	1955	Metropolitan deconcentration
Cwmbran	United Kingdom	1949	Industrial
Cyberjaya	Malaysia	1997	Industrial
Dandeli	India	1930s	Industrial
Daqing City	China	1959	Industrial
Daxing District	China	1957	Metropolitan deconcentration
Delicias	Mexico	1933	Industrial
Deltona	United States	1963	Metropolitan deconcentration
Diamond Bar	United States	1964	Metropolitan deconcentration
Dimitrovgrad	Bulgaria	1947	Industrial
Dimona	Israel	1951	Industrial
Dodoma	Tanzania	1975	Capital
Dolgoprudny	Russia	1931	Industrial
Domododevo	Russia	1900	Industrial
Dubna	Russia	1956	Military/research
Durgapur	India	1950	Industrial
Dushanbe	Tajikistan	1930	Capital
Dzerzhinsk	Russia	1941	Industrial
Dzerzhynsk	Ukraine	1938	Industrial
East Kilbride	United Kingdom	1947	Metropolitan deconcentration
Eilat	Israel	1951	Industrial
El Obour City	Egypt	1982	Industrial
Elblag	Poland	1945	Reconstruction
Elektrostal	Russia	1938	Industrial
Elk Grove Village	United States	1964	Industrial
Ennerdale	South Africa	1974	Resettlement
Erechim	Brazil	1918	Industrial
Erin Mills	Canada	1953	Metropolitan deconcentration
Erzincan	Turkey	1939	Reconstruction
Evry	France	1965	Industrial
Fanling/Sheung Shui	China/Hong Kong	1979	Metropolitan deconcentration
Faridabad	India	1949	Industrial
Farsta	Sweden	1959	Metropolitan deconcentration
Fifteenth of May City	Egypt	1978	Metropolitan deconcentration
Flower Mound New Town	United States	1968	Metropolitan deconcentration
Fort McMurray	Canada	1974	Industrial
Foster City	United States	1963	Metropolitan deconcentration

Original Name	Country	Date Started	Purpose
Foumbot	Cameroon	1965	Industrial
Fryazino	Russia	1938	Military/research
Fuladshahr	Iran	1964	Industrial
Gaborone	Botswana	1964	Capital
Gachsaran	Iran	1955	Industrial
Gandhidham	India	1950	Resettlement
Gandhinagar	India	1967	Capital
Gary	United States	1907	Industrial
Gdynia	Poland	1920	Industrial
Ghaziabad	India	1976	Metropolitan deconcentration
Gheorghe Gheorghiu-Dej	Romania	1952	Industrial
Glenrothes	United Kingdom	1948	Industrial
Goiana	Brazil	1937	Capital
Greater Noida	India	1991	Metropolitan deconcentration
Gulshan Thana	Bangladesh	1972	Metropolitan deconcentration
Gumi	South Korea	1973	Industrial
Gungahlin	Australia	1991	Metropolitan deconcentration
Guragon	India	1970s	Industrial
Gwacheon	South Korea	1979	Metropolitan deconcentration
Haarlemmermeer	Netherlands	1960	Metropolitan deconcentration
Habana del Este	Cuba	1959	Metropolitan deconcentration
Hadera	Israel	1951	Industrial
Hammarsdale/Mpumalanga	South Africa	1962	Industrial
Harlow	United Kingdom	1947	Metropolitan deconcentration
Hashtgerd	Iran	1988	Metropolitan deconcentration
Hasselby-Vallingby	Sweden	1954	Metropolitan deconcentration
Hatfield	United Kingdom	1948	Metropolitan deconcentration
Havirov	Czech Republic	1955	Industrial
Heliopolis	Egypt	1905	Metropolitan deconcentration
Hemel Hempstead	United Kingdom	1947	Metropolitan deconcentration
Hong Gai	Vietnam	1980	Industrial
Hoogvliet	Netherlands	1951	Metropolitan deconcentration
Hougang New Town	Singapore	1977	Metropolitan deconcentration
Houten	Netherlands	1970	Metropolitan deconcentration
Hoyerswerda	Germany	1955	Industrial
Huambo	Angola	1912	Industrial
Hunedoara	Romania	1952	Industrial
Hyderabad HITEC City	India	1998	Industrial
Illichivsk	Ukraine	1952	Industrial
Ilsan	South Korea	1990	Metropolitan deconcentration
Irvine	United Kingdom	1966	Metropolitan deconcentration
Irvine	United States	1960	Metropolitan deconcentration
Islamabad	Pakistan	1961	Capital
Izberbash	Russia	1932	Industrial

Original Name	Country	Date Started	Purpose
Izumi Park Town	Japan	1972	Metropolitan deconcentration
Jamshedpur	India	1945	Industrial
Jamsil	South Korea	1974	Metropolitan deconcentration
Jauharabad	Pakistan	1953	Capital
Jebel Ali	Dubai	1977	Industrial
Jiading (District?)	China	1959	Metropolitan deconcentration
Jimei District	China	1992	Industrial
Jinja	Uganda	1952	Industrial
Jinshan New Town	China	1972	Industrial
Jizni Mesto	Czech Republic	1975	Metropolitan deconcentration
Joondalup	Australia	1980s	Metropolitan deconcentration
Jōsō New Town	Japan	1971	Metropolitan deconcentration
Jubail	Saudi Arabia	1975	Industrial
Jungdong	South Korea	1990	Metropolitan deconcentration
Jurong	Singapore	1960	Industrial
Kachkanar	Russia	1957	Industrial
Kafue	Zambia	1967	Industrial
Kallang/Whampoa	Singapore	1959	Metropolitan deconcentration
Kalyani	India	1950	Metropolitan deconcentration
Kampala	Uganda	1913	Capital
Kan	Iran	1975	Metropolitan deconcentration
Kanata	Canada	1964	Industrial
Kansai Science City	Japan	1978	Military/research
Kapchagay	Kazakhstan	1960	Industrial
Karagandy	Kazakhstan	1934	Industrial
Karmiel	Israel	1964	Industrial
Kashima Port Industrial Town	Japan	1962	Industrial
Kaspiysk	Russia	1932	Military/research
Kebayoran Baru	Indonesia	1944	Metropolitan deconcentration
Kelamayi City	China	1958	Industrial
Kemerovo	Russia	1918	Industrial
Kenkyu-Gakuen	Japan	1968	Satellite
Khayelitsha	South Africa	1983	Metropolitan deconcentration
Kingsport	United States	1916	Industrial
Kingwood	United States	1971	Metropolitan deconcentration
Kirovo-Chepetsk	Russia	1935	Industrial
Kiryat-Gat	Israel	1955	Resettlement
Kisumu	Kenya	1910	Industrial
Kitahiroshima	Japan	1996	Metropolitan deconcentration
Kizilyurt	Russia	1963	Industrial
Kohoku New Town	Japan	1969	Metropolitan deconcentration
Kohtle-Jarve	Estonia	1970	Industrial
Komsomolsk-on-Amur	Russia	1932	Industrial
Komsomolsk-on-Dnieper	Ukraine	1961	Industrial

Original Name	Country	Date Started	Purpose
Kopeysk	Russia	1928	Industrial
Korangi	Pakistan	1958	Resettlement
Korba	India	1950	Industrial
Kotovsk	Russia	1912	Industrial
Kozoji New Town	Japan	1965	Metropolitan deconcentration
Krasnokamensk	Russia	1967	Industrial
Krasnokamsk	Russia	1929	Industrial
Krasnoznamensk	Russia	1981	Industrial
Kremlyov	Russia	1939	Military/research
Kryvyi Rih	Ukraine	1926	Industrial
Kumertau	Russia	1948	Industrial
Kurchatov	Russia	1968	Industrial
Kuwait City	Kuwait	1951	Capital
Kwinana	Australia	1953	Metropolitan deconcentration
Kwun Tong	China/Hong Kong	1953	Metropolitan deconcentration/Industrial
Kyzyl	Russia	1914	Industrial
Laguna Niguel	United States	1959	Metropolitan deconcentration
Lake Havasu City	United States	1964	Military/research
Langqi Town	China	1997	Industrial
Las Colinas	United States	1973	Industrial
Lauderhill	United States	1959	Metropolitan deconcentration
Lázaro Cárdenas	Mexico	1940s	Industrial
Lelystad	Netherlands	1960	Capital
Lesnoy	Russia	1954	Military/research
Lesozavodsk	Russia	1932	Military/research
Letchworth Garden City	United Kingdom	1903	Metropolitan deconcentration
Lilongwe	Malawi	1947	Capital
Linkou New Town	Taiwan	1967	Metropolitan deconcentration
Lippo Karawaci	Indonesia	1993	Metropolitan deconcentration
Littoria	Italy	1932	Metropolitan deconcentration
Livingston	United Kingdom	1962	Metropolitan deconcentration
Lobnya	Russia	1902	Metropolitan deconcentration
Londonderry Derry	United Kingdom	1969	Metropolitan deconcentration
Londrina	Brazil	1929	Industrial
Longview	United States	1923	Industrial
Lusaka	Zambia	1935	Capital
Ma'ale Adumim	Israel	1991	Metropolitan deconcentration
Magadan	Russia	1929	Industrial
Magnitogorsk	Russia	1929	Industrial
Makati	Philippines	1952	Industrial
Malvern	Canada	1953	Metropolitan deconcentration
Margate	United States	1955	Metropolitan deconcentration
Marine Parade Estate	Singapore	1970	Metropolitan deconcentration
Maringá	Brazil	1947	Industrial

Original Name	Country	Date Started	Purpose
Marl	Germany	1914	Industrial
Marne-la-Valleé	France	1966	Metropolitan deconcentration
Mbalmayo	Cameroon	1965	Industrial
Meadowvale	Canada	1968	Metropolitan deconcentration
Melun-Sénart	France	1965	Metropolitan deconcentration
Mill Woods	Canada	1969	Metropolitan deconcentration
Milton Keynes	United Kingdom	1967	Metropolitan deconcentration
Mingachevir	Azerbaijan	1946	Industrial
Minhang	China	1959	Industrial
Mirnyj	Russia	1955	Industrial
Mirpur City	Pakistan	1960s	Industrial
Mission Viejo	United States	1960s	Metropolitan deconcentration
Mitchells Plain	South Africa	1973	Metropolitan deconcentration
Miyun District	China	1958	Industrial
Modi'in	Israel	1990	Metropolitan deconcentration
Mohali	India	1975	Industrial
Monchegorsk	Russia	1937	Industrial
Montgomery Village	United States	1962	Metropolitan deconcentration
Murmansk	Russia	1916	Industrial
Nahariyya	Israel	1934	Resettlement
Nakhodka	Russia	1950	Industrial
Nāngal	India	1948	Industrial
Narita New Town	Japan	1968	Industrial
Navapolatsk	Belarus	1958	Metropolitan deconcentration
Navi Mumbai	India	1970	Metropolitan deconcentration
Nazareth Illit	Israel	1954	Resettlement
Nazimabad	Pakistan	1950	Metropolitan deconcentration
Nee Soon	Singapore	1974	Industrial
Neftekamsk	Russia	1957	Industrial
Neryungri	Russia	1975	Industrial
New Borg El-Arab City	Egypt	1979	Metropolitan deconcentration
New Cairo City	Egypt	1995	Metropolitan deconcentration
New Delhi	India	1911	Capital
New Kanpur City	India	1997	Satellite
New Songdo City	South Korea	1996	Metropolitan deconcentration
New Town, Kolkata	India	1965	Metropolitan deconcentration
Newcastle/Madadeni-Osizweni	South Africa	1972	Industrial
Neyveli	India	1956	Industrial
Nieuwegein	Netherlands	1971	Metropolitan deconcentration
Nizhnevartovsk	Russia	1909	Industrial
Noida (New Okhla Industrial Development Authority)	India	1976	Industrial
Norilsk	Russia	1935	Industrial
North Lantau	China/Hong Kong	1992	Metropolitan deconcentration
North Nazimabad	Pakistan	1958	Metropolitan deconcentration

Original Name	Country	Date Started	Purpose
Northampton	United Kingdom	1968	Metropolitan deconcentration
Northglenn	United States	1960s	Metropolitan deconcentration
Nova Gorica	Slovenia	1947	Military/research
Nova Kakhovka	Ukraine	1951	Industrial
Nove Mesto	Slovakia	1961	Metropolitan deconcentration
Novi Belgrad	Serbia	1950	Metropolitan deconcentration
Novodvinsk	Russia	1936	Industrial
Novokuybyshevsk	Russia	1952	Industrial
Novokuznetsk	Russia	1931	Industrial
Novomoskovsk	Russia	1931	Industrial
Novoshakhtinsk	Russia	1939	Industrial
Novotroitsk	Russia	1940	Industrial
Novouralsk	Russia	1941	Military/research
Novovolynsk	Ukraine	1950	Industrial
Novovoronezh	Russia	1957	Industrial
Novy Urengoy	Russia	1975	Industrial
Nowa Huta	Poland	1949	Industrial
Nowe Tychy	Poland	1947	Industrial
Nubaria	Egypt	1986	Metropolitan deconcentration
Nyeri	Kenya	1910	Industrial
Obninsk	Russia	1956	Industrial
Oktyabrsky	Russia	1946	Industrial
Olmaliq	Uzbekistan	1930	Metropolitan deconcentration
Orléansville	Algeria	1954	Reconstruction
Orsk	Russia	1930	Industrial
Osinniki	Russia	1926	Industrial
Ozyorsk	Russia	1945	Industrial
Palm Coast	United States	1969	Metropolitan deconcentration
Palmas	Brazil	1990	Capital
Pardis	Iran	1991	Metropolitan deconcentration
Pasir Ris New Town	Singapore	1997	Metropolitan deconcentration
Peach Tree City	United States	1960	Metropolitan deconcentration
Pechora	Russia	1940	Military/research
Petaling-Jaya	Malaysia	1954	Metropolitan deconcentration
Peterborough	United Kingdom	1967	Metropolitan deconcentration
Pijnacker-Nootdorp	Netherlands	1976	Metropolitan deconcentration
Pimpri-Chinchwad	India	1970	Industrial
Pohang	South Korea	1968	Industrial
Poladshahr	Iran	1962	Metropolitan deconcentration
Pomezia	Italy	1939	Metropolitan deconcentration
Porirua	New Zealand	1948	Metropolitan deconcentration
Port Charlotte	United States	1964	Metropolitan deconcentration
Port Malabar	United States	1959	Metropolitan deconcentration
Port St. Lucie	United States	1958	Metropolitan deconcentration

Original Name	Country	Date Started	Purpose
Portmore	Jamaica	1965	Metropolitan deconcentration
Poruba	Czech Republic	1950	Metropolitan deconcentration
Prokopyevsk	Russia	1918	Industrial
Punggol	Singapore	1996	Metropolitan deconcentration
Purmerend	Netherlands	1965	Metropolitan deconcentration
Putrajaya	Malaysia	1995	Capital
Pyeongchon	South Korea	1989	Metropolitan deconcentration
Pyongyang	North Korea	1953	Capital
Qingdao Xihai'an New Area	China	1985	Industrial
Queenstown	Singapore	1949	Industrial
Quezon City	Philippines	1938	Capital
Raduzhny	Russia	1985	Industrial
Ranch Bernado	United States	1964	Metropolitan deconcentration
Rancho Mission Viejo	United States	1963	Metropolitan deconcentration
Rancho Santa Margarita	United States	1986	Metropolitan deconcentration
Ra's Lanuf	Libya	1984	Industrial
Redditch	United Kingdom	1964	Metropolitan deconcentration
Reforma Chipas	Mexico	1970s	Industrial
Resita	Romania	1953	Industrial
Reston	United States	1963	Metropolitan deconcentration
Richards Bay	South Africa	1971	Industrial
Richland	United States	1943	Military/research
Rinkeby-Kista	Sweden	1970s	Metropolitan deconcentration
Rives de l'Etang de Berre	France	1971	Industrial
Riyadh	Saudi Arabia	1953	Capital
Rostock	Germany	1971	Reconstruction
Rourkela Industrial Township	India	1955	Industrial
Runcorn	United Kingdom	1964	Metropolitan deconcentration
Rustavi	Georgia	1948	Industrial
Ryugasaki New Town	Japan	1971	Metropolitan deconcentration
Sadat City	Egypt	1975	Metropolitan deconcentration
Saint-Quentin-en-Yvelines	France	1970	Industrial
Salavat	Russia	1949	Industrial
Salihorsk	Belarus	1949	Industrial
Salzgitter	Germany	1938	Industrial
Sanandaj New Town	Iran	1958	Industrial
Sanbon	South Korea	1989	Metropolitan deconcentration
Sapporo	Japan	1922	Capital
Sarcelles	France	1955	Metropolitan deconcentration
Sasolburg	South Africa	1951	Industrial
Sayansk	Russia	1970	Industrial
Schwedt	Germany	1959	Industrial
Secunda	South Africa	1976	Industrial
Seishin New Town	Japan	1972	Metropolitan deconcentration

Original Name	Country	Date Started	Purpose
Sembawang New Town	Singapore	1938	Military/research
Senboku New Town	Japan	1965	Metropolitan deconcentration
Sengkang New Town	Singapore	1970	Metropolitan deconcentration
Senri New Town	Japan	1964	Metropolitan deconcentration
Seongnam	South Korea	1968	Metropolitan deconcentration
Serangoon New Town	Singapore	1997	Metropolitan deconcentration
Sertolovo	Russia	1936	Military/research
Severodvinsk	Russia	1936	Military/research
Severomorsk	Russia	1951	Military/research
Seversk	Russia	1949	Military/research
Sha Tin	China/Hong Kong	1965	Metropolitan deconcentration
Shah Alam	Malaysia	1963	Capital
Sharm-el-Sheikh	Egypt	1967	Capital
Sharpstown	United States	1955	Metropolitan deconcentration
Shcherbinka	Russia	1975	Industrial
Shekou Industrial District	China	1979	Industrial
Shevchenko	Kazakhstan	1963	Industrial
Shidami Human Science Town	Japan	1989	Military/research
Shihezi	China	1954	Military/research
Shuangdun	China	1996	Metropolitan deconcentration
Sibay	Russia	1913	Industrial
Sindri	India	1944	Industrial
Sinop	Brazil	1972	Industrial
Sixth of October City	Egypt	1979	Metropolitan deconcentration
Skärholmen	Sweden	1967	Metropolitan deconcentration
Skarpnäck	Sweden	1950	Metropolitan deconcentration
Skellefteå	Sweden	1967	Metropolitan deconcentration
Skelmersdale	United Kingdom	1961	Metropolitan deconcentration
Skopje	Macedonia	1965	Reconstruction
Slavgorod	Russia	1910	Military/research
Sosnovy Bor	Russia	1958	Industrial
Spijkenisse	Netherlands	1962 & 1976	Metropolitan deconcentration
Spring Hill	United States	1967	Metropolitan deconcentration
St. Charles Communities	United States	1970	Metropolitan deconcentration
Stalowa Wola	Poland	1937 and 1950	Industrial
Stavropol	Russia	1955	Industrial
Stevenage	United Kingdom	1946	Metropolitan deconcentration
Stupino	Russia	1939	Industrial
Suma New Town	Japan	1970s	Metropolitan deconcentration
Summerlin	United States	1990	Metropolitan deconcentration
Sumqayit	Azerbaijan	1939	Industrial
Sun City	United States	1959	Metropolitan deconcentration
Suzhou Science & Technology Town	China	1993	Industrial
Svobodnyj	Russia	1912	Industrial

Original Name	Country	Date Started	Purpose
Sztalinvaros	Hungary	1949	Industrial
Tai Po	China/Hong Kong	1979	Industrial
Tallaght	Ireland	1967	Metropolitan deconcentration
Talnakh	Russia	1960	Industrial
Tama Den'entoshi	Japan	1953	Metropolitan deconcentration
Tama New Town	Japan	1965	Metropolitan deconcentration
Tampines	Singapore	1978	Metropolitan deconcentration
Tarnowskie Góry	Poland	1946	Industrial
Tatabánya	Hungary	1947	Industrial
Tayshet	Russia	1937	Industrial
Telford	United Kingdom	1963	Metropolitan deconcentration
Telok Blangah	Singapore	1970	Industrial
Tema	Ghana	1956	Industrial
Temirtau	Kazakhstan	1945	Industrial
Tenth of Ramadan City	Egypt	1977	Metropolitan deconcentration
Thamesmead	United Kingdom	1967	Metropolitan deconcentration
Thika	Kenya	1947	Metropolitan deconcentration
Thousand Oaks	United States	1964	Metropolitan deconcentration
Tiberias	Israel	1951	Resettlement
Tin Shui Wai	China/Hong Kong	1982	Metropolitan deconcentration
Toa Payoh	Singapore	1966	Industrial
Tolyatti	Russia	1964	Industrial
Tomakomai	Japan	1952	Industrial
Tres Cantos	Spain	1975	Metropolitan deconcentration
Tryokhgorny	Russia	1952	Military/research
Tseung Kwan O	China/Hong Kong	1982	Metropolitan deconcentration
Tsuen Wan	China/Hong Kong	1961	Metropolitan deconcentration/Industrial
Tsukuba Science City	Japan	1976	Military/research
Tuen Mun	China/Hong Kong	1965	Metropolitan deconcentration
Tuggeranong	Australia	1986	Metropolitan deconcentration
Tung Chung	China	1993	Metropolitan deconcentration
Tynda	Russia	1907	Industrial
Uchaly	Russia	1963	Industrial
Ukhta	Russia	1929	Industrial
Ulhasnagar	India	1950	Resettlement
Ulsan	South Korea	1962	Industrial
Uray	Russia	1922	Industrial
Urayasu	Japan	1962, 1975	Metropolitan deconcentration
Usinsk	Russia	1966	Industrial
Uttara Model Town	Bangladesh	1965	Metropolitan deconcentration
Valencia	United States	1960	Metropolitan deconcentration
Vanderbij Park	South Africa	1943	Industrial
Vantaa	Finland	1974	Metropolitan deconcentration

Original Name	Country	Date Started	Purpose
Ventanilla	Peru	1961	Industrial
Vidnoye	Russia	1949	Industrial
Viladecans	Spain	1996	Metropolitan deconcentration
Villeneuve d'Ascq	France	1970	Industrial
Vitrolles	France	1973	Industrial
Volgodonsk	Russia	1975	Industrial
Volta Redonda	Brazil	1941	Industrial
Volzhsky	Russia	1951	Industrial
Vorkuta	Russia	1947	Industrial
Warrington	United Kingdom	1968	Metropolitan deconcentration
Washington	United Kingdom	1964	Metropolitan deconcentration
Welkom	South Africa	1948	Industrial
Welwyn Garden City	United Kingdom	1920	Metropolitan deconcentration
Westlake Village	United States	1968	Metropolitan deconcentration
Witbank	South Africa	1951	Industrial
Woden Valley	Australia	1962	Metropolitan deconcentration
Wolfsburg	Germany	1937	Industrial
Woodlands	Singapore	1971	Metropolitan deconcentration
The Woodlands (Texas)	United States	1974	Metropolitan deconcentration
Xiasha District	China	1990	Industrial
Xinwu District	China	1992	Industrial
Yamoussoukro	Ivory Coast	1983	Capital
Yanbu	Saudi Arabia	1975	Industrial
Yubileyny	Russia	1972	Industrial
Yuen Long	China/Hong Kong	1978	Metropolitan deconcentration
Zaporizhia	Ukraine	1928	Industrial
Zarechny	Russia	1958	Military/research
Zelenogorsk	Russia	1956	Military/research
Zelenograd	Russia	1956	Military/research
Zheleznogorsk	Russia	1957	Industrial
Zhigulyovsk	Russia	1949	Industrial
Zhodzina	Belarus	1963	Industrial
Zhukovsky	Russia	1956	Industrial
Zoetermeer	Netherlands	1965	Metropolitan deconcentration
Zouérat	Mauritania	1960s	Industrial

Table A.2. Inventory of Twenty-First-Century New Towns

Original Name	Country	Date Started	Purpose
8City	South Korea	2012	Resort
Aamby Valley City	India	2000s	Resort
Abuja Centenary City	Nigeria	2014	Metropolitan deconcentration
Aerotropolis	Kenya	2013	Industrial
Al Noor	Djibouti	2007	Metropolitan deconcentration
Amaravati	India	2015	Capital

Original Name	Country	Date Started	Purpose
Amboseli New Town	Kenya	2013	Resort
Anting	China	2002	Industrial
Appolonia City (City of Light)	Ghana	2013	Industrial
AURIC (Aurangabad Industrial City)	India	2016	Industrial
Beibei District	China	2006	Industrial
Binh Duong New City	Vietnam	2005	Industrial
Binhu New District	China	2006	Metropolitan deconcentration
Binjiang New Area	China	2003	Metropolitan deconcentration
Blue City, The	Oman	2010	Resort
Boughzoul	Algeria	2010	Capital
Bouinan	Algeria	2012	Industrial
CamKo	Cambodia	2005	Metropolitan deconcentration
Caofeidian Area Tangshan Bay Eco-City	China	2007	Industrial
Caucuaco	Angola	2008	Metropolitan deconcentration
Changping New Town	China	2004	Industrial
Chapelton	United Kingdom	2011	Metropolitan deconcentration
Chenggong New District	China	2003	Metropolitan deconcentration
Chongming New City	China	2002	Metropolitan deconcentration
Cuntan New City	China	2008	Industrial
Dahej	India	2012	Industrial
Dai Phuoc Lotus	Vietnam	2010	Metropolitan deconcentration
Daybreak	United States	2005	Metropolitan deconcentration
Defense Housing Authority (DHA) City Karachi	Pakistan	2009	Metropolitan deconcentration
Dholera	India	2009	Industrial
Dianbu	China	2006	Metropolitan deconcentration
Dianshanhu New City	China	2002	Metropolitan deconcentration
Dongqian Lake Tourist Holiday Resort Area	China	2001	Resort
Dongtan 1	South Korea	2001	Metropolitan deconcentration
Dongtan 2	South Korea	2008	Metropolitan deconcentration
Eastmark	United States	2013	Metropolitan deconcentration
Ebbsfleet	United Kingdom	2014	Metropolitan deconcentration
Educity Iskandar	Malaysia	2007	Military/research
Eko Atlantic Economic City	Nigeria	2003	Industrial
Fangshan New Town	China	2004	Metropolitan deconcentration
Fengcheng Town	China	2002	Metropolitan deconcentration
Fengjing Town	China	2002	Metropolitan deconcentration
Gaoqiao	China	2001	Metropolitan deconcentration
Geniland New Town	Democratic Republic of Congo	2012	Metropolitan deconcentration
Grand Wisata	Indonesia	2009	Metropolitan deconcentration
Guangzhou Higher Education Mega Center	China	2001	Metropolitan deconcentration

Original Name	Country	Date Started	Purpose
Gujarat International Finance Tec-City (GIFT)	India	2007	Industrial
Hacienda Eco-City	Kenya	2008	Resort
Hanoi New Town	Vietnam	2008	Metropolitan deconcentration
Hassi Messaoud New Town	Algeria	2006	Industrial
Hitobito New Town	Japan	2004	Metropolitan deconcentration
Huishan New Town	China	2001	Industrial
Hutai New Town	China	2007	
Jazan Economic City	Saudi Arabia	2006	Industrial
Jinan Western New Town (University Valley of Changqing)	China	2005	Military/research
Jing Jin City	China	2004	Metropolitan deconcentration
Jinghai New Town	China	2004	Industrial
Jinnan New Town	China	2004	Metropolitan deconcentration
Kangbashi New District	China	2000	Metropolitan deconcentration
Khed City	India	2006	Industrial
Kigamboni New City	Tanzania	2011	Metropolitan deconcentration
Kilamba	Angola	2011	Metropolitan deconcentration
King Abdullah Economic City	Saudi Arabia	2005	Industrial
King City	Ghana	2013	Industrial
Kintélé	Congo	2012	Metropolitan deconcentration
Kiswishi	Democratic Republic of Congo	2014	Metropolitan deconcentration
Knowledge Economic City	Saudi Arabia	2006	Industrial
Knowledge-Health City	Kenya	2011	Industrial
Konza Technology City	Kenya	2009	Industrial
La Cité du Fleuve	Democratic Republic of Congo	2008	Metropolitan deconcentration
Lavasa	India	2000s	Metropolitan deconcentration
Lekki	Nigeria	2016	Industrial
Leogane	Haiti	2010	Reconstruction
Liangjiang New Area	China	2010	Industrial
Liangzhu New Town	China	2006	Metropolitan deconcentration
Linping New Town	China	2001	Metropolitan deconcentration
Lingang. See Nanhui New City			
Liti Chengshi	China	2012	
Luodian	China	2002	Metropolitan deconcentration
Lusail City	Qatar	2010	Metropolitan deconcentration
Magarpatta	India	2000	Industrial
Manesar-Bawal	India	2012	Industrial
Masdar City	United Arab Emirates	2006	Military/research
Meixi Lake New International City	China	2007	Metropolitan deconcentration
Mesa del Sol	United States	2007	Metropolitan deconcentration

Original Name	Country	Date Started	Purpose
Modderfontein	South Africa	2009	Metropolitan deconcentration
Nanhui New City (formerly Lingang)	China	2002	Industrial
Nanqiao New City	China	2002	Metropolitan deconcentration
Nansha New Area	China	2012	Industrial
Naya Raipur	India	2006	Capital
Naypyidaw	Myanmar	2005	Capital
New Capital	Egypt	2015	Capital
New Harare	Zimbabwe	2013	Capital
New Moscow	Russia	2012	Metropolitan deconcentration
Nha Be	Vietnam	2008	Metropolitan deconcentration
Northstowe	United Kingdom	2005	Metropolitan deconcentration
OneHub Chennai	India	2015	Industrial
Pagcor Entertainment City	Philippines	2009	Resort
Panchkula	India	2001	Military/research
Pangyo	South Korea	2003	Metropolitan deconcentration
Pingshan New District	China	2009	Industrial
PlanIT Valley	Portugal	2008	Industrial
Prince Abdulaziz bin Musaid Economic City	Saudi Arabia	2009	Industrial
Pujiang	China	2002	Metropolitan deconcentration
Qianhai New District	China	2010	Industrial
Rajarhat	India	2005	Industrial
Rancho Sahuarita	United States	2002	Metropolitan deconcentration
Rawabi	Palestine	2010	Resettlement
Rublyovo-Arkhangelskoye	Russia	2009	Metropolitan deconcentration
Saadiyat Island	United Arab Emirates	2004	Resort
Sejong City	South Korea	2002	Capital
Shunyi	China	2004	Industrial
Sidi Abdellah	Algeria	2008	Military/research
Sino-Singapore Guangzhou Knowledge City	China	2009	Industrial
Skolkovo	Russia	2010	Military/research
Sobha Hi-Tech City	India	2007	Military/research
Songjiang	China	2002	Metropolitan deconcentration
Sports City	Kenya	2011	Industrial
Springfield Lakes	Australia	2000	Metropolitan deconcentration
Taihu New Town	China	2001	Industrial
Taiping New Town	China	2003	Metropolitan deconcentration
Tamansour	Morocco		Metropolitan deconcentration
Tamesna	Morocco	2007	Metropolitan deconcentration
Tangye New District	China	2003	Metropolitan deconcentration
Tatu City	Kenya	2010	Industrial
Tianjin Eco-City, Sino-Singapore	China	2007	Metropolitan deconcentration

Original Name	Country	Date Started	Purpose
Tongzhou New City	China	2005	Metropolitan deconcentration
Trans Ganga	India	2012	Industrial
Transport New Town	Kenya	2011	Industrial
Tsukuba Express Town	Japan	2005	Metropolitan deconcentration
Verrado	United States	2004	
Vikram Udyogpuri	India	2014	Military/research
Vikramaditya Knowledge City	India	2014	Military/research
Wenjiang District	China	2002	Metropolitan deconcentration
Xidong New Town	China	2009	Industrial
Xindu District	China	2001	Metropolitan deconcentration
Xiyong	China	2006	Industrial
Yachay City of Knowledge	Ecuador	2012	Military/research
Yizhuang	China	2005	Industrial
Zango	Angola	2006	Resettlement
Zhengdong New Area	China	2001	Metropolitan deconcentration
Zhujiajiao	China	2001	Metropolitan deconcentration
Zhujiang New Town	China	2003	Metropolitan deconcentration

Table A.3. Classic New Towns and New Neighborhoods

Original Name	Country	Date Started	Purpose
Alcoa	United States	1917	Industrial
Atlantic Station	United States	1999	Redevelopment
Auroville	India	1968	Experimental township
Baldwin Park	United States	1997	Redevelopment
Battery Park City	United States	1960s	Redevelopment
Belo Horizonte	Brazil	1893	Capital
Bournville	United Kingdom	1895	Industrial
Carbonia	Italy	1938	Industrial
Celebration	United States	1994	Metropolitan deconcentration/Resort
Country Club District	United States	1907	Metropolitan deconcentration
Daceyville	Australia	1912	Metropolitan deconcentration
Dalian/Dalny	China	1899	Industrial
Denenchōfu	Japan	1922	Metropolitan deconcentration
Don Mills	Canada	1952	Metropolitan deconcentration
East Tilbury	United Kingdom	1932	Industrial
Elizabeth	Australia	1957	Metropolitan deconcentration
Forest Hills Gardens	United States	1909	Metropolitan deconcentration
Goodyear Heights	United States	1912	Industrial
Greenbelt	United States	1937	Metropolitan deconcentration
Greendale	United States	1938	Metropolitan deconcentration
Greenhills	United States	1938	Metropolitan deconcentration
Hammarby Sjostad	Sweden	1999	Metropolitan deconcentration
Hampstead Garden Suburb	United Kingdom	1906	Metropolitan deconcentration

Original Name	Country	Date Started	Purpose
Hellerau	Germany	1908	Industrial
Hershey	United States	1900	Industrial
Lake Nona	United States	1996	Metropolitan deconcentration
Lakewood Ranch	United States	1995	Metropolitan deconcentration
La Plata	Argentina	1882	Capital
Levittown	United States	1947	Metropolitan deconcentration
Levittown	United States	1951	Metropolitan deconcentration
Llewellyn Park	United States	1857	Metropolitan deconcentration
Logis-Floreal	Belgium	1922	Metropolitan deconcentration
Los Alamos	United States	1942	Military/research
Lynch	United States	1917	Industrial
Maria Elena	Chile	1926	Industrial
Märsta	Sweden	1964	Metropolitan deconcentration
Mount Royal	Canada	1910	Metropolitan deconcentration
New Albany	United States	1985	Metropolitan deconcentration
Newton Aycliffe	United Kingdom	1947	Metropolitan deconcentration
Oak Ridge	United States	1947	Military/research
Palmerston	Australia	1971	Metropolitan deconcentration
Palos Verdes Estates	United States	1913	Metropolitan deconcentration
Park Forest	United States	1948	
Peterlee	United Kingdom	1948	Metropolitan deconcentration
Pinelands	South Africa	1919	Metropolitan deconcentration
Port Sunlight	United Kingdom	1888	Industrial
Poundbury	United Kingdom	1989	Metropolitan deconcentration
Pretoria	South Africa	1855	Capital
Pullman	United States	1880	Industrial
Radburn	United States	1928	Metropolitan deconcentration
Riverside	United States	1869	Metropolitan deconcentration
Roland Park	United States	1891	Metropolitan deconcentration
Rosyth Garden City	United Kingdom	1915	Metropolitan deconcentration
Sabaudia	Italy	1933	Experimental
Saltaire	United Kingdom	1851	Industrial
Santa Ana	Argentina	1889	Industrial
Sea Ranch, The	United States	1962	Resort
Seaside	United States	1979	Resort
Skarholmen	Sweden	1960s	Metropolitan deconcentration
Southern Village	United States	1994	Experimental
Stapleton	United States	1991	Redevelopment
Tapiola	Finland	1952	Metropolitan deconcentration
Terramor	United States	1999	Experimental
Vila Piloto	Brazil	1961	Industrial
Wythenshawe	United Kingdom	1926	Metropolitan deconcentration
Yorkship Village	United States	1918	Industrial
Zlín	Czech Republic	1923	Industrial

References

Abou-Zeid, A. 1979. "New Towns and Rural Development in Egypt." *Africa: Journal of the International African Institute* 49, no. 3: 283–90.

AECOM. 2004. *Verrado Master Plan*. Los Angeles: AECOM.

———. 2005. *Verrado Phase 1 Design Guidelines*. Scottsdale, AZ: AECOM.

———. 2007. *Rancho Mission Viejo PA1 Master Plan*. Irvine, CA: AECOM.

———. 2009. *Alphaville Urbanismo Master Plan*. Irvine, CA: AECOM.

———. 2010a. *Canon Station Fairfield, California Master Plan SSIM Analysis*. Irvine, CA: AECOM.

———. 2010b. *Jurong Lake Master Plan*. Singapore: AECOM.

———. 2011a. *Marina Bay SSIM Analysis*. Irvine, CA: AECOM.

———. 2011b. *Tongzhou New Town Concept Studies*. Los Angeles: AECOM.

———. 2012. *Marina Bay Sustainability Master Plan*. Irvine, CA: AECOM.

———. 2014. *Transit Technology Costs—Hillsborough County*. Accessed March 22, 2016. http://www.hillsboroughcounty.org/DocumentCenter/View/12668.

Alberti, M. 1999. "Urban Patterns and Environmental Performance: What Do We Know?" *Journal of Planning Education and Research* 19, no. 2: 151–63.

Aldridge, M. 1979. *The British New Towns: A Programme Without a Policy*. London: Routledge and Kegan Paul.

Alexander, A. 2009. *Britain's New Towns: Garden Cities to Sustainable Communities*. London: Routledge.

Alexander, C. 1965. "A City Is Not a Tree." *Architectural Forum* 1221, no. 1: 58–62.

Alexander, G. 1989. "Dilemmas of Group Autonomy: Residential Associations and Community." *Cornell Law Review* 75, no. 1: 1–61.

Alexander, I. 1979. *Office Location and Public Policy*. London: Longman.

Almeida, H. 2009. "Angola Says Luanda's Housing Shortage Is Critical." Reuters. Last modified July 31, 2009. http://www.reuters.com/article/idUSLV623806.

Alonso, W. 1970. "What are New Towns For?" *Urban Studies* 7, no. 1: 37–55.

Alonso, W. 1977. "The Mirage of New Towns." In *New Towns and the Suburban Dream*, edited by I. Allen, 175–87. Port Washington, NY: Kennikat.

Al-Rabwa. 2006. "Villas." Accessed August 22, 2016. http://www.al-rabwa.com/Villas.htm.

Amati, M., and R. Freestone. 2014. "Trans-National Promotion of British and American Planning Practice in the 1940s." *Planning Theory and Practice* 15, no. 3: 370–85.

American Planning Association, Orion Planning + Design, Placeways and University of California, San Diego. 2016. "Innovations in Planning and Public Engagement for Community Resilience. Task 3—Scenario Planning Model Report." Accessed November 7, 2016. https://www.planning.org/media/document/9109463/.

American Public Transportation Association. 2004. "Community Partners Join UTA to Advance Light Rail Project." *Passenger Transport*. Accessed March 24, 2016. http://www.apta.com/passengertransport/Documents/archive_614.htm.

Andelman, R., R. Board, L. Carman, R. Cummins, A. Ferriss, P. Friedman, A. Michalos, et al. 1998.

Quality of Life Definition and Terminology: A Discussion Document from the International Society of Quality of Life Studies. Blacksburg, VA: International Society of Quality of Life Studies.

Anis-Ur-Rahmaan, T. A., and T. A. Fadaak. 1991. "New Towns in Saudi Arabia." *Habitat International* 15, nos. 1/2: 167–79.

Apgar, M. 1971. "Systems Management in the New City: Columbia, Maryland." In *New Tools for Urban Management*, edited by R. S. Rosenbloom and J. R. Russell, 157–220. Boston: Harvard Business School Division of Research.

———. 2015. *Placemaking: Innovations in New Communities*. Washington, DC: Royal Institute of Chartered Surveyors and Urban Land Institute.

Appolonia City. 2016. "A Contemporary Urban Oasis." Accessed August 20, 2016. http://www.appolonia.com.gh.

Archer, R. W. 1969. "From New Towns to Metrotowns and Regional Cities." *American Journal of Economics and Sociology* 28, no. 4: 385–98.

Ashworth, G. 1973. "New Towns." In *Encyclopedia of Planning*, by G. Ashworth, 67–68. London: Barrie and Jenkins.

Associated Press. 2002. "Next Big UTA Project Uncertain Daily Herald." Accessed March 19, 2016. http://www.heraldextra.com/news/local/next-big-uta-project-uncertain/article_1b01d32f-5c46-5a54-b703-dc085o121c7e.html.

Attali, J. 2008. "Rapport de la Commission pour la libération de la croissance française." Paris: La Documentation française. Accessed January 2018. http://www.ladocumentationfrancaise.fr/var/storage/rapports-publics/084000041.pdf.

Bae, N. J. 2008. "A Study on the Conflict Management in New Town Project." PhD diss., Kyungwon University.

Baeten, J.-P. 2010. *Inventory of the Archives of the International New Towns Association, 1976–2004*. Almere: International New Towns Association.

Bardo, J. W. 1977. "Social Class, Age, Sex, Mother-Daughter Role Relationships, and Community Satisfaction in a British New Town." *Journal of Social Psychology* 103, no. 2: 251–55.

Bardo, J. W., and D. J. Bardo. 1983. "A Re-Examination of Subjective Components of Community Satisfaction in a British New Town." *Journal of Social Psychology* 120, no. 1: 35–43.

Barth, B. 2016. "Let's Beat It." *Landscape Architecture Magazine* 106, no. 10: 132–51.

Beatley, T. 2009. *Planning for Coastal Resilience: Best Practices for Calamitous Times*. Washington, DC: Island.

Beauregard, R. A. 2006. *When America Became Suburban*. Minneapolis: University of Minnesota Press.

Beijing Tongzhou Government Statistical Yearbook. 2010. Beijing: China Statistics Press.

Beito, D. T. 1990. "The Formation of Urban Infrastructure Through Nongovernmental Planning: The Private Places of St. Louis, 1869–1920." *Journal of Urban History* 16, no. 3: 263–303.

Berg, J. 2007. "De tweede jeugd van Almere." *Blauwe Kamer* 4:34–41.

Berkman, L. 1987. "Bren Tells Court About Irvine Co.'s Troubles." *Los Angeles Times*, October 27. http://articles.latimes.com/1987-10-27/business/fi-16590_1_chairman-donald-l-bren.

Berlin, R. 2013. "Amenities Survey—2013 Capital Region Community Development District South-Wood." *Capital Region Community Development District*. Accessed April 2, 2016. http://www.capitalregioncdd.com/PDF/Amenities Survey Final for Website.pdf.

Bernhardt, C. 2005. "Planning Urbanization and Urban Growth in the Socialist Period: The Case of East German New Towns, 1945–1989." *Journal of Urban History* 32, no. 1: 104–19.

Beveridge, C. E., and C. F. Hoffman. 1987. *The Master List of Design Projects of the Olmsted Firm 1857–1950*. Boston: National and Massachusetts Associations for Olmsted Parks.

Bhattacharya, R., and K. Sanyal. 2011. "Bypassing the Squalor: New Towns, Immaterial Labour and Exclusion in Post-Colonial Urbanization." *Economic and Political Weekly* 46, no. 31: 41–48.

Biddulph, M. 2000. "Villages Don't Make a City." *Journal of Urban Design* 5, no. 1: 65–82.

Birnbaum, H. 1973. "Tsukuba: Japan Makes a Major Commitment to the Future." *Mosaic* 4, no. 2: 24–29.

Bisoee, A. 2014. "Thumbs Up to Tata Township." *Telegraph*, September 11. https://www.telegraph india.com/india/thumbs-up-to-tata-township/cid/1579175

Blakely, E. J., and A. Carbonell. 2012. *Resilient Coastal City Regions: Planning for Climate Change in the United States and Australia*. Cambridge, MA: Lincoln Institute of Land Policy.

Blakely, E. J., and M. G. Snyder. 1997. *Fortress America: Gated Communities in the United States*. Washington, DC: Brookings Institution Press.

Bloom, N. 2001. *Suburban Alchemy: 1960s New Towns and Transformation of the American Dream*. Columbus: Ohio State University Press.

Borut, A. 1976. "A Framework for Financing New Town Development." *Urban Land* 35, no. 7: 18–19.

Bottles, S. L. 1987. *Los Angeles and the Automobile: The Making of the Modern City*. Berkeley: University of California Press.

Bowers, P. 2014. "New Interactive Map Shows Effects of Sea Level Rise on Charleston: Here Comes the Ocean." *Charleston City Paper*, August 13. http://www.charlestoncitypaper.com/charleston /new-interactive-map-shows-effects-of-sea-level-rise-on-charleston/Content?oid=4972978.

Branch, M. C. 1983. *Comprehensive Planning: General Theory and Principles*. Pacific Palisades, CA: Palisades.

Breckenfeld, G. 1971. *Columbia and the New Cities*. New York: Washburn.

Bristow, M. R. 1989. *Hong Kong's New Towns: A Selective Review*. New York: Oxford University Press.

Brooks, R. O. 1974. *New Towns and Communal Values: A Case Study of Columbia, Maryland*. New York: Praeger.

Brown, I. 2011. "Elements of Green Infrastructure." Presentation, Annual Meeting of the American Society of Landscape Architects, Phoenix, October 1.

Buckingham. J. S. [1849] 2011. *National Evils and Practical Remedies, with The Plan of a Model Town*. Cambridge: Cambridge University Press.

Burby, R. J., and S. F. Weiss. 1976. *New Communities U.S.A.* Lexington, MA: Lexington Books.

Burkhart, L. C. 1981. *Old Values in a New Town: The Politics of Race and Class in Columbia, Maryland*. New York: Praeger.

Burnett, R. 2009. "UCF's Medical School's Debut Is Just the Beginning." *Orlando Sentinel*, August 2. https://www.orlandosentinel.com/news/os-xpm-2009-08-02-orl-ucf-medical-city -vision-080209-story.html.

Burnham, D., and D. Bennett. 1909. *Plan of Chicago*. Chicago: Commercial Club of Chicago.

Business Standard. 2008. "Lavasa Lake City near Completion." *Business Standard*, October 13. https://www.business-standard.com/article/beyond-business/lavasa-lake-city-near-completion -108101301057_1.html.

Cabannes, Y., and P. Ross. 2014. *21st Century Garden Cities of To-Morrow: A Manifesto*. Morrisville, N.C.: Lulu.com Press.

Cagle, M. R. 2009. "The Woodlands, Once a Logging Camp." *Woodlands Lifestyles and Homes*. Last modified May 2009. http://www.woodlandslifestylesandhomes.com/may9history.htm.

Calthorpe, P., and W. Fulton. 2001. *The Regional City: Planning for the End of Sprawl*. Washington, DC: Island.

Campanella, T. J. 2008. *The Concrete Dragon: China's Urban Revolution and What It Means for the World*. Princeton, NJ: Princeton Architectural Press.

Campbell, A., and P. Converse. 1972. *The Human Meaning of Social Change*. New York: Russell Sage Foundation.

Campbell, A., R. Converse, and W. Rodgers. 1976. *The Quality of American Life: Perceptions, Evaluations, and Satisfactions*. New York: Russell Sage Foundation.

Caprotti, F. 2007. "Destructive Creation: Fascist Urban Planning, Architecture and New Towns in the Pontine Marshes." *Journal of Historical Geography* 33, no. 3: 651–79.

Carmichael, M. 2014. "Top Amenities by Generation." *John Burns Real Estate Consulting*, June 9. Accessed April 3, 2016. http://realestateconsulting.com/top-amenities-by-generation/.

Carson, R. 1962. *Silent Spring*. Boston: Houghton Mifflin.

Castells, M. 1992. "The World Has Changed: Can Planning Change?" *Landscape and Urban Planning* 22, no. 1: 73–78.

Castells, M., L. Goh, and R. Yin-Wang Kwok. 1990. *The Shek Kip Mei Syndrome: Economic Development and Public Housing in Hong Kong and Singapore*. London: Pion.

Castells, M., and P. Hall. 1994. *Technopoles of the World: The Making of 21st Century Industrial Complexes*. London: Routledge.

Caulfield, G. 2016. *Lake Nona Medical City*. Orlando: Tavistock Development Corporation.

CCIM Institute. 2012. *Advanced Market Analysis for Commercial Real Estate*. Chicago: CCIM Institute.

Center for Livable Cities. 2015. *Urban Systems Studies: Built by Singapore, from Slums to Sustainable Development*. Singapore: Center for Livable Cities.

Cervero, R. 1989. "Jobs-Housing Balancing and Regional Mobility." *Journal of the American Planning Association* 55, no. 2: 136–50.

Cervero, R., and M. Duncan. 2006. "Which Reduces Vehicle Travel More: Jobs-Housing Balance or Retail-Housing Mixing?" *Journal of the American Planning Association* 72, no. 4: 475–90.

Chadha, S. 2014. "Lavasa to Lodha: Is the Revival in Real Estate IPOs for Real?" *Firstpost*, July 15. https://www.firstpost.com/business/real-estate/lavasa-to-lodha-is-the-revival-in-real-estate-ipos-for-real-2010421.html

China National Bureau of Statistics. 2013. *Daxing District, Yizhuang*. Beijing: National Bureau of Statistics of P.R. of China.

Chohan, U. W. 2014. *The Ubiquitous City—Songdo*. Montreal: McGill University Press.

City of Mesa. 2014. "2014 Job Center Report." Accessed February 3, 2016. http://geo.azmag.gov/services/employment2014/Reports.html?jobCenter=ME_8#.

Clapp, J. A. 1970. "The New Town Concept: Private Trends and Public Response." In *Exchange Bibliography*, 122. Monticello, IL: Council of Planning Librarians.

———. 1971. *New Towns and Urban Policy: Planning Metropolitan Growth*. New York: Dunellen.

Clapson, M. 1997. *Invincible Green Suburbs, Brave New Towns: Social Change and Urban Dispersal in Post-War Britain*. Manchester: Manchester University Press.

Clawson, M. 1968. *The Land System of the United States*. Lincoln: University of Nebraska Press.

Collings, M. N.d. "From Lavasa, Exploring Business Models for New Cities." *New Cities Foundation*. Accessed June 30, 2015. http://www.newcitiesfoundation.org/blog-new-city-business-models-a-roundtable-in-lavasa-india/.

Collinson, P. 2011. "Self-Build: It's Time to Go Dutch." *Guardian*, November 25. https://www.theguardian.com/money/2011/nov/25/self-build-go-dutch.

Community Associations Institute. 2016. *Large Scale Associations Survey Results June 2016*. Falls Church, VA: Foundation for Community Association Research.

———. 2017. "Community Associations in the United States, Alexandria, Virginia." *Community Associations Institute*. Last updated 2017. https://www.caionline.org/AboutCommunityAssociations/Pages/StatisticalInformation.aspx.

Corden, C. 1977. *Planned Cities: New Towns in Britain and America*. Beverly Hills, CA: Sage.

Correa, F. 2016. *Beyond the City: Re Extraction Urbanism in South America*. Austin: University of Texas Press.

Counties USA: A Directory of United States Counties. 2006. 3rd ed. Detroit, MI: Omnigraphics.

Crabtree, J. S. 2015. "Welcome to Jamshedpur, India's Steel Citadel." *Financial Times*, November 10 https://www.ft.com/content/c3035e70-7d79-11e5-98fb-5a6d4728f74e.

Crewe, K., and A. Forsyth. 2011. "Compactness and Connection in Environmental Design: Insights from Ecoburbs and Ecocities for Design with Nature." *Environment and Planning B* 38, no. 2: 267–88.

Crimson Architectural Historians. 2012. "The Banality of Good: Six Decades of New Towns, Architects, Money and Politics." *Crimson Architectural Historians*, August 28. https://www.crimsonweb.org/spip.php?article132.

Croese, S. 2012. "One Million Houses? China's Engagement in Angola's National Reconstruction."

In *China and Angola: A Marriage of Convenience?* edited by A. Alves and M. Power, 124–44. Cape Town: Pambazuka.

Cropper, V., and B. Brown. 2001. "New Urban and Standard Suburban Subdivisions: Evaluating Psychological and Social Goals." *Journal of the American Planning Association* 67, no. 4: 402–19.

Cullingworth, J. B. 1979. *Environmental Planning, 1939–1969*. Vol. 3, *New Towns Policy*. London: H. M. Stationery Office.

Cupers, K. 2014. *The Social Project: Housing Postwar France*. Minneapolis: University of Minnesota Press.

Daily News Egypt. 2015. "Weekly Average Salary Reached EGP 806 in 2014: CAPMAS." Accessed August 22, 2016. http://www.dailynewsegypt.com/2015/05/13/weekly-average-salary-reached -egp-806-in-2014-capmas/.

Daniels, P. W. 1975. *Office Location: An Urban and Regional Study*. London: Bell.

Debrezion, G., E. Pels, and P. Rietveld. 2007. "The Impact of Railway Stations on Residential and Commercial Property Value: A Meta-Analysis." *Journal of Real Estate Finance Economics* 35, no. 2: 161–80.

Deng, F. F., and Y. Huang. 2004. "Uneven Land Reform and Urban Sprawl in China: The Case of Beijing." *Progress in Planning* 61:211–36.

den Hartog, H., ed. 2010. *Shanghai New Towns: Searching for Community and Identity in a Sprawling Metropolis*. Rotterdam: 010 Publishers.

Ding, C., S. Fu, and J. Zhou. 2013. *Vanke Liangzhu New Town*. Tokyo: Shinkenchiku.

DiPasquale, D., and W. Wheaton. 1996. "Econometric Analysis of Office and Industrial Markets." In *Urban Economics and Real Estate Markets*, chapter 12. Englewood Cliffs, NJ: Prentice-Hall.

DMB Associates. 2014. "Apple's Deal in Mesa at Eastmark Honored as Top Deal by Site Selection and Business Facilities Magazines." News release, June 27. Accessed February 3, 2016. https:// dmbinc.com/apples-deal-in-mesa-at-eastmark-honored-as-top-deal-by-site-selection-and-busi ness-facilities-magazines/.

———. 2015. "Victory District Disclosure Statement." *Verrado—a Planned Community*. July 31. Accessed April 12, 2016. http://www.verrado.net/Assets/Verrado Digital Assets/Governance /Victory District/Disclosures/VDA MDS 07–31–15.pdf.

———. 2016. "Verrado FAQ." *Verrado*. Accessed April 6, 2016. https://www.verrado.com/faq.

Dobbs, D., and H. Lyndon. 2012. "Comparative Examination of New Start Light Rail Transit, Light Railway, and Bus Rapid Transit Services Opened from 2000." Presentation, TRB/APTA Joint Light Rail Transit Conference, Salt Lake City, November 12.

Donzelot, F. 2004. "La ville à trois vitesses: Relégation, péri-urbanisation, gentrification." *Revue Esprit*. Last updated March 2004. http://www.esprit.presse.fr/article/donzelot-jacques /la-ville-a-trois-vitesses-relegation-periurbanisation-gentrification-7903.

Ducom, E. 2008. "Tama New Town, West of Tokyo: Analysis of a Shrinking Suburb." *Landscape and Urban Planning*, January, 1–35.

Durham, R. L. 1967. Editorial, *Washington Post*, November. Quoted in Gombach Group, Reston— Overview, *Living Places*. Last updated 2017. http://www.livingplaces.com/VA/Fairfax_County /Reston.html.

Ebbing, W. 2016. President of New Albany Company memorandum, May 2.

Ecocity Builders. 2016. *Eco-Cities Emerging*. Accessed June 17, 2016. http://ecocitiesemerging.org/.

Economist. 2011. "Company Towns: The Universal Provider." *Economist, Schumpeter Blog*, January 19. https://www.economist.com/blogs/schumpeter/2011/01/company_towns.

———. 2016. "Far and Few Between: Africa's Middle Class." Retrieved June 6, 2016. http://www .economist.com/news/middle-east-and-africa/21676774-africans-are-mainly-rich-or-poor-not -middle-class-should-worry.

EDAW. 2002. *Sustainability Study for Rancho San Benito*. Irvine, CA: EDAW.

———. 2004. *Ladera Village 5 Master Plan*. Irvine, CA: EDAW.

Egypt New Urban Communities Authority. N.d. "Sheikh Zayed City." Retrieved August 22, 2016. http://www.newcities.gov.eg/english/New_Communities/Zayed/default.aspx.

Eichler, E., and M. Kaplan. 1967. *The Community Builders*. Berkeley: University of California Press.

Ekers, M., P. Hamel, and R. Keil. 2012. "Governing Suburbia: Modalities and Mechanisms of Suburban Governance." *Regional Studies* 46, no. 3: 405–22.

Eko Atlantic. 2016. "About Eko Atlantic." Retrieved August 20, 2016. http://www.ekoatlantic.com.

Eng, T. S. 1996. "Character and Identity in Singapore New Towns: Planner and Resident Perspectives." *Habitat International* 20, no. 2: 279–94.

Erbsen, C. E. 1966. "Brazil's New Pilot City." *Hartford Courant*, June 19.

European Commission, Directorate General for Regional Policy. 2011. *Cities of Tomorrow: Challenges, Visions, Ways Forward*. Brussels: European Union.

European New Towns Platform. 2006. "Contextual Analysis of Six New Towns." NEWTASC INTERREG IIIB program. Brussels.

———. 2015. "News and Events." Accessed January 2015. http://www.pilotcities.eu/.

Eurostat. 2015. *Eurostat Regional Yearbook 2015*. Luxembourg: European Commission.

Evans, H., and L. Rodwin. 1979. "The New Towns Program and Why It Failed." *Public Interest* 56 (Summer): 90–107.

Ewing, R. 1991. *Developing Successful New Communities*. Washington, DC: Urban Land *Institute*.

———. 1997. "Is Los Angeles-Style Sprawl Desirable?" *Journal of the American Planning Association* 63, no. 1: 107–26.

———. 2000. *"There's a Hybrid in Your Future: Tomorrow's Development Will Look Like Today's Only More So." Planning,* November, 18–21.

Ewing, R., and K. Bartholomew. 2013. Pedestrian- and Transit-Oriented Design. Washington, DC: Urban Land Institute and American Planning Association.

Ewing, R., and R. Cervero. 2010. "Travel and the Built Environment: A Meta-Analysis." *Journal of the American Planning Association* 76, no. 3: 265–94.

Ewing, R., M. DeAnna, C. Heflin, and D. R. Porter. 1996. *Best Development Practices*. Chicago: APA Planners.

Ewing, R., and S. Hamidi. 2014. *Measuring Urban Sprawl and Validating Sprawl Measures*. Washington, DC: National Institutes of Health and Smart Growth America.

Ewing, R., Tian, G., Lyons, T., and Terzano, K. 2017. "Trip and Parking Generation at Transit-Oriented Developments: Five U.S. Case Studies." *Landscape and Urban Planning* 160: 69–78.

Ex-Service Man, J47485 [pseud.]. 1934. *A Hundred New Towns?* Letchworth, U.K.: J. M. Dent.

Fahmi, W. S., 2008. "The Right to the City: Stakeholder Perspectives of Greater Cairo Metropolitan Communities." In *World Cities and Urban Form: Fragmented, Polycentric, Sustainable?* by M. Jenks, D. Kozak, and P. Takkanon. 269–92. Abingdon, U.K.: Routledge.

Fava, S. 1973. "The Pop Sociology of Suburbs and New Towns." *American Studies* 14, no. 1: 121–33.

Federal Emergency Management Agency (FEMA). 2014. "For Communities Plagued by Repeated Flooding, Property Acquisition May Be the Answer." Accessed June 9, 2016. https://www.fema .gov/news-release/2014/05/28/communities-plagued-repeated-flooding-property-acquisition -may-be-answer.

Federal Housing Administration. 1963. *Planned Unit Development with a Homes Association*. Land Planning Bulletin no 6. Washington, DC: Federal Housing Administration.

Federal Housing Administration and Urban Land Institute. 1964. *The Homes Association Handbook*. Technical Bulletin no. 50. Washington, DC: Urban Land Institute.

Feng, J., Y. Zhou, and F. Wu. 2008. "New Trends of Suburbanization in Beijing Since 1990: From Government-Led to Market-Oriented." *Regional Studies* 42, no. 1: 83–99.

Fennell, L. A. 2013. "The Problem of Resource Access." *Harvard Law Review* 126, no. 6: 1471–530.

Fernandes, W., and V. Paranjpye. 1997. "Hundred Years of Displacement in India: Is the Rehabilitation Policy an Adequate Response?" In *Rehabilitation Policy and Law in India: A Right to Livelihood*, by W. Fernandes and V. Paranjpye, 1–34. New Delhi: Indian Social Institute.

Fink, A. 1966. *Time and the Terraced Land*. Berkeley, CA: Howell North Books.

Finley, W. E. 1969. "A Fresh Start." In *The New City*, edited by D. Canty, 163–67. New York: Frederick A. Praeger.

Firman, T. 2004. "New Town Development in Jakarta Metropolitan Region: A Perspective of Spatial Segregation." *Habitat International* 28, no. 3: 349–68.

Fishman, Robert. 1987. *Bourgeois Utopias: The Rise and Fall of Suburbia*. New York: Basic Books.

Flynn, J. 1987. "Owning Irvine Calif. Isn't What It Used to Be." *Business Week*, March. no. 2988: 80–82.

Fontanella-Khan, J., and J. Lamont. 2010. "Indian Nod to Float Modern-Day Hill Station." *Financial Times*, November 19. https://www.ft.com/content/3ffe3a0c-f40f-11df-886b-00144feab49a.

Foo, T. S. 2000. "Subjective Assessment of Urban Quality of Life in Singapore (1997–1998)." *Habitat International* 24, no. 1: 31–49.

Forest City Stapleton. 2016. "Stapleton Denver Named Number Four Best-Selling Master Planned Community in Nation." News release, February 1. Accessed April 10, 2016. http://www.stapletondenver.com/wp-content/uploads/2016/02/MPCRankingRelease.pdf.

Forsyth, A. 2002. "Planning Lessons from Three U.S. New Towns of the 1960s and 1970s: Irvine, Columbia, and the Woodlands." *Journal of the American Planning Association* 68, no. 4: 387–415.

———. 2003. "New Towns." In *Encyclopedia of Community*, edited by K. Christensen and D. Levinson. Thousand Oaks, CA: Sage.

———. 2005. *Reforming Suburbia: The Planned Communities of Irvine, Columbia, and The Woodlands*. Berkeley: University of California Press.

———. 2011. "Planned Communities and New Towns." In *Urban Design: Roots, Influences, and Trends; The Routledge Companion to Urban Design*, edited by T. Banerjee and A. Loukaitou-Sideris, 365–75. New York: Routledge.

———. 2014a. "Alternative Forms of the High Technology District: Corridors, Clumps, Cores, Campuses, Subdivisions, and Sites." *Environment and Planning C* 32, no. 5: 809–23.

———. 2014b. "Global Suburbs and the Transition Century: Physical Suburbs in the Long Term." *Urban Design International* 19, no. 4: 259–73.

Forsyth, A., and K. Crewe. 2009a. "New Visions for Suburbia: Reassessing Aesthetics and Place-Making in Modernism, Imageability, and New Urbanism." *Journal of Urban Design* 14, no. 4: 415–38.

———. 2009b. "A Typology of Comprehensive Designed Communities Since the Second World War." *Landscape Journal* 28:57–78.

———. 2010. "Suburban Technopoles as Places: The International Campus-Garden-Suburb Style." *Urban Design International* 15, no. 3: 165–82.

———. 2011. "Finding Common Ground in the Metropolis: Planned Residential Enclaves as Connection or Exclusion?" *Journal of Architectural and Planning Research* 28, no. 1: 58–75.

Fouchier, V. 2010a. "New Towns: Drawing Lessons from the Past to Better Anticipate the Future." Paper presented at New Medina Project Conference, Val-Maubuée, Marne-la-Vallée, January.

———. 2010b. "Villes nouvelles! Comment tirer les leçons du passé pour anticiper le futur." Paper presented at Conference des Villes Nouvelles aux Villes Durables, Marseille, France, February.

Foundation for Community Association Research. 2012. *Statistical Review: 2012; For U.S. Homeowners Associations, Condominium Communities and Housing Cooperatives*. Alexandria, VA: Community Associations Institute.

Franzese, P. 2000. "Neighborhoods: Common Interest Communities; Standards of Review and Review of Standards. *Washington University Journal of Law and Policy* 3, no. 1: 663–97.

Freemark, Y. 2014. "Have U.S. Light Rail Systems Been Worth the Investment?" *Atlantic*, April 10. Accessed July 23, 2016. http://www.citylab.com/commute/2014/04/have-us-light-rail-systems-been-worth-investment/8838/.

Freestone, R. 2000. "Utopias." In *Design Professionals and the Built Environment*, edited by P. Knox and P. Ozolins, 179–90. New York: John Wiley.

———. 2012. "Futures Thinking in Planning Education and Research." *Journal for Education in the Built Environment* 7, no. 1: 8–38.

———. 2013. "Back to the Future." In *Made in Australia: The Future of Australian Cities*, edited by R. Weller and J. Bolleter, 237–44. Perth: University of Western Australia Press.

———. 2016. "A Brief History of New Towns." Paper presented at New Towns conference, Harvard University, Cambridge, MA.

Freestone, R., and E. Liu, eds. 2016. *Place and Placelessness Revisited*. London: Routledge.

Freudenberg, R., E. Calvin, L. Tolkoff, and D. Brawley. 2016. *Buy-In for Buyouts: The Case for Managed Retreat from Flood Zones*. Policy Focus Report Series. Cambridge, MA: Lincoln Institute of Land Policy.

Frey, B. 2001. "A Utopia? Government Without Territorial Monopoly." *Journal of Theoretical and Institutional Economics* 157:162–75.

Frug, G. E. 1980. "The City as a Legal Concept." *Harvard Law Review* 93: 1059–154.

———. 1999. "City Making." In *Building Communities Without Walls*, 32–35. Princeton, NJ: Princeton University Press.

Gaborit, P. 2010. *European New Towns Image, Identities, Future Perspectives*. Brussels: Peter Lang.

———. 2012. *New Medinas: From New Towns to Sustainable Cities*. Brussels: Peter Lang.

———, ed. 2014. *European and Asian Sustainable Towns: New Towns and Satellite Cities in Their Metropolises*. Brussels: Peter Lang.

Gaborit, P., and J. Nguyen. 2009. *New Towns Study*. Brussels: ENTP Publications.

Gaborit, P., and L. Van Leuwen. 2004. "Les Villes Nouvelles en Europe: De la ville pilote à la ville durable." *Pouvoirs Locaux* 60, no. 1: 20–23.

Gadugah, N. 2015. "Building a City in Accra: The Ambitious Plan at Appolonia." *My Joy Online*. Retrieved September 4, 2016. http://www.myjoyonline.com/business/2015/August-12th /building-a-city-in-accra-the-ambitious-plan-at-appolonia.php.

Galantay, E. Y. 1975. *New Towns: Antiquity to the Present*. New York: G. Braziller.

Galatas, R., and j. Barlow. 2004. *The Woodlands: The Inside Story of Creating a Better Hometown*. Washington, DC: Urban Land Institute.

Gale International. 2007. "Songdo IBD Subject of Largest Financing in Korean History." Press release, November 2.

Gans, H. 1963. "Effects of the Move from City to Suburb." In *The Urban Condition*, edited by L. Duhl, 184–98. New York: Basic Books.

———. 1967. *The Levittowners*. New York: Pantheon Books, Random House.

Garcés Feliu, E. 1989. "Las Ciudades del Salitre: Un studio de las oficinas salitreras." *ARQ* 13 (August): 2–13.

———. 2010. *Las Ciudades del Cobre*. Santiago: Ediciones Universidad Catolica de Chile.

Garreau, J. 1991. *Edge City: Life on the New Frontier*. New York: Doubleday.

Garvin, A. 2002. "Country Club District." In *Great Planned Communities*, edited by J. A. Gause, 24–25. Washington DC: Urban Land Institute.

———. 2013. *The American City: What Works, What Doesn't*. 3rd ed. New York: McGraw-Hill Education.

Gelézeau, V. 2007. *Apartment Republic*. Translated by HeaYon Gil. Seoul: Humatinas.

Gillis, J. 2016. "Flooding of Coast, Caused by Global Warming, Has Already Begun." *New York Times*, September 3. http://www.nytimes.com/2016/09/04/science/flooding-of-coast-caused -by-global-warming-has-already-begun.html?_r=0.

Glaeser. E. 2011. *Triumph of the City*. London: Penguin.

Godschalk, D. R. 1967. "Comparative New Community Design." *Journal of the American Institute of Planners* 33, no. 6: 371–87.

———. 2003. "Urban Hazard Mitigation: Creating Resilient Cities." *Natural Hazards Review* 4, no. 3: 136–43.

———. 2004. "Land Use Planning Challenges: Coping with Conflicts in Visions of Sustainable Development and Livable Communities." *Journal of the American Planning Association* 70, no. 1: 5–13.

———. 2009. "Review of *To-Morrow: A Peaceful Path to Real Reform* by Ebenezer Howard." *Journal of the American Planning Association* 75, no. 2: 264.

Godschalk, D. R., T. Y. Beatley, P. Berke, D. J. Brower, E. J. Kaiser, C. C. Bohl, and R. M. Goebel. 1999. *Natural Hazard Mitigation: Recasting Disaster Policy and Planning*. Washington, DC: Island.

Godschalk, D. R., A. Rose, E. Mittler, K. Porter, and C. T. West. 2009. "Estimating the Value of Foresight: Aggregate Analysis of Natural Hazard Mitigation Benefits and Costs." *Environmental Planning and Management* 52, no. 6: 739–56.

Golany, G. 1973. *New Towns Planning and Development: A World-Wide Bibliography*. Washington DC: ULI-Urban Land Institute.

———. 1976. *New Town Planning: Principles and Practice*. New York: John Wiley.

Golubchikov, O., and N. A. Phelps. 2011. "The Political Economy of Place at the Post-Socialist Urban Periphery: Governing Growth on the Edge of Moscow." *Transactions of the Institute of British Geographers* 36, no. 3: 425–40.

Gordon, H., and P. Molin. 1972. *Man Bara Anpassar Sig Helt Enkelt*. Stockholm: Pan Norstedts.

Grant, J. 2006. *Planning the Good Community: New Urbanism in Theory and Practice*. London: Routledge.

———. 2010. *Multi-Functional Urban Green Infrastructure*. Briefing report. London: Chartered Institution of Water and Environmental Management.

Gray, E. 2014. "An Exciting Array of New Shopping and Dining Options in South Jordan." *Daybreak Utah*. News release, October 9. Accessed March 24, 2016. http://www.daybreakutah.com/whats-happening/shopping-dining/an-exciting-array-of-new-shopping-dining-options-in-south-jordan/.

Greer, G. E., and P. T. Kolbe. 2003. *Investment Analysis for Real Estate Decisions*. La Crosse, WI: Dearborn Real Estate Education.

Griffin, Nathaniel. 1974. *Irvine: The Genesis of a New Community*. Washington, DC: ULI-Urban Land Institute.

Grubisich, T., and P. McCandless. 2006. *Reston: The First Twenty Years*. Reston, VA: Reston.

Guan, C. 2016. "High-Rise Buildings and Their Accessibility to Public Transit: The Case of Shanghai." Unpublished manuscript.

Guan, C., and P. G. Rowe. 2016. "The Concept of Urban Intensity and China's Townization Policy: Cases from Zhejiang Province." *Cities* 55:22–41.

Gulf Reston, Inc. 1970. *Brief History of Reston, Virginia 1970*. Reston, VA: Gulf Reston.

Gulick, M., and J. A. Barefoot. 2013. "DMB Unveils Vision for Victory, Verrado's Next Generation Community for 55." *DMB Associates*. News release, October 16. Accessed April 2, 2016. https://dmbinc.com/dmb-associates-unveils-vision-for-victory-verrados-next-generation-community-for-55/.

———. 2015. "Verrado Named Best Place to Retire." *DMB Associates*. News release, July 21. Accessed April 6, 2016. https://dmbinc.com/verrado-best-place-to-retire/.

Hall, P. 1989. "Summary." In *TCPA Annual Conference on British Towns and the Quality of Life Proceedings*, 13.1–13.4. London: Town and Country Planning Association.

———. 1980. "Outline Prospectus for a Third Garden City." *Town and Country Planning*, January, 33.

———. 2002. *Cities of Tomorrow: An Intellectual History of Urban Planning and Design in the Twentieth Century*. 3rd ed. Oxford: Blackwell.

———. 2014. *Cities of Tomorrow: An Intellectual History of Urban Planning and Design Since 1880*. 4th ed. Oxford: Wiley-Blackwell.

Hall, P., and N. Falk. 2014. *Good Cities, Better Lives: How Europe Discovered the Lost Art of Urbanism*. London: Routledge.

Hall, P., and C. Ward. 1998. *Sociable Cities: The Legacy of Ebenezer Howard*. Chichester, U.K.: John Wiley and Sons.

———, eds. 2014. *Sociable Cities: The 21st-Century Reinvention of the Garden City*. 2nd ed. London: Routledge.

Hamer, D. 1990. *New Towns in the New World: Images and Perceptions of the Nineteenth-Century Urban Frontier*. New York: Columbia University Press.

Hamidi, S., K. Kittrell, and R. Ewing. 2015. "Value of Transit as Reflected in U.S. Single Family Home Premiums: A Meta-Analysis." *Transportation Research Record: Journal of the Transportation Research Board* 2543, no. 12: 108–15.

Hammar-Klose, E., and E. Thieler. 2001. "National Assessment of Coastal Vulnerability to Future Sea-Level Rise: Preliminary Results for the US Atlantic, Pacific and Gulf of Mexico Coasts." *U.S. Geological Survey*. Accessed June 9, 2016. https://nca2014.globalchange.gov/highlights /regions/southeast/graphics/vulnerability-sea-level-rise.

Han, J. 2014. *Toa Payoh New Town*. Singapore: Infopedia—National Library Board.

Hardy, D. 1991a. *From Garden Cities to New Towns: Campaigning for Town and Country Planning, 1899–1946*. London: E. and F. N. Spon.

———. 1991b. *From New Towns to Green Politics: Campaigning for Town and Country Planning, 1946–1990*. London: E. and F. N. Spon.

———. 2008. *Cities That Don't Cost the Earth*. London: Town and Country Planning Association.

Harlow Renaissance Ltd. 2007. *Learning from Dutch New Towns and Suburbs: Report of the Harlow Renaissance Study Tour*. March. http://urbed.coop/sites/default/files/Report_1.pdf.

Harvey, D. 1978. "The Urban Process Under Capitalism." *International Journal of Urban and Regional Research* 2, nos. 1–3: 101–31.

Hashas, M. H. 2004. "Residents' Attachment to New Urbanist Versus Conventional Suburban Developments." PhD diss., North Carolina State University, College of Design.

Hauk, M. L. 2015. *Postwar Residential New Towns in Japan: Constructing Modernism*. St. Louis: Washington University Open Scholarship.

Hayes, J. 1993. *Tsuen Wan and Its People: Growth of a New Town*. New York: Oxford University Press.

———. 2012. *The Great Difference: Hong Kong's New Territories and Its People, 1898–2004*. Hong Kong: Hong Kong University Press.

Healey P., and T. Shaw. 1994. "Changing Meanings of 'Environment' in the British Planning System." *Transactions of the Institute of British Geographers* 19, no. 4: 425–38.

Healey, P., and R. Upton. 2010. *Crossing Borders: International Exchanges and Planning Practices*. London: Routledge.

Hegazy, I. R., and W. S. Moustafa. 2013. "Toward Revitalization of New Towns in Egypt Case Study: Sixth of October." *International Journal of Sustainable Built Environment* 2, no. 1: 10–18.

Heine, B., ed. 2000. *African Languages: An Introduction*. Cambridge: Cambridge University Press.

Henry, C. 2012. "Songdo International Business District." *Arch Daily*, March 14. https://www.arch daily.com/118790/songdo-international-business-district-kpf.

Hillman, A. 1975. "New Communities: Are Residents Satisfied?" *Sociological Focus* 8, no. 2: 161–71.

Holzheu, T., R. Lechner, and G. Turner. 2015. "Underinsurance of Property Risks: Closing the Gap." In *Sigma Series,* no 5, edited by K. Karl and P. Ronke. Zurich: Swiss Reinsurance. PDF available at: https://www.swissre.com/institute/research/sigma-research/sigma-2015-05.html

Hong Kong Census and Statistics Department. 1977. *Hong Kong By-Census 1976—Main Report*. Vol. 2, *Tables*. Hong Kong: Census and Statistics Department, HKSAR Government.

———. 1982. *Hong Kong Census 1981—Main Report*. Hong Kong: Census and Statistics Department, HKSAR Government.

———. 1984. "Special Survey of Transport Characteristics, Hong Kong Monthly Digest of Statistics." Last updated June 16, 2012. www.censtatd.gov.hk/hkstat/sub/sp130.jsp?productCode =FA100255.

———. 1987. *Hong Kong By-Census 1986—Main Report*. Vol. 2, *Tables*. Hong Kong: Census and Statistics Department, HKSAR Government.

———. 1993. *Hong Kong Census 1991—Main Report*. Hong Kong: Census and Statistics Department, HKSAR Government.

———. 1997. *1996 Population By-Census—Main Tables*. Hong Kong: Census and Statistics Department, HKSAR Government.

———. 2002. *2001 Population Census—Main Tables*. Hong Kong: Census and Statistics Department, HKSAR Government.

———. 2012. *2011 Population Census—Main Report*. Hong Kong: Census and Statistics Department, HKSAR Government.

———. 2015a. *Population and Household Statistics Analyzed by District*. Hong Kong: Census and Statistics Department, HKSAR Government.

———. 2015b. "Table E009: Number of Establishments and Persons Engaged (Other Than Those in the Civil Service) Analysed by Industry Section and Tertiary Planning Unit (TPU)." Last updated April 15, 2015. http://www.censtatd.gov.hk/hkstat/sub/sp452.jsp?productCode=D5250006.

———. 2015c. "Working Population by New Town and Industry, 2011." Last updated June 1, 2015. http://www.census2011.gov.hk/en/main-table/H119.html.

Hong Kong Civil Engineering and Development Department. 2016. *Hong Kong: The Facts; New Towns, New Development Areas and Urban Developments*. Hong Kong: HKSAR Government.

Hong Kong Department of Social Work and Social Administration. 2008. *A Study on Tim Shui Wai New Town*. Hong Kong: Department of Social Work and Social Administration.

Hong Kong Industrial Estates Corporation. 1982. *Annual Report 1981/82*. Hong Kong: Hong Kong Industrial Estates Corporation.

Hong Kong Information Services Department. 2000. *Hong Kong*. Hong Kong: Government of Hong Kong.

Hong Kong Lands and Works Branch. 1984. *NTDD—a Decade of Progress*. Hong Kong: Lands and Works Branch, New Territories Development Department.

Hong Kong Lands Department. 1984. *Town Planning in Hong Kong*. Hong Kong: Lands Department, Town Planning Division.

Hong Kong Legislative Council. 2007. *Progress Report on the Implementation of the Pilot Transport Support Scheme*. LC Paper no. CB(2)253/07–08(01). Hong Kong: Hong Kong Legislative Council.

———. 2015. *Legislative Council Panel on Manpower Work Incentive Transport Subsidy Scheme*. LC Paper no. CB(2)798/14–15(05). Hong Kong: Legislative Council.

Hong Kong Planning Department. 2002. *Planning with Vision Pamphlets (Sai Kung, Islands, Tseung Kwan O, Sha Tin, Tuen Mun, Tai Po, Yuen Long, Fanling/Sheung Shui)*. Hong Kong: Planning Department, HKSAR Government.

———. 2015. *Summary of Statistics: Tim Shui Wai*. Hong Kong: Government of the Hong Kong Special Administrative Region.

Hong Kong Transport Department. 1997. *Third Comprehensive Transport Study*. Hong Kong: Transport Department, HKSAR Government.

———. 2014. *Travel Characteristics Survey 2011*. Hong Kong: Transport Department, HKSAR Government.

Hopkins, L. D., and M. A. Zapata. 2007. *Engaging the Future: Forecasts, Scenarios, Plans, and Projects*. Cambridge, MA: Lincoln Institute of Land Policy.

Horowitz, J. 2008. *Argentina's Radical Party and Popular Mobilization, 1916–1930*. University Park: Penn State University Press.

Houghton, D. S. 1976. "Resident Satisfaction in an Australian New Town: Kwinana, Western Australia." *Australian Journal of Social Issues* 11, no. 4: 263–75.

Housing and Development Board, Singapore. 1970. *First Decade in Public Housing, 1960–69*. Singapore: Housing and Development Board,

———. 2013. *HDB Annual Report, 2012–2013, Key Statistics*. Singapore: Housing and Development Board.

Housing Finance Information Network. 2016. "Arab Republic of Egypt." *HOFINET*. Retrieved August 30, 2016. http://hofinet.org/countries/country.aspx?regionID=5&id=51.

Howard, E. [1898] 2003. *Tomorrow: A Peaceful Path to Real Reform*. London: Swan Sonnenschein. Reprinted, and edited by P. Hall, D. Hardy, and C. Ward. London: Routledge. Citations refer to Routledge edition.

———. 1902. *Garden Cities of To-Morrow*. London: Swan Sonnenschein.

Hsing, Y. T. 2010. *The Great Urban Transformation: Politics of Land and Property in China*. Oxford: Oxford University Press.

Huat, C. B. 2011. "Singapore as Model: Planning Innovations, Knowledge Experts." In *Worlding Cities: Asian Experiments and the Art of Being Global*, edited by A. Roy and A. Ong, 29–54. New York: Wiley-Blackwell.

Huis, F. 1985. "Er is met deze stad iets merkwaardigs aan de hand." *De Almare*, November 30.

Hyatt, A. G. 2004. *Transition: How Community Associations Assume Independence*. Alexandria, VA: Community Associations Press.

Hyatt, W. S., and S. F. French. 1998. *Community Association Law: Cases and Materials on Common Interest Communities*. Durham, NC: Carolina Academic Press.

International New Town Institute. 2010. *Data Browser*. Hong Kong: International New Town Institute.

Irvine Company. 2016. *Irvine Ranch Master Plan*. Newport Beach, CA: Irvine Company.

Iyer, P. V. 2011. "The Environment Ministry Does Not Have Measurable Standards. So How Do You Know What and Whom to Deal With?" *Indian Express*, January 29. Accessed January 2018. http://indianexpress.com/article/news-archive/web/the-environment-ministry-does-not-have-measurable-standards-so-how-do-you-know-what-and-whom-to-deal-with/.

Jackson, C. 2010. "University of Utah Health Care and Kennecott Land Break Ground on New Specialty Center in South Jordan's Daybreak Community." *Daybreak*. News release, July 27. Accessed March 24, 2016. http://www.daybreakutah.com/whats-happening/press-release/university-of-utah-health-care-and-kennecott-land-break-ground-on-new-specialty-center-in-south-jordans-daybreak-community/.

Jacobs, J. [1961] 1993. *The Death and Life of Great American Cities*. New York: Random House. Reprint, New York: Modern Library. Citations refer to the Modern Library edition.

Jacquemin, A. R. A. 1999. *Urban Development and New Towns in the Third World: Lessons from the New Bombay Experience*. Aldershot, U.K.: Ashgate.

Jamshedpur Utilities and Services Company. N.d. "Profile." http://www.juscoltd.com/jusco.asp.

Jenson, J. 2002. "Identifying the Links: Social Cohesion and Culture." *Canadian Journal of Communication* 27, no. 2. http://www.cjc-online.ca/index.php/journal/article/view/1289/1309.

Jie, L. 2015. "New Town Development in an Entrepreneurial City: The Case of Shanghai." PhD diss., University of Hong Kong.

Joo, Y. M. 2013. "New Town Developments in Korea: Then and Now." In *Urban Megaprojects: A Worldwide View*, by G. del C. Santamaría, 3–26. Bingley, U.K.: Emerald.

Jorgensen, A., J. Hitchmough, and N. Dunnett. 2007. "Woodland as a Setting for Housing-Appreciation and Fear and the Contribution to Residential Satisfaction and Place Identity in Warrington New Town, UK." *Landscape and Urban Planning* 79, nos. 3–4: 273–87.

Joshi, R. 2009. "Integrated Townships as a Policy Response to Changing Supply and Demand Dynamics of Urban Growth." In *India Infrastructure Report 2009*, by Infrastructure Development Finance Company, 167–75. New Delhi: Oxford University Press.

Juarez-Dappe, P. 2010. *When Sugar Ruled: Economy and Society in Northwestern Argentina, Tucuman, 1876–1916*. Athens: Ohio University Press.

Jung, I. 2013. *Architecture and Urbanism in Modern Korea*. Honolulu: University of Hawaii Press.

Kafkoula, K. 2009. "New Towns." In *International Encyclopedia of Human Geography*, edited by R. Kitchin and N. Thrift, 428–37. Amsterdam: Elsevier.

Kahn, J., and D. Bachman. 2016. "Top 50 Master Planned Communities of 2015." *John Burns Real Estate Consulting Newsletter*, January. Accessed April 4, 2016. http://realestateconsulting.com/wp-content/uploads/2016/01/JBREC-Top50-MPC_Survey_Newsletter_2015.pdf.

Kang, Y. R. 2000. "The Socio-Spatial Characteristics of Middle Class's Suburb." *Journal of Geography* 36:1–31.

Keeton, R. 2011. *Rising in the East: Contemporary New Towns in Asia*. Amsterdam: SUN Architecture.

Keil, R. 2018. *Suburban Planet: Making the World Urban from the Outside In*. Cambridge: Polity Press.

Keung, J. K. 1985. "Government Intervention and Housing Policy in Hong Kong." *Third World Planning Review* 7, no. 1: 23–44.

Kim, H., M. Jo, B. Choi, D. Kim, G. Lee, C. Byun, W. Lee, et. al. 1993. *The Impact of New Town Developments in Seoul Metropolitan Region on Residential Mobility and Population Change*. Seoul: Korea Research Institute for Human Settlements.

Kim, J. 2001. "Sense of Community in Neotraditional and Conventional Suburban Developments: A Comparative Case Study of Kentlands and Orchard Village." PhD diss., University of Michigan, Ann Arbor.

Kim, J., and S.-C. Choe. 1997. *Seoul: The Making of a Metropolis*. New York: Wiley.

King, R. 2008. *Kuala Lumpur and Putrajaya: Negotiating Urban Space in Malaysia*. Kuala Lumpur: Nias Press.

Kingswood Villas. 2018. "Introduction—Kingswood Villas." *Kingswood Villas*. Accessed February 2018. http://www.kingswood.com.hk.

Kladnik, A. 2005. "Town Development in the European Socialist Countries after World War II." Paper presented at the 2005 ENTP Conference.

Klijn, E. H. 1995. "De stille revolutie in de volkshuisvesting,' Blad Bestuurskunde. Themanummer bestuurlijke reorganisaties: De dadendrang van de kabinetten-Lubbers." *Bestuurskunde* 4, no. 2: 53–61.

Kling, R., S. Olin, and M. Poster, eds. 1995. *Post-Suburban California: The Transformation of Orange County Since World War II*. Berkeley: University of California Press.

Knox, P. L. 2008. *Metroburbia, USA*. New Brunswick, NJ: Rutgers University Press.

Koh, C., and J. Park. 1993. *The Impact of New Town Developments in Seoul Metropolitan Region on Residential Mobility and Population Change*. Seoul: Korea Research Institute for Human Settlements.

Kohn Pedersen Fox. N.d. "New Songdo City: Songdo International Business District. Projects—Master Plan." *KPF*. Accessed June 2016. https://www.kpf.com/projects/new-songdo-city.

Kolbert, E. 2015. "The Siege of Miami: As Temperatures Climb, So, Too Will Sea Levels. *New Yorker*, December 21–28, 42–50.

Konza Techno City. 2016. "Investors Information." Retrieved August 20, 2016. http://www.konza city.go.ke.

Korea Land and Housing Corporation. 2003. Photo. Bundang Newtown Area.

Korea Land Corporation. 1997. *Bundang New Town Development*. Seoul: Korea Land Corporation.
———. 1999. *Land Development Business Report: Completion in 1997*. Seoul: Korea Land Corporation.

Korea Ministry of Land, Infrastructure and Transport. 2016. "New Town Introduction." Accessed March 15, 2016. https://www.molit.go.kr/USR/policyData/m_34681/dtl?id=523.

Korea Statistical Information Service. 2016. "Economy/Corporate Business (Company)—Census on Establishments." 9th rev. http://kosis.kr/eng/statisticsList/statisticsList_01List.jsp?vwcd =MT_ETITLE&parentId=B.

Kundu, A., G. K. Misra, and R. Meher. 1986. *Location of Public Enterprises and Regional Development*. New Delhi: Concept.

Kun-Hyuck, A., and Y.-T. Ohn. 1997. *Urbanization in South Korea and Its Policy Responses*. Seoul: Seoul Urban Institute.

Lai, L., 1999. "Reflections on the Abercrombie Report of 1948: A Strategic Plan for Colonial Hong Kong." *Town Planning Review* 70, no. 1: 61–86.

Lang, J. T. 1994. *Urban Design: The American Experience*. New York: Van Nostrand Reinhold.

Lang, R. E. and J. B. LeFurgy. 2007. *Boomburbs: The Rise of America's Accidental Cities*. Washington, DC: Brookings Institution Press.

Langford, L. C., and G. Bell. 1975. "Federally Sponsored New Towns of the Seventies." *Growth and Change* 6, no. 4: 24–31.

Lansing, J. B., R. W. Marans, and R. B. Zehner. 1970. *Planned Residential Environments.* Ann Arbor: University of Michigan, Survey Research Center.

Larue, T., and B. Martin. 2016. "MPC Survey—Mid-Year Update." *Robert Charles Lesser and Co.,* July 7. http://www.rclco.com/advisory-mpc-survey-2016-midyear.

Larue, T., and C. Pawelek. 2016. "The Top-Selling Master-Planned Communities of 2015." *Robert Charles Lesser and Co.,* January 5. http://www.rclco.com/advisory-top-selling-mpcs-2015.

Lau, J. C. Y. 2010. "The Influence of Suburbanization on the Access to Employment of Workers in the New Towns: A Case Study of Tin Shui Wai, Hong Kong." *Habitat International* 34, no. 1: 38–45.

Lavasa Corporation Limited. 2014. "Lake City's 2014 Draft Red Herring Prospectus." June 30. http://www.cmlinks.com/pub/dp/dp34370.pdf.

Lavasa Investor [pseud.]. 2015. "Lavasa Is the Highway to Hell." Last updated February 2, 2015. http://cityoflavasa.blogspot.in.

Law, C. K., Y. C. Wong, E. Chui, K. M. Lee, Y. Y. Pong, R. Yu, and V. Lee. 2009. *A Study on Tin Shui Wai New Town.* Hong Kong: Department of Social Work and Social Administration, University of Hong Kong.

Leavitt, P. 2015. "Eastmark Among U.S. Top 10 for Home Sales." *Arizona Republic,* July 15. Accessed March 9, 2016. http://www.azcentral.com/story/news/local/mesa/2015/07/15/eastmark-among-us-top-home-sales/30207333/.

Leccese M., and K. McCormick, eds. 1999. *The Charter of the New Urbanism.* New York: McGraw-Hill.

Lee, B. H. 2012. *Korean Version of New Town Development.* Seoul: Korea Research Institute for Human Settlements.

Lee, C., and K. Ahn. 2005. "Five New Towns in the Seoul Metropolitan Area and Their Attractions in Non-Working Trips: Implications on Self-Containment of New Towns." *Habitat International* 29, no. 4: 647–66.

Lee, G. 1999. *Public Concept of Land Ownership and New Town.* Seoul: Samsung Economic Research Institute.

Lee, J., and N. Yip. 2006. "Public Housing and Family Life in East Asia: Housing History and Social Change in Hong Kong, 1953–1990." *Journal of Family History* 31, no. 1: 66–82.

Lehrer, U. A. 1994. "Images of the Periphery: The Architecture of Flex Space in Switzerland." *Environment and Planning D: Society and Space* 12, no. 2: 187–205.

Leon, C. 2016. "Our Story—Rancho Sahuarita Community." *Rancho Sahuarita Community.* Accessed July 25, 2016. http://www.ranchosahuarita.com/community/vision/.

Leopold, A. 1949. *A Sand County Almanac.* Oxford: Oxford University Press.

Leung, W. T. 1980. "Hong Kong's New Towns Programme: A Social Perspective." In *Hong Kong: Dilemmas of Growth,* edited by C. K. Leung, J. W. Cushman, and G. Wang, 375–95. Hong Kong: University of Hong Kong, Centre of Asian Studies.

Levey, R. 2007. "Lake Nona Entitlement History." Presentation, Orlando City Council, Orlando, FL, October 30.

Li, Y., and F. L. Wu. 2012. "Towards New Regionalism? Case Study of Changing Regional Governance in the Yangtze River Delta." *Asia Pacific Viewpoint* 53, no. 2: 178–95.

Lin, G. C. S., and F. Yi. 2011. "Urbanization of Capital or Capitalization on Urban Land? Land Development and Local Public Finance in Urbanizing China." *Urban Geography* 32, no. 1: 50–79.

Lindelauf, H. 1988. "Almere Almaar mooier!" *ABP Wereld,* October.

Llewellyn, M. 2004. "Producing and Experiencing Harlow: Neighbourhood Units and Narratives of New Town Life 1947–53." *Planning Perspectives* 19, no. 2: 155–74.

Low, S. 2003. "Behind the Gates: Life, Security, and the Pursuit of Happiness in Fortress America." London: Routledge.

Lu, D. J. 1997. *Japan: A Documentary History*. Armonk, NY: Sharpe.

Luanda Urban Poverty Programme. 2010. "Angolan Context." *LUPP*. Last updated 2010. http://dw.angonet.org/luppangola.org/angolanContext.html.

Lupton, M. 1993. "Ennerdale New Town, South Africa: The Social Limits to Urban Design." *Geo-Journal* 30, no. 1: 37–44.

Lyndon, D., and J. Alinder. 2004. *The Sea Ranch*. New York: Princeton Architectural Press.

Malaysia Department of Statistics. 2015. *Population and Housing Census of Malaysia*. Kuala Lumpur: Department of Statistics.

Maller, C., M. Townsend, A. Pryor, P. Brown, and L. St. Leger. 2005. "Healthy Nature, Healthy People: Contact with Nature as an Upstream Health Promotion Intervention for Populations." *Health Promotion International* 21, no. 1: 45–54.

Manzo, L. C., and P. Devine-Wright. 2013. *Place Attachment: Advances in Theory, Methods and Applications*. Abingdon, U.K.: Routledge.

Marans, R. W. 2003. "Understanding Environmental Quality Through Quality of Life Studies: The 2001 DAS and Its Use of Subjective and Objective Indicators." *Landscape and Urban Planning* 65, no. 1: 73–83.

Marans, R. W., and B. S. Kweon. 2011. "The Quality of Life in Metro Detroit at the Beginning of the Millennium." In *Investigating Quality of Urban Life: Theory, Methods, and Empirical Research*, edited by R. W. Marans, and R. Stimson, 163–183. Dordrecht, Netherlands: Springer.

Marans, R. W., and W. Rodgers. 1975. "Toward an Understanding of Community Satisfaction." In *Metropolitan America in Contemporary Perspective*, edited by A. Hawley and V. Rock, 299–352. New York: Halsted.

Marans, R. W., and R. Stimson, eds. 2011. *Investigating Quality of Urban Life: Theory, Methods, and Empirical Research*. Dordrecht, Netherlands: Springer.

McAllister, G. 1946. "Planning New Towns." *The Spectator*, 5 April, p. 8.

McCabe, B. C. 2011. "Homeowners Associations as Private Governments: What We Know, What We Don't Know, and Why It Matters." *Public Administration Review* 71, no. 4: 535–42.

McCrea, R., J. Western, and R. J. Stimson. 2011. "Modeling Determinants of Subjective QOUL at Different Geographic Scales: The Case of the Brisbane-SEQ Region." In *Investigating Quality of Urban Life: Theory, Methods, and Empirical Research*, edited by R. W. Marans and R. J. Stimson, 347–68. Dordrecht, Netherlands: Springer.

McFadden, R. D. 2015. "Robert E. Simon Jr., Who Created a Town, Reston, VA, Dies at 101." *New York Times*, September 21. Retrieved January 2018. https://www.nytimes.com/2015/09/22/realestate/communities/robert-e-simon-jr-founder-of-reston-va-dies-at-101.html.

McHarg, I. 1969. *Design with Nature*. Garden City, NY: Natural History.

McKenzie, E. 1994. *Privatopia: Homeowner Associations and the Rise of Residential Private Government*. New Haven, CT: Yale University Press.

———. 2011. *Beyond Privatopia: Rethinking Residential Private Government*. Washington, DC: Urban Institute Press.

McMahon, E. T., and M. A. Benedict. 2012. *Green Infrastructure: Linking Landscapes and Communities*. Washington DC: Island Press.

McNamara, K. 1948. "A Selected List of References on the Planning of New Towns." *Journal of the American Institute of Planners* 14, no. 3: 36–37.

McNeill, D. 2009. "New Songdo City: At Limits of the Far East." *Independent*, June 21. http://www.independent.co.uk/news/world/asia/new-songdo-city-atlantis-of-the-far-east-1712252.html.

Meadows, D. L., J. Randers, and W. W. Behrens. 1972. *The Limits to Growth: A Report for the Club of Rome's Project on the Predicament of Mankind*. New York: Universe Books.

Meerow, S., J. P. Newell, and M. Stults. 2016. "Defining Urban Resilience: A Review." *Landscape and Urban Planning* 147:38–49.

Melber, H., ed. 2016. *The Rise of Africa's Middle Class*. London: Zed Books.

Meller, H., and H. Porfyriou. 2016. *Planting New Towns in Europe in the Interwar Years: Experiments and Dreams for Future Societies*. Newcastle-upon-Tyne, U.K.: Cambridge Scholars.

Meng, T. E. E. 2016. "Punggol's New Mall Opens, but Old Woes Remain." *TODAYonline*, April 19. https://www.todayonline.com/singapore/punggols-new-mall-opens-old-woes-remain.

Menon, N., and S. Mitra. 2009. "Special Economic Zones: The Rationale." In *Special Economic Zones: Promise, Performance and Pending Issues*, by Center for Policy Research, 3–38. New Delhi: Center for Policy Research.

Mercado, L. 2003. *El Ingenio Santa Lucia en Tucuman: Los Primeros Habitantes*. Buenos Aires: Umbilicus Mundi.

Merlin, P. 1971. *New Towns: Regional Planning and Development*. London: Methuen.

———. 2005. "New Towns britanniques et Villes Nouvelles françaises: De la conception à l'achève-ment." In *International Conference on New Towns Report*, by Ministry of Housing and Urban Development of Iran, 139–48. Tehran: Ministry of Housing and Urban Development of Iran.

Milton Keynes Council. 2016. "Milton Keynes Future 2050 Report." *Milton Keynes Futures 2050 Commission*. Last updated 2016. http://www.mkfutures2050.com/read-our-report.

Min Joo, Y. 2013. "Chapter 1 New Town Developments in Korea: Then and Now." In *Urban Megaprojects: A Worldwide View*, ed del G. Cerro Santamaría, 3–25. Bingley, U.K.: Emerald.

Moore, W. E., and E. B. Sheldon. 1968. *Indicators of Social Change: Concepts and Measurements*. New York: Russell Sage Foundation.

Morgan, D. 1982. *The Palos Verdes Story*. Palos Verdes Estates, CA: Review Publications.

Morrison, T. 2015. *Unbuilt Utopian Cities 1460 to 1900: Reconstructing Their Architecture and Political Philosophy*. Surrey, U.K.: Ashgate.

Morisset, L. K. 2011. "Nonfiction Utopia: Arvida, Cité Industrielle Made Real." *Journal for the Society of the Study of Architecture in Canada* 36, no. 1: 3–40.

Mouchly, E., and R. Peiser. 1993. "Lessons for Value Creation in Master-Planned Communities and Large-Scale Mixed-Use Projects." *Urban Land*, August, 16–20.

Mukhopadhyay, P., and K. C. Pradhan. 2009. "Location of SEZs and Policy Benefits: What Does the Data Say?" In *Special Economic Zones: Promise, Performance and Pending Issues*, by Center for Policy Research, 61–84. New Delhi: Center for Policy Research.

Mulligan, G., J. Carruthers, and M. Cahill. 2004. "Urban Quality of Life and Public Policy: A Survey." *Contributions to Economic Analysis* 266:729–802.

Mumford, L. 1977. "Introduction." In *New Towns: Their Origins, Achievements, and Progress*, 3rd ed., edited by F. J. Osborn and A. Whittick, xiii–xvii. London: Leonard Hill.

Municipality of Almere. 2008. *De Almere Principles: Voor een ecologisch, sociaal en economisch duurzame toekomst van Almere 2030*. Almere: Gemeente Almere.

———. 2014. *De staat van de stad*. Almere: Gemeente Almere.

———. N.d. "Floriade 2022." http://floriade.almere.nl/en/. Access date November 1, 2018.

Municipality of Almere, Teun Koolhaas Associates (TKA), and Goudappel and Coffeng. *Concept Ruimtestudie Westflank van Almere* (Almere-Pampus). Almere, Netherlands: Gemeente Almere.

MVRDV. 2011. "Masterplan for Oosterwold." *MVRDV Projects*. Accessed January 2018. https://www.mvrdv.nl/projects/oosterwold.

Na, J.-J. 2012. "In Financial Pinch, Incheon Under Pressure to Downsize Asaid Plans." *Korea Times*, March 4. Accessed January 2018. http://www.koreatimes.co.kr/www/news/nation/2012/04/113_108358.html.

Nakanishi, H., H. Sinclair, and J. Lintern. 2013. "Measuring Quality of Life: An Integrated Evaluation of Built Environment." Paper presented at the 13th International Conference on Computers in Urban Planning and Urban Management, Utrecht, Netherlands.

Nakazawa, H. 2011. "Aged Newtown Problems on Greater Tokyo Outskirts." Paper presented at Session 25: Changing Urban Geographies of Growth and Decline, Research Committee 21 Conference, University of Amsterdam, Amsterdam, Netherlands, July 7–9.

Nam, I.-S. 2013. "South Korea's $35 Billion 'Labor of Love': Developer Struggles to Build a City from Scratch." *Wall Street Journal*, December 6. https://www.wsj.com/articles/no-headline-available-1386092653.

National Association of Home Builders (NAHB). 2016. "Three Community Amenities Topping Home Buyer Wish Lists." *NAHB Now*, February 22. Accessed April 2, 2016. http://nahbnow .com/2016/02/3-community-amenities-that-top-all-home-buyers-wish-lists/.

National Association of Realtors. 2015. *Community and Transportation Preferences Survey*, July 23. Accessed April 8, 2016. http://www.realtor.org/sites/default/files/reports/2015/nar-psu-2015 -poll-report.pdf.

National Geographic. 2013. "If All the Ice Melted." *National Geographic*, September, spec. issue, "Rising Seas: How They Are Affecting Our Coastlines." Accessed March 25, 2016. http://ngm .nationalgeographic.com/2013/09/rising-seas/if-ice-melted-map.

National Oceanic and Atmospheric Administration (NOAA). 2016. *Climate Explorer*. Accessed June 17, 2016. http://toolkit.climate.gov/tools/climate-explorer.

National Office for the IJsselmeerpolders. 1975. *Cultuurrijp*, September. Zeewold, Netherlands: Rijksdienst voor de IJsselmeerpolders.

National Research Council. 2014. *Reducing Coastal Risk on the East and Gulf Coasts*. Washington, DC: National Academy of Sciences Press.

Nelson, G. 2013. "Mesa GM Site Reborn as a Housing Development." *Arizona Republic*, May 13. Accessed March 20, 2016. http://www.azcentral.com/community/mesa/articles/20130429 mesa-gm-site-housing-development.html.

Nelson, R. H. 1977. *Zoning and Property Rights*. Cambridge, MA: MIT Press.

———. 2003. "The Rise of the Private Neighborhood Association: A Constitutional Revolution in Local Government." In *The Property Tax, Land Use and Land Use Regulation*, edited by D. Netzer, 209– 72. Northampton, MA: Edward Elgar in association with the Lincoln Institute of Land Policy.

———. 2005a. "In Defense of Religious Neighborhood Associations." *Philosophy and Public Policy Quarterly* 25, no. 4: 10–16.

———. 2005b. *Private Neighborhoods and the Transformation of Local Government*. Washington, DC: Urban Institute Press.

———. 2009. "The Puzzle of Local Double Taxation: Why Do Private Community Associations Exist?" *Independent Review* 13, no. 3: 345–65.

———. 2011. "Homeowners Associations in Historical Perspective." *Public Administration Review* 71, no. 4: 546–49.

Netherlands Social and Cultural Planning Office. 2001. *New Towns Development*. The Hague, Netherlands: Netherlands Social and Cultural Planning Office.

Netherlands Ministry of Housing, Spatial Planning and the Environment (VROM). 1989. *Volkshuisvesting in de Jaren negentig*. Van bouwen naar wonen, The Hague: SDU.Neuman, M. 2005. "The Compact City Fallacy." *Journal of Planning Education and Research* 25, no. 1: 11–26.

New Townsmen [pseud.]. 1918. *New Towns After the War: An Argument for Garden Cities*. London: J. M. Dent and Sons.

Nissim, R. 2011. *Land Administration and Practice in Hong Kong*. 3rd ed. Hong Kong: Hong Kong University Press.

Noss, R. 2016. "Announcing the World's 36th Biodiversity Hotspot: The North American Coastal Plain." Accessed March 28, 2016. http://www.cepf.net/news/top_stories/Pages/Announcing -the-Worlds-36th-Biodiversity-Hotspot.aspx.

Nozeman, F. 1990. "Dutch New Towns: Triumph or Disaster." *Tijdschrift voor Economische and Sociale Geographie* 81, no. 2: 149–55.

Oakerson, R. J. 1999. *Governing Local Public Economies: Creating the Civic Metropolis*. Oakland, CA: Institute of Contemporary Studies Press.

Ogilvy, A. A. 1968. "The Self-Contained New Town: Employment and Population." *Town Planning Review* 39, no. 10: 38–54.

Ogino, C. 2004. "Making of Most Preferred '8th School District' of Gangnam, Korea: A Case Study of Place Identity Formation." *Journal of Geography* 58:1–207.

Oh, S., and D. Yim. 2014. *50 Years of Planned Cities in Seoul Metropolitan Area 1961–2010*. Anyang, South Korea: Architecture and Urban Research Institute.

O'Kelly, M. E., and W. Lee. 2004. "Disaggregate Journey-to-Work Data: Implications for Excess Commuting and Jobs-Housing Balance." *Environment and Planning A* 37, no. 12: 2233–52.

Oldenburg, R. 1989. *The Great Good Place*. New York: Paragon House.

Olds, K. 2001. *Globalization and Urban Change: Capital, Culture, and Pacific Rim Mega Projects*. Oxford: Oxford University Press.

Olmsted, Vaux, and Co. 1992. "Preliminary Report upon the Proposed Suburban Village at Riverside, Near Chicago." Quoted in *The Papers of Frederick Law Olmsted*, vol. 6, by D. Schuyler and J. T. Censer, 273–290. Baltimore: Johns Hopkins University Press.

Olson, M. 1965. *The Logic of Collective Action: Public Goods and the Theory of Groups*. Cambridge, MA: Harvard University Press.

Omar, D. B. 2008. "Development Strategy and Physical Characteristics of New Towns in Malaysia." *Asian Social Science* 4, no. 9: 50–55.

———. 2009. "Assessing Residents' Quality of Life in Malaysian New Towns." *Asian Social Science* 5, no. 6: 1911–2017.

Oosterman, A., ed. 2012. "City in a Box." *Volume Magazine* 34. Amsterdam: Archis Foundation.

Orueta, F. D., and S. S. Fainstein. 2008. "The New Mega-Projects: Genesis and Impacts." *International Journal of Urban and Regional Research* 32, no. 4: 759–67.

Osborn, F. J. 1965. "Preface." In *Garden Cities of To-Morrow*, by E. Howard, 9–28. Cambridge, MA: MIT Press.

———. 1974. "New Towns." In *Encyclopaedia of Urban Planning*, by A. Whittick, 730–34. New York: McGraw-Hill.

Osborn, F. J., and A. Whittick. 1963. *The New Towns: The Answer to Megalopolis*. New York: McGraw-Hill.

———. 1977. *The New Towns: The Answer to Megalopolis*. 3rd ed. London: Leonard Hill.

Oxford Brookes University, Department of Planning. 2006. *Transferrable Lessons from the New Towns*. London: Department for Communities and Local Government.

Padawangi, R. 2010. "The Planned Suburbanization of a City-State: Singapore's New Towns." In *Suburbanization in Global Society: Research in Urban Sociology*, edited by M. Clapson and R. Hutchison, 293–317. Bingley, U.K.: Emerald.

Parker, B., and R. Unwin. 1906. *Hampstead Garden Suburb, London, Plan*. London.

Parnell, S., and E. Pieterse, eds. 2014. *Africa's Urban Revolution*. London: Zed Books.

Pasveer, Th., F.H. van der Veen, J.J.P. Scheek, and J.A. Wezenaar. 1973. *Notitie Werkgroep maatschappelijke aspekten management*. Projektburo Almere, 8 maart. (City Archive Almere/Collection Han Wezenaar).

Peck, J. 2011. "Neoliberal Suburbanism: Frontier Space." *Urban Geography* 32, no. 6: 884–919.

Peiser, R. 1984. "Financial Feasibility Models in New Town Development: Risk Evaluation in the United States." *Town Planning Review* 55, no. 1: 75–90.

Peiser, R., and A. Chang. 1999. "Is It Possible to Build Financially Successful New Towns? The Milton Keynes Experience." *Urban Studies* 36, no. 100: 1679–703.

Peiser, R., and G. Yu. 1998. "Reston Re-Visited." *Lusk Review for Real Estate Development* 4, no. 1: 44–53.

Percival, T., and P. Waley. 2012. "Articulating Intra-Asian Urbanism: The Production of Satellite Cities in Phnom Penh." *Urban Studies* 49, no. 13: 2873–88.

Perroux, F. 1970. "Note sur la notion de pôle de croissance: Économie appliquée." As translated in *Regional Economics*, edited by D. L. McKee, R. D. Dean, and W. H. Leahy, 93–103. New York: Free Press.

Perry, C. [1929] 1998. *The Neighborhood Unit*. New York: Regional Plan Association. Reprinted, and edited by T. Press, London: Routledge/Thoemmes Press.

Phelps, N., and F. Wu, eds. 2011. *International Perspectives on Suburbanization: A Post-Suburban World?* Basingstoke, U.K.: Palgrave Macmillan.

Phillips, D. R. 1987. "Social Services and Community Facilities in the Hong Kong New Towns." In *New Towns in East and Southeast Asia—Planning and Development*, edited by D. R. Phillips and A. G. O. Yeh, 82–106. Hong Kong: Oxford University Press.

Phillips, D. R., K. H. C. Cheng, A. G. O. Yeh, and O. L. Siu. 2010. "Person-Environment (P-E) Fit Models And Psychological Well-Being Among Older Persons in Hong Kong." *Environment and Behavior* 42, no. 2: 221–42.

Phillips, D. R., and A. G. O. Yeh, eds. 1987. *New Towns in East and Southeast Asia—Planning and Development*. Hong Kong: Oxford University Press.

Phillips, E. E. 2016. "Panama Canal Fuels U.S. Building Frenzy." *Wall Street Journal*, June 24, B1.

Pieterse, E. 2015. "Africa's Urban Imperatives." In *Cape Town: Densification as a Cure for a Segregated City*, edited by M. Provoost, 10–25. Rotterdam: NAI010 Publishers.

Pilkey, O. H., and K. C. Pilkey. 2011. *Global Climate Change: A Primer*. Durham, NC: Duke University Press.

Planning Commission, Government of India. 2012. *Five Year Plans*. http://planningcommission .nic.in/plans/planrel/fiveyr/welcome.html.

Plas, J. M., and S. E. Lewis. 1999. "Environmental Factors and Sense of Community in a Planned Town." *American Journal of Community Psychology* 24, no. 1: 109–43.

Polefka, S. 2013. "Moving Out of Harm's Way: Energy and Environment News." *Center for American Progress*, December 12. Accessed June 9, 2016. https://www.americanprogress.org/issues /green/report/2013/12/12/81046/moving-out-of-harms-way/.

Polletta, M. 2015. "Mesa's Eastmark, a 'City Within a City,' Gaining Traction." *Arizona Republic*. July 15. Accessed March 19, 2016. http://www.azcentral.com/story/news/local/mesa/2014/07 /01/eastmark-city-within-city-gaining-traction/11832051/.

Popenoe, D. 1977. *The Suburban Environment: Sweden and the United States*. Chicago: University of Chicago Press.

Pow, C.-P. 2009. *Gated Communities in China: Class, Privilege and the Moral Politics of the Good Life*. Abingdon, U.K.: Routledge.

Prince, E. 1995. "Postscript on New Towns: The End of an Era." *Proceedings of the Institution of Civil Engineers—Municipal Engineer* 109, no. 2: 67–78.

Provoost, M. 2010. "New Towns for the 21st Century: The Planned vs. the Unplanned City." In *New Towns for the 21st Century*, edited by M. Provoost, 6–27. Amsterdam: Idea Books.

Provoost, M., and W. Vanstiphout. 2011. "Introduction." In *Rising in the East: Contemporary New Towns in Asia*, edited by R. Keeton, 9–42. Amsterdam: SUN Architecture.

Pruntel, H. 2013. "Lammers, Johan Christiaan Jan (1931–2000)." In *Biografisch Woordenboek van Nederland*. Last updated December 11, 2013. http://resources.huygens.knaw.nl/bwn1880-2000 /lemmata/bwn6/lammers.

Pryor, E. G. 1978. "Redevelopment and New Towns in Hong Kong." In *Housing in Hong Kong: A MultiDisciplineary Study*, edited by L. S. K. Wong, 266–86. Hong Kong: Heinemann.

Public Result. 2012. "Evaluatie en advies uitvoeringsagenda Ortega gemeenten." The Hague: Public Result B. V. http://www.publicresult.nl/wp-content/uploads/2011/01/Evaluatie-uitvoerings agenda-Ortega-gemeenten.pdf.

Purdom, C. B. 1925. *The Building of Satellite Towns*. London: J. M. Dent.

Randazzo, R., and G. Nelson. 2013. "After Years of False Starts, Eastmark Is Ready for Apple." *Arizona Republic*, November 6. Accessed February 3, 2016. http://www.azcentral.com/community /mesa/articles/20131104after-years-false-startseastmark-ready-apple.html.

Ravindran, S. 2015. "Is India's 100 Smart Cities Project a Recipe for Social Apartheid?" *Guardian*, May 7. https://www.theguardian.com/cities/2015/may/07/india-100-smart-cities-project-social-apartheid.

Reagor, C. 2012. "7 Builders Commit to Mesa's Eastmark." *Arizona Republic*, June 28. Accessed February 6, 2016. http://www.azcentral.com/business/realestate/articles/20120626mesa -builders-commit-eastmark.html.

Redvers, L. 2012. "Angola's Chinese Ghost Town." *BBC News*, July 3. http://www.bbc.com/news /world-africa-18646243.

Reich, R. 1991. "Secession of the Successful." *New York Times Magazine*, January 20, Section 6: 16.

Reiner, T. A. 1963. *The Place of the Ideal Community in Urban Planning*. Philadelphia: University of Pennsylvania Press.

Reingold, J. 2014. "How to Build a Great American City." *Fortune*, June 12. http://fortune.com/2014/06/12/lake-nona-florida/.

Reston Museum. 2018. "A Brief History of Reston." Accessed February 1, 2018. https://www.reston museum.org/reston-history.

Richards, J. M. 1953. "Failure of the New Towns." *Architectural Review* 114 (July): 28–32.

Richardson, H. 1996. *Reston Town Center Celebrates Its 20th Anniversary*. Reston, VA: Reston Community Center.

Rio Tinto. 2009. "Rio Tinto Companies in the Salt Lake Valley Release Annual Sustainable Development Report." *Rio Tinto*. News release, March 4. Accessed March 19, 2016. http://www.kennecott.com/library/media/Rio Tinto companies in the Salt Lake Valley release SD report 05.04.09.pdf.

Riverside Improvement Company. 1871. *Riverside in 1871 with Description of Its Improvements Together with Some Engravings of Views and Buildings*. Originally printed by D. and C. H. Blakely, Chicago, 1871, and reprinted by the Frederick Law Olmsted Society of Riverside in 1981.

Robinson, A. J. 1975. *Economics and New Towns: A Comparative Study of the United States, the United Kingdom, and Australia*. New York: Praeger.

Robles, S., L. M. Ross, and R. M. Sharpe. 2012. "Residential Futures—Thought Provoking Ideas on What's Next for Master-Planned Communities." *Urban Land Institute—Terwilliger Center for Housing*. Accessed April 2, 2016. http://uli.org/wp-content/uploads/ULI-Documents/resident_futures_web_F.pdf.

Rodwin, L. 1945. "Garden Cities and the Metropolis." *Journal of Land Economics and Public Utilities* 21 (August): 268–84.

———. 1956. *The British New Towns Policy: Problems and Implications*. Cambridge, MA: Harvard University Press.

Rose, A., K. Porter, N. Dash, J. Bouabid, C. Huyck, J. C. Whitehead, D. Shaw, et al. 2007. "Benefit-Cost Analysis of FEMA Hazard Mitigation Grants." *Natural Hazard Review* 8, no. 4: 97–111.

Rosenblatt, T., L. Cheshire, and G. Lawrence. 2009. "Social Interaction and Sense of Community in a Master Planned Community." *Housing, Theory and Society* 26, no. 2: 122–42.

Roullier, J.-E., and M. Apgar. 1976. "France: The Focus on Innovation." In *New Perspectives on Community Development*, edited by M. Apgar, 59–74. London: McGraw-Hill.

Rouse, J. 1968. *The Rouse Company Annual Report*. Columbia, MD: Rouse.

———. 1976. "Progress in Community Development: The Columbia Experience." In *New Perspectives on Community Development*, edited by M. Apgar, 157–220. London: McGraw-Hill.

Rowe, J., and R. Kahn. 1998. *Successful Aging*. New York: Pantheon/Random House.

———. 2015. "Successful Aging 2.0: Conceptual Expansions for the 21st Century." *Journals of Gerontology, Series B: Psychological Sciences and Social Sciences* 70, no. 4: 593–96.

Rowe, P. G. 2005a. *East Asia Modern: Shaping the Contemporary City*. London: Reaktion.

———. 2005b. Hong Kong—New Territories, New Towns. *Abitare* 450 (May): 118–25.

Rowe, P. G., A. Forsyth, and H. Y. Kan. 2016. *China's Urban Communities: Concepts, Contexts and Well-Being*. Basel: Birkhauser.

Roy, A., and A. Ong. 2011. *Worlding Cities: Asian Experiments and the Art of Being Global*. Hoboken, NJ: Wiley-Blackwell.

Ruggeri, D. 2009. "Constructing Identity in Master Planned Utopia: The Case of Irvine New Town." PhD diss., University of California, Berkeley.

Rumbach, A. 2014. "Do New Towns Increase Disaster Risk? Evidence from Kolkata, India." *Habitat International* 43 (July): 117–24.

Salomons, I. 1975. "De valse start van Almere." *Plan* no. 2: 12–20.

Sanchez Roman, J. A. 2005. "La Industria Azucarera en Argentina (1860–1914): El Mercado Interno en una Economia Exportadora." *Revista de Indias* 65, no. 233: 142–72.

Sanyal, B. 2005. *Comparative Planning Cultures*. New York: Routledge.

Savills Research. 2010. "Briefing Bundang Office Sector." *Savills*, March. http://pdf.savills.asia/asia

-pacific-research/korea-research/korea-sub-market-briefing/2010–03-bundang-office-market
-briefing-2h-2009-en.pdf.

Schiffer, J. R. 1991. "State Policy and Economic Growth: A Note on the Hong Kong Model." *International Journal of Urban and Regional Research* 15, no. 2: 180–96.

Schriener, J. 1998. "Old Denver Airport Razing Near." *Engineering News-Record* 240, no. 2: 20.

Schroeder, H. W. 1996. "Ecology of the Heart: Understanding How People Experience Natural Environments." In *Natural Resource Management: The Human Dimension*, edited by A. W. Ewert, 13–27. Boulder, CO: Westview.

Schwab, J. C., ed. 2014. *PAS Report 576: Planning for Post-Disaster Recovery; Next Generation*. Chicago: American Planning Association.

Seattle Department of Transportation. 1998. "Denver RTD Light Rail Case Study." In *Case Studies of Transit Oriented Development*, 29–37. Accessed April 10, 2016. http://www.seattle.gov/transportation/SAP/TOD_Case_Studies/Denver_RTD.pdf.

Seetha. 2006. "Saying 'Tata' to Good Governance." *Daily News and Analysis (DNA) India*, November 18. http://www.dnaindia.com/analysis/comment-saying-tata-to-good-governance-1064785.

Segel, A., B. Blaser, G. Garza, A. Kim, J. Richard, and A. M. Murphy. 2012. "New Songdo City." *Harvard Business School Case 9–206–019*. Boston: Harvard Business School. Available at: http://encarnation.com/site/HBS_CASE_STUDY_files/HBS,%20New%20Songdo%20Case_1.pdf

Seoul Metropolitan Government. 2017. *Seoul Population Statistics*. Seoul: Seoul Metropolitan Government.

Shatkin, G. 2011. "Planning Privatopolis: Representation and Contestation in the Development of Urban Integrated Mega-Projects." In *Worlding Cities: Asian Experiments and the Art of Being Global*, edited by A. Roy and O. Aihwa, 77–97. New York: Wiley-Blackwell.

She, W., J. Chen, and H. Wang. 2016. "Affordable Housing Policy in China: New Developments and New Challenges." *Habitat International* 54:224–33.

Shen, J., and F. Wu. 2012. "Restless Urban Landscapes in China: A Case Study of Three Projects in Shanghai." *Journal of Urban Affairs* 34, no. 3: 255–77.

———. 2013. "Moving to the Suburbs: Demand-Side Driving Forces of Suburban Growth in China." *Environment and Planning A* 45, no. 8: 1823–44.

———. 2019. "Paving the Way to Growth: Transit-Oriented Development as a Financing Instrument for Shanghai's Post-Suburbanization." *Urban Geography*, online first.

Shepard, W. 2015. *Ghost Cities of China: The story of Cities Without People in the World's Most Populated Country*. London: Zed Books.

Shepherd, I. D. H., and C. J. Thomas. 1980. "Urban Consumer Behaviour." In *Retail Geography*, edited by J. A. Dawson., 18–94. London: Croom Helm.

Shi, Y., and Y. Chen. 2015. "New City Planning and Construction in Shanghai: Retrospective and Prospective." *International Journal of Urban Sciences* 20, no. 1: 49–72.

Shui, L. 2008. "The Harbor of Beijing: Tongzhou and the Grand Canal in the Ming Dynasty." *Research on Waterborne Transportation* 2008, no. 3: 42–48.

Sieb Organization. 2016. *Eastmark, Mesa, Arizona Case Study: Live in Synchronicity*. Accessed February 3, 2016. http://sieb.com/case-study/eastmark/.

Siegel, S. 2006. "The Public Role in Establishing Private Residential Communities: Towards a New Formulation of Local Government Land Use Policies That Eliminate the Legal Requirements to Privatize New Communities in the United States." *Urban Lawyer* 38, no. 4: 859–948.

Sies, M., I. Gournay, and Freestone, R., eds. 2019. *Iconic Planned Communities and the Challenge of Change*. Philadelphia: University of Pennsylvania Press.

Silva, C. N., ed. 2015a. *Urban Planning in Sub-Saharan Africa: Colonial and Post-Colonial Planning Cultures*. New York: Routledge.

———, ed. 2015b. *Urban Planning in Lusophone Africa Countries*. Farnham, U.K.: Ashgate.

Sims, D. 2014. *Egypt's Desert Dreams*. Cairo: American University in Cairo Press.

Sims, R. 2001. *Japanese Political History Since the Meiji Restoration: 1868–2000*. New York: Palgrave.

Singapore Department of Statistics. 2015a. *Planning Areas in Singapore—Statistics, Locations, and Areas: Punggol Planning Area.* Singapore: Ministry of Trade and Industry.

———. 2015b. *Planning Areas in Singapore—Statistics, Locations, and Areas: Toa Payoh.* Singapore: Ministry of Trade and Industry.

———. 2015c. *Population Trends.* Singapore: Ministry of Trade and Industry.

Singapore National Parks. 2016. *Punggol Waterway Park.* Singapore: National Parks Board.

Sivaramakrishnan, K. C. 1976–77. *New Towns in India: A Report on a Study of Selected New Towns in the Eastern Region.* Calcutta: Indian Institute of Management.

———. 2009. "Special Economic Zones: Issues of Urban Growth and Management." In *Special Economic Zones: Promise, Performance and Pending Issues,* 93–114. New Delhi: Center for Policy Research.

Social Value UK. 2016. *Social Return on Investment—for Social Investing.* Retrieved March 21, 2016. http://socialvalueuk.org/what-is-sroi.

Sorensen, A. 2002. *The Making of Urban Japan: Cities and Planning from Edo to the Twenty-First Century.* London: Routledge.

Spirn, A. 1984. *The Granite Garden: Urban Nature and Human Design.* New York: Basic Books.

Stapleton Redevelopment Foundation. 1995. *Stapleton Development Plan.* Denver, CO: Stapleton Redevelopment Foundation.

Stein, C. 1939. "The Case for New Towns." *Planners Journal* 5, no. 2: 39–44.

———. 1951. *Toward New Towns for America.* Liverpool: Liverpool University Press.

———. 1957. *Toward New Towns for America.* New York: Reinhold.

———. 1966. *Towards New Towns for America.* 2nd ed. Cambridge, MA: MIT Press.

Steinberg, R. 1985. "Large Hydroelectric Projects and Brazilian Politics." *Revista Geografica* 101:29–44.

Steinhardt, N. S. 1999. *Chinese Imperial Planning.* Honolulu: University of Hawaii Press.

Stoker, P., and R. Ewing. 2014. "Job-Worker Balance and Income Match in the United States." *Housing Policy Debate* 24, no. 2: 485–97.

Stokols, A. 2014. "Songdo Style: How Wise Is Korea's 'Smart City'?" *Korea JoongAng Daily*, August 26. http://koreajoongangdaily.joins.com/news/article/Article.aspx?aid=2994022

Stowe, E., and J. Rehfuss. 1975. "Federal New Towns Policy: Muddling Through at the Local Level." *Public Administration Review* 35, no. 3: 222–28.

Straits Times. 1966. "Toa Payoh: The First Tenants Move In." *Straits Times*, June 21, 6.

Strong, A. L. 1971. *Planned Urban Environments: Sweden, Finland, Israel, the Netherlands, France.* Baltimore: Johns Hopkins University Press.

Sturgis, D. 2016. "Autonomous Mobility and Urban Form." Presentation, Irvine Company, Newport Beach, CA, May 20.

Sutcliffe, A. 1981. *The History of Urban and Regional Planning: An Annotated Bibliography.* London: Mansell.

Sze, J. 2015. *Fantasy Islands: Chinese Dreams and Ecological Fears in an Age of Climate Crisis.* Oakland: University of California Press.

Takahashi, N. 1981. "A New Concept in Building: Tsukuba Academic New Town." *Ekistics* 48, no. 289: 304.

Talen, E. 1999. "Sense of Community and Neighbourhood Form: An Assessment of the Social Doctrine of New Urbanism." *Urban Studies* 36, no. 8: 1361–79.

Tan, X. 2010. "New-Town Policy and Development in China." *Chinese Economy* 43, no. 3: 47–58.

Tanabe, H. 1978. "Problems of the New Towns in Japan." *Geo Journal* 2, no. 1: 39–46.

Tao, R., F. B. Su, M. X. Liu, and G. Z. Cao. 2010. "Land Leasing and Local Public Finance in China's Regional Development: Evidence from Prefecture-Level Cities." *Urban Studies* 47, no. 10: 2217–36.

Teaford, J. C. 1975. *The Municipal Revolution in America: Origins of Modern Urban Government, 1650–1825.* Chicago: University of Chicago Press.

Telegraph, India. 2016. "Maiden Meeting On Industrial Town." *Telegraph, India*, December 20. https://www.telegraphindia.com/1161220/jsp/jharkhand/story_125616.jsp.

Tennenbaum, R., ed. 1996. *Creating a New City: Columbia Maryland*. Columbia, Md.: Partners in Community Building and Perry Publishing.

Te Raa, B. 1989. *Van gevaarlijke binnenzee tot Almere*. The Hague: SDU Utigeverij.

Thieler, E. R. 2000. "National Assessment of Coastal Vulnerability to Future Sea-Level Rise." USGS Fact Sheet FS-076–00. Woods Hole, MA: U.S. Geological Survey.

Thomas, R. 1969. *London's New Towns: A Study of Self Contained and Balanced Communities*. London: Political and Economic Planning.

Thomas, R., and P. Cresswell. 1973. *The New Town Idea*. Milton Keynes, U.K.: Open University Press.

Tolan, C. 2014. "Cities of the Future? Indian PM Pushes Plan for 100 'Smart Cities.'" CNN, July 18. http://www.cnn.com/2014/07/18/world/asia/india-modi-smart-cities/index.html.

Tongzhou Municipal Local History Office. 2003. *Tongzhou Zhi—the History of Tongzhou*. Beijing: Beijing Publishing House.

Town and Country Planning Association (TCPA). 1989. "British Towns and the Quality of Life." Paper presented at the 1989 Annual Town and Country Planning Association Conference, London.

———. 2007. *Best Practice in Urban Extensions and New Settlements*. London: Town and Country Planning Association.

———. 2008. *The Essential Role of Green Infrastructure: Eco-Towns Green Infrastructure Worksheet*, September. Oldham, U.K.: RAP Spiderweb. https://www.tcpa.org.uk/Handlers/Download .ashx?IDMF=dd06b21d-6d41–4c4e-bec5–4f29a192f0c6.

———. 2011. *Re-Imagining Garden Cities for the 21st Century*. London: Town and Country Planning Association.

———. 2012a. *Creating Garden Cities and Suburbs Today*. London: Town and Country Planning Association.

———. 2012b. "The New Towns: Their Problems and Future." Memorandum submitted by the Town and Country Planning Association to the U.K. House of Commons, 2012.

———. 2014a. *New Towns Act 2015?* London: Town and Country Planning Association.

———. 2014b. *New Towns and Garden Cities—Lessons for Tomorrow*. London: Town and Country Planning Association.

———. 2017. *Guide 1: Locating and Consenting new Garden Cities*. Garden City Standards for the 21st Century: Practical Guides for Creating Successful New Communities. London: Town and Country Planning Association. Trevisan, R. 2014. "An Overview of Brazilian New Cities in the 20th Century." In conference proceedings, *20th Century New Towns: Archetypes and Uncertainties*, edited by P. Marcolin, and J. Flores, 411–25. Porto, Portugal, Escola Superior Artística do Porto (ESAP), May 22–24, 2014. Porto: Escola Superior Artisitica do Porto.

Tsang, S. 2007. *A Modern History of Hong Kong*. London: I. B. Tauris.

Tuppen, J. N. 1979. "New Towns in the Paris Region: An Appraisal." *Town Planning Review* 50, no. 1: 55–70.

Turok, I. 1990. "Public Investment and Privatization in the New Towns: A Financial Assessment of Bracknell." *Environment and Planning A* 22, no. 10: 1323–36.

Tzoulas, K., K. Korpela, S. Venn, V. Yli-Pelkonen, A. Kazmierczyk, J. Niemela, J., and P. James. 2007. "Promoting Ecosystem Health and Human Health in Urban Areas Using Green Infrastructure: A Literature Review." *Landscape and Urban Planning* 81, no. 3: 167–78.

Underhill, J. 1990. "Soviet New Towns, Planning and National Urban Policy: Shaping the Face of Soviet Cities." *Town Planning Review* 61, no. 3: 263–85.

U.K. Department for Communities and Local Government (DCLG). 2006. *Transferable Lessons from the New Towns*. London: Department for Communities and Local Government.

U.S. Census Bureau. 2011. "Historical Census of Housing Tables." Last updated October 31, 2011. https://www.census.gov/hhes/www/housing/census/historic/owner.html.

U.S. Global Change Research Program. 2009. *Global Climate Change Impacts in the United States*. Cambridge: Cambridge University Press.

U.S. Government, 2016: "Steps to Resilience." *U.S. Climate Resilience Toolkit*. Accessed June 17, 2016. https://toolkit.climate.gov/#steps.

U.N. Habitat. 2013. *State of the World's Cities 2012/2013: Prosperity of Cities*. New York: Routledge.

United Nations. 2014. *World Urbanization Prospects*. Revised 2014 ed. New York: U.N. Department of Economic and Social Affairs.

University of Georgia, Carl Vinson Institute of Government. N.d. *A Brief Summary of Municipal Incorporation Procedures by State*. Athens: University of Georgia.

University of Strathclyde. 1967. *Cumbernauld 67: A Household Survey and Report, Occasional Paper No. 1*. Glasgow: University of Strathclyde.

———. 1970. *East Kilbride 70: An Economic and Social Survey*. Glasgow: University of Strathclyde.

Unwin, R. 1912. *Nothing Gained by Overcrowding*. London: P. S. King and Son.

Urban Land Institute. 1992. *Planned Communities, New Towns, and Resort Communities in the United States and Canada*. Washington, DC: ULI-Urban Land Institute.

———. 2004. "Stapleton." *Development Case Studies* 34, no. 4. Washington, DC: Urban Land Institute. Accessed April 10, 2016. http://casestudies.uli.org/wp-content/uploads/sites/98/2015/12/C034004.pdf.

———. 2007. "Daybreak." *Development Case Studies* 37, no. 24. Washington, DC: Urban Land Institute. Accessed March 25, 2016. http://casestudies.uli.org/wp-content/uploads/sites/98/2015/12/C037024.pdf.

———. 2015. *America in 2015: A ULI Survey of Views on Housing, Transportation, and Community*. Washington, DC: Urban Land Institute, 2015.

URBED. 2014. "Wolfson Economics Prize 2014." *URBED*, online blog, September 4. http://urbed.coop/wolfson-economic-prize.

Van der Wahl, C. 1997. *In Praise of Common Sense: Planning the Ordinary; A Physical Planning History of the New Towns in the IJsselmeerpolders*. Rotterdam: 010 Publishers.

van Duijn, N., and F. Huis. 2004. "Raad van Overleg 1977–1978." *Almere City Archive*, http://almerebestuurd.nl/Bestuur_Anecdotes.html, Accessed 2016.

Vanke Hangzhou. 2016. *Liangzhu New Town Land Use and Neighborhood Composition*. Archival data. Hangzhou, P.R. of China: China Vanke.

van Wijnen, J. F. 1993. "Wat is er nou tegen een beetje corruptie?" *Vrij Nederland*, July 24, 6–8.

Vasoo, S. 1988. "The Development of New Towns in Hong Kong and Singapore: Some Social Consequences." *International Social Work* 31, no. 2: 115–33.

Viet, J. 1960. *New Towns: A Selected Annotated Bibliography*. Paris: UNESCO.

Voicu, I., and V. Been. 2008. "The Effects of Community Gardens on Neighboring Property Values." *Real Estate Economics* 36, no. 2: 241–83.

Wakeman, R. 2014a. "Rethinking Postwar Planning History." *Planning Perspectives* 29, no. 2: 153–63.

———. 2014b. "Was There an ideal Socialist City? Socialist New Towns as Modern Dreamscapes." In *Transnationalism and the German City*, edited by J. M. Diefendorf and J. Ward, 105–24. London: Palgrave Macmillan.

———. 2016. *Practicing Utopia: An Intellectual History of the New Town Movement*. Chicago: University of Chicago Press.

Walters, J., B. Bochner, and R. Ewing. 2013. "Getting Trip Generation Right: Eliminating the Bias Against Mixed Use Development." *Planning Advisory Service Memo Series*, May. Accessed July 24, 2016. http://www.fehrandpeers.com/wp-content/uploads/2013/07/APA_PAS_May2013_GettingTripGenRight.pdf.

Wang, L., R. Kundu, and X. Chen. 2010. "Building for What and Whom? New Town Development as Planned Suburbanization in China and India." In *Suburbanization in Global Society*, edited by M. Clapson and R. Hutchison, 319–45. Bingley: Emerald Group.

Wang, L. H., and A. G. O. Yeh. 1987. "Public Housing-Led New Town Development: Hong Kong and Singapore." *Third World Planning Review* 9, no. 1: 41–63.

———, eds. 1993. *Keep a City Moving: Urban Transport Management in Hong Kong*. Tokyo: Asian

Productivity Organization. Translated and published in Chinese. Beijing: China Architecture and Building Press.

Wang, Y.-W., and T. Heath. 2010. "Towards Garden City Wonderlands: New Town Planning in 1950s Taiwan." *Planning Perspectives* 25, no. 2: 141–69.

Ward, A., ed. 2006. *Reston Town Center: A Downtown for the 21st Century*. Washington, DC: Academy Press.

Ward, S. V., ed. 1992. *The Garden City: Past, Present and Future*. London: E. and F. N. Spon.

———. 2000. "Re-Examining the International Diffusion of Planning." In *Urban Planning in a Changing World: The Twentieth Century Experience*, edited by R. Freestone, 40–60. London: Routledge.

———. 2002. *Planning the Twentieth-Century City*. Chichester, U.K.: John Wiley.

———. 2015. "Introduction." In *The Garden City Movement Up-to-Date*, by E. G. Culpin, vii–xxvii. London: Routledge.

———. 2016. *The Peaceful Path: Building Garden Cities and New Towns*. Hatfield, U.K.: University of Hertfordshire Press.

Warwick, E. 2015. "Policy to Reality: Evaluating the Evidence Trajectory for English Eco-Towns." *Building Research and Information* 43, no. 4: 486–98.

Waterman, T. 2016. "There's Room: In the New Battle Strategy, the Dutch Give Some Ground Back to the Water." *Landscape Architecture Magazine*, June, 119–35.

Watson A. G. 1991. *New Towns in Perspective in England*. In *New Towns in Perspective*, International New Towns Association, 11. London: INTA Press .

Webster, D., J. Cai, L. Miller, and B. Luo. 2003. *Emerging Third Stage Peri-Urbanization: Functional Specialization in the Hangzhou Peri-Urban Region*. Stanford, CA: Asia Pacific Research Center.

Weller, R., and J. Bolleter. 2013. *Made in Australia: The Future of Australian Cities*. Perth: University of Western Australia Press.

Wells, N., and K. Rollings. 2012. "The Natural Environment: Influences on Human Health and Function." In *The Oxford Handbook of Environmental and Conservation Psychology*, edited by Susan Clayton, 509–23. Oxford: Oxford University Press.

Welsh, F. 1993. *A History of Hong Kong*. London: Harper.

WHA Architects. 2004. *Ladera Ranch Avendale Guidelines*. Santa Ana, CA: WHA Architects.

———. *Verrado Phase 1 Design Guidelines*. Santa Ana, CA: WHA Architects.

Wheaton, W., and R. Torto. 1990. "An Investment Model of the Demand and Supply for Industrial Real Estate." *AREUEA Journal* 18, no. 4: 530–47.

Whelan, R. 1984. "New Towns: An Idea Whose Time Has Passed?" *Journal of Urban History* 10, no. 2: 195–209.

Wilburn, M., and R. Gladstone. 1972. *Optimizing Development Profits in Large Scale Real Estate Projects*. Urban Land Institute Technical Bulletin 67. Washington, DC: Urban Land Institute.

Wilbur Smith Associates. 2009. "South Carolina State Rail Plan 2008 Update." Accessed June 26, 2016. http://www.palmettorailways.com/pdfs/SC_State_Rail_Plan_2008_Part_1_Executive _Summary_Wilbur_Smith_Associates_2009r.pdf.

Williamson, L. 2013. "Tomorrow's Cities: Just How Smart Is Songdo?" *BBC News*, September 2, 2013. http://www.bbc.com/news/technology-23757738.

Willmott, P. 1962. "Housing Density and Town Design in a New Town: A Pilot Study at Stevenage." *Town Planning Review* 33, no. 2: 115–27.

———. 1964. "East Kilbride and Stevenage: Some Characteristics of a Scottish and an English New Town." *Town Planning Review* 34, no. 4: 307–16.

———. 1967. "Social Research and New Communities." *Journal of the American Planning Association* 33, no. 6: 387–97.

Winton, A. 2009. *Ground Control: Fear and Happiness in the Twenty-First Century City*. London: Penguin.

Worley, W. S. 1990. *J. C. Nichols and the Shaping of Kansas City: Innovation in Planned Residential Communities*. Columbia: University of Missouri Press.

Wu, A. 2012. "The Silver New China: Opportunities in Developing Senior Housing in China." Master's thesis, Harvard University, Graduate School of Design.

Wu, A., and C. Guan. 2011. "Senior Housing in China: What Foreign Investors Should Know." Unpublished manuscript.

Wu, F. 2005. "Rediscovering the 'Gate' Under Market Transition: From Work-Unit Compounds to Commodity Housing Enclaves." *Housing Studies* 20, no. 2: 235–54.

———. 2010. "Gated and Packaged Suburbia: Packaging and Branding Chinese Suburban Residential Development." *Cities* 27, no. 5: 385–96.

———. 2015. *Planning for Growth: Urban and Regional Planning in China*. London: Routledge.

———. 2016. "Emerging Chinese Cities: Implications for Global Urban Studies." *Professional Geographer* 68, no. 2: 338–48.

———. 2018. "Planning Centrality, Market Instruments: Governing Chinese Urban Transformation Under State Entrepreneurialism." *Urban Studies* 55, no. 7: 1383–1399.

Wu, F., and N. A. Phelps. 2011. "(Post)suburban Development and State Entrepreneurialism in Beijing's Outer Suburbs." *Environment and Planning A* 43, no. 2: 410–30.

Wu, F., and J. Shen. 2015. "Suburban Development and Governance in China." In *Suburban Governance: A Global View*, edited by P. Hamel and R. Keil, 303–24. Toronto: University of Toronto Press.

Wu, F., and A. G. O. Yeh. 1999. "Urban Spatial Structure in a Transitional Economy: The Case of Guangzhou, China." *Journal of the American Planning Association* 65, no. 4: 377–94.

Wu, F., F. Z. Zhang, and C. Webster. 2013. "Informality and the Development and Demolition of Urban Villages in the Chinese Peri-Urban Area." *Urban Studies* 50, no. 10: 1919–34.

Xu, J., A. Yeh, and F. L. Wu. 2009. "Land Commodification: New Land Development and Politics in China Since the Late 1990s." *International Journal of Urban and Regional Research* 33, no. 4: 890–913.

Xue, C. Q. L., Y. Wang, and L. Tsai. 2013. "Building New Towns in China: A Case Study of Zhengdong New District." *Cities* 30, no. 1: 223–32.

Xue, P. 2006. "The Merchants of Chang'an in the Sui and Tang Dynasties." *Frontier of History in China* 1, no. 2: 254–75.

Yeh, A. G. O. 1987. "Spatial Impacts of New Town Development in Hong Kong." In *New Towns in East and Southeast Asia—Planning and Development*, edited by D. R. Phillips and A. G. O. Yeh, 59–81. Hong Kong: Oxford University Press.

———. 1990. "Unfair Housing Subsidy and Public Housing in Hong Kong." *Environment and Planning C: Government and Policy* 8, no. 4: 439–54.

———. 1997. "Economic Restructuring and Land Use Planning in Hong Kong." *Land Use Policy* 14, no. 1: 25–39.

———. 2002. "Further Cooperation Between Hong Kong and the Pearl River Delta in Creating a More Competitive Region." In *Building a Competitive Pearl River Delta Region: Cooperation, Coordination and Planning*, edited by A. G. O. Yeh, Y. S. Lee, T. Lee, and N. D. Sze, 319–45. Hong Kong: Centre of Urban Planning and Environmental Management.

———. 2003. "Public Housing and New Town Development." In *Fifty Years of Public Housing in Hong Kong: A Golden Jubilee Review and Appraisal*, edited by Y.-M. Yeung, 85–107. Hong Kong: Chinese University Press.

Yeh, A. G. O., P. R. Hills, and K. W. Ng, eds. 2001. *Modern Transport in Hong Kong for the 21st Century*. Hong Kong: University of Hong Kong, Centre of Urban Planning and Environmental Management.

Yeh, A. G. O., and H. Q. Yuan. 1987. "Satellite Town Development in China: Problems and Prospects." *Tijdschrift voor Economische en Sociale Geografie* 78, no. 3: 190–200.

Zamani, B., and M. Arefi. 2013. "Iranian New Towns and Their Urban Management Issues: A Critical Review of Influential Actors and Factors." *Cities* 30, no. 1: 105–12.

Zehner, R. B. 1977. *Indicators of the Quality of Life in New Communities*. Cambridge, MA: Ballinger.

Zhang, L. 2010. *In Search of Paradise: Middle-Class Living in a Chinese Metropolis.* Ithaca, NY: Cornell University Press.

Zhang, T. 2000. "Land Market Forces and Government's Role in Sprawl." *Cities* 17, no. 2: 123–35.

Zhou, J. 2012. "Urban Vitality in Dutch and Chinese New Towns: A Comparative Study Between Almere and Tongzhou." *Architecture and the Built Environment* 3:1-432.

Zhou, Y., and L. J. C. Ma. 2000. "Economic Restructuring and Suburbanization in China." *Urban Geography* 21, no. 3: 205–36.

Zipporah, A. 2014. "A Photographic History of Bonifaco Global City." *Zipwatch*, October 9. Accessed January 2018. https://www.zipmatch.com/blog/photographic-history-of-bonifacio -global-city/.

Contributors

Sandy Apgar, an award-winning consultant and author of pioneering articles on real estate and urban development, launched and led the Army's Residential Communities Initiative and is a senior advisor at the Center for Strategic and International Studies. A former partner of McKinsey & Company and the Boston Consulting Group, he has advised clients on over 600 projects in thirteen countries and holds a U.S. patent for a real estate evaluation methodology.

Sai Balakrishnan is an assistant professor of urban planning at the Harvard Graduate School of Design. Balakrishnan has also worked as an urban planner in the United States, India, and the United Arab Emirates, and as a consultant to the U.N.-HABITAT in Nairobi, Kenya.

JaapJan Berg is architectural historian and works as an independent researcher and journalist in the field of architecture and spatial planning. He also works as a project manager and researcher for the International New Town Institute (INTI).

Paul Buckhurst, a principal of Perkins Eastman Architects, has more than forty years of experience in urban planning, urban design, and architecture. He has worked on a variety of development and design projects, including new city and community plans in Canada, Brazil, Egypt, China, Vietnam, and Saudi Arabia.

Felipe Correa is the Vincent and Eleanor Shea Professor and the chair of Architecture at UVA School of Architecture. Correa is a cofounder and director of the South America Project (SAP), a transcontinental applied research network that proactively endorses the role of design within rapidly transforming geographies of the South American continent.

Carl Duke is the vice president of underwriting at Property Reserve, Incorporated. Since 2005, Duke has managed numerous large communities across the country at various stages of the entitlement and development life cycle.

Reid Ewing is a professor in the Department of City and Metropolitan Planning at the University of Utah. His eight books include *Best Development Practices*, listed by the American Planning Association (APA) as one of the one hundred "essential" books in planning over the past one hundred years.

Ann Forsyth, trained in planning and architecture, is the Ruth and Frank Stanton Professor of Urban Planning at Harvard University. Forsyth's works include analyses of the success of planned alternatives to sprawl, particularly exploring the tensions between social and ecological values in urban design.

Robert Freestone is a professor of planning in the Faculty of Built Environment at the University of New South Wales, Australia in Sydney. His research interests are in urban planning history, metropolitan change, heritage conservation, and planning education.

Shikyo Fu is a chief planner of China Vanke. He served as the chief architect for the Vanke Liangzhu New Town. His research interest is in new towns development in China and Japan.

Pascaline Gaborit has more than fifteen years of work experience in the area of towns and cities cooperation, as former director of the European New Towns and Pilot Cities' Platform (ENTP). She is currently working for the Global Relations Forum, a think tank of Asian and European experts.

Elie Gamburg, a director at Kohn Pedersen Fox, has experience creating innovative designs for cities, institutions, companies, and developers. His work includes an array of project types internationally, across multiple scales and sectors.

Alexander Garvin is currently president and CEO of AGA Public Realm Strategists, Incorporated, a planning and design firm in New York City, and is also an adjunct professor of urban planning and management at Yale University. Garvin is the author of *The American City: What Works, What Doesn't*, now in its third edition.

David Godschalk, FAICP, was Stephen Baxter Professor Emeritus of City and Regional Planning at the University of North Carolina, Chapel Hill. Godschalk coauthored the popular text *Urban Land Use Planning* and has written, researched, and consulted on planning for resilience, growth management, land-use planning, hazard mitigation, and dispute resolution.

Tony Green is managing partner of The Pinehills, the award-winning, thirty-two-hundred-acre new village center in Plymouth, Massachusetts. In January 2016, the National Association of Home Builders named The Pinehills "Community of the Year" at the Best in American Living Awards.

ChengHe Guan is an assistant professor of urban design at New York University Shanghai. He was the Harold A. Pollman Fellow in Real Estate and Urban Development at the Harvard Graduate School of Design. Guan's research interest is on urban design, urban form, and urban simulation. He specializes in spatial analysis, regional urban growth modeling, and quantitative research methodologies.

Rachel Keeton is an urban researcher specializing in contemporary new towns and a global initiative fellow in urbanism at TU Delft. She is the author of *Rising in the East: Contemporary New Towns in Asia* (SUN, 2011) and co-editor of *To Build a City in Africa: A History and a Manual* (Nai010, 2019). Her current research aims to develop and test a series of adaptive planning and design principles for future African New Towns.

Steven Kellenberg is founder of Kellenberg Studio and past senior vice president of community planning for the Irvine Company, developer of the Irvine Ranch in Orange County, California. He has over thirty-five years of experience in new community design, having worked globally on a number of new towns in North America, Asia, the Middle East, and South America. He has coauthored two books with the Urban Land Institute and is adjunct associate professor in the University of Southern California Master of Real Estate Program.

Kyung Min Kim is an associate dean of Graduate School of Environmental Studies at Seoul National University. His major research area is global real estate market analysis, and he has published several books and a variety of newspaper serials. Since 2017, he has been the chair of the Social Innovation Committee of the Ministry of Interior and Safety, South Korea.

Gene Kohn is the chairman of Kohn Pedersen Fox Associates, a firm he cofounded in 1976. He has worked globally, and his achievements have been recognized with numerous prestigious awards.

Todd Mansfield is president and chief executive officer of Crescent Communities. As president of Disney's Celebration Company, he led the team that initiated development of the five-thousand-acre town of Celebration and was involved in the planning and execution of Val d'Europe, the transit-oriented town east of Paris.

Robert W. Marans is a research professor at the Institute for Social Research and professor emeritus of architecture and urban planning in the Taubman College of Architecture and Urban Planning at the University of Michigan. He has conducted numerous studies on communities, neighborhoods, housing, parks, and recreation.

Robert H. Nelson was a professor at the University of Maryland and the author of more than one hundred journal articles and edited book chapters and ten books. He worked in the Office of Policy Analysis of the Office of the Secretary of the Interior from 1975 to 1993.

Pike Oliver is the founder and managing member of Urbanexus, LLC, and a lecturer in the Runstad Department of Real Estate at the University of Washington. For three decades, he worked on planned communities at the Irvine Ranch and other properties in western North America and abroad.

Richard Peiser has been the Michael D. Spear Professor of Real Estate Development at Harvard University's Graduate School of Design since 1998. Peiser's primary research has focused on understanding real estate developers' responses to the marketplace and to the institutional environment in which they operate, particularly in the areas of urban redevelopment, affordable housing, and suburban sprawl.

Michelle Provoost is an architectural historian. In 1994, she cofounded the office of Crimson Architectural Historians. Since 2008 she has been the director of the International New Town Institute in Rotterdam, the Netherlands.

Peter G. Rowe is Raymond Garbe Professor of Architecture and Urban Design, and Harvard University Distinguished Service Professor. Rowe's research and consulting are extensive, diverse, and international in scope, including cultural interpretation and design, the relationship of urban form to issues of economic development, historic conservation, housing provision, and resource sustainability.

Jongpil Ryu is a real estate professional from South Korea who studied real estate at Cornell University, focusing on real estate finance, market analysis, and global real estate capital flows.

Andrew Stokols is a PhD student at MIT in the Department of Urban Studies and Planning and received a master's in urban planning from the Harvard Graduate School of Design. His research lies at the intersection of urban design and macroeconomic forces, exploring how spatial trends such as the concentration of economic activity in "superstar cities" have fueled the rise of global populism.

Adam Tanaka is a senior analyst at HR&A Advisors and a lecturer in urban planning and design at the Harvard Graduate School of Design. His research, teaching, and professional practice focus on the challenges and opportunities of public-private real estate development, with a particular emphasis on affordable housing in U.S. cities.

Jamie von Klemperer is president and design principal at Kohn Pedersen Fox Associates. His work ranges in scale from a house to a city, and he contributes closely to these efforts from conception to completion.

Fulong Wu is Bartlett Professor of Planning at University College London. His research interests include urban development in China and its social and sustainable challenges. He has recently published a book, *Planning for Growth: Urban and Regional Planning in China* (2015). He is an editor of *International Journal of Urban and Regional Research*.

Ying Xu is a postdoctoral fellow at the Institute for Social Research, University of Michigan. Her research interests cover environmental change in urban China and its implications for the quality of life of diverse populations.

Anthony Gar-On Yeh is Chan To-Hann Professor in Urban Planning and Design, Chair of the Department of Urban Planning and Design, and director of GIS Research Centre at the University of Hong Kong. His research interests include new towns, land-use planning, GIS, and urban planning and development in Hong Kong, China, and Southeast Asia.

Chaobin Zhou is a deputy general manager at China Vanke. His expertise is in real estate development and real property finance. Zhou is currently in charge of a community development project with six super-high-rise towers.

Index

Page numbers in bold refer to figures.

American Institute of Architects, 298

American Planning Association (APA), 88, 89

Amersfoort, Netherlands, 375

Amsterdam, the Netherlands, 256–257

Ando, Tadao, 172, 173

Angola, 280, 281–286

Apgar, Sandy, **312, 314, 315, 322,** 434

Apple, 94

Appolonia City, Ghana, 280

Argentina, 263–266, 275

Article 243Q (India constitutional governance provision), 224–225, 229

artist communities, 135–136

arts and cultural centers, 170–172, **173,** 245–247, 354–355, 358

ARUP engineers, 351

Asia, new towns in, 23, 329–330; Asian financial crisis, 359; community satisfaction in, 49. *See also* East and Southeast Asia, new towns as response to urban expansion in; individual location

Australia, new towns in, 22, 50, 388; Canberra, 9, 48, 433; community satisfaction in, 48; map of new towns in, 431

automobiles, 80–81, 337–338; dependency on, 95, 163, 236; driverless cars, 334, 369–370, 419–420; European new towns, 236, 241; Lingang, 163; reducing impact of, 369, 381; Sheikh Zayed, 287. *See also* transit and transportation

Bahrain, new towns in, 381

balanced communities (income level balance), 188–189. *See also* income

balanced communities (jobs-housing balance). *See* jobs-housing balance

"The Banality of Good" exhibition (Venice Biennale), 23

bankruptcy, of U.S. planned communities, 60, 63, 75, 82

Bartholomew, Harland, 26

Basildon, U.K., **234,** 243, 246

beach renourishment projects, 397–398

Beijing, China, 119, 132–137, 150; 2005–20 Master Plan, 134–135; Tongzhou, 133–136; Yizhuang, 136–137. *See also* China, new towns compared

Belgium, 232

Bell, G., 28

Belo Horizonte, 17

Benedict, M. A., **374**

benefit-cost analyses, 398–399, 408

benefits of new towns, 32–33, 35–38; unproven, 38–39. *See also* motivations

Best Development Practices: Doing the Right Thing and Making Money at the Same Time (APA and ULI), 88

Best in American Living Awards, 341

bicycle travel, 237, 391–392, 420

bin Sultan al Nahyan, Sheikh Zayed, 286

biodiversity, 372, **373, 375,** 405–406

Blakely, E. J., 69

bond funding, 21, 77, 79, 88–89, 318

Bournville Village Trust, 25

Bracknell, 295

Brainerd, Harry Beardslee, 267

Branch, M. C., 27

branding. *See* marketing

Brazil, 263, 270–273, 275; Brasilia 2, 368

Breheny, Michael, 24

Bren, Donald, 300–301

Britain, new towns in, 232, 309, 327, 395, 401, 404–405, 409; "British Towns and Quality of Life" conference, 43; community satisfaction in, 46–47; Department for Communities and Local Government, 295; Eco-Town Program, 374–375; Greater London Plan, 395; lessons learned, 295; New Towns Act (1946), 16, 19, 21–22, 24–28; private developers in, 190, 207–208; self-contained new towns, 231; Singapore and, British new towns as model, 143, 145; studies of, 46; suburbs for working class, 157; Tama New Town and, British new towns as model, 121; Town and Country Planning Association (TCPA), 16, 25, 43, 374; Urban Development Services Unit, 29. *See also* United Kingdom, European new towns comparisons

Brown, Isaac, 50, **375**

Buckingham, James Silk, 17

builders, 306, 337–338; guild, 321–322, 325–326; warranty program, 325

built environment, importance of, 45, 53–54, 158, 165, 216, 309. *See also* design layouts

Bulgaria, new towns in, 234

Bundang, South Korea, 139–**140,** 200–215, **210,** 306; branding and marketing, 212; centralized government authority, 200–201, 211; commercial development, 140, 206, 209–210, 213–215; design layout, 140, 205, 206, 209–212; financial activity summary (table), 213, 214; Five Korean New Towns comparisons (table), 203; focused planning, 200–201, 211–212; housing prices,

climate change, regional development and, 394–409; adaptations of Howard's model, 395–396. *See also* coastal region new town systems; sea-level rise

cluster cities, 319

coastal region new town systems, 400, 403–406; flood insurance, 400, 408, 409n1; planning stages, 404–405; roles and responsibilities, 403–404. *See also* climate change; sea-level rise

colonialism, 17, 19; African new towns and, 278; colonial settlements, 37–38

Columbia, Maryland, 20–21, 47, 59, **62**, 79, **85, 307**, 371; Columbia Association, 321, 323; Columbia Economic Model, 313; Columbia Foundation, 318; curvilinear layout, 69; "D variables" in, 89; open space in, 63, 78, 84–85; organization and management of, 309–310, 317–318, 327; racial diversity, 86–87; residential demand, 82; site acquisition, 74; site development costs, 75; transit and transportation, 95

Comissão Interestadual da Bacia Paraná-Uruguay (CIBPU), 270

commercial districts and development, 318, 342–345, 354; Bundang, 140, 206, 209–210, 213–215; Europe, comparative analysis, 244–245; Hong Kong, 191–199; Liangzhu, 170–171, 173, 178; in neighborhood unit design concept, 211; Pangyo, 215; Park Avenue CBD, 358; Songdo, 142; South Korea, general, 206; Tokyo, 121; Tongzhou, 134, 135; Yizhuang, 137. *See also* commuting; finance districts and employment; industrial districts and development; jobs-housing balance; mixed-use districts and development; office districts and employment; residential districts and development; retail districts and employment; self-sufficiency and self-containment goals

Commission for New Towns, **307**

common properties, 323–324

communication, importance of, 312–313, 323

communities: activities in, 319; community association (CA), 321–325; Community Associations Institute (CAI), 105; Community Development Block Grant program, 400; community-scale planning, 317; development districts, 344; intentional, 15, 379; livability of, 45; organizations, 320–321, 344; residents' council, 324; satisfaction, 44–49, 53–54, 55n3; sense of community, 37, 46, 49–51, 53–54, 126, 178, 324, 341–342; single-use, 10

community facilities and amenities. *See* amenities and public services; home owners' associations; open space and parkland

commuter rail. *See* transit and transportation

commuting: automobile dependency, U.S., 95; cost of, Hong Kong subsidizing, 196–197; Hong Kong, comparative analysis, 194–195; reducing congestion, Hong Kong, 194; reducing congestion, Tongzhou-Beijing, 135; reducing time, China, 164–165; reducing time, Hong Kong, 186; reducing time, U.S., 85, 90–91; Sheikh Zayed-Cairo, 287–288; Tama-Tokyo, 122, 123; Tin Shui Wai, 196–197; Tongzhou-Beijing, 135; Tsukuba-Tokyo, 125; VMT metric, 90–91, 363, 365–366. *See also* automobiles; jobs-housing balance; roadways, design and use of; transit and transportation

compact city approach, 385–387, 389–391

Companhia Energética de São Paulo (CESP), 270, 272–273

competitive advantage, 318

comprehensive planning, 8, 10, 12, 36–37, 294, 301, 402, 404–405; phased new towns, 7, 347, 411–412, 414–415, 421

concentric circle form, 395

condominiums, 111, 211

Congrès Internationaux d'Architecture Moderne (CIAM), 278

Connecticut General, 299, 307

connectivity, 363, 367–371, **373,** 374–375, 384; autonomous vehicles, 370; new frontiers in, 369–370; optimal multinodal framework-using spatial analytics, 365–367; sustainable mobility as master plan framework, 367–368; trails, 372

Connery, John, 341

construction of new towns and planned communities (physical construction issues): builders, 306, 321–322, 325–326, 337–338; developers' role, 207–208; Tsukuba City, 125–126

conventional, incremental, real estate ventures, U.S., 84–87, 104

conventional communities, comparison of new towns to, 45–49, 51, 54

Converse, R., 44–46

co-operative commonwealths, 18

copper industry, 269, 274

Le Corbusier, 18, 390

Corden, C., 22

cores and centers, 363–367, 383–384; central activity core, 363; central governmental administration, 351; city center, 330, 331; district center, 330, 331; golden mean methodology, 364–365; growth center plans (the Netherlands), 232–233, 262n2; multicenter plan, 331; town centers, 298, 300, 335, 342–345, 381, 416

corporations. *See* developers, private; home owners' associations; municipal incorporation

Correa, Felipe, 434

corridors, 366–367, **374,** 376–377, 395, 406–407

Country Club District, Missouri, 59, **61, 74,** 78, 79, **83–84**

Crescent Communities (developer), 302, 342–345; Celebration, Florida, 343–345; commercial development and new town centers, 342–343

Crewe, K., 15

critiques of new towns, 21–22, 26–27, 32, 38–41, 389, 418. *See also* segregation, socio-spatial

Cropper, V., 50

cul-de-sac layout, 67, 69, 70, **71, 76,** 89

culture. *See* arts and cultural centers

Cumberland, Scotland, 11

Cumbernauld, 27–28

curvilinear layout, 67, **68–69,** 139, 286

Czech Republic, new towns in, 234

Daceyville Garden Suburb, 388

Dalny, 17

Dan Cutrona Photography, **335**

Danielak, Silvia, 434

Daybreak, Utah, 89, 95–96, 103

debt, 154; debt service, 77, 79, 88–89

decision making. *See* Almere, the Netherlands, governance history; governance; voting

defining new towns, 8–10, 12, 32–33, 55n1, 88, 231, 432–433; by ENTP, 231; suburban sprawl, compared, 89

de Gaulle, Charles, 20

Delhi, India, 412

Delouvrier master plan, 395

demographics. *See* families; population demographics

Den-en Toshi, Japan, 388

density. *See* population density

Denver Park Creek Metropolitan District, **373**

design layouts, 11, 27–29, 36–37, 48, 351–352, 359, 381, 419–420; architectural features, 72, 73, 78, 146, 252, 283; architectural standards, 325–326; Beaux-Arts design structure, 378; Bundang, 140, 205, 206, 209–212; in Chinese new towns (as "mega" urban projects), 153; core and pe-

riphery model, 168–169; effect on identity and affiliation, 50; focal vs. background architecture, 381; form of individual new towns, 395; "good bones," 379–380, 384; innovations in, 332–334; Kilamba, 283, 285; Liangzhu, 168–169; Lingang, 162; Maria Elena, 267; neighborhood unit design concept, 210–211, 271; Punggol, 148; resource extraction towns, 264–269, 271–272, 274–275; Santa Ana, 264–265; Shanghai townscape strategy, 159; Sha Tin, 128–130; Sheikh Zayed, 286; Singapore, 144–146, 148; Songjiang, 41, 155–157, 160–161, 415; streets designed to tell a story, 380–381; Tama New Town, 122–123; Tin Shui Wai, 130–131; Toa Payoh, 145–146; Tongzhou, 134–135; Tsukuba City, 125–126; urban design framework, 379–381, 384; Vila Piloto, 271–272; Yizhuang, 136–137. *See also* garden city movement; jobs-housing balance; suburbs, layouts in U.S.

design phase. *See* phasing development; planning phase

Design with Nature (McHarg), 175

destination accessibility issues ("D" variable), 89. *See also* roadways, design and use of; transit and transportation

developers: local, 360; role of, 310, 326; vision of, 310–311, 345, 418

developers, challenges for. *See* financing; infrastructure development; land use diversity issue ("D variable"); phasing development; problems in U.S. planned communities; residential demand; site issues; transit

developers, China: Liangzhu, 169–174, 176–178; Lingang, 156, 161–163; Narada, 169, 170, 176; public-private intersections, 134, 152, 154–156, 177; Songjiang, 160–161; Vanke, 169–174, 176–178

developers, private, 12, 20–21, 313–314, 351, 401, 404, 419; Britain, 190, 207–208; financing new towns, 295–297, 302–305, 308n4; Ghana, 280; Lavasa, 219; property and services management by, 174, 221–224

developers, private, in U.S., 59, 63, 65–66, 97–98, 113; DMB Associates, 93–94, 101–102; revenue for, 66, 79–80, 88; site acquisition by, 74, 79–80; The Woodlands, 175

developers, public (state-led), 314, 327, 391, 402, 415, 417–418; Africa, general/comparative analysis, 279–280; Almere (RIJP), 250–255; China, 154; Chinese developers assist in Angola, 282–283;

balance; self-sufficiency and self-containment goals

EDAW, **369**

Ede, Netherlands, 432–433

edge cities, 152, 157, 319, 371

education. *See* schools

Edwards, A. Trystan, 18

EF-5 tornado, 398

Egypt, 278, 280, 281, 286–288, 290n2

ekistics methodology, 29

elevated buildings, 397–398

employment. *See* jobs and employment

employment-based new towns. *See* economic and research reasons

engineered systems, 351

England. *See* Britain; United Kingdom, European new towns comparisons

enterprise, holistic, 309

entitlements, 186, 335

entrepreneurial stewardship, 313

environmental issues, 385–393; Almere, 260; biodiversity, 372, 373, 375, 405–406; carbon footprint, 363–367, 372–373, 420; carbon sequestration, 372–373; China new towns and, 155; compact city approach, 385–387, 389–391; conservation, 36; ecological systems, role in urban communities, 371; ecology of the heart, 391; Europe, comparative analysis, 231, 236–237, 241–243; flooding, 248n3, 400, 407–408, 409n1; garbage collection and recycling, 391; greenhouse gases (GHG), 363, 365–367, 372–373; habitat and ecosystem protection, 386; heat island effect, 372–373, 375; Milton Keynes and, 236–237, 242, 243; natural systems education, 377; pollution, 386; preservation management, 349; progress, 351; resilient new towns approach, 385–387, 392–393; Sino-Singapore Tianjin Eco-City, 156; support systems, 386; wildlife movement, 372, 375–377; the Woodlands design, 175. *See also* climate change; eco-places; garden city movement; open space and parkland; sustainability

equity, social, 30, 103, 372, 417. *See also* social issues

Etablissement Public d'Aménagement (EPA), 304, **307**, 308n8

Ethiopia, new towns in, 279

Europe, new towns compared, 230–248; amenities and public services, 235, 238–239; arts and culture, 245–247; budget cuts, 233–234; community satisfaction in, 48; Eastern Europe,

232, 234–235, 238; end of new town creation, 247–248; environmental issues, 231, 236–237, 241–243; financing issues, 231, 233–236, 242, 245–246; first, second, and third generation towns (table), 233; housing types and prices, 235, 237, 238; industrial expansion and, 231, 232, 234–235; jobs-housing balance, 237, 244–245; local governance, 231, 235, 237, 244; locations (table), 235; map of, 425; motivations and influences, 230–232, 234–235, 237; planning and management methods, 235; population issues, 231, 232, 234, 235, 237–238, 241; public opinion, 242–243; research studies, 230; sense of community, 49–50; social issues, 238–240; table, 232; transit and transportation, 235–237, 241; unemployment, 239–240. *See also* France, European new towns comparisons; the Netherlands, European new towns comparisons; United Kingdom, European new towns comparisons

European and Asian Sustainable Towns: Satellite Towns in their Metropolises (EAST) project, 230

European New Towns and Pilot Cities Platform (ENTP), 230–231

Ewing, Reid, 434

expansion, urban, 9, 23, 421, 432–433. *See also* East and Southeast Asia, new towns as response to urban expansion in; India, new towns in

Ex-Service Man J47485 (Edwards), 18

extensions, city. *See* expansion, urban

Falk, N., 30

fallacies: completed cities, 82–83; completed planning, 83–84; self-sufficient cities, 83

families and households, 44–45, 47, 132, 210–212, 236–238, 310; childcare, 238, 279, 322, 365; children, 39, 48, 51, 53, 105, 175, 197, 210, 222, 286, 317; parents, 39, 210, 387, 420; youth, 39, 53, 239. *See also* age; population demographics

Fanling/Sheung Shui (Hong Kong), 127, 183, 184, 192–195

Fashion Island, Newport Beach, 347

feasibility analysis, 366, 378–379, 404, 408

Fehr and Peers (consulting firm), 364

Ferguson, Lena, 312

FHA (Federal Housing Administration) insurance, 82, 110, 118n2

finance districts and employment, 121, 135, 191–193, 213–214

financial access to real estate. *See* housing prices

financing new towns and planned communities, 12, 293–308; Africa, general, 279, 280, 288; Almere, 255, 257; assistance programs, 403; bonds, 21, 77, 79, 88–89, 318; British literature review, 295–296, 308n2; budget multiplier, 328; Bundang, 205, 207–209, 212; capital appreciation, 316–317; case studies, 296, 297–304; Cergy-Pontoise, 303–304, 308nn5–8; China, general, 152–154, 156, 157, 164, 165, 178–179; Europe, comparative analysis, 231, 233–236, 242, 245–246; failure, reasons for, 306–307; foreign direct investment, 359, 360; global financial crisis, 303; India, general, 216, 217, 227; investment return, sources and measures of, 316–317; Jamshedpur, 222, 224; Kilamba, 284–285; Lavasa, 218–219, 224; Liangzhu, 169, 172, 174, 176, 178–179; loans, 296–299, 301, 305–306, 340, 415; Milton Keynes, 175, 207–208; the Netherlands, 233–234; outcomes, 304–308; resource extraction towns, South America, 269, 270, 273, 275; sequencing of cash sources, availability, and requirements, 315; Sheikh Zayed, 286; Singapore, 144; Songdo, 142, 302–303, 308n4; Songjiang, 155, 160–161; South Korea, comparative analysis, 203; stability, 418–419; Tama New Town, 123; viability, 12. *See also* developers; infrastructure development; revenue

financing U.S. planned communities, 59–60, 73, 90; amenities, 77–79, 84–85, 88–89, 99–100, 102, 103; bankruptcy, 60, 63, 75, 82; capital investments, 60, 63, 74, 77, 79, 84; Columbia, 299; "community district" payments, 77; debt service, 77, 79, 88–89; development and infrastructure costs, 75–79; Greensprings assisted living community model, 117–118; home owners' associations and, 106, 113–115; infrastructure development, 73, 75–77, 79–80, 88, 92, 97, 100; Irvine, 300–301; national economic factors, 81–82, 92, 93; residential construction costs, 79–80; Reston, 297–298; site acquisition, 74, 79, 88–89; transit and transportation, 95–98; U.S. literature review, 296–297; The Woodlands, 175, 301–302, 308n3

Finland, new towns in, 244

Finley, William, 63

First World Towers, 359

Five New Towns Development Plan (South Korea), 201, 203, 211. *See also* Bundang, South Korea; South Korea, new towns in

flexibility, importance of, 100, 401, 414, 419; in local governance, 104, 108–109; regulatory, 108–109, 337–338, 360; Songdo plan deviations, 143; in transit development, 96, 98, 103; zoning, 93–94

flood insurance, 400, 408, 409n1

floor area ratio (FAR), 176–177, 188, 203

Floréal, Belgium, 388

Flower Mound New Town, Texas, 325

food production, 343, 391–392

Ford, Henry II, 300

Forest City (developer), 97–98, 103n5

Forest Hills Gardens, 388

Forsyth, Ann, 15, 27, 47–48, 50, **389–390, 392, 414–415,** 434

Fortune (magazine), 20

Foundation for Housing Almere, 253

France, 20, 22, 303–304, 320, 395

France, European new towns comparisons, 232, 235; arts and culture, 245–247; environmental issues, 243; financing and budget cuts, 233–234; housing prices, 238; social issues, 239, 240; transit, 236

Freestone, Robert, 12, 434

Frieling, Dirk, 254

Fu, Shikyo, 175

future of new towns, 12, 410–421; changing purposes, 410–414; coordinators, 418–419; end of new town creation in Europe, 247–248; new towns *versus* new-town-style planning innovations, 419–420; styles, 411, 414–418; twenty-first-century trends and implications, 410–412, 433–434

Gaborit, Pascaline, 433

Galantay, E. Y., 22

Galatas, Roger, 302, 311, 316–317, 326, 328n1

Gale International (developer), 141–142, 303, **307,** 351

Gangnam, South Korea, 200–202, 212–214

garden city movement, 43, **364,** 371, 385–389, 395, 432; African new towns and, 278; Almere influenced by, 252; approach, 248n2, 385–389; Chinese new towns and, 167, 177; eastern European new towns, 234; Garden Cities Association (Garden City Association), 17–18, 43; history of, 17, 24–26, 30

Gardens by the Bay urban park, 377

Garnier, Tony, 18

409; influence of, 24–26, 248n3. *See also* garden city movement

Howard Research and Development Corporation (HRD), 299

Hsing, Y. T., 153

hubs, 374–375, **377**

Huis, Frits, 256

Hungary, new towns in, 234

Hurricanes Irene and Sandy, 400

hybrid developments, 89

hydroelectric energy (Brazil), 270–273

ideal city, concept of, 15–16, 32–33, 350. *See also* socialist new town models; utopianism

identity, of place, 44, 49–50, 55n3, 242–243, 379

Ihla Solteira, Brazil, 272–273

IIRSA (Initiative for the Integration of Regional Infrastructure in South America), 275

Ikeda Hayato, 120

L'île d'Abeau, France, 232

Ile de France region, 303–304

Ilsan, South Korea, 201–203

implementation strategy, 418

Incheon, South Korea, 302–303, **307**, 352–354

inclusion (and exclusion) criteria, 433; age-restricted communities, 102, 109, 116; local governance of, 109, 116

income: Bundang, 212; commuting costs and travel subsidizing, 196–197; Ghana, average gross annual salary, 280; Great Recession, 92–94, 101, 337, 339–340; income-balanced communities, Hong Kong new towns, 188–189; income-homogenous communities, 116; Kilamba, 285; from land sales, China, 154; low-income households, 49; public housing ceiling tests, Hong Kong, 185; Sheikh Zayed, 287; socio-spatial segregation and, 281, 287–289; Tin Shui Wai, 132, 196. *See also* housing prices; jobs and employment; social class

incremental real estate ventures, traditional, 84–87, 104

independence, of new towns. *See* self-sufficiency

India, new towns in, 216–229, 433; map, 427; new "new towns," 216–219, 221–224, 226–227; satellite towns, 216; steel townships (old "new towns"), 216–218, 220–222, 224–228; urbanization needs, 219; U.S., compared, 228–229. *See also* Jamshedpur and Lavasa, India, compared

industrial districts and development (and industry-motivated expansion), 6, 10, 17, 412;

advancement in, 351; Beijing, 132–134, 136; Bundang, 213; China, 152–153, 156–158, 164–165; complexes, 300; development of, 41; Europe, comparative analysis, 231, 232, 234–235; growth centers, 433; Hong Kong new towns, 130, 182, 189–194, 197–198; India, 216–218, 220–222, 224–228, 229; Japan, 121; Lingang, 161–162; rail's importance to, 265–266, 269; regenerated industrial zones, 23; Shanghai, 159; Songjiang, 160–161; South Korea, 138, 200. *See also* commercial districts and development; mixed-use districts and development; residential districts and development; resource extraction towns (South America)

inequality, 411–412. *See also* social issues

informal housing and informal sectors: Africa, 277, 279, 282–283, 285, 287–290; China, 155, 158; India, 226, 227; South Korea, 138. *See also* housing types; income; social class

information technology: Africa, 279; internet, community-wide, 344; smart cities, 216–217, 220, 227, 248, 433; smart technologies, 358–359

infrastructure development, 298, 340–341, 404–405; Almere, 253, 260; Bundang, 203, 204, 207, 209, 213, 215; China, financing, 154, 157, 158, 164, 165; comprehensive, 421; configuration of, 146, 167, 271–272, 289; cost of, 295–296, 298–299, 301–302, 319, 344–345; Europe, for aging populations, 238; Europe, population density and, 235; IIRSA plan, 275; information technology, 217, 279; Jamshedpur and Lavasa, compared, 221–224, 226; Kilamba, 283; by KLC in Bundang, 203, 204, 207, 209; maintenance of, 105, 143, 174, 238; planning, 391; Putrajaya, 149; removal, from abandoned sites, 94; Singapore, 143–144, 146; Songdo, 141, 142; storm water management, 372, 375–377, 391–392; U.S., comparative analysis, 73–79, 81, 97; U.S., difficulties of, 73–78, 81, 97; U.S., financing, 73, 75–77, 79–80, 88, 92, 97, 100; Vila Piloto, 270–272. *See also* amenities and public services; phasing development; roadways, design and use of; transit and transportation

Ingenio de Santa Ana (Santa Ana Sugar Mill, Argentina), 263–266

instant new towns, 7, 411, 415, 417, 421

insurance: FHA, 82, 110, 118n2; flood, 400, 408, 409n1; home owners, 82; insurance companies provide startup capital for planned communities, 79; Teachers Insurance Annuity Association, 299, 307

Integrated Housing Development Program (IHDP), 279

intentional communities, 15, 379

intentional urban space, 378–384; (un)intentional space, 383; neighborhood crafting toolbox, 380–381; the third place, 381–383

international networks, 29, 303, 353–354; International Federation for Housing and Planning, 18; International Garden Cities and Town Planning Association, 18; International New Towns Association, 22, 29–30; The International New Towns Institute, 432; International Urban Development Association, 30

international practice, reflections from, 329–360; on higher density and mixed-use development, 329–331; on innovations, new towns as testing grounds for, 332–334; on new political centers and smaller new towns, 331–332. *See also* Crescent Communities; Irvine, California; Kohn Pedersen Fox (KPF); The Pinehills

interstate highway corridors, 406–407

interventionist state approach, European new towns, 231–233, 237

inventory of new towns (Appendix 2), **4–5**, 6, **33–35**, 41, **432–451**; classic new towns and new neighborhoods, 433, 450–451; countries with more than five new towns, 4, 34, 42n1; countries with more than three in golden age, 5; inventory of twenty-first-century new towns, 433–434, 446–450; main inventory of twentieth-century new towns with populations over 30,000, 432–446; methods, 434; overview, 432–434; starts, 33–35

investment in new towns and planned communities. *See* financing new towns and planned communities

Irvine, California, 20–21, 47, 50, 325; Business Center, 300–301; city council, 349; early retail development, 345–348, 350; governance, 348–350; Irvine Company, 300–301, 307, 346–350, 377; Irvine family, 300–301; Irvine Ranch, 345–350, 375, 377, 433–434; Irvine Spectrum, 300; University of California, 346–347

Isle de Jean Charles, Louisiana, 400

Italy, new towns in, 232

Jacobs, Jane, 26

Jacquemin, A. R. A., 27

Jamshedpur and Lavasa, India, compared, 217–227; amenities and public services provision, 221–224; developers, public-private issues, 217–228; governance and jurisdiction, 217–219, 225–228; location, 217, 220–221; size, 217; table, 217

Jamshedpur Utilities and Services Company (JUSCO), 221–222, 224, 228

Japan, new towns in, 119–126, 150, 151; fifty-year bonds, 318; map, 429; Tama New Town, 121–123; Tsukuba City, 121, 124–126

J. C. Nichols Company, 74

Jeffery Open Space Trail (JOST) corridor, 377

Jiading new town, China, 155, 156

Jinan, China, 331–332

JMB Realty, **307**

jobs and employment, 10, 36–38, 363, 383; Bundang, 213; Europe, comparative analysis, 244–245; Hong Kong, comparative analysis, 190–196, 198–199; Hong Kong economic restructuring (table), 190; Hong Kong employment distribution (table), 192–193; Hong Kong fails to decentralize, 190, 198–199; Jamshedpur and Lavasa, compared, 118, 222, 226; in Japan, 120, 121; Kilamba, 285; Sha Tin, 128, 192–193; steel townships, 218, 222; targeted population/jobs ratio, 304; Tin Shui Wai, 132; Tongzhou, 135–136; U.S., comparative analysis, 63, 65, 85, 86, 91, 103; worker housing, 66, 265, 271, 273–274. *See also* commuting; income; unemployment

jobs-housing balance: Bundang, 209; Europe, general/comparative analysis, 237, 244–245; Hong Kong, comparative analysis, 128, 186, 189–198; Japan, 120; Kilamba, 285; Milton Keynes, 236, 240; Tin Shui Wai, 196–197; U.S., general/comparative analysis, 85–86, 89–95, 102–103. *See also* commuting; design layouts; mixed-use districts and development; transit and transportation

Johns Hopkins University medical institutions, 327

John Wayne Airport area, 301

de Jonge, P. M. M., 256–257

Joongdong, South Korea, 201–203

jurisdiction issues. *See* governance

Jurong Lake District, Singapore, 365

Kan, Har Ye, 434

Kato, Araki, 271–272

Keeton, Rachel, 15, 434

Kellenberg, Steven, **370**

Kelly, Daniel, 103nn12–13

Kennecott Utah Copper, 96

Kentlands, Maryland, 72, 73, 378

Kenya, new towns in, 279, 281, 288

Kilamba, Angola, 280–286, **282, 283**

Kim, J., 50

Kim, Kyung Min, 434

Kingsport, 20

Kohn Pedersen Fox (KPF), 141–142, 350–360; on connectivity, 352–353; on lifestyle, 354–357; on policy, 359–360; on sustainability, 358–359; on variety, 357–358

Konzo Techno City, Kenya, 281, 288

Koolhaas, Rem, 251, 257

Korea, new towns in, 353–354, 395; Korea Research Institute for Human Settlements, 203–204; map of, 429

Korea Land Corporation (KLC), 203, 205–212, 215nn1–2; compensation for existing land owners, 205; land sales revenue, 207, 208; rapid land acquisition for Bundang, 205, 207, 208, 211, 212; site acquisition issues, 204–205; site distribution decisions, 205–207. *See also* Bundang, South Korea

Kowloon, China, 128

Kubitschek, Juscelino, 270

Kweon, B. S., 44

Kwinana, 48

Kwun Tong, Hong Kong, 182

Laguna Beach, 347

Lake Forest, Illinois, 67

Lake Nona (Orlando, Florida), 89, 91–92, 102–103

Lakewood Ranch, Florida, 95

Lammers, Han, 254, 255

land: acquisition, 219, 334–335; assembly, 404; costs, 331, 342; development model, 315; division, efficient system of, 367; eminent domain, 401; finger annexation, 348, 350; Land Acquisition, Rehabilitation, and Resettlement Act (LARRA, India), 219; Land and Technical Management Agency of the Parisian Region, 304; localized shortages, 421; management system, China, 155, 165, 174; new, 413; ownership, 120, 219–220, 300–301, 304, 307–308, 345; per person, 11; plan, 343–344; scarcity, 8, 411, 413; values, 374. *See also* land reclamation; land use; site acquisition and land purchasing

landdrost role, Almere, 250–254, 262n1

land reclamation: Hong Kong new towns, 183, 185; Lingang, 155; the Netherlands, 233, 235, 246; Songdo, 141; Tin Shui Wai, 130, 183

landscape analyses, 391

land use, 364–365, 391, 405. *See also* agricultural land; commercial districts and development; industrial districts and development; mixed-use districts and development; residential districts and development

land use diversity issue ("D variable"), 89. *See also* jobs-housing balance

Lang, Robert, 112

Langford, L. C., 28

language issues, 433–434

Las Vegas, Nevada, 111–112

Lau, J. C. Y., 196

Laurence, Christopher, 370

Lavasa, India. *See* Jamshedpur and Lavasa, India, compared

Lavasa Corporation Limited (LCL), 219, 222–224, 226–228

Lavasa New Town, Pune, India, 333–334

law and legal issues: India, 120, 219–221, 224–225, 229; regulatory flexibility, 108–109, 337–338, 360; Sea Ranch litigation and occupancy, 83, 84

law and legal issues, corporate organization of new towns, 107–116; historical origins of, 109–111; municipal *vs.* nonprofit incorporation of new towns, 112–116; permitting process, 337–338; recent changing patterns of, 111–112. *See also* home owners' associations; municipal incorporation

layouts. *See* design layouts

Leccese, M., 73

LEED-rated buildings, 359

Leefbaar Almere (Netherlands political party), 251, 256–259

Lee Kwan Yew, 143

LeFurgy, Jennifer, 112

leisure activities. *See* amenities and public services; open space and parkland

Leisure World, 348

Lelystad, the Netherlands, 233, 235–236, 240

lessons learned, 12–13; best practices, 88, 294; from British New Town Program, 295; from Irvine Ranch, 345–350; from Songdo, 350–360

Letchworth Garden City, U.K., 17, 295, **386,** 388, **389**

Letter A/B land exchange entitlements system (Hong Kong), 186

Levitt, Alfred, 63

Levitt, William, 63

perimeter block, 357

Perkins Eastman Architects, 329, **330, 332**

Perry, Clarence, 210

PERT (program evaluation and review technique), 299

phasing development, 7, 294, 347, 411–412, 414–415, 421, 433; amenities as difficult up-front expense, U.S., 77–79, 84–85, 88–89, 99–100, 102, 103; amenities *vs.* population issues, Hong Kong, 197–198; employment *vs.* population issues, Liangzhu, 178; employment *vs.* population issues, U.S., 91; Hong Kong, comparative analysis, 127, 197–198; Kilamba, 283; Liangzhu, 171, 176, 178; site acquisition, KLC, Bundang, 206, 208–209, 211; site acquisition, U.S., 74, 80, 97; Tin Shui Wai, 131; transit and transportation, Hong Kong, 197–198; transit and transportation, importance of timing, 95–97, 103; transit and transportation, U.S., 98; transitional periods, governance during, 106, 112–113. *See also* amenities and public services; financing new towns and planned communities; infrastructure development; planning phase; residential demand; transit and transportation

philanthropy, 295, 302, 388, 404

the Philippines, new towns in, 119, 149

Pieterse, Edgar, 278

Pilgrim Hall Museum, 341

The Pinehills, Plymouth, Massachusetts, 334–342; The Market, 338, 340; marketing, 338–339; market research, 337; Old Sandwich Road, 334, 336; permitting, 337–338; planning, 338; recession and recovery, 339–340; reputation, recognition, and community, 341–342; Stonebridge Club, 339; Summerhouse, 337–338, 338–339; utilities and association management, 340–341; the Village Green, 335–337

place-making, 344, 379; place-based conditions, 44; placelessness, 29

planned retreat, 411, 412, 420–421; building consensus, 401, 409n2; calculus, 399; developing receiving areas, 400–401; federal buyouts of at-risk property, 398–400, 409n1; pros and cons, 401–403

Planned-Unit Development with a Homes Association (FHA), 111

planning, 338, 378; diffusion studies in, 28–29; innovations in, 332–334, 419–420; overdetermined, 414; principles of, 48; scenario, 401; unplanned informal development, 413–414

planning phase, 60; Almere, 252–254; Bundang, focused planning, 200–201, 211–212; China, comparative analysis, 152, 155; completion fallacy, 82–83; disassembly intentions for Vila Piloto, 272; Europe, interventionist state approach, 231–233, 237; Europe, no new plans, 247–248; Hong Kong new towns, 182–183, 185–186, 190, 196–199; Lingang, 162; Tsukuba City, 125–126; U.S., general/comparative analysis, 66–73

Plan of Chicago (Burnham and Bennett), 82

Plater-Zyberk, Elizabeth, 73

platooning, autonomous car, 370

Plymouth Plantation, 341

Poland, new towns in, 234

policy, 28, 352. *See also* law and legal issues

political aims, 37–38, 149, 331–332

Pontine Marshes, 19

population demographics, 7–8, 10, 36–37, 319; amenities surveys, U.S., 99–100; China suburbs, general, 157–158; demographic mix, 299, 342–343, 417, 420; effects of change, 330, 381–383, 411–413, 420; housing needs based on, Europe, 237–238; Kilamba, 284; racial diversity, 46, 86–87; Tama New Town, 123. *See also* age; income; social class

population density, 299, 335, 340, 367–368; China, general/comparative analysis, 153, 154, 163, 164; environmental issues, 241; Europe, comparative analysis, 231, 235, 237–238, 241; golden mean methodology, 363–365; gradient, 357–358; high, 329–331, 389–391; Hong Kong, comparative analysis, 127–128, 130, 186–187; leveraging adjacent urban, 352–353; Liangzhu, 168–169, 173, 178; lower, 391–392; metropolitan densification, 389; mixed, 357–358; the Netherlands, 255; Punggol, 147; Singapore, 145, 147; South Korea, comparative analysis, 203; as sustainability framework, 358–359; Tama New Town, 122; urban shrinkage, 411–412. *See also* size and scale of planned communities

population growth, 411–412; Africa, UN projections, 277; Europe, general, 237–238; Hong Kong, general/comparative analysis, 126, 187; Japan, 120–121; Lingang, 161; Singapore, 143; Songjiang, 161; Urban Growth and New Community Act in (1970), 52, 296

population numbers: Almere, 236; Europe, comparative analysis (table), 232; Hong Kong, comparative analysis, 127–128, 130, 184–185;

railroads: resource extraction and, 265–266, 269; in U.S., 73, 80, 81

rail transit. *See* commuting; transit and transportation

Rancho Mission Viejo, California, 369, 375

Rancho Sahuarita (Tucson, Arizona), 100–**101**, 103, 103n9

Rancho Santa Margarita, California, 34, 89

rapid sales, 305–306

real estate cycles, 37, 305, 308

reasons for new towns. *See* motivations

recessions, economic, 298–299, 302, 305, 339–340

reclaimed land. *See* land reclamation

recreational facilities. *See* amenities and public services; open space and parkland

rectilinear layout, **67**, 69

redevelopment, 97, 415–417, 421

redistribution goals. *See* population redistribution, as new town motivation

refugees. *See* resettlement

regional development, 402; cities, 15–16, 22; new town concentrations, 395–396; planning and transportation agencies, 403; strategy, instruments of, 395. *See also* climate change, regional development and

Regional Organ Amsterdam (ROA), 257

Regional Planning Association of America (RPAA), 18, 388

regulations. *See* governance; law and legal issues

Reiner, T. A., 15, 18

Rendeavour (developer), 280

rent prices. *See* housing prices

resettlement of residents, 216, 393; Bundang, 204–205; Hong Kong, 185–187; refugees, 7–8, 412, 420; Resettlement Administration, 18; wars and refugees, 120, 216, 231, 282, 284. *See also* climate change

residential construction, private residences: Almere, 259–260; financing, in U.S., 79–80

residential demand: African middle class and, 280; Bundang, 208, 209; Hong Kong public housing, 187, 197; transit and transportation and, 80–81, 83, 209; U.S., comparative analysis, 73, 74, 80–84, 89

residential districts and development: Bundang, 140, 210–211; China, general, 153, 154; Liangzhu, 170–171, 178; neighborhood unit design concept, 210–211, 271; Shanghai, 159; South Korea, general, 206. *See also* commercial districts and development; design layouts; dormitory

towns; industrial districts and development; jobs-housing balance; mixed-use districts and development

residential valuations, 342

residents, government participation by. *See* Almere, the Netherlands, governance history; governance

residents' advisory groups, 321–322, 324–325, 337, 341

resilience, 402; agencies, 398; resilient new towns approach, 385–387, 392–393; social, 392–393. *See also* climate change, regional development and

resource extraction towns (South America), 263–275, 421; Chile, 274; design layouts, 264–269, 271–272, 274–275; IIRSA plan for, 275; map of, 424; Maria Elena, 263, 267–269, 275; *vs.* mining hotel model, 274; Santa Ana, 263–266, 275; Vila Piloto, 263, 270–273, 275

Reston, Virginia, 20, 47, **59,** 63–64, 75, 78, 82–84, 371; "D variables" in, 89; financing, 79–80, 86, 297–298, 307; organization and management of, 311, 322; plan changes, 82–83; Reston Land Corporation, 298; transit and transportation, 83, 95

resurgence of new town model, 35, 40–42

retail districts and employment: Bundang, 206, 213; Hong Kong, 191–197; Irvine, 345–348, 350; Lavasa, 223; Liangzhu, 173, 177–178; Songdo, 142; specialty retail, 347; Tongzhou, 134. *See also* commercial districts and development

retirement homes, retirement communities, senior housing, 102, 109, 116, 118, 433; in Liangzhu, 172–173, 178, 180. *See also* age

revenue: Almere, 255; Liangzhu, 176; South Korea, 142, 207, 208; U.S. planned communities, 65–66, 74, 78–80, 83, 88. *See also* financing new towns and planned communities

RIJP (National Office for the IJsselmeerpolders, the Netherlands), 250–255

Riverside, Illinois, 59, 60, **61, 75, 81,** 451; curvilinear layout, 68; as financial failure, 79, 81, 86; residential demand, 80; Riverside Improvement Company, 60; site acquisition, 73

roadways, design and use of: Bundang, KLC and, 203, 209; corridors, 366–367, 374, 376–377, 395, 406–407; Europe, comparative analysis, 235–237; highway access to Reston, 83; jurisdiction issues, U.S., 106, 117; Lingang, 163; neighborhood unit design concept, 210, 272;

roadways, design and use of (*continued*)
site development costs, U.S., 75–76; subsidized through land sales, in China, 154; suburban layouts, U.S., 66–73, 77, 78, 84–85; Vila Piloto, 272; Yizhuang, 137. *See also* commuting; infrastructure development; transit and transportation
Robertson, Jaquelin, 65
Robinson, A. J., 21
Rockefeller family, 273
Rodgers, W., 44–46
Rodwin, Lloyd, 26–27
Roh Tae-Woo, 203–204
Roth, Eric, **339**
Rouse, James, 20, 36, 299, **307**, 311
Rouse Company, 63, 74, 79, 299, 310
Rowe, Peter, 434
Ruggeri, D., 50
Russia, new towns in, 6, 19, 26, 33, 248n5, 433
Sacramento, California, 366–367; Sacramento–San Joaquin River delta system, 397
Sadat, Anwar, 278, 290n2
Sanbon, South Korea, 201, 202, 203
San Francisco, California, 366–367
Santa Ana, Argentina, 263–266, **265**, 275, 348, 350
Sant'Elia, Antonio, 18
satellite communities, 11, 33, 319, 329–332, 388, 412, 433; Beijing, 132; China, consolidation of, 158–159; history of, 16, 20, 23; Hong Kong, 182; India, 216; Seoul new towns as, 138. *See also* East and Southeast Asia, new towns as response to urban expansion in
scenario planning, 401
schools and education, 355, 357; access to, 238, 285, 290n15; Bundang, 140, 210, 212; as community anchors, 91, 92; Jamshedpur and Lavasa, compared, 221, 222, 224; Kilamba, 185; Liangzhu, 180; in neighborhood unit design concept, 211; New Albany, 78; shortage of (Tuen Mun), 197; Tama New Town, 122–123; Tsukuba City as academic-centered new town, 124–126; University of California, 300, 346–347; University of Michigan (U-M) study, 45, 47; University of North Carolina (UNC) study, 45, 47–48, 52, 54
Schroeder, H. W., 391
sea-level rise, strategic adaptation to, 397–408; ad hoc rebuilding, drawbacks of, 402–403; coping with sea-level rise, 397; developing a coastal region new town system, 403–405; example application: southeast region, 405–406; planned

retreat, 397–403, 409nn1–2; projections, 396; relocating Charleston, 407–408, 409nn3–5; sea-level rise projections, 396; vulnerable coastal areas, 397–398. *See also* climate change; coastal region new town systems
The Sea Ranch, California, 59, **64**, 65, 73, 79, 82; litigation and occupancy issues, 83, 84; open space in, 70, 76, 78
Seaside, Florida, 21, 50, 73, 378
seawalls, 397–398
Secretariat of Urban Regeneration Major Operations, 304
segregation: gentrification, 27, 227–228; socio-spatial, 281, 287–289
self-sufficiency and self-containment goals, 8–9, 33; Almere, participatory government, 251, 259–261; Asia, general, 150; Bundang, 139, 140, 209, 213–215; Europe, comparative analysis, 231; fallacy of, 83; Hong Kong, comparative analysis, 183, 186, 189–197, 199; Jamshedpur, 218; Liangzhu, 176; Maria Elena, 268–269; Punggol, 148; Tin Shui Wai, 130; Toa Payoh, 145
senior housing. *See* age; retirement homes, retirement communities, senior housing
Seoul, South Korea, 200–202, 211, 302–303, 352–353, 355–356, 358
Shaefer, Gavin, 383
Shanghai, China, 20, 23–24, 155, 158–163, 395
Sharpe, Robert, 100
Sha Tin, Hong Kong, 127–130, **129**, 194–195; characteristics of, 184; employment in, 128, 192–193; Ma On Shan extension, 183; transit and transportation, 129–130, 198. *See also* Hong Kong, new towns in
Sheikh Zayed City, Egypt, 280, 281, 286–288
Shi, Y., 24
Shinkenchiku (architectural magazine), 180n1
side-by-side developments, 132–133, 149
sidewalks, 77, 237. *See also* pedestrian travel; walkability
Silkin, John, 22
Silkin, Lewis, 22
Silkingrad. *See* Stevenage
Simon, Robert E., 63, 80
Simon, Robert E. Jr., 20, 297–298, **307**, 311
Sims, David, 286
Singapore, new towns in, 20, 29, 50, 119, 143–149, **144**, 151, 413; Central Business District, 367; Pungol, 147–149; Toa Payoh, 145–147; Urban Redevelopment Authority (URA), 367

United States (U.S.) (*continued*)
Department of Housing and Urban Development (HUD), 21, 301, 400, 403; Eastmark (Mesa, Arizona), 92–93, 103; Federal Emergency Management Agency (FEMA), 399–400, 403; federal programs, 66; financial motivations for, private development of, 59, 65–66; greenbelt towns, 26–27; jobs-housing balance, 85–86, 90–91; Lake Nona (Orlando, Florida), 89, 91–92, 102–103; map of new towns in, 423; Medical City, Florida, 91–93; new communities program, 27; population issues, 60, 63, 65, 73, 84, 99–100; Post Office, 338; Rancho Sahuarita (Tucson, Arizona), 100–101, 103; Southeast region, 405–406; Stapleton, Colorado, 89, 95, 97–98, 103; Title VII communities, 28, 296, 301–302, 304, 317–318, 327; TOD for, 366; Urban Growth and New Communities Act (1970), 52, 296. *See also* climate change, regional development and; developers, private, in U.S.; financing U.S. planned communities; governance, in U.S. new towns; home owners' associations; open space and parkland, in U.S.; problems in U.S. planned communities; site issues, U.S. planned communities; suburbs, layouts in U.S.; transit and transportation, U.S.; individual location

universities. *See* schools

Unwin, Raymond, 26, **371,** 378

upper class, 205, 209, 212, 287. *See also* social class

urban development, as inseparable from non-urban, 169

urbanism, 73; high-modernist, 20; new urbanism, 21, 24–25, 48, 50, 334, 378–379

urbanization: Indian new towns, 219; peri-urbanization, 248n1. *See also* Africa, new towns in; Jamshedpur and Lavasa, India, compared

Urban Land Institute (ULI), 9–10, 89, 110, 118n2; *Best Development Practices,* 88; study, 2015, 94; survey of planned communities, 1992, 65–66

urban renewal, 30–31, 313

urban riots, 21

Utah Transit Authority (UTA), 96

utilities. *See* infrastructure development

utopianism, 14–17, 218, 227, 230, 268, 274. *See also* ideal city; socialist new town models

Uxcester (fictional city), 24

Vallee, Jeff, **336**

Vällingby, Sweden, 41, 247, **414**

Valmeyer, Illinois, 398

Vanderlip, Frank, 60

Vanke (Chinese developer), 169–174, 176–178, 180n1

Le Vaudreuil, France, 232, 304

Vaux, Calvert, 68, 75

Venezuela, new towns in, 273

Venice, Florida, 378

Venice Biennale (Italy), 23

Verrado, Arizona, 347–348, 350, 380; South Town Center, 348; Victory, 101–103

Victoria (unbuilt utopian city), 17

Vila Piloto, Brazil, 263, 270–273, **271,** 275

villages, residential, 298, 300, 334–335, 346–347

Villeneuve d'Ascq, France, 232

Ville Radieuse (Le Corbusier), 18

villes nouvelles program (France), 20, 22, 232, 320

Vinex growth centers plan (the Netherlands), 233

VMT (vehicle miles traveled) metric, 90–91, 363, 365–366. *See also* commuting; jobs-housing balance

Volkshuisvesting in de jaren negentig (Public Housing in the 1990s), 256

voting: Almere ACA elections, 251, 254, 257; home owners' associations, 107–109, 113, 115. *See also* governance

Wakeman, R., 19

walkability, 334, 358, 367, 381, 390, 420. *See also* pedestrian travel

Walt Disney Company, 343–345

Wang Shi, 172

wars and refugees, effects on new town development, 120, 216, 231, 282, 284, 290n1

Washington Post (newspaper), 298

Waterman, T., 409n2

Watson, Raymond, 300

wealth. *See* income; social class

Welwyn Garden City, 295, 388

West Antarctica ice sheet, 396

Westerterp, Tjerk, 253

Wexner, Les, 65, 82

Whittick, Arnold, 3, 28, 432, 434

wildlife movement, 372, 375–377

William Pereira and Associates, 300

Willmott, P., 50

Wolfson Economics Prize, 24

Woodbridge Village Association, 349

The Woodlands, Texas, 47, 66, **305, 307,** 329–330, 391–392; "D variables" in, 89; future of new towns, 416, 417, 419; history of new towns, 21,

28; Liangzhu, compared, 175–176; local governance of, 117; organization and management of, 311, 316–318, 322, 326–327; site design, 371, 386; transit and transportation, 95; The Woodlands Corporation, 302, 316–317

worker housing, 66, 273–274, 420; Santa Ana, 265; Venezuela and Standard Oil, 273; Vila Piloto, 271. *See also* jobs and employment; resource extraction towns (South America)

working class, 157, 161, 239, 290. *See also* social class

worlding of urban space, 23

World War II, 28–29, 33, 120, 388, 394

Wright, Henry, 63, 76, 388

Wright, Scott, 224

Xi Jinping, 283

Yizhuang, Beijing, 136–**137**

youth. *See* families and households

youth housing (Sheikh Zayed), 287–288, 290n14

Yuen Long, Hong Kong, 183; commuting, 194–195; employment distribution in, 192–193; industry in, 191; map, 184

Yuen Long South (YLS), 185

Zaragoza, Spain, 375

Zhejiang Narada Real Estate Group (Narada), 169

Zhou, J., 49

Zoetermeer, the Netherlands, 240–243, 246

zoning, 335; code, 297–298; Euclidean, 378; flexibility in, 93–94; form-based, 378; income homogeneity through, 116; Zone d'Aménagement Différée (ZAD), 304, 308n7. *See also* commercial districts and development; industrial districts and development; mixed-use districts and development; residential districts and development

Acknowledgments

We would like to thank the authors who wrote chapters and also attended a workshop to present and refine the pieces. Vanke Incorporated's Chengdu office provided funding for the book, including a workshop for authors held at Harvard University in September 2016. We appreciate Vanke's interest in the global practices of new town development and particularly thank Chaobin Zhou, our contact person at Vanke. Series editors Eugenie L. Birch and Susan M. Wachter provided very valuable support, as did Peter Agree and Robert Lockhart of Penn Press. Various students and scholars assisted in checking the inventory in Appendix 2, and we outline their contributions in the introduction to that section. Additional assistance, beyond that for the inventory, came from Lena Ferguson, Antara Tandon, Andrew Stokols, Deni Lopez, Kevin Chong, Edward Lamson, YingYing Lu, and Adam Tanaka; postdoctoral scholar ChengHe Guan provided advice throughout the project, and postdoctoral scholar Har Ye Kan helped with the inventory and final manuscript.